Texas Veterans of Czech Ancestry

BY
The Czech Heritage Society of Texas

EAKIN PRESS Austin, Texas

FIRST EDITION

Published in the United States of America
By Eakin Press
A Division of Sunbelt Media, Inc.
P.O. Drawer 90159 Austin, Texas 78709-0159
email: eakinpub@sig.net
website: www.eakinpress.com

2 3 4 5 6 7 8 9

1-57168-344-5

LIABILITY

The information in this book should not be used as the final authority for the information found in it. Typographical errors may have been made. Handwriting may have been misread. Mistakes may have been commited. All information received has been included to the best of the ability of the volunteers who have worked on the project. The Czech Heritage Society of Texas is not liable for errors, discrepancies or omissions contained in the material.

Library of Congress Cataloging-in-Publication Data

Texas veterans of Czech ancestry / by the Czech Heritage Society of Texas—1st ed.
p. cm.
ISBN 1-57168-344-5
1. Czech Americans—Texas Biography Dictionaries. 2. Veterans—Texas Biography Dictionaries. 3. Texas Biography Dictionaries. I. Czech Heritage Society of Texas.
F395.B67T49 1999
920'.00929186073—dc21 99-38310
[B] CIP

DEDICATION

No greater sacrifice can be made by the citizens of a nation than to serve in its Armed Forces in times of war and peace. The Czech Heritage Society of Texas proudly honors and pays tribute to those Texans of Czech ancestry who accepted the call to arms, serving courageously to help provide freedom for the United States of America from the time of the Civil War to the present.

This book is dedicated to all Texas veterans of Czech ancestry who have served in the Armed Forces of the United States, especially those men and women who so nobly gave their lives in defending their country. Their heroic efforts should never be forgotten; hence this documentation of their service is a lasting written legacy, providing an account of their patriotic support of freedom and democracy and their commitment as citizens of the United States of America.

Carolyn Sumbera Meiners

ACKNOWLEDGMENTS

We gratefully acknowledge all the Czech Heritage Society of Texas volunteers who were instrumental in publishing this book. Victor Peter initially conceived the idea in 1986 and began collecting information. He was encouraged by Albert J. Blaha, founder of the Czech Heritage Society of Texas. In 1993 a committee was formed to finish gathering and compiling information. Chaired by Ed Baca (Galveston County Chapter), the committee members were Dorothy Bujnoch (Lavaca County Chapter), Jodie Feltman Wright and Bob Biskup (Bexar County Chapter), Carolyn Meiners and Helen Mikus (Fayette County Chapter), Willa Mae Cervenka, Richard Gaidusek, Bo Jaska, and Rudy Stanislav (McLennan-Hill Counties Chapter), and Jim Vrazel (Harris County Chapter).

In 1998, the project was picked up again. State President Anna Krpec, Frank Mikula (McLennan-Hill Counties Chapter), and Bennie and Jackie Marek (Harris County Chapter) sorted all the materials and determined what steps needed to be taken to finish the project. Countless hours were spent by Fort Bend County Chapter members Pat Parma, Robert Roesner, Jerome and Aurelia Cerny, Vicky Matocha, Mary Spacek, Mary Jane Kocurek, and Anna Krpec preparing the manuscript and photos for publishing.

Over the course of the project, proofreading has been done by Alice Maffei (Galveston County Chapter), Mildred Targac (Victoria County Chapter), Helen Mikus (Fayette County Chapter), Mary Spacek, and Jerome and Aurelia Cerny (Fort Bend County Chapter), and Anna Krpec (Harris County Chapter).

Final proofing and correlating photos to text was done by Anna Krpec and Marjorie Matula (Victoria County Chapter), and Richard Pavlasek, James Gerick, and Leo Dornak (Travis-Williamson Counties Chapter).

Special thanks to Robert Roesner for his work in compiling a complete list of all 2,565 names with corresponding photo numbers. He made corrections and entries to the manuscript delivered to Eakin Press. Mr. Roesner then worked with Pat Parma and Jerome and Aurelia Cerny for two days compiling a mailing list from the original biographies.

Victor Peter and Albert Blaha would have been proud of the many volunteers who so generously gave many hours to finish this project, and they would have been pleased with this final result of their vision.

We sincerely appreciate Ed Eakin and the staff at Eakin Press for their patience and guidance.

We thank JoAnn Cernosek in Houston, Texas for her work in typing the biographies into a manuscript.

Anna Wheeler Krpec
State President 1996-1999

INTRODUCTION

A few of the early Czech immigrants served in the Confederate Army during the Civil War, although this conflict proved to be a dilemma for them. Many had immigrated to escape military conscription, and most did not agree with the issues of the war, especially slavery and "brother fighting brother." Their descendants, however, willingly volunteered for U. S. military duty during World War I, because this war brought them the opportunity to combine patriotism for their adopted country with their desire for a free and independent Czech state. Their dream became a reality when the democratic state of Czechoslovakia was created after the war. Czech nationalism in Texas was quite popular until the time of World War II, which was again wholeheartedly supported by Texas Czechs. Their interest in the liberation of Czechoslovakia from Nazi domination combined with their support of American participation in the efforts of World War II were compelling reasons for their loyal response to the call of duty. Texas Czechs continued to serve their country in subsequent wars and conflicts, bravely upholding their belief in a democratic nation.

Carolyn Sumbera Meiners

Adamcik, Adolph C., son of Adolph and Henrietta Muras Adamcik, was born Aug. 4, 1927, in La Grange, TX. Attended Radhost School near La Grange. Enlisted in the U.S. Marine Corps in Houston, TX. Stationed at Marine Training Center, San Diego, CA. Honorably discharged Aug. 21, 1946 at Treasure Island, CA. Home of record: Lancaster, TX

Adamcik, Albert Julius, son of Joe Victor and Therezie Marek Adamcik, was born on Mar. 3, 1893, in Ammannsville, Fayette Co., TX. Enlisted in the U.S. Army Corps during WWI. Was with the American Expeditionary Force, serving as Pfc., HQ Co., 18th Infantry. Theater of Operations: Europe. Fought battles in France. WOUNDED IN ACTION on Jul. 19, 1918, near Soissons, France. Medals: Silver Star, Purple Heart, and WWI Victory Medal. Honorably discharged, 1919. Married Clara Effie Orsak on Jul. 18, 1928. Children: Albert, Georgia, and Neal Adamcik. Occupation: accountant until his retirement. Died June 20, 1954 in Houston, Harris Co., TX, and is buried in El Campo, TX.

Adamcik, Charlie Frank, son of Adolph F. and Lena Vacek Adamcik, was born on July 24, 1915, in La Grange, TX. Attended school in Radhost, Ammannsville, and Hostyn, TX, near La Grange. Enlisted in U.S. Navy, Dallas, TX on Mar. 16, 1945. Rank: Seaman First Class. Was in Casu 33 in California. Awarded World War II Victory Medal. Honorably discharged Nov. 12, 1945, San Pedro, CA. Married Julie Jurecka on Jan. 29, 1940. Children: Cathey Adamcik Daboub and Patricia Adamcik Patak. Home of record: Dallas, TX.

Adamcik, Edwin Allen, son of Adolph F. and Lena Vacek Adamcik, was born on Oct. 20, 1922, in La Grange, TX. Enlisted in U.S. Navy on Nov. 6, 1942, Houston, TX. Rank: USNR.V6 Seaman First Class. Shipwrecked off the coast of Scotland while serving on board the ship, *William M. Welch*. Honorably discharged Sept. 26, 1944 at the U.S. Naval Hospital in New Orleans, LA. Died May 28, 1983.

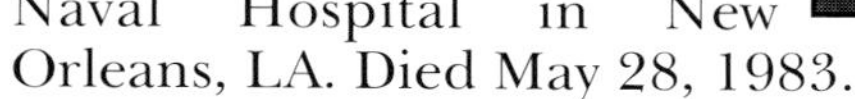

Adamcik, Eustace Edward, son of Joseph V. and Theresia Marek Adamcik, was born on Sept. 2, 1894. in Ammannsville, TX. Education: grammar school through ninth grade in Ammannsville. Attended Massey Business College. Enlisted in the U.S. Army Corps in 1918 at El Campo, TX. Theater of Operations: Europe (served in France). Went overseas with the American Expeditionary Forces. Medals: European Theater of Operations Campaign Medal, WWI Victory Medal, among others. Honorably discharged in 1919. Celebrated 101st birthday on Sept. 2, 1995, at home of record in El Campo, TX.

Adamcik, Leon A., son of Adolph and Lena Vacek Adamcik, was born on Dec. 1, 1918 in La Grange, TX. Joined the U.S. Marine Corps on July 12, 1940. Trained at Camp Pendleton, CA. Served in the Pacific War Zone from July 1, 1942–Sept. 4, 1944. Rank: T/Sgt. Battles: Tarawa, Guadalcanal, Saipan. Discharged Sept. 29, 1945, at Camp Pendleton, CA.

Adamcik, Merrill Travis, son of Lewis Victor and Lillie Lucy Peterka Adamcik, was born on Aug. 17, 1936, in El Campo, TX. Texas A&M graduate with a Bachelor of Science degree. Entered U.S. Army Corps from Texas A&M. Assigned to Ft. Sill,

OK. Served overseas in Germany (1960–1963), Viet Nam (1965–1966 and 1968–1969), and in Korea in 1974. Fought in six campaigns in Viet Nam. Flew CV-2 (Caribou) Aircraft for Special Forces and CH-47 Helicopter for 101st Airborne Division. Had over 4,000 flying hours. Awards and decorations include: Senior Army Aviation Badge, BSS with OLC, Meritorious Service Medal with OLC, Air Medal with eleven OLC, Army Commendation Medal, National Defense Service Medal, Korean Meritorious Service Medal, Viet Nam Service Medal with silver and BSS, RVN Gallantry Cross with Palm and Republic of Viet Nam Campaign Medal. Graduate of Army Command and General Staff College. Retired June 30, 1978, Ft. Hood, TX, as Lt. Colonel, after 20 years' service in the Artillery Branch, with Aviation and Nuclear Weapons Specialties. Home of record: Louise, TX.

Adamcik, Neal Eugene, son of Albert J. and Clara Effie Orsak Adamcik, was born in Houston, TX, on Apr. 18, 1947. Attended the University of Houston and Sam Houston State University. Entered the army in 1969 and trained at Fort Polk, Louisiana. Served in the United States and Viet Nam. Medals: NSM, Overseas Ribbon, Viet Nam Service Medal, Expert M-14, M-16, M-60, M-79 and .45 Pistol. Discharged June 30, 1971.

Adamek, Calvin Coolidge, son of Joe Frank and Emilie Dusek Adamek, attended Elk School in Elk, TX. Enlisted in the U.S. Army Corps on Oct. 18, 1948, in Waco, TX. Served in the Korean War. Medals: U.N. Service Medal, Korean Service Medal, BSS and Meritorious Unit Commendation. Rank: Staff Sgt. Discharged Sept. 1950.

Adamek, John, of Taylor, TX, member of American Legion Post # 282, Granger, TX, WWII Veteran, deceased.

Adamek, Richard Lee, son of Calvin and Olga Adamek, was born in Waco, TX on Mar. 6, 1953. Graduate of Mart High School. Enlisted in the army in Waco, TX, in May 1971. Rank: Spec. 5. Served in Viet Nam Conflict and received the Good Conduct Medal and Commendation Medal. Discharged June 6, 1976.

Albrecht, Gerald C., son of Marvin H. Albrecht, Sr. and Evelyn Berkovsky Albrecht, was born on Oct. 23, 1940, in Rosenberg, TX. Received a BBA degree from the University of Houston (1965). Enlisted in the U.S. Air Force in Houston, TX, on Jan. 17, 1966. Served in Germany with the 6910th Security Wing, USAFSS. Discharged July 10, 1969. Reserve discharge date Nov. 16, 1971. Home of record: Houston, TX.

Ancinec, Henry Joseph, son of Frank and Mary Cisar Ancinec, was born on Sept. 15, 1916, in Houston, TX. B.A. from San Diego State University and an M.A. (equivalency). Received a General Secondary Teaching Credential in California. Enlisted in the U.S. Navy on Dec. 11, 1943, in Houston, TX. Served in the China Service, Asiatic-Pacific (three Battle Stars), Southwest Pacific (two Battle Stars), American Theater (Pre-Pearl, one Star). Battles: Manila, Bataan-Corregidor, Macassar Strait, Java Sea, Bali, Coral Sea, Solomon Islands (Guadalcanal Campaign). Medals: Commendation Ribbon, Army Distinguished Unit Badge, Submarine Combat, two Stars, Good Conduct one Star, American Campaign one Star, WWII Victory, National Defense, Korean Service, United Nations, Philippine Defense three Stars, Purple Heart. WOUNDED IN ACTION in Bataan, reported MISSING IN ACTION. Discharged Sept. 1, 1956, after twenty years of military service.

Ancinec, Joseph, Jr., son of Joseph Ancinec, Sr. and Rose Dusek Ancinec, was born on Sept. 22, 1927, in Red Ranger, Bell Co., TX. Education:

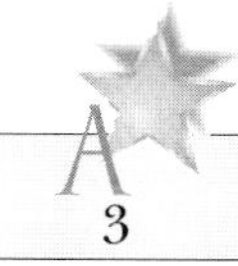

high school, Littlefield, TX. Enlisted in U.S. Army at Ft. Bliss, TX, during WWII. Medals: ASR, WWII Victory Ribbon. Honorably discharged on Nov. 20, 1946. Private, assigned to DEML, AUS. Home of record: Plains, TX. Submitted by Bessie Sisson of Brownfield, TX.

Ancinec, Stanley Eugene, son of Joseph Ancinec, Sr. and Rose Dusek Ancinec, was born on Nov. 14, 1929, Red Ranger, Bell Co., TX. Graduated high school, Whitharral, TX. Enlisted, WWII, U.S. Army Corps. Rank: Corporal. ETO. Medals: Army OCC, Germany. Honorably discharged Jan. 19, 1953. Home of record: Loop, TX. Submitted by Bessie Sisson of Brownsville, TX.

Anders, George A., son of Ludvik J. and Katherine Kaluza Anders, was born on Oct. 17, 1923, in Schulenburg, TX. Education: St. Edward School, Dubina, TX; high school, Crowley, TX. Enlisted in the Army at Ft. Sam Houston, TX. Served with the 16th Armored Division, 3rd Army,

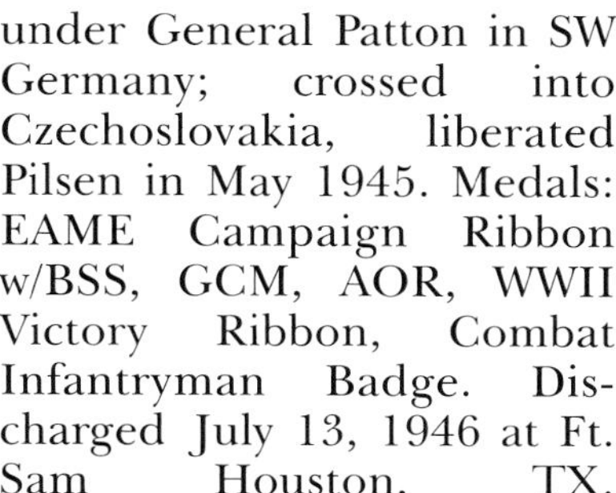

under General Patton in SW Germany; crossed into Czechoslovakia, liberated Pilsen in May 1945. Medals: EAME Campaign Ribbon w/BSS, GCM, AOR, WWII Victory Ribbon, Combat Infantryman Badge. Discharged July 13, 1946 at Ft. Sam Houston, TX.

Aug, Edward F., son of Frank and Mary Kalas, was born on Oct. 1, 1916, in East Bernard, TX. Attended grade school there. Served in the Asiatic-Pacific Theater of Operations during WWII. Japanese PRISONER OF WAR for four years. Suffered shrapnel wounds in both shoulder and leg. Awards and decorations: American Defense Service Medal, American Campaign Medal, Asiatic-Pacific Campaign Medal with campaign star, Good Conduct Medal, Distinguished Unit Citation, Purple Heart, seven Overseas Service Bars, and six Service Stripes. Separated from service Jan. 22, 1946.

Aug, Edward J., son of Edward F. and Josephine Aug, was born on Feb. 18, 1949 in El Campo, TX. Graduated from high school. Enlisted in the U. S. Air Force at Houston, TX, during the Viet Nam Conflict. Stationed at Carswell, AFB, Ft. Worth, TX, and at Lowing AFB in Caribou, Maine. Awards and decorations: Small Arms Expert Marksmanship Ribbon and the National Defense Service Medal. Separated from service Oct. 16, 1972. Home of record: Louise, TX.

B

Babik, Joe, served 2 yrs, 11 months in U.S. Army.

Baca, Arnold, son of Joe O. and Louisa Krenek Baca (daughter of Joseph Krenek) of Fayetteville, TX. Attended Fayetteville High School. Entered the U.S. Army Corps in 1942. Trained at Camp Barkley, TX. Awarded the GCM. Honorably discharged in 1943. Died Sept. 21, 1969. Interred at Fayetteville Catholic Cemetery, Fayetteville, TX.

Baca, Clarence John, son of John R. and Mary Zelesky Baca, was born on Feb. 9, 1920, in Fayetteville, TX. Education: Graduated from Fayetteville High School. Attended Texas A&M for two years (1939–1941). In 1933, he joined the Baca Band. He was 13. John R. Baca was the Band Leader. Clarence has his band in Houston, TX, under the name of Clarence Baca Band, which started in 1964. Enlisted in U.S. Navy, December 1943 in Houston, Harris Co., TX. Sent to N.T.S., San Diego, CA; Administration and Military Com. USNRB, San Diego, CA. Was in the Pacific Theater of Operations. USS LST 477, 13 months sea duty. Landed with the 3rd and 4th Marines at Iwo Jima on Feb. 19, 1945. A Japanese bomb and a Kamikaze plane hit the USS LST 477, off the coast of Iwo Jima. Honorably discharged in December 1946 at Pelican Island. Married Anna Lou Schroeder in Las Vegas, NV, on Nov. 8, 1994. Home of record: Houston, TX.

Baca, Edward A., son of Joe O. and Louisa Krenek Baca (daughter of Joseph Krenek) of Fayetteville, TX. Graduated from Fayetteville High School. Entered U.S. Army Corps, 1942. "My training was at Camp Roberts, California and Camp Pickett, VA. Saw action in Italy and Sicily and was awarded the GCM, Purple Heart, and ET Ribbon with Battle Star." Pvt. Baca was WOUNDED IN ACTION in Salerno, 1943; discharged in 1944. Married Elizabeth Belota. Two children: Edward and Rita. Played in the John Baca Band for many years and became the band leader in the early '50s. Home of record: La Grange, TX.

Baca, Eugene J., son of Lad and Georgie Baca of Granger, TX, was born on Feb. 25, 1947, in La Grange, Fayette Co., TX. When he was 5 years old, he moved with his family to Granger, TX, where he attended Sts. Cyril & Methodius Catholic School for 8 years. He graduated from Granger High School. Enlisted in the U.S. Army Corps on May 23, 1966, in San Antonio, Bexar Co., TX. First year of enlistment was spent at Ft. Polk, LA, Ft. Bliss, TX, Ft. Gordon, GA, and Ft. Hood, TX. Spent following two years in the Pacific Theater of Operation with the 513th Military Police Detachment, under the 13th Military Police Company in Bangkok, Thailand. Sgt. Baca was honorably discharged on May 23, 1969. Medals: National Defense Service Medal, Viet Nam Service Medal, Viet Nam Campaign Medal, Army Commendation Medal. Married; two children. Home of record: Austin, TX.

Baca, John Charles, son of Mr. and Mrs. Lee Edward Baca, was born on Dec. 23, 1952, in Brenham, TX. He graduated from Waltrip High School, Houston, TX, in 1974. Worked at S&B Engineering making blueprints and designing maps for two years. Enlisted in the U.S. Army Corps, Mar. 19, 1976, Houston, TX. Basic Training, Ft. Jackson, SC, transferred to Ft. Gorden, GA (580-72E20 Telecommunications Center) for 11 weeks. He learned how to break

down, make up, and send out messages. Sent to Frankfurt, Germany, assigned to a unit which was attached to the German Army, 83rd U.S. Artillery Detachment at Montabaur. Stayed there for 3½ years, working with communications. Duty position title was Communication Center Crypto Clerk. Released from active duty on Mar. 22, 1980; rank SP4; honorable discharge.

Baca, Lee Edward, Sr., son of Mr. and Mrs. John Baca, was born Apr. 13, 1927, Fayetteville, TX. Graduated from Fayetteville High School, May 1945. Played full-time in his father's band, the John Baca Band. Drafted on July 18, 1945. Entered U.S. Army Corps, Ft. Sam Houston, San Antonio, TX. Transferred to Camp Wolters, near Mineral Wells, TX, for basic training. On Jan. 19, 1946, left for European Theater of Operations. After landing in England, men were split up. Mr. Baca arrived on Jan. 28, 1946, at Headquarters Area Command, Vienna, Austria. Obtained T-4 status (Technician 4th Grade). At this time, war was over, Vienna Area Command was an alliance between the USA, Russia, France, and England. This is where he met his good friend, Larry York, from North Carolina. On the way home, he contracted meningitis in Bremerhaven, Germany, was sent to a hospital in Germany from Nov. 23 until Dec. 13, 1946. After he began to recuperate, he left by boat on Dec. 25, 1946, for USA. After arriving at Ft. Dix, NJ on Jan. 3, 1947, he received an honorable discharge on Jan. 6, 1947. Recorded discharge was made in LaGrange, TX, courthouse, Feb. 14, 1947.

Bacak, Anton A., Jr., son of Anton Bacak, Sr. and Rosie Barak Bacak, was born on Jan. 9, 1920, in West, McLennan Co., TX (fourth child). Fall 1925, moved to Jourdanton, Atascosa Co., TX, attended elementary school in Jourdanton, TX. Lived on a farm near Jourdanton and worked as Deputy Sheriff. Enlisted in the U.S. Army Air Corps on June 14, 1945 at Ft. Sam Houston, TX. Served during World War II in the Asiatic-Pacific Theater of Operations with the Japan Occupational Forces as a Sgt. in the Headquarters and Base Service Squadron, 63rd Air Service Group. Military awards and decorations include the World War II Victory Medal, Army of Occupation Medal, and Asiatic-Pacific Campaign Medal. Separated from service on Mar. 9, 1947, at Camp Beale, CA. Honorably discharged Apr. 21, 1947. Came back to Jourdanton, TX, and went to work for the Atascosa Co., TX, Sheriff's Office. Married Opal Mae Phillips. They had five children. Retired from the State of Texas Alcohol Beverage Commission. Member of St. Ignatius Catholic Church, Austin, TX. Member of KJT and the American Legion. Home of record: Austin, TX.

Bacak, Fred, son of Anton Bacak, Sr. and Rosie Barak Bacak, was born on July 25, 1913 (second child), in West, McLennan Co., TX, and attended St. Mary's School in West, TX, Tokyo County School in McLennan Co., TX. Fall 1925 moved to Jourdanton, Atascosa Co., TX, and attended elementary school there. Inducted into the U.S. Army at Ft. Sam Houston, TX, on Feb. 25, 1942. Went into the Signal Corps AUS Co. B 439th Heavy Construction Battalion, became Chief Line Foreman. Departed for EAME on July 1, 1942, arriving there July 13, 1942. The Battalion moved to GO 33 WD 45, Algeria French Morocco, Tunisia, Sicily Naples-Foggia-Rome-Arno, Northern Rhineland Central Europe. In all this time, he came through without a scratch! Served during World War II in the European, African, and Middle Eastern Theater of Operations with Company B, 439th Signal Battalion (Heavy Construction) and attained the rank of Technical Sgt. Military awards and decorations include the BSS Medal GO 5 Hq. 9th T A C, Jan. 9, 1945, Good Conduct Medal, and American Defense Service Medal, along with the European African Middle Eastern Campaign Medal with nine Bronze Campaign Stars. Released from service on Oct. 3, 1945. Farmed with his parents after the war. Member of St. Matthew's Catholic Parish, KJT, Knights of Columbus, VFW #4853. Home of record: Jourdanton, TX.

Bacak, Ignac A., Jr., son of Ignac Bacak, Sr. and wife, Klish Bacak, was born on Feb. 13, 1917, in West, TX. Attended St. Mary's Catholic School at West. Enlisted in U.S. Army on Nov. 20, 1940, in Dallas, TX. Served during World War II as a Mortar Gunner Orderly (Cavalry), with the rank of Pfc. until his discharge on Feb. 28, 1944, at Bushnell General Hospital, Brigham City, UT. Home of record: Ennis, TX.

Bajer, Jimmie J., son of Frank Bajer, Sr. and Julie Kucera Bajer, was born on Sept. 1, 1931, in Goldson, TX. Educated at St. Mary's Catholic School, West, TX. Enlisted in the U.S. Army on July 7, 1952, at Ft. Sam Houston, TX. Assigned to the 6th Armored Division and fought in the Korean War. Medals received: Korean Service Medal w/2 bronze campaign stars, UN Service Medal, and the National Defense Service Medal. Honorably discharged Apr. 7, 1954. Home of record: Waco, TX.

Bajer, Ludwik J., son of Mr. and Mrs. Frank Bajer, West, TX. Entered U.S. Navy, 1945. Attained rank of F1/C. Served in South Pacific during WWII. Awarded Good Conduct Medal.

Balusek, Larry V., son of Mr. and Mrs. Louis V. Balusek, was born on Aug. 3, 1947, in Refugio, TX. Attended college for two years. Enlisted at Ft. Sam Houston, TX. Fought in the Tet Offensive, Viet Nam. Awards received: BSS and Good Conduct Medal. Honorably discharged June 7, 1969. Home of Record: Rockport, TX.

Balusek, Louis Victor, Sr., son of Henry Joseph Balusek, Sr. and Rosie Hubka Balusek, was born on Nov. 1, 1920, in Shiner, TX. Entered military service on Sept. 9, 1942 at Ft. Sam Houston, San Antonio, TX. Fought in the Rhineland in Central Europe. Awards include: American Theater Campaign Medal, EAME Campaign Medal with two BSS, GCM Medal, WWII Victory Ribbon, one Service Stripe, and two Overseas Service Bars. Honorably discharged Jan. 28, 1946.

Barak, Emil Anton, was born July 14, 1917. Served in U.S. Army Corps during WWII. Died Sept. 7, 1985. Buried in Waco Memorial Park Cemetery, Waco, McLennan Co., TX.

Baros, Adolph, son of John and Emilie Malina Baros, was born on Apr. 11, 1919, in Shiner, TX. Enlisted in the service in Houston, TX, and served as a Chief Radioman, Submarine Force. Discharged Dec. 23, 1945. Medals: American Theater, American Defense, and the Good Conduct Medal. Lives in Houston, TX.

Baros, Joe, son of Vinc and Apolena Micek Baros, was born on June 24, 1888, in Sweet Home, TX. First grade education. Enlisted in U.S. Army Corps on May 28, 1918, San Antonio, TX. Served with the American Expeditionary Force from Aug. 26, 1918 to May 11, 1919. Served with 64th Infantry, 14th Infantry Brigade, and 7th Division in France. Died on Dec. 6, 1973. Submitter of information: daughter, Mrs. Julius Matusek, Wharton, TX.

Barta, Charlie J., son of Mr. and Mrs. Alfred Barta, was born on Jan. 24, 1922, Gonzales Co., TX. Inducted into the U.S. Army Corps on Oct. 13, 1942, to serve his country. Fulfilled this obligation with pride and valor from Oct. 13, 1942 until Nov. 21, 1945, when he received an honorable discharge. Served in the Aleutian Islands from Nov. 1942 until Sept. 1944. Served from Dec. 1944 until Nov. 1945 in the China, Burma, and India area. Married his sweetheart, Sylvia Socah, on Oct. 7, 1944. Home of record: San Angelo, TX.

Barta, Rudolf L., son of Vinc and Theresa Niegelbauer Barta, was born in Praha, TX, on January 12, 1919. Attended school in Komensky, TX. Entered the Army on March 20, 1942. Stationed at Camp Barkley and Fort Dix. Attained rank of

Pfc. Sent to England with the 90th Division. KILLED IN ACTION in the invasion of Normandy, France, on June 16, 1944. Received the Purple Heart posthumously, and was buried in France, but later sent home to be buried with honors in the Veterans' Plot in Praha, TX, in July 1948.

Barton, Albert, son of Mr. and Mrs. Henry Barton, entered Army Air Corps in 1944. Served in England during WWII. Attained rank of S/Sgt. Awarded European Theater Ribbon w/2 Battle Stars, three Oak Leaf Clusters and Air Medal, WWII Victory Medal. Honorably discharged 1946, Waco, TX.

Barton, Alton W., son of Mr. and Mrs. Henry Barton, Waco, TX. Entered U.S. Navy in 1944. Attained rank of Lt. Served in Asiatic-Pacific Theater of Operations during WWII. Awarded Asiatic-Pacific Ribbon w/2 Battle Stars.

Barton, Aug, of West, TX, veteran of WWII.

Barton, Ben, COL 359 Infantry, WWI, born Nov. 5, 1895. Attained rank of Pfc. Died May 26, 1966. Buried in West Brethren Cemetery, West, TX.

Barton, Bennie A., son of Victor and Rosalie Barton, was born on July 11, 1916, in Port Lavaca, TX. Education: tenth grade. Enlisted in U.S. Army Corps, February 11, 1937, in Dallas, TX. C Co., 1st Infantry Regt., Ft. Frances E. Warren, WY; Ft. Sam Houston, TX. Assigned to G Co, 9th Infantry Regt. Reenlisted Feb. 14, 1940, for C Btry, 8th Field Artl. Btln., HI Dept. 1941. HHC, 19th Inf. Regt., Schoffield Barracks, Dec. 7, 1941, during Pearl Harbor attack. With C Brty, 89th Field Artillery in 1942. Asiatic-Pacific Theater of Operations. Medals: Asiatic Pacific Campaign with four BSS, Philippine Liberation with one BSS, GCM, American Defense Service with one BSS, WWII Victory, and Army of Occupation. In 1946, Occupation Duty in Germany with C Battery, 33rd Field Artillery Battalion. Assigned to HHC, 4th Armored, Ft. Hood, TX in 1954. In 1957 became active in the 4th Armd. Div. Changed location with 2nd Armd. Div., Copenhagen. 1960, 87th Ordnance Co G.S. Ft. Hood, TX. 1961, 87th Ordnance Co., ordered to Germany during Berlin Crisis. Stationed at Ansback, Germany. Retired June 20, 1962. Home of record: Killeen, TX.

Barton, Daniel A., son of Reverend and Mrs. Joseph Barton. Graduated from high school in Granger, TX. Enlisted in Army Air Corps in 1942. Trained at Daniel Field, GA, and SC. Rank: Private. Asiatic-Pacific Theater of Operations. Teletype Operator. Served in New Guinea and Leyte, Philippines, where he was in battle eight days when he was KILLED IN ACTION on November 12, 1944. Awarded Purple Heart and Presidential Citation. Buried in Granger, Williamson Co., TX.

Barton, Eddie H., of West, TX, 37th Bombardment.

Barton, Edmund J., was born Jan. 17, 1925. Served U.S. Army Corps, WWII. Rank: Pfc. Died Sept. 27, 1988. Buried West Brethren Cemetery, West, TX.

Barton, Erwin, of West, TX, WWII veteran.

Barton, Erwin W., son of Joe and Annie Pauler Barton, was born Dec. 10, 1931, in Dubina, Fayette Co., TX. Graduated from Schulenburg High School, Schulenburg, TX, and Lee College. Served in U.S. Army Corps, 1953 through 1955, both overseas and stateside. Retired as a Member of the Texas House of Representatives, where he was Chairman of Human Services Committee. Also served on the Higher Education and Liquor Regulation Committees. Married Helen Schoener in 1953. They have three daughters: Denise (Barton) Metzgar, Donna (Barton) Tarrance and Carol (Barton) Jetter, and five grandchildren. Also retired from Simpson Paper Company. Died Feb. 1, 1997. Buried in Grand View Memorial Park, Pasadena, TX.

Barton, Fred H., son of Mr. and Mrs. J. E. Barton, WWII Veteran, entered U.S. Army Corps in 1942. Served in EAME Theater of Operations. Awarded American Theater Campaign Ribbon, EAME Theater Campaign Ribbon with two BSS, and WWII Victory Ribbon, Good Conduct Medal, and five Overseas Bars. Honorably discharged 1945.

Barton, Frank John, 1CL MGBN 83rd Division. attained rank of Private, buried in St. Mary's Catholic Cemetery, West, TX.

Barton, Jerry, of West, TX, served in 143d Infantry. WWII veteran.

Barton, Jesse J. was born June 16, 1914, in Port Lavaca, TX, to Victor and Rosalie Drgac Barton. Attended school in West, TX, and at Lee College in Baytown, TX. Enlisted in the Army on March 3, 1941, in Houston, TX. Assigned to Second Armored Division, 67th Armored Regiment, with occupational specialty of Cook No. 60. While stationed in Tennessee, was badly burned when a gasoline stove exploded. Stayed in the hospital over six months. Went overseas in November 1942. Rank: TEC 4. Was in the following battles and campaigns: Tunisia, Sicily, Normandy, Northern France, Rhineland, Ardennes (Battle of the Bulge), Central Europe GO 33 WD 45. Medals received: American Defense Service, Good Conduct, and EAME Campaign with seven BSS. Discharged July 5, 1945, at Fort Sam Houston, TX. Went to work with the Exxon Refinery, Baytown, TX. Married Marie Peter of Weinert, TX, on Nov. 10, 1945. Retired from Exxon in 1972. Moved to ranch in Jacksonville, TX. In 1980, moved to Mt. Vernon, TX. One son: Freddie J. Barton, DVM, who lives in Mt. Vernon, TX. Home of record: Mt. Vernon, TX.

Barton, Lambert S., son of Mr. and Mrs. E. L. Barton, West, TX. Entered U.S. Navy, 1945. Trained in San Diego, CA. Attained rank of HA 2/C.

Barton, Raymond V., son of Mr. and Mrs. Joe Barton, Bellmead, TX. Entered U.S. Army Corps, 1939. Served in European Theater of Operations during WWII. Action in Africa and Italy. Awarded BSS w/OLC, Medical Badge, Bronze Arrowhead, Pre-Pearl Harbor Ribbon, WWII Victory Medal. Attained rank of S/Sgt. Honorably discharged 1945.

Barton, Robert L., son of Mr. and Mrs. Rudolph Barton, Abbott, TX. Entered U.S. Army Corps 1940. Assigned to EAME during WWII. Served in France. Awarded BSS, two Citations, European Theater Campaign Medal, Pre-Pearl Harbor Ribbon, and Combat Medical Badge, Good Conduct Medal. Attained rank of first Lt. prior to honorable discharge 1945.

Barton, Theodore, son of Reverend and Mrs. Joseph Barton. Attended high school in Granger, TX. Attended Texas and Southwestern Universities. Entered U.S. Army Air Corps in 1941. Trained in Texas and Washington. Rank: Lt. Served in Hawaii and Guadalcanal. Medals: Air Medal and Purple Heart. Was married. KILLED IN ACTION on February 13, 1943, in the Solomon Islands. Buried in Moravian Cemetery, Granger, Williamson Co., TX.

Barton, Willie B., born July 8, 1911, of West, TX. Served in U.S. Army Corps during WWII. Attained rank of Sfc. Died Oct. 16, 1992. Buried in St. Mary's Catholic Cemetery, West, TX.

Barton, Wilton T., son of Mr. and Mrs. John E. Barton, Waco, TX. Entered U.S. Army Corps, 1942, during WWII. Served in the Asiatic-Pacific Theater of Operations. Attained rank of Corporal. WOUNDED IN ACTION in Asiatic-Pacific Theater 1944. Medals: American Theater Campaign Ribbon, Asiatic-Pacific Campaign Ribbon with two BSS, Philippine Liberation Ribbon with one BSS, Purple Heart.

Bartos, Edward J., was born in 1918. Pilot in U.S. Army Air Corps, WWII. Died on Aug. 9, 1962. Buried at Holy Cross Catholic Cemetery, Granger, TX.

Bartos, Henry D., son of John B. and Eleanora Bezdicek Bartos, was born on December 13, 1923, Hungerford, Wharton Co., TX. Graduate of East Bernard High School in East Bernard, TX, class of 1941. Spent 1943-1944 in the Army Specialized Training Program at Indiana University, Bloomington, IN. Enlisted in U.S. Army Corps, 1943, at Ft. Sam Houston, Bexar Co., TX. Theater of Operations: EAME. Europe, France, Germany, and Luxembourg, Belgium. Battles: Normandy Invasion (landed on Omaha Beach), Battle of Ardennes Forest, Rhineland Campaign, Battle of the Bulge, Bastogne, Belgium. Attained rank of Sergeant. Recommended for Battlefield Promotion to 2nd Lieutenant. Medals: Overseas Medal, American Theater Campaign Medal, EAME Campaign Medal with three BSS, Good Conduct Medal, and BSS Medal awarded per General Orders #3, Hq. XII Corps, attached to General George Patton's Third Army. Honorably discharged November 1, 1945. Home of record: Houston, TX.

Bartos, Louis, was born in 1915. Veteran of WWII. Died in 1972. Buried at Holy Cross Catholic Cemetery in Granger, TX.

Bartos, Simon John, son of John J. and Annie Janik Bartos, was born on October 29, 1934, in East Bernard, TX. Graduated from East Bernard High School in 1953. Attended Fort Bend Business College in Rosenberg, TX, Wharton County Junior College, Wharton, TX, and Houston Community College, Houston, TX. Enlisted in the U.S. Army on March 23, 1954, in Wharton, TX. Completed basic training at Fort Bliss, TX, and advanced training in automatic weapons and supply at Fort Sill, Oklahoma, as an SP3. Honorably discharged March 23, 1956, at Fort Sill. Home of record: Rosenberg, TX.

Bartosh, Bennie A., WWII veteran. Member of American Legion Post No. 282, Granger, TX.

Bartosh, Edward Frank, son of Edmund and Amelia Stasny Bartosh, was born on Feb. 4, 1908, in Granger, Williamson Co., TX. Educated through eighth grade, Macedonia School, Granger, TX. Enlisted Feb. 16, 1942, Abilene, TX, U.S. Army Corps. Attained rank of Staff Sgt. Military Occupation: Artillery Observer. Theater of Operations: Europe. Battles: Normandy Beach. Medals: Bronze Service Arrowhead, EOT Campaign Medal and Ribbon w/BSS, WWII Victory Medal and Ribbon. Honorably discharged Nov. 15, 1945. Married Christine Albina Drozd. Civilian Occupation: Farmer. Retired in 1966. Hobbies: Fishing and playing dominoes. Member of American Legion Post No. 282, Granger, TX, Now deceased. Submitted by adopted son, Roman Stasny, Taylor, TX.

Bartosh, Edward J., son of Valentine and Phelomina Bartosh, was born in 1894 in Granger, TX. Attended school in Granger. Served in World War I. Expert craftsman of furniture making. Married Bertie Bartosh; no children. Edward did have two sisters: Marcella Bartosh and Martha Bartosh, and three brothers: Timothy, William and Emil Bartosh. Recipient of the 50 Year Gold Merit Cross From the KJT of Granger #53. Died Aug. 18, 1962. Interred in the cemetery at Durant, OK.

Bartosh, Edward V. was born on July 27, 1928, in Prince, TX. Entered service Dec. 7, 1948, in San Antonio, TX. Served as Seaman Apprentice in the Pacific Theater on the ship *APD Begor 127*. Discharged from service Aug. 8, 1949, in San Diego, CA. Home of record: Pleasanton, TX.

Bartosh, Emil Joseph, was born on Aug. 2, 1914, in Granger, TX, to Emil A. and Maria P. Parma Bartosh. Attended Sts. Cyril & Methodius Catholic School, Granger High School, and Baylor College in Waco, TX. Enlisted in the Army on Jan. 23, 1942 at Duncan Field, San Antonio, TX, as a Private. Commissioned a 2nd Lt. on Dec. 23, 1942. Theater of Operation: Southwest Pacific. Fought in Luzon Southern Philippines, Western Pacific, and New Guinea Battles. Medals include: American Theater Service, Philippine Liberation Ribbon, WWII Victory, and Asiatic Pacific Theater service with two BSS. Discharged with rank of Major on July 13, 1946, at Fort MacArthur, CA. Home of record: Granger, TX.

Bartosh, Eugene, Penelope, TX, Asiatic-Pacific Theater, WWII veteran.

Bartosh, F. J., member of American Legion Post No. 282, Granger, TX, WWII military veteran.

Bartosh, Felix, Granger, TX, WWII veteran.

Bartosh, Gilbert, U.S. Navy. Served in U.S. Armed Forces after WWII, Granger, TX.

Bartosh, James Edward, son of Timothy D. and Christine S. Stavinoha Bartosh, was born on Nov. 25, 1931, Temple, Bell Co., TX. Graduated, class of 1949, Granger High School; St. Mary's University, class of 1954. Commissioned in U.S. Army as 1st Lt. on June 15, 1954; active at Ft. Hood TX. Military Occupation: Artillery Commander. Received honorable discharge from service in June 1956. Civilian Occupation: Machine Operator (Babeco) Married Patricia Kovar. Children: James

Edward, Jr., Denise, Timothy, Jane, and Claire. Hobbies include hunting and working in his shop.

Bartosh, Jerry E., was born Sept. 19, 1928. Served in the U.S. Army Corps during Korean conflict. Attained rank of Sgt. Died July 21, 1978. Buried in St. Mary's Catholic Cemetery, West, TX.

Bartosh, Lad J., member American Legion Post No. 282, Granger, TX, WWII Veteran.

Bartosh, L. R., Jr., member American Legion Post No. 282, Granger, TX, WWII Veteran.

Bartosh, Richard Frank, son of Charles B. and Anastasia Stasny Bartosh, was born Dec. 13, 1924. Graduated from Granger High School May 1943, and Texas A&M College in College Station, Feb. 1951. Enlisted in the Navy June 8, 1943 in San Antonio. Theater of operations: American Area Campaign and the Asiatic Pacific Area. Awarded the World War II Victory Medal. Discharged May 3, 1946. Married Cornelia M. Zett; has one daughter. Home of record: Taylor, TX.

Bartosh, Robert A., son of Raymond and Bessie Bartosh, was born on Oct. 18, 1914, in Ammannsville, TX. Educated through fifth grade. Enlisted U.S. Army on Jan. 25, 1941, in San Antonio, TX. Attained rank of S/Sgt, 36th Div. Co. D, 142nd Infantry. Served in European Theater Of Operations. Battles: North Africa, Salerno, Anzio Beach, San Pietro, Cassino, Rapido River, Montelimar. Annihilated the German 19th Army. Germans were driven across Santa Marie Pass, Bosges Mountains. Fought in Naples, Foggia, Rome, Arno, Southern France, Rhineland, Central Europe, Austria, Africa. Medals: American Defense, GCM, EAME Campaign with five BSS, and Bronze Arrowhead. Honorably discharged July 31, 1945. Farmer; worked for Lone Star Brewery, San Antonio, TX, for 25 years. Married Anastasia Pawelek. Daughters: Florence and Jeanette. Son, Richard. Lives at Retana Manor Nursing Home, Jourdanton, TX.

Bartosh, Roman J., AAL, son of Edmund D. and Emillie Stasney Bartosh, was born on April 4, 1905, in Granger, Williamson Co., TX. Education: Sts. Cyril & Methodius elementary; Graduated from Granger High School, 1925. Received BA degree from University of Texas in 1929. Received an Exchange Scholarship and was an Instructor of International Education, University of Texas to University of Prague, Czechoslovakia, for one year. Travelled extensively as student tourist. Returned to University of Texas, obtained license to practice law on May 18, 1934. Joined the U.S. Army on June 17, 1942, in Taylor, Williamson Co., TX. Honorably discharged on October 3, 1942, with rank of private. Was in Citizens Military Training Camp, June 15–July 14, 1927; TX Natl. Guard, Sept. 26, 1929–Sept. 22, 1931. Married Marie T. Stiba; two children: Joseph S. and Louise. Hobbies: Hunting and fishing. Member of St. Mary's Catholic Church, Taylor, TX, Knights of Columbus, Knights of the Holy Sepulchre, Catholic Workman; KJT Lodge, American Legion, Former President of Nasinec Publishing Co., Granger, TX. Retired Sept. 1978. Died Dec. 9, 1982. Buried Taylor, Williamson Co., TX. Submitted by son, Joseph S. Bartosh, Austin, TX.

Bartosh, Timothy Daniel, son of Timothy D. and Christine Stavinoha Bartosh, was born on June 16, 1929, Temple, Bell Co., TX. Education: Granger High School, St. Mary's University, U.S. Naval Academy, 1952. Commander in U.S. Navy. Place of orders: Oceana, VA. Military Occupation: Pilot. Theater of Operations: American. Died: June 15, 1954. Buried at Arlington National Cemetery, Washington, D.C. One child: Cathy Bartosh. Submitted by James Bartosh, Taylor, TX.

Bartosh, Vladin, son of Karl and Johanna Kurecka Bartos, was born on June 29, 1894, in Ammannsville, Fayette Co., TX. Educated in Ammannsville, TX. Enlisted in U.S. Army Corps during WWI, on July 22, 1917 at La Grange, Fayette Co., TX. Assigned to Co. M. Rank: Pvt. Theater of Operations: Europe, mainly France. Reported MISSING IN ACTION in France. Married Mary Millie Kaderka. Children: Elizabeth Agnes Bartosh and Georgie Marie Bartosh. Hobbies include fishing, playing dominoes, and dancing. Civilian Occupations: farmer, grocer, wrecking yard and tavern owner.

Retired 1959. Died July 7, 1986, in Granger, Williamson Co., TX. Buried Holy Cross Cemetery.

Bartosh, Walter Lad, Sr., son of Edward and Marie Bartosh, was born on February 7, 1925, Granger, Williamson Co., TX. Education: high school and officer training–two years TCU, TX, and Tulane, LA. Enlisted 1943 in San Antonio, TX in the U.S. Navy, Hedron F.A.W. No. 14 (Personnel Office). Theater of Operations: Asiatic-Pacific. Military Occupation: Photographer. Photographic Squadron, stationed in Guam. Took pictures of invasions of Iwo Jima and Okinawa. Medals: Asiatic-Pacific Theater Campaign Ribbon with BSS, WWII Victory Ribbon. Attained rank of Yeoman 2/C prior to honorable discharge in June 1946. Civilian occupation: electric motor mechanic. Retired February 7, 1990. Married Laverne Pasemann. Children: Don, Mary, Walter Lad Jr., Tina, and Allen. Hobbies are hunting and fishing. Home of record: Austin, TX.

Bartosh, William Frank, son of William and Hermina Dubil Bartosh, was born September 19, 1922, in Granger, TX, at home. During WWII, enlisted in A.A.F. in 1942 and received an honorable discharge in 1945. Served in South Pacific, Australia, New Zealand, New Guinea. While there in his foxhole, he got word that his older sister, Edith Bartosh (who had been married only one month) died of leukemia on July 4, 1942. After his return from service, he studied dentistry at Marquette University, in Wisconsin, opening his office in Corpus Christi, TX. He is now retired. Home of record: Corpus Christi, where he resides with his wife, Ruth Ziegler Bartosh, whom he met while studying dentistry in Wisconsin.

Bartz, Logan Edward, son of Ed Frank and Nova Ella Lange Bartz, was born on July 1, 1931, in Bartlett, Bell Co., TX. Education: Graduate, Holland, TX, High School, class of 1950; Southwest Texas University, B.S. in Education, class of 1958. Enlisted March 4, 1951, U.S. Army Corps, Temple, TX. Military Occupation: Radar Technician–Mechanic, Motor Division. Theater of Operations: European. Served in Germany. Medals: Good Conduct Medal. Attained rank of Sgt. prior to honorable discharge in March 1954. Civilian Occupation: Teacher. Retired 1986. Hobbies: Tennis, fishing, traveling. Was married. Two children: Michael L. Bartz and Susan Bartz McLaughlin. Home of record: Round Rock, TX.

Bayer, Jesse S., son of Method "Mat" and Stella Simersky Bayer, was born on March 4, 1921, in Floresville, TX. Graduated Floresville High School. Enlisted US AAC, Oct. 30, 1942, San Antonio, TX; active duty Jan. 30, 1943. Graduated, Nav./ 2nd Lt, Apr. 22, 1944, Nav. School, San Marcos, TX. U.S. Air Corps, 8th AF, July 1944. 30 combat missions out of England over Germany as Sqrdn. Lead Nav. and Group Lead Nav. in the Flying Fortress (B-17) Bombers. Promoted twice in combat, achieved rank of Captain on March 30, 1945. Battles: N. France, Ardennes, Rhineland, Central Europe. Medals: DFC, Ore with four OLC, EAME Campaign w/4 BSS, WWII Victory. Qualified in Arms: .45 calibre pistol marksman. Honorably discharged on July 9, 1945 at Ft. Sam Houston, TX. Home of Record: Floresville, TX.

Bayer, Jim Anton, son of William and Lydia Blinka Bayer, was born on Feb. 16, 1920, in Deanville, TX. Educated: Dime Box High School, Dime Box, TX; Blinn Junior College, Brenham, TX. Enlisted in Marine Corps on Oct. 9, 1940, in Austin, Travis Co., TX. Promoted to Pfc. April 28, 1941, Corporal on Jan. 28, 1942, Sergeant (Org) on Aug. 5, 1943, Sergeant (Temp, Aug. 5, 1943. Weapons qualifications: Marksman (rifle), Expert (pistol). Special military qualifications: Intelligence, NCO in Foreign Service. Embarked from San Diego, CA, on June 9, 1942; disembarked at Tulagi, Solomon Islands, on Aug. 8, 1942; embarked to Pearl Harbor, T.H., Dec. 6, 1943, disembarked San Diego CA, Dec. 13, 1943. WOUNDED IN ACTION–received gunshot wound on the right side of head. Participated in the Battle of the Solomon Islands, Aug. 7–9, 1942; on Tulagi Island, Aug. 8, 1942 to Oct. 28, 1942; on Guadalcanal Island, Oct. 29, 1942 to Jan. 31, 1943. In active operations at Tarawa, Atoll, Gilbert Islands, Nov. 20, 1943. Honorably discharged on Nov. 8, 1944 at Pocatello, Idaho, upon report of medical survey for disability. Medals and Citations: Presidential Unit Citation for outstanding performance in combat (bloodiest battle in Marine Corps history) during seizure and occupation of Japanese-held atoll of Tarawa, Gilbert

Islands (spent more time on the front lines than any other Marine Regiment in its history). Presidential Unit Citation ribbon bar with two stars, American Defense Service Medal, American Campaign Medal, Asiatic Pacific Campaign Medal with three BSS, Victory Medal. Married Julia Ann Paul. Three children: Cynthia Bayer Krenek, Jimmy A. Bayer, and Don E. Bayer. Home of record: Dime Box, TX.

Beal, John Robert/see Bil, John Robert

Beal, Leroy Joseph, son of John Robert and Clara Wagner Beal, was born on July 14, 1928, in Yoakum, TX. Enlisted July 14, 1946. Served in the Korean War in the 187th Airborne RCT. Received the Korean Ribbon with three stars and the Purple Heart after being WOUNDED IN ACTION on Feb. 13, 1951. Had two combat parachute jumps. Honorably discharged Nov. 1969, as retired M/Sgt., U.S. Army Corps.

Becan, Jaromir Joseph, son of Joseph and Alouise/Aloisie Slovak Becan, was born May 2, 1918, Dallas, TX. Education: O. M. Roberts Elemementary; St. Edwards Academy, Dallas, TX; Mt. Carmel Academy, J. P. Elder and Northside High Schools, Ft. Worth, TX. Enlisted, TX Natl. Guard, member, 144th Inf, 36th Division. Attained rank of Tech 4th Radio Oper. Served in Harbor Defense, WA, OR, CA, NC. Theater of Operations: EAME, 3103rd Signal Service Btln, attained the rank of Cpl (T/4). Campaigns: Rhineland, N. France, Central Europe, Ardennes, was part of a sensational escape during this battle: Alsace. Medals: EAME Campaign Medal with four BSS, American Campaign Medal, WWII Victory Medal, GCM. Discharged, Ft. Sam Houston, TX, Sept. 7, 1945. Married Willie Mae Hejl, West, TX. Four children, eleven grandchildren. Home of record: Ft. Worth, TX.

Becan, Robert Alois, was born Apr. 18, 1927, Dallas, TX, son of Joseph H. Becan (who was born on Jan. 3, 1893, at Zalesy, Ukraine, Russia) and came to Texas with parents in 1906. Joseph's parents came from Czechoslovakia, originally. (Robert's Mother, Alouise/Aloisie Slovak, was born May 10, 1897, in Schradice, Moravia, Czechoslovakia—came to TX by herself in 1913 at age 15). Educated in Catholic and public schools in TX. Enlisted in U.S. Marine Corps, Dallas, TX. Boot Camp, Parris Island, SC; Secondary Camp, LeJuen, NC; Special Training, Camp Pendleton, CA. Theater of Operations: Asiatic Pacific. Attained rank of Cpl. Was in Guam, occupation of Japan, North China. Guam. Occ of Japan; North China. Refurbished Jeeps in San Francisco, CA, Warehouse in Barstow, CA, guarded ammo depot in OK. Medals: Asiatic-Pacific Campaign, Japanese Occupation, China Service, WWII Victory, GCT III-96, MATT I-131. Honorably discharged May 10, 1949. Married Bernice Bordovsky on Oct. 26, 1948, in La Grange, TX; one daughter and nine grandchildren. Worked with the Boy Scouts of America for over 15 years. Retired from GM, Arlington, TX, after 37 years. Loves camping in the woods. Home of record: Ft. Worth, TX.

Becker, Oscar J. was born on Nov. 18, 1910, in Crosby, TX, to John Aug and Rosie Kristinek Becker. Attended grade school in the Crosby area. Joined the Army in Houston, TX. Was a machine gunner 605 in the Northern Solomons, Southern Philippines. Received an Asiatic-Pacific Campaign Medal with two BSS, Good Conduct, Philippine Liberation Medal with one BSS, four Overseas Service Bars, and the Victory Medal. Discharged Nov. 15, 1945. Died Jan. 1, 1974.

Bednar, Charles Vincent, son of Vincent and Emily Anna Bednar, was born Dec. 19, 1920, in Houston, Harris Co., TX. Graduated from the University of Houston, 1943. Enlisted in the Army Medical Corps on Feb. 12, 1943, Houston, TX. Theater of Operations: ETO, 28 Medical Laboratory, 3 Medical Laboratory—Pacific Theater of Operations. Engaged in battles in Germany, the Rhineland. Medals: GCM, American Campaign, WWII Victory Medal, ETO with battle star for Rhineland, Asiatic-Pacific Campaign, Army of Occupation with clasp for Germany and clasp for Japan. Honorably discharged June 1946. Home of record: Houston, TX.

Bednarek, Frank, son of Frank D. and Agnes M. Kossa Bednarek, was born on Nov. 21, 1912, in Fayette Co., TX. Grade school: Engle, TX. High school: Schulenburg, TX. Graduated from TX A&M in 1935. Commissioned a 2nd Lt. in U.S. Army Corps Reserve. Began active duty in May 1941. Attained rank of Colonel. Received regular army commission in 1945. Was on active duty until January 1968. Served in S.W. Pacific (New Guinea and Philippines) Theater of Operations. Post War assignments: Staff Officer, Office of Asst. Chief of Staff G4; Dept. of Army and Office of Asst. Secretary of Defense (Supply and Logistics), Washington, D.C. Other duties: Service with U.S. Naval forces in London, England. Headquarters, 8th U.S. Army and United Nations Command, Korea. Medals include: BSS and Legion of Merit, Asiatic-Pacific Campaign Medal, Army of Occupation Medal (Japan), National Defense Service Medal. Retired from active duty in January,1968. With the University of Maryland for approximately ten years. Frank and Irene Bednarek have four children. Home of record: Alexandria, VA. This submission was by Colonel Frank Bednarek, through encouragement from his sister, Mary Bednarek Pederson of Houston, TX.

Bedrich, Jerry Lee, son of Frank J. and Theresa Bedrich, was born on Nov. 30, 1922, in Temple, Bell Co., TX. Educated at Casey Grade School. Enlisted in U.S. Army Corps on January 14, 1943 at Ft. Sam Houston, TX. Theater of Operations: EAME. Fought in Africa and Italy. Medals: WWII Victory Medal, Atlantic Medal, Good Conduct Medal, EAME Campaign Medal with BSS, Marksman Pistol, Rifle Badge. Attained rank of Sgt. prior to receiving honorable discharge on March 1, 1946. Married Jeanette; three children. Civilian Occupation: Farmer. Worked at Used Tractor Dealer Co. Owner of David B. Auction Service. Collector of antique "one-row" farm tools. Home of record: Temple, TX.

Belota, C. J. "Clement," son of Mr. and Mrs. John Belota of Plum, TX. Attended Plum High School. Entered the Army in 1942; trained in California. Served in New Guinea and Philippines as a Sergeant. Awarded GCM and AD Ribbons. Discharged in 1945. Married Lydia Evanicky.

Belota, Fred A., son of Mr. and Mrs. John Belota of Plum, TX. Attended La Grange High School. Entered the Army in 1941; trained in New Jersey and California. Served in Australia and New Guinea as a T/4. Awarded AP, AD Ribbons, and GCM with 1 Battle Star. Discharged in 1945.

Belota, Leonard L., son of Mr. and Mrs. Louis Belota, was born on Dec. 25, 1920, in La Grange, TX. Educated at Mt. Carmel and Diamond Hill High Schools. Enlisted in U.S. Army Corps in July 1939 at Dallas, TX. Theater of Operations: Asiatic-Pacific, July 1939; USA, Nov. 9, 1941; Asiatic Pacific, June 8, 1942; USA, Nov. 11, 1943; Asiatic Pacific Nov. 30, 1943. Medals: GCM, American Defense Service Medal, Asiatic Pacific Campaign Medal, EAME with one BSS. Attained rank of Corporal with Coast Artillery. Served six years in the Philippines, Alaska, and European theater. Returned home to wife, Agnes, in Ft. Worth in 1945. Submitted by James Belota of Arlington, TX.

Belunek, Joe A., son of Michael and Josephine Vesely Belunek, was born on Jan. 20, 1921, in Frydek, Austin Co., TX. Graduated from Sealy High School in Sealy, TX. Enlisted in the service on Sept. 29, 1942, in Houston, TX. Military Occupation: Medic (103rd Medical Battalion). Theater of Operations: EAME. From July 23, 1944, to May 9, 1945, he was in Normandy, Northern France, Belgium, Luxembourg and Germany. The remainder of time was served in Central Europe; Rhineland, Ardennes, Normandy, Northern France. Medals: EAME Campaign Medal with five BSS, Good Conduct Medal, WWII Victory Medal. Honorably discharged Sept. 18, 1945. Name is listed on the monument which was erected by St. Mary's Catholic Parish in Frydek, TX in honor of 75 men who valiantly served their country during WWII from 1941–1945, who were all parishioners of the church, and who all returned safely from the war. Civilian Occupation: Merchant, Rancher, Farmer. No wife listed, though he had one daughter, Janice Ann Belunek Roberts. Hobby was ranching. Died Oct. 10, 1976, in Frydek, Austin Co., TX. Submitted by Annie Pavlicek of Sealy, TX.

Beran, Anton Andrew, was born on Nov. 30, 1914, in Fayetteville, TX to Anton Beran and Louisa Pavlicek Beran. He enlisted in the Army and served as a Cannoneer 845 in the Rhineland, Central Europe, Northern France, and Normandy. Private First Class Beran received the EAME Campaign medal with four BSS and the Good Conduct medal. He was discharged from the service on Oct. 11, 1945, at Maxey, TX. He died on September 2, 1967 and is buried at St. John's Catholic Cemetery in Fayetteville, TX.

Beran, Bettie Barbara, daughter of Joe Lee and Bessie Pivonka Beran, was born in Caldwell, TX on Sept. 3, 1919. Attended Red Hallow School in Caldwell, Caldwell High School, and Providence Hospital School of Nursing in Waco, TX. Joined the Navy Nurse Corps in Corpus at Corpus Christi, TX. Rank: Ensign. During WWII, served in the following locations: U.S. Naval Hospital, Long Beach, CA, U.S.N. Special Hospital, CA, U.S. Naval Hospital, Corpus Christi, TX. Honorably discharged Jan. 20, 1946.

Beran, Frank Herny, Jr., son of Frank Beran, Sr. and Louise Petrash Beran, was born on Sept. 5, 1922, in East Bernard, TX. Educated at East Bernard schools. During WWII, enlisted at San Diego, CA. Attained rank of Corporal. Theater of Operations: China, Burma, India. Was a truck driver and chauffeur for VIP dignitaries. Medals and Awards received: Asiatic Pacific Service Medal, BSS, GCM Medal and Clasp, UD Medal. Honorably discharged Oct. 1945. Died Feb. 9, 1976. Buried with full military honors on Feb. 12, 1976, at Mt. Olivet Cemetery, Dickinson, TX.

Beran, Frank Herny, III, "Frankie," son of Frank Herny Beran, Jr. and Georgia Kolenovsky Beran, was born on March 11, 1947, in East Bernard, TX. Educated: Holy Cross Catholic Elementary School, East Bernard. Kirwin High School, Galveston, TX. Enlisted in U.S. Marine Corps at Camp Pendleton, San Diego, CA. Theater of Operation: Viet Nam, Co K, 34th Bn, 8th Marine Regt., 3rd Marine Division. Battles fought: Quang Tri Province, West of Dong Ha, S. Viet Nam. Medals received: Rifle Sharpshooter, Service Medal, Good Conduct Medal. Fought in areas of Hills, Battlefields of Viet Nam. On May 20, 1967, was assigned Assistant Machine Gunner, Weapons Platoon of Company K. Was in Operation Hickory on that fateful day. His family received the message KILLED IN ACTION on June 5, 1967. Received full military honors at burial in Mt. Olivet Cemetery in Dickinson, TX. Information submitted by Gold Star Mother, Georgia Kolenovsky Beran. Home of record: Galveston, TX.

Beran, L. Walter, held rank of Lt., Granger, TX, WWII Veteran.

Beseda, Chad Christopher, son of Larry and Twyla Nicholson Beseda, was born on March 23, 1970, Levelland, Hockley Co., TX. Graduated from Whiteface High School in Whiteface, TX, in 1988. Enlisted in Amarillo, Deaf Smith, TX. Attained rank of E-3. Theater of Operations: Desert Storm. Stationed at Charleston, SC, and Ft. Hood, GA. Received two medals. Honorably discharged Jan. 30, 1992. Married Jill Tallent. Children: Kelsei and Chase. Employed with Beseda Grain Co., Whiteface, TX. Home of record: Whiteface, TX.

Beseda, David Todd, son of Larry Beseda and Twyla Nicholson, was born Sept. 3, 1965, Levelland, Hockley Co., TX. Graduated from Whiteface High School in Whiteface, TX. Enlisted in military service, Amarillo, Deaf Smith Co., TX. Attained rank of E-4. Theater of Operations: Desert Storm. Stationed in Las Vegas, NV and Saudi Arabia. Received four medals. Honorably discharged Jan. 25, 1992. Employed by Beseda Grain Company. Home of record: Whiteface, TX.

Beseda, Frank Edward, born Aug. 18, 1903. Served in the U.S. Navy. Attained rank of Seaman 2nd/C. Died Sept. 14, 1989. Buried in St. Mary's Catholic Cemetery, West, TX.

Beseda, James Ray, son of Joseph Henry Beseda and Mollie Ruzicka, was born on May 1, 1945, Dallas, Dallas Co., TX. Graduate of Morton High School, Morton, TX in 1963. Received BBA in Accounting in 1967 from Texas Tech University, Lubbock, TX. Enlisted in the U.S. Navy at Albuquerque, NM as a commissioned officer, Lt. Jr. Grade. Theater of Operations: Viet Nam. Received the Viet Nam Service Medal and two others. Was serving in North Korea, when the USS *Pueblo* was seized. Served on an Oil Tanker (USS *Caliente*). Honorably discharged July 31, 1970. Married Jane Stewart. Employed with U.S. Customs. Home of record: Playa Del Rey, CA.

Beseda, John Frank, Jr., son of John Frank Beseda, Sr. and Sophie Makovy Beseda, was born on Aug. 27, 1919, in Abbott, Hill Co., TX. Educated in Brookin schools. Enlisted in the U.S. Army Air Corps during WWII. Johnie was a tail-gunner on a B-24 Bomber. His plane was a lead plane when it was hit by a German ME-109 Fighter over enemy territory. He was captured on April 22, 1944, and held at Stalag XVII-B, BK 38B, as a PRISONER OF WAR until the end of the war on May 3, 1945. Medals: Received Air Medal with two OLC, Prisoner of War Medal, EAME Campaign Medal, and WWII Victory Medal. Attained rank of Staff Sgt. Died on March 9, 1963. Buried in Abbott, Hill, TX.

Beseda, Maitland, of West, TX. Military veteran.

Beyer, Westin Edwin "Sonny," son of Edwin R. Beyer and Claudia Ann Brunner, was born on October 31, 1932, in Schwertner, Williamson Co., TX. Educated at Holy Trinity Catholic School, three years; Schwertner Elementary, five years. Graduate of Bartlett High School, Bartlett, TX, in 1949. Enlisted U.S. Army Corps on March 17, 1953 at San Antonio, TX, during Korean War. Military Occupation: Missile Specialist–Radar. Stationed at White Sands, NM. Medals: National Defense and Good Conduct. Attained rank of Corporal. Honorably Discharged. Civilian Occupation: Electronics. Retired 1985. Married Patricia Ann Urbanek. Children: Kathy, Susan, Sherry. Home of record: Austin, TX.

Bezdek, Eddie, of West TX. Stationed in FL. Military veteran.

Bezdek, Louis J., Jr., son of Louis J. Bezdek, Sr. and Mary Soukup Bezdek, was born on Jan. 9, 1936, at 400 S. Washington St., West, TX. Educated at St. Mary's Catholic School, West, TX, from 1942–1950. Attended West High School from 1950–1954. Attended 4 C College in Waco, TX from 1955–1956. Enlisted in the U.S. Army Corps in 1957 at Dallas, TX. Basic Training in Infantry at Ft. Chaffee, AR., Signal Corps, Ft. Gordon, GA, 3rd Missile Battalion, 57th Artillery, Ft. MacArthur, CA. Honorably discharged Aug. 2, 1961.

Bezdek, Louis Joseph, Sr., son of Joseph Frank Bezdek, Sr. and Marie Sulak Bezdek, was born on February 28, 1897, in Cottonwood, McLennan Co., TX. Educated at West Elementary School, West, TX, St. Mary's Parochial School, La Porte, TX, St. Mary's Seminary, La Porte, TX, Toby's

Practical Business College, Waco, TX, 4-C College, Waco, McLennan Co., TX. Enlisted March 27, 1917, at Waco, TX, U.S. Army Corps, during WWI. Theater of Operations: Europe–2nd Army Infantry Division. Rank: Cpl. Assigned to Co. B, 9th Infantry, U.S. Reg. A, 2nd Civ. 1. Served in Eastern France. Battles: Chateau Therry, St. Mihiel, Meusse Argonne, Aisne Marne, Belleauwood. Received Silver Star, Purple Heart, and Victory Medal Aesne Marne, St. Michael, and Meuse Argonne. Suffered shrapnel wounds from machine gun fire and bayonet wounds on Oct. 4, 1918, at Belleau Wood. Honorably discharged April 17, 1919, at Camp Bowie, TX. Disabled veteran, medical disabilities. Served as Commander and Service Officer in the American Legion, West Post. Provided vital assistance and guidance to countless veterans in the local area. Married Mary Soukup of West, TX. Children: Louis Joseph Bezdek, Jr. and Willie Mae Bezdek Hutyra. Died Feb. 20, 1988, at Temple VA Hospital in Temple, TX. Buried in St. Mary's Catholic Cemetery, West, TX, American Legion Honor Guard. Organizations: West-American Legion Post #478; Veterans of Foreign Wars #4819; Waco–Disabled American Veterans. Last home of record: West, TX. Submitted by Willie Mae Bezdek Hutyra of Ft. Worth, TX.

Bigon, Josef "Joe" E., Jr., son of Josef E. Bigon Sr. and Regina Jelesnansky (of Lidicku, Austria) was born on Feb. 3, 1891, in Lidicku, Austria (naturalized citizen). Served in the U.S. Army Corps during WWI. Married Martha M. Bartosh (daughter of Valentine Bartosh and Filomena Vacek of Granger), at Sts. Cyril & Methodius Catholic Church. In 1928, proprietor of a Temple, TX, bakery on N. Main St. Was a TB patient in Thompson's Sanatarium, Kerrville, TX, Veteran's Hospital #93, and several other places. After seven and a half years of illness, died at home in Granger, TX, on Oct. 27, 1937. Buried with military honors at Holy Cross Catholic Cemetery in Granger, TX. Martha died on March 3, 1946, at the State Hospital in Austin, TX, and is buried next to Josef.

Bil, John Robert (John Robert Beal), son of Joseph Frank Bil and Rosa Paprs, was born at Val Mezerici, Moravia, May 11, 1891. Inducted into military service on July 25, 1918, at Columbus, TX. Served with the American Expeditionary Force in France. Honorably discharged at Camp Bowie, TX, on Feb. 25, 1919. Married Clara Wagner. Died Oct. 20, 1963.

Bilek, Emil Frank, son of Emil W. Bilek and Frances Stokr Bilek, was born on July 24, 1921, in El Campo, Wharton Co., TX. Inducted into military service during WWII on Feb. 5, 1943, in Houston, TX. Theater of Operation: China, Burma, India. Medals: American Theater Campaign Ribbon, Asiatic Pacific Campaign Ribbon with one BSS, Good Conduct Medal, WWII Victory Ribbon, one Service Stripe, one Overseas Service stripe, one Overseas Service Bar. Never Wounded!! Honorably discharged March 15, 1946. Home of record: El Campo, TX.

Bilek, Emil W., son of John Bilek and Marie Lizicar Bilek, was born on Nov. 17, 1892, in Dubina, TX. Served in WWI. Inducted into military service on July 24, 1918, at Camp Travis, TX. Received no wounds. Honorably discharged Feb. 24, 1919. Died Sept. 4, 1967. Buried in St. John Catholic Cemetery, Taiton, TX.

Bily, Jerry Allen, son of Miroslav Bily and Elizabeth Agnes "Alice" Bartosh, was born on Dec. 6, 1947, in Houston, Harris Co., TX. Educated at Browning Elementary, 1954–59, Hogg Jr. High, 1959–62, Reagan High, 1962–66, University of Texas, 1966–70. Enlisted in U.S. Army Corps on Oct. 18, 1970,

in Houston, TX. Military Occupation: Finance Specialist. Theater of Operations: American. Honorably discharged March 1972. Rank: Sergeant. Married Deborah Jane Horsley. Children: Mike Bruce Olbrich Bily; Lindsey Leigh Bily; Erin Elaine Bily. Hobbies: Hunting, fishing, reading, and gardening. Home of record: Sugarland, TX. Submitted by Elizabeth Agnes (Alice) Bartosh Bily.

Bily, John Eugene, son of Miroslav Bily and Elizabeth Agnes "Alice" Bartosh, was born on March 12, 1944, in Orange, TX. Educated at Browning Elementary, 1949-1956, Hogg Jr. High, 1956-1959, Reagan High, 1959-1963. Some college in service. Graduated from University of Houston in 1970. Enlisted, Houston, Harris Co., TX, on March 1, 1964, in U.S. Air Force. Attained rank of Sgt. Theater of Operations: S.E. Asia. Honorably discharged Dec. 21, 1967. Married Melinda Michalle Sour Bily. Children: Daniel Miroslav, Devin Richard, John Austin, Guy Hunter. Hobbies: Hunting, scuba diving, fishing and traveling. Civilian occupation: Home Builder. Home of record: Bellaire, TX. Submitted by Elizabeth A. Bily.

Biskup, Alfred Joe, son of Will Biskup and Ida Ondrej Biskup, was born on Dec. 21, 1919 at Cameron, TX. Attended both Catholic and public elementary schools and Yoe High School in Cameron, TX. Enlisted in the U.S. Army on Oct. 14, 1939, at Ft. Sam Houston, TX. Served in the European, African, and Middle Eastern Theater of Operations as a U.S. Army Medical Corpsman in the 3rd Medical Battalion in WWII. Attained the rank of Technical Corporal. Served in the European, African, and Middle-Eastern Theater of Operations for two and a half years and participated in the Algeria-French Morocco, Tunisia, Sicily, Naples-Foggia, Anzio, Rome-Arno, Southern France, Rhineland, and Central Europe campaigns. Awards and decorations include the American Defense Service Medal, European African Middle Eastern Campaign Medal with eight campaign stars and one arrowhead, Good Conduct Medal, World War II Victory Medal, Distinguished Unit Badge, and the French Croix de la Guerre with Palm. Discharged July 27, 1945, at Ft. Sam Houston, TX. Was living and working in Galveston, TX, at the time of the Texas city disaster. Volunteered and assisted in the evacuation of patients from Texas City to medical facilities in Galveston, TX. Married Mary Josephine Pinkman of Wichita Falls, TX, on June 16, 1946, at Cameron, TX. Children: Ida Mary, Ruth, Kitty Jo, Agnes Ann, Alfred Joe, Jr. Biskup. In the late 1940s, went to work with uncle and two cousins in the plumbing business in Wichita Falls, until retirement. A long time resident of Wichita Falls. Died May 1, 1994. Interred at Crestview Memorial Park in Wichita Falls, TX.

Biskup, Emil, son of Fred and Rosie Biskup, was born on Aug. 16, 1913, in Cameron, TX, and attended Yoe High School at Cameron, TX. Inducted into the U.S. Army at Camp Wolters, TX on March 21, 1942 during WWII. Served as a Squad Leader in the 213th Replacement Company, 11th Replacement Depot, Indio, CA. Attained rank of Sgt. Honorably discharged Nov. 25, 1943, at Indio, CA. Lived in Cameron, TX, and worked as a carpenter until death on Feb. 26, 1979 at the Veterans Administration Hospital in Temple, TX.

Biskup, Robert L., son of Will and Ida Biskup, was born Sept. 16, 1934, Cameron, TX. Attended Texas A&M, where he received a ROTC commission of 2nd Lt., May 23, 1958; went to active duty station at Ft. Benning, GA, Oct. 11, 1958. Involved in four campaigns in Viet Nam. After 26 years of active duty in the grade of LTC, Robert retired July 1, 1984. Medals: Army Commendation w/1 OLC, Meritorious Service with three OLC, Joint Service Commendation, Bronze Star with one OLC, National Defense Service, Viet Nam Service, Viet Nam Campaign, Overseas Service Medal, and Army Service Ribbon. Married Marie Josephine Rochen on June 27, 1959, Frydek, TX. Lives in San Antonio, TX. Children: Theresa Marie Biskup Engelstad, Robert Laurence Biskup, and Bruce Allen Biskup.

Biskup, Robert Lawrence, son of Robert Lee and Marie Josephine Rochen Biskup, was born on May 14, 1963, in Verdun, France. During his father's military service, he attended schools in TX, NC, KS, VA, GA, and MD, and overseas in Iran. Graduated from Cole High School at Ft. Sam Houston, TX in 1981. Attended the U.S. Military

Academy at West Point, New York and was commissioned as a Second Lieutenant in the Corps of Engineers upon his graduation in 1985. Served in overseas assignments in Korea and Kuwait. Stateside assignments included Ft. Hood, TX, Ft. Carson, CO, Ft. Leonard Wood, MO. Separated from the military service in July 1994 with the grade of Captain and is in the U.S. Army Active Reserves. Married Debra Gail Hixon. One son: Joel Brandon Biskup. Pursuing career in civil engineering and is a construction project engineer. He is an avid collector of model cars, enjoys tinkering with automobiles, and is active in outdoor activities specifically, skiing. Last known home of record was Colorado Springs, CO.

Blaha, Daniel T., son of Mr. and Mrs. J. F. Blaha, was born in TX. Educated at Granger High School. Enlisted in USMC in 1943. Completed basic training in San Diego, CA. Theater of Operations: American. Attained rank of Sgt.

Blaha, Jodie T., son of Mr. and Mrs. Walter J. Blaha, Granger, TX. Attended Granger High School. Enlisted U.S. Army Corps, 1944; basic training at Camp Hood. Theater of Operations: Asiatic-Pacific. Campaigns in Saipan, Okinawa and Philippines. Medals: Combat Badge, APO, BSS, Philippine Liberation Medal, Good Conduct Medal and WWII Victory Ribbons. Attained rank of Pfc. Home of record: Granger, TX

Blaha, Raymond T., son of Mr. and Mrs. J. F. Blaha, of Granger, TX. Educated at Granger High School. Enlisted in U.S. Army Corps in 1945. Basic training at Camp Fannin and at Ft. Benning, GA. Theater of Operations: American. Attained rank of Pfc.

Blaha, William Daniel, born May 8, 1912. Served country valiantly during WWII. Attained rank of Tech/Sgt, U.S. Army Corps. Died Aug. 23, 1980. Buried in West Brethren Cemetery, West, TX.

Blahuta, Alvin H., son of Mr. and Mrs. Alois Blahuta, West, TX, was born July 8, 1919, West, TX. Joined U.S. Army Corps in 1937. After two years, received honorable discharge. Joined the U.S. Marine Corps in 1939. Assigned as guard at U.S. Embassy in Peking, China. At that time, Japan already controlled China, and soon after the bombing of Pearl Harbor on Dec. 7, 1941, the Japanese surrounded the U.S. Embassy and captured the 150 Marines. Blahuta was a PRISONER OF WAR for about four years. He stayed out of the Marines for two and a half years, then reenlisted and completed his 20 years of service in 1960. Awarded a POW Service Medal. Mr. Blahuta did not want to go into detail on the Marines' treatment in the prison camp; he did say it was "total brutality," from the first day to the last. Toward the end of the war, their meals consisted of seaweed and kelp. The Japanese captors delighted in marching prisoners of war through the streets to the ridicule of those watching. On May 29, 1988, he was honored in his home town, West, TX, when he received the Prisoner of War Medal. West Mayor, William F. Pareya, proclaimed the day as "Alvin Blahuta Day." Attained the rank of Master Sgt. prior to his retirement.

Blahuta, Charles A., son of Charles A. Blahuta, Sr. (1886–1974) and Louise Picha Blahuta (1893–1966), was born on May 29, 1931, West, TX. Enlisted in the U.S. Marine Corps on June 24, 1949. Served in the Infantry. WOUNDED IN ACTION on Sept. 13, 1951, and was awarded a Purple Heart. Honorably discharged April 4, 1952. Home of record: West, TX.

Blahuta, George, West, TX. WWII PRISONER OF WAR.

Blahuta, Joseph E., son of Joe and Maria Chromack Blahuta, was born on Sept. 22, 1891, at Moravia, Lavaca Co., TX. Attended elementary school in Moravia, TX. Enlisted during WWI and served as a member of Company M, 143rd Infantry. Attained the rank of Corporal. Served with the American Expeditionary Forces in France from July 11, 1918 to May 31, 1919. Participated in the Meuse-Argonne Campaign. Discharged June 14, 1919, at Camp Bowie, TX. Married Justine Motal, daughter of Thomas and Frances Motal, in 1917. Children: three daughters and a son. Farmed at Moravia and Ganado, TX. Preceded in death by his wife, Justine. Subsequently married Lillie Matula, widow, in 1948. Died March 19, 1969, at Ganado, TX.

Blazek, Frank Joseph, son of Louis L. and Rosa Huschke Blazek, was born on March 14, 1931, in Ennis, TX. Graduated from Southmayd High School, Southmayd, TX. Enlisted in U.S. Army Corps and went through basic training in El Paso, TX. Stationed at Ft. Mead, MD,

and at Ft. Dix, NJ, with guided missile unit to track radar and guard coasts. Served in Korean War, received Sharp Shooter and Good Conduct Medals. Honorably discharged Dec. 6, 1955, Ft. Meade, MD. Rank: Corporal. Home of record: Ennis, TX.

Blazek, George T., son of Henry and Frances Blazek, was born on April 1, 1909, in Smetana, Brazos Co., TX. Graduated from Bryan High in 1927. Attended TX A&M. Enlisted in the US Army Corps on March 6, 1942, at Ft. Sam Houston, TX. Had three hundred days combat duty with the 5th Army, 88th Infantry, "Blue Devil" Division, Italy. Medals: EAME Campaign with three Battle Stars, Combat Inf. Badge, Purple Heart, BSS. Honorably discharged Jan. 11, 1946. Married Dorothy Mae Reif of San Antonio, TX. Member of St. Joseph Catholic Church. Home of record: Bryan, TX.

Blazek, Lawrence J., son of Laddie J. Blazek and Annie J. Pilcik, was born on Aug. 9, 1929, in Nelsonville, Austin Co., TX. Educated at Nelsonville, Bellville High Schools, Blinn College, Sam Houston State, University of Houston. Enlisted in U.S. Air Force on July 17, 1947, at Houston, TX. Attained rank of Staff Sgt. Military Occupation: Motor Vehicle Sgt. Theater of Operations: American. Stationed at Fairbanks, AK. In 1951, during the Korean War, Russian planes entered Alaskan Air Space, and Staff Sgt. Blazek was alerted for active combat duty. The incident was quietly resolved. Honorably discharged July 16, 1952. Married Irene A. Sodolak. Children: Debbie K. Blazek, Larry W. Blazek, Michael C. Blazek, and Pat A. Blazek. Civilian Occupation: Ranching, Service manager of a Ford dealership. Earned Ford Medallion Manager Award in 1984, 1985, and 1986. Hobbies: Fishing and hunting. Home of record: Sealy, TX.

Blinka, Adolf, member of SPJST Lodge 20, Granger, TX. Served in U.S. Armed Forces during WWI, 1917–1918.

Bludau, Joseph Bernard, Jr., son of Joseph Bernard Bludau, Sr. and Bernadina Grahinaim Bludau, was born on Nov. 3, 1915, in Hallettsville, TX. Inducted into service Feb. 13, 1945, at Fort Sam Houston, TX. Rank: S/Sgt. Served in the Asiatic-Pacific as a Supply Clerk with the 759th Engineer Parts Supply Company. Separated from service July 3, 1946. Medals: Asiatic-Pacific Campaign Ribbon, Good Conduct Medal, Victory Ribbon, one Overseas Service Bar. Died Sept. 24, 1974. Buried in Sacred Heart Cemetery, Hallettsville, TX.

Bludau, Joseph Bernard, III, son of Joseph Bernard Bludau, Jr. and Alice Margaret Sobotik Bludau, was born on March 12, 1946, in Hallettsville, TX. Education: high school, Electronics Technical School, and Texas A&M. Earned a BS degree in Animal Science. Was a Corporal in the Marine Corps in 1967 and transferred to Marine Corps Reserve on June 30, 1968, with Hq. Co, 9th MAB. Terminal date of reserve was July 4, 1972. Medals: National Defense Service Medal, Viet Nam Service Medal with one Star. Home of record: Hallettsville, TX.

Bogar, Louis, son of John Bogar and Anna Kutra, was born on June 3, 1931, in Sealy, Austin Co., TX. Attended Sealy High School, Sealy, TX, through the 11th grade. Received GED in 1952. Enlisted in U.S. Navy on July 12, 1948, at San Diego, CA. Military Occupation: Machinist Engine Room Throttle Man, mine sweeping. Served on the USS *Carmick* (DMS 33). Was in the Korean War for 13 months. Medals: Korean Conflict Medal, European Theater Medal, Good Conduct Medal. Married (1) Dorothy Mixon (deceased); married (2) Jean West; adopted girls, Theresa Bogar Burton and Belinda Bogar Ladas. Hobby is fishing. Retired in June 1993. Served 1948–1952, in U.S. Navy. Home of record: Ponte Verda Beach, FL.

Bogar, William Thomas, son of Paul Frank Bogar and Mary Annie Gavranovic, was born on Dec. 7, 1924, in Frydek, Austin Co., TX. Enlisted on July 26, 1943. Theater of Operations: EAME. Fought at Normandy, Northern France; Ardennes, Rhineland, Central Europe (Plizen, Czechoslovakia). Medals: EAME Campaign Ribbon with five

BSS, Good Conduct Medal, two Overseas Service Bars; WWII Victory Ribbon. Honorably discharged Nov. 8, 1945. Married Henrietta Mary Rohan on April 22, 1946. Children: Jacqualyn Bogar Stewart, Francis "Skip" Bogar, and Marilyn Bogar Zaskoda. Civilian Occupation: County Clerk, Austin Co., TX. 4th Degree Knights of Columbus. Name is on a monument which was erected because the prayers of the parishioners were fulfilled, as the 75 men who were members of St. Mary's Catholic Parish, Frydek, TX, returned home from honorably serving their country during WWII, 1941–1945. Home of record: Bellville, TX.

Bohac, A. L., of Bartlett, TX. WWII veteran. Member of American Legion Post No. 282.

Bohac, Albert C., of West, TX, served in the U.S. Army Corps, 434th Infantry, during WWII. Theater of Operations: Asiatic-Pacific.

Bohac, Albin N., son of John F. Bohac and Alosie Naizer Bohac, was born on Dec. 11, 1921. Attended Sts. Cyril & Methodius School in Granger, TX, and Granger High School. Enlisted in the U.S. Army Air Corps at Ft. Sam Houston, TX, on July 14, 1942, during WWII. Attained rank of Corporal before separation from service on Dec. 22, 1943. Was a farmer until his retirement in 1988. Married Agnes Hajda. Member of American Legion Post No. 282. Last known home of record: Granger, TX.

Bohac, Aug, son of Joseph and Mary Hajda Bohac, was born on Sept. 6, 1896, in Skidmore, TX. Received an eighth grade education. Enlisted in the army on Sept. 5, 1918, at Camp Travis, San Antonio, Bexar Co., TX, during WWI. Rank: Private. Assigned to the European Theater of Operations, fighting with the American Expeditionary Forces in Germany and France. Honorably discharged Nov. 26, 1918. Died on Aug. 24, 1961, in Skidmore, TX. Survived by widow, Georgia Bohac, whose home of record is Skidmore, TX.

Bohac, Charles James "Chuck," son of James and Mary Bohac, was born on Jan. 28, 1923, Schuyler, NE. Educated at Kimball High School, NE. Attended Blinn College, Brenham, TX. Enlisted in U.S. Army Corps, Ft. Warren, WY. Rank: Pfc. Theater of Operations: Asiatic-Pacific. Fought in battles at New Guinea, Leyte. Medals: APTC Ribbon with two BSS, Purple Heart, Parachute Wings, Expert Infantry Badge, GCM. WOUNDED IN ACTION on Dec. 15, 1944 on Mahonag Island. Honorably discharged Sept. 8, 1945. Died Oct. 3, 1993.

Bohac, Edmund, Jr., son of Mr. and Mrs. Edmund Bohac, Sr., was born in 1889. WWI veteran. Died in 1970. Buried in Holy Cross Catholic Cemetery, Granger, TX.

Bohac, Joe J., of Bartlett, TX. WWII veteran. Member of American Legion Post No. 282.

Bohac, Johnnie F., of Bartlett, TX. WWII veteran. Member of American Legion Post No. 282.

Bohac, Josef John, son of Joe N. Bohac and Olga Cervenka, was born on March 30, 1930, Granger, TX. Member of Sts. Cyril & Methodius Catholic Church, Granger, TX. Attended Sts. Cyril & Methodius Elementary School for eight years. Graduate of Granger Public High School. Enlisted in U.S. Army, at Georgetown, TX, and received basic training at Ft. Riley, Kansas. Stationed overseas in Germany. Rank: Pvt. Married with six children and two grandchildren. Farmed in Granger, TX, and is presently farming in Bartlett, TX. Member of KJT Lodge, American Legion, RVOS. Home of record: Bartlett, TX.

Bohuslav, Robert V., son of Tom F. and Mary Migl Bohuslav, was born on Oct. 18, 1922, in Komensky, TX. Attended Komensky School and worked on the family ranch in West, TX. Entered the Army Infantry at Fort Sam Houston and received training at Camp Wolters. Rank: Pfc. Sent to North Africa, landing in Posteum, Italy, serving in the 5th Army, 36th Infantry Division where he manned a Bazooka gun. The division, made up of TX military men, fought at the battle of Cassino. KILLED IN ACTION on Feb. 3, 1944. Received two Purple Hearts among other awards. Buried in the Praha Cemetery. Submitted with love by his sister, Elsie Bohuslav Darilek of Texas City, TX.

Bordovsky, Adolf D., son of Mr. and Mrs. A. Bordovsky, Mart, TX, entered U.S. Army Corps, 1932. Served in Hawaii. Awarded the Pre-Pearl Harbor Ribbon. WWII veteran. Attained rank of Chief Warrant Officer prior to honorable discharge.

Bordovsky, John Stephen, II, son of John Stephen Bordovsky and Frances Mikulenka Bordovsky, was born on Aug. 29, 1908, in Hallettsville, TX. Enlisted in U.S. Army Corps in 1932 at Ft. Sam Houston, TX. Served with the 2nd Division of the horse-drawn field artillery unit. Was part of a cadre sent to Paris, TX, in 1943 to form the 102nd Division. Was on Enewitok in the South Pacific, where the atomic bomb was tested during WWII. Also served and fought in the Korea conflict. Honorably discharged May 10, 1951. Rank: CWO. Was proud of being a Czech-American, serving in the Army, and was a very good, charitable, Catholic, searching out the poor and sick, making life easier for them. Was President of the local KJT Society at one time. Died Dec. 6, 1986. Buried in St. Jerome's Cemetery, San Antonio, TX. This information is presented lovingly by his surviving widow, Mrs. John S. Bordovsky II, whose home of record is San Antonio, TX.

Bordovsky, Robert Edward, son of Mr. and Mrs. A. Bordovsky, was born on Sept. 10, 1910, at Mart, TX. Educated at Hallsbury Rural School, Hallsbury, TX. Enlisted in the US Army Corps in 1943. Trained at Camp Fannin. Theater of Operations: EAME–North Africa and Europe. Medals: Combat Infantry Badge, Purple Heart. KILLED IN ACTION on Sept. 24, 1944, at Florence, Italy, and buried there. Interred 4½ years later at Holy Cross Catholic Cemetery, Waco, McLennan Co., TX. Submitted by sister, Frances Bordovsky Morris of Waco, TX.

Bordovsky, Theodore, son of Mr. and Mrs. A. Bordovsky, Mart, TX, entered U.S. Navy, 1944. Theater of Operations: Asiatic-Pacific. Saw action in the Pacific during WWII. Awarded Asiatic-Pacific Theater Campaign Ribbon; Philippine Liberation Medal; American Theater Campaign Ribbon and WWII Victory Ribbon. Honorably discharged 1946, having attained rank of MO MM 3/C.

Boudny, Alfred Louis, son of Mr. and Mrs. A. L. Boudny of Taylor, TX. Educated at Coupland High School. Enlisted U.S. Navy, 1942. Went through boot camp in San Diego, CA. Theater of Operations: Asiatic-Pacific. Assigned to USS *New Mexico*, campaigns in Aleutians Islands, Gilbert Islands, Marshall Islands, Bismarck, Archipelago, Marianas Islands, Philippine Islands and Ryukyus. Medals: APO with nine Bronze Battle Stars, AD Ribbon, BSS Ribbon. Rank: RdM 2/c. Home of record: Coupland, TX.

Brandesky, Albert C., son of Mr. and Mrs. Fred Brandesky, of Nueces Co., TX, was born about 1923, served in U.S. Army Corps, Pacific Theater of Operations during WWII. Died a few years ago. Submitted by Erwin E. Krejci, Corpus Christi, TX.

Bravenec, Joe Lee/see Schiller, Joe Lee (name was legally changed to Schiller).

Brnovak, Frank, son of Anton and Mary Brnovak, was born on Jan. 16, 1918, in Airville, Bell Co., TX. Educated at Thompson School, Bell Co., TX. Enlisted at Sweetwater, Nolan Co., TX, during WWII. Theater of Operation: European Theater, Corporal in 602nd Tank Destroyer Division. Fought with valor in battles in Northern France; Rhineland, Central Europe. WOUNDED IN ACTION. Medals: GCM Medal, Purple Heart, American Theater Stars, WWII Victory Ribbon, two Over Seas Stripes, one Service Stripe. Pulled M.P. duty while waiting to return home for an honorable discharge on Dec. 24, 1945. Home of record: Merkel, TX.

Brom, Victor F., son of Mr. and Mrs. Jim Brom,

was born on Feb. 19, 1918. Attended Moulton High, Moulton, TX, for one year. Enlisted in the military for active service, on Oct. 8, 1941 at Houston, TX. Sgt. Brom was stationed in the Pacific on Gilbert Island "Tarawa." He was a gun crew Sgt. in Battery D 811th A.A.A. (A.W.) Battalion. Honorably discharged Oct. 18, 1945. Home of record: Deer Park, TX.

Brosch, Daniel J. Jr., of Granger, TX. WWII veteran. Member of American Legion Post No 282, Granger, TX.

Brosch, Daniel J., Sr., of Granger, TX. WWII veteran. Member of American Legion Post No 282, Granger, TX.

Brosch, Ladd, Granger, TX. WWII Veteran.

Brosch, Sylvester, of Granger, TX. WWII veteran. Member of American Legion Post No 282, Granger, TX.

Brosch, Vladimir L., of Granger, TX. WWII veteran. Member of American Legion Post No 282, Granger, TX.

Brown, Thomas Lee, son of Ervin Lee Brown, Sr. and Hattie Lacik Brown, was born on Feb. 8, 1961, Waxahachie, Ellis Co., TX. Graduated from Red Oak High School on May 25, 1976. Enlisted in U.S. Navy on Dec. 19, 1980. Reported to U.S. Naval Base, Orlando, Florida, for basic training. Served three years as a Seaman aboard the USS *Tripoli*, a Helicopter Carrier. In 1984, as Petty Officer 2nd Class, participated in a joint effort to clear the Red Sea and Gulf of Suez of mines which had damaged 17 ships. Served three years as Aviation Electrician's Mate First Class aboard the USS *Guadalcanal*. At the present time, is serving three years at the Naval Air Station in Jacksonville, FL, as Master Chief of his shop and in Search and Rescue aboard a helicopter, when needed.

Brownshadel, Elton J., son of Louis Brownshadel and Rosie Horecka Brownshadel, was born on Sept. 25, 1918, in Hungerford, TX. Graduated from Wharton High School in 1936. Attended the University of TX and entered the U.S. Army Air Corps as a cadet on Aug. 8, 1942. Flight training included locations at Gaines Field, Uvalde, TX, Randolph Field, TX, and Brooks Field, San Antonio, TX. Received commission and pilot's wings on April 22, 1943. Served in NC, GA, CA, and Cambridge, England. KILLED IN ACTION on D-Day, June 6, 1944, in a P-51 crash over London, England. Buried in U.S. Military Cemetery in Cambridge, England. Was married to Dorothy Brown, Austin, TX, in 1943. One daughter: Trudy Faye Brownshadel Callihan.

Brownshadel, Gilbert, son of Louis Brownshadel and Rosie Horecka Brownshadel, was born on Sept. 22, 1920, in Hungerford, TX. Graduated from Wharton High School in 1938. Entered the Army in 1942 and was honorably discharged in 1946. Lived in Houston for many years and died there on Sept. 17, 1981. Buried in Memorial Oaks Cemetery Mausoleum, Katy Freeway, Houston, TX.

Broz, Lad L., Granger, TX, WWII Veteran.

Brunner, Leo A., son of Mr. and Mrs. J. R. Brunner. Graduate of Granger High School in Granger, TX. Enlisted in U.S. Army Corps in 1943. Took basic training at Camp Robinson, AR. Theater of Operations: American and Asiatic-Pacific. Medals: American Theater of Operations Campaign Ribbon, Asiatic-Pacific Theater of Operations Campaign Ribbon with one BSS, Good Conduct Medal, WWII Victory Ribbon. Honorably discharged in 1946.

Brunner, William F., son of Mr. and Mrs. J. R. Brunner of Granger, TX. Graduated Granger High School. Enlisted U.S. Army Corps in 1944. Took basic training at Camp Wolters. Theater of Operations: EAME. Medals: WWII Victory Ribbon, EAME Campaign Ribbon with one BSS. Attained rank of Pfc. Home of record: Granger, TX.

Bubenik, Charles Gilbert, son of Bohumil Bubenik and Marie Kusak, was born on Oct. 22, 1913, in Moulton, TX. Educated at Moulton

Elementary, TX (third grade). Inducted in the U.S. Navy during WWII on March 11, 1944, San Antonio, TX. Attained rank of 1st Gunner's Mate. Boot Camp, March 13, 1944, Naval Training Station, San Diego, CA. May 4, 1944, Armed Guard, Destroyer Base, San Diego, CA; June 7, 1944, assigned to ship, USS *Alcoa Pioneer*. Theater of Operations: Asiatic-Pacific. Served at Fiji, Pearl Harbor, Philippines, New Guinea, etc. On Oct. 31 and on Nov. 2, 1944, ship was attacked by an enemy submarine. On Nov. 19, 1944, a Kamekazi Japanese plane crashed on USS *Alcoa Pioneer*, in the Philippines. WOUNDED IN ACTION. Was transferred from ship to hospital at Treasure Island, CA. on Feb. 8, 1945, and arrived on April 7, 1945 for treatment of back injury. Medals: Asiatic-Pacific Theater Campaign Medal with BSS, Purple Heart, WWII Victory Ribbon (among others). Honorably discharged. Married Vlasta Mach of Shiner, TX. Died April 11, 1972. Interred at Greenlawn Cemetery, Rosenberg, TX. Submitted by daughter, Margie Ann Bubenik, Houston, TX.

Buchala, Louis, served in U.S. Army Corps during WWII.

Buchholz, Ransom R., son of Mr. and Mrs. F. E. Buchholz, of Georgetown, Williamson Co., TX. Graduate of: Georgetown High School, Southwestern University, and Vanderbilt University and Medical School. Entered U.S. Army Medical Corps in 1943. Basic training at Carlisle Bks., PA. Theater of Operations: EAME. Served in England, Normandy, Belgium and ETO. Medals: EAME Campaign Ribbon w/4 BSS, ETO Ribbon, WWII Victory Ribbon w/1 BSS. Honorably discharged in 1945, attaining the rank of Major.

Bujnoch, George E., son of George and Apolena (Miculek) Bujnoch, was born July 20, 1928 in Hallettsville, TX. Attended Thompson School in Lavaca Co., TX. Enlisted at Fort Sam Houston, San Antonio. Served in Korea. Discharged Sept. 3, 1956. Married Dorothy Grafe in Hallettsville on Nov. 24, 1952; two children. Home of record: Hallettsville, TX.

Bujnoch, Marvin J., son of Mr. and Mrs. Victor A. Bujnoch, was born on April 1, 1953. Enlisted in the Army on Aug. 3, 1972 at Fort Sam Houston, San Antonio, TX. Stationed in Germany during the Viet Nam War. Rank: Sgt. Received Good Conduct and Expert M-16 Rifle Medals. Discharged Aug. 2, 1978. Home of record is Hallettsville, TX.

Bures, George Joseph, son of Charles A. Bures and Gabriela Fojtik Bures, was born on Feb. 22, 1919, in Weimar, TX. Educated at Louise High School, Louise, TX. Enlisted U.S. Air Force, Ft. Sam Houston, TX. Honorably discharged Nov. 6, 1945, in Amarillo, Deaf Smith, TX, with the rank of Master Sgt. "The picture was taken late Dec. 1941, Edward Air Force Base, Muroc, CA. I was one of the Flight Engineers in the 2nd Reconnaissance Squadron. There were 13 B-24 Liberators in this squadron carrying out reconnaissance missions over the Pacific Ocean, and down the Southern Pacific Coast, after the Pearl Harbor attack." Medals received: American Theater Service Medal with one BSS, Good Conduct Medal, American Defense Medal. Home of record: Lincoln, NE.

Bures, James Anthony, son of Eugene A. Bures and Margaret Franta, was born on April 4, 1951, in El Campo, TX. Graduated El Campo High School, 1969; Wharton Jr. College, Wharton, TX; Del Mar College, Corpus Christi, TX. Enlisted on Feb. 18, 1970, Houston, Harris Co., TX in the U.S. Navy. Stationed NATTC, Orlando, FL; V.T. 28–Corpus Christi Naval Air Station, Corpus Christi, TX. Honorably discharged Feb. 15, 1974. Attained rank of E-4. Married Connie McMahon. Two children. Civilian Occupation: Civil Service Employee, Aviation Hydraulics Mechanic, Naval Air Station, Corpus Christi, TX. Home of record: Corpus Christi, TX. Submitted by mother, Margaret Franta Bures of El Campo, TX.

Bures, James William, son of Joseph and Frances Bures, was born on Sept. 3, 1895, in Weimar, Colorado Co., TX. Education: fifth grade. Enlisted in U.S. Army Corps during WWI, with the American Expeditionary Forces, European Theater of Operations. Among Medals received: WWI Victory Medal. Fought in France. Honorably discharged at end of WWI. Civilian occupation: owned grocery store. Married Frances Trojcak; three children. Died Feb. 5, 1966. Buried in the Catholic Cemetery at Nada, TX. Submitted by Margaret Franta Bures of El Campo, TX.

Burge, Charlie Elzner, son of Henry C. and Agnes Elzner Burge, was born on July 16, 1951, in Caripito, Estado Monagas, Venezuela. Has a BBA and MS in Business Education. Enlisted in Oct. 1975 in San Antonio and currently holds the rank of Lieutenant Commander in the Navy. Served in Desert Shield and Desert Storm and on three ships as Supply Officer: USS *Compass Island*, USS *Denver*, and USS *South Carolina*. Medals: Defense Meritorious Service Medal, Navy Commendation Medal, Joint Meritorious Unit Award, Navy Unit Commendation, Meritorious Unit Commendation, National Defense Service Medal, Southwest Asia Medal w/1 BSS, Sea Service Deployment Ribbon with two BSS, Navy and Marine Corps Overseas Service Ribbon with one BSS, Drug Enforcement Operations Ribbon, Kuwait Liberation Medal w/Gold Palm, Expert Pistol Shot Medal. Two command tours: DSCAPRO General Electric New England, Lynn, MA and Fleet Industrial and Supply Center, Naval Station Ingleside, TX. Currently on active duty. Home of record: Nahant, ME.

Buxkamper, Joseph, son of Mr. Buxkamper and Frances Janish Buxkamper, was born on Sept. 19, 1916, (Lone Oak) Ellinger, Fayette Co., TX. Enlisted in U.S. Army Corps during WWII. Attained rank of Staff Sergeant. Died Sept. 9, 1985. Submitted by Emil F. Petter, Wharton, TX.

Cadan, Richard P., served in the U.S. Army Corps, between Korean and Viet Nam Wars. Stationed stateside, achieved rank of E-5 prior to honorable discharge. Hometown: Granger, TX.

Carpenter, Warren, son of Mr. Carpenter and Mrs. Hecl Carpenter, of Granger, TX, is a Desert Storm U.S. Armed Forces veteran.

Carpenter, Travis, son of Mr. Carpenter and Mrs. Hecl Carpenter, of Granger, TX, is a Desert Storm U.S. Armed Forces veteran.

Cechan, Frank, military service veteran. Home of record: Dallas, TX.

Cechan, Henry, son of Henry A. and Antonie M. Cechan, was born on Oct. 1, 1924, in Dallas, TX. Went through elementary and high school and on to attain a college education. During WWII, he enlisted in the U.S. Navy at Dallas, TX. Rank: Machinist Mate 2nd/C. Was in the South Pacific Theater of Operations stationed aboard the USS *Houston*. Battles: Marshall Islands, Guam, Siapan, Iwo Jima, 1st and 2nd Battles of Philippine Islands. Medals and awards: American Theater Medal, Asiatic Pacific Medal, Purple Heart, Presidential Citation. WOUNDED IN ACTION in the second Battle of Philippines. Honorably discharged. Home of record: Dallas, TX.

Cejka, Abdon S., son of Fred G. and Annie E. Cejka, was born on May 3, 1932. Graduated from high school and attended South Texas Junior College and the University of Houston, Houston, TX. Enlisted in the U.S. Army at Ft. Sam Houston, TX on March 12, 1953, during the Korean Conflict. Basic training at Camp Breckinridge, KY. Served as infantryman in Hawaii and Korea, attaining rank of Corporal. Awards and decorations include the National Defense Service Medal, United Nations Service Medal, Korean Service Medal, and Good Conduct Medal. Separated from service Feb. 24, 1955 at Ft. Bliss in El Paso, TX. Home of record: Houston, TX.

Cejka, Alfonse H., son of Fred G. and Annie E. Cejka, was born on April 27, 1927. During WWII, was drafted into the U.S. Army before finishing high school. Received high school diploma after military service. Inducted into the service at Ft. Sam Houston, TX, on July 23, 1945. Basic training at Ft. Hood, TX. Served in Berlin, Germany, as Honor Guard at the four powers (U.S., England, France, and Russia) meeting hall. Separated from service Jan. 18, 1947, at Ft. Bragg, NC. Home of record: Hallettsville, TX.

Cejka, Fred George, son of Mr. and Mrs. Cejka, was born on Jan. 1, 1898. Everyone in family, except for one sister and himself, were born in Czechoslovakia. Family arrived in New York, moved to NE; as result of crop failure due to cold weather and insects, the family moved to TX, settling at Honey Creek, near Sublime, south of Weimar. Entered the U.S. Navy in 1916. Served as a musician during WWI. Stationed in U.S. for entire tour of duty, at Newport News, VA, and San Diego, CA. Suffered loss of right eye in an accident. Separated from service in 1918. Attended Texas A&M College. Farmed near Hallettsville, TX. Married Annie Cejka in 1924; four children: Alfonse H., Abdon S., Lucy C. Kloppenburg, and Rita M. Wachel Cejka. Died Oct. 1, 1960. Interred in Sacred Heart Cemetery, Hallettsville, TX.

Cepak, Albert J., was born Nov. 20, 1895. Served in U.S. Army Corps during WWI as MUS 3/CL in HQ Co. 109th Eng. R.S. Died Jan. 26, 1957. Buried in Lady Fatima Cemetery, Abbott, TX.

Cepak, Benedict, son of Mr. and Mrs. Albert Cepak, Abbott, TX. Served during Korean War, 1955–1957. Rank: Pfc. Awarded Good Conduct Medal prior to his honorable discharge. Married Mary Ann Mikula in Waco, TX.

Cepak, Edward Wesley, was born Aug. 29, 1924.

Served in U.S. Army Corps, WWII, F1. Died July 25, 1972. Buried in St. Mary's Catholic Cemetery, West, TX.

Cepak, Elbert J., served in WWI, of West, TX, 366 1030 Engineer, attained rank of Pvt.

Cepak, John Henry, born Jan. 3, 1897. Served during WWI: Pvt III SM TN 36 Div. Died Feb. 22, 1919.

Cepak, Marvin L., son of Louis Cepak and Christine Bezdek, was born Jan. 13, 1936, Penelope, TX. Education: High school and several trade courses. Enlisted March 1957, U.S. Armed Forces, Hillsboro, TX. Released March 1959, three years active reserve, extended during Cuban Crisis. Theater of Operations: USA. Rank: SP4. Medals and honors: Expert Rifle and Good Conduct Medals. Civilian Occupation: Industrial Maintenance and Repair. Played in several polka bands; presently playing in Dallas Czech Concert Orchestra. Has several in-plant inventions and labor-saving devices. Chosen Chamber of Commerce Employee for Quarter. Home of record: Waxahachie, TX.

Cepazc, Moneen, military service veteran. Home of record: Waya, TX.

Cepica, Fred E., son of Raymond L. Cepica and Julia M. Hrabal Cepica, was born on Sept. 24, 1929, in Penelope, TX. Graduated from Abbott High School and from Portland State University, Portland, OR. Enlisted in USAF, Lackland AFB, TX, on Sept. 10, 1950. Rank: S/Sgt. in Northern Air Defense Command. Medals: GCM; Northern Air Defense Command. Honorably discharged Sept. 10, 1954. In the summer of 1952, Naknek, AL, while serving two years there, S/Sgt. Cepica and three other Airmen, would-be fishermen, ventured across barren tundra to try luck in Pike Lake, small landlocked body of water located in the middle of nowhere. The sun *does* shine in Alaska! Within ½ hr., they had caught all the pike they could carry and headed back to camp. "Mosquitoes and deer flies, we thought they laid low 'til the sun went away—not these critters. Doubt they'd had a meal or contact with humans for who knows how long. They crawled under our protective hat nets and chewed and chewed and chewed!!! Walking on tundra was like being on a trampoline—more than two miles. Our water supply from small canteens was soon exhausted, as well as we. Doggedly stubborn and determined, I wasn't about to drop my prize, but I admit that I lightened the load and lagged behind the others. Reaching the Naknek River, I literally fell into the water, clothes and all, filled my belly with polluted water; I reached camp, dumped my catch in the mess hall, with instructions to wake me for the evening meal. Then I slept, probably through dinner. I hope the fish were good. That was a long time ago." Home of record: Portland, OR.

Cernik, Joseph, see Chernik, Joseph.

Cernosek, Anna M., born in West, TX. Graduated from Providence Hospital School of Nursing with an R.N. degree. Entered U.S. Army Nurse Corps, 1944, during WWII. Served in European Theater of Operations. Awarded two Battle Stars. Attained rank of Lt., prior to honorable discharge, 1946.

Cernosek, Benjamin Francis, son of John F. and Johana Lednicky Cernosek, was born Oct. 28, 1917, Ammannsville, Fayette Co., TX. Education: St. Mary's, Ross High School, West High, and Federal School of Modern Illustrating in Minneapolis, MN. Enlisted in U.S. Army Air Corps Nov. 6, 1941 in Dallas, TX, a month before Pearl Harbor. Trained as Air Craft mechanic. Rank: Tech Sgt. Assigned as Crew Chief to the Warhawk Group of the 12th Air Force. The Unit was 318th Fighter Sqdn. and was assigned to North Africa and Italy, Jan. 12, 1943. The group flew P-40s, P-47s and P-51s for two and a half years in Europe during WWII. It was the only fighter group in the Mediterranean Theater that averaged more than one aerial victory for each combat mission flown. It was also the first AAF unit to fly combat missions from a Soviet base. Went stateside on June 7, 1945. Medals: Presidential Distinguished Unit Citation w/1 OLC, Good Conduct, American Defense Service, EAME Campaign w/8 BBSs, WWII Victory, American Defense and Pre-Pearl Harbor. Honorably discharged July 13, 1945. Married Edith S. Gerik on Nov. 14, 1955. Children: Mary Rose, David Bernard and Benjamin Francis, Jr. Occupation: Karlik and Cernosek Construction Co., Cernosek

Construction Co., partner in Western Auto, and owner of House of Flowers. Coach/sponsor West Youth Baseball-Softball League, K.C. Choir, member of zoning board in West, active member, Church of the Assumption, Knights of Columbus, KJT and VFW. Home of record: West, TX.

Cernosek, Benjamin Franklin "Bennie," son of Vaclav Anton "Jim" Cernosek and Annie Martha Vacek, was born June 21, 1929, Weimar, Colorado Co., TX. St. Michael's Elementary School and Weimar High School Graduate. Married Jeanette Cernosek. Enlisted in U.S. Army Corps, Jan. 18, 1951, San Antonio, TX. Basic training at Ft. Bliss, TX. Assigned to Germany. Honorably discharged Jan. 1953. Married Juanita Cernosek. Children: Randy, Julia, Dana, one granddaughter. Died July 18, 1986, Houston, TX. Buried with military honors in the Houston National Cemetery, Space L-26-44. Also survived by four brothers and two sisters. Submitted by brother, Johnny Cernosek of Houston, TX.

Cernosek, Bernard C., son of Johnny F. Cernosek and Jeannette J. Podsednik Cernosek, was born on Sept. 26, 1968. Attended Good Shepherd School, Garland, TX, North Garland High School, Garland, TX, Texas A&M, College Station, TX. Enlisted in the U.S. Marine Corps on Dec. 20, 1991. Rank: 1st Lieutenant. Stationed at Pensacola Naval Station, FL, in pilot training.

Cernosek, Bernard David., son of John F. and Johana Lednicky Cernosek, was born Nov. 21, 1919, Ammannsville, Fayette Co., TX. Education: St. Mary's, Ross High School, West High and Texas A&M. Lettered two years on the West High School football team and was an active member and officer in the FFA. Majored in landscape architecture at Texas A&M. Enlisted in the U.S. Army Corps Apr. 1, 1942, Bryan, TX, and was sent to Camp Shelby, MS for basic training. Transferred to OTS at Ft. Sill, OK, graduating as 2nd Lt. in the Artillery July 1943. Assigned as field artillery instructor. Transferred to Army Air Corps Feb. 25, 1944, for pilot training. Received wings and qualification to fly twin-engine aircraft Feb. 1, 1945. Served tour in Alaska Nov. 1, 1944 to Oct. 10 1946. Assigned as Base Communications Officer at Holloman AFB, NM. Married Lenora "Taddy" Kellnar Aug. 9, 1952. Sent to Japan Mar. 15, 1953, in support of the Korean War. Assigned to the 815th TRP. CARR. SQ. At Ashiya AB flying C-119s "Flying Box Car." In the early morning of June 23, 1953, he took off from Ashiya with a full load of supplies for the troops in Korea. Shortly after take off, he lost power in one engine. Unable to maintain altitude, the plane crashed into the Sea of Japan. No survivors were found. Listed as KILLED IN ACTION June 23, 1953, just 34 days before the Korean truce was signed. Decorations: Purple Heart, Air Medal, American Defense, American Campaign, Asiatic-Pacific Campaign, WWII Victory and Korean Service Medal. Buried May 26, 1954 in St. Mary's Catholic Cemetery, West, TX.

Cernosek, Cyril W., son of Mr. and Mrs. John Cernosek, was born Feb. 3, 1931. Attended St. Mary's School in West, TX, and Aquilla High School. Entered service Nov. 1948. Served during Korean War. Air Force Communication. Rank: S/Sgt. Awarded numerous medals. Discharged Sept. 1952. Home of record: West, TX.

Cernosek, Glenn Joseph, son of Johnny Jerry Cernosek and Evelyn E. Barton Baker, was born on Oct. 1, 1950, Weimar, Colorado Co., TX. Educated at Our Lady of Mt. Carmel Catholic Elementary School, San Jacinto High School, San Jacinto Jr. College, University of Houston. Enlisted in U.S. Naval Reserve, Oct. 1967 in Houston, Harris Co., TX. Basic training at San Diego, CA. Other places stationed: Great Lakes, IL; Galveston, TX; Vallejo, CA; Corpus Christi, TX. Viet Nam veteran. Battles fought: PBR's, River Division 553, NSAD Binh Thuy, Viet Nam. Rank: Gunner's Mate, 3rd Class/GMG3. "The week of Survival School we received for training, before going to Viet Nam was one of the most interesting events in military service." WOUNDED IN ACTION at Binh Thuy, Viet Nam. Sent to an overseas hospital, then back to the states to a hospital in Corpus Christi, TX. Received medical retirement on Sept. 1, 1973. Married Gloria Goldsby; one daughter: Stephanie Lynn Cernosek. The marriage ended in a divorce. Occupation: artist and commercial printing consultant; has a gallery in Jackson Hole, WY. Married Deborah A. Harris on Jan. 27, 1990, in Houston, TX. Children: Michael Joseph and

Brandon James. Favorite pastime is hiking. Home of record: Ft. Collins, CO.

Cernosek, James George, son of Vaclav Anton "Jim" Cernosek and Annie Martha Vacek, was born on April 23, 1932, in Weimar, Colorado Co., TX. Education: St. Michael's Catholic Elementary School–8 years. Graduated from Weimar High School in 1950. Employed with GMAC, Houston, TX, as Mail and Stock Clerk. Enlisted in U.S. Air Force on April 4, 1951, in Houston, Harris Co., TX. Basic training at Lackland AFB, San Antonio, TX, and at Sheppard AFB, Wichita Falls, TX. Rank: Airman 1st Class. Technical School, Electronics, Keesler AFB, Biloxi, MS. Graduated from Shoran Radar School. Transferred to Barksdale AFB, Shreveport, LA. Assigned to 52nd Troop Carrier Squadron (TAC). On Jan. 1, 1953, left for Kadena AFB, Okinawa. Line Chief for Shoran Bombing System on B-29s that bombed North Korea. After Korean War, transferred to Donaldson AFB, Greenville, SC, in Oct. 1953. Radio Technician on airplanes at Donaldson until honorably discharged Jan. 15, 1955. Decorations and Medals: Korean Service Medal, United Nations Service Medal, National Defense Service Medal, Good Conduct Medal, Carbine Excellent Sharpshooter Badge, Carbine 30 Sharpshooter badge. Children: four daughters, two sons. Runs and owns Houston Electronics. Home of record: Houston, TX.

Cernosek, John Herbert, son of Johnny Jerry Cernosek and Evelyn E. Barton Baker, was born on Sept. 27, 1948, in Schulenburg, TX. Education: Our Lady of Mt. Carmel Catholic Elementary School, Milby High School, Houston, TX. Enlisted in U.S. Naval Reserve in 1966 at Houston, TX. Called to active duty in 1967. Shipped to Sasebo, Japan; served three years in Mobil Navy Post Office as Postal Clerk. Rank: E-5. In 1970, another postal clerk jumped ship with a *huge* payroll. John followed him through Viet Nam, into Subic Bay in the Philippine Islands, spent three weeks in Bangkok, Thailand, aboard a U.S. Naval spy ship. The scoundrel eluded John and the Navy and evidently retired over there; never came back to the States. John was flown back in a Naval helicopter to Sasebo. Separated from active duty at San Diego CA, and went back into Naval Reserve. Spent final year of Naval Reserve duty in Houston, TX, and was honorably discharged in 1971. Enjoyed seeing "a lot of the world he had never seen before, during his tour of duty. It was different." John is a supervisor with Brown and Root Construction. Has two grown sons, Wesley and Robert Cernosek, one granddaughter. John and his fiancee, Gwen Pogue Plant plan to be married soon. Home of record: Houston, TX.

Cernosek, Johnny F., son of John F. and Anne Mae Karlik Cernosek, was born on July 19, 1933. Attended St. Mary's Catholic School, West, TX, Aquilla High School, Aquilla, TX, and Texas Technological College. Enlisted in the U.S. Air Force on Oct. 2, 1951. Rank: Sgt. Served with the 39th Fighter Intep Squadron as an aircraft mechanic at Yokota and Johnson Air Force Bases. Honorably discharged Sept. 30, 1955. Married Jeannette J. Podsednik. Children: John David, Theresa Ann, Mary Kathleen, Jean Marie, and Bernard C. Cernosek. Graduated from college in 1961. Employed by Lone Star Gas Company as an Engineer, until retirement, in March 1994. Home of record: West, TX.

Cernosek, Johnny Jerry, son of Vaclav Anton "Jim" and Annie Martha Vacek Cernosek, was born on April 7, 1924, in Ammannsville, Fayette Co., TX. Attended 1st grade, Catholic school, Ammannsville, TX. Family moved to Weimar, Colorado Co., TX. Attended St. Michael's Catholic Elementary School. Graduated from Weimar Public High School in 1942. Attended University of Houston, Houston, Harris Co., TX. Enlisted in U.S. Army Reserve on Nov. 4, 1942, at San Antonio, TX. Entry into active service was on Jan. 28, 1943. Basic Training: Camp Kohler, Sacramento, CA. Assigned to 826th Amphibious Tract Battalion, Infantry. Military occupations: Lineman telephone and telegraph 238. Theater of operations: American Theater and Asiatic Pacific Theater. Battles and Campaigns: New Guinea, South Philippines (Liberation), Luzon. Military qualifications: Marksman Rifle. Decorations and Citations: American Theater Ribbon, Asiatic Pacific Theater Ribbon, Philippine Liberation Ribbon, Good Conduct Medal, WWII Victory Medal. Rank: T/5. Continental USA service: 1 year, 1 month, 2 days; foreign service: 2 years and 28 days. Departed for overseas on Nov. 24, 1943, for S.W. Pacific-Asiatic; arrived Dec. 10, 1943. Departed overseas, Dec. 8, 1945. Honorably discharged Jan. 3, 1946, Ft. Bliss, El Paso, TX. Married Evelyn Barton on July 15, 1947. Children: John H., Glenn J., Larry G., Debra A., Tamera A., Don A.; 18 grandchildren, three great grandchildren. Evelyn predeceased Johnny. Married JoAnn Robison on May 26, 1985; two stepchildren: Homer E. Roderick and Reecea A. Roderick Henderson. Retired as packaging supervisor from Nabisco Brands, Inc., on Nov. 21, 1985, in Houston, TX. Registered member of Our Lady of Mt. Carmel Catholic Church, Houston, TX, member of VFW, Pearland, TX, member of American Legion Post 594, Houston, TX, Member of DAV, Pearland, TX, Knights of Columbus #4577, Houston, TX. Home is in Houston, TX.

Cernosek, Leo Raymond "Leroy," son of Vaclav Anton and Annie Martha Vacek Cernosek, was born on Dec. 27, 1925, in Ammannsville, Fayette Co., TX. Education: St. Michael's Catholic Elementary School. Graduated Weimar High School, Weimar, TX, 1944. Inducted into U.S. Army Corps, June 6, 1944, Ft. Sam Houston, TX. Assigned to 84th Infantry Division, 335th Battalion, Company K. Boot Camp, Ft. Hood, Killeen, TX, transferred to Camp Chaffee, Ft. Smith, AR. Received Anti-Tank training, Camp Gruber, Muskogee, OK. Sent to Port of Embarkation, Boston, Mass. Departed the States Dec. 24, 1944, and arrived in Glasgow, Scotland on Dec. 29, 1944. Theater of Operations: European Theater including Rhineland and Central Europe. Battles: Rhineland, Central Europe GO 105, WD 45. General Eisenhower, Commanding Officer, asked him what he made in marksmanship on the Rifle Range. Leroy told him Sharpshooter. Eisenhower told him in a few days he would be an expert!!! Spent one year and two months overseas during WWII. Arrived stateside NY on March 25, 1946. Medals and awards: EAME Campaign Ribbon with two BSS, Good Conduct Medal, WWII Victory Ribbon, two Overseas Service Bars, Combat Infantry Badge; Sharpshooter Badge. Honorably discharged May 27, 1946, at Ft. Sam Houston, TX. Civilian Occupation: Laundry Deliveryman for Laundry/Dry Cleaners, San Antonio, TX. Moved to Houston, TX in 1952 and worked for Lone Star Beer Distributors for 22 years, until 1974. Was Harris County Commissioner for 14 years. Retired Jan. 1988. Married Emilie Demel on Jan. 28, 1950; four children, eight grandchildren. Home of record: Weimar, TX.

Cernosek, Robert R., enlisted in U.S. Army Corps in TX in 1942 during WWII. Basic training at Ft. Sam Houston, TX. Received further training at Camp Swift, TX. Assigned to Medical Detachment. Honorably discharged 1943.

Cernosek, Sidney Jerome, son of Vaclav Anton and Annie Martha Vacek Cernosek, was born on May 2, 1920, in Schulenburg, Fayette Co., TX. Educated in Ammannsville and Weimar, TX. Enlisted in U.S. Army Corps on Oct. 14, 1940 at Ft. Sam Houston, TX. Assigned to Headquarters Detachment Station Complement SCU 1464. Theater of Operations: Continental U.S.A.; Military Occupational Specialty: Carpenter, General 050. Rank: Technical Sgt. Medals and decorations: American Service Medal, WWII Victory Medal, Lapel Button for Marksmanship w/ SS Rifle. Served during WWII for 4 years, 3 months, 25 days. Honorably discharged Nov. 9, 1945, Ft. McPherson, GA. Married Martha Petrash, daughter of Jim V. Petrash and Sophie Hluchanek on April 12, 1942, San Antonio, Bexar Co., TX. Children: one daughter and two sons, five grandchildren, four great grandchildren. Died Feb. 8, 1978, San Antonio, TX, the result of an automobile wreck. Buried with full military honors at the National Cemetery, Ft. Sam Houston, TX. Widow's home of record: San Antonio, TX. Submitted by daughter, JoAnn Cernosek Koenig of San Antonio, TX.

Cernosek, Silvin Jerome, son of Vaclav Anton Cernosek and Annie Martha Vacek, was born on Sept. 3, 1921, Schulenburg, Fayette Co., TX. Educated: Ammannsville and Weimar, TX. Enlisted in U.S. Army Corps on July 19, 1944, at Ft. Sam Houston, TX. Assigned to 9956th T.S.U., San Francisco, CA. Was Carpenter General 050 and Expert Infantryman. Medals and Decorations: Good Conduct Medal, American Campaign Medal, WWII Victory Medal, Lapel Button, ASR. Served in the military service for 1 year, 11 months, and 5 days in the American Theater of Operations. Honorably discharged June 23, 1946, at Camp Beale, CA. Semi-retired from civil service. Married Dorothy Petrash on June 14, 1941, San Antonio, TX. Children: one daughter and one son, four grandchildren. Home of record: San Antonio, TX. Submitted by niece, JoAnn Cernosek Koenig of San Antonio, TX.

Cernosek, Vaclav Anton "Jim," son of Jan. A. (immigrant from Czechoslovakia, 1880) and Aneska "Agnes" Sobotik Cernosek, was born on Sept. 25, 1895, in Bluff, Fayette Co., TX.

Educated in Ammannsville, Fayette Co., TX. Also attended business school. Enlisted in U.S. Army Corps on Oct. 9, 1917. Served with the American Expeditionary Forces from June 12, 1918, through Dec. 20, 1918. Assigned to Co. L, 360th Infantry. Theater of Operations: Europe. WOUNDED IN ACTION in France, shrapnel wound to the head, resulting in a gold plate replacing part of his skull. Honorably discharged Feb. 21, 1919. Medals: WWI Victory Medal among other honors. Discharge papers state: "Has brown eyes, black hair, ruddy complexion, 5'8" in height. Vocation: farmer." Member of St. John's Catholic Church in Ammannsville, TX. Married Annie Martha Vacek on his return from U.S. Army Corps on July 19, 1919. Moved to Weimar. Children: six sons and two daughters; all of whom lived to maturity and reared families. Active member of St. Michael's Catholic Church. Member DAV; American Legion and VFW, SPJST. Died April 4, 1978. Interred at the St. Michael's Catholic Mausoleum. Eldest son, Sidney, preceded him in death on Feb. 8, 1978, the same year. Jim's fifth son, Benjamin, died on July 18, 1986. At this compilation, 1996, all six of his other children are living. Lovingly submitted in honor of his father by his son, Johnny J. Cernosek whose home of record is Houston, TX.

Cervenka, Adolph J., son of Louis and Julia Tobolka Cervenka, was born on May 10, 1897, in Granger, TX. Attended Macedonia Grade School and Sts. Cyril & Methodius Catholic School. Served during WWI with AEF in France as a member of MTC Repair Unit, U.S. Army. Married Angeline Rozacky. Occupation: farmer. Enjoyed hunting and fishing. Died July 23, 1955. Interred at Capitol Hills Gardens, Austin, TX.

Cervenka, Alan Ray, son of Raymond A. and Martha Kocurek Cervenka, was born on Aug. 13, 1953, in Houston, TX. Enlisted in the U.S. Marine Corps in 1972. Rank: Col. Served in the Viet Nam Conflict. Honorably discharged in 1974. Married Debbie Cervenka; two children. Occupation: attorney-at-law. Home of record: Sugarland, TX.

Cervenka, Albert, served in U.S. Armed Forces after WWII. Granger, TX.

Cervenka, Arnold Victor, son of Louis and Julia Tobolka Cervenka, was born on July 21, 1910, in Granger, Williamson Co., TX. Attended Macedonia Grade School and the Catholic elementary school in La Porte, TX, for two years. Served in the U.S. Army from Oct. 17, 1929 through Oct. 16, 1930. Enlisted in the U.S. Army at Ft. Sam Houston, TX during WWII. Served stateside as Clerk General. Rank: Pfc. Discharged Oct. 1945. Occupation: farmer. Named Outstanding Farmer from Texas in 1949. Enjoyed hunting and dancing. Married Hattie Rozacky. Children: Joyce Marie Cervenka Repadomsch and Robert E. Lee Cervenka. Died Sept. 9, 1963. Buried at Calvary Cemetery in Granger, TX.

Cervenka, Clement E., son of Will J. (immigrant, 1914) and Annie Smajstrla Cervenka, was born on Nov. 23, 1926, in West, TX. Attended Leggott Elementary and West High School. Enlisted in U.S. Army on June 27, 1945, at Dallas, TX. Served 18 years with paratrooper divisions; 11th Airborne, Airb Reg Cbt Team, 101st Airb. Div. Assigned to U.S. Army Hqtrs Com Viet Nam, U.S. Army Med Com Japan, U.S. Army Primary Heli Ctr, Ft. Wolters, TX, U.S. Army Troop Support Ag, Ft. Lee, VA, var non Major units. Rank: Sgt. Major. Medals: BSS, Meritorious Service, Asia Pac, Natl. Defense w/OLC, WWII Victory, Pres Unit Cit, Army Comm w/OLC, GCM 2/9 Awards, Occ Japan, Comb Inf, Korea Service, Korean Presi Unit Citation, UN Service, Viet Nam Service, Viet Nam Cam 2/60 Device, Glider Wings, and M/Parach Wings. Retired from the U.S. Army on Aug. 1, 1975, after 30 years' service. Married Mildred. Home of record: Burleson, TX.

Cervenka, Dan G., of Taylor, TX. WWII veteran. Navy: C.A.S.U. 37. Member of American Legion Post No 282, Granger, TX.

Cervenka, Frank A., son of Mr. and Mrs. William Cervenka, was born on Oct. 4, 1917, in Granger, Williamson Co., TX. Graduated from Granger, TX, High School. Enlisted in U.S. Army Corps,

1941, Granger, TX. Basic training at Ft. Sam Houston, TX. Theater of Operations: EAME and American. Served during WWII in Algeria, French Morocco, Tunisia, Naples, and Foggia. Medals: EAME Campaign Medal w/3 BSS, American Defense Service Medal, WWII Victory Medal. Honorably discharged 1945. Married Elizabeth. Died Aug. 23, 1983. Buried at Holy Cross Catholic Cemetery in Granger, TX. Was a member of American Legion Post No. 282, Granger, TX.

Cervenka, Frank T., of Dallas. WWII Veteran. Member of American Legion Post No. 282, Granger, TX. Deceased.

Cervenka, Joe Albert, son of Joe K. and Agnes Kubacak Cervenka, was born on Dec. 4, 1917, in Granger, Williamson Co., TX. Education: seventh grade. Enlisted in U.S. Army Corps on March 19, 1942, at Ft. Sam Houston, TX. Rank: S/Sgt. Infantry. Heavy Mortar Crewman 1607. Theaters of Operation: American and EAME. Battles: Ardennes, Rhineland, Central Europe. Medals: Good Conduct Medal, American Theater Campaign Medal, EAME Theater Campaign Medal with three BSS, three overseas service bars, one service stripe, WWII Victory Medal. Honorably discharged Oct. 30, 1945. Married Vlasta Fojtik. Children: Gloria Cervenka Steglich, Bobby J. Cervenka, and Monica Cervenka Schwitzer. Owned and operated service station. Died Sept. 23, 1986. Buried in Granger, Williamson Co., TX. Submitted by widow, Vlasta Cervenka, Granger, TX.

Cervenka, Joe R., of Granger, TX. WWII veteran. Member of American Legion Post No. 282, Granger, TX. Deceased.

Cervenka, Joseph Arnold, son of Josef and Anna Matus Cervenka, was born on May 2, 1895, in Fayetteville, TX. Education: Cortes School, Roznov, TX, Massey Business College, Houston, TX. Enlisted during WWI in the U.S. Army Corps on May 25, 1918, at LaGrange, TX. Assigned to 36th Division. Theater of Operations: Europe. Left Camp Bowie, TX, for Port of Embarkation in July 1918. Arrived in France in August for training. Put in front lines in Meuse-Argonne Offensive for Oct. 1918 Offensive. Discharged March 17, 1919—all within one year! Married Lottie Vaudak. Died on Aug. 28, 1971. Submitted by Lee Roy Cervenka, Lake Jackson, TX.

Cervenka, Lee Roy, son of Joseph and Lottie Vaudak Cervenka, was born on Dec. 16, 1931, in Houston, TX. Education: Texas A&M–BS and ME. Commissioned 1st Lt. in June 1953 upon graduation from Texas A&M. Korean War Armistice in July 1954. Worked at Dow Chemical Co. for one year before receiving orders to active duty. Assigned to the Technical Escort Detachment to escort chemical and biological agents plus some rocket fuels all over the world. Place of orders: Ft. McClellan, AL, June 1, 1954. Honorably discharged June 20, 1961. Home of record: Lake Jackson, TX.

Cervenka, Louis F., son of Mr. and Mrs. William Cervenka. Graduate of Granger, TX, High School. Enlisted in U.S. Army Corps in 1939 at Granger, TX. Basic training at Ft. Sam Houston, TX. Theater of Operations: Asiatic-Pacific. Served in Central Pacific, Luzon, Philippines. Rank: Sgt. Medals and awards: American Defense Medal, Asiatic-Pacific Campaign Ribbon with four BSS, Philippine Liberation Ribbon with two BSS. Honorably discharged 1945. Member of American Legion Post No. 282, Granger, TX. Lives in Granger, TX.

Cervenka, Norman Louis, son of Albert and Otilie Ann Kocurek Cervenka, was born on April 2, 1935, in Granger, Williamson Co., TX. Graduate of Granger, TX, High School, 1953. Attended University of Texas, Austin, TX–BSCE; Georgia Institute of Technology–MSCE. Commissioned on May 30, 1958, University of Texas, Austin, TX. U.S. Navy. Rank: Commander. Civil Engineer Corps. Theater of Operations: Japan, Lebanon, Viet Nam. Battles: Viet Nam, two tours. First resident officer in charge of construction for the Orlando, FL, Naval Training Center, Officer in Charge of Advance Party to establish a Seabee camp in Viet Nam. Decorations and Awards: Viet Nam Service Medal with two BSS and Fleet

Combat Insignia, National Defense Medal, Viet Nam Campaign Medal with Device (1960–), Republic of Viet Nam Meritorious Unit Citation. Retired Nov. 1978. Occupation: Construction Engineer. Married Judith J. Windsor. Children: Cathy Lynn and Holly Ann. Hobby: travel. Home of record: Winter Park, FL.

Cervenka, Richard L., son of Louis F. and Sallie M. Reisner Cervenka, was born on March 14, 1948, in Taylor, TX. Education: high school; Associates Degree in Mgmt. from Temple Jr. College. During the Viet Nam Conflict, enlisted in the Navy at USN Reserve Center, Austin, TX, in Nov. 1965. Two tours of duty in Viet Nam waters (total of 15 months) aboard the USS *St. Paul* (CA73), 6th Fleet Flagship. Medals: National Defense Service Medal, Presidential Unit Citation, and Navy Unit Citation. Separated from service Nov. 1971. Occupation: Machinist. Hobbies are yard work and fishing. Married Miss Vanek. Children: Robert J. and Jennifer L. Home of record: Granger, TX.

Cervenka, Richard P., of Georgetown, TX. WWII veteran—Navy: U.S.S. *Clarion* A.K. 172. Member of American Legion Post No 282, Granger, TX.

Cervenka, Robert J., West, TX. WWII veteran, U.S. Army Corps.

Cervenka, Robert J., son of Mr. and Mrs. Robert Cervenka, West, TX. Attended West High School. Entered Coast Guard, 1943. Trained in Florida. Awarded GCM, American Theater and WWII Victory Ribbon. Rank: SP 1/C M. Honorably discharged 1946.

Cervenka, Rudolf, served in U.S. Armed Forces during WWI. Member of SPJST Lodge 20, Granger, TX.

Cervenka, Rudolph Joe, son of Rudolph William and Mary L. Poncik Cervenka, was born on Jan. 13, 1922, in Sparks, Bell Co., TX. Graduate of George West High School, 1940, George West, TX. Enlisted in US Navy in June 1942 in Houston, TX. Boot camp, San Diego, CA. Assigned to the Amphibious Force. Assigned to the last Landing Ship Tank (LST475) built in Vancouver WA, by Kaiser Shipyard in March 1943. Served aboard the LST475 until the end of WWII. Rank: Motor Machinist 1st Class. Theater of Operations: Asiatic-Pacific. Took part in all major invasions from Lae, New Guinea, to Luzon and Borneo. Returned stateside Oct. 1, 1945. Transferred to Washington, D.C. Married June E. Liese of Almonesson, NJ, on Nov. 3, 1945. Children: R. W. "Sonny" Cervenka of Corpus Christi, TX, and Robert Cervenka of San Antonio, TX. Honorably discharged Dec. 14, 1945, at Camp Wallace, TX. Employed by Dept. of Defense. Retired in 1977 as aircraft engine tester, Corpus Christi, TX. Member of SPJST Lodge # 66, Waco, TX. Home of record: Rusk, TX.

Cervenka, Rudolph William. WWI veteran. Married Mary L. Poncik, Bell Co., TX.

Cervenka, Wilfred J., son of Will J. (immigrant, 1914) and Annie Smajstrla Cervenka, was born on March 3, 1925, in West, TX. Attended Leggott Elementary and West High School and 4-C Business College, Waco, TX. Enlisted in U.S. Army on Sept. 11. 1943 at Camp Wolters, TX. Received training at Camp Bruber, OK, in the 42nd, Rainbow Division Infantry; Camp Phillips, Kansas 79th, Lorrine Division Infantry. Theater of Operation: European Theater. Battles: Normandy, Northern France and Germany. WOUNDED IN ACTION on Jan. 6, 1945, in Germany. Medals: Sharpshooter, Combat Infantry Badge, Good Conduct Ribbon, Unit Citation, European Theater Operation with three BSS, Purple Heart and WWII V.E. Ribbon. Honorably discharged Jan. 16, 1946, at Camp Fannin, TX. Lived in Waco, TX, until death on Sept. 12, 1993. Buried in St. Mary's Cemetery, West, TX.

Cervenka, Willie L. WWII veteran. Member of American Legion Post No 282, Granger, TX.

Ceska, Frank J., son of Frank and Julie Jaska Ceska, was born Aug. 11, 1910, in Tours, TX. Education: Waco, McLennan Co., TX. Entered Armed Services at Camp Bowie, TX, on March 4,

1942. Was a Pfc. Co C, 818th Tank Destroyer Btln, 3rd Army. Theater of Operations: EAME. Campaigns: Rhineland and Ardennes, Alsace (Battle of the Bulge); KILLED IN ACTION on Dec. 20, 1944. Awards: Purple Heart, European African Middle Eastern Campaign with two stars. Interred in military cemetery in Nice, France. Was returned to U.S. in 1948 and interred in St. Mary's Cemetery, Waco, TX.

Chabisek, Herman, of Texas. Served in France.

Chada, Leo J., was born Oct. 3, 1906. Served in U.S. Army Corps during WWII. Troop F, 106 Cavalry. Died Apr. 3, 1963. Buried in St. Mary's Cemetery, West, TX.

Chaka, Edmund M., son of Mr. and Mrs. Frank J. Chaka, was born on May 30, 1919. Education: high school. Enlisted in U.S. Army Corps, 1941. Theater of Operation: Europe. Tours of duty: England, France, Belgium, Czechoslovakia. Medals and awards: Good Citizenship Award, Unit Citation, five Battle Stars. Honorably discharged in 1945. Married Zora M. Klatt; four sons, five grandchildren. Home of record: Wharton, TX. Submitted by Mr. and Mrs. Jerry Fabrygel, Needville, TX.

Chaloupka, Adolph J., son of Frank and Pauline Bucek Chaloupka, was born in 1896 in Sweet Home, TX. Enlisted in the Army, Dec. 12, 1917, at Ft. Sam Houston, TX. Rank: Pfc. Assigned to the 22nd Balloon Company, gas demolition group. Discharged July 24, 1919. Married Elen Olsen; three children. Both died in 1932; buried in Yoakum Catholic Cemetery.

Chaloupka, Alfred F., son of William and Josephine Berkovsky Chaloupka, was born 1920, at Sweet Home, TX. Education: high school. Enlisted at Fort Sam Houston, TX. Rank: Technician Fifth Grade. Participated in battles in the East Indies and New Guinea. Discharged July 13, 1945. Medals: Asiatic-Pacific Campaign with two BSS, Distinguished Unit Citation with one Oak Leaf Cluster, Good Conduct, American Defense Service Medal. Died July 28, 1956.

Chaloupka, Charles Anthony, son of Frank J. and Annie Pekar Chaloupka, was born on Jan. 28, 1928, in Yoakum, TX. Enlisted in U.S. Army Corps at San Antonio, TX, stationed at Ft. Sill, OK. Corporal Chaloupka served in the Korean War before being honorably discharged at Ft. Hood, TX. Home of record: Hallettsville, TX.

Chaloupka, David Wayne, son of Sam and Irene Dornak Chaloupka, was born March 29, 1954, at Shiner, TX, and attended Sam Houston School, Houston, TX. Enlisted in the U.S. Air Force at Houston, TX. Rank: Sgt. Served in Viet Nam during the Viet Nam Conflict. Discharged from the U.S. Air Force at Bergstrom AFB, TX, on April 27, 1976. Home of record: Schulenburg, TX.

Chaloupka, Frankie A., son of Mr. and Mrs. Chaloupka, was born in Hallettsville, TX. Attended Reagan High School, Houston, TX. Enlisted in Houston, TX. Served in Viet Nam Conflict. Rank: E-5. Honorably discharged at Ft. Louis, WA. Home of record: Schulenburg, TX.

Chaloupka, George James, son of Frank J. and Annie Pekar Chaloupka, was born on April 14, 1919, in Sweet Home, TX. Attended Straten School. Enlisted at Fort Sam Houston, TX, on March 21, 1942. Rank: Tec 5. Assigned to 744th Truck Battalion. Battles: Normandy, Northern France, Ardennes, Rhineland, Central Europe. Discharged on Nov. 11, 1945 at Camp Fannin, TX. Medals: American Theater Campaign, EAME Campaign w/5 BSS, GCM, BSS, WWII Victory and Rifle Marksman. Died Aug. 19, 1979.

Chaloupka, Phillip Emil, son of Frank J. and Annie Pekar Chaloupka, was born on Jan. 6, 1921, Sweet Home, TX. Education: Straten School. Enlisted at Ft. Sam Houston, TX on Oct. 9, 1942. Rank: Pfc. Assigned to Cav with 823rd Tank Destroyer Btln. Battles: Northern France, Normandy. WOUNDED IN ACTION Aug. 28, 1944, France. Honorably discharged Aug. 27, 1945, Hosp Ctr, Camp Carson, Colorado. Medals: EAME Ribbon with two BSS, Purple Heart, Good Conduct Ribbon and Rifle M1 MKM. Died on Aug. 31, 1987.

Chaloupka, Samuel Alfred, son of Frank and Annie Pekar Chaloupka, was born on Nov. 3,

1925, Yoakum, TX. Education: Stratton-Vysehrad School. WWII, enlisted in Navy, San Antonio, TX. Rank: S/M 3/C. Theater of Operations: EAME and Asiatic-Pacific. Honorably discharged April 11, 1946, Camp Wallace, TX. Home of record: Schulenburg, TX.

Chaloupka, Willie J., Jr., son of Willie and Josie Chaloupka, Sr., was born on Feb. 23, 1928, Sweet Home, TX. Graduated high school. Enlisted NRS, San Antonio, TX. Received WWII Victory Medal. Discharged Aug. 8, 1947. Died Dec. 7, 1983. Submitted by his widow, Lillie M. Chaloupka. Home of record: Hallettsville, TX.

Chalupa, Jerry, was born on March 22, 1920, in Taylor, TX. Graduate of Taylor High School, Taylor, TX, 1938. Attended business college, Austin, TX, 1939. Inducted into U.S. Army Air Corps in Oct. 1941 at Ft. Sam Houston, TX. Basic training: Camp Grant, Rockfort, IL. Assigned to Medical Corps. Transferred to Kelly Field and San Antonio Aviation Cadet Training Center, TX. Attended special school for Medical Technician, William Beaumont General Hospital, El Paso, TX, in Aug. 1942. Selected to initial cadre of 1st Air Commando Grp, Nov. 1943. Flew to India. Served as Medical Tech, Hailakandi and Asanol, 1943-44 and with 5th Fighter Sqdn., 1944-45. Rank: Staff Sgt. Medals: American Defense Service Medal; American Theater Campaign Medal, Asiatic Pacific Campaign Medal with two stars and Distinguished Unit Badge. Honorably discharged: 1945. Employed by the Steck Co. as printer, one year pre-war and 27 years Post WWII, Austin, TX. Ambassador College, Pasadena, CA, and Big Sandy, TX, for 20 years, until retirement. Married Georgie. Children: David and Dana, two granddaughters. Home of record: Big Sandy, TX.

Charbula, Arnold, son of Ladislav J. and Della Bartosh Charbula, was born May 8, 1925, in Schulenburg, TX. Education: St. John's Catholic Parochial School, Ammannsville, TX, and Pecan Catholic Parochial School, Holman, TX, through 9th grade. Inducted into U.S. Army Corps on Aug. 12, 1943, at Ft. Sam Houston, TX. Theater of Operation: EAME. Arrived Naples, Northern Italy, May 1944. Assigned to 91st Infantry Div., 361st Combat Infantry Regt. "We landed at Anzio Beachhead on June 1, 1944. Went into combat zone June 4, 1944, Rome-Arno River and Northern Apennines, including Gothic line and numerous small towns and villages–Florence, Longhorn, Leaning Tower of Pisa." WOUNDED IN ACTION Sept. 1944, on Gothic Line. Medals: Purple Heart, American Theater Ribbon, EAME Theater Ribbon with two BSS; WWII Victory Medal, Good Conduct Medal, Combat Infantry Badge. Honorably discharged Dec. 6, 1945, SAD-AAF Personal Distribution Command Center, San Antonio, TX. Owns and operates Superior Motor Parts of El Campo, TX, with his son, Gary Charbula. Home of record: El Campo, TX.

Charbula, Eugene G., son of Robert and Millie Marek Charbula, was born Sept. 6, 1920, Ammannsville, TX. Education: Swiss Alp. Enlisted during WWII, Jan. 8, 1942, Houston, Harris Co., TX, in U.S. Navy. Theater of Operations: EAME; Asiatic-Pacific; American. Battles: Anti-Aircraft Gunner, European, African, Middle East Area–Asiatic-Pacific Area, American Area. Medals: three BSS. Rank: Seaman First Class. Honorably discharged Oct. 27, 1945. Married Anita Nikel, Nov. 26, 1945. Children: one son, Robert Charbula, Sr., one daughter, Darlene Charbula (Evanicky). Two grandsons: Robert Charbula, Jr. and William Marak. Died Nov. 13, 1992. Buried at St. John the Baptist Catholic Church Cemetery.

Chasak, Edward F., son of Mr. and Mrs. Joe B. Chasak, was born in Taylor, TX. Graduate of St. Mary's Catholic High School. Enlisted in U.S. Army Air Corps, Williamson Co., TX, 1942. Basic training at Foster Field, TX. Further training Matagorda Island, TX. Rank: S/Sgt. Honorably discharged 1945.

Chasek, Erwin T., son of Mr. and Mrs. Joe B.

Chasek, born Taylor, TX. Education: Taylor, TX. Enlisted U.S. Army Corps, 1939. Basic training at Ft. Russell, TX. Further training at Camp Bowie, TX. Theater of Operations during WWII: EAME. Served in North Africa, Sicily and Italy. Medals: EAME Campaign Medal, ETO Ribbon w/5 BSS. Honorably discharged 1945. Married Gladys McDonald of Durham, NC. Listed hometown: Taylor, TX.

Chernik, Joseph, son of Thomas and Rozina Martinek Cernik, was born on Feb. 4, 1887, Ellinger, TX. Education: grade four, Santa Anna School, Colorado Co., TX. Father died, and as eldest child, Joseph took over the reins of the family. Enlisted in U.S. Army Corps, Columbus, TX, June 25, 1918. Assigned to Co. 165 DB, 14th Veterinary Hospital Unit. Served in European Theater of Operations (France), WWI, from Oct. 14, 1918–Dec. 28, 1918. Awarded WWI Victory Medal. Honorably discharged Feb. 8, 1919, Camp Bowie, TX. Died Feb. 1969. Buried at LaGrange City Cemetery, LaGrange, TX. Submitted by Mrs. Ben Hrachovy, Columbus, TX.

Chervenka, Calvin C., son of Mr. and Mrs. Cervenka, was born Jan. 6, 1925. Education: high school and University of Texas, Austin, TX. B.S. in Aerospace Engineering and M.S. in Mechanical Engineering. Member of U.S. Army Air Corps, Infantry, Field Artillery, 38th Infantry Division. Theater of Operations: USA and Philippine Islands. Retired Aerospace/Mechanical Engineer. Married Mildred M. Lucien. College Instructor, Dallas, TX, Physics, English, Math and Czech Language. Home of record: Dallas, TX.

Chevanec, John, Granger, TX, WWII veteran.

Chilek, Joseph Fredrick, son of Fred F. and Mary Vinklarek Chilek, was born June 27, 1920, Hochheim, Dewitt Co., TX. Education: Hochheim Country School. Inducted into U.S. Army Air Corps on June 23, 1941. Basic training in Albuquerque, NM. In Oct. 1941, sailed off to the Philippine Islands, landing at Clark Field. Theater of Operation: Asiatic-Pacific. Battles: Luzon and Mindanao. Reported MISSING IN ACTION after the Battle of Mindanao on May 26, 1942, while serving in the U.S. Army Air corps, 440th Ordnance Company. In 1945, his mother received a telegram that Joseph was KILLED IN ACTION at the Battle of Mindanao on May 26, 1942. Joseph never got a furlough before going overseas—never got to come home at all. Medals: Purple Heart, Good Conduct, Asiatic-Pacific Campaign with a BSS, WWII Victory. Submitted by his sister, Otelia Chilek Mudd of Yoakum, TX.

Chilson, Josephine Ruzicka, daughter of Henry and Albina Ruzicka Chilson, was born Feb. 2, 1922, Ft. Worth, Tarrant, TX. Education: high school graduate and one year college. Enlisted in U.S. Armed Forces, during WWII, Nov. 26, 1942, Washington, D.C. Rank: Yeoman First Class (Y1C). Theater of Operations: Jacksonville, FL. Medals: WWII Victory Medal; American Theater Campaign Medal. Honorably discharged Oct. 27, 1945. Home of record: Hampton, VA.

Chovanec, Henry L., son of Peter and Annie Petter Chovanec, was born July 3, 1914, Fayetteville, Fayette Co., TX. Education: high school and University of Texas, Austin, TX. Received commission as 1st Lt. at University of TX. Assigned to 321st AAF Bomb Sqdn., U.S. Army Air Corps. Theater of Operations: Philippine Islands. Fought in WWII. KILLED IN ACTION April 30, 1943. Submitted by Emil F. Petter, Wharton, TX.

Chovanec, Joe F., was born April 8, 1908, Was a Private in U.S. Army Corps, WWII. Member of American Legion Post No 282, Granger, TX. Died Aug. 13, 1980. Buried Holy Cross Catholic Cemetery, Granger, TX.

Chovanec, John, Jr., son of John Chovanec, Sr. and Katherine Kawulok (both parents immigrants, born in Reka, Czechoslovakia), was born Sept. 22, 1922 in Danbury, Brazoria Co., TX. He graduated from Danbury High School in May, 1940. Prior to his enlistment, he was employed as an aircraft mechanic by Lockheed Aircraft Company, was living in Burbank, CA. Enlisted in the U.S. Army Air Corps in Los Angeles, CA, on Jan. 28, 1944. Staff Sgt. Chovanec served in the

Pacific and fought in the skies over Tokyo, Japan. His aircraft was at a base on Tinian Island in the Mariana Islands. On Feb. 10, 1945, he was a rear gunner on a B-29 aircraft, which failed to return from a bombing mission to Nakajima Aircraft Factory located in Ota, Japan. Staff Sgt. Chovanec was declared MISSING IN ACTION on Feb. 12, 1945 and was reported KILLED IN ACTION two years later. He was awarded the Purple Heart and Air Medal. He was survived by his parents, one brother, Adolph Chovanec of Corpus Christi, TX, one sister, Annie Chovanec of Danbury, TX, and his wife, Cletice Payne Chovanec of Los Angeles, CA. John Chovanec, Sr., immigrated to Texas in 1912. Katherine Kawulok immigrated to Texas in 1921. Both became naturalized citizens of the U.S.A. Lovingly submitted in John, Jr.'s memory, by S/Sgt. Chovanec's sister, Annie Chovanec, whose home of record is Danbury, TX.

Chudej, Albin, West, TX, WWII military veteran, PRISONER OF WAR.

Chudej, Albin F., West, TX. WWII veteran, military service. WOUNDED IN ACTION, Germany.

Chudej, Alton Emil, son of Eddie and Agnes Chromcak Chudej, was born on Dec. 9, 1937 in Hallettsville, Lavaca Co., TX. Education: Moravia School through tenth grade, GED in Army. He enlisted in the service at Gonzales, TX on Aug. 16, 1961. His Basic Training was taken at Ft. Jackson, SC. His remaining training was taken at Ft. Leonard Wood, MO. He attained rank of SP/4, was honorably discharged on Aug. 16, 1967. Medals and decorations: expert rifle medal, expert carbine medal and GCM. Assigned to 554th Engineer Battalion. Married Gayenell Grones, on Oct. 29, 1961. Children: Laurie Chudej Leer, Janell Marie Chudej, Chris Edward Chudej, and Gary Alton Chudej. One granddaughter: Kelsey Marie Leer. Employed with Hoffer Truck Company as truck mechanic since Feb. 1964. Home of record: Hallettsville, TX.

Chudej, Ambrose John, was born Dec. 7, 1896, served in the U.S. Army Corps during WWI, attained rank of Private. Died July 4, 1971. Buried in St. Mary's Cemetery, West, TX.

Chudej, Andrew, West, TX, WWII military veteran.

Chudej, Benjamine F., West, TX, military veteran, Asiatic-Pacific Theater of Operations.

Chudej, Eddie E., son of Matthew and Caroline Kuchar Chudej, was born Jan. 8, 1895 in Hallettsville, Lavaca Co., TX. Education: Boethel School through 6th grade. Enlisted in U.S. National Guard on July 21, 1917, in Moravia, TX. Reported to LaGrange, TX, under draft of President Wilson on Aug. 5, 1917. Fought in AEF, France, Meuse-Argonne Offensive, Champagne, France, Oct. 6–Oct. 29, 1918. Honorable discharge on June 14, 1919. Married Agnes Cromcak on Jan. 11, 1921, was blessed with four children: Marvin Chudej, Virginia Chudej Spaeth, deceased, Vernon Chudej, Alton Chudej. As a civilian, his occupation was farmer. He also served as Constable of Precinct 2, Moravia, TX, for 32 years, prior to his retirement. He died on Feb. 9, 1974, and is buried at Moravia Catholic Cemetery, Moravia, TX. Submitted by Alton Chudej, Hallettsville, TX.

Chudej, Edwin, was born Sept. 16, 1925, married Evelyn Macon, served in the U.S. Army Corps, during WWII, attaining rank of Pfc. Died June 16, 1985, buried in St. Mary's Cemetery, West, TX

Chudej, Frank J., son of Joe and Vera Cadre Chudej, was born in 1894 in Buckholts, TX. Entered the service in 1917 during WWI as a Pfc. in Co. D, 133rd M.G. Battalion as a machine gunner. He was involved in the Meuse-Argonne Offensive and the Canitgny Offensive in Oct. 1918. He received the Victory Medal for the Meuse-Argonne Offensive. After his discharge from the service, he married Louise Pivoda and they had two children. Frank worked for the Southern Pacific Railroad in Houston until his retirement. He died in 1968.

Chudej, Henry John, attained rank of Pfc. during WWII. ER. ARMOR VSAR.

Chudej, Henry W., son of Frank and Louise Pivoda Chudej, was born in 1918 in Houston, TX. Served one year peacetime duty, married Rose Swonke on Nov. 23, 1941. He was assigned to the 304th Signal Operating Battalion. Made Staff Sgt. during WWII. Theater of Operation: Asiatic-Pacific. Honorably discharged, received Japanese cavalry sword as a war souvenir. He returned to his job with Houston Lighting and Power in Rosenberg, TX where he and his wife raised four children.

Chudej, Joseph R., of West, TX, WWII military veteran, 8th Bomber Squadron.

Chudej, Louis, of West, TX, WWII military veteran, ETO.

Chudej, Louis V., was born Feb. 13, 1922, attained rank of Pfc. in U.S. Army Corps during WWII. Died May 4, 1992, buried in St. Mary's Cemetery, West, TX.

Chudej, Marvin George, son of Eddie and Agnes Chromcak Chudej, was born on Sept. 22, 1924, Hallettsville, TX. Education: 10th grade. Volunteered for the USMC on Jan. 18, 1943. Pvt. Chudej was assigned to Company A, 1st Battalion, 2nd Marines NS. Fought in the South Pacific, was KILLED IN ACTION on Nov. 20, 1943 at Betio Island, Tarawa Atoll, Gilbert Islands. Remains never recovered. Medals: Asiatic-Pacific Campaign Medal and Purple Heart. His memorial marker lies next to the graves of his parents in the Moravia, TX Catholic Cemetery.

Chudej, Tony A., son of Mr. and Mrs. A. J. Chudej, married Mary Jan. Bartosh, Waco, TX. Entered U.S. Navy, during WWII, 1944. Served in Philippines, Hawaii, Tarawa, Iwo Jima, Okinawa. Awarded AD and PL. Assigned to an auxiliary minesweeper. The USS *Ardent* AM34 played part in sinking of Japanese Submarines 1–12, one of the deadliest submarines in action by the Japanese during the WWII. Ironically, SM 3/C Chudej signed on with the Navy hoping for an assignment aboard a submarine. But, Chudej stated, "That's what I wanted." He passed every test they gave him, but he had a crooked tooth that failed him. To this day, Tony Chudej can't understand why a crooked tooth disqualified him from submarine duty, but he is not complaining, after seeing what the submarines went through and all that, he was thankful it didn't happen. He said he was glad to be on the ocean, instead of under it. He got to see the world. Honorably discharged in 1947. Resides with his wife in Waco, TX.

Chupik, Charlie J., Sr., son of Stephan and Marie Skrla Chupik, was born Oct. 25, 1909, West, TX. Inducted into the U.S. Army Corps on Jan. 8, 1942, at Ft. Sam Houston, TX. He was with Company E, 234th Armored Eng. Battalion. Rank: Pfc. WOUNDED IN ACTION. Medals: EAME Campaign, ADS, Purple Heart, GCM, Rifle Qual. Honorably discharged on Aug. 2, 1945 at Longview, TX. He married Mary Vaja. Home of record: Houston, TX.

Ciesleivicz, Charlie, served in U.S. Navy during WWII. His name is on monument which was erected because of all the prayers of the parishioners were fulfilled as all 75 men returned from serving in WWII. Grotto and monument erected to honor all these 75 men who were members of St. Mary's Catholic Parish, Frydek, TX and who honorably served their country during WWII, 1941-1945.

Ciesleivicz, Joseph, served in U.S. Navy during WWII. His name is on monument which was erected because of all the prayers of the parishioners were fulfilled as all 75 men returned from serving in WWII. Grotto and monument erected to honor all these 75 men who were members of St. Mary's Catholic Parish, Frydek, TX and who honorably served their country during WWII, 1941-1945.

Cinek, Alfons J., son of Mr. and Mrs. J. P. Cinek,

of West, TX. Entered Army Air Corps in 1942 during WWII. Served European Theater, awarded E.T. Ribbon w/5 Battle Stars. Discharged 1945, having attained rank of T/5.

Cmerek, John C., son of Joseph and Agnes Kubacak Cmerek , was born on July 2, 1916 in Corn Hill, Williamson Co., TX. He attended Grade School at Walburg, TX. He enlisted in the U.S. Army at Austin, TX on Sept. 18, 1940. During WWII, he served in the Asiatic-Pacific Theater of Operations at Guam as a member of the 204th General Hospital as Mess NCO Cook. He was separated from the Service on Oct. 10, 1945 at Ft. Sam Houston, TX. He subsequently enlisted into the U.S. Army and served with Headquarters, 98th General Hospital in Europe at Munich, Germany. His awards and decorations include the American Defense Service Medal, Asiatic-Pacific Campaign Medal with campaign star, Good Conduct Medal, Service Stripe, and six Overseas Bars. His second separation from the Service occurred at Camp Kilmer, NJ on April 1, 1949. After his military service, he became a farmer/barber who enjoyed bowling and gardening. He married Hattie Rozacky. Home of record, Granger, TX. Member of American Legion Post No 282, Granger, TX, WWII military veteran.

Cmerek, Laddie Joe, was born Sept. 21, 1940, died Feb. 11, 1988, buried Calvary Catholic Cem., Granger, TX. Served in U.S. Army during WWII.

Cmerek, Louis, son of Mr. and Mrs. Mathilda Cmerek, was born in Taylor, TX. Education: Graduate, Taylor High School. Enlisted in U.S. Army Corps in 1943 at Granger, TX. Received his basic training at Camp Callan, CA. Theater of Operations: Asiatic-Pacific, WWII. Served in Australia; New Guinea; Philippines and Japan. Medals: Asiatic-Pacific Campaign Ribbon with three BSS, one Bronze Arrowhead, WWII Victory Medal. Discharged honorably in 1946, having attained rank of Pfc.

Cmerek, Rudolph S., son of Joseph and Agnes Kubacak Cmerek, was born April 19, 1919, at Corn Hill, Williamson Co., TX. Education: Walburg, TX. He enlisted in the U.S. Army on April 9, 1942, at Houston, TX. Received basic training at Ft. Lewis, WA. Served in both the Asiatic-Pacific and American Theaters of Operation with tours of duty in the Aleutian Islands and Amchitka Island. He was in Alaska as a member of Company C, 71st Infantry. As a Utility Repairman, he was primarily responsible for maintaining runways and keeping them free of ice and snow. Medals: American Theater Campaign Medal, Asiatic-Pacific Campaign Medal, WWII Victory Ribbon. Honorably discharged on Nov. 20, 1945, rank of Pfc. Civilian Occupation: farming. Died on July 20, 1983. Interred in Holy Trinity Cemetery at Corn Hill, Williamson Co., TX.

Cmerek, Victor A., son of Mr and Mrs. Frank Cmerek, was born in Granger, TX. Education: Palacky School, Granger, TX. Married Angeline Zrubek. Entered U.S. Army Corps, 1942, Granger, TX. Received basic training at Camp Barkeley. Theater of Operations: EAME and American. Campaigns in England, France and Germany. Medals: WWII Victory Medal, American Theater Campaign Medal, EAME Campaign Medal w/3 BSS, Purple Heart. WOUNDED IN ACTION, 1944, France. Honorably discharged, 1945. Granger, TX, WWII Veteran.

Cocek, Amos E., son of Mr. and Mrs. Eugene Cocek of West, TX. Education: Attended West High School. Entered Service March, 1941. Served in Atlantic Theater. Served on two Aircraft Carriers: USS *Randolph*; USS *Kearsarge* in the North Atlantic Casu Unit. Awards: GCM; WWII Victory Medal; American Defense Medal. Attained rank of AMM 3/C before honorable discharge 1947. Married Mary Ann Cocek.

Cocek, Bernard, of West, TX, military veteran, WWII.

Cocek, Fred F., son of Mr. and Mrs. Frank Cocek, West, TX. Entered Seabees, 1943, during WWII. Served in Hawaii. Honorably Discharged 1945, having attained rank of S 1/C. Married Georgia Nemecek.

Cocek, Jerry Wilford, son of Eugene Cocek and Mary Gerik, was born Jan. 30, 1927, in West, TX. Education: Finished two years of high school,

West, TX. Enlisted in U.S. Army Air Corps on May 21, 1945 at Ft. Sam Houston, TX. Theater of Operations: EAME. Locations served: Sheppard Field, TX, Chanute Field, IL, Clark Field, Philippine Islands. Medals: Asiatic Pacific Campaign Medal, WWII Victory Medal, Philippine Independence Ribbon. Rank: Corporal. Honorably discharged Dec. 8, 1946. General Contractor, specializing in concrete and tile setting. Home of record: West, TX.

Cocek, William E., Medical Technician, WWII. 36th Division. Served in Central Europe Campaign. PRISONER OF WAR, Germany. Honorable discharged in 1946, having attained rank of Pfc. Home of record: West, TX.

Cocek, Willie, was born June 26, 1897. Served in the Armed Services during WWI in the 141st Infantry. Died June 2, 1965, Buried in St. Mary's Cemetery, West, TX.

Coker, Delbert E., son of Willie Lee and Vlasta Shimek Coker, was born on Jan. 1, 1933, in Baytown, TX. Graduated from high school. Enlisted in the Army at Baytown, TX on March 11, 1953. Theater of Operations: Germany. Discharged Jan. 25, 1955. Home of record: Baytown, TX.

Courtade, Mary (Horak), daughter of Joe and Lillie Cernoch Horak, was born Aug. 14, 1921, Dubina, TX. Education: Schulenberg Elementary; Griffin School, Mt. Calm, TX. Graduated from Penelope TX High School, 1941. Enlisted during WWII in WAAC, Feb. 26, 1943 and in WAC Oct. 13, 1943. Theater of Operations: American. Medals: Good Conduct; WAAC American Theater; WWII Victory Medal. Took basic training at Ft. Damoies, IO. Stationed at Marana Air Force Base AZ, May to Aug. 1943. Took discharge Aug. 18, 1943, reenlisted Oct. 13, 1943, sent to Ft. Oglethorpe GA; then Daytona Beach FL, Dec. 1943 to Camp Wolters, Mineral Wells, TX. Honorably discharged Jan. 3, 1946, Ft. Sam Houston, San Antonio, TX. Home of record: Mart, TX.

Covanec, John, was born Sept. 12, 1915. Served in WWII as Sp. 5, U.S. Army Corps. Died July 1, 1978. Buried at Holy Cross Catholic Cemetery in Granger, TX.

Ctvrtlik, Albert B., was born Aug. 8, 1895, served in the U.S. Army Corps during WWI, attained rank of Corporal. Died July 4, 1974, buried in St. Mary's Cemetery, West, TX.

Cuba, Daniel B., son of Mr. and Mrs. John L. Cuba, was born June 4, 1907, in Taylor, Williamson Co., TX. Attended Taylor High School and Tyler Business College. Was connected with the Texas Oil Company prior to his voluntary enlistment into the Armed Forces. Entered the U.S. Army Air Corps on Jan. 24, 1941. Trained at Randolph Field, San Antonio, Bexar Co., TX. Later served at Mather Field, CA, and with the 3017th Army Air Force B. U. in Hobbs, NM. Rank: S/Sgt. Awards: WWII Victory and American Defense Ribbons. Honorably discharged on Sept. 19, 1944, at El Paso, TX. Lived in Taylor, Williamson Co., TX. Died and buried in Taylor, TX.

Cuba, Edwin J., son of Mr. and Mrs. John L. Cuba, was born on Aug. 19, 1909, in Taylor, Williamson Co., TX. Attended Taylor High School. Volunteered on Sept. 30, 1940, for the U.S. Army Corps, assigned to Field Artillery. Basic training, Ft. Sam Houston, TX. Theater of Operations: EAME. T/Sgt. Cuba served from Jan. 1944 to June 1945 in the Italian Campaign at Rome to Arno River, Apennines Mts. on to Po

Valley into the Alps. Medals: Military Valor Cross (from Italian Govt), Legion of Merit Medal, ETO Ribbon with three BSS, Pre-Pearl Harbor Medal, WWII Victory Medal. Honorably discharged in June 1945. Lived in Taylor, TX, married Martha Blaha, had two daughters, Edwina and Ruth Ellen. Died in 1955 and is buried in Taylor, Williamson Co., TX. Submitted by his sister, Mrs. Daniel J. Svoboda of Victoria, TX.

Cuba, Leonel F., son of Mr. and Mrs. John L. Cuba, was born May 25, 1922, in Taylor, Williamson Co., TX. Attended Taylor High School. Aided his country by farming, prior to volunteering on Nov. 4, 1942 for the U.S. Army Air Corps. Pfc. Cuba entered service at Ft. Sam Houston, San Antonio, TX; received basic training there and was stationed at Randolph Field. He served his total duty in the United States at various Air Fields. His awards include: WWII Victory Medal, American Defense, American Theater Ribbons. Honorably discharged on Feb. 1, 1946, Lowry Field, CO. He is one of John Cuba's four sons who served. Employed by Victoria Machine Works. Home of record: Victoria, TX. Submitted by sister, Mrs. Daniel J. Svoboda, Victoria, TX.

Cuba, Marvin Lee, son of Mr. and Mrs. John L. Cuba, was born on June 10, 1927, in Taylor, Williamson Co., TX. Graduated Taylor High School, 1944. Volunteered June 30, 1945, for the United States Navy. Theater of Operations: Asiatic-Pacific. Trained and was graduated from the Naval Training School, Radar Operators, Point Loma, San Diego, CA, as Seaman 2nd Class. Later promoted to Seaman 1st Class. Seaman Cuba is the youngest son of John L. Cuba, and brother of Daniel, Edwin and Leonel Cuba, who all served their country during WWII. Honorably discharged. Home of record: Taylor, TX. Submitted by sister, Mrs. Daniel J. Svoboda, Victoria, TX.

Cuba, Oldrich J., son of John and Rosie Cuba, was born on March 16, 1922, in Megargel, TX. Education: Graduated Megargel High School. Enlisted in U.S. Army Air Corps on Oct. 26, 1942, Dallas, Dallas, TX. Theater of Operations: American. Medals: American Theater Campaign Medal, GCM, WWII Victory Medal. Sgt. Cuba was an Aerial Engineer for 36 months on B-24, B-29, B-17, C-54 and C-47. He had many hours of flight time, was kept in U.S. to help train student pilots and the ferrying of airplanes coming back from overseas to Kingmon, AZ. He was a member of KJT. He died on Aug. 29, 1982, from leukemia. Submitted by widow, Mrs. O. J. Cuba. Home of record: Duncan, Stephens Co., OK.

D

Danek, Louis A., son of Mr. and Mrs. Louis Danek of West, TX. Served at Camp Polk, LA; Camp Hood, TX. Tank Battalion, WWII. Injury, Medical Discharge, attained rank of Private. Died Jan. 19, 1994, buried St. Mary's Cemetery, West, TX.

Danek, Rudolph, Jr., son of Rudolph Danek, Sr. and Mary Danek, was born in Taylor, Williamson Co., TX. Married Mamie Ann Meyer. Enlisted in U.S. Army Corps in 1942, assigned to Field Artillery. Received basic training at Ft. Warren, WY. Other training in CA, OK, GA, IN. Theaters of Operation: American and EAME. Served in Campaigns in France, Germany and Belgium. Medals: EAME Campaign Medal, ETO Ribbon w/2 BSS, American Theater Ribbon, WWII Victory Medal, Good Conduct Medal. Honorably discharged in 1945.

Darilek, Anton, son of Adolf and Bessie Darilek, was born on Aug. 8, 1917 in Flatonia, TX. Fourth grade education. Entered the U.S. Army in Feb. 1940. Rank: Cpl. (Sp.); gun crewman, light artillery, MM Howitzer. Battles: Central Europe, Rhineland, Naples-Foggia, Rome-Arno and Southern France. WOUNDED IN ACTION. Medals: GCM, ADS, EAME w/5 BSS, Purple Heart, Arrowhead. Discharged July 1, 1945. Home of record: Hallettsville, TX.

Darilek, Edwin F., son of John A. and Agnes Machart Darilek, was born on Aug. 13, 1916, Henkhaus, Lavaca Co., TX. Education: public schools and Draughons' Business College. Worked for Red and White Stores, Lufkin, TX. Inducted into the U.S. Army Corps on March 21, 1942 at Ft. Sam Houston, TX. Airplane Mechanic, Sheppard Field, TX and Boeing Aircraft Co., Seattle, WA. Was on transport ship to Oran, Africa, on March 21, 1942, w/15th Air Force, 346th Sqdn, B-17 Airplane, mechanic. Battles: Sicily, Europe, Rome-Arno, Northern France, Normandy, Balkans, Tunisia, Naples-Foggia. Ancestors (Darilek and Machart) immigrated from Churdin, Landskrown, Hermanica, Czechoslovakia in 1877. Mother's family also came from the Hermanica area. Currently retired, serving on City Council, Chamber of Commerce, American Legion and delivering noon meal to shut-ins in Moulton, Old Moulton, Komensky, and Moravia, TX, five days a week. Been in partnership with brother for 32 years. Home of record: Shiner, TX.

Darilek, Edward H., son of Tom J. and Albina Hanslik Darilek, was born on Dec. 4, 1919, in Witting, Lavaca Co., TX (near Moulton). Education: Witting Schools. Worked on family farm until 1941. In 1941, joined U.S. Army Air Corps, San Antonio, TX. Attended Aircraft Mechanic School, Keesler Field, Biloxi, MS, and additional training in Indianapolis, IN. After training, was transferred to Reykjavik, Iceland, served as crew chief on P-38s, one of which was the first to be recorded for shooting down a German Focke-Wolf 200K Kurier near Iceland. After two years in Iceland, transferred to Scotland, then to Walton Field in England as a Mosquito and B-17 Flying Fortress crew chief T/Sgt. These Mosquitoes were used for photographic reconnaissance filming German targets by day and night to scout the way for the 8th Air Force; then Belgium as an aircraft crew chief in the 8th Air Force, 50th Fighter Squadron, 654th Bomber Group, WWII. In Aug. 1945, Edward returned to USA. Medals received: American Defense Ribbon, GCM and Ribbon, EAME Campaign Medal w/6 BSS for participation of his unit in the aerial warfare over Western Europe. On Oct. 8, 1945, he married Elsie Marie Bohuslav. They have one son, Glenn Thomas, and three daughters: Darlene Marie, Barbara Jean, and Joyce Eileen. Moved to Galveston, TX, and to

LaMarque, TX. In 1954 they settled in Texas City, TX. Edward worked for Marathon Oil for 35 years and retired as an accountant in 1979. His hobbies include playing accordion and violin, singing and playing with Czech Heritage Singers with whom he recorded two albums. Is an active member of Knights of Columbus No. 5236, LaMarque, TX, Secy. of KJT, LaMarque. Served as President of RVOS, Democratic Precinct Chairman for 40 years and Treasurer of Marathon Oil Company Credit Union. Member of VFW in LaMarque, TX.

Darilek, Kenneth R., son of Mr. and Mrs. Anton Darilek, was born on Dec. 28, 1948, in Hallettsville, TX. He graduated from high school in Hallettsville. He enlisted in San Antonio and was a Sp. 5. He was an ordnance mechanic. He fought in Viet Nam. His medals were: National Defense Service Medal, Viet Nam Service Medal, Viet Nam Campaign Medal, Army Commendation Medal, and Good Conduct Medal. He was discharged on Feb. 2, 1971. He lives in Victoria, TX.

David, Daniel R., son of Robert K. and Adelle Michna David. Born Jan. 13, 1930 in Granger, Williamson Co., TX. Educated at Circleville Grammar, and Granger High School. Enlisted in the Army Sept. 8, 1948 in Austin, TX. He was an administrative specialist in the post-WWII era, Korean Conflict and Viet Nam. Awarded BSS for merit, C1B, E1B, Commendation Medal (7 awards) in Korea and the Viet Nam Service Medal. Learned seven languages, visited Australia in 1969. Discharged July 2, 1972 with the rank of 1st Sgt, E-8. Married Corinne Turner. Plays the accordion. Residence: Pineville, SC.

David, Edward John, was born on Aug. 8, 1928 and died on Oct. 13, 1952, buried Holy Cross Catholic Cemetery, Granger, TX. Served during WWII, Pfc., Military Police Detective.

David, Ferdinand J., son of Ferdinand and Frantiska Pajdl David, was born on March 17, 1895, Moravia, TX. Sometime after 1900, the family moved to Marak, Milam Co., TX. Ferdinand was drafted there, served as Private, WWI, assigned to the 315th Artillery, U.S. Army Corps. Private David never made it to the battlefields. He died of pneumonia on Feb. 5, 1918, at Ft. Sam Houston, San Antonio, Bexar Co., TX, and is buried in Marak, TX. Submitted by great-niece Kathy Dunn, San Angelo, TX.

David, James Everett, was born June 16, 1941. Education: BBA (General Business), Texas A&M University, 1964. Received an honorable discharge from the U.S. Army Corps Reserves. Married Laura Ann Gallia, and they have three children. Employed by Placid Oil Company. Home of record: Dallas, TX 75238.

David, John, was born on May 14, 1896. Member of SPJST Lodge 20, Granger, TX. Served in U.S. Armed Forces during WWI. Died on June 2, 1961, and is buried in Holy Cross Catholic Cemetery in Granger, TX. Married Lillian. Enlisted in U.S. Army Corps, WWI, Pvt, Btry D, 131 Field Artillery.

David, Julius, Granger, TX, WWII Veteran.

David, Klementa/Clement J., son of Joe and Julia Blazek David, was born Aug. 7, 1918, Georgetown, Williamson Co., TX. Education: Graduate, Corn Hill High School. Enlisted U.S. Army Corps in 1942. Took basic training at Camp Wolters, TX. Served in AK and Aleutians. Theater of Operations: Asiatic-Pacific. Medals: Asiatic-Pacific Campaign Ribbon w/1 BSS; Good Conduct Medal. Honorably discharged in 1944. Died on Dec. 10, 1944, and is buried in Corn Hill, Williamson Co., TX.

David, Theofil John, son of Emil Paul and Frieda Krnavek David, was born in Granger, Williamson Co., TX. Education: Macedonia School, Granger, TX, Cornhill, TX Catholic School. Enlisted in U.S. Army Corps in Texas and was stationed at Camp Barkley, Abilene, TX. American Theater of Operation. Honorably discharged in 1919. Married Emily Straka. Died August 1975. Buried at Holy Cross Cemetery, Granger, Williamson Co., TX. Submitted by Alice Heselmeyer, Taylor, TX.

Demek, Arnold, son of Mr. and Mrs. A. Demek,

West, TX. Attended West High School. Entered U.S. Army Corps, 1940. Trained at Kelly Field, Brooks Field and Independence Field, Kansas. Served during WWII. Attained rank of T/Sgt. before being honorably discharged in 1945.

Divin, Adolph, West, TX, 36th Division, WWII veteran.

Divin, George was born Sept. 9, 1912. Served in the U.S. Armed Forces during WWII as a Private. Buried in St. Mary's Cemetery, West, TX.

Divin, Louis, West, TX, WWII veteran.

Dlabaj, Bobby Gene, son of Charlie and Julie Dvoracek Dlabaj, was born Aug. 19, 1948 in Dallas, TX. Attended school through the 10th grade. Entered the Army on June 5, 1969 and received basic training at Ford Ord, California. Rank: Spec 4. Sent to Viet Nam in Oct. 1969, to Cambodia, Cameron Bay, and Da Nang. Left Viet Nam in August 1970. Discharged on Feb. 3, 1973 in Dallas, TX.

Dlabaj, Charlie A., son of John and Aloise Bedrich Dlabaj, was born on Feb. 15, 1915 in Kaufman, TX. Completed school through the 4th grade and entered the Army on May 1, 1945. Rank: Private. Was an Aircraft Assembler and fought in WWII. Received the Victory Medal before discharge on Oct. 30, 1945 at Fort Knox, Kentucky. Died on Aug. 10, 1970.

Dlabaj, Eddie J., son of John and Aloise Bedrich Dlabaj, was born May 8, 1921 in Kaufman, TX. Attended school through the sixth grade. Entered the Army Air Force on Feb. 20, 1936 in Ennis, TX. Rank: S/Sgt. Served with 1153rd Army Air Force Base in Brazil as 1st Cook and fought in WWII. Received a WWII Victory Ribbon and Good Conduct Medal. Died in 1986.

Dlabaj, Joe S., son of John and Aloise Bedrich Dlabaj, was born Feb. 15, 1919 in Ennis, TX. Attended school through the 5th grade and enlisted on Feb. 13, 1942 in Ennis, TX. Rank: Pfc. Theater of Operations included Africa, Italy, France, and Germany in WWII. Received the EAME Campaign medal with seven BSS and five Overseas Stars. Discharged Oct. 14, 1945. Died Jan. 19, 1982.

Dlabaj, Leo C., son of Charlie and Julie Dvoracek Dlabaj, was born July 15, 1942 in Ennis, TX. Attended school through the eleventh grade and entered the Army on Jan. 4, 1966 in Dallas, TX. Rank: Spec 4. Stationed at Ft. Polk, LA, AIT Redstone, AL and White Sands, NM. Discharged on Jan. 3, 1986 at Ft. Bliss, TX. Home of record: Mesquite, TX.

Dlabaj, Raymond S., son of John and Aloise Bedrich Dlabaj, was born on July 25, 1930 in Ennis, TX. Schooling went through the eighth grade. Entered the Army at Ennis, TX and was in Boot Camp at Fort Knox, KY. Rank: Corporal. Theater of Operations was in Korea as 1st Cook supervising kitchen serving 200 to 400 troops. Fought in Battery A 76th AAA–AW Battalion Korea. Received the Korean Service with two BSS, UN Service, National Defense and Good Conduct Medals. Discharged on Jan. 20, 1954 at Fort Bliss, TX. Home of record: Ennis, TX.

Dlabaja, Anton John, son of Mr. and Mrs. Anton Dlabaja. Attended West High School. Entered U.S. Army Corps, 1941. Served N. Africa, France, Italy. Awarded GCM and ET Ribbon. WOUNDED IN ACTION, Italy, 1944. KILLED IN ACTION, 1944, Italy, during WWII.

Dlabaja, Rudolph V., West, TX, WWII veteran, U.S. Army Corps, Infantry. Theater of Operations: Asiatic-Pacific.

Dlabaja, Victor, served in U.S. Army Corps, Infantry, in European Theater, England and France. WOUNDED IN ACTION. Awarded Purple Heart. Attained rank of Pfc.

Dlouhy, Floyd E., served in U.S. Navy during WWII. Buried Holy Cross Cemetery, Granger, Williamson Co., TX. Hometown was Granger, TX.

Dobecka, Arnold, son of Frank and Lillian Macik Dobecka, was born Aug. 18, 1934, Carrollton, TX. Education, Grapevine, TX. Enlisted at Dallas, TX, on Feb. 11, 1958. Sent to Ft. Bliss, El Paso, TX. Rank: Spc 4. Served in European Theater of Operations in Germany and France. Honorably discharged on Feb. 9, 1960. Home of record: Ennis, TX.

Dobecka, Johnny Robert, Jr., Coppell, TX, son of Johnny Robert and Vickie Marie Cervenka Dobecka, Sr. Graduated from Coppell High School in 1964. Enlisted in the Army in Dallas, TX. Served three years in Viet Nam, where he was involved in many battles, and Turkey. Awarded many medals, including a Purple Heart Cluster for being WOUNDED TWICE in 1977 and 1978. Discharged at rank of E6. Married Vicki Kay Crow, has one daughter. Residence is Grapevine, TX.

Dobecka, John Robert, Sr., son of Frank Paul and Mary Niazer Dobecka, was born Sept. 17, 1917. Attended school in Carrollton, TX. Enlisted in the Army at Camp Wolters. Theater of Operations: Asiatic Pacific and Philippine Islands during WWII. WOUNDED THREE TIMES. Rank: Sgt. Medals: Purple Heart with two Oak Leaf Clusters, the Asiatic-Pacific with two BSS, Philippine Liberation with BSS and Good Conduct. Discharged May 21, 1945. Married Vickie Cervenka and has six children. Residence is Coppell, TX.

Dobecka, Marvin Frank, son of Frank and Lillian Macik Dobecka, was born on April 30, 1942, Mesquite, Dallas Co., TX. Education: Grapevine Public School, University of Texas at Arlington, Abilene, TX, Christian College. Drafted into U.S. Army Corps on Jan. 21, 1964, Dallas, TX. Basic Training was at Ft. Polk, LA, Military Police School, Ft. Gordon, GA. Served his country at Ft. Sill, OK. Rank: SP 4. Honorably discharged on Jan. 20, 1966. Home of record: McKinney, TX.

Dobias, Francis J., was born on Feb. 12, 1902. Ordained on Dec. 20, 1930. Served in U.S. Army Corps as Catholic chaplain during WWII. Rank: Captain. Died on June 26, 1961. Buried in Holy Cross Catholic Cemetery in Granger, TX. Hometown was Granger, TX.

Dobias, Jerry F., was born on Jan. 2, 1928. Served during WWII in the U.S. Army Corps, Co H, 21 Infantry. Rank: Pfc. Died on June 12, 1961. Buried in Holy Cross Catholic Cemetery in Granger TX. Hometown was Granger, TX.

Doenges, Viola (Kolos), daughter of Josef and Anezka Kolos, was born Apr. 18, 1921, Hallettsville, TX. Education: St. Joseph's Catholic School, Yoakum, TX; University of Texas, Austin, TX. Enlisted in U.S. Armed Forces, Aug. 5, 1943, Ft. Sam Houston, San Antonio, TX, during WWII. Rank: Sgt. Stationed in Newport News, VA, which was a port of embarkation. Thousands of GIs left from there for overseas service. Honorably discharged Jan. 24, 1946. Home of record: Houston, TX.

Dolezal, Alphonse F., son of Mr. and Mrs. Frank Dolezal. Attended school in Ross, TX. Entered service in 1943. Served in Czechoslovakia, England, France and Germany. Awarded five Battle Stars, one Bronze Arrowhead, Good Conduct Medal and three overseas bars. Rank: Pfc. Honorably discharged in 1945. Married Mary Slay.

Dolezal, Charlie F., son of Frank and Elizabeth Pokorny Dolezal, was born June 11, 1923, Weimar,

Colorado Co., TX. Education: Live Oak Public School, through third grade, near Weimar, TX. Parents immigrated from Obristvi, Melnik, Czechoslovakia in 1906, landing in Galveston, TX. In 1908, moved to Fayette Co., TX, near Dubina, and lived there until 1920, then bought a farm in the Borden Community, near Weimar, TX, where Charlie was reared. Enlisted in US Army Corps on Sept. 23, 1942, Houston, TX, and was assigned to Company M, 350th Infantry. Battles: Casa Blanca, Rome, Arno, North Apennines-Po Valley. Medals and Decorations: Combat Infantryman Badge, GCM, EAME Ribbon, American Theater Ribbon, WWII Victory. Honorably discharged on Nov. 1, 1945, Camp Bowie, TX. Rank: Pfc. Died at Wagner General Hospital, Palacios, TX, on June 14, 1977. Buried in St. Michael's Catholic Cemetery, Weimar, TX. Submitted by Annie Dolezal, Palacios, TX.

Dolezal, Edwin D., son of Thomas Anton and Frances Lahodny Dolezal, was born on July 14, 1929, Shiner, TX. Graduated from high school. Enlisted in the U.S. Navy on July 3, 1947, in Houston, Harris Co., TX. Stations and Ships: NAS, Alameda, CA, USS *Oriskany* (CVA-34), NAS, Kingsville, TX, NAVCOMSTA., Adae, AK, VT-31, NAS, Corpus Christi, TX. Medals and Awards: GCM (6 Awards), Korean Service Medal w/2 BSS, China Service Medal, Navy Occupation Medal, National Defense Medal, United Nations Service Medal, Korean Presidential Unit Citation, Expert Pistol Shot Medal. Date of Retirement: Mar. 1, 1977. Home of record, Kingsland, TX.

Dolezal, Thomas Anton, son of Anton and Julia Castka Dolezal, was born on Dec. 17, 1898 in Flatonia, Fayetteville Co., TX. Educated through third grade in rural schools in Shiner and Sweet Home, TX. Enlisted in the Army on June 15, 1917 at Houston, TX. Rank: Pfc. Assigned to Q.M.C. Detachment G.H.Q. Theater of Operations: Europe. Battles: Belleau Wood, Argonne Forest. Served in France as a truck driver and at one time chauffeured for General Pershing. Awarded the WWI Victory Metal and entitled to wear three gold chevrons. Honorably discharged at Mitchell Field, NY on July 8, 1919. Married Frances Lahodny. Was a blacksmith and welder in Shiner, TX for 37 years. Died on Feb. 23, 1986.

Dolezal, Victor, son of Frank and Elizabeth Pokorny Dolezal, was born Aug. 7, 1907, in Galveston, TX. Parents immigrated from Obristvi, Melnik, Czechoslovakia to USA in 1906, landing in Galveston, TX. They moved in 1908 to Fayette Co., TX, settling near Dubina, where they lived until 1920. The family bought a farm in the Borden community near Weimar, TX, where Victor was reared. Education: Dubina and Weimar, TX, grammar schools. Enlisted in the Army on March 20, 1942, at Ft. Sam Houston, TX. Assigned to Company L, 359th Infantry, 90th Division, U.S. Army Corps. Rank: Pfc. Battles: Invasion of France, D-Day, June 6, 1944. WOUNDED IN ACTION on June 13, 1944, near San Lo, France. Medals and decorations: Purple Heart, Combat Infantryman Badge, European-African Theater Ribbon, GCM. Honorably discharged on Oct. 23, 1944 at Brooke General Hospital, Ft. Sam Houston, TX. Married Annie Jurasek on June 25, 1946 at St. Peter's Catholic Church in Blessing, TX. Children: Helen and Billy. Died at his home in Palacios, TX, on Nov. 18, 1967, and is buried in St. John's Catholic Cemetery, Taiton, TX (near El Campo). Submitted in loving memory by his widow, Annie Jurasek Dolezal, Palacios, TX.

Dolezel, Marvin A., entered U.S. Army Corps, 1944, during WWII. Trained at Camp Wolters, TX. Rank: Pfc. Served European Theater. Awarded GCM, EAME Ribbon and two BSS. Honorably discharged 1946. Married Juanita Dolezel. Home of record: Waco, TX.

Dolezalek, James Edward, son of Edward and Bessie Martinek Dolezalek, was born Oct. 17, 1947, Wilson Jones Hospital, Sherman, TX. Education: S and S Sadler–South Mayd.; Grayson County College; Southeastern State Teachers College, Durant, OK. Enlisted at Dallas, TX, U.S.

Army Corps. Rank: Sgt. Theater of Operations: Viet Nam. WOUNDED IN ACTION. Medals: Purple Heart, Combat Infantry Badge, Army Accommodation, Good Conduct, Viet Nam Campaign. Honorably discharged 1969. Married Johnnie. Children: Jamie, James Jr., Jennifer, Jeremy. Two grandchildren: Zeke and Sebastian. Occupation: Employed by General Telephone Co. of Sherman, TX. Home of record: Sherman, TX.

Dornak, Henry, son of Cyril and Mary Pesl Dornak, was born on Aug. 1, 1918, in Cistern, TX. Enlisted during WWII on Feb. 20, 1942, at Gonzales, TX. Theater of Operations: Europe. Honorably discharged on Feb. 24, 1946. Home of record: Moulton, TX. Submitted by Evelyn Vecera, Bellaire, TX.

Doskocil, Joe Lee, son of Joe and Matilda Manak Doskocil, was born Dec. 20, 1923, Cyclone, TX. Educated Cyclone, TX. Enlisted in 1942 at Ft. Sam Houston, San Antonio, TX, in the U.S. Army Corps. Rifleman. Rank: Sgt. Theater of Operations: European. Battles: Germany and France. Medals: WWII Victory Medal, European Theater of Operations w/2 BSS, GCM, one Overseas Service Bar. Honorable discharged July 29, 1946, San Antonio, TX. Died Feb. 29, 1988. Submitted by Geraldine Doskocil, Temple, TX.

Dostacik, Ernest A., son of Mr. and Mrs. Alois Dostacik, was born in Flatonia, TX on Dec. 5, 1920. Graduated from Flatonia High School. Entered the army in 1942 in San Antonio. Assigned as an ammunition server in Company C, 409th Infantry. Campaigns: Sicilian, Naples-Foggia, Rome-Arno, Southern France, Northern France, Ardennes, Rhineland, and Central Europe. Medals: EAME Campaign with eight BSS. one Bronze Arrowhead, Good Conduct, one Service Stripe, four Overseas Service Bars. Discharged on Oct. 18. 1945. Died on Nov. 27, 1983. Information supplied by his sister, Mrs. Vlasta Niemann of Victoria, TX.

Dostalik, Frank, served in U.S. Armed Forces during WWI. Member of SPJST Lodge 20, Granger, TX.

Dostalik, Henry, served in U.S. Armed Forces during WWI. Member of SPJST Lodge 20, Granger, TX.

Drastata, John J., son of Mr. and Mrs. Charles Drastata of Taiton, TX, was born on Jan. 6, 1932, in El Campo, TX. Enlisted in U.S. Army Corps on Dec. 11, 1952. Theater of Operations: Korean War. Assigned to Infantry, 2nd Division, Ft. Hood, TX. Participated in Korean War, 1953, 1954 on Papsan Mountain, was gunner, 50 caliber machine gun. Medals: Presidential Unit Citation, Korean Service w/1 BSS, UN Service, NDS, C.I. Badge. Honorably discharged on Dec. 10, 1954. Home of record: Allen, TX.

Drexler, Joe L., son of John A. and Agnes Recek Drexler, was born Feb. 26, 1928, St. Mary's, TX. Education: Stacy School. Enlisted in the U.S. Army in Texas. Rank: Cpl. Fought in Korean War. Honorably discharged. Married, one daughter: Ann Marie Drexler. Died on Jan. 1, 1989 and is buried in St. Mary's Cemetery, TX. Submitted by niece, Shirley Moczygemba, Yorktown, TX.

Drexler, Leon James, son of Louis J. and Rosie Christen Drexler, was born July 2, 1944, Hallettsville, TX. Education: high school. Enlisted in 1965, U.S. Army Reserves. Became active in U.S. Army Corps during Viet Nam. Assigned to Engineer Battalion. Rank: E-5 Sgt. Honorably discharged on Dec. 5, 1969, in Washington, D.C. Married. Children: Jeffery (deceased), Jerry, Jackie, Leon James Jr., and John. Home of record: Luling, TX. Submitted by Shirley Moczygemba, Yorktown, TX.

Dreyer, Joe Rudolph, Jr., son of Joe Rudolph Dreyer, Sr. and Annie Bell Clepper Dreyer, was born June 23, 1930, Goose Creek, TX. Education: high school, Lee College. Enlisted U.S. Navy on Sept. 18, 1950, Houston, TX. Boot camp, San Diego, CA, transferred to Moffet Field, Naval Air Station, CA. Rank: Aviation Machinist 3rd Class. Attached to Composite Sqdn VC-3. All enlistment was served there except for a nine month detachment w/Fox-Baker Company, Naval Air Station, Atsugi, Japan. Medals: National Defense, United Nations, Korean Service, Good Conduct. Honorably discharged on July 2, 1954. Married Sylvia Maxine Guillote, had three children, five grandchildren as of Dec. 1993. Returned to printing industry, Solvay Polymer, in Deer Park TX. Retired in 1988.

Dreyer, Ladis B., son of William and Anna Marek Dreyer, was born on April 3, 1909 in Milam Co., TX. Education in Meeks and Brenham, TX. Served in Okinawa on Supply Dump Duty and in USNR in Houston, TX, from April 1944 to Jan. 1946. Rank: Seaman First Class. Married Irene Voigt Dreyer. Children: a son and a daughter. Retired carpenter. Home of record: Lorena, TX.

Dreyfuss, Cecelia Anne (Stiborik), daughter of Antonin and Cecelia Capak-Najvar Stiborik, was born in Taylor, TX. Educated at Barnard College and Columbia College. Ph.D. from the University of Michigan. Enlisted at Fort Sam Houston, TX, on Oct. 21, 1942, with her sister Mary. Theaters of operation: United States, 8th Air Force HQ, High Wycombe, England and France. Discharged at Fort Sam Houston, TX in Nov. 1945. Currently resides in Ann Arbor, MI.

Drgac, Hubert J., son of Walter J. and Anna Langer Drgac, was born on Jan. 30, 1930, Burleson Co., TX. Enlisted on June 29, 1951, during Korean War, at San Angelo, TX. Discharged early due to death of brother in plane crash. Came home to help father in dairy business. Honorably discharged on Oct. 30, 1952. Married Noemi Helen Michalik. Four sons. All of family is involved in farming and ranching in West, TX. All enjoy hunting. Home of record: San Angelo, TX.

Driska, Benny, served in U.S. Army Corps, WWII. Achieved rank of Sgt. before honorable discharge. Hometown: Granger, TX.

Driska, Harry, served in the U.S. Army Corps, WWII. Achieved rank of Sgt. before honorable discharge. Hometown: Granger, TX.

Driska, John A., was born on Feb. 5, 1912. WWII veteran; Cpl, 39 AAF Air Depot GP. Died Dec. 1, 1950. Buried at Holy Cross Catholic Cemetery, Granger, TX.

Driska, Walter J., served in the U.S. Army Corps, WWII. Achieved rank of Sgt. before honorable discharge. Member of American Legion Post No 282, Granger, TX. Hometown: Granger, TX.

Drlik, Raymond, son of Leo and Rosie Prihoda Drlik, was born on Nov. 30, 1936 in Garwood, TX. His education was at Garwood High School. He enlisted at Columbus, TX. His theater of operation was Europe. He received the Good Conduct Medal. He was discharged in 1962 and currently resides in Garwood, TX.

Drozd, Albert, Granger, TX, WWII Veteran.

Drozd, Charles Joseph, son of John Drozd, Jr. (immigrated to Lavaca Co., TX from Moravia, Czechoslovakia) and Clara Svrcek Drozd, was born June 5, 1912 in Moravia, Lavaca Co., TX. Educated at Komensky and Pagel settlement schools. Seven brothers, five sisters. Enlisted at Ft. Sam Houston, TX, on Dec. 7, 1942. Boot Camp training was at Camp Sibert, AL, and at Camp

Rucker, AL for one year. Rank: Staff Sergeant. 4th HQ and HQ Detachment Special Troops 2nd Army, 87th Chemical Battalion. Battles: Normandy, Northern France, Ardennes, Rhineland, and Central Europe. Served in the Rhine Bulge in Frankfort and Hamburg, Germany as Chief Cook for 18 months. Medals: EAME Campaign w/5 BSS, Good Conduct, Distinguished Unit Badge, Purple Heart. WOUNDED IN ACTION at the Rhine Battle of the Bulge. Honorably discharged on Oct. 14, 1945, Thomasville, Georgia. Employed by Texaco, Inc. for 18 years. Married Adela Hanslik on Oct. 27, 1936, at Sacred Heart Catholic Church, Hallettsville, TX, by Msgr. Anthony Drozd. Member of VFW No. 382, American Legion, SPJST, Knights of Columbus, Hallettsville Volunteer Fire Dept., and Sacred Heart Catholic Church. Was also a rancher. Enjoyed hunting, fishing, and dancing. Died at the age of 50 years on Jan. 7, 1963, at Renger Memorial Hospital, following a prolonged illness. Buried in Sacred Heart Cemetery with full military honors. Information supplied by his widow, Adela Pohl, Hallettsville, TX.

Drozd, Daniel J., son of Mr. and Mrs. John L. Drozd, was born in Granger, Williamson Co., TX. Graduate, Granger, TX, High School. Enlisted in 1944 in the Merchant Marines. Basic training was at St. Petersburg, FL. Theater of Operations: Asiatic-Pacific. Served in Panama, Carolines, Marshalls, and Philippines. Medals: Asiatic- Pacific Campaign Ribbon, WWII Victory Ribbon. Honorably discharged in 1945. Hometown, Granger, TX.

Drozd, Henry J., son of Henry F. and Agnes M. Vasek Drozd, was born on March 4, 1937, in Ennis, TX. Education: St. John's Catholic School, Ennis, TX. St. John's Seminary, San Antonio, TX, Assumption Seminary, San Antonio, TX, University of Dallas, Irving, TX, North American College, Rome, Italy, Gregorian University, Rome, Italy, United States Army Chaplain School, Brooklyn, NY, United States Army Airborne School, Ft. Benning, GA, Long Island University, Brooklyn, NY, Webster College, St. Louis, MO, Command and General Staff College, Ft. Leavenworth, KS, California Family Studies Center, Burbank, CA, Azusa Pacific University, Azusa CA. Rank: Lt. Col., U.S. Army Corps. Theaters of Operation: Kingdom of Saudi Arabia. Campaigns: Desert Shield, Desert Storm. Medals: Liberation, Overseas Service Ribbons (3), Army Service Ribbon, Armed Forces Reserve, BSS (3), National Defense Service (2), Army Commendation (5), Meritorious Service, Legion of Merit, BSS, Master Parachutist. Spent many hours during tour of duty at Dahran Air Base in Saudi Arabia picking up hundreds of thousands of "any soldier" mail. Currently is a priest in the Diocese of Dallas. Home of record: Hunter Army Airfield, Savannah, GA.

Drozd, Jerry T., son of Theodore J. and Mary Gallia Drozd, was born May 4, 1925, Penelope, TX. Education: grammar school, Massey, TX; high school, Bynum TX. Enlisted in Hillsboro, TX, in 1944. Theater of Operations: Central Europe. Served in Infantry as Truck Driver. Battles: Rhineland GO 105 and WD 45 in Central Europe. Medals: European Theater of Operations w/2 BSS, GCM, Purple Heart, two Overseas Service Bars, WWII Victory Ribbon. WOUNDED IN ACTION, Rhineland, Germany, on April 25, 1945. Honorably discharged on July 15, 1946. Married Ida Hutyra Matus. Died Jan. 8, 1994. Submitted by his widow, Ida Drozd of West, TX.

Drozd, John, of Granger, TX, WWII veteran, was a member of American Legion Post No. 282, Granger, TX. Deceased.

Drozd, John L., served in the U.S. Army Corps, WWI. Hometown, Granger, TX. Deceased.

Drozd, Leo Martin, son of Theodore J. and Mary Gallia Drozd, was born Jan. 30, 1924, Penelope, TX. Education: Massey Grammar School, Hill, TX; Bynum High School, Hill, TX. Enlisted in Dec. 1942 at Hillsboro, TX. Served with Co. B, 300th Engineer Battalion in the European

Theater of Operations. Medals: Good Conduct, American Campaign, European Campaign, Purple Heart. MISSING IN ACTION, June 19, 1944. Declared KILLED IN ACTION on June 19, 1945, while in service on ship that exploded from hitting a mine landing in Normandy in Europe.

Drozd, Theodore J., son of John and Anna Cernosek Drozd, was born Oct. 30, 1894, in Praha, Flatonia, TX. Education: grammar school. Enlisted in the Army Corps on Aug. 27, 1918, Hillsboro, Hill, TX. Rank: Pvt. Served in the American Expeditionary Forces in the Panama Canal from Oct. 18, 1918 through May 8, 1919, during WWI. Theater of Operation: Panama Canal. Awarded WWI Victory Medal. Honorably discharged May 20, 1919. Married Mary Gallia. Died on Aug. 15, 1974 at the age of 79 years. Submitted by Ida Drozd, West, TX.

Drozd, Thomas Julius, was born March 31, 1922. Veteran of WWII, Tec 5, U.S. Army. Died Oct. 31, 1969. Buried at Holy Cross Catholic Cemetery, Granger, TX.

Drozda, Alvin F., son of Mr. and Mrs. Frank Drozda, was born in Taylor, Williamson Co., TX. Graduate, Taylor High School, TX. Enlisted in the USMC in 1940. Received basic training at San Diego, CA, and Camp Pendleton, CA. Rank: 1st Sgt. Theater of Operations: Asiatic-Pacific. Campaigns: Guadalcanal, Vangunu, New Georgia, Guam, Emirau Era, Okinawa. WOUNDED IN ACTION in 1945 in Japan. Medals: Asiatic-Pacific Campaign Ribbon w/4 BSS, American Defense, National Defense, Navy Unit Commendation Ribbons, Purple Heart. Honorably discharged.

Dubcak, Joe Daniel, son of Joe and Julia Dubcak, was born Nov. 11, 1930, Rogers, TX. Education: Rogers High School, Rogers, TX. Enlisted in the Air Force in Nov. 1951 at Waco, TX. Rank: S/Sgt. Was in North East Air Command. Medals: National Defense and Good Conduct. Honorably discharged on Nov. 22, 1955. Married Irene; two daughters. Home of record: Temple, TX.

Dubec, Henry, was born on July 18, 1917. WWII veteran. Pvt., Co. B, 80 Inf. Training Battalion. Died Oct. 9, 1958. Buried at Holy Cross Catholic Cemetery, Granger, TX.

Dudek, Eugene M., son of Mr. and Mrs. John Dudek, Waco, TX, entered Army Air Corps, 1942, trained in Texas, Mississippi, Louisiana and Utah. Served during WWII. Attained rank of Sgt. before honorable discharge in 1945.

Dudek, Fred B., son of Mr. and Mrs. John Dudek, Waco, TX. Entered U.S. Army Corps, 1941. Served during WWII in European Theater. WOUNDED IN ACTION, Battle of Roha. Awarded Purple Heart, three Battle Stars, Presidential Citation and European Theater Ribbon. Attained rank of Sgt. prior to honorable discharge in 1945.

Dudek, John Francis, son of Mr. and Mrs. John Dudek. Entered Army Air Corps, 1943. Served on Guam. Awarded GCM, WWII Victory Medal, Asiatic-Pacific Campaign Ribbons. Attained rank of S/Sgt. prior to honorable discharge in 1946.

Dudek, Raymond P., son of Mr. and Mrs. John Dudek, Waco, TX. Entered U.S. Marine Corps, 1940. Served in Asiatic-Pacific Theater of Operations on Marshalls, Guam, and Solomons during WWII. WOUNDED IN ACTION on Guam, 1944. Awarded Purple Heart, Presidential Citation, three Battle Stars and Asiatic-Pacific Campaign Ribbon. Attained rank of Sgt.

Dudek, Rosalie, daughter of Mr. and Mrs. John Dudek, Waco, TX. Education: attended Academy of Sacred Heart. Entered WAVES during WWII in 1943. Trained in New York, Norman, OK and St. Louis, MO. Attained rank of SP 2/C prior to honorable discharge, 1945.

Dujka, Milan, son of Jan. and Anna Dujka, was born Feb. 12, 1915 in Skidmore, TX. Graduated from Ross High School in Ross, TX. Joined the National Guard in Oct. 1940. Mobilized into the 36th Division in Nov. and trained in Brownwood, TX, and in FL and MA. Sailed for North Africa on April 1, 1943 and made an amphibious landing on Nov. 9, 1943, in Salerno, Italy, where he fought at Alto Villa, San Pietro, and Rapido River. Also made an amphibious landing at Anzio and fought his way home through Rome. Rotated home as a

Staff Sergeant in June 1944 and was discharged in Feb. 1945. Received the Silver Star for gallantry in action for saving many lives at the Battle of Rapido River. Other medals include European Theater of Operation, Marksman and Combat Infantryman. Home of record: Ross, TX.

Dukatnik, Clarence, son of Emil Dukatnik and Agnes, was born Oct. 18, 1951, enlisted in U.S.A.F. Spent four years in Air Force, 17 years in U.S. Army Corps. M/Sgt NCO with 101st Airborne Division, moved into Iraqi, entered Saudi Arabia in the direction of Baghdad, at the Euphrates River. The 101st turned toward Basra, helping capture Iraqis at the Euphrates River.

Dukatnik, Emil, son of Vince and Mary Lugo Dukatnik, was born Oct. 15, 1910, Temple, TX. Education: Red Ranger School through sixth grade. Inducted into U.S. Army Corps at Abilene, TX, on Dec. 5, 1942. Assigned to 9th Army, 406th Infantry, Company F. Military Occupation Specialty-Basic 521. Combat Infantryman, Badge 20, Nov. 1944. Battles: Rhineland, Central Europe, GO 33 WD 45. Medals: American Theater Campaign, EAME Campaign w/2 BSS, Good Conduct, Lapel button issued for ASR Score–57, Purple Heart Per WD Ltr. to Hq. 232nd (US) Sta. Hospital, May 22, 1945, WWII Victory Ribbon, one Service Stripe, one Overseas Service Bar. WOUNDED IN ACTION, EAME, Feb. 27, 1945. Date of embarkation, destination EAME Sept. 12, 1944. Foreign Service: 8 months, 27 days. Total Service, 2 years, 3 months, 7 days. Honorably discharged Dec. 1, 1945, at Ft. Sam Houston, TX. Married Agnes. Two sons: Alfred Dukatnik, born Oct. 7, 1945, died Oct. 12, 1991, and Clarence Dukatnik, born Oct. 18, 1951. Home of record: Haskell, TX.

Dulak, Edwin Aug, son of Aug and Mary Morris Dulak, was born March 1, 1921 in Moulton, Lavaca Co., TX. Education: high school, West and Waco, TX. Baylor University, three years, Waco, TX. Commissioned as an officer in the Naval Reserves in May 1942 at the Naval Air Station at Grand Prairie, TX. Rank: Captain. Dive Bomber Pilot during WWII. Served in the South Pacific. Honorably discharged Nov. 1945. Re-enlisted, joining the U.S. Marine Corps Air Force in April 1947. Second in Command at Lowery Field in Colorado. Was transporting old dive bombers from Florida to Colorado when plane crashed into the ground in a heavy, heavy fog. No instruments or radio were working in the plane. KILLED WHILE IN THE SERVICE OF HIS COUNTRY on May 10, 1947. Medals: Asiatic-Pacific Theater Campaign w/BSS, Distinguished Flying Cross, WWII Victory. Married Margaret Rook of Waco, TX. One daughter: Eddie Margaret Dulak, born on June 17, 1947. His widow and his daughter live in Waco, TX. Daughter married Steve Massey; two children: Gabrielle (14) and Christopher (7).

Dulak, Ernest, son of Constance and Pauline Cinek Dulak, was born July 26, 1918, at West, TX. Educated at Axtell, TX, and Waco Academy. Enlisted at Fort Sam Houston, TX, in July 1936, U.S. Army Corps. Rank: Sgt. Second Infantry Division, 12th Field Artillery and "C" Battery. Battles: Normandy (D-Day+1), Brest, Belgian Bulge, Leipzig and Tinchecray. Medals: Good Conduct and five Battle Stars. Discharged in July 1945 at Fort Sam Houston, TX. Married Lillie Winkler. Home of record: Waco, TX area.

Duron, Bobby, son of John Joseph Dusek. Home of record: Dallas, TX.

Dusek, Alfonse, of Houston, TX. Military Service: WWII.

Dusek, Darwin, Granger, TX, WWII Veteran.

Dusek, David L., son of Lumir F. and Frankie L. Garlitz Dusek, was born Dec. 28, 1946 in Stephenville, TX. Attended Littlefield High School in Littlefield, TX. Enlisted in the U.S. Air Force in Sept. 1966 at Lubbock, TX. Retired from the U.S. Air Force in Oct. 1986 with the rank of Master Sgt., after twenty years of active service.

Medals: NCO Professional Military Educational Graduate Ribbon, Air Force Longevity Service Award with four bronze oak leaf clusters, Air Force Overseas Tour Ribbon, Air Force Outstanding Unit Award with bronze oak leaf cluster, and Air Force Good Conduct with silver oak leaf cluster. Home of record: Waco, TX.

Dusek, Dennis, son of John Joseph Dusek, U.S. Armed Forces Veteran, Peacetime, after WWII.

Dusek, Edwin, son of Joseph and Anna Lavre Dusek, was born Oct. 22, 1885. Served in the U.S. Army during WWI as a Private in an Army Ordnance Unit. Died on Aug. 23, 1937 and is interred in the SPJST Cemetery at Holland, Bell Co., TX.

Dusek, Edwin, son of John Joseph Dusek, U.S. Armed Forces, WWII veteran.

Dusek, Jerome, son of John Joseph Dusek, U.S. Armed Forces, WWII veteran.

Dusek, Jerry, attained rank of Sgt., Granger, TX, WWII veteran.

Dusek, Joe D., son of Mr. and Mrs. C. V. Dusek, was born in Granger, Williamson Co., TX. Graduate of Granger High School. Enlisted in U.S. Army Corps, 1941. Basic training Ft. Leonard Wood, MO. Commissioned 1st Lt., Sept. 1943, Brisbane, Australia. Theater of Operations: Asiatic-Pacific. Campaigns in S.W. Pacific, East Indies, Papaun, New Guinea, Philippines. Medals: Asiatic-Pacific Campaign Ribbon w/4 BSS, American Defense Medal, American Theater Campaign Ribbon, Philippine Liberation Ribbon w/1 BSS, Pres. Unit Citation. Honorable discharge, 1945. Granger, TX.

Dusek, John, son of John Joseph Dusek, U.S. Armed Forces, WWII veteran.

Dusek, John Joseph, son of John George Dusek and Anna Faltysek, was born Aug. 8, 1894, in Cermna, Bohemia. Completed fourth grade. Enlisted in the U.S. Navy during WWI at Houston, TX. Rank: Musician Second Class. Was in the Atlantic Fleet on the USS *Pennsylvania*. Was in the U.S. Navy Band conducted by John Philip Sousa. Received the Good Conduct Medal. Discharged on June 24, 1919. Six sons, all of whom served in the military: Alfonse, Jerome, and John in WWII; Edwin and Dennis in peacetime; Stanley in the Korean War. Died on July 12, 1978.

Dusek, Lumir Francis, son of Frank D. and Anna Dusek, was born Nov. 24, 1916, in Rogers, Bell Co., TX. Attended John Tarleton College in Stephenville and college in Huntsville, earning a BS degree. Enlisted in the Navy at San Angelo, TX. Rank: RM3C. Theater of Operations: Pacific USNTS, San Diego, CA, USS *Brown* (DD546), RS, San Francisco, CA, SCTS, Terminal Island, CA, and USNH, Long Beach, CA. Battles: Carolinas, Marianas, Pelileu, Formosa, and Luzon in the Philippines. Hospitalized in Jan. 1945 for battle fatigue. Discharged on May 29, 1945 with disability pension. Died March 31, 1987.

Dusek, Stanley, son of John Joseph Dusek, U.S. Armed Forces, Korean War veteran.

Dvoracek, Charles Frank, son of Charles and Otillie Bezdek Dvoracek, was born Dec. 16, 1917, in West, TX. Attended West High School and Texas Tech University in Lubbock. Entered the Navy in 1942. Trained in San Diego, CA. Rank: Lt. Served in Guadalcanal, Gilberts, Marshalls, Carolines, Iwo Jima, Philippines, and Japan. Medals: American Theater Service, Asiatic-Pacific Service, and Philippines Liberation ribbons. Discharged in 1945. Married Laura Shope in San Francisco. One daughter and one son who is deceased. Served in the Naval Reserve after WWII and later worked with the Civil Service in Okalona, AR. Farmed after retirement. Home of record: Okalona, AR.

Dvoracek, Frank Louis, son of Charles and Otillie Bezdek Dvoracek, was born Aug. 20, 1919, in West, TX. Attended West High School. Enlisted in the Army in 1942. Trained at Camp Barkeley and in El Paso. Stationed in CA. Rank: Sgt. Discharged in 1945. Married Sabina Grabarczyk; two sons and one daughter. Worked as a tool and die designer in South Bend, IN, and later as a farm equipment plant manager in Ossea, WI.

Dvoracek, Herman Joseph, son of Charles and Otillie Bezdek Dvoracek, was born Feb. 2, 1930 in West, TX. Attended West High School and the University of Texas in Austin. Enlisted in the service and received his training at Fort Smith, AR. Stationed in Japan and briefly in Korea at the end of the war. After discharge, completed degree in Petroleum Engineering and was employed by Mobile Oil Company. Married Sarah Frances Brown; a son and a daughter. Home of record: New Orleans, Louisiana.

Dvorak, Aug. E. "Goober," of Penelope and West, TX, WWII veteran.

Dvorak, Frank, son of Thomas and Frantiska Dvorak, was born Oct. 8, 1897, in Vienna, Austria. Attended grades 1-5 in Austria and the sixth grade in East Bernard, TX. Left Texas during WWI and went to Europe via New York to join the Czech Legionnaires. Rank: Pvt. Fought with the Slovak 21st Regiment in France and participated in the Alsace and Bois Q Argonne Campaigns. Discharged on Oct. 9, 1919 in Prague, Czechoslovakia, and returned to the Richmond, TX, area.

Dybala, Bernard Frank, son of William and Julie Novosad Dybala, was born Nov. 8, 1925, Fayetteville, TX. Education: St. John's Catholic Elementary School and Fayetteville High School. Inducted into service about 1943 at Ft. Sam Houston, TX. Attended Cook and Bake School, Ft. Sam Houston, TX. Rank: TEC 4. Theater of Operations: America. Medals: Good Conduct, American Theater Campaign Ribbon, WWII Victory Ribbon. Honorably discharged Aug. 16, 1946. Married Mary Baca; five children. Home of record: Rosenberg, TX. Submitted by brother, Joseph John Dybala of Fayetteville, TX.

Dybala, John F., son of Rudolph and Frances Volcik Dybala, was born Feb. 26, 1917, Fayetteville, TX. Education: Ross Prairie Elementary, Ellinger, TX and Red Square High School, Ganado, TX; Carpentry Academy, Houston, TX. Enlisted in the U.S. Army Corps, Ganado, TX, in June 1942. Rank: S/Sgt. Theater of Operations: American and European. Battles: Rhineland G033 WD45. Medals: GCM Medal, BSS, WWII Victory Medal, Purple Heart. WOUNDED IN ACTION. Honorably discharged on June 20, 1946. Married Annie Pasteka in April 1951. Two daughters: Clare and Marie. Employed as carpenter foreman. Hobbies: played drums, trumpet, dulcimer, with various orchestras and SPJST Lodge #88 Concert Orchestra. Died July 11, 1986. Buried in Resurrection, South Park Cemetery, Pearland, TX. Submitted by Annie Dybala, whose home of record is Houston, TX.

Dybala, Joseph John, son of William and Julie Novosad Dybala, was born March 11, 1921, Fayetteville, TX. Education: St. John's Catholic Elementary School and Fayetteville High School. Inducted about 1942 at Ft. Sam Houston, TX. Rank: Pvt. Theater of Operations: America. Medals: American Theater Ribbon among others. Honorably discharged Aug. 10, 1943. Home of record: Fayetteville, TX.

Dybala, Rudolph Rehor, son of Rudolph Edward and Frances Volcik Dybala, was born March 12, 1909, Fayetteville, TX. Education: Ross Prairie Grammar School and Ellinger High School, Ellinger, TX, graduating in 1927. Awarded a two year Temporary Teacher Certificate, qualifying him to teach in grammar and high schools in TX. Previously a farmer and carpenter. At the beginning of WWII, worked in U.S. Defense Plants in TX and LA, and under Civil Service as a Carpenter Foreman, Ellington Field, Harris Co., TX. Inducted into the U.S. Army Corps in Jan.

1944, serving in the European Theater of Operations in Northern France as subsistence NCO with Replacement and Deployment Center Unit. Medals: GCM, Victory Ribbon, three overseas Service Bars, EAME Campaign Ribbon w/1 BSS and Rifle Expert Badge. Honorably discharged on May 2, 1946 at Ft. Sam Houston, TX. Died on Jan. 7, 1986. Buried in Rosewood Memorial Park, Humble, TX. Was a talented musician, music teacher, band and orchestra leader in the 1930s. Also was a member of the American Legion Band of Houston, TX. On Jan. 21, 1949 he married Gladys Naplava, a Czech girl, the daughter of John Naplava and Annie Adamek. Four daughters and two sons. Blessed with six grandchildren before he died; four more came later.

Dykowski, Alvin J., of Granger, TX, member of American Legion Post No 282, Granger, TX, WWII veteran.

Dykowski, Edward E., of Granger, TX, member of American Legion Post No 282, Granger, TX, WWII veteran.

Dykowski, John, of Taylor, TX, member of American Legion Post No 282, Granger, TX, WWII veteran.

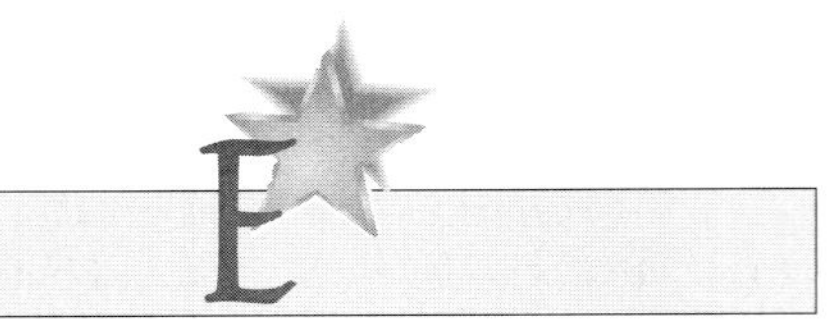

Elick, Victor, member of SPJST Lodge 20, Granger, TX; served in U.S. Army Corps during WWI. Hometown, Granger, TX. Deceased.

Elliott, James Curtis, son of Elmer Ernest (deceased Sept. 18, 1965) and Evelyn Margie David Elliott, was born Feb. 18, 1957, Taylor, Williamson County, TX. Education: St. Mary's, Taylor, TX, 1963-1967; Taylor Middle and High School. Graduate, class of 1975. Enlisted on Sept. 15, 1975 in the U.S. Air Force, San Antonio, TX. Attained rank of Tech Sgt. Military Occupation: Nuclear Weapons Specialist. Theater of Operations: American. Battles: Gulf War. Medals: Air Force Commendation Medal; Meritorious Service Medal; Good Conduct Medal w/4 OLC. Served one year in Turkey as Instructor. In Air Force now. Married Geri Lynn Bush. Hobbies: all sports—golf, darts, soft ball, etc. Stationed at submission of information: Denver, CO 80231. Submitted by Evelyn Elliott, Taylor, TX.

Elsik, Alvin Jerry, son of Emil and Frances Simecek Elsik, was born Nov. 12, 1918, Oeanaville, TX. Education: Oenaville, TX, public schools; graduated high school there. Enlisted in U.S. Army Corps on Oct. 8, 1941, Ft. Sill, OK, prior to start of WWII. Boot camp, Camp Callan, CA. Served in Iceland, England, France, Belgium and Germany. Theater of Operations: EAME. Medals: American Defense Service Medal, EAME Campaign Medal w/3 BSS, Good Conduct Medal. Honorably discharged on Oct. 20, 1945. Died on Jan. 9, 1991, Dallas, TX. Buried, Grove Hill Cemetery, Dallas, TX. Submitted by Libbie Elsik of Dallas, TX.

Elsik, Johnnie Edwin, son of Emil and Frances Elsik, was born Aug. 25, 1916, Oenaville, Bell County, TX. Education: Oenaville High School. Enlisted U.S. Army Corps, Ft. Sam Houston, TX, attained rank of T/Sgt. Theater of Operations: Europe. Battles and Campaigns: Normandy, Northern France, Ardennes, Rhineland, Central Europe. Medals: WWII Victory, EAME Campaign w/5 BSS, American Defense Service, American Theater Campaign, GCM. Honorably discharged on Nov. 11, 1945. Married Lillian Salac on Nov. 27, 1945 in Cyclone, TX. Was a retired farmer and electrician at the time of his death on Sept. 19, 1992. Buried in St. Joseph's Catholic Cemetery, Cyclone, TX. Submitted by daughter, Marie E. Elsik, Temple, TX, lovingly, in his memory.

Elzner, Agnes (Burge), daughter of Frantisek Elzner, married Henry C. Burge, served during World War II in the U.S. Cadet Nurse Corps from Aug. 31, 1944 until her discharge on Sept. 31, 1947. Thanks to Agnes for submitting most of the Elzner family information. Her home of record is Kerrville, TX.

Elzner, Edwin, Army, WWII, son of Stephen Elzner.

Elzner, Emil E., son of Frantisek Elzner, served in the U.S. Navy during World War I. Deceased.

Elzner, Frank, son of Frantisek Elzner, served with the U.S. Armed Forces during World War II. Deceased

Elzner, Frank, Army, WWI, son of Frank Elzner.

Elzner, Franklin, U.S. Army Corps. Home of record: Malin, OR.

Elzner, Jerry Louis, son of Frantisek "Frank" and Agnes Popelka Elzner, was born July 14, 1925, St. Paul, TX. Education: high school, college. Enlisted in Corpus Christi, TX, 1945. Assigned to Co. M, 15th Infantry Rgt., 3rd Inf. Division. Theaters of Operation: European and Korean. Assigned to Intelligence and Investigations: seven and a half years, Europe; four years, Alaska; one year, Korea. Medals: BSS, GCM, ETO, WWII

Victory, Korean Occupation, UN Defense. U.S. Army retired, 1966, 21 years. Rank, S/Sgt. Married Milly Elzner. Home of record is Corpus Christi, TX.

Elzner, Larry, son of Jerry Louis and Milly Elzner, is on active duty with the U.S. Navy. Home of record: Corpus Christi, TX.

Elzner, Lincoln, U.S. Navy. Home of record: Malin, OR.

Elzner, Peter, Jr., son of Peter and Anne Elzner. Served with the U.S. Army during the Korean Conflict.

Elzner, Stephen, son of Frantisek Elzner, served with the U.S. Navy during World War I. Deceased.

Elzner, Timothy, son of Jerry Louis and Milly Elzner, served with the U.S. Army.

Ermis, William Joseph, son of John and Marie Horak Ermis, was born Aug. 26, 1891, McLennan Co., TX. Graduated Brantley-Draughon Business College, Ft. Worth, TX. Married Bertha Janek, on May 14, 1918. Enlisted in U.S. Army Corps, May 27, 1918, Waco, TX. Sgt. Med. Dept, 165th Depot Brig, Inf, Camp Travis, TX. Honorably discharged on Nov. 21, 1918. In 1919, he entered Postal Service and was a letter carrier for 31 years. Retired in 1950. Built three houses in Ft. Worth, TX, for his family's use. Was a constant builder and investor in real estate. Deacon, Elder, elected to Elder Emeritus of his church. Member Masonic Lodge. Bertha was active in Eastern Star. Died on Dec. 28, 1969, Ft. Worth, TX. Buried Mt. Olivet Cemetery, Ft. Worth, TX. Survived by two daughters: Lillian Ermis Allen and Artie Ray Ermis Collier. Lovingly submitted to his memory by daughter, Lillian Ermis Allen of Bedford, TX.

Fabrygel, Anton J., son of Mr. and Mrs. Louis Fabrygel, was born July 6, 1931, Midfield, TX. Graduate of Blessing High School, Blessing, TX. Enlisted U.S. Navy on July 14, 1948, Houston, TX. Rank: CO 3. Boarded troop train to San Diego, CA. Basic training at the U.S. Navy Co. 290 Training Center, San Diego, CA. Assigned to Commander Service Force Pacific Fleet located in Pearl Harbor, HI. Assigned to confidential and secret files as a files clerk. In 1951, transferred to the C.B.'s training school, Port Hueneme, CA. Then to N.O.B. Guam, where he joined the 103 NCB for a year. Later assigned to Public Works, where he served as Security Chief for six months. Medals: Good Conduct, Korean Campaign Ribbon, Marksmanship w/Carbine Rifle. Honorably discharged on June 24, 1953. Married for 26 years; two children. Member SBJST Lodge #88, 25 years; American Legion Post #560, 33 years. Home of record: Houston, TX.

Fabrygel, Christian B., Jr., son of Christian B. Fabrygel, Sr. and Emily Zboril Fabrygel, was born April 4, 1932 in Matagorda Co., TX. Attended West Columbia School and entered the Army on Dec. 1, 1955 at Angleton, TX. Theater of Operations were USA and Alaska. Rank: Spec. 4th Class. Medals: Good Conduct, Sharpshooter. Discharged on Sept. 3, 1957. Married Shirley Cravens on March 4, 1960; two children. Resides in West Columbia, TX.

Fabrygel, Jerome Jerry, son of Christian B. Fabrygel, Sr. and Emily Zboril Fabrygel, was born April 5, 1936 in Markham, Matagorda Co., TX. Attended Columbia schools and received his GED in 1955. Enlisted in the Army in Angleton on Oct. 18, 1956. Rank: E4. Served with the Armored Division in Europe and fought in the Lebanese Conflict. He received a Good Conduct Medal and was discharged on Oct. 17, 1958. Married to Joe Ann Stancliff; three children and three grandchildren. Employed with Gulf Sulphur, Newgulf, for the past 20 years. Home of record : Needville, TX.

Fabrygel, Louis John, Sr., son of Anton and Anna Sitka Fabrygel, was born Dec. 15, 1897, Hallettsville, Lavaca Co., TX. Attended Brown School in Hallettsville, Lavaca Co., TX. Enlisted in the Army at San Antonio, on July 5, 1917. Rank: Pfc. Served with the Defensive Sector, US Army, Europe. Assigned to Co. E, 5th Am. Tr. Red Diamond. Theater of Operations: AEF. Left the U.S. on May 27, 1918. Arrived in France on June 6, 1918. St. Die 8/5/18–8/24/18; St. Mihiel 9/23/18–-10/16/18; Meuse Argonne 9/17/18–11/11/1918. Medals: St. Mihel-Meuse Argonne-Defensive Sector and Bronze Victory B. Honorably discharged on Aug. 2, 1919. Married Catherine/ Katherine Florus (living 12/30/93); seven children. During WWII, employed by the Civil Service at Camp Helen in Palacios, TX. After the war, worked for Gulf Sulphur Company at Matagorda, and then went into rice farming in the Blessing, Matagorda Co., TX, area. Lifetime member of Cecil Lee American Legion Post 649 in Blessing, TX. Hobbies: fishing and hunting. Died on Jan. 24, 1989, Blessing, TX. Buried in St. Peter's Catholic Cemetery, Blessing, TX. Submitted by daughter, Rose F. Fabrygel Williamson, Bay City, TX.

Fabrygel, Wilbert Leo Daniel, attended West Columbia School. Enlisted in the Army on Nov. 1, 1951 at Angleton, TX. Rank: Sgt. E-5. Served in the U.S. and Germany. Medals: Good Conduct and Sharpshooter. Discharged on Oct. 31, 1963. Resides in West Columbia, TX.

Fajkus, Lenard John, son of John and Caroline Fajkus, was born May 11, 1925, Wallis, TX. Attended schools in Beasley-Cottonwood area, near Rosenberg, TX. Enlisted in U.S. Navy, Dec. 10, 1943, Houston, TX. Sent to Naval Air Station in Corpus Christi, TX; on to San Bruno, CA; then to Island of Samar in the Philippines in 1945, serving in the Asiatic-Pacific Theater. Rank: Coxswain (T). Battalion responsible for unloading ammunition at the ammunition depot in the Philippines. Honorably discharged on Jan. 26, 1946, Camp Wallace, TX. Married Lillie Novosad of Sealy TX. Two sons: Harvey and Lenard, two daughters, Rosalie Chernohorsky and Alice Ann Divin, four grandchildren. Retired. Enjoys gardening, fishing and raising rabbits. Home of Record: Beasley, TX.

Fajkus, Simon, son of John and Caroline Fajkus, was born May 23, 1920, Orchard, TX. Educated in Wallis-Tavener and Beasley, TX, areas. Entered U.S. Army on May 6, 1941. Served during WWII in the 46th Engineers Construction Battalion as a general carpenter. Rank:Tec 5. Left the US on Jan. 23, 1942 for Asiatic-Pacific Campaign. Battles: East Indies islands of New Guinea and the Southern Philippines. Medals: Asiatic-Pacific Campaign Ribbon w/4 BSS, Philippine Liberation Ribbon w/2 BSS, and Good Conduct. Honorably discharged on May 29, 1945, Ft. Sam Houston, TX. Died on Jan. 31, 1990. Survived by wife, Janet (Sykora) Fajkus and two sons, Rodney and Carroll.

Fajkus, Sylvester, son of John and Caroline Fajkus, was born Dec. 29, 1915, Tavener Community, near Wallis, TX. Educated in Wallis-Tavener and Beasley, TX, areas. Inducted into the U.S. Army Corps during WWII, Apr. 9, 1943, Houston, TX. 955th Air Engineers Sqdn, construction carpenter. Rank: Sgt. Embarked for overseas duty in the EAME Theater, Dec. 24, 1943. Rome-Arno, Italy, Campaign. Medals: EAME Campaign w/1 BSS for action in North Africa, Good Conduct, WWII Victory. Honorably discharged Dec. 9, 1945 at Camp Fannin, TX. Married Ella Raska; three sons: Clement, Larry and Richard James (deceased Sept. 8, 1992); one daughter: Carrie Ann Kinnison; and eight grandchildren.

Faltisek, Alvin Fred, son of John and Mary Zalman Faltistek, was born May 30, 1910, Hermleigh, TX. Attended Baursville School, Baursville, TX. Enlisted in 1936, U.S. Army Corps, Ft. Sam Houston, TX. Served nine years. Machine Gun Sgt. (605). Military qualifications: Ex Rifle, MM Pistol, Carbine Rifle. Assigned to posts in TX, KY, FL, and LA, but mostly at Ft. Bragg, NC. 34th F.A. Bn. 9th Div. Trained soldiers for overseas duties until sent to France. Married Lisette Winkenwerder on Oct. 5, 1940; daughter Joycelyn, son Harvey. Settled on a farm north of Moulton, TX. Retired from farm, moved to the city of Moulton, where everyone knew him as "Scoup" Faltisek. Died Jan. 12, 1984. Buried: Moulton, TX. Submitted by his daughter, Joycelyn Faltisek Marquis, whose home of record is Omaha, NE.

Faltisek, Emil William, son of Frank and Francis Chernohorsky Faltisek, was born Dec. 1, 1894, three miles west of Industry, TX. Attended school nearby. He always said he went to "4th grade, 4th page." Enlisted in 1918, LaGrange, TX, during WWI. Assigned to Amer. Expeditionary Forces, Co. L, 360 Infantry, 90 Division. Served in France and Germany. Honorably discharged June 21, 1919. Married Helen Keprta on Aug. 8, 1923, Hungerford, TX; five daughters, one son. Owned and operated a grocery store in East Bernard, TX, in 1920s. Also farmed for several years. In 1946, became manager and cotton buyer for East Bernard Farmers Co-op. Retired in 1964, but worked for Tavener Gin as cotton broker. Hobbies: trapped and sold furs for many years; telling stories about his experiences in WWI to his children, grandchildren, and many friends. Submitted by Mrs. Thomas Krenek, East Bernard, TX.

Faraziel, Charlie, *please see* Frazier, Charlie.

Farek, Ann, Axtell, TX, entered the WAVES, 1942. Graduate of Texas University, trained in Seattle, WA, attained rank of Lt. prior to honorable discharge, 1946.

Farek, Marvin J., Sr., son of Joe J. and Annie Amy Morris Farek, was born Sep. 8, 1921, in Axtell,

TX. Education: Waco High School and National School of Business. Enlisted in Army Air Corps in Fort Worth, TX, on Jan. 29, 1941. Rank: Technical Sgt. Theater of Operations: European and American. Served in the 780th Bomb Squadron, 465 Bomb Group in Italy. Battles: Southern France, Rhineland, Rome-Arno, Northern France, Northern Apennines, Po Valley, and Air Combat Balkans. Medals: Soldiers, Good Conduct, American Defense, European Campaign with seven BSS, American Campaigns, Victory, and Distinguished Unit Badge with Oak Leaf Cluster. Discharged at Fort Sam Houston, TX, on Sept. 28, 1945. Home of record: Corpus Christi TX.

Farek, Lee Roy, son of Emil and Lillie Farek, was born March 1, 1930, Flatonia, TX. Attended Flatonia High; A. A. degree in management. Enlisted Houston, TX. Served in Korea (Inchon Landing). Medals: Occupation, National Defense, Korea, Viet Nam, Good Conduct. Retired Nov. 17, 1967. Home of record: Pollock Pines, CA.

Farek, Robert L., son of Mr. and Mrs. Frank Farek, Elk, Axtell, TX. Entered U.S. Army Corps, 1942, during WWII. Served in Pacific. Rank: Cpl. Honorably discharged 1945.

Fee, Clarence, January 1942 through July 1945, served in Air Force during WWII. Name on monument erected by St. Mary's Catholic Parish, Frydek, TX.

Feldtman, Robert W., son of Floyd and Mary Jo Rippel Feldtman, was born Aug. 8, 1946, Harlingen, TX. Graduated Edinburg High School; Pan American Univ., 1968; Univ. of TX Medical Branch, Galveston, 1972; entered USAF while in medical school. Rank: Col. Military education: Surgical residency, Wilford Hall USAF MC, 1972-77; Aerospace Medicine, Brooks AFB; Air Command and Staff College and Air War College. Surgeon, USAF Academy, Colorado Springs, CO. 11th USAF Contingency Hospital in 1988, Wilford Hall during Panama Crisis and Operation Desert Storm. Volunteered during Desert Shield as a surgeon at Davis-Monthan AFB in Arizona. Received Amos Pollard Award, Wilford Hall, and the Air Force Commendation Award. Made commander of the 11th USAF Contingency Hospital in June 1993. Has been a pilot since 1975, holding multi-engine, instrument, and commercial ratings. Flies regularly with USAF and Texas National Guard units. Has over 1,400 hours as Pilot-in-Command. As a civilian, did thoracic residency with Dr. Michael DeBakey, including surgery at Kin Faisal Hospital in Saudi Arabia. Since 1983, has had practice in Houston, TX, performing thousands of general, thoracic, and cardiovascular operations. Married Susan; two grown daughters. Home of record: Houston, TX. Submitted by Jody Rippel Feldtman of San Antonio, TX.

Fiala, Raymond W., member of American Legion Post No 282, Granger, TX. WWII veteran.

Filer, William James, son of Joseph Henry and Anna Beseda Filer, was born in Tours, TX, on Sept. 24, 1922. Educated at Waco High School. Enlisted in the Navy in Houston, TX. Theater of operation: South Pacific. Discharged on Oct. 1, 1945. Home of record: Waco, TX.

Filla, Joe R., son of Mr. and Mrs. John Filla, born in Taylor, Williamson Co., TX. Education: Thrall schools. Enlisted U.S.M.C., 1943 in TX. Basic training at San Diego, CA. Medals: Asiatic-Pacific Campaign Ribbon, WWII Victory. Rank: Pfc. Honorably discharged 1946.

Filla, John J., Jr., son of Mr. and Mrs. John J. Filla, Sr., was born in Taylor, Williamson Co., TX. Educated in Thrall schools. Enlisted in U.S. Army Corps, 1942. Basic training, Camp Barkley, TX. KILLED IN ACTION, 1944, France. Medals: EAME Campaign, Purple Heart.

Firasek, Benjamin J., son of John and Mary Firasek, was born Aug. 21, 1920, Praha, TX. Education: high school. Enlisted in U.S. Army Corps on Aug. 6, 1941, at Randolph Field, TX. Rank: Staff Sgt. Medals: GCM, Sharpshooter Carbine, and American De-

fense. Honorably discharged Dec. 19, 1945. Home of record: Penelope, TX.

Foit, Joe R., son of Mr. and Mrs. Joseph Foit, West, TX. Graduated Ross High School. Entered U.S. Army Corps, 1940. Rank: Pfc. Served in North Africa and Italy. WOUNDED IN ACTION, Italy, 1944. Awarded Purple Heart, Infantry Combat Badge w/2 Battle Stars. Honorably discharged in 1945. Married Josephine Barton.

Foit, William A., of West, TX, WWII veteran. Served in Italy.

Fojtik, Albert A., Jr., son of Mr. and Mrs. Albert A. Fojtik, Sr., was born Sept. 20, 1926. Veteran WWII. S/Sgt, Inst. Sq AF. Died Jan. 7, 1958. Buried Holy Cross Catholic Cemetery, Granger, TX.

Fojtik, Albert C., was born July 30, 1926. Served in U.S. Army Corps during WWII. Died May 26, 1983. Buried Calvary Catholic Cem., Granger, TX.

Fojtik, Calvin Lee, son of Louis and Emma Fojtik, was born Jan. 13, 1926, Needville, TX. Educated in Damon, TX. Enlisted at Camp Swift in U.S. Army Corps. With Army Water Point in Korea. Medals: GCM and Rifle Marksmanship, among others. Honorably discharged in 1946. Married wife, Mary Ann; three sons: Calvin Jr., Gary, and Larry. Retired from Highway Dept. after 27 years. Submitted by mother Emma Fojtik, who was born in 1902. She was 91 years old at time information was submitted at Damon, TX.

Fojtik, Edmond Joseph, son of Louis and Emma Fojtik, was born Oct. 1, 1922, Needville, TX. Education: Damon, TX. Enlisted at Ft. Clayton. Assigned to Coast Artillery; was in the Panama Canal Zone. Honorably discharged, but with nervous condition. Married wife, Alice, who predeceased him of cancer in 1985. Two children, David, born 1950, and Joann, born 1951. Died on Dec. 7, 1991. Submitted by mother Emma Fojtik.

Fojtik, Jerome Frank, son of John Anton Fojtik (son of Louis Fojtik and Mary Horak) and Julia Fojtik (daughter of John J. Fojtik and Johanna Miculka), was born May 12, 1921. KILLED IN ACTION. Lost at sea during WWII, between Nov. 29, 1944, and Dec. 5, 1944.

Fojtik, Willie, of Taylor, TX, member of American Legion Post No 282, Granger, TX. WWII veteran.

Foyt, Anton, son of Frank and Annie Hanicak Foyt, was born Oct. 21, 1918 in Beaumont, TX. Graduated high school and later earned B.A. degree from University of Texas in 1940. Entered the U.S. Army at Ft. Sam Houston, TX, during WWII. Theater of Operations: European, African, and Middle Eastern. Member of the U.S. Army Intelligence Corps. Rank: Tech. Sgt. Participated in military campaigns in Normandy, Northern France, Adrennes, Alsace, Rhineland, and Central Europe. Medals: BSS, European African Middle Eastern Campaign with five campaign stars. "My most memorable military event was to have been a part of the security team provided for President Harry Truman, Marshal Joseph Stalin and Prime Minister Winston Churchill, Potsdam Conference on July 17, 1945, following Germany's defeat in WWII." Released from the service on Oct. 25, 1945. Home of record: Wichita Falls, TX.

Foyt, John, son of Frank and Annie Hanicak Foyt, was born April 16, 1924, in Runge, TX. Attended Edna High School at Edna, TX, and Texas A&M, College Station, TX. Enlisted at Edna, TX, during WWII. Rank: 1st Sgt. in the U.S. Army Air Corps. American Theater of Operations. Medals: American Campaign , WWII Victory, and Good Conduct. Discharged Feb. 1945. Died on Oct. 18, 1970.

Foyt, Pauline M., daughter of Frank and Annie Hanicak Foyt, was born Nov. 8, 1921 in Bessmay, TX. Graduate of Edna High School. Attained BA degree plus one year of graduate studies at the University of Texas, Austin, TX. American Theater of Operations during WWII. Enlisted in the U.S. Navy at Houston, TX. Received basic training at Norfolk, VA. Attended Radar Operators School at Virginia Beach, VA. Served in CONUS at the 5th Naval District and attained the rank of SK1C. U.S. Navy. Discharged March 18, 1946. Home of record: San Antonio, Bexar Co., TX.

Foytek, Clarence J., son of Jerry E. and Sophie Matocha Foytik, was born Dec. 20, 1924, near Damon, in Ft. Bend Co., TX. Attended Richmond High School and enlisted in the Army Air Force on Dec. 3, 1942 at San Antonio, TX. Rank: Corporal. Asiatic-Pacific Theater in WWII. Fought in Southern Philippines, China Air Offense, Japan, Eastern Mandates, and Ryukyus as Turret Machine Gunner on B-24 Liberator plane. Medals: Good Conduct, WWII Victory, Asiatic-Pacific with five Good Conducts, WWII Victory, Asiatic-Pacific with five BSS and Aerial Gunner and Instructor Wings. Discharged on Oct. 2, 1945 at Ft. Bliss, TX. Served in the Air Force Reserves for five years. Promoted to T/Sgt. Fought in the Korean War. Discharged in 1958. Married Jo Ann Sebesta on Oct. 21, 1961; five children: Clarence Jr., David, Dale, Brian, and Cheryl. Member of the American Legion Post 271, St. Michael's Catholic Church, and SPJST. Home of record: Needville, TX.

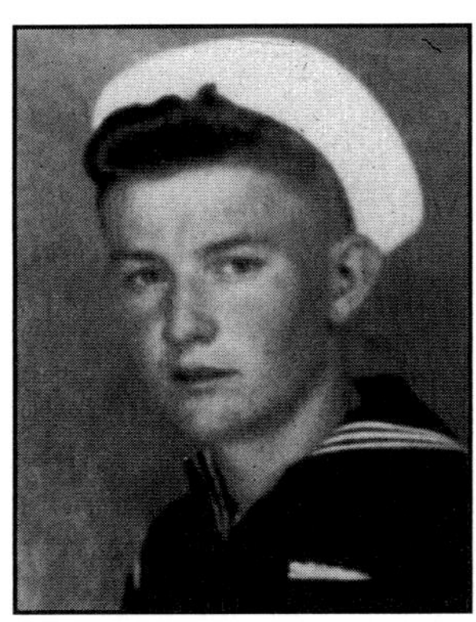

Foytek, Domin Jerry, son of Jerry E. Foytik, Sr. and Sophie Matocha Foytik, was born Feb. 7, 1927 in Ft. Bend Co. near Damon, TX. Attended Needville High School in Needville, TX. Enlisted in the Navy on Jan. 5, 1945 at Houston, TX. Stationed in San Diego, CA, aboard the USS *Manila Bay* aircraft carrier and on the battleship *Missouri* in Japan and Okinawa. Rank: S 1/C. Medals: Asiatic-Pacific Campaign with one BSS and a Victory Medal. Discharged in June 1946 at Boston, MA. Served in the Air Force Reserves and was promoted to S/Sgt. Married Dorothy Stavinoha; three daughters: Dorothy, Deborah, and Donna. Died on Oct. 21, 1979 and is buried at Greenlawn Memorial Cemetery in Rosenberg, TX.

Foytek, Elheart Edwin, son of Jerry E. Foytik, Sr. and Sophie Matocha Foytik, was born Sept. 14, 1921, near Damon, Ft. Bend Co., TX. He graduated from Richmond High School in Richmond, and from Aircraft Mechanic and Flight Chief School. Enlisted in the Air Force on Aug. 2, 1941 at Houston, TX. Rank: M/Sgt. Was in the Korean War in Japan in 1950, and served in the combat support group in London, England, in 1963. Worked in the Aero Space Program at Brooks Field in San Antonio, TX, in the radiology laboratory. Retired Jan. 1, 1968. Medals: Defense Ribbon, Good Conduct, and Air Force Commendation Medals along with WWII, Viet Nam, and Korean Campaign Ribbons. Married Peggy Bayes on May 21, 1952; three children: Paul, Susan, and Julie. Home of record: San Antonio, TX.

Foytik, Jerry E., Sr., son of Frank Foytik, Sr. and Theresa Kupcak Foytik, was born Jan. 9, 1895 in La Grange, Fayette Co., TX. Enlisted in the Army June 25, 1918 at La Grange, TX. Rank: Pfc. Served in France and fought in WWI, receiving a France Liberation Medal. Discharged on July 9, 1919, at Camp Bowie, Ft. Worth, TX. Married Sophie Matocha; five children: Elheart, Clarence, Jerry Jr., Domin, Irene, and Franklin; and 24 grandchildren. Member of Holy Rosary Catholic Church in Rosenberg, and American Legion Post 271, Rosenberg, TX, for 50 years.

Foytik, Jerry John, Jr., son of Jerry E. Foytik, Sr. and Sophie Matocha Foytik, was born May 16, 1930, in Damon, Ft. Bend Co., TX. Graduated from Needville High School and the University of Kentucky, receiving BS degree. Enlisted in the Air Force on Oct. 25, 1950, in Houston, TX. Rank: S/Sgt. Stationed in San Antonio, TX. Served during the Korean War, receiving the American Defense and Good Conduct Medals. Discharged on Oct. 25, 1954 at Lackland Air Force Base, San Antonio, TX. Married Geneva; nine children. Home of record: Old Hickory, TN.

Foytik, Joseph W., was born Aug. 3, 1894. Served in U.S. Army Corps during WWI. Died Feb. 10, 1964. Buried in St. Mary's Cemetery, West, TX.

Franta, Alvin Albert, son of Rudolph and Hermina Marek Franta, was born on Nov. 22, 1923 in Crosby, TX. Educated at Crosby High School and Houston Business College. Enlisted at Fort Sam Houston, TX. Rank: Sgt. Served at the Halloran General Hospital on Staten Island, NY. Discharged on Nov. 25, 1946. Resides in Crosby, TX.

Franta, Joseph Robert, Jr., son of Joseph Robert Franta, Sr., and Gussie Matula, was born Oct. 1, 1922, Hallettsville, TX. Graduated Hallettsville High School, 1939. Enlisted in USAF, Victoria, TX, during WWII. Theater of Operations: Panama Canal Zone. Rank: Staff Sgt. Honorably discharged 1942. Occupation: concrete construction. Died March 27, 1960, Hallettsville, TX. Buried in Sacred Heart Catholic Cem., Hallettsville, TX. Submitted by Margaret Franta Bures of El Campo, TX.

Franta, Louis James, son of Joseph Robert Franta, Sr. and Gussie Matula, was born Jan. 11, 1925, Hallettsville, TX. Graduated Hallettsville High, 1939. Enlisted in U.S. Navy 1943, Victoria, TX. Rank: RM 3/C. Theater of Operations: Philippine Islands (Pacific). Radio Operator/Minesweeper. Honorably discharged Nov. 1951. Married Dorothy Ploch; two children. Employed as Linotype Operator. Retired. Home of record: Karnes City, TX. Submitted by Margaret Franta Bures of El Campo, TX.

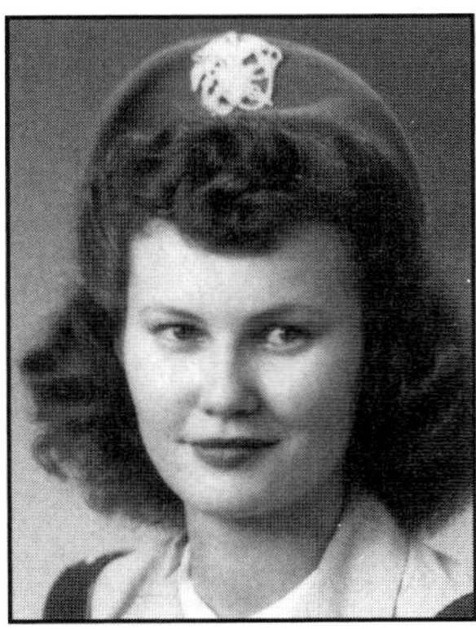

Franta, Margaret D., daughter of Joseph Robert Franta, Sr. and Gussie Matula, was born on July 5, 1926, Hallettsville, TX. Graduate of Hallettsville High School, 1942; Victoria Jr. College, and St. Joseph School of Nursing, Houston, TX, 1946. Enrolled in U.S. Cadet Nurse Corps on March 15, 1944, and went to school through Sept. 1946. WWII ended before graduation. Married Eugene A. Bures in Jan. 1949; eight children. Home of record: El Campo, TX.

Frazier/Faraziel, Charlie, son of Joseph and Frances "Fannie" Laznovsky Faraziel/Frazier, was born Jan. 19, 1913, Ennis, TX. Education: Graduated Ennis High School, 1930. His mother died at an early age, he was reared in home of Uncle and Aunt, Joe Rada and Bessie Laznovsky Rada. Entered U.S. Army Corps, 1942, received training in Louisiana, KY and PA. Theater of Operations: EAME. Battles: WWII-Battle of the Bulge, England, France, Belgium, Germany. KILLED IN ACTION on Jan. 13, 1945, during Battle of the Bulge. Charlie was the first of WWII dead to be returned to Ennis, TX for reburial. Funeral Services and Military Reburial was at Myrtle Cemetery, Ennis, TX, Nov. 25, 1947. Medals received: Purple Heart, Good Conduct Medal, WWII Victory Medal, Presidential Citation. Submitted by Sylvia J. Laznovsky, Ennis, TX.

Fridel, Emil J., son of Joe A. and Ella Mladenka Fridel. Attended La Vega Grammar School, Bellmead, TX, Riesel High, Riesel, TX, Baylor University, Waco, TX. Enlisted in U.S. Air Force, Kelly Field, San Antonio, TX. Highest enlisted rank was Sgt. Commissioned 2nd Lt., 1942. Theater of Operations included European African Middle East, Persian Gulf Command (Iran 1943-44); France (1945). Captain Fridel was also at Rhineland and received European African Middle East Campaign Medal with one BSS, American Campaign, WWII Victory Medal. Honorably discharged on Jan. 14, 1946 at Ft. Sam Houston, San Antonio, TX. Employed by General Tire and Rubber Co., Waco TX, 1946-47, and as Supt. for Postal Operations in West, TX until retirement. Emil married Pearl Deiterman of West, TX on May 12, 1947. Home of record: West, TX.

Fronek, Joe, of Holland, Bell Co., TX. Attended Granger Catholic Church, Granger, TX. WWII veteran.

Gaida, Daniel L., Granger, TX. WWII veteran. Navy: State of MD. Member of American Legion Post No. 282. Hometown, Granger, TX.

Gaida, Edward J., son of Joe and Annie Martinets Gaida, was born Oct. 20, 1923. Graduated from high school at Granger, TX. Attended Texas A&M for one year. Graduate of Southwestern University. Enlisted in the U.S. Army Air Corps during WWII. Served in the European, African, and Middle Eastern Theater of Operations as a B-24 Bomber crew member. Rank: Staff Sgt. Medals: European African Middle Eastern Campaign, American Campaign, Air Medal with five oak leaf clusters, Good Conduct, and the WWII Victory. Separated from service on Nov. 21, 1945. Married Hattie Martinets; two children. Member of American Legion Post No. 282, Granger, TX. Died May 26, 1983. Buried Calvary Catholic Cemetery, Granger, TX.

Gaidusek, Johnnie Joe, Sr., son of Joe and Marie Zatopek Gaidusek, was born on Aug. 23, 1925 in West, TX. Educated at West High School. Enlisted in the Navy in San Diego, CA on Dec. 7, 1943. Rank: MO MM 3/C. Served in the South Pacific.

Gaidusek, Richard J., son of John and Marcella Oslick Gaidusek, was born Sept. 12, 1932, Chicago, IL. Attended West High School, West, TX; University of Maryland. Served in Texas National Guard, 1949-1950, HQS Company, 143 HCT Regt, 36th Div. Enlisted U.S. Navy, Mar. 29, 1951, Chicago, IL. Rank: E-8. Locations served: Great Lakes TC, IL; NTC, San Diego, CA; Imperial Beach Radio Station, Imperial Beach, CA; Adak, Aleutian Islands; Yokosuka and Kamiseya, Japan; Washington, DC; Bremerhaven, Germany; Cyprus (2 Wireless Regt., Royal Signal Corps; SS-343, Clamagove; NSA Ft. George G. Mead, MD; Karamursel, Turkey; GCHQ, Chettenham, England; Rota, Spain; various Aircraft Carriers as operational necessity dictated; flying with VQ-2. Medals: Joint Services Commendation; GCM (8 Awards); Occupation; Unit Commendation; Korean; U.N.; National DeBose, etc. Honorably discharged Sept. 16, 1975. Semi-retired; has own tax preparation business. Home of record: West, TX.

Gaiser, Ernest A., son of Henry and Mary Rendek Gaiser, was born Nov. 6, 1920, West, TX. Education: St. Mary's Catholic Parochial School and West High School, West, TX. Graduated May 1939. Enlisted in U.S. Army Air Corps, Sept. 1940. Stationed at Brooks Field, TX. Embarkation from there to England, served with 8th Air Force. WOUNDED IN ACTION, explosion in England. Married Evelyn Vanzura on Nov. 4, 1944. Spent 28 months in England. Honorably discharged in 1945. Re-enlisted in U.S. Air Force, May 1948, Corpus Christi, TX. Sent to Camp Leroy Johnson, LA, Ft. Sam Houston, TX; Korea; Ellington AFB, TX; Connally AFB, TX. Then back to England for three years. Retired July 1964, McGuire Air Field, Trenton, NJ, as Staff Sgt after over 20 years of service. Medals: Good Conduct, Air Force Longevity Service Award, National Defense Service, United Nations Service; Korean Service. Two children, four grandchildren, one great-grandchild. Died on July 25, 1980. Lovingly submitted by his sister, Eleanor Gaiser Dennis, West, TX.

Gaiser, Henry Lewis "Buster," son of Christian Henry and Mary Rendek Gaiser, was born on Jan. 17, 1917, West, TX. Attended St. Mary's Catholic School and West High School, West, TX. Enlisted in U.S. Army Corps, Ft. Sam Houston, TX, on Sept. 1, 1936. Was at Ft. Clark until Feb. 28, 1939.

Rank: Pfc. A Troop, 5th Cavalry; 1st Horse Cavalry, 12th Cav. Div; transferred to the Army Air Corps on Feb. 28, 1939. Org. 1804th Ordnance Co. Aviation, Brooks Field, TX. Theater of Operations: Asiatic-Pacific. Rank: M/Sgt. Supply and Mess Sgt.; Australia, New Guinea, Biak, Owi Islands. 5th AF during WWII, Battles: D-Day, Leyte Island, Philippine Islands, WOUNDED IN ACTION. Honorably discharged May 30, 1945. Enlisted in U.S. Army Corps on Dec. 7, 1949; I Co, 34th Reg., 24th Inf Div, Japan for initial landing. Korea, July 1, 1950. Battles: 17 in Puson Perimeter, from July 4, 1950-July 20, 1950; WOUNDED IN ACTION three times, PRISONER OF WAR, N. Koreans, 3½ yrs; listed MISSING IN ACTION, in 119 mile "Tiger Death March." While in Korea, was WOUNDED IN ACTION by grenade shrapnel. While a PRISONER OF WAR, was stabbed 21 times in the stomach, had back broken, lost 104 lbs. of original weight of 175 lbs; then prisoner of Chinese. Released on Oct. 22, 1953. Medals: Purple Heart w/1 OLC, Distinguished Unit Emblem, Prisoner of War, Good Conduct, American Defense Service, American Campaign, Asiatic Pacific Campaign w/1 BSS, WWII Victory, Army of Occupation w/Japan Clasp, National Defense Service, Korean Service w/2 Silver Stars, Combat Infantry Badge, Philippine Liberation w/BSS, ROK Presidential Unit Citation, United Nations. Honorably discharged Nov. 1953. Lived in Pasadena, TX, 1957 to 1983. Retired as letter carrier for Postal Service, 1972. Back to West, TX, 1983. Member of St. Mary's Catholic Church and VFW Post 4819 of West. Died Nov. 2, 1991. Buried St. Mary's Catholic Church, West, TX. Survivors include son Mark Gaiser of Deer Park, TX; brothers John R. Gaiser and Willie J. Gaiser, Dallas, TX; sisters, Eileen Gaiser Dennis (Mrs. O.R.) and Joyce Gaiser Eddy (Mrs. Marvin), West, TX; nieces and nephews. Home of record: West, TX. Submitted by son Mark Gaiser of Deer Park, TX.

Gaiser, John R., son of Henry and Mary Rendek Gaiser. Education: St. Mary's Catholic Parochial School and West High School, West, TX. Received GED certificate in service. Worked during the war on government machines. Had two deferments. Enlisted in the U.S. Navy, March 29, 1944, Waco, TX. Service in NTC, San Diego, CA; USS *Alcyone* (AKA-7). Stationed on cargo ship in Japan for 10 months, supplying troops. Medals: American Area Campaign, Asiatic Pacific Area, WWII Victory. Honorably discharged on July 29, 1946. Married Theresa Matysek in 1968. One son and two daughters from a prior marriage. Civilian occupation, building maintenance for S. H. Lynch and Co. for 33 years. Retired in 1987. Home of record: Dallas, TX. Submitted by sister Eleanora Gaiser Dennis, West, TX.

Gaiser, Willie J., son of Henry and Mary Rendek Gaiser. Education: St. Mary's Catholic Parochial School and West High School, West, TX, graduated in 1937. Enlisted U.S. Army Corps, April 19, 1942. Sent to Brooks Field, TX. Basic training at Joseph T. Robinson Camp, North Little Rock, AR, 11 months. Battles and Campaigns: Aleutian Islands, New Guinea, South Philippines and Japan. Medals: American Theater Campaign, Asiatic Pacific Campaign w/3 BSS, Good Conduct, WWII Victory Ribbon, one service stripe, four overseas service bars. Honorably discharged Dec. 10, 1945, Ft. Sam Houston, TX, w/rank of 1st Sgt. Was in Medical Corps. Married Rudy Rejcek of Abbott, TX, on Oct. 5, 1942, Base Chapel, Camp Gordon, GA. Two sons, one daughter, five grandsons and one great-granddaughter. Civilian Occupation: worked in construction, Fox and Jacobs, Dallas, TX. Retired. Home of record: Dallas, TX. Submitted by sister, Eleanora Gaiser Dennis, West, TX.

Gajdosik, Jerry J., son of Charlie and Janie Bucanek Gajdosik, was born on Sept. 11, 1913 in West, TX. Attended West Convent School in West, TX and Liberty School in Tours, TX. Enlisted in the U.S. Army at Ft. Sam Houston, TX, on Feb. 3, 1942, during WWII. After training at Camp Barkeley, TX, Camp Chaffee, AR, and Camp Campbell, KY, he served in the European,

African, and Middle Eastern Theater of Operations, in France, Germany, and Czechoslovakia. Awards and decorations: European-African-Middle Eastern Campaign Medal with three campaign stars and the Good Conduct Medal. Separated from the service on Oct. 20,1945 with the rank of Tech. Sgt. Married Evelyn Girard on Nov. 18, 1941, in West, TX. Three children: one son and two daughters. Last known home of record: West, TX.

Gajdosik, Louis J., son of Mr. and Mrs. Charles Gajdosik, husband of Margie Chudej. Entered U.S. Army Corps in 1942, served during WWII, trained Camp Bowie, TX; Camp Blanding, FL and Camp Edwards, Mass. Served in North Africa and Italy. Awarded GCM, WWII Victory Ribbon, E.T.O. Ribbon w/2 Battle Stars; one Bronze Arrowhead, Purple Heart and combat Infantry Badge. WOUNDED IN ACTION, Cassino, Italy, 1944. Attained rank of Pfc prior to honorable discharge, 1945.

Gajdosik, Rudolph A., attended grammar school, West, TX. Entered U.S. Army Corps, 1942, trained in Washington, California and Camp Adair, OR. Served in Philippines and Ryukyus. Awarded A.T. Ribbon w/2 BSS and Bronze Arrowhead and P.L. w/2 BSS. Attained rank of Pfc prior to honorable discharge in 1946.

Gajewski, Edward, served in Air Force during WWII, name on monument which was erected by St. Mary's Catholic Parish, Frydek, Tx.

Gajewski, Pete, served in U.S. Army Corps WWII, name on monument which was erected by St. Mary's Catholic parish, Frydek, Tx.

Galetka, Edwin H., son of John and Therese Mikush Galetka, was born Dec. 6, 1923, Hallettsville, Lavaca Co., TX. Education: Boethel School. PFC Galetka served in U.S. Army Corps, WWII, 3rd Infantry, 2nd Headquarters, Co. 3rd Battalion, fought in Germany, Berlin. Medals: Good Conduct Medal and Overseas Bar. Honorably discharged on Nov. 6, 1946. Married Erma Stonequist; two daughters: Shirley Galetka Dennel and Patricia Galetka Denny. Home of record: Needville, TX.

Galetka, Emil O., son of John and Therese Mikush Galetka, was born Dec. 28, 1921, Hallettsville, Lavaca Co., TX. Education, Boethel School through ninth grade. Enlisted on Oct. 9, 1942, San Antonio, Bexar, TX. Active Service on Oct. 24, 1942, in the U.S. Army Corps. Corporal Galetka was assigned to Company M, 160th Infantry. Theater of Operations included Bismarck Archipelago, Southern Philippines, Luzon. Battles fought in were: New Britain Island and Philippine Islands. Medals received: Combat and Infantry Badges, Asiatic Pacific Theater Campaign Ribbon w/3 BSS, Philippine Liberation Ribbon w/1 star, GCM, WWII Victory Ribbon, one Service Stripe and five overseas bars. Honorably discharged on Nov. 16, 1945. He was a barber, is semi-retired. Home of record: Lake Jackson, Brazoria, TX.

Galetka, Hilmer R., son of John and Therese Mikush Galetka, was born Sept. 25, 1927, Hallettsville, Lavaca, TX. Education: Boethel School through ninth grade and Baldwin's Business College. Pvt. Galetka enlisted on Jan. 10, 1946, Ft. Sam Houston, TX; served with Co. A, 2nd Basic Training Battalion. Honorably discharged on May 17, 1946, Madigan Hospital Center, Ft. Lewis, WA. Married Gaye Ann Fahrenthold on Nov. 22, 1965. Civilian occupation: Jackson Farm Machinery Co. and Paul's Supply, Hallettsville, TX. Retired. Home of record: Hallettsville, TX.

Galetka, Julius M., son of John and Therese Mikush Galetka, was born May 29, 1916, Hallettsville, Lavaca Co., TX. Education: Boethel School. Enlisted Feb. 12, 1942, U.S. Army Corps, assigned to Company A, 340th Engineer (C) Battalion. Technician 5th Grade Galetka fought in the battles of New Guinea and Luzon. Medals: WWII Victory Ribbon, American Theater Campaign Medal, Asiatic Pacific Campaign Medal w/2 BSS, GCM,

Distinguished Unit Badge, one Service Stripe, six Overseas Service Bars. Honorably discharged on Dec. 6, 1945, Ft. Sam Houston, TX. Is a retired farmer. Home of record: Hallettsville, TX.

Galetka, Victor F., son of John and Therese Mikush Galetka, was born Aug. 8, 1913, Hallettsville, Lavaca Co., TX. Education: Boethel School. Entered U.S. Army, March 20, 1942, Ft. Sam Houston, TX. Rank: Pfc. Assigned to 75th Field Artillery Battalion. Fought in North Opinion Po Valley. Medals: EAME Campaign Medal w/2 BSS, Asiatic Pacific Theater Campaign Medal, GCM, one Service Stripe and three overseas Service Bars. Honorably discharged Oct. 24, 1945, Ft. Sam Houston, TX. Maintenance worker for Lavaca Co., TX, precinct, and was a farmer. Retired. Home of record: Hallettsville, TX. Submitted by Alton E. Chudej, Hallettsville, TX.

Gallia, Alois Joseph, son of Augin Johann and Frances Anna Hanzelka Gallia, was born Nov. 20, 1921, Hill Co., TX. Inducted into U.S. Army Corps, Hill Co., TX, Nov. 23, 1942, during WWII, assigned to 104th Timberwolf Infantry Division, Co. H., 413th Infantry. Rank: S/Sgt. Theater of Operations: Europe. Landed in Cherbourg, France on Sept. 7, 1944; was in Belgium and Holland from Oct. 23, 1944–Nov. 8, 1944; Siegfried Line to Rhine, Nov. 8, 1944–March 7, 1945; Central Germany, March 21, 1945–April 21, 1945; Junction w/Russians, April 26, 1945; 195 consecutive days in front line combat. Honorably discharged on Dec. 4, 1945. Married Eleanor Maria Baca; three children, six grandchildren. Retired in 1986. Home of record: Dallas, TX.

Gallia, Aug. John, son of Augin Johann and Frances Anna Hanzelka Gallia, was born June 27, 1924, Hill Co., TX. Attended high school, Penelope, TX. Served in U.S. Army Corps, WWII, 3½ years. Honorably discharged at end of war. Retired carpenter. Married Cecilia Marek; one daughter. Home of record: Mesquite, TX. Submitted by Sister Cornelia M. Knezek, SSCJ.

Gallia, Charles Alois, son of Augin Johann and Frances Anna Hanzelka Gallia, was born Oct. 18, 1918, TX. Attended Brigmann public schools. Married Mildred M. Lucien; two children. Enlisted in U.S. Army Corps during WWII. Assigned to Anti-Aircraft (3 years), in Richmond, CA and El Paso, TX. Honorably discharged 1946. Died Dec. 2, 1967, Dallas, TX. Buried Calvary Hill Cemetery, Dallas, TX. Submitted by Sister Cornelia M. Knezek, SSCJ, of Amarillo, TX.

Gallia, Edward J., son of Antone and Annie Mensik Gallia, was born March 17, 1930, Penelope, TX. Attended public schools in Bynum, TX, graduating from high school in 1948. Married Martha Ann Supak Nov. 7, 1953; one daughter, Margaret. Enlisted in 1948 in U.S. Air Force. Served in Japan and Korea. Released from active duty in July 1952. Enlisted in the Texas Air National Guard on Dec. 7, 1952, Hensley Field, Dallas, TX, and became a full time technician. His first assignment was in Air Operations with subsequent assignments in Air Administration and Personnel Management, advancing to the position of Chief, Consolidated Base Personnel. Rank: Captain. Awarded the National Defense Service Medal, Army Occupation Medal (Japan), Korean Service Medal w/3 BSS, United Nations Service Medal, GCM, Air Force Reserve Medal, Air Reserve Forces Meritorious Service Ribbon, the Air Force Outstanding Unit Award, and (posthumously) the Air Force Commendation Medal. Died Dec. 21, 1970. Submitted by Mrs. Martha Willis. Home of record: Midlothian, TX.

Gallia, Marvin Henry, son of Henry A. and Christine A. Dvorak Gallia, was born May 18, 1944, Penelope, Hill Co., TX. Attended Penelope Grade School, Gaston Junior High, Dallas, TX, Bryan Adams High School (graduated 1962), Dallas, TX; University of Texas, Arlington; Draughon's Business College, Drafting. Enlisted in Texas Air National Guard, Hensley Field, Dallas, TX, attained rank of S/Sgt. Was at Lackland AFB, Amarillo AFB, Hensley Field, Dallas, TX. Medals: SAEMR; AFOUA; ARFMSR. Honorably discharged on Oct. 23, 1970. Occupation, Manifest Shipping Systems Operator. Married Sharon Tedesco; one daughter, Ashley. Home of record: Dallas, TX. Submitted by Sister Cornelia M. Knezek, SSCJ, Amarillo, TX.

Gavenda, Victor, son of Steven and Wincensia Salek Gavenda, was born Nov. 20, 1901, in the

Providence community near Caldwell, Tx. Educated in the Providence school. Enlisted in the Navy on April 20, 1921 in Houston, Tx. Member of the Electoral Mission during the Nicaraguan Revolution of 1926-1931. Chief Gunners Mate on the destroyer *Benson* and participated in the capture of Fedala and Casablanca, French Morocco on the destroyer *Tillman*. He was Ordnance Division Officer and Diving Officer on the ship *Luzon* at Fuma-Fti, Ellice Islands, and Kwajalein, Marshall Islands, Guam, Saipan and the Marianas. His medals are the Good Conduct Medal with three Stars, Second Nicaraguan Campaign Medal, Expert Rifleman Medal, American Defense Medal, American Theater Medal, European Theater Medal, China Service Medal, and the World War l Victory Medal. He died on Aug. 30, 1968 and is buried in the New Tabor Cemetery near Caldwell, Tx. Information was submitted by his niece, Mildred Skrabanek Hejl, Temple, Tx.

Genzer, Alfons J., son of Raymond and Frances Kadlecek Genzer, was born Oct. 7, 1917, Ammannsville, TX. Education: Flatonia, TX; Edinburgh, TX and Corpus Christi College Academy. Enlisted Ft. Sam Houston, TX. Served in WWII with the 3rd Armored Division, Sgt. Hq Co. 45th Medical Division. Theater of Operations: European. Served in Normandy Invasion, Battle of the Bulge and other battles that took place in Germany, Belgium, Luxenburg, Holland. His outfit was first to crack the Siegfried Line. Received five battle stars; the Good Conduct Medal and American Defense Ribbon. Honorably discharged 1945. Before entering service, was in produce and feed business with his father. Married Elizabeth Ermis in 1941; two children: Carolyn and Alfons J., Jr. Hobbies: hunting, fishing and tennis. Died Jan. 24, 1966, car accident, Round Top, TX. Buried in St. Rose Catholic Cemetery, Schulenburg, TX. Submitted with love and affection by his sister Judith Genzer Fillip, Dickinson, TX.

Gerick, Adolph Anton, son of Vinc Karl "VK" and Anna Kocian Gerick, was born June 13, 1892. Education: elementary schools in Fayette Co., TX and Rahe Technical (Auto and Tractor) College in Kansas City, MO, 1922. Enlisted in U.S. Army Corps, April 26, 1918, Weinert, Haskell Co., TX. Theater of Operation: Europe. Assigned to American Expeditionary Force, Co. M, 360th Infantry Div. Battles: Villiers-En-Haye, St. Michiel, Puvenelle, Meuse-Argonne. Medals: WWI Victory, GCM and Purple Heart. WOUNDED IN ACTION. Honorably discharged June 21, 1919, having attained rank of Corporal. Civilian occupation: farmer/blacksmith, retired 1964. Married Annie Rafay Gerick; five children: James Gerick, Edwin Gerick, Annette Gerick Maloy, Milam Gerick, Mary Lou Gerick Ludwig. Hobbies were fishing and hunting. Died March 22, 1969. Buried: Bartlett City Cemetery, Bartlett, Williamson Co., TX. This information submitted by his son, James Gerick. Home of record: Austin, TX.

Gerick, Edwin, West, TX, WWII veteran, U.S. Army Air Corps.

Gerick, James Adolph, son of Adolph Anton and Annie Rafay Gerick, was born Aug. 5, 1926, Weinert, Haskell Co., TX. Education: Texas Tech, BBA, Aug. 1950; graduate work, University of OK and University of NM, while in USAF. Entered active duty July 11, 1953, Vance AFB, Enid, OK. Military Duty: two years, Administrative Officer; balance of career as government staff auditor. Theater of Operation: Japan/Korea, Italy and Southeast Asia. Medals: National Defense Service, Armed Forces Reserve, Viet Nam Service, AF Outstanding Unit Award and Small Arms Expert Marksmanship Ribbon. Retired from USAF Reserve, Aug. 5, 1986 as a Lt. Colonel. Civilian Occupation: Auditor/Accountant-State Government, Retired Sept. 30, 1993. Married Virginia Raffaela Macri Gerick; one son, James Ray Gerick. Hobbies: gardening, photography and travelling. Home of record: Austin, TX.

Gerik, Alfred E., son of Frank and Lydia Milberger Gerik, was born Oct. 12, 1924, in West, TX. Enlisted in the U.S. Army Air Corps on Oct.

12, 1942, during WWII. Attained the rank of Staff Sgt. and served as Crew Chief and Flight Engineer aboard U.S. Army Air Corps aircraft in the American Theater of Operations. Awards and decorations include the American Campaign Medal and WWII Victory Medal. Released from service on Feb. 16, 1946. Married Nita McPherson in 1948; four children.

Gerik, Bernard Jim, son of Jim and Hattie Cocek Gerik, was born Sept. 1, 1928, West, TX. Education: Sacred Heart Academy, Waco, TX; South Waco Junior High; Waco High School; Pierce College, Canoga Park CA. Enlisted in U.S. Navy on June 1947, Waco, TX. Served NTS, San Diego, CA; Jacksonville, FL, Moffett Field; Sunnyvale, CA, Hickam Field and Barbers Point N.A.S., Honolulu, Oahu, Hawaii. Rank: Aviation Electronics Tech. Second Class. Honorably discharged June 1952, Alameda Naval Air Station, Alameda, CA. Retired from Rockwell International, Rocket-Dyne Division, development and testing of rocket engines for moon landing and space shuttle main engines. Home of record: Canoga Park, CA.

Gerik, Daniel J., was born July 19, 1934. Served in the U.S. Army Corps during Korean Conflict, attaining rank of SP-4. Died Feb. 24, 1993. Buried in St. Mary's Cemetery, West, TX.

Gerik, Emil Joe, was born Feb. 25, 1892. Served in U.S. Army Corps during WWI. Died Nov. 10, 1984. Buried in Lady Fatima Cemetery, Abbott, TX.

Gerik, Frank G., son of Joseph and Otillie Settlemeyer Gerik, was born Oct. 10, 1895 at West, TX. Drafted during WWI on July 25, 1918, and served as a Pvt. in the 31st Company, 165th Depot Brigade, 117th MGBW, 83rd Division. His unit was part of the American Expeditionary Forces in France from Aug. 24, 1918 until Jan. 21, 1919. Returned to the U.S. on Feb. 8, 1919, and was assigned to the 34 Company, 165th Depot Brigade for separation. Discharged on Feb. 13, 1919. Awards and decorations include the Bronze Victory Button issued in 1920. Married Lydia Milberger at St. Mary's Catholic Church in West, TX, on Oct. 16, 1920; two sons: John Lee and Alfred E. Frank. Died Feb. 14, 1987.

Gerik, Frank J., son of Mr. and Mrs. Max Gerik, West, TX. Entered Army Air Corps in 1942, during WWII. Served in England and France. Awarded: GCM; WWII Victory Ribbon; E.T. w/6 Battle Stars and Presidential Citation. Attained rank of Cpl. prior to honorable discharge, 1945.

Gerik, Fred, son of Mr. and Mrs. Max Gerik, West, TX. Attended West High School. Entered U.S. Army, 1944. Trained at Ft. Bliss, TX and Fort Ord, CA. Served in Pacific and Hawaii. Awarded GCM and WWII Victory Ribbon.

Gerik, Henry L., West, TX, WWII veteran, U.S. Army Air Corps.

Gerik, Jerry C., West TX, WWII veteran; U.S. Army Air Corps. Theater of Operations: Asiatic-Pacific.

Gerik, John Lee, son of Frank and Lydia Milberger Gerik was born Aug. 10, 1921 in West, TX. Enlisted in the U.S. Army Air Corps in Jan. 1942, during WWII. Attained the rank of Tech. Sgt. and served with the 752nd Bomber Squadron as an aerial gunner in the European, African, and Middle Eastern Theater of Operations. Participated in aerial campaigns in the Rhineland, Ardennes, Alsace, and Northern France. Awards and decorations include the European African Middle Eastern Campaign Medal, Air Medal with four oak leaf clusters, and Good Conduct Medal. Discharged from the service on June 26, 1945. John, now deceased, married Jo Ann Smajstrla and they had five children.

Gerik, Raymond E., served in Army Air Force during WWII. Attained rank of Cpl. prior to honorable discharge in 1946.

Gerik, Raymond J., son of Mr. and Mrs. J. Gerik, West, TX. Entered Army Air Force, 1943, during WWII. Served in E.T. and Italy. Awards: EAME w/1 Silver Star; WWII Victory Ribbon; GCM; Air Medal w/1 OLC. Attained rank of S/Sgt. prior to honorable discharge, 1945.

Gerlich, Benny, military service veteran. Home of record: Dallas, TX.

Gerlich, Felix William, son of Aug. D. and Estelle Jansky Gerlich, was born May 8, 1923, Ennis, Ellis Co., TX. Graduated St. John's Catholic High School, Ennis, TX. Inducted in U.S. Army Corps, Jan. 18, 1943. Discharged March 22, 1946, Ft.

Bliss, TX. Decorations: American Theater Medal, WWII Victory Medal, Asiatic Pacific Theater Medal, GCM. Continental Service: 1 year, 3 months, 11 days; foreign service: 1 year, 10 months, 24 days. Self-employed, never married. Died Dec. 1, 1982, age 59, VA Medical Center, Marlin, TX, Cause of death: myocardial infarction and atherosclerosis. Buried Dec. 4, 1982, St. Joseph's Catholic Cemetery, Ennis, Ellis Co., TX. Submitted by Herbert E. Gerlich, brother, of Santa Maria, CA.

Gerlich, Fred, Sgt. WWII veteran, West, TX.

Gerlich, Georgie, of West, TX, WWII veteran, U.S. Women's Army Corps.

Gerlich, Henry W., military service veteran. Home of record: Abbot, TX.

Gerlich, Herbert E., son of Aug. D. and Estelle Jansky Gerlich, was born June 7, 1926, Ennis, Ellis Co., TX. Graduated St. John's Catholic High School, Ennis, Ellis, TX; Hancock College, Santa Maria, Santa Barbara, CA. Inducted in U.S. Army Corps, Sept. 7, 1944, Ft. Sam Houston, TX. Discharged Oct. 31, 1945. Military Occupation: Rifleman, Combat Infantryman. Campaign: Rhineland Central Europe, WOUNDED IN ACTION, Rhineland, Germany. Decorations: two BSS, Rhineland; Central Europe, EAME Ribbon; Combat Infantry Badge. Discharged, convenience of government to enlist in Regular Army. 2nd induction: Nov. 1, 1945-RCTG Camp, NY, France. Discharged Oct. 26, 1946, Ft. Sam Houston, TX. Military occupation: Chaplain's Asst. for 5th Constabulary Regiment, Augsburg, Germany. Decorations: Army of Occupation Ribbon, Germany; WWII Victory Ribbon; Overseas Service Bar. 3rd induction in the Reserve: Oct. 22, 1946, Ft. Sam Houston, TX. Discharged Oct. 21, 1949. 4th induction: Sept. 6, 1950, Fort Ord, CA. Discharged: Feb. 3, 1951, Camp Roberts CA. Military Occupation: Clerk Typist, HQ Co., 7th Army Division. Married; two children, three granddaughters.

Gerlich, Rheinhardt, Lt., WWII veteran of West, TX.

Gerlich, R. W., son of Mr. and Mrs. Louis Gerlich, West, TX. Entered U.S. Army Corps, 1942, during WWII. Served in E.T. Awards: E.T. w/5 Battle Stars; Pres. Citation; Merit Unit Award Cluster; Belgium Fourraquerre. Attained rank of Captain prior to honorable discharge, 1945.

Gerlich, Robert H., was born Mar. 1, 1925. Served in the Army Air Corp during WWII, attaining rank of Sgt. Died Nov. 1, 1946. Buried in St. Mary's Cemetery, West, TX.

Gerlich, William F., son of Mr. and Mrs. Louis Gerlich, West, TX. Entered U.S. Navy 1942, during WWII. Served in Battles of Attu and Atlantic. Attained rank of GM 3/C prior to honorable discharge, 1945.

Girard, Henry John, son of Will J. and Julia Beseda Girard, was born Aug. 24, 1920, West, TX. Attended West High School, West, TX, Baylor University, and Texas A&M. Enlisted in U.S. Air Force, March 7, 1940, Randolph Field, TX. Theater of Operations: American Theater, Asiatic Pacific Theater, CBI (China, Burma, India). Flew 152 missions over "The Hump" between China and India. Medals: DFC with OLC, Distinguished Unit Badge (Pres. Cit.), Asiatic Pacific Campaign, American Defense, American Campaign, WWII Victory. Honorably discharged Nov. 20, 1951, Westover AFB, MA. Rank: Major. Employed by Chance Vought, Dallas, TX, as Aerospace Engineer, and Hayes Aircraft Corp., Birmingham, AL, as Flight Test Pilot, and Aerospace Engineer with Dept. of Defense in Washington, D.C. Retired Dec. 31, 1977. Home of record: West, TX.

Girard, Louis V., son of Will J. and Julia Beseda Girard, was born Dec., 1921, West, TX. Attended West High School, West, TX and Texas A&M. Enlisted in the RCAF, Canada, transferred to the U.S. Army Corps A7, 1942. 1st Lt. Girard was stationed in England and Africa, fought many battles over Germany as co-pilot and pilot of B-24s. Medals: DFC, Purple Heart, Air Medal with two OLC. 1st Lt. Girard was KILLED IN ACTION over Ploseti, Rumania, Aug. 1943.

Girard, William C., son of Mrs Julia Girard, West, TX, husband of Ruth Greenhill. Graduate of West High School. Entered Army Air Corp in 1942, trained in California, Pennsylvania, Florida. Awards: GCM; WWII Victory Medal and A.T. Ribbons. Attained rank of Pfc prior to honorable discharge, 1946.

Gitzinger, Benjamin Alonzo, son of J.W.and Annie Adamak Gitzinger, was born on June 19, 1897, Wesley, Tx. Entered the army on April 1, 1930 in Portland, Oregon. Rank: Sgt., Co. C 115th Engineer Battalion. Served in WWII and Korea. Awards: Victory Medal and Occupation Medal. Honorably discharged May 31, 1952, at Percy Jones Hospital, Battle Creek, MI. Died in 1970 in Crosby, TX. Information submitted by his niece, Naomi Gilbreath of Beaumont, TX.

Gorubec, Jerry B., was born April 30, 1933. Sp. 2 Co. B 141 Armd, Sig BN. Served in U.S. Armed Forces since WWII. Died Nov. 17, 1965. Buried Holy Cross Cemetery, Granger, Williamson Co., TX.

Green, Brice P., Jr., son of Brice P. Green, Sr. and Josephine Zernicek Green, was born Ju y 19, 1948 in Galveston, TX. Joined the Navy on Oct. 22, 1966 and while on active duty served on two nuclear submarines in the Engineering Department. Discharged Dec. 12, 1973. Married Brenda Downing on Aug. 2, 1986; one child: Jamie Lynn. Home of record: El Campo, TX.

Gregurek, Aug, son of John and Maria Cada Gregurek, was born Oct. 20, 1909, at Sealy, TX. Enlisted in AAF in San Antonio, TX, on Sept. 30, 1942. Rank: Cpl. Attended a service school at Chanute Field, IL. Served as an AP Power Plant Mechanic at Foster Field Air Base in Victoria, TX. Received a Good Conduct Medal and was discharged. Member of Ganado Concert Band in the early 1900s. Died on Oct. 9, 1945, in Nightingale Hospital, El Campo, TX, from complications from severe burns he received in an accident on the job. Buried in Ganado Catholic Cemetery.

Gregurek, Edwin, son of Mr. and Mrs. Joseph Gregurek, Ganado, TX. Served in the military during peacetime.

Gregurek, James, son of Mr. and Mrs. Joseph Gregurek, Ganado, TX. Served in the military during peacetime.

Gregurek, Joseph, was born April 21, 1895. Served in the U.S. Army Corps, WWI, Texas Infantry, Co. G 127 Infantry. Rank: Pvt. Served in American Expeditionary Forces. Died June 15, 1959. Buried St. Mary's Catholic Cemetery, Frydek, Austin Co., TX.

Gregurek, Joseph, son of John and Maria "Mary" Cada Gregurek, was born March 13, 1897, Passovire, Czechoslovakia, became a U.S. Citizen on Dec. 4, 1916. He had a lower school education. Enlisted June 11, 1917, Camp Nicholas, LA. Honorably discharged Jan. 18, 1919, Camp Beauegass, LA. Served as a Musician in the 3rd Class Hq. Co., 29th Infantry, Regular Army, WWI. Died on June 18, 1970. Buried in Ganado Catholic Cemetery. Submitted by daughter Josephine Gregurek Machac of Victoria, TX.

Gregurek, Marcell, eldest son of Mr. and Mrs. Joseph Gregurek, served in military service during WWII, was WOUNDED IN ACTION. Received Purple Heart and WWII Victory Medal. Ganado, TX.

Grere, Willie was born in the New Ulm, TX, area. Served with the American Expeditionary Forces in France during WWI as a member of the U.S. Army. Interred in Sts. Peter and Paul Cemetery in Frelsburg, TX.

Grieger, Adolf A., son of Mr. and Mrs. F. C. Grieger, was born in Taylor, Williamson Co., TX. Education: Taylor High School. Enlisted U.S. Navy, 1945. Basic training: San Diego, CA. Advanced training, NV. Attained rank of S2/c before honorable discharge.

Grieger, Elias R., son of Mr. and Mrs. F. C. Grieger, born in Taylor, Williamson Co., TX. Education: Taylor High School. Enlisted in U.S. Army Corps, 1944. Basic training, Camp Fannin and Ft. Benning, GA. Theater of Operations: Asiatic-Pacific. Served in the Philippine Islands. WOUNDED IN ACTION, 1945, Negroes Island. Medals: Combat Inf. Badge, Purple Heart, Philippine Liberation Ribbon w/1 BSS, Good Conduct Medal. Attained rank of Pfc., before honorable discharge.

Grieger, Fred B., son of Mr. and Mrs. F. C. Grieger, Taylor, TX. Education: Taylor High School. Enlisted U.S. Army Air Corps, 1943. Basic training, St. Petersburg, FL, TX, and CA. Theater of Operations: CBI. Medals: CBI Campaign Medal, American Theater Campaign Medal, WWII Victory Medal. Attained rank of Sgt. before honorable discharge. Submitted by Dorothy Bohoc.

Grieger, Gilbert J., son of Mr. and Mrs. J. E. Grieger, Hutto, TX. Education: Hare High School. Enlisted in U.S. Navy, 1943. Basic training, Corpus Christi, TX. Theaters of Operations: CBI, Asiatic-Pacific, American. Attained rank of S1/c before honorable discharge.

Grimm, Joseph E., son of Herman and Rosie Grimm, was born May 2, 1931, Tours, TX. Education: St. Martin's Elementary, West High School, Baylor University. Enlisted on July 7, 1948, West, TX. Served in Guam, MI, Korea. Medals: Good Conduct, Korea War. Honorably discharged June 25, 1952. Rank: Class A Storekeeper. Civilian occupation: Owner, Insurance Agency. Home of record: West, TX.

Grmela, Albert W., West, TX, WWII veteran. USMC. West, TX.

Grmela, Joseph "Joe," Jr., son of Joseph and Marie Michna Grmela of Czechoslovakia, was born May 24, 1905, Abbott, TX. Education: St. Mary's Catholic School, West, TX. Inducted in U.S. Army Corps, Hillsboro, Hill Co., TX on Feb. 18, 1942. Went into training at Camp Robinson, AR, then to Ft. Ord, CA, before being shipped to the Pacific Theater of Operations on the Island of New Guinea in the Solomon Islands. Rank: Pfc. KILLED IN ACTION July 28, 1943, defending the Air Base Munda. Medals: Purple Heart, Military Merit for bravery. American Legion Post No. 478, West, TX, gave him a military service on July 9, 1948. Submitted by niece Henrietta Grmela Schindler.

Grones, Anthony Charles "Tony," son of Emil and Selma Galetka Grones, was born Jan. 7, 1950, Hallettsville, Lavaca Co., TX. Education: Hallettsville ISD; Victoria College; Texas A&M, Kingsville (electrical engineer); University of Houston, Victoria, TX. Enlisted July 17, 1968, U.S. Army Reserves, Victoria, TX. Honorably discharged on April 7, 1974, Victoria, TX. Made Victoria, TX home for past 20 years. Professional electrical engineer w/Alcoa in Point Comfort for 20 years. Married Maureen Wagner, who is math instructor at Victoria High School; four children: Scott Anthony, Eric Kyle, Melissa Gail, Jill Marie. Enjoys family and spends many hours with them. Hobby is being a very proud father. Home of record: Victoria, TX.

Grones, Daniel Emil, son of Emil and Selma Galetka Grones, was born June 3, 1937, Hallettsville, Lavaca Co., TX. Graduated 1955, Hallettsville High School, and Victoria Junior College, Victoria, TX. Entered U.S. Army Corps, Sept. 27, 1959, Victoria, TX. Served six months active duty at Ft. Dix, NJ, remainder of his term in U.S. Army Reserves, until being honorably discharged on Aug. 30, 1965. Rank: Pvt. E-2. Received Good Conduct Medal. Married Charlene Sevcik, Sept. 29, 1962; three children: Dana Grones Gleinser, Randall Grones, and Amy Grones. After serving 35 years, retired from U.S. Postal Service on Jan. 3, 1993. Died Dec. 3, 1993, at the age of 56 years. Interred in Memory Gardens, Victoria, TX. Submitted in his honor in loving memory by his widow, Charlene Sevcik Grones of Victoria, TX.

Grones, Jim, son of Paul and Rosie Grossman Grones, was born Jan. 4, 1897, Frenstat, TX. Served during WWI in 2M Corps; Depot Wagon Co #3; Auxiliary Remount Depot #329; U.S. Army. Inducted Sept. 5, 1918, West, TX. Honorably discharged from Camp Travis, TX, May 21, 1919, having attained rank of Pfc. Married Albina Kucera; one son and one daughter. Civilian occupation:

farmer. Lived in the Menlow Community, near Aquilla, TX, for the most of his life following discharge from Army. Died June 20, 1962.

Grones, Melvin J., son of Emil J. and Selma Galetka Grones, was born Jan. 9, 1936, Hallettsville, Lavaca Co., TX. Graduated Hallettsville High School, 1954; Undergraduate, Texas A&I University, 1959; Graduate, Central Michigan University, 1978; commissioned 2nd Lt., Texas A&I University, Regular U.S. Army Signal Corps. Theater of Operations: CONUS–Ft Monmouth, N.J.; NORAD, Ft. Leavenworth; Pentagon JCS, MacDill AFB; USARPAC–Korea; USARPAC–Viet Nam; USARPAC–Hawaii; USAREUR–Germany. Retired 1980, as Lt. Colonel. Currently employed by Valero Energy Corp., San Antonio, TX. Married Patricia H. Grones. Children: Leah Grones Raney (spouse of Dr. Rance W. Raney), Matthew J. Grones. Home of record: Seguin, TX.

Grones, Paul Jerry, son of Louis and Emilie Gerlich Grones, was born June 23, 1926, West, TX. Education: through tenth grade, Ross, Aquilla, and West, TX. Enlisted U.S. Army Corps, Dallas, TX, Aug. 22, 1944. Theater of Operations: European. Military Occupation: Rifleman and Truck Driver. Battles: Germany–Rhineland; Central Europe. Medals: Rifleman Sharpshooter Badge; Combat Infantryman Badge; Good Conduct Medal; EOT Campaign Medal w/BSS; WWII Victory Medal; ribbons. Attained rank of Corporal prior to honorable discharge on July 8, 1946, San Antonio, TX. Married Peggy Blaschke; four children, three grandchildren. Employed as machinist for MKT Railroad, and carpentry and construction for Bell Helicopter. Semi-retired, does tractor repair and shop work. Home of record: Elm Mott, TX.

Grones, Royce Gene, son of Emil J. and Selma Galetka Grones, was born Feb. 10, 1945, Hallettsville, TX. Education: Hallettsvile High School; Associate of Arts, Victoria Junior College, Victoria, TX; Bachelor of Arts, University of Texas, Austin, TX; Master of Arts, Central Michigan University, Mt. Pleasant, MI; MBA, Southern Methodist University, Dallas, TX. Enlisted Lackland AFB, TX, U.S.A.F. Rank: Col. Theater of Operations: Viet Nam Conflict; Operation Desert Storm. Battles fought in: Viet Nam Conflict and Desert Storm. Medals and Awards: Legion of Merit, BSS, Meritorious Service Medal w/2 OLC, Air Medal w/2 OLC, Joint Service Commendation Medal, Air Force Commendation Medal w/1 OLC; Joint Meritorious Unit Award, Air Force Outstanding Unit Award w/7 OLC, Air Force Organizational Excellence Award, Combat Readiness Medal, National Defense Service Medal w/1 BSS, Viet Nam Service Medal, Air Force Longevity Service Award Ribbon w/4 OLC, Small Arms Expert Marksmanship Ribbon, Air Force Training Ribbon, S.W. Asia Service Medal w/2 OLC, Republic of Viet Nam Gallantry Cross w/Palm, Kuwait Liberation Medal. Other events: 102 Combat Sorties, 650 Flight Hours Combat Time, USAF Test Pilot School Graduate w/over 6,500 flight hours in more than 65 Aircraft Types/Models.

Gully, Clement Henry, son of Thomas E. and Mary E. Krenek Gully, was born Nov. 29, 1915, Fayetteville, TX. Education: grade school. Enlisted in U.S. Army, Jan. 11, 1943, Ft. Sam Houston, TX; Basic training, Santa Monica and Long Beach, CA. Assigned as M.P. to Co. B, 777th MPBN, Daugherty Airbase, Anita, CA. Feb. 28, 1943, overseas from NY with 576 Ord Ammo Co on HMS *Britannia* and landed Liverpool, England. June 10, 1943, 576th landed on Omaha Beach, part of General Patton's 3rd Army. Dec. 1944, Co. supplied ammo to 1st Army, during Battle of the Bulge. 576th travelled to Omaha Beach, Diesdorf, LeMans, Frankfort, Munich, Tittling, Czechoslovakian border. Medals: four Battle BSS, GCM, Sharpshooter Marksmanship. Honorably discharged in 1946. Married Olga. Home of record: Gully, Fayetteville Co., TX.

Gully, Daniel John, son of Thomas E. and Mary

E. Krenek Gully, was born Sept. 9, 1917, Fayetteville, TX. Graduated Fayetteville High, TX, May 22, 1936, Draughon's Business College, Houston, TX, May 31, 1938. Volunteered June 19, 1941, Houston, TX, U.S. Navy. Trained, USNTS, San Diego, CA. Assigned to submarines U.S.S. *Sturgeon*, USS *Seal* and USS *Harder*. Main bases of operation: Pearl Harbor, Hawaii, and from southern, eastern, northern coasts of Australia. Commendation Ribbon Citation reads in part: "During 2nd War Patrol of the USS *Sturgeon* . . . Gull's exceptional skill . . . and proficiency . . . resulted in sinking of three enemy ships, totalling 20,600 tons. . . ." The Presidential Legion of Merit Citation reads, in part: "For exceptional meritorious conduct . . . as Radar Operator of the USS *Harder* during the Fifth War Patrol . . . in enemy waters . . . rendered valuable assistance to Gully's commanding officer in launching . . . attacks which resulted in the sinking of five . . . Japanese destroyers . . . and successful evasion of enemy counter measures." Most decorated sub in WWII, #46. "The five patrols of the USS *Harder* resulted in the sinking of enemy shipping totalling over 80,000 tons." On Aug. 5, 1944, the USS *Harder* was ordered on its 6th War Patrol, along with the USS *Haddo*, to ". . . harass and destroy Japanese shipping. . . ." along the eastern coast of the Philippines in the South China Sea. While engaging enemy shipping on Aug. 24, 1944, the USS *Harder* was listed MISSING IN ACTION. Commander of the USS *Haddo* logged "By 0955, breakup noise faded out." No survivors from the USS *Harder*! Medals: American Campaign, European, African, Middle Eastern Campaign, Asiatic-Pacific Campaign, GCM, Submarine Combat Insignia, Ribbon Bar w/Star of Pres Unit Cit, Meritorious Conduct, Freedom, Legion of Merit w/Combat "V," Purple Heart, Submarine Bar w/3 BSS, Commendation Ribbon, Ancient Order of the Deep. Submitted in his memory by sister-in-law and brother, Clement and Olga J. Gully, whose home of record is Fayetteville, TX.

Hacznijski, Steve, Jr., served three years in U.S. Army Corps during WWII. Name is on monument which was erected by St. Mary's Catholic Parishioners in Frydek, Tx.

Hafernik, Bennie, son of Frank and Emma Hafernik. Theater of Operations included Europe during WWII and Korea.

Hafernik, Johnny, son of Frank and Emma Hafernik.

Hafernik, William, son of Frank and Emma Hafernik. Born in 1908 in Honkhaus, TX. Theater of Operations was the Far East. Fought in the Battle of Pearl Harbor. Died 1990.

Haidek, Larry F., son of Frank George and Eddie May Lucus Haidek, was born Oct. 10, 1943 in West, TX. Graduated from West High School and completed Hill Junior College. Also attended Grossmont Community College, all in TX. During the Viet Nam Conflict he enlisted in the U.S. Navy and served aboard the USS *Bridget* DE-1024 in the coastal waters of Viet Nam. Attained the grade of E5, (RM2-Radioman 2nd Class). Awards and decorations include the Viet Nam Service Medal, Viet Nam Campaign Medal, and Good Conduct Medal. Separated from the service Feb. 2, 1970. Last known home of record: Glendale, AZ.

Haidek, Louis, West, TX, WWII Military Veteran.

Haidusek, Alois Daniel, son of Louis and Mary Cocek Haidusek, was born July 9, 1926, West, TX. Education: Graduate: St. Mary's Catholic Elementary School, West, TX; West High School; Hill Jr. College, Hillsboro, TX; Baylor University, Waco, TX–BBA Degree. Enlisted in U.S. Navy, Dallas, TX, July 10, 1943. Served on USAT MAUI (Transport) and USS *Takanis Bay* #89 (aircraft carrier) in the Asiatic-Pacific Theater of Operations. Made four crossings to Manila, when crossing the equator, remembers thinking when Sr. Alfred tried to teach us about the equator in the fourth grade, he didn't pay attention, as he thought it was so far away, he would never need to know what it meant, or where it was! On his second trip to Manila, he watched as General Douglas MacArthur landed on the beach and made his historical statement, "I have returned!" and thinking he was a little late. While in Manila, he learned that Emil "Hoot" Hutyra of West, TX, was stationed at Clarke AFB. He hitchhiked there about 200 miles, only to learn Hoot had been transferred the night before. He returned to his ship, then found Hoot only a half block away! He also met with Aug. Barton of West, TX on his third trip to Manila. Alois married Henrietta Ann Hykel; they had five children. Henrietta died on July 9, 1978. Alois later married Joann Hornberger, widow of Mr. Burns. Alois is owner and President of Cedar Hills Memorial Park, Ft. Worth, TX. Their "unusual hobby" is keeping up with their 24 grandchildren and two great grandchildren! Home of record: Ft. Worth, TX.

Haidusek, Augustin, was born Sept. 19, 1845, Mysi, Czechoslovakia, immigrated to USA on Nov. 1, 1856, and to Fayette County, TX, on Nov. 29,

1856. Served in Confederate Army, 1864-1865; School Teacher, 1872, 1873; Mayor of LaGrange, TX, 1875-1878; member of Texas Legislature,1880-1884. Fayette County Judge, 1884-1890. Publisher of *Svoboda*, 1885-1927; Director of Texas A&M College, 1901-1907. Died Sept. 29, 1929, La Grange, TX. Presented by Reverend Emil Vinklarek, Schulenburg, TX.

Haisler, Eugene Allen, son of L. B. and Bertha Vanacek Haisler, was born Nov. 21, 1933 at Temple, TX. Attended schools at Deanville, TX, and Rosebud, TX. Enlisted in the U.S. Army at Dallas, TX in 1955. Assigned to Ft. Carson, CO, and also overseas to Paris, France before his separation from active service in 1957. Subsequently served two years in the TX National Guard. He and his wife, Dorothy, and son, Haisler Allan, live on a farm in Cyclone, TX. Active as a home builder, paint contractor, and farmer. He and his family are members of the Ocker Brethren Church. Last listed address was Burlington, TX.

Hajda, Albert Frank, son of Frank and Annie Nemec Hajda, was born April 1, 1929, Granger, Williamson Co., TX. Graduate, Granger High School. Enlisted in U.S. Army Corps, Feb. 12, 1951, Ft. Sam Houston, TX. Military Occupation: Interrogator and Translator. Theater of Operations: ECON. Medals: Citation for work in Czech language handling Czech refugees and dissenters. Helped with Freedom Train at Czech and German Border, 1951. Attained rank of Cpl. Married Marie Gola; five children: Mark, Rosanne, Karen, Amy, Cindy. Retired from military on Dec. 22, 1992, after 41 years of service. Civilian Occupation: Custom Cabinets. Hobby: Community service. Home of record: Granger, TX.

Hajda, Frank, served in U.S. Armed Forces during WWII. Married Annie Nemec, of Granger, TX.

Hajda, Joe D., born Nov. 21, 1925. WWII veteran. SI–USNR. Member of American Legion Post No. 282, Granger, TX. Died Dec. 21, 1956. Buried in Holy Cross Catholic Cemetery, Granger, TX.

Hajda, Johnnie Dan, son of Mr. and Mrs. Cyril Hajda, Granger, TX. Education: Granger High School. Enlisted in U.S. Army Corps, 1942. Basic training, Camp Barkeley, Camp Butner, NC, and Camp Young, CA. Theaters of Operations: Asiatic-Pacific; American. Campaigns in New Guinea and Philippines. Medals: ATO w/3 BSS; APO Ribbon w/2 BSS; Good Conduct Medal; WWII Victory Ribbon. Attained rank of Pvt. before honorable discharge. Married Matilda Skrahak. Member American Legion Post No. 282, Granger, TX.

Hajda, Rudolph Alois, son of Frank and Annie Hajda, was born June 5, 1926. Attended high school at Granger, TX. Enlisted in the U.S. Army at Ft. Sam Houston, TX, 1944, during WWII. Basic training at Camp Hood, TX. Served in the Asiatic-Pacific Theater of Operations and participated in campaigns in the Philippine Islands and in the occupation of Japan. Awards and decorations include the Asiatic Pacific Campaign Medal, Good Conduct Medal, Army of Occupation Medal, WWII Victory Medal, Philippine Liberation Ribbon, and two Overseas Service Bars. Separated from the Service as Technical Corporal (T-5) on Nov. 17, 1946. Resides in Granger, Williamson Co., TX. Works as a bridge foreman for Williamson Co. Married Alice Matula; four children: Patrick, Gary, Rick, and Melissa. Enjoys building toys for his grandchildren and gardening. Member American Legion Post No. 282, Granger, TX.

Hajda, Vaclav J., Sr., son of Louis and Rosie Nemec Hajda. Born Apr. 22, 1923. Attended Sts. Cyril & Methodius School in Granger, TX. Enlisted at Ft. Sam Houston in the Army Infantry. Served in Northern France and the Rhineland, WOUNDED IN ACTION. Decorations include: two Bronze Campaign Stars, Combat Infantryman Badge, Purple Heart, Victory Ribbon, American Theatre Ribbon, Good Conduct Ribbon, European African Middle Eastern Theatre Ribbon. Discharged Jan. 10, 1946. Member American Legion Post No. 282, Granger, TX. Married Margie Kurten, two sons and two daughters.

Hajda, Wesley Joe, Jr., son of Vaclav John and

Margaret Kurtin Hadja, was born Jan. 19, 1947 in Taylor, Williamson, TX. Graduated from Granger High School, Granger, TX, in 1965, Temple Junior College, Temple, TX, in 1966, and attended the University of TX, Austin, TX. Enlisted in the Texas National Guard in March 1969, during the Viet Nam Conflict. Served at Camp Mabry, Austin, TX, as an Equipment, Storage, and Supply (Airborne) NCO and attained the rank of Sgt. Separated from the service in March 1975. Married Henrietta Tomasek; two children: David and Julia. Last known home of record: Granger, TX.

Hajek, Albin B., was born Feb. 8, 1928. Served in U.S. Army during WWII. Died June 19, 1975. Buried in Lady Fatima Cemetery, Abbott, TX.

Hajek, Anton, son of Henry and Mary Kotrlik Hajek, was born Jan. 17, 1896 in Fortran, Victoria Co., TX. Attended elementary school in Victoria Co., TX. Enlisted in the armed services at Hallettsville, TX during WWI and served in the American Expeditionary Forces in France as a member of the 325th Machine Gun Company, 82nd Infantry. WOUNDED IN ACTION in France and was presented the Purple Heart. Discharged from the service in May 1919. Married Jane Migl.

Hajek, Benjamin F., son of Anton and Jane Migl Hajek, was born Sept. 17, 1931 in Shiner, TX. Graduated high school. Earned a BS degree from Texas A&M in 1958, and PhD from Auburn, AL, in 1964. Served in the U.S. Armed Forces in Germany as a member of the Occupational Forces. Discharged from the service on Dec. 19, 1953. Last known home of record: Auburn, AL.

Hajek, John Frank, son of Emil T. and Lillie Ennis Hajek, was born Apr. 19, 1925 in Shiner, TX. Graduated high school. Attended college for 3½ years. Enlisted in the armed services at Ft. Sam Houston, TX, during WWII. Served in the European, African, and Middle Eastern Theater of Operations. Participated in the Ardennes-Alsace Campaign, specifically, in the Battle of the Bulge. Discharged from the service on Dec. 10, 1945. Home of record: Austin, TX.

Hajek, Reynold L., son of Mr. and Mrs. A. J. Hajek, Abbott, TX. Entered U.S. Army Corp, 1943. Served in Italy, Corsica, France, Germany, Luzon and Japan. WOUNDED IN ACTION, 1944, France. Awards: EAME Ribbon; Camp Medal w/5 BSS; Combat Infantry Badge; Asiatic-Pacific Ribbon; Philippine Liberation; GCM; Purple Heart; WWII Victory Ribbon w/4 overseas bars. Attained rank of T/5 prior to honorable discharge, 1945.

Hajek, William John, was born June 24, 1921, served in the U.S. Coast Guard RES, during WWII, attained rank of S1. Died Oct. 8, 1965, buried in St. Mary's Cemetery, West, TX.

Hajovsky, Adolph G., son of Adolph A. and Josephine Kocurek Hajovsky, was born Apr. 23, 1942, Caldwell, TX. Graduated from Caldwell High School, 1960; University of Texas, Austin, TX, Degree and Commission, 1964. 1st Lt., U.S. Army, in University of Texas, Austin, ROTC. Served in U.S. Army Area Support Command, Chicago, IL, 1965; Republic of Viet Nam, 1966. Operation Masher, 1966; Operation Whitewing, 1966; Operation Bluebeard, 1966. Awards and Decorations: BSS Medal, National Defense Service Medal, Viet Nam Service Medal, Viet Nam Campaign Medal, Republic of Viet Nam Gallantry Cross w/Palm, Unit Citation Badge. May 21, 1970, U.S. Army Reserve Corps, Houston, TX. Home of record: Cameron, TX.

Halamik, Laddie, WWII veteran, West, TX.

Haluzan, Aug, Granger, TX. Member of American Legion Post No. 282, Granger, TX. WWII veteran.

Hammonds, Allan, son of Charley and Regina Zaskoda Hammonds was born in March 1952 and served in the U.S. Army during the Viet Nam Conflict. Died in Nov. 1981 in Ft. Worth, TX. Interred at Rosehill Cemetery in Ft. Worth, Tarrant, TX.

Hanacik, Henry John, Jr., son of Henry John and

Lena Pauline Spinn Hanacik, Sr., Taylor, TX. Born Sept. 11 1926, in Temple, Bell Co., TX. Graduate of Taylor High School. Enlisted in U.S. Army Corps Jan. 2, 1945 at Ft. Sam Houston, TX. Assigned to Battery C, 57th Field Artillery Battalion. Served in Okinawa and Korea. Achieved the rank of Sergeant. Decorations included: Asiatic-Pacific Campaign Ribbon, Good Conduct Medal, Victory Ribbon, Army of Occupation Ribbon (Japan), two Overseas Service Bars. Discharged Nov. 29, 1946. Married Mary Ann Martinka, had four children. Died Jan. 3, 1986, and is buried in Weir, Williamson Co., TX.

Hanak, Otto, Jr., son of Mr. and Mrs. Otto Hanak, Sr., was born Mar. 14, 1921, West, TX. Attended Leggott School. Served in the U.S. Armed Forces during WWII, Asiatic-Pacific Theater, in Pacific and Japan. Attained rank of T-5 prior to honorable discharge in 1947. Married Pauline Freyer.

Hanna, Clarence Milton "Chad," son of Frank and Mary Pechacek Hanna was born June 18, 1920, in Fayette Co., TX. Graduated from high school, and earned 150 college credits. Member of the U.S. Marine Corps during WWII, initially in enlisted status and later as commissioned officer. Served in both the American and the Asiatic-Pacific Theaters of Operations. Participated in military operations at Tarawa, Marianna, and Okinawa. Awards and decorations include Asiatic-Pacific Campaign Medal, American Campaign Medal, WWII Victory Medal, and Good Conduct Medal. Released from active duty on Aug. 31, 1962. Last known home of record: Fountain Valley, CA.

Hanslik, Adolph R., son of Frank and Mary Hanslik, was born Mar. 22, 1917, Hallettsville, TX. Attended business college. Enlisted in the U.S. Army at Ft. Sam Houston, TX, during WWII. Served in the European, African and Middle Eastern Theater of Operations and attained the rank of Sgt. Many awards and decorations. Separated from the service on Oct. 8, 1945. Last known home of record: Lubbock, TX.

Hanus, Alton, son of Vaclav and Marie Jurecek Hanus, was born Aug. 24, 1924 in Skidmore, TX. Attended elementary school in Bee Co., TX, near Olmos, TX. Enlisted in the U.S. Army at Ft. Sam Houston, TX, during WWII. Served in the Asiatic-Pacific Theater of Operations and attained the rank of Sgt. Participated in the Luzon Campaign in the Philippine Islands. Awards and decorations include the Asiatic-Pacific Campaign Medal with campaign star, WWII Victory Medal, Good Conduct Medal, Philippine Liberation Ribbon, and the Combat Infantryman Badge. Discharged from the service at Ft. Sam Houston, TX on Nov. 24, 1946. Home of record: Waco, TX.

Hanys, Marvin O., son of Otto and Albina Kacir Hanys, was born Mar. 26, 1924, in Yoakum, TX. High school education. Enlisted on Sept. 11, 1942, at Foster Field, Victoria, TX, and as T/Sgt participated in battles in New Guinea, South Philippines and Luzon. Discharged Oct. 7, 1945. Medals: three BSS, Air Medal and three Oak Leaf Clusters, Good Conduct Medal. Died July 9, 1979.

Hanzelka, Alphonse T., son of Mr. and Mrs. Hanzelka. Graduate of Taylor High School, TX. Enlisted U.S. Army Air Corps, 1942. Basic training, Sheppard Field, TX. Further training, CA. Theater of Operations: ETO. Medals: ETO Ribbon w/6 BSS; BSS and CC Ribbons. Attained rank of M/Sgt. before honorable discharge. Married Doris Marie Speegle, Taylor, TX. Home of record: Granger, TX.

Hanzelka, Raymond J., West, TX, WWII veteran, ETO.

Hanzlicek, Johnny Walter, son of Mr. and Mrs. John Hanzlicek of West, TX. Entered U.S. Army Corps, 1944. Theater of Operations: European. WOUNDED IN ACTION, France, 1944. Awards: Purple Heart, GCM and European Theater Ribbon. Attained rank of Pvt. prior to honorable discharge in 1946.

Hatka, Louis, Granger, TX, WWII veteran.

Hatka, Otis R., son of Lillian Hatka, Granger, TX. Attended Texas A&M. Enlisted in U.S. Army, 1942, during WWII. Basic training, Ft. Benning, GA. Theater of Operation: Asiatic-Pacific. Served in campaigns in Hawaii; New Caledonia; New

Hebrides; Fiji; Solomons; Guadalcanal. WOUNDED IN ACTION, 1942. Medals: Asiatic-Pacific Campaign Ribbon and Purple Heart. Honorably discharged, 1943. Rank: 1st Lt. Buried Holy Cross Catholic Cemetery, Granger, TX.

Havelka, Emil Edward, son of John Joe and Mary Hattie Kohoutek Havelka born Oct. 28, 1925, Corn Hill, Williamson, TX. Education: Holy Trinity School; Schwertner High; graduated from Jarrell, TX, High School. Enlisted in U.S. Army Air Corps, 1944. Basic training, Sheppard Field, TX, and Sioux City, Iowa; Military Occupation: Nose Gunner; Theater of Operations: EAME. Served in Germany. Medals: two Silver Flying Medal; Good Conduct Medal; Presidential Citation; Purple Heart. Attained rank of S/Sgt. MISSING IN ACTION, March 21, 1944; declared KILLED IN ACTION, March 21, 1945. Hobbies: Art and sports; loved animals. Submitted by Eileen Rosipal of Austin, TX.

Havelka, Johnnie S., son of Mr. and Mrs. Louis Havelka, Bartlett, TX. Graduate, Bartlett High School. Enlisted U.S. Army Air Corps, 1944. Basic training, Kelly Field. Theater of Operations: American. Honorable discharge, 1944. Rank: Pvt. Married Emily Valenta.

Havelka, Louis John, born Dec. 31 1912. Served in the United States Coast Guard Merchant Marine aboard merchant vessels between Dec. 7, 1941, and Aug. 15, 1945. Home of record: Houston, TX.

Havran, Edward F., son of Adolph Havran and Julia Jasek, was born Feb. 19, 1921, Weinert, TX. Graduated Weinert High School, Texas Tech University. Enlisted Lubbock and Knox City, TX. Theater of Operations: 8th Air Force/401st Bomb Group; European Theater of Operations. Battles: Air battle of Europe; Northern France, 35 combat missions over ETO. Not wounded, but hit by flack. Medals: Air Medal w/4 Oakleaf Clusters, Silver Cluster, Bronze Battle Star Northern France. Assigned to retired reserve May 8, 1972. Served as replacement in NATO in Europe. Home of record: Colleyville, TX.

Havran, Elo J., son of Joseph and Kathryn Supak Havran, was born Oct. 15, 1914 in Ganado, TX. Attended high school and subsequently served in the U.S. Army as a Medical Corpsman from 1935 to 1939 at Ft. Sam Houston in San Antonio, TX. Was in the Reserves and called back to duty during WWII where he served as an instructor for Medical Corps Recruits until discharge from the service in Dec. 1945. Died July 2, 1984.

Havran, Jerome J., son of Joseph and Kathryn Supak Havran, was born Oct. 16, 1902 in Fayetteville, TX. Attended high school and in the 1920s served in the U.S. Army at San Antonio, TX. Drafted in 1944, during WWII, and served a few months. Discharged in 1945 due to his age. Died Dec. 28, 1968.

Havran, Jerry James, son of Anton Marvin and Annie Marie Havran, was born Jan. 24, 1930 in Fayetteville, TX. GED at Sealy, TX, High School. Attended the University of Houston, TX, for three years, majoring in diesel engineering. Enlisted in the U.S. Navy at Houston in Jan. 1948. Participated in naval operations at Pusan, Inchon, and Wonsan during the Korean Conflict. Awards and decorations include the Korean Service Medal, United Nations Service Medal, National Defense Service Medal, and Good Conduct Medal. Discharged from the Navy on Dec. 22, 1951. Home of record: Houston, TX.

Havran, Laddie Louis, son of Anton Marvin and Annie Marie Havran, was born Apr. 7, 1926 in Ellinger, TX. Graduated from Sealy, TX, High School, and subsequently attended business college in Houston, TX. Enlisted in the U.S. Army Air Corps at Houston on Jan. 29, 1944, during WWII, and served in the American Theater of Operations as a flight crew member. Awards and decorations include the American Campaign Medal and WWII Victory Medal. Discharged from the service on Nov. 14, 1945. Home of record: Sealy, TX.

Havran, Oswald A., son of Joseph and Kathryn Supak Havran, was born Feb. 29, 1924 at Ganado, TX. Graduated from high school and attended the University of Houston, TX, prior to his enlistment in the U.S. Navy during WWII. Served in the Asiatic-Pacific Theater of Operations as a member of a

Naval Air Wing. Awards and decorations include the Asiatic-Pacific Campaign Medal and WWII Victory Medal. Discharged from the service on Jan. 31, 1946. Home of record: Houston, TX.

Havranek, Ernest Raymond, son of Mr. and Mrs. Anton Havranek, was born Oct. 27, 1923, Bellmead, TX. Volunteered for service Sept. 15, 1941. Assigned to U.S. Marine Corps, 4th Division. Trained at San Diego, CA; Elliott, CA. Served overseas Jan. 10, 1944, through Oct. 11, 1945, Asiatic-Pacific Theater of Operations: Marshall; Marianas, Hawaiian; Volcano Islands; Iwo Jima; Roi Namur. Awards: Presidential Unit Citation w/1 Star; Asiatic-Pacific w/3 Stars; WWII Victory Medal; American Defense Medal. Attained rank of Corporal prior to honorable discharge Oct. 29, 1945.

Havranek, Richard Joe, son of Mr. and Mrs. Anton Havranek, was born Aug. 6, 1920, Bellmead, TX. Volunteered for service May 1940. Was assigned to U.S. Army Corps, 36th Division, 155th Field Artillery. Trained at Camp Bowie, Brownwood, TX; on maneuvers in LA. Served overseas Apr. 10, 1942, through Jan. 4, 1946, in the European Theater of Operations: North Africa; Sicily; Italy; Salerno; Tunisia; Napolis. Decorations: American Defense Medal; ETO Campaign Medal; WWII Victory Ribbon and all citations and medals merited by the 36th Division. Attained rank of Sgt. prior to honorable discharge Jan. 27, 1946.

Havranek, Rudolf Anton, son of Mr. and Mrs. Anton Havranek, was born July 21, 1918, Bellmead, TX. Attended Waco Junior High School. Volunteered for service Oct. 1943. Assigned to U.S. Marine Corps, Replacement Battalion. Trained at San Diego, CA. Served overseas from Mar. 3, 1944, through Aug. 12, 1944, Honolulu and Oahu, Hawaii during WWII, in the Asiatic-Pacific Theater. Awards: Asiatic-Pacific Theater Campaign Medal; Good Conduct Medal; American Defense Medal; WWII Victory Ribbon. Attained rank of Corporal prior to honorable discharge, Nov. 17, 1945.

Havranek, Willie Rudy, son of Mr. and Mrs. Anton Havranek, was born Jan. 16, 1925, Bellmead, TX. Volunteered for service Sept. 4, 1943; assigned to U.S. Marine Corps, 34d Amphibious Battalion and 2nd Defense Bn. Trained at San Diego, CA. Served overseas Dec. 23, 1943, through Nov. 8, 1945, in Asiatic-Pacific Theater of Operations: Okinawa, Ryukyus, Hawaii, Gilberts, Marshall, Perry Marianas Islands, Saipan and Guam. Awards: Presidential Unit Citation, Asiatic-Pacific Theater Campaign Medal; U.S. Navy Unit Citation and WWII Victory Medal. Attained rank of Corporal prior to honorable discharge Feb. 1946.

Havrda, Erwin, son of Joseph and Carrie Havrda, was born May 1, 1934, at Schulenburg, TX. Graduated from Schulenburg High School in 1953. Obtained two years of college GED and studied at the University of Washington for one year and at the University of TX, Austin, TX for a half year. Enlisted in the U.S. Air Force in 1953 at Lackland AFB, TX, during the Korean Conflict. Served in Korea, Newfoundland, Viet Nam, England, Spain, and Alaska. Temporary duty stints in Italy, Germany, Greece, and Turkey. Awards and decorations include the Korean Service Medal, Viet Nam Service Medal, National Defense Service Medal, Air Force Achievement Medal, Meritorious Service Medal, Air Force Commendation Medal with two Oak Leaf Clusters, Good Conduct Medal, Presidential Unit Citation, Air Force Outstanding Unit Award, and Air Force Overseas Ribbon. Selected as the outstanding airman of the year. Active in military sports programs and participated in baseball, fast pitch, and slow pitch softball for 18 years, earning numerous awards including USAF All Star status four times, MVP in 1961, two no-hit games, and USAF Championship Teams '66, '67, '68, and '70. Retired as Senior Master Sgt. after 21 years of service on Aug. 30, 1974. Married Sharlene Havrda; four children: Davene, Joseph, Nancy, and Sherry. Last known home of record: Schulenburg, TX.

Hawkins, Charles D., son of Joseph F. and Hedwig M. Machard Hawkins, was born Jan. 21, 1945 at Corpus Christi, TX. Graduated from high school. Drafted into the U.S. Army at San Antonio, TX, during the Viet Nam Conflict. Served in the Me Quon Delta and attained the rank of Specialist 4. Separated from the service in June 1967 at Oakland, CA. Home of record: Hebbronville, TX.

Hegar, Joseph Adolph, son of Reverend Joseph P. and Mary Mikulencak Hegar, was born Oct. 15, 1915, Granger, Williamson Co., TX. Education: TX public schools; Mary Harding Baylor College, Belton, TX; University of TX, Austin, TX; Signal Corps Officer Candidate School, Ft. Monmouth, NJ; Sig. Corps Co. Advanced Course, Ft. Monmouth, NJ; Command and General Staff School, Ft. Leavenworth, KS. Enlisted Feb. 27, 1942, Dodd Field, Ft. Sam Houston, TX. Theater of Operation: Asiatic-Pacific; Korea; Japan; U.S. Army, Europe. Battles: Korea. Medals: Legion of Merit; BSS w/2 OLC; Army Commendation w/1 OLC; American Defense Service; American Campaign; Asiatic-Pacific Theater Campaign; WWII Victory; National Defense Service w/1 OLC; Korean Service w/3 Campaign Stars; Armed Forces Reserve; United Nations Service; Republic of Korea Presidential Unit Citation; Meritorious Unit Citation; Eight (8) Overseas Duty Stripes; Dept. of Army Genl. Staff ID Badge. Military Department: Army, Component: USAR, Branch: Signal Corps and General Staff. Married Lucille E. Bolf, Floresville, TX; one daughter: Rebecca.

Hegar, Marvin W., attended West High School, West, TX. Entered U.S. Navy, 1945; trained in San Diego and Holtville, CA. Served in Asiatic-Pacific Theater of Operations, Pacific and Japan. Attained rank of S2/C prior to honorable discharge in 1946. Married Irene Merenda.

Hejl, Alvin Joe, son of Joe Vince and Sophie Shiller Hejl, was born Nov. 29, 1914, Taylor, Williamson Co., TX. Education: public schools, Taylor, TX; Nixon Clay Business College, Austin, TX. Enlisted Aug. 18, 1941, Ft. Sam Houston, TX; assigned to 1st Armored Div., U.S. Army Corps, Cryptograph Tech. Overseas June 11, 1942, ETO. Battles: Tunisian, Naples-Foggia, Rome-Arno, Algeria-French Morocco, North Apennines, Po Valley. Medals: six BSS and one Bronze Arrowhead; American Defense Service; GCM; WWII Victory. Rank: Tec 4. Honorably discharged Aug. 23, 1945. Home of record: Taylor, TX. Submitted by sister, Leona Hejl.

Hejl, Edmond H., was born Mar. 30, 1912. Drafted into the Army Nov. 23, 1943 at Wills Point, TX. Reported for military duty Dec. 14, 1943, at Ft. Sam Houston in San Antonio, TX. After 17 weeks of basic training in the Army Engineers at Camp Abbott, OR, transferred June 1944 to Ft. Lewis, WA. Sailed from San Francisco to Hawaii on Apr. 12, 1945, the same day President Franklin Roosevelt died. Stationed at Ft. Shafter out of Honolulu, Hawaii. Served as an anti-aircraft, Master Gunner, with the rank of Staff Sergeant. Discharged Jan. 24, 1946, at Camp Fannin, Tyler, TX. Submitted by spouse, Milady H. Hejl.

Hejl, Emil F., was born Nov. 27, 1916. Served in the U.S. Armed Forces during WWII, attaining rank of Pfc. Died Dec. 8, 1992, buried St. Mary's Cemetery, West, TX.

Hejl, Hubert A., son of William and Rosalie Hejl, was born at Snook, TX about 1910. Education: seventh grade. Enlisted during WWII, U.S. Army Corps. Theater of Operations: Europe. Medals: WWII Victory, Good Conduct, EAME Campaign. Honorably discharged about 1946. One of four sons of William and Rosalie Hejl to serve. Date of death, unknown, if deceased. Submitted by Edwin L. Hlavaty of Caldwell, TX.

Hejl, John Bryce, son of John Bohuslav and Lillie Kopecky Hejl, was born Mar. 12, 1923, Temple, Bell Co., TX. Education: Baker Elementary, University Jr. High, Austin High, Austin, TX; graduated in 1942. Enlisted in U.S. Navy, Sept. 16, 1942, Houston, Harris Co., TX. Attained rank of Seaman, S/1. Theater of Operations: Asiatic-Pacific. Military occupation: N.A.S. Ground Crew; later, gunnery division on Submarine. Medals: American Theater Campaign; Asiatic-Pacific Campaign; WWII Victory; Submarine Combat. Honorably discharged Feb. 12, 1946. Married LaVerne Louise Heine; four children: John Bruce, William Daniel, Janice Louise, and Diane Elaine. Civilian occupation: State Employee, Texas Highway Dept. and University of Texas. Retired Aug. 31, 1986. Hobbies include woodworking, metalworking, welding, metal detecting, and hunting.

Hejl, Robert Delman, son of John Bohuslav and

Lillie Libusa Kopecky Hejl, was born Dec. 6, 1925, Austin, Travis, TX. Education: Austin High School; Travis Co. Voc School, graduated 1950, NYA Radio School; Univ of TX. During WWII, enlisted U.S. Navy, Mar. 3, 1943, Austin, TX. Served in the Asiatic-Pacific Theater of Operations in the U.S. Navy aboard the USS *Hickox*, DD 673. Boarded the USS *Hickox* on Dec. 6, 1943, and sailed for the Pacific on Dec. 7, 1943. Served as a radioman and 20 mm gunner on the Destroyer USS *Hickox*, DD-673. Attained the rank of Seaman 1/C. The USS *Hickox* provided screening missions for Task Forces 38 and 58 in an area in the Pacific Ocean which stretched from New Guinea to the Aleutian Islands with only the order to "Destroy the Enemy." The USS *Hickox* was credited with the sinking of two Japanese cargo ships, downing three enemy planes, rescuing downed pilots, taking 22 men off the fantail of the devastated aircraft carrier *Franklin*, and rescuing about 90 of the Aircraft Carrier *Franklin*'s crew from the sea after a kamikaze attack. While in the area around Okinawa on "coffin corner" (Radar Picket Duty) the USS *Hickox* under kamikaze attacks for five months; sent to the China Sea on a decoy communications mission in 1944, nearly sunk by typhoon. The U.S. ships: *Hull*, *Spence*, *Monaghan* sank with heavy losses. Battles: Marshal Islands, Truk, Marcus Islands, Marianas Islands, Yap, Palaus Islands, Bonin Islands, Formosa, Philippines, Japan, Iwo Jima, Okinawa, Leyte Gulf and others. Medals: GCM, Asiatic-Pacific Campaign w/11 campaign stars, Philippine Liberation Ribbon, and Navy Unit Citation. Honorably discharged Feb. 26, 1946, Camp Wallace, TX. Children: Mollie Elizabeth; Robert Cyril Jerome, Steven Anthony, Vincent Jay, and Herman Mark Hejl. Occupation: Farmer, rancher, salvage specialist, never plans to retire. Hobbies: Archeology, antiquities, woodworking, metalworking, winemaking, ecology, wild life preservation. For 36 years, undercover agent, government intelligence. Home of record: Manchaca, TX.

Hejl, Walter R., son of William and Rosalie Hejl, was born Feb. 27, 1916, Snook, TX. Education: seventhth grade. Drafted U.S. Army, Ft. Sam Houston, TX, 1941. Attained rank of Tech Sgt-5 during WWII. Theater of Operations: EAME. Engineer. Battles: Italy, Germany. WOUNDED IN ACTION, Germany. Medals: Purple Heart; GCM; Marksmanship; EAME w/5 BSS. Honorably discharged, Oct, 1945. One of four sons of William and Rosalie Hejl to serve in WWII. Home of record, Houston, TX. Submitted by Edwin L. Hlavaty, Caldwell, TX.

Hejl, Willie E., son of William and Rosalie Hejl, was born June 13, 1908, Snook, TX. Graduated seventh grade. Drafted Ft. Sam Houston, TX, 1941, U.S. Army Corps. Theater of Operations: EAME. Battles: Central Europe, Naples-Foggia, France, Rhineland. WOUNDED IN ACTION, Oct. 14, 1943. Honorably discharged as Pfc., Oct. 22, 1945, disabled American veteran. Medals: Service Ribbon W/1 Silver Star; Purple Heart w/OLC; Good Conduct; WWII Victory. One of four sons of William and Rosalie Hejl to serve in WWII. Home of record: Caldwell, TX. Submitted by Edwin L. Hlavaty, Caldwell TX.

Hejny, Joe B., son of Frank L. and Anna Martinek Hejny, was born Sept. 21, 1912 at Telico, TX. Attended Telico schools. Enlisted in the U.S. Marine Corps on Apr. 12, 1945, during WWII, and trained at Parris Island, SC, and Camp LeJeune, NC. Served with the 3rd Marine Division in Tiensin, China. Honorably discharged July 6, 1946. Married Stacie Trojacek in 1934. Died May 24, 1978, and is interred in St. Joseph Cemetery in Ennis, TX.

Hejny, Joseph H., son of Frank and Rosie Honza Hejny, was born Feb. 12, 1913, in Ennis, TX. Attended Ennis High School. Enlisted in Dallas, TX. Rank: Pfc. Served in the 1st Cavalry at Ft. D.A. Russell, Marfa, TX, from Aug. 17, 1931, until Jan. 1933 when the Cavalry was abandoned and all personnel were moved to Ft. Knox, KY and became the 1st Cavalry Mechanized. Received discharge at Ft. Knox on Aug. 17, 1934. Reenlisted in the Air Force at Randolph Field, TX, on Oct. 22, 1934, and served three years, receiving discharge Oct. 23, 1937. Home of record: Duncanville, TX.

Hejny, Raymond Frank, only son of Frank W. and Lillie Skrivanek Hejny, was born May 31, 1930 at Ennis, TX. Attended Telico elementary and high schools prior to enlisting into the U.S. Marine Corps at Dallas, TX during the Korean Conflict. Served in Korea and participated in the Munsan-Ni Campaign where he was KILLED IN ACTION on Mar. 27, 1953. Awards and decorations include the Purple Heart, National Defense Service Medal, Korean Service Medal, United Nations Service Medal, Gold Star Lapel Button, Korean Presidential Unit Citation, and the 1st Marine Division Service Award.

Hejtmancik, James Harold, son of Rudolph Joseph and Millie Frances Jurcak Hejtmancik, was born Sept. 3, 1922, Dime Box, TX. Graduated from Giddings High School. Received BA from University of Texas, Austin, TX, and an M.D. from University of Texas Medical Branch, Galveston, TX. Enlisted in U.S. Army, at Galveston, TX, was Pfc. ASTP, 1943-1945; then received orders, Ft. Sam Houston, San Antonio, TX, 1st Lt. Medical Corps, Air Training Command, Geiger Field, WA and Ft. Francis E. Warren, WY, 1945–1948. Honorably discharged July 1948. Home of record: Jasper, TX.

Hejtmancik, Milton Rudolph, son of Rudolph Joseph and Millie Frances Jurcak, was born Sept. 27, 1919, Caldwell, TX. Public High School. B.A., Univ. of TX in 1939, Graduate School, Physics, 1940; M.D. Univ. of TX Medical Branch 1943. Enlisted in the Army at Galveston, TX. Entered into active service at Carlisle Barracks, PA, June 2, 1944; Medical Corp, European Theater; evacuation, general hospitals, France, Germany, Austria. This was as a general medical officer, with specialty in Neuropsychiatry. Last duty station was Glasenbach, Austria, where he was CO of the 62nd Field Hospital. "Our hospital was in a German schoolhouse at Rheinau, three miles from Mannheim, when Gen. George Patton was critically injured in a jeep accident. We were alerted by phone that Patton was being brought to us, and we frantically labored to make a suitable place for him. But minute after minute passed, and there was no sign of Patton. We found later he had been taken to the station hospital in Heidelberg. We were very much relieved. It was not that we did not admire Patton, but he was rough on doctors, especially those in the 3rd Army." Discharged Aug. 16, 1946 at Fort Sam Houston, TX. He married Myrtle Lou Erwin, Aug. 21, 1943. She died June 29, 1975. Married Myrtle McCormick, Nov. 27, 1976; three children: Kelly Erwin, Milton Rudolph, Jr., and Peggy Lou. Served on the faculty of Univ. of TX Medical Branch, 1946-1980. Retired as Professor of Medicine and Director of Heart Station. Home of record: Hammond, LA.

Hejtmancik, Rudolph Joseph, son of Josef and Frances Krupa Hejtmancik, born Oct. 23, 1893, Dime Box, TX. Education: S.W. Texas State College, San Marcos, TX; University of Texas, Austin, TX. Volunteered for U.S. Army Corps, 1918, inducted at Camp Mabry, Austin, TX. Served during WWI, U.S. Army 1918-1919, Kelly Field, San Antonio, TX. Honorably discharged, 1919, San Antonio, TX. Married Aug. 15, 1917, Millie Frances Jurcak; three children: Milton Rudolph, James Harold, and Grace Hejtmancik Ward. Taught school at Hranice, Old Dime Box, New Dime Box; Co. School Superintendent, Lee Co., TX, for over 40 years. Died Nov. 3, 1982. Interred at City Cemetery, Giddings, TX.

Hejtmanek, Frank Henry, son of Frank J. and Albina Wetzel Hejtmanek, was born Aug. 24, 1920 in Blessing, TX. Graduated from high school and attended the University of TX for two years. Enlisted in the U.S. Navy at Bay City, TX, during WWII. Served in the Asiatic-Pacific Theater of Operations as an Ensign. Discharged from the service on Mar. 16, 1946. Latest home of record: Pasadena, TX.

Hejtmanek, George William, Sr., son of Frank Joseph and Albina Wetzel Hejtmanek, was born Feb. 14, 1928 in the El Maton community, Matagora Co., TX. Graduated from Blessing High School in May, 1945. Attended Wharton Junior College and University of Texas. Enlisted in the Army May 1945. Basic training at Ft. Sam

Houston, San Antonio, TX, and Pharmacy School at Brooke General Hospital. Served as Pharmacist at Bruns General Hospital, Santa Fe, NM and Murphy General Hospital in Walthan, MA. Discharged Mar. 20, 1947 at the rank of T-5. Married Dovie Lee Spoor in June 1948; three children. Home of record: Palacios, TX.

Helona, Stanley J., was born Oct. 3, 1921. Served in the U.S. Army Corps during WWII, attaining rank of Corporal. Died June 15, 1988. Buried in St. Mary's Cemetery, West, TX.

Hercheck, Edward A., son of Leo and Carrie Shulak Herchek, was born May 23, 1917 in Mt. Olive, Lavaca Co., TX. Attended Mt. Olive Elementary; business college in Yoakum, TX. Inducted in the Army Mar. 12, 1941, in Houston, TX. Rank: Sgt. Stationed at Camp Bowie, TX, Aberdeen Ordnance Proving Ground, MD, Camp Swift, TX, Camp Stoneman, CA. Foreign service was HQ South Pacific Base Command (SOPACBA-COM) in Noumea, New Caledonia, and Luzon, Philippine Islands, and HQ Kobe Base, Honshu, Japan. Battle: Luzon. Medals: American Defense, one BSS, Philippine Liberation, Good Conduct, Victory Ribbon, one Service Stripe, and four Overseas Service Bars. Discharged Nov. 28, 1945, at Fort Sam Houston, TX. Home of record: Seguin, TX.

Herman, Bohumil Benedict, son of Arnost and Frances Motal Herman, was born Aug. 16, 1912, in Sweet Home, TX. Enlisted at San Antonio, TX, 1945, in the U.S. Army Corps. Sent to Ft. Sill, Lawton, OK. The war ended by the time basic training was finished. Honorably discharged. Died Dec. 10, 1973.

Herman, Ladislav Blase, son of Arnost and Frances Motal Herman, was born Sept. 2, 1915, at Sweet Home, TX. Entered the U.S. Army Corps, Nov. 11, 1941 at San Antonio, TX. Served in Cuba and Asiatic-Pacific Theater. Sent to the Pacific with the 449th Heavy Bombardment Group and returned Dec. 24, 1945. Medals: American Defense, American Theater Campaign, Asiatic Pacific Theater Campaign, Good Conduct and Victory. Honorably discharged Jan. 3, 1946, San Antonio, TX. Home of record: Spring, TX.

Herman, Richard Lee, son of Ladislav Herman and Mildred Piter Herman, was born Oct. 25, 1946, in St. Louis, Missouri. Entered the Air Force at Houston, TX. Fought in Viet Nam with the 31st Tactical FTR. WG. (PACAF). Medals: National Defense Service, Air Force, Good Conduct, Viet Nam Service, Viet Nam Commendation, and Air Force Outstanding Unit. Discharged Jan. 10, 1969. Home of record: Houston, TX.

Herman, Stanley Martin Hubert, son of Arnost Herman and Frances Motal Herman, was born Nov. 8, 1922, in Hallettsville, Lavaca Co., TX. Enlisted in the U.S. Navy at Corpus Christi, TX, 1942. Sent to the Pacific. Received Victory, Good Conduct and Asiatic-Pacific Medals. Discharged Feb. 18, 1946. Died Jan. 29, 1982.

Hermis, Henry R., son of Emil Hermis and Francis, was born June 24, 1929, Schulenburg, TX. Education: Engle and Flatonia, TX. Enlisted Ft. Sam Houston, TX during Korean War. Basic training, St. Louis, MO, further training Obisco, CA and Japan. Assigned to 26 Signal Corp. Was in Wont Ju; Switch-Korea and Battle Korea. Medals: BSS, Good Conduct, Korea Service. Married Rita Barta; three children: Henry, Jr., Dennis, Carolyn

Hermis Kubeczka. Hobby is taking care of farm and cattle. Home of record: Houston, TX, and farm home in Ammannsville, TX.

Hermis, Walter J., son of Fred and Martha Hermis, was born Jan. 7, 1940, Schulenburg, TX. Education: High School, Schulenburg, TX. Enlisted U.S. Coast Guard, Houston, TX, about 1958. Rank-Fireman E-4. Theater of Operations: American. Gout. Island, Alameda, CA, USCG. Played in U.S. Coast Guard Band. Home of record: Schulenburg, TX.

Hetmer, Frank, son of Joe and Annie Hetmer, was born Apr. 30, 1923, Ennis, TX. Education at Kaufman (Lone-Star), TX. Enlisted in U.S. Navy at Terrell, TX, WWII. Theater of Operations: Asiatic-Pacific. Battles: Gilbert, Kiska, Kwajalein, Saipan, and Tention Islands. Stationed on USS *J. Franklin Bell*. Honorably discharged Jan. 3, 1946. Married Bessie Jaska, 1947; two children: David Hetmer and Peggy Hetmer Snapka. Died July 13, 1981. Submitted by his widow, Bessie Hetmer Johnson of Ennis, TX.

Hilsher, Alfred L., son of Charles A. Hilsher, Sr. and Albina Halamicek Hilsher, was born Dec. 5, 1912, at (Roznov) Fayetteville, TX. Class salutatorian at La Grange High School. Attended Draughon's Business College for two years before going to La Salle Extension College to study business accounting and law. Inducted in the Army Nov. 18, 1943, at Ind. Station, Houston, TX. Rank: Pfc. Served with Patton's Third Army as a Cannoneer #44 and fought in Northern France, Ardennes, Rhineland, and Central Europe Campaigns. WOUNDED IN ACTION, Apr. 1, 1945. Awarded the Purple Heart, EAME medal with four BSS, and Combat Infantryman Badge. Discharged Dec. 4, 1945. Died Dec. 31, 1976. Home of record: Houston, TX.

Hilsher, Charlie A., Jr., son of Charles A. Hilsher, Sr. and Albina Halamicek Hilsher, was born Sept. 8, 1917, in Fayetteville, TX. Graduated from high school and attended business college. Inducted into the Armed Services at Houston, TX, during WWII and served in CONUS until his separation on Feb. 12, 1946. Awards and decorations include the WWII Victory Medal. Died Oct. 21, 1956.

Hilsher, John A., son of Charles A. Hilsher, Sr. and Albina Halamicek Hilsher, was born Sept. 8, 1917, in Fayetteville, TX. Graduated from high school. Attended business college and majored in accounting and business administration. Enlisted in the U.S. Army Air Corps at San Antonio, TX, during WWII. Served in the Asiatic-Pacific Theater of Operations as a member of the 312th Bombardment Squadron. Participated in the New Guinea, Bismarck Archipelago, Leyte, Luzon, Southern Philippines, and Ryukus (Okinawa) Campaigns. Awards and decorations include the Asiatic-Pacific Campaign Medal, Distinguished Unit Citation, and Good Conduct Medal. Separated from the service on Oct. 21, 1945, at Ft. Bliss, TX. Home of record: Fayetteville, TX.

Hlavaty, Andrew, was born Nov. 17, 1914. Served in the U.S. Army Corps during WWII, attaining rank of T/Sgt. Died Dec. 23, 1983. Buried in St. Mary's Cemetery, West, TX.

Hlavaty, Edwin L., son of Walter R. and Matilda Hlavaty, was born Dec. 30, 1931, Caldwell, TX. Education: Junior College. Enlisted U.S. Army Corps, Ft. Bliss, El Paso, TX, about 1949. Attained rank of Tech Sgt. Theater of Operation: Europe. Awards: American Occupation of Germany Medal; Good Conduct Medal. Honorably dischargd Nov. 3, 1962. Home of record: Caldwell, TX.

Hlavaty, Frank J., son of Joseph F. Hlavaty, Sr. and Johanna Gerik Hlavaty (one of four sons and three daughters), was born Aug. 2, 1895, Fayetteville, TX. Finished eighth grade; enlisted in the U.S. Army Corps, Hillsboro, Hill Co., TX, Apr. 27, 1918. Rank: Pvt. Was in France during WWI, machine gunner in Co. B, 245th MG Battalion, 90th Division., T and O. Fought in the Battles of San Miguel, Argonne Muese, Puoennelle, Prenny. Awards: Bronze Victory Button and French Epaulet. Served in the Army of Occupation. Honorably discharged, Camp Bowie, TX, June 23, 1919. Home of record: West, TX.

Hlavaty, Jim A., was born Jan. 15, 1891. Served in the U.S. Army Corps during WWI. Died Oct. 31, 1986. Buried in St. Mary's Cemetery, West, TX.

Hlavenka, Andrew A., son of Mr. and Mrs. Anton Hlavenka, West, TX. Entered U.S. Navy in 1943, during WWII. Served in the Asiatic-Pacific Theater of Operations. Awards: American Theater Campaign Medal; Asiatic-Pacific Theater Campaign Medal; Good Conduct Medal; WWII Victory PL Ribbon, and one Battle Star. Attained rank of S1/C prior to honorable discharge, 1946.

Hlavenka, August J., son of Anton and Mary Hlavenka, was born Jan. 23, 1919, in Tours, TX. Attended St. Martin's Catholic School at Tours, TX. Enlisted in the U.S. Army at Dallas, TX, during WWII. Served in both the American and European, African, and Middle Eastern Theaters of Operations and attained the rank of Corporal. Participated in the Normandy, Northern France, Rhineland, Central Europe, and Ardennes: Alsace ("Battle of the Bulge") Campaigns. Awards and decorations: European African Middle Eastern Campaign Medal with five campaign stars, American Campaign Medal, WWII Victory Medal, Good Conduct Medal, Presidential Unit Citation, and the Belgian Furegere. Discharged from the service on Nov. 6, 1945. Home of record: Dallas, TX.

Hlavenka, Willie T., attended West High School, West, TX. Entered U.S. Army Corps, 1946, trained at Aberdeen, MD.

Hlavinka, Edward F., son of Frank Hlavinka and Maria Kalas, was born Oct. 1, 1916, East Bernard, TX. Educated through fifth grade. Enlisted in U.S. Armed Forces during WWII, San Antonio, TX. Theater of Operations: Asiatic-Pacific for seven years. Japanese PRISONER OF WAR for four years. Awards: American Defense Service Medal, American Theater Campaign Medal, Asiatic-Pacific Campaign Medal w/1 BSS, Philippine Defense Medal w/1 BSS, Good Conduct Medal, seven Overseas Service Bars, six Service Stripes, Lapel Button, Distinguished Unit Badge, Purple Heart. WOUNDED IN ACTION: shrapnel wounds, shoulder and leg. Honorably discharged Jan. 22, 1946. Died Apr. 24, 1978. Submitted by son and daughter-in-law, Edward J. and Deborah Hlavinka of Louise, TX.

Hlavinka, Edward J., son of Edward F. and Josephine Hlavinka, was born Feb. 18, 1949, El Campo, TX. Education: High School, 12 years. Enlisted about 1968 in USAF, Houston, TX. Stationed at Carswell AFB, Ft. Worth, TX, and Loring AFB, Caribou, ME. Medals: Small Arms Expert Marksmanship Ribbon, National Defense Service Medal. Honorably discharged Oct. 16, 1972. Married Deborah. Home of record: Louise, TX.

Hlavinka, Frank Vaclav, son of Frank and Maria Svoboda Hlavinka, was born Mar. 25, 1896, Ostravanky, Moravia, Austria-Hungary. Left Ostravanky to attend a tailoring school in Vienna, Austria, as a young man. Then emigrated to the USA in 1914. Enlisted in U.S. Army Corps in 1917, serving during WWI in Company F, 57th Infantry, 15th Division. Stationed at Camp Logan, Houston, TX. Honorably discharged 1919, Camp Bowie, San Antonio, TX. Rank: Pvt. Award: WWI Victory Medal. Lived in Minnesota and Oregon, working in a sawmill and on a farm. Married Marie Hlavinka in 1922. Resided in Scappoose, OR, until 1925. Returned to Texas and lived in East Bernard, for the remainder of his life, farming cotton and grain, operating a furniture and hardware store. Died May 7, 1958, Schuhmann Hospital, East Bernard. Buried in the Holy Cross Cemetery. Survived by wife Marie, son Joe

Hlavinka, daughter Lucille Hlavinka Ferguson, five grandchildren, 10 great-grandchildren. Daughter Patricia Hlavinka Viaclovsky died Nov. 12, 1990.

Hlavinka, Hattie Dorothy Masek, see Masek, Hattie Dorothy.

Hlavinka, Joseph Charles, Jr., son of Joseph Charles and Annie C. Hlavinka, was born Nov. 28, 1934, East Bernard, TX. Education: East Bernard High School, Texas A&M University. Enlisted in USAF, Lackland AFB, San Antonio, TX, Aug. 2, 1956. Rank: Captain. Theater of Operations: Navigator-Bombardier, 341st Bomb Wing. Battles: Combat Ready Crew on B-47. Separated from active duty, Aug. 6, 1959. Served in USAF Reserve until Aug. 2, 1966. Home of record: East Bernard, TX.

Hlavinka, Joseph Henry, son of Frank and Marie Hlavinka, was born July 13, 1923, Scappoose, OR. Education: East Bernard Grammar and University of Houston, Houston, TX. Enlisted in U.S. Navy about 1942 in TX. Theater of Operations: Asiatic-Pacific, served in China, Japan, and Korea. Decorations and Medals: WWII Victory Medal, Korean Service Medal, Navy Occupation Medal, Good Conduct Medal, Asiatic-Pacific Campaign Medal, American Theater Campaign Medal. Was on the USS *Mindonao*, ARG3, when the USS *Mount Hood* exploded on Nov. 10, 1944, approximately 8:50 A.M. USS *Mindonao* had 33 holes in its side from 1' to 10' in diameter. Total of 383 people were killed–372 wounded in the explosion. USS *Mindonao* had 180 casualties. 36 other large ships and 56 smaller craft were damaged. Served in Japan at Yokahama Naval shipyard and construction Battalion NAS at Sugi, Japan. Honorably discharged Dec. 22, 1951, San Diego, CA. Rank: MEW 2nd Class. Married Hattie Dorothy Masek; one son Don. Home of record: Kerrville, TX.

Hlozek, Charlie T., son of Alois and Marie Balajka Hlozek, was born Oct. 12, 1916, Cistern, TX. Education: completed 6th grade, 1931, Blessing, TX. Enlisted in U.S. Army Corps, Jan. 21, 1941, Recruiting Station, Houston, TX. Assigned 250th Quartermaster Depot Company, Heavy Mortar 607. European Theater of Operations. Decorations and Citations: American Defense Service Medal, EAME Campaign Medal w/5 BSS; GCM; Distinguished Service Medal; GO 32 Hq 2nd Inf, 1 Feb. 1945; 1 Service Stripe; three overseas service bars; Lapel Button issued ASR Score (2 Sept. 1945)-96, Combat Infantryman's Badge, Aug. 8, 1944. Battles and Campaigns: Normandy, Northern France, Ardennes, Rhineland, Central Europe GO 33 WD 45. Married Marie Filip on July 22, 1947. They met while stationed in Czechoslovakia during WWII. Honorably discharged Oct. 21, 1945. Home of record: El Campo, TX.

Hnatek, John O., son of Joseph and Vlasta Shiller Hnatek, was born Nov. 18, 1924, Dacosta, TX. Attended Victoria High School and Victoria Junior College, 1948. Graduated from University of Texas, Austin, TX, B.B.A. degree. Later became a Certified Public Accountant. Inducted into U.S. Army Corps, Ft. Sam Houston, San Antonio, TX. Rank: Corporal. Theater of Operations, Europe. Fought in Normandy, Brittany and the Rhineland. Awards: GCM, BSS, and Purple Heart. Honorably discharged Feb. 26, 1946. Prominent Victoria businessman, associated with the CPA firm of Rofoff and Hnatek. Member of the Lions Club, TSCPA, and SPJST. Married Faye Marie Nichols, 1951, who is an artist and an active worker in Womens' Clubs and the Church. Two children: Jan Faye Hnatek West, a high school teacher and girls basketball coach in Zavalla, TX, married James E. West, college graduate, landscape artist; Joe David Hnatek, M.D., practicing anesthesiology, Bryan, TX, married Lynn Pentecost, M.D., a doctor in Family Practice. Joe David and Lynn have two children: Sarah, 3 years, 10 months, and Joshua, seven months. John and Faye Marie's home of record: Victoria, TX. Submitted by only sister, Margaret Hnatek, Dacosta, TX.

Hobizal, George L., son of Tom J. and Albina Mares Hobizal, was born Sept. 13, 1931, in Flatonia, TX. Attended Flatonia Elementary School and graduated from Flatonia High School in 1949. Enlisted in the U.S. Air Force on Mar. 17, 1951, during Korean Conflict. Basic training at Lackland Air Force Base in San Antonio, TX. Attended electronics school in Biloxi, MS, and graduated as a radar technician. Spent 31 months

overseas at Iwakuni, Japan, as a radar technician. Discharged from the service on Jan. 15, 1955 and attended the University of Texas under the GI assistance program. In Oct. of 1960 opened a TV sales store and service business and operated it for 25 years. Also purchased a Radio Shack store in LaGrange, TX, and sold it in 1990. Married Cora Walker of Schulenburg, TX; two sons: Marcel Ray and Myron Duane. Served on the Weimar, TX, City Council for five years. Home of record: Weimar, TX.

Hodnett, Gregory Todd, son of Mickey Wilton and Carolyn Zijicek Hodnett, was born Dec. 11, 1969, in Austin, TX. Graduated from Crockett High School, Austin, TX, in 1988, and attended the University of TX, Austin, TX, prior to his acceptance to the U.S. Military Academy at West Point, New York in 1989. Commissioned at the Academy in 1993 as an Infantry Officer. Hobbies include fishing, hunting, and sports. Home of record: Ft. Hood, TX.

Holasek, Joseph F., was born Oct. 30, 1898, of West, TX. Entered the U.S. Armed Services during WWI. Served in the European Theater of Operations. WOUNDED IN ACTION in France.

Holecek, George R., son of Mr. and Mrs. J. J. Holecek, was born Apr. 17, 1914, West, TX. Entered U.S. Army Corps, 1941. Served in the Asiatic-Pacific Theater of Operations: Fuji; Guadalcanal; N. Georgia; Bouganville; Philippines; Luzon. Awards: American Defense Medal; Asiatic-Pacific Theater Campaign Ribbon w/3 BSS; P.L. w/1 star; GCM and Combat Infantry Badge. Attained rank of Sgt. prior to his honorable discharge, 1945.

Holecek, George, Tours, TX, WWII veteran, U.S. Army Corps, 37th Infantry. Theater of Operations: Asiatic-Pacific.

Holecek, Henry John, son of Mr. and Mrs. J. Holecek, served in the U.S. Navy during WWII. Also served in Pearl Harbor and Japan. Attained rank of S1/C prior to his honorable discharge, 1945.

Holecek, Roman A., son of Andrew and Katie Holecek, was born Mar. 5, 1918, at Tours, TX. Attended St. Martin's Catholic School at Tours, TX, and Santa Clara High School, Santa Clara, CA. Enlisted in the U.S. Army at Waco, TX, during WWII. Served in the European, African, and Middle Eastern Theater of Operations as a Pfc. Participated in the Tunisia, Sicily, Naples-Foggia, and Rome-Arno Campaigns. Awards and decorations: European-African-Middle Eastern Campaign Medal with four campaign stars. Discharged from the service at Ft. Sam Houston, TX. Home of record: West, TX.

Holecek, Victor Jake, son of Andrew and Katherine Wolf Holecek, was born July 24, 1913, in Tours, McLennan Co., TX. Attended St. Martin's Catholic School, Tours, and Waco High School in Waco, and 4C Business College in Waco. Enlisted in the Army at Fort Sam Houston, San Antonio, TX. Rank: S/Sgt. Awards: Good Conduct and Rifle and Bayonet medals. Discharged Jan. 1946 at Westover Field, MA. Home of record: Austin, TX.

Holecek, Vince L., son of Mr. and Mrs. J. J. Holecek, of West, TX. Entered U.S. Army Corps, 1942. Served in Iran and Persian Gulf. Awarded Good Conduct Medal. Attained rank of T/5 prior to honorable discharge, 1945.

Holub, Albert John, son of Peter F. and Annie Gallia Holub, was born Aug. 24, 1921, Wallis, TX. Graduated Wallis High School, 1939; Blinn College. Enlisted: Ft. Sam Houston, as Engineer Unit Commander. Served overseas 22 months w/360th Engineer Regiment in England and France and Co. C in European Theater of Operations. Honorably discharged Apr. 1, 1953. Died June 1, 1987. Buried Forest Park Cemetery,

Garden of Gethsemane, Houston, TX. Submitted by Evelyn Vecera, Bellaire, TX.

Holub, Andrew H., son of Albert and Marie Macek Holub, was born Nov. 29, 1917, El Campo, Wharton Co., TX. Education: Louise Elementary and El Campo High School, class of 1936. Enlisted June 11, 1942, Houston, TX, U.S. Army Corps. Pacific Theater of Operations. Involved in Air Offensive in Japan. Specialty was Electrical Mechanic. Medals: Air Offensive Japan, Eastern Mandate; Electrical Mechanic, and Expert Rifle; Asiatic Pacific Campaign Medal; WWII Victory Ribbon, one Service Stripe, one Overseas Service Bar. Rank: S/Sgt. 680th Bombardment Sqdn. Honorably discharged Feb. 10, 1946. Home of record: Pasadena, TX. Submitted by Lillian B. Mikulec, Buckholts, TX.

Holub, Edwin Eugene, son of Mr. and Mrs. John Holub. Entered U.S. Army Corps, 1943 during WWII. Theater of Operations: Asiatic-Pacific: Philippines; Leyte; Luzon; Japan. Awards: GCM; American Theater and Asiatic-Pacific Ribbons; Philippine Liberation Ribbon w/1 battle star. Attained rank of Corporal prior to honorable discharge, 1946.

Holub, Emil "Pat," son of John Holub, Sr. and Franciska Orsak Holub, was born Mar. 24, 1913, Fairchild, TX. Education: grades 1 and 2, Needville, TX; Grade 3, Beasley, TX. Enlisted in Navy Seabees, Houston, TX, May 3, 1942. Rank: 1st Class Gunner's Mate (Co B, Plant. 6). Assigned to NTS, Great Lakes, IL; USNCB, USNCTC, Norfolk, VA (Camp Allen, VA) by train NW route to Bremerton Navy Yard, June 24, 1942 (chipped paint on USS *Nevada*, salvaged from Pearl Harbor–left July 9, 1942, on USS *Chaumont*, a Navy transport to the Aleutians, Dutch Harbor, Alaska, from Aug. 13, 1943–June 4, 1944. Camp Parks, CA; Honolulu, Hawaii; Saipan, Tinian, Iwo Jima. Emil was one of 25 men with Chief Ellis who was detached from 8th and assigned to 8th Marine Field Supply Depot as equipment operators. They went in on the invasion with the Marines. Theirs was to be the hazardous job of handling cranes, bulldozers, and trucks which were to bring supplies from the ships to the front lines. Each of these men were given official commendations. Honorably discharged Oct. 29, 1945, Camp Wallace, TX. 80 years of age, at 12/15/93. Lives in Houston, TX, and Rosenberg, TX. Married Martha Grunwald; daughter Brenda. Occupation:1946–1977, carpenter specializing in acoustical ceiling installation. May 20, 1933-June 30 1934, in the Civilian Conservation Corps, forestry division. Home of record: Houston, TX.

Holub, Eugene J., son of Emil J. and Julia Jurena Holub, was born May 12, 1915, at Moulton, TX. Attended the Komensky School near Moulton, TX, and graduated from Shiner High School, Shiner, TX. After a short enlistment in the U.S. Army Air Corps at Randolph Air Base, TX, he attended and graduated from Southwest State Teachers College at San Marcos, TX. Taught school for two years before going to Washington, DC, as a member of Representative J. J. Mansfield's Congressional Staff. Later went to work as a civil servant at Corpus Christi, TX, where he was at the outbreak of WWII when he again volunteered for service in the U.S. Army Air Corps. Served in the U. S Army Air Corps during WWII as bomber crew member and attained the rank of Sgt. Served in the European, African, and Middle Eastern Theater of Operations, conducting bombing missions into mainland Europe from bases in England. On Apr. 19, 1945, Eugene and his fellow crew members were declared MISSING IN ACTION on a flight mission to Normandy, France. Awards and decorations include the Air Medal with Oak Leaf Cluster, Purple Heart, Presidential Unit Citation, European-African-Middle Eastern Campaign Medal with three campaign stars, and WWII Victory Medal.

Holub, Jerome, son of Emil J. and Julia Jurena Holub, was born Aug. 2, 1918. Attended Komensky High School near Moulton, TX. Enlisted in the U.S. Army on Sept. 8, 1937, and served with the 15th Field Artillery. After three years he enlisted into the U.S. Army Air Corps on Sept. 16, 1940, and subsequently was stationed at Ellington Field near Houston, TX, until 1945. In

May 1945, he was sent to the Asiatic-Pacific Theater of Operations and served in India, Burma, and China as a member of the 319th Troop Carrier Squadron. Separated from the service in Dec. 1945 at Ft. Bliss, TX. Enlisted into U.S. Army Air Corps in Jan. 1946, and was stationed at Lake Charles, LA. Sent to Japan in 1947 and served with the occupation forces as a member of the 3rd Bomb Group, 84th Bomb Squadron. Returned to CONUS and assigned to Offutt Air Base, NE, as a member of 3802nd Air Base Wing until his retirement with over 22 years of service in July 1959 as a Master Sgt. Awards and decorations include the National Defense Service Medal, American Campaign Medal, Asiatic-Pacific Campaign Medal with campaign star, WWII Victory Medal, Good Conduct Medal with Silver Loop, Army of Occupation Medal (Japan), Army Air Force Crew Member Badge, and Army Air Force Technician Badge. Resides in San Antonio, TX.

Holub, John Robert, son of Martin and Veronica Holub, was born Nov. 14, 1893, Dubina, Fayette, TX. Education: completed eighth grade, Schulenberg, TX. Enlisted Apr. 19, 1917, Houston, TX, during WWI, U.S. Navy. Theater of Operation: Atlantic Ocean. Stationed aboard USS *Yankton*. Rank: Fireman 1st Class. Honorably discharged Jan. 9, 1920, on USS *Yankton*. Married Anna Kana. Member of SPJST Lodge 20, Granger, TX. Died Sept. 24, 1985. Submitted by son, Vojt John Holub of San Antonio, TX.

Holub, Johnnie, son of Ed and Frances Mencik Holub, was born June 19, 1922 in Penelope, TX. Attended school in Penelope, TX. Enlisted in the U.S. Army on Sept. 18, 1942, during WWII, at Waco, TX. Served as a Military Policeman at Blackland Air Base, Waco, TX, and with the 2nd Air Force at Harvard, NE. Was separated from the service on Jan. 2, 1946, Randolph Field in San Antonio, TX. Home of record: Waco, TX.

Holub, Vojt John, son of John and Anna Kana Holub, was born Mar. 28, 1924, LaGrange, TX. Education: Fowlerton High School, Fowlerton, TX. Enlisted Cotulla, LaSalle, TX, July 13, 1944, U.S. Army Corps. Theater of Operation: Europe. Battles: final battle before surrender. Medals: European Theater of Operations Campaign Medal, GCM; Infantry Badge; Expert Rifleman Badge. Honorably discharged as Technical/4 Sgt. June 27, 1946. Home of record: San Antonio, TX.

Holubec, Aug W., member of SPJST Lodge 20, Granger, TX; served in U.S. Armed Forces during WWI.

Holubec, Cleo James, son of Julius Alex and Sophie Trlicek Holubec, was born Apr. 15, 1930, La Grange, Fayette, TX. Graduated from La Grange High, 1947; University of TX, Austin, TX, with BBA degree, 1953. Enlisted in U.S. Air Force, Lackland AFB, San Antonio, Bexar Co., TX, Mar. 1, 1952. Basic training, Lackland AFB. Assigned to Career Guidance School at Lowry AFB, Denver, CO. Assigned to 4th Air Force at Hamilton AFB, CA, working with overseas assignments for personnel before being transferred to attend Cryptographic School, Scott AFB, IL. Assigned to Security Service as cryptographer, Elmendorf AFB, Anchorage, AK for 21 months. Honorably discharged, Parks AFB, CA, Dec. 22, 1955. Rank: Airman First Class. Medals: National Defense Service, and Good Conduct. Married Saphronia Louise Clegg, Oct. 12, 1954, Houston, TX; three children: Robert, Ann, and Paul. Retired from Union Oil Co. of California after 30 years' employment. Home of record: Bellaire, TX.

Holubec, Edward W., son of Joe and Albina Holubec, was born Dec. 14, 1919, Rowena, TX. Graduated Ballinger High, Ballinger, TX. Enlisted in U.S. Air Force, Ft. Sam Houston, San Antonio, Bexar Co., TX, Nov. 6, 1941. Assigned to

the 348th A.A.F. Base Unit as A.P. Maintenance. Tech. 570. Awards: American Defense Ribbon, American Theater Ribbon, Victory Medal, Good Conduct Medal. Honorably discharged, A.A.A. Separation Base, Barksdale, LA, Dec. 18, 1945. Rank: Tech. Sgt. Died on Nov. 19, 1985. Interred at St. Joseph Cemetery, Rowena, TX.

Holubec, Frank George, son of John J. and Frances Roznovak Holubec, was born Nov. 25, 1923 in Bee Co., TX. Education includes a Graduate Gemologist degree. Enlisted into the U.S. Navy on Oct. 27, 1942, during WWII. Served in the Asiatic-Pacific Theater of Operations and attained the rank of Aviation Machinist's Mate (I) First Class. Awards and decorations include the Asiatic-Pacific Campaign Medal and WWII Victory Medal. Discharged from the service on Mar. 2, 1946. Latest home of record: Spring, TX.

Holubec, Henry Peter, son of Joseph and Agnes Polacek Holubec, was born Mar. 16, 1891, Kurtin/Bryan, Brazos, TX. Served in U.S. Army Corps, WWI. Married Antonia Frances Kalas; five children: Joseph Sydney, Frank Henry, Valeria Dorothy Holubec Pavelka, John Evangelist, and Georgia Josephine Holubec Beran. Civilian Occupation: Farming and Ranching. Died Aug. 27, 1967. Buried Mt. Calvary Cemetery, Bryan, Brazos Co., TX. Submitted by John G. Pavelka, Granger, TX.

Holubeck, J. J., son of Mr. and Mrs. Joe Holubeck, Taylor, TX. Enlisted U.S. Navy, 1942. Basic training, San Diego, CA. Served in New Hebrides on USS *Enterprise*, 30 months overseas in South Pacific. Honorably discharged 1945.

Holubeck, M. J., son of Mr. and Mrs. John Holubeck, Taylor, TX. Enlisted U.S. Navy in 1943, during WWII. Basic Training, San Diego, CA. Further training, Norfolk, VA, and Ft. Pierce, FL. Assigned to USS *Briscoe*. Theaters of Operations: American; European, Asiatic-Pacific. Campaigns: North Africa, Italy, France, and South Pacific. Awards: American Theater Campaign Ribbon; European Theater Campaign Ribbon; Asiatic-Pacific Theater Ribbon and Philippine Liberation Medal. Rank: MoMM 2/c prior to honorable discharge, 1946.

Holy, Bill, West, TX, WWII Military Veteran.

Holy, Joe, son of Joe and Lillian Holy, of West, TX. Served in the U.S. Army Corps during WWII, attaining rank of Pfc. Married Loraine Grones.

Holy, Raymond, son of Joe and Lillian Holy, West, TX. Attended schools in West, TX. Served in U.S. Army Corps, WWII. Married Marcella Novatny.

Holy, William J., of West, TX. Entered U.S. Army, 1942. Served in USA. Awards: American Theater Campaign Medal, Good Conduct Medal, WWII Victory Ribbon. Attained rank of Private prior to honorable discharge, 1943.

Honza, Adolph F., son of Charlie and Annie Haskovec Honza, was born May 30, 1923, in Ennis, TX. Graduated from high school and attended the Southwest Aeronautical Institute of Dallas TX. Enlisted into the U.S. Army at Camp Wolters, Mineral Wells, TX, during WWII. Served with the 11th Airborne Division as a Light Motor Crewman on Gliders. Subsequently served in the Asiatic-Pacific Theater of Operations as Military Policeman in Headquarters Company. Participated in the New Guinea, Southern Philippines, and Luzon Campaigns and attained the rank of Sgt. Awards and decorations: American Campaign Medal, Asiatic-Pacific Campaign Medal with three campaign stars and one arrowhead, Philippine Liberation Ribbon with one campaign star, Good Conduct Medal, Expert Infantryman Badge, Distinguished Unit Badge, WWII Victory Medal, and three Overseas Service Bars. Separated from the service on Jan. 10, 1946. Died July 29, 1985. Interred at St. Joseph Cemetery, Ennis, TX. Wife, Alice Honza, survives him. Her home of record: Ennis TX.

Honza, Willie F., son of Willie and Mary Horak Honza, was born Mar. 29, 1932, in Ennis, TX. Attended St. John's Catholic High School in Ennis, TX. Enlisted in the Armed Service at San Antonio, TX, during the Korean Conflict. Discharged from the service on Jan. 19, 1955. Home of record: Dallas, TX.

Horak, Charlie Louis, Jr., son of Charlie Louis

Horak, Sr. and Annie Zbranek Horak, was born Mar. 27, 1913 in Granger, TX. Attended school at Friendship, TX. Enlisted in the U.S. Army at Brownwood, TX, in 1942, during WWII. Served in the European, African, and Middle Eastern Theater of Operations as a member of Company E, 143rd Infantry, 36th Division. Participated in military campaigns in North Africa and Italy. MISSING IN ACTION at Salerno, Italy, and later declared DECEASED on Sept. 19, 1943. Awards and decorations include the EAME Campaign Medal and the Purple Heart. Home of record: Granger, TX.

Horak, Emil R., son of Mr. Horak and Miss Skhrak Horak, born Feb. 2, 1921, Granger, TX, where he completed school through sixth grade. Enlisted in U.S. Air Force, Dallas, Dallas, TX, Oct. 23, 1942. Assigned to 2526th AAF Base Unit and 1521st AAF BU APO 953 as Airplane and Engine Mechanic 747. Pistol Marksman; Carbine Marksman; Carbine Sharpshooter. Some awards received: Good Conduct Medal and WWII Victory Medal. Honorably discharged Camp Beale, CA, Dec. 28, 1946. Rank: Sgt. Died Oct. 7, 1975.

Horak, Eugene Charles, son of Charles Horak and Anna Drozd, was born Jan. 3, 1924, Penelope, TX. Education: Penelope Grade School and Penelope High School. Enlisted in U.S. Armed Forces, Dec. 13, 1942, Dallas, TX, during WWII. Took Aviation Mechanic School, attained rank of AMM/1C. Theater of Operations: Asiatic-Pacific. Awards and Decorations: American Campaign Ribbon and Asiatic Pacific Campaign Ribbon. Honorably discharged Nov. 3, 1945. Married Marie Mikulik. Home of record: West, TX.

Horak, Mary, (see Courtade, Mary).

Horak, Joe, son of Joe and Marie Habrnal Horak, was born Aug. 8, 1892 in Dubina, TX. Attended the Catholic elementary school at Dubina, TX. Enlisted in the U.S. Army at Camp Travis, TX, on May 26, 1918, during WWI. Served with the American Expeditionary Forces in France as a Pvt. from Aug. 12, 1918 to June 14, 1919. Participated in the Meuse-Argonne Campaign, specifically in the Verdun area which was the scene of fierce trench warfare and heavy casualties on both sides during WWI. Was not wounded, but suffered an acute appendicitis attack while in France. Discharged from the service on June 25, 1919, at Camp Bowie, TX. Previously enlisted into the U.S. Army on Oct. 17, 1916, at Port Arthur, TX, but had been honorably discharged for dependent reasons (Hardship Discharge) on July 6, 1917. Also participated in WWII as a member of the Texas State Guard at Hilllsboro, TX, from 1941 through 1944. Died Aug. 6, 1981.

Horak, Joe Henry, Granger, TX, WWII veteran. Navy: U.S.S. *Selfridge*.

Horak, Joseph Charles, son of Joseph H. and Georgie M. Rychlid Horak, was born Nov. 15, 1947, in Taylor, Williamson Co., TX. Graduated from Granger High School, Granger, TX, in 1968 and attended Temple Junior College, Temple, TX. Enlisted in the U.S. Army Reserves at Austin, TX in May 1968, during the Viet Nam Conflict, and attained the rank of Sgt. Separated from the Reserves in May 1974. Sales Manager in Granger, TX, and likes to hunt and fish. Married Monica Ann Kaderka; three step-children: Kim, Judy, and Dwayne Justice. Latest home of record: Granger, TX.

Horak, Joseph Henry, son of Charles L. and Annie Zbranek Horak, was born Dec. 17, 1918, in El Campo, Wharton Co., TX. Attended schools in Friendship and Granger, TX. Joined the U.S.Navy on Apr. 11, 1940, in San Diego, CA, and was at Pearl Harbor when War WWII started. Chief Machinist Mate. Served in the American;

Asiatic-Pacific; European, African, and Middle Eastern Theaters of Operations. Ship was torpedoed at Midway. Although it suffered substantial damage and loss of one-third of its crew, it managed to limp into the San Francisco Naval Shipyard for repairs. Awards and decorations include the WWII Victory Medal, American Campaign Medal, American Defense Service Medal, European African Middle Eastern Campaign Medal, and Asiatic Pacific Campaign Medal. Separated from the service on Apr. 10, 1946. Employed by Alcoa and retired in 1977. Married Georgie M. Rychlik; three children: Joseph C. Horak, Jeannette A. Horak Henry, and Darwin J. Horak. Enjoyed gardening and doing carpentry work. Died Mar. 13, 1988, and is interred at Granger, TX. Was a Member of American Legion Post No. 282, Granger, TX.

Horak, Marvin Daniel, son of Charles Louis and Annie Zbranek Horak, was born Jan. 22, 1929, in Granger, TX. Graduated from Granger High School. Earned a bachelor's degree at the University of Texas, Austin, TX, a master's degree from Stephen F. Austin University, Nacogdoches, TX. Enlisted in the U.S. Navy on July 13, 1947, at San Diego, CA. Tour in the Pacific area included Asia, Philippine Islands, China, and Korea. Participated in the Inchon Invasion, Wonson, and Chongjin Campaigns during Korean War. Awards and decorations include the Good Conduct Medal, Navy Occupation Service Medal with Asian Clasp, China Service Medal, National Defense Service Medal, Korean Service Medal with three campaign stars, United Nations Service Medal, Republic of Korea Presidential Unit Citation, Navy Combat Action Ribbon, and Navy Overseas Service Ribbon. Separated from the service on June 30, 1952. Taught mathematics at the junior college level until his retirement in May 1992. Married Jo Ann Stratton; two children: Debra Lynn Horak Stelling; Kimberly Dawn Horak. Enjoys doing woodwork. Home of record: Freeport, TX.

Horak, Raymond F., son of Mr. and Mrs. A. J. Horak, Granger, TX. Attended Granger High School. Enlisted in U.S. Navy, 1945. Basic training, San Diego, CA. Post Office Duty in San Francisco. Served at Seattle, WA.

Horecka, Benedict R., son of Ignac J. and Bertha Till Horecka, was born Mar. 20, 1926, Hallettsville, Lavaca Co., TX. Education: Breslaw Grammar and Komensky High School. Enlisted in U.S. Navy, Aug. 11, 1944, San Antonio, TX. Theater of Operations: Asiatic-Pacific. Served one year on USS *Chanago* (Aircraft Carrier). Medals: Asiatic-Pacific Theater Campaign Medal w/BSS; WWII Victory Medal (among others). Honorably discharged Mar. 5, 1946 after having attained rank of S 1/C. Went to trade school for two years, then employed by Alcoa for 36 years until retirement in 1985. Enjoyed gardening and raising cattle on farm near Moravia, TX. Died Nov. 23, 1987, Port Lavaca, TX. Survived by widow Edna, daughter Linda, granddaughter Tonia, and brother George. Submitted by brother, George Horecka, Victoria, TX.

Horecka, George A., son of Ignac J. and Bertha Till, Horecka was born Feb. 14, 1924, Hallettsville, TX. Education: Breslau Grammar, Komensky High School. Enlisted Feb. 25, 1945, during WWII, San Antonio, TX, U.S. Army Corps. Rank: Sr. Master Sgt. (E-8). Theater of Operations: EAME. Battles: Northern France; Rhineland; Central Europe; Southern Europe. Assigned to Medical Detachment, 324th Infantry Regt, 44th Infantry Div., at Ft. Lewis, WA. Sent to LA for maneuvers, and to Camp Phillips, KS, before embarkation for combat in France and Germany w/7th U.S. Army. Awards: EAME Theater Campaign Medal w/1 BSS; Medical Combat Badge; Good Conduct Medal w/1 Silver Loop; American Theater Medal; WWII Victory Medal; Meritorious Service Plaque; Occupation Medal of Germany; National Defense Service Medal; AFLS Service Award w/3 bronze OLC and BSS for Heroic Action. Reenlisted in the U.S. Army Air Corps. Assignments: Victoria, TX, Recruiting Service, Nov. 1945–May 1951; Goodfellow AFB, TX, 1st Sgt., May 1951–Sept. 1952; Foster AFB, TX, Personnel Sgt. Major, Sept. 1952–May 1956; Orlando AFB, FL, Personnel Sgt. Major, May 1956–May 1959; Sembach AB, Germany, Personnel Sgt.

Major, May 1959–May 1962; Seymour AFB, NC, Personnel Sgt. Major, May 1962–Nov. 1963. Retired Nov. 1, 1963 w/21 years service. Returned to Victoria, TX, where he lives with wife, Katherine (married 47 years). Have one daughter, Patricia Horecka Barber, one grandson, Zachary George Barber. One brother, Benedict, who died Nov, 1987. Was employed for 29 years as sales counselor for a Chevrolet dealership in Victoria. Home of record: Victoria, TX.

Hornak, John, of West, TX, WWII veteran, U.S. Army Air Corps.

Horsak, Ollie L., son of Louis F. and Millie Popp Horsak, was born Aug. 23, 1917, West, TX. Attended St. Mary's Catholic School and West High School in West, TX. Enlisted at Ind. Sta., Camp Wolters, TX. Rank: Cpl. Fought at Ardennes Rhineland Central Europe, Battle of the Bulge and Battle of Bastogne. Awards: EAME Campaign Ribbon with three BSS, Good Conduct, Purple Heart with one OLC, Distinguished Unit Badge, Victory Ribbon one Service Stripe and two Overseas Service Bars. WOUNDED IN ACTION Dec. 7, 1944 and again Jan. 19, 1945. Discharged Mar. 13, 1946 at Fort Sam Houston, TX. Home of record: Waco, TX.

Horsak, Rudolf, served in U.S. Armed Forces during WWI. Member of SPJST Lodge 20, Granger, TX.

Hosak, Method, served three years in U.S. Army Corps during WWII.

Hosek, Alexander, son of Joseph and Anna Hosek, was born Feb. 26, 1921, Milam Co., TX. Enlisted U.S. Army Corps, during WWII, Ft. Sam Houston, TX. Theater of Operations: Asiatic-Pacific. Assigned to 469th Infantry Battalion of MacArthur's 6th Army. Battles: New Guinea, New Britain, and two Philippines. Awards: Asiatic-Pacific Theater Campaign Medal w/4 BSS; Philippine Liberation Medal w/2 BSS; American Defense Medal; WWII Victory Medal; Good Conduct Medal; Ribbons. Attained rank of Corporal, 1/c before honorable discharge, Dec. 1945. Married 49 years to Geraldine. Worked as millwright for PPG Industries, Corpus Christi, TX, before retirement. Hobbies: working in yard and gardening. Home of record: Rockdale, TX. Submitted by wife, Geraldine Hosek of Rockdale, TX.

Hosek, Elvin T., son of Tom and Anastacia Hosek, was born Dec. 27, 1913, at Granger, TX. Attended Reagan High School in Houston, TX. Inducted into the U.S. Army at Houston, TX, on June 5, 1942, during WWII. Served in the European, African, and Middle Eastern Theater of Operations as a member of the U.S. Medical Corps in the 168th General Hospital. Attained the rank of First Sgt. Separated from the service on Jan. 24, 1946. Died Oct. 14, 1965.

Hosek, Jerry Andrew, son of Joseph and Anna Hosek, was born Aug. 15, 1929, Cameron, TX. Education was through eighth grade. Enlisted in Dallas, TX, about 1948. Basic training in San Diego, CA. Trained at Camp Pendleton, CA. Assigned to Korean Theater of Operations, 1st Marine Infantry Division. WOUNDED IN ACTION in winter of 1953. Honorably discharged Nov. 1953. Married Peggy Dreher; two grown daughters: Debbie Hosek Ament and Karen Hosek Butschek. Employed 33 years with Aluminum Company of America, located in Rockdale, TX. Retired in 1987. Home of record: Rockdale, TX.

Hosek, Jerry J., son of Louis and Anna Kraft Hosek, was born Jan. 10, 1933, Dallas, TX. Graduated and received commission at Texas A&M University, College Station, TX. Enlisted College Station, TX, June 1955, USAF, Veterinary Corps. Assigned to: Montgomery, AL, and St. John's, Newfoundland, Canada. Honorably discharged Aug. 1957. Veterinarian, retired private practice. Currently director Czech Educational Foundation; Member SPJST #130; Sokol Zizka, Dallas; TX Vet Med Assn; Am Vet Med Assn; Dallas Co. Vet Med Assn.

Former director: Dallas Co. Farm Bureau; Republic Bank, Carrollton; Texas Vet Med Assn; European Christian College, Vienna, Austria; Emergency Animal Clinic, Dallas, TX; Deacon, church of Christ. Home of record: Dallas, TX.

Hosek, Louis O., Jr., son of Louis O. Hosek, Sr. and Anna Kraft, was born Aug. 26, 1930, Dallas, TX. Education: High School. Enlisted Aug. 1, 1948, Dallas, TX, U.S. Marine Corps. Began as a Pvt., retired as a Capt., holding every enlisted and commissioned rank along the way, proving it can be done!!! This won unfaltering admiration and trust of his men. Locations served: China, Japan, Philippines, Okinawa, Guam, Korea, Viet Nam, Lebanon, and all Marine stations in USA. Battles: all major Marine engagements in 1951, Korea; all major Marine 1st Division engagements, Viet Nam, 1965. Medals: BSS, Purple Heart, Letter Commendation, Good Conduct, Expeditionary USMC, Viet Nam Cross of Gallantry, Presidential Unit Citation, Korean Presidential Citation, Viet Nam Presidential Unit Citation, United Nations Service Medal, China Service Medal, National Defense Medal. WOUNDED IN ACTION, Korea, 1951. Retired from USMC Aug. 1, 1969. Civilian Occupation: Retired Hwy. Dept. Material Inspection. Member of SPJST Lodge #92, Ft. Worth, TX. Submitted by brother, Dr. Jerry J. Hosek, Dallas, TX.

Hosek, Louis O., Sr., of Granger, TX, served in U.S. Armed Forces, WWI. Married Anna Kraft. Member of SPJST Lodge #20, Granger, TX.

Houdek, Stanley, Jr., son of Stanley Houdek, Sr. and Bettie Danek Houdek, was born July 4, 1921, Ennis, TX. Graduated Ennis High School. Enlisted U.S. Army Air Corps, Mineral Wells, TX, Aug. 24, 1942. Theater of Operations: European–Air Offensive. Battles: 30 missions, 8th Air Force, from England; Radio Operator, Gunner, B-17, Flying Fortress, H Bomb. Medals: Distinguished Flying Cross, Air Medal w/4 OLC, Good Conduct Medal, ETO Service Medal, WWII Victory Ribbon. Honorably discharged Oct. 2, 1945. Married Jeanette; two children: Larry Houdek and Betty Ann Houdek Mullins. Home of record: Ennis, TX.

Hrabal, Alfons, Jr., was born July 30, 1932. Served in U.S. Army Corps during Korean Conflict, attaining rank of Corporal. Died Oct. 31, 1984. Buried in St. Mary's Cemetery, West, TX.

Hrabal, Eugene, was born Feb. 1929. Served in U.S. Navy during WWII, attained rank of Seaman. Died Sept. 5, 1990. Buried in St. Mary's Cemetery, West, TX.

Hrabina, Johnie F., son of John and Mary Hrabina, was born Dec. 9, 1911, Ennis, TX. Education: Telico Public School, Telico, TX. Enlisted U.S. Army Corps, 1943, Mineral Wells, TX, WWII, assigned to 143rd Ord. Bttln, 3289 Base Depot, supplied 1st and 3rd Armies, rebuilt engines and power trains. Rank: Tech. Sgt., Theater of Operations: EAMS. Battles: Battle of the Bulge, Liege and Bastogne. Awards: EAME Campaign Medal w/BSS, WWII Victory Medal, among others. Honorably discharged Jan. 1946. Two brothers in military service: Emil Hrabina, deceased, and Louis Hrabina of Baytown, TX. Married Dolfie; one daughter: Judy Hrabina. Retired from hardware and gift retail business. Hobby is restoration of antique furniture. Home of record: Ennis, TX.

Hrachovy, Charlie Edward, son of Charlie and Vlasta Juris Hrachovy, was born Sept. 14, 1928, in Temple, TX. Attended Yoe High School, Cameron, TX. Enlisted in the U.S. Army on Dec. 14, 1950, Dallas, TX. Served overseas in Germany and attained the rank of Corporal. Awards: Army of Occupation Medal. Separated from the service on Oct. 8, 1956. Retired and enjoys fishing and gardening. Married Vallie Mae Pomkal; three children: Doris Ann Hrachovy Vanicek; Dorothy Hrachovy Morton; Delores Hrachovy Staff. Home of record: Cameron, TX.

Hrachovy, Joe C., son of Joe M. and Rosie Holub

Hrachovy, was born Sept. 18, 1928. Attended Swiss Alp and Ellinger Public Schools and LaGrange, TX, High School. Enlisted in the U.S. Marine Corps at the Recruit Depot in San Diego, CA on Sept. 8, 1948. Served in Korea during the Korean Conflict, and participated in the Defense of Pusan Perimeter, Inchon Invasion, Wonsan Invasion of North Korea, and Guerilla Warfare in South Korea. Awards include the Presidential Unit Citation, Good Conduct Medal, National Defense Service Medal, Korean Service Medal, and United Nations Service Medal. Although he was not wounded, his feet were frostbitten. Separated from the service at Camp Lejeune, NC, on Aug. 15, 1952. Home of record: Missouri City, TX.

Hrachovy, Rudolph Edward "Hracha," son of Joseph and Ludmila Stephen Hrachovy, was born Oct. 13, 1913, in Temple, TX. Attended schools in Bell Co. at both Red Range and Meeks, TX. Enlisted in the U.S. Army June 14, 1939, at Ft. Sam Houston, TX. Served in the European, African, and Middle Eastern Theater of Operations during WWII as an Infantryman in Headquarters Company, 3rd Battalion, 410th Infantry. Participated in the Northern France, Ardennes: Alsace, and Rhineland campaigns. In a letter to his family after the war while he was still in the service he stated that he found it hard to believe that he had survived. His unit had to assault Hill 118, a German pillbox installation and site where German Tiger tanks could and did attack allied troops with devastating results. In the assault on the hill, the allies lost 118 men to 1 German, hence the name for the hill. Still to come were two more major battles, Germany and the Battle of the Bulge. The going was tough; coping not only with the enemy; but also with ice, snow, and miserable cold. Sleeping in muddy foxholes for weeks at a time was almost unbearable. Awards include the American Defense Service Medal, EAME Campaign Medal with four campaign stars, Good Conduct Medal, Combat Infantryman Badge, two Service Stripes, and two Overseas Bars. Separated from the Army but reenlisted in the Air Force from which he retired on Sept. 30, 1960 with the rank of Sgt. Worked as airplane and engine mechanic. Married Dorothy Sofia Slavik; five children: Gloria Jean Hrachovy Hunter, Carolyn Sue Hrachovy Avalon, Rudy Wayne Hrachovy, Vanek Marie Hrachovy Schmidt, Donna Louise Hrachovy Bierschwale. Hobbies are fishing, hunting, and gardening. Home of record: Cibolo, TX.

Hrachovy, Rudolph Joe, son of Charlie and Vlasta Juris Hrachovy, was born on Apr. 10, 1945 in Cameron, TX. Attended Ada Henderson Elementary School and Yoe High School in Cameron, TX. Served in the U.S. Army during the period Mar. 17, 1966 to Mar. 16, 1972 as a Pershing Missile Crewman. Married Bernice Miklajewski; two children: Michelle Lynn and Jennifer Kay Hrachovy. Hobbies are hunting and fishing. Home of record: Temple, TX.

Hrbacek, Raymond Jerry, son of George and Hermina Konvieka Hrbacek, was born Feb. 3, 1922, La Grange, Fayette, TX. Education: 7th grade, Bridge Valley School. Enlisted Nov. 30, 1942, U.S. Navy, Armed Guard, Houston, TX. Rank: Petty Officer, 3rd Class. Theater of Operations: Atlantic and Pacific Oceans on SS *Carole Lombard* and SS *Sea Ray*. Honorably discharged Jan. 4, 1946, Camp Wallace, TX. Married Addie Wolf, who died on Apr. 30, 1992. One daughter: Leah Ann Hrbacek Failla; grandchildren: Melinda, Sandre, Joanna, and James Failla. Occupation: Retired gravel pit plant operator and truck driver. Hobbies: Fishing and sports, especially baseball! Home of record: LaGrange TX. Submitted by Carolyn Meiners of LaGrange, TX.

Hrna, Edward L., son of Frank and Annie Hrna, was born June 21, 1926, 4½ miles west of Floresville, TX. Education: Wehmann School. Enlisted in U.S. Army Corps, June 1944, shortly after 18th birthday. Assigned to the 78th Division of the 311th Infantry, Company I. Rank: Pvt. KILLED IN ACTION in Keoningstadt, Germany, Mar. 16, 1945 by machine gun fire. Died instantly early one

morning while in front line of battle. Survived by parents and two brothers: Alvin and Julius of Floresville, TX. Buried in the Sacred Heart Catholic Cemetery, Floresville, TX. Interred in his final resting place Dec. 4, 1947. Submitted by niece, Shirley Hrna Bienik, Floresville, TX.

Hrna, Julius Frank, son of Frank and Annie Hrna, was born Dec. 3, 1921, Taylor, TX. Education: eight years grammar school, one year high school. Enlisted in U.S. Army Corps, May 29, 1942, San Antonio, TX. Military Occupation: Medium Tank Crewman 2736. Military Qualification: Expert 90 Cal Thompson Submachine Gun, Mar. 28, 1944; Motor Vehicle Drivers Badge, Jan. 19, 1944. Theater of Operation: EAME. Battles and Campaigns: Normandy GO 33 WD 45; Northern France GO 33 WD 45; Central Europe GO 40 WD 45; Sicily GO 33 WD 45; Rhineland GO 40 WD 45. Assigned to Co. A 82d Armored Reconnaissance Battalion. WOUNDED IN ACTION in the European Theater in Germany, Nov. 26, 1944. Attained rank of T-5. Tour of duty overseas WWII started Dec. 12, 1942, ended June 19, 1945. Foreign service, 2 years 6 months 16 days. Continental service, seven months, 13 days. Medals: Purple Heart, GO 24 107th Gen Hosp, Dec. 9, 1944; Good Conduct Medal GO 38 Wm Beaumont; EAME Service Medal, Gen Hosp, July 16, 1945. Honorably discharged Sept. 27, 1945, Brooke Convalescent Hospital, Ft. Sam Houston, TX. Married Christine Felux; three children: David and Don Hrna, Shirley Hrna Bienek, who reside in Floresville, TX. Was a carpenter and a farmer all his life. Enjoyed fishing and hunting and being with his four grandsons. Julius and Christine are deceased. Submitted by daughter Shirley Bienik.

Hrncir, Charles Leonard, son of Charles Rudolf and Ida Vlasta Gallia Hrncir, was born Sept. 25, 1922, Komensky, Lavaca Co., TX. Education: Hallettsville High School; B.A.-Economics, Texas A&M; commissioned Major, U.S. Marine Corps Reserve; enlisted, San Antonio, TX, as a Pvt. in U.S. Marine Corps, Dec. 1942. Went to San Diego, CA for boot camp. After boot camp, was made Drill Instructor. Sent to Officers Training School in Quantico, VA. Received commission as 2nd Lt., June 1943, Quantico, VA. 3rd in class of 144. Completed Reserve Officers' School, sent to USMC Recruit Depot as Recruit Battalion Commander and then, Theater of Operations, Asiatic-Pacific, to USMC Fleet Marine Dept. of Pacific, San Francisco, CA, and U.S. Naval Air Station as a Barracks Commander and Horse Marine Commander. Sent to 5th Amphibious Corps as Company C Commander, Military Police Battalion, then became Acting Provost Marshall of the city of 700,000 Japanese, one Army Division, a Marine Brigade, and 18 POW camps that had Korean personnel interred. Captured a group of Japanese General Officers and returned them to MacArthur's Headquarters. Released to inactive duty on Apr. 4, 1946, recalled July 1950 for the Korean War. Served at Camp Pendleton, CA, 2nd Training Regiment as Officer in Charge of night fighting, preparing men for combat. Released from active duty, Sept. 1951 as Major. Retired FMF. Married Marilyn C. McGehearty, Jan. 21, 1946; six children. Received B.S. degree in Economics at A&M in 1949. Retired from Sears Roebuck and Co as Sears General Manager of Kansas City Area; Vice President of Austin, TX, Bank; Marketing Instructor-Austin Community College; President Austin Chamber of Commerce; President Capital City A&M Club; President, Retail Merchants Association of Greater Kansas City Area; Knight Commander of Knights of Holy Sepulchre; Listed in "Who's Who in Finance and Industry." Working on family and parish histories, and cattle ranch. Home of record: Austin, TX.

Hrncir, Charles Rudolph, son of John Frank Hrncir and Josephina Morris, was born Sept. 12, 1897, Moravia, TX. Earned B.S. at Sam Houston State Teachers College; C.R. in Student Army Training Corps, Fall 1918, Bugler and Barber, Company A. Honorably discharged 1919. Teacher, Breslau, Falfurias; Principal, Komensky, Sweet Home; Vocational Ag. teacher, Sweet Home; Hallettsville and Sacred Heart High School; farmer, dairyman, owner of Exxon station, Hallettsville; District Deputy of Knights of

Columbus; Eucharistic Minister; received Archbishop Award. Bugler, American Legion; Lions Club. Married Ida Vlasta Gallia, daughter of Squire (J.P.) Valentin Gallia and Frances Horak. Four children: one daughter and three sons, all college graduates; one son-WWII and Korean War, USMC; one son, WWII, USA; one son, Viet Nam War, USA, Retired Colonel, USA. Died Nov. 13, 1987, Hallettsville, TX, age 90 years. Submitted by son, Charles L. Hrncir, Austin, TX.

Hrncir, Edith M., daughter of Frank K. and Frances Rektorik Hrncir, born Feb. 13, 1915, Moulton, Lavaca Co., TX. Graduated from Moulton High, 1934; Registered Nurse at Seton Hospital, Austin, TX. Enlisted at Ft. Sam Houston, San Antonio, Bexar Co., TX. Theater of Operations included Camp Wallis, TX, 172nd Station Hospital, Brisbane Australia, New Guinea. Honorably discharged and retired July 31, 1946. Rank: 2nd Lt. Home of record: Moulton, Lavaca Co., TX

Hrncir, Lambert A., son of Louis F. and Marie S. Morkovsky Hrncir, was born Aug. 21, 1931, Nada, TX. Earned B.S. in Civil Engineering Jan. 1957 from University of Texas at Austin, TX. Attained Rank of Cpl. after enlisting in U.S. Army Corps, Sept. 14, 1950, San Antonio, TX. Basic training, Ft. Ord, CA; Advanced Basic: Ft. Belvoir, VA. Korean Service P and A Platoon, HQ Co., 2nd Battalion, 7th Infantry Regiment, 3rd Infantry Div. Theater of Operations: Korea. Campaigns: 1st U.N. Counteroffensive; CCF Offensive; U.N. Summer-Fall Offensive; Second Korean Winter. Awards: Combat Infantry Badge; Korean Service Medal 2/4 Battle Service Stars; United Nations Service Medal. Honorably discharged Sept. 13, 1953, Ft. Hood, TX. Occupation: Structural Engineer; Registered Professional Engineer State of Texas. Married Betty Jean Blaschke, Feb. 1957; four sons. Home of record: Houston, TX.

Hrncir, Oran T. "Doc," son of Charles R. and Ida V. Gallia Hrncir, was born Nov. 25, 1932, Hallettsville, TX. Education: Sacred Heart Catholic School, Hallettsville, TX; graduated Hallettsville High School, 1950. Graduated Texas A&M, where he received B.S. degree, May 1954. Commissioned 2nd Lt., U.S. Army Corps, Quartermaster, Ft. Lee, VA, Oct. 22, 1954. Attended Basic Quartermaster Officers' Course and Artillery Associate Officers' Course. Graduated from Quartermaster Advanced Course and the Command and General Staff College, Inspector General Orientation Course. Key assignments: Company Commander, 1960-1962; Battalion Commander, 1970-1972. Rank: Col. Command assignments include Quartermaster Field Maintenance Co. and the Supply and Transport Battalion, 1st Infantry Division. Overseas tours include two tours in Viet Nam and two tours in Europe; Federal Republic of Germany, 1959-1962 and 1976-1979; Republic of Viet Nam, 1966-1967 and 1972-1973. Staff assignments include Director of Logistics, Military Assistance Command Studies Observation Group; Plans Officer, Deputy Chief of Staff Logistics, Dept. of the Army; Director of Services Division, Army-Air Force Exchange Service-Europe and for five years at TCATA, served as the Deputy Chief of Staff, Logistics; Director of Instrumentation and Special Assistant to the Chief of Staff. Awards include: Legion of Merit W/OLC, BSS Medal w/OLC, Meritorious Service Medal w/3 OLC, Air Medal, Joint Service Commendation Medal w/2 OLC, Humanitarian Service Medal, National Defense Service Medal, Army Service Medal, Overseas Service Medal 2/Numeral I, Viet Nam Service Medal w/4 BSS, Republic of Viet Nam Campaign Medal w/60 Device, Meritorious Unit Commendation w/1 OLC, Viet Namese Cross of Gallantry w/Silver Star, Viet Namese Cross of Gallantry w/Palm, Republic of Viet Nam Armed Forces Honor Medal. III Corps and Fort Hood Commanding General Award for Public Service. Retired as Colonel. Married Lea Norris; four children: Lisa Hrncir, Tina Hrncir, Glee Hrncir, John Hrncir, and eight grandchildren. Home of record: Copperas Cove, TX.

Hrncir, Oscar J., son of Mr. and Mrs. R. E. Hrncir, was born on July 20, 1923, in Robstown, TX. Attended Robstown public schools and earned B.A. degree from Texas A&I College, Kingsville, TX. Enlisted in the U.S. Army at Ft.

Sam Houston, TX during WWII. Served in the European, African, and Middle Eastern Theater of Operations and participated in campaigns in Southern France, at the Rhine crossing, and Ruhr Valley. Awards include the European-African-Middle Eastern Campaign Medal, Combat Infantryman Badge, and Presidential Unit Citation. Separated from service in July 1946, with the rank of Corporal. School teacher for more than 30 years, and also a farmer and an artist. Married Vanek Hrncir, also a teacher; two daughters: Dr. Elizabeth Hrncir at the University of Viriginia, and Elaine Hrncir Sells, in Istanbul, Turkey. Home of record: Robstown, TX.

Hrncir, Richard Bernard, son of John Hrncir and Josephine Morris Hrncir, was born Apr. 3, 1914, Moravia, TX. Attended schools in Moravia and Schulenberg, TX; graduated from Southwest State Teacher College, San Marcos, TX. Taught school in Rocky Hill and Bois d'Arc School in Lavaca Co., TX, and Tavener School in East Bernard, TX. USAAF during WWII, 1942. Commissioned 2nd Lt. Discharged from active duty in 1945, in Reserves. Returned to teaching, Ft. Bend Co., TX. Recalled in 1951 during the Korean Conflict. Reassigned in 1952 to Foster Field, TX, Bolling AFB, Washington, D.C.; Ft. George G. Meade, MD, tours to Japan, Melbourne, Australia, Taiwan, Okinawa, Singapore, Hong Kong, Philippines, Guam. Honorably discharged as Major. Returned to teaching, Lamar Consolidated School, Rosenberg, TX. Retired in 1973. Married Elizabeth Lou Arlt, from Wharton, TX; daughter Betty Jo. Elizabeth died while being stationed in England. Second marriage to Agnes Valenta from Corn Hill, Jarrell, TX; two daughters: Louise Ann and Catherine Marie. Died Dec. 10, 1982. Buried Green Lawn Cemetery, Rosenberg, TX. submitted by A. M. Hrncir of Round Rock, TX.

Hrncir, Wilson R., son of Rudolph and Agnes Rektorik Hrncir, was born Dec. 16, 1918, Moravia, TX. Graduated from Robstown High, 1936. Enlisted in U.S. Army Corps, May 6, 1941, Ft. Sam Houston, San Antonio, TX. Theater of Operation was Europe. Tank Commander, G Co., 32nd Armored Regiment of 3rd Armored Div. Fought in Normandy, Northern France, Ardennes, Central Europe, Rhineland. Awards: Purple Heart; American Defense Service Medal, EAME Campaign Medal with five BSS. WOUNDED IN ACTION when first tank was hit in France. Lost two more tanks: one in Belgium, one in Germany. Honorably discharged, Ft. Sam Houston, San Antonio, TX, Oct. 9, 1945. Rank: Sgt. Home of record: Robstown, TX.

Hromadka, Eugene A., was born May 7, 1926. Served in U.S. Army Corps during WWII. Died May 31, 1987; buried in St. Mary's Cemetery, West, TX.

Hromadka, Raymond J., son of Joseph and Mary Koval Hromadka, was born July 12, 1924, in Hill Co., TX. Attended high school. Enlisted in the U.S. Army at Camp Wolters, TX, during WWII. Served in the European, African, and Middle Eastern Theater of Operations as member of the 3rd Army in the 398th Engineer Battalion, General Service Div. Attained rank of Tech. Sgt. Participated in three campaigns, including the Ardennes: Alsace (Battle of the Bulge), France. Awards include the European African Middle Eastern Campaign Medal with three campaign stars, Good Conduct Medal, and WWII Victory Medal. Separated from the service on Sept. 10, 1945. Home of record: West, TX.

Hromcik, Rudolph John, son of John and Kathern Valick Hromcik, was born Dec. 25, 1917, in Bell Co., TX. Attended St. Cyril's Catholic School in Cameron, TX. Enlisted in the U.S. Army at Dallas, TX, on Oct. 24, 1942. Served in both the American and Asiatic-Pacific Theaters of Operations. Attained the rank of Sgt. Participated in and WOUNDED IN ACTION IN the Philippine Liberation Campaign at Leyte. Awards include the Purple Heart, Asiatic-Pacific Campaign Medal with one campaign star and one bronze arrowhead, American Campaign Medal, WWII Victory Medal, and the Combat Infantryman Badge. Discharged from service at William Beaumont General Hospital, El Paso, TX, on Nov. 11, 1945. Died July 20, 1986. Submitted lovingly in his memory by his widow, Mrs. Rudolph Hromcik, Ft. Worth, TX.

Hromcik, Stanley J., son of John and Kathern Valick Hromcik, was born May 1, 1910, in East St. Louis, IL. Attended Little River School in Bell Co., TX. Inducted into the U.S. Army at Ft. Sam Houston, TX, during WWII. Served in both the American and European, African, and Middle Eastern Theaters of Operations. Awards include the American Campaign Medal, European-African-Middle Eastern Campaign Medal with campaign star, Good Conduct Medal, and WWII Victory Medal. Separated from the service at Ft. Sam Houston, TX, on Jan. 12, 1946. Died Sept. 11, 1980.

Hruska, Darwin A., Granger, TX, WWII veteran.

Hruska, Ed. J., served in U.S. Armed Forces during WWI. Member of SPJST Lodge 20, Granger, TX.

Hruska, John Joe, the son of Stepan and Lesikar Hruska, was born June 8, 1916, in Cyclone, TX. Attended Red Ranger Elementary School. Enlisted at Kelly Air Base, San Antonio, TX, Nov. 1941, U.S. Army Air Force and served until Dec. 14, 1945. Rank: Cpl. 591st, 672nd, 64th Army Air Force Bands at Kessler Air Base in MS, Dale Mabry Field in FL, Stutgaart Air Base in AR, and Andrews Field, Washington, DC. Played the trumpet and bass horn. Duty was to play taps for soldiers who died in training and for those who died overseas. Awarded the Carbine Marksmanship and Good Conduct Medals. Married Vlasta Mikeska in 1944; one daughter. Was a farmer and carpenter. Now retired, and living on a farm near Temple, TX.

Hruska, John Lee, was born Apr. 29, 1912, West, TX. Served in the U.S. Armed Forces during WWII, attaining the rank of S/Sgt. Married Helen Sula. Died Feb. 17, 1988; buried in St. Mary's Cemetery, West, TX.

Hubalek, Jerome, son of Emil and Carrie Janceka Hubalek, was born Mar. 8, 1921, in Victoria Co., TX. Graduated from Ganado, TX, High School. Earned B.S. degree from Texas A&I, and Master of Education degree from the University of Houston. Enlisted in the U.S. Navy during WWII on Apr. 6, 1942, and served aboard the AO-2 USS *Maumee,* the AO-97 USS *Allagash* in the Atlantic, Mediterranean, and Caribbean, attaining the rank of Lt./jg. Released from active duty on May 11, 1946. Retired from teaching after 36 years as a teacher and principal. A 50-year-member of the SPJST. Home of record: Austin, TX.

Hudec, Benjamin, was born Nov. 22, 1910, in TX. Served in U.S. Army Corps, WWII. Attained rank of Pfc. Died Dec. 22, 1984; buried Corn Hill, Williamson Co., TX.

Hudec, Joseph J., son of Joseph and Mary Wolf Hudec, was born Apr. 7, 1892. Served in U.S. Army during WWI as Bugler. Died Jan. 1, 1986; buried Corn Hill, Williamson Co., TX.

Hudek, Joe, son of Mr. and Mrs. A. Bordovsky, Mart, TX. Attended Riesel High and Draughon's Business College. Entered AAC, 1942, during WWII. Trained in SD and TN. Served in Bahama Islands and South Caicos. Attained rank of Sgt.

Huff, Louis J., son of Mr. and Mrs. Joe J. Huff, Granger, TX. Enlisted in U.S. Army Corps, 1941. Basic training, Camp Bowie. Served in ETO, 29th Infantry Division for three years. WOUNDED IN ACTION in France, 1944. Awards: Purple Heart, ETO Ribbon w/4 BSS; one Bronze Arrowhead; Combat Infantry Medal, and Good Conduct Medal. Attained rank of T/Sgt. before honorable discharge, 1945. Married Frances Jezisek. Home of record: Granger, TX.

Huggins, Patrick James, son of Joseph Martin and Frances Anatolia Zernick Huggins, was born Jan. 11, 1947, in Bay City, TX. Drafted into the Army in July 1966, and was a Specialist 4 E-4 in Battery C, 2nd Battalion, 19th Artillery. Served from Dec. 1966 through Dec. 1967 in Viet Nam. Hospitalized for two months in Oklahoma with hepatitis after returning home. Decorated with the Soldier's Medal for Heroic Service near Dak To, Viet Nam. Had been serving as a cook when a fire broke out in the battery area. He exposed himself to explosions as he attempted to extinguish the fire and although WOUNDED IN ACTION, he kept fighting the fire. Also received the Good Conduct Medal and the BSS for meritorious service of duty in Viet Nam. Discharged from active duty in July 1968. Married Sally Lucille Bard in 1970; one son: Brian Patrick, who was born July 30, 1979. Home of record: El Campo, TX.

Hunka, Leo Joe, son of Mr. and Mrs. Frank Hunka (born in Czechoslovakia), was born June 6, 1911, Granger, TX. Educated in Circleville, TX, Public School. Joe was the U.S. Navy's first recruit after the Japanese attacked Pearl Harbor on Dec. 7, 1941. Enlisted in San Angelo, TX. Trained in San Diego, CA, and Norfolk, VA. Theater of Operations: EAME. Served in South America and Palawan Island. Awards: AP, ET, AT, PI Ribbons; one BSS; Good Conduct Medal; WWII Victory Medal. Honorably discharged Oct. 1945, as a Chief Petty Officer. Then served 19 years in Naval Reserves. Died July 12, 1985. Submitted lovingly in his memory by his widow, Lady Edna Hunka of San Angelo, TX.

Hurta, Edward O., son of Charles C. and Carrie Lesikar Hurta, was born Sept. 28, 1919, in Taylor, TX. Enlisted in the U.S. Army Corps, Taylor, TX, Mar. 18, 1942. Served in the European Theater (France and Germany) with the 5th Armored Div. and 772nd Tank Battalion. Awards: American Campaign, European African Middle Eastern, American Defense Campaign. Honorably discharged Nov. 1945. Home of record: Temple, TX.

Husak, John Joe, son of John and Anna Trampota Husak, was born Oct. 11, 1893, in Fayetteville, TX. Attended elementary school in Fayetteville, TX. Served as a member of the 32nd Company, 8th Battalion, 165th Depot Brigade at Camp Travis, TX. Awarded the WWI Victory Medal. Separated from the service on Dec. 31, 1918, at Camp Travis. Active member of the American Legion Post at West, TX, the SPJST Lodge at Ross, TX, and an Elder at the West Brethren Church. Died on May 26, 1964, and is interred at the West Brethren Cemetery at West, TX.

Husak, Johnny R., son of John J. and Julia Lastovica Husak, was born Oct. 23, 1931, at West, TX. Attended Leggett Elementary School and West High School at West, TX, and Baylor University at Waco, TX. John began military career at Lackland AFB, San Antonio, TX. Assigned to the 474th Tactical Fighter Wing in Takli, Thailand, supporting operations in Viet Nam. Flew B-47, B-52, FB-111, KC-135, F-111, C-118, C-119, C-47, C-54, SA-16, T-6, T-33, and T-29 aircraft. Awards include the Meritorious Service Medal and the Air Force Commendation Medal. Retired from the service as a Lt. Col. on June 30, 1982, at Barksdale AFB, LA. Home of record: Haughton, LA.

Husak, Leo John, son of John J. and Julia Lastovica Husak, was born Aug. 9, 1923, at West, TX. Attended Leggett Elementary School and West High School at West, TX. Enlisted in the U.S. Army at Camp Wolters, TX, during WWII. Served in the European, African, and Middle Eastern Theater of Operations as a member of the 8th Infantry, 78th Lightning Division. Attained the rank of Staff Sgt. Participated in the Rhineland Campaign, where he was initially reported as MISSING IN ACTION, and subsequently reported as KILLED IN ACTION on Jan. 30, 1945, in Germany. Awards include the Purple Heart and the European-African-Middle Eastern Campaign Medal. Member of the West Brethren Church, the Future Farmers of America, and the SPJST. A memorial plaque stands in his honor at the West Brethren Church Cemetery, West, TX. Buried in West Brethren Cemetery, West, TX.

Hutyra, Angelene, West, TX, WWII veteran, U.S. Women's Army Corps (WAC).

Hutyra, Edwin Anton, son of Vinc Joseph and Christine Marie Ondrej Hutyra, was born Jan. 21, 1924, West, McLennan, TX. Education: Oak Valley and Tokyo Elementary; Aquilla High School, Hill Co. Junior College, Hillsboro, TX; Baylor University, Waco, TX; University of Houston, Houston, TX. Enlisted in U.S. Army Corps, during WWII, Mar. 9, 1943, Dallas TX. Stationed at Camp Wolters, TX; Ft. Leonard Wood, MO; Camp Gruber, OK. Theater of Operations: Asiatic Pacific, 32nd Army Infantry Division. Battles: New Guinea, Leyte, Luzon. WOUNDED IN ACTION, Apr. 28, 1945, by shrapnel, causing loss of right eye. Awards: Purple Heart, BSS Medal, three BSS for New Guinea, Leyte and Luzon Campaigns, Philippine Liberation w/2 BSS, Philippine Presidential Unit Citation Badge, GCM, WWII Victory Medal. Honorably discharged Nov. 24, 1945, Ft. Sam Houston, TX. Belonged to American Association of Bioanalysts; ISCLT; West Veterans of Foreign Wars #4819, Charter Member, 1st Commander and District Commander; American Legion #478; Ft. Worth Disabled American Veterans #020; Knights of Columbus #759. Married Willie Mae Bezdek; five children: Deborah, Rosemary, Linda, Veronica, Catherine. Employed as Medical Lab Supervisor. Died Mar. 10, 1983, Ft. Worth, TX. Buried in St. Mary's Catholic Cemetery, West, TX, with full Military Honor Guard from Fort Hood, Killeen, TX. Submitted lovingly in his memory by his wife, Willie Mae Hutyra, whose home of record is Ft. Worth, TX.

Hutyra, Emil Joseph, son of Emil C. and Frances Katherine Pavlica Hutyra, was born Feb. 6, 1926, Karnes City, TX. Education: West High School, West, TX; TSTI, Waco, TX. Enlisted U.S. Air Force, Mar. 14, 1944, Dallas, TX. Served in USAF, WWII, Korean War, 1950-1951, USAF Reserve. Theater of Operations: Asiatic-Pacific, American, Korean. Awards: Asiatic-Pacific Campaign Medal, three BSS, Good Conduct Medal. Honorably discharged June 1945. Reenlisted. Retired as Master Sgt., 1986. Home of record: West, TX.

Hutyra, Ernest R., son of Mr. and Mrs. John V. Hutyra, West, TX. Entered U.S. Army Corps, 1943, during WWII. Served in France and Germany. Awarded Purple Heart, GCM and Inf. Badge. WOUNDED IN ACTION, Germany, 1944. Attained rank of Sgt. prior to honorable discharge, 1945.

Hutyra, Henry E., was born Apr. 25, 1922. Served in the U.S. Army Corps, WWII, attaining rank of Tec/4. Died Oct. 10, 1981; buried in St. Mary's Cemetery, West, TX.

Hutyra, Jerry Emil, son of Emil and Marilyn Grimm Hutyra, was born Oct. 19, 1951, in Waco, TX. Attended the Texas State Technical Institute at Waco and Tarleton State University at Stephenville, TX. Enlisted in the U.S. Air Force and received basic training at Lackland AFB, TX. Served in CONUS and overseas in Germany until release from active duty on July 29, 1974. Remained active in the Air Force Reserves as a member of the 301st Communications Squadron at Carswell Air Force Base, Ft. Worth, TX. Worked as an electronics instructor at the Texas State Technical Institute in Waco, TX. Active in the American Legion, having served as District Vice-Commander, District Commander, and Division Commander. Home of record: West, TX.

Hutyra, Louis, was born June 18, 1892, of West, TX. Served in the U.S. Army Corps, Co. F, 360th Infantry, WWI. Attained rank of Sgt. Died June 28, 1970; buried in St. Mary's Cemetery, West, TX.

Hutyra, Raymond J., was born Aug. 30, 1934. Served in the U.S. Air Force. Attained rank of A 1/C. Died Dec. 19, 1990; buried in St. Mary's Cemetery, West, TX.

Hutyra, Robert Vincent, son of Vinc J. and Christine Ondrej Hutyra, was born Dec. 28, 1918, West, TX. Grade school education. Enlisted U.S. Army, attained rank of Pfc., Sept. 1940, West, TX. Theater of Operations: EAME. Served as a medic with the 143rd Infantry Medical Det., 36th Div, North Africa and Italy during Apr. 10, 1942 through June 15, 1945. Awards: Combat Inf. Badge, Combat Med. badge, two Purple Hearts,

BSS, American Defense Medal, EAME Campaign Medal, Honorable Service Medal, American Campaign Medal, Good Conduct Medal, WWII Victory Medal, Army Service Medal w/3 BSS. WOUNDED IN ACTION TWICE. Honorably discharged June 15, 1945. Civilian Occupation: Retired VA Hospital Medical Lab Tech. Catholic, married Elizabeth Macicek; three children, all living. Home of record: West, TX.

Hutyra, Thomas Stephen, son of Emil and Marilyn Grimm Hutyra, was born Sept. 18, 1953, in Waco, TX. Graduated West High School and attended Texas State Technical Institute at Waco, TX. Enlisted in the U.S. Air Force at Dallas, TX, on Nov. 14, 1972, and undertook basic training at Lackland AFB, TX. Stationed at three CONUS Air Force installations and overseas at Karamursel, Turkey. Discharged from the service on Nov. 13, 1978. Married Janice Ann Poehls, May 27, 1978; three children. Home of record: West, TX.

Huzarevich, Julian Eli, was born in Ft. Worth, TX. During WWII, served in the European, African, and Middle Eastern Theater of Operations in the U.S. Army Air Corps as a member of 8th Bomber Squadron and was the unit's lead navigator. Awards: Purple Heart and the Distinguished Flying Cross. Attended the University of Texas at Austin, TX, and graduated with honors in 1947. Employed as a Petroleum Engineer for Standard Oil Company and Atlantic Richfield Oil Company in Kuwait until retirement in the early 1970s. Member of the Exes for more than 40 years, and a member of SPJST. Died Aug. 20, 1987. Interred at Mount Olivet Cemetery.

Hykel, Cyril M., was born July 4, 1919. Served in the U.S. Army Corps during WWII, attaining rank of Sgt. Died Oct. 10, 1990; buried in St. Mary's Cemetery, West, TX.

Hykel, Harry Lee, son of Edward and Vlasta Hykel, born Aug. 13, 1931, West, TX. Education: grade school and some high school. Enlisted July 6, 1952, Dallas, TX. Theater of Operation: Korea. Awards: National Defense Service Medal, Korean Service Medal w/2 Service Stars, U.N. Service Medal, Korean Occupation Medal, GCM, Merit Unit Commendation, Presidential Citation for Meritorious Service. Honorably discharged May 17, 1954. Retired from civilian occupation. Home of record: West, TX.

Hyzak, Frankie Edward, son of John and Cecilia Hyzak, was born Dec. 28, 1940, at Taylor, TX. Attended Sts. Cyril & Methodius School in Granger, TX, St. Mary's School in Taylor, TX, and Austin School of Electronics in Austin, TX. Enlisted in the U.S. Army, San Antonio, TX, during the Viet Nam Conflict. Served with the 7th Army in Europe as a member of Headquarters Battery, 5th Battalion, 77th Artillery, attaining the rank of Specialist 5C. Honor Graduate in his class at Redstone Arsenal in Huntsville, AL. Discharged from the service on May 3, 1966, at Ft. Hamilton, NY. Home of record: Austin, TX.

Jakubik, Eugene Wesley, son of Emil and Tony Trojacek Jakubik, was born July 22, 1930, Ennis, Ellis, TX. Educated through the tenth grade. Enlisted in Ennis TX; attained rank of Pfc. Theaters of Operation: European and Korean. Battles: Enchon, Korea. Awards: Purple Heart, Combat Infantry Badge, Korean Service Medal w/3 BSS. WOUNDED IN ACTION, feet froze while fighting. Honorably discharged Mar. 14, 1953. Home of record: Ennis, TX.

Jakubik, Emil A., was born Feb. 11, 1926. Served in the U.S. Army Corps during WWII, attaining rank of Pvt. Married Judy Sykora. Died Nov. 16, 1975; buried in St. Mary's Cemetery, West, TX.

Jakubik, Hubert Henry, son of Henry and Christine Orsak Jakubik, was born Feb. 11, 1932, Snook, TX. Education: 12 years public school. Enlisted Giddings, TX, U.S. Army Corps. Attained rank of Cpl. Theater of Operations: Europe. Served in Germany. Awards: American Occupation of Germany Medal, Good Conduct Medal, NSSM. Honorably discharged Feb. 2, 1955. Died Sept. 7, 1983. Submitted by Benjamin L. Marek, Houston, TX.

Jamek, Edward Alois, attended S.F. Austin High. Entered U.S. Navy, 1942, during WWII. Served in Philippines and Japan. Attained rank of SSML 2/C.

Janac, Albert A., son of Joe L. and Theresa Sebasta Janac, was born Oct. 15, 1923, Sheldon, TX. Graduated from Snook High School. Enlisted in the Armed Services in Caldwell, TX. Rank: Pfc. Served in the European Theater of Operations during WWII. Was in the Battle of the Bulge. Served one year of Occupation Duty. Honorably discharged May 22, 1946. Died Mar. 3, 1985.

Janac, Edwin Joe, son of Joe Ludwig and Teresie F. Sebesta Janac, was born Feb. 26, 1913 in Merle, Burleson Co., TX. Attended Snook School, Caldwell High School, and A&M. Enlisted in the Army Oct. 19, 1943, in Harris Co., TX. Rank: T-4. Served at Ft. Sill, OK. Discharged on Feb. 1, 1946 at Camp Fannin. Awarded the Good Conduct Medal, and received an honorable discharge.

Janac, Joe Thomas, son of Joe L. and Theresa Sebesta Janac, was born Sept. 13, 1918, Crosby, TX. Attended Washington and Snook schools. Enlisted U.S. Army, Caldwell, TX. Rank: Pfc. Served with the C K 32nd Infantry Motorized Division in the Pacific Theater during WWII. KILLED IN ACTION May 20, 1943, at the front in the Aleutian Islands. Was awarded, posthumously, the Purple Heart.

Janac, Joe Rosser, son of Edwin Joe and Annie Rosser Janac, was born on May 10, 1945, in Lawton, OK. Attended Snook High School and A&M University. Joined the service in Giddings, TX, in Oct. 1965. Rank: E-2. Served in Viet Nam and was awarded the Good Conduct Medal. Received a honorable discharge in Sept. 1967.

Janacek, Edward Jerome, son of Frank and Mary Janacek, was born July 3, 1924, Hostyn, TX. Joined U.S. Navy, Apr. 30, 1943. Served in the

South Pacific during WWII. Battles serving on the USS *Guadalupe*: Pacific Raids, Marcus Islands, Tarawa Islands Raids, Gilbert Islands, Asiatic Pacific Raids, Truk, Palou, Yap, Ulithi, Moleai, Marianas Operation, Western Carolines Operation, Philippine Islands, Leyte, Luzan, Formosa. Awards: American Area Campaign Ribbon, Asiatic Pacific Area Campaign Ribbon, BSS on Asiatic Pacific Area Campaign Ribbon, Philippine Liberation Ribbon. Honorably discharged Nov. 29, 1945.

Janack, Vinc, son of Adolph and Barbara Kristynik Janack, was born Jan. 21, 1896, in Ellinger, TX, and attended school there. Was inducted into the Armed Service at Wharton, TX, on Dec. 20, 1917, during WWI. Served in the U.S. Coast Artillery, 23rd Band at Galveston, TX, and attained the rank of Second Class. Discharged at Ft. Crockett, TX, on Dec. 12, 1918. Married Justina Koelen, in Rosenberg, TX, on May 25, 1938. He and his brother, Arthur Janack, owned and operated Janack Brothers Men's Store in Rosenberg, TX, for many years. Died in Richmond, TX, on Oct. 12, 1961, and is interred at West Gethsemane (Greenlawn Memorial Park) in Rosenberg, TX.

Janak, Clarence, son of Mr. and Mrs. F. I. Janak, Granger, TX. Graduate of Granger High School and Texas A&M. Enlisted in Coast Guard, 1942. Basic training, Camp Harahan, New Orleans, LA. American Theater of Operation during WWII. Served in LA and TX. Attained rank of Sp. (F) 3/c before honorable discharge, 1945.

Janak, Edward F., was born Oct. 4, 1905; died Oct. 15, 1954; buried Calvary Catholic Cem., Granger, TX. Tec 5 DEML–WWII.

Janak, Frankie A., Jr., son of Mr. and Mrs. F. I. Janak of Granger, TX. Graduate of Granger High and Texas A&M. Enlisted in Coast Guard, 1942; basic training, Camp Harahan, New Orleans, LA. Theater of Operations: American. Served in LA and TX. Served during WWII. Attained rank of Sp(F) 3/c before honorable discharge in 1945.

Janak, Johnnie, served his country in U.S. Armed Forces during WWII. Hometown was Granger, TX. Deceased.

Janak, Matilda A., daughter of Nicholas and Elizabeth Satsky Janak, was born Mar. 19, 1917, Wied, Hallettsville, TX. Education: Sacred Heart Elementary, member of Hallettsville graduating class of 1935. In 1937 began nursing studies, State Hospital, San Antonio, TX. Graduated as R.N. from Robert B. Green Hospital. Enlisted in Red Cross Army Reserves. Commissioned in the Regular Army; Fitzsimmons General Hospital, Denver, CO, 1st assignment, Apr. 1941. Rank: Major. Theater of Operations: EAME, His Majesty's Transport *Mauritania* w/316th Station Hospital, U.S. Army Medical Dept, Sept. 12, 1943. 1st Station: "Camp Stover, near Newton Abbot, Devon; 2nd Station: Cowglen Military Hospital, Pollockshaws, Glasgow, Scotland. 1950, to Japan with the 141st General Hospital. Aug. 1951, Korea, to join the 8055th Mobile Surgical Unit, nursing postoperative patients, 38th Parallel. Replaced 1952. Awards: American Defense Service Medal, EAME Campaign Medal, American Theater Medal, five Overseas Bars, Army of Occupation Medal, Korean Service Medal, United Nations Service Medal, National Defense Service Medal. While stationed at Valley Forge General Hospital, Phoenixille, PA, after more than 20 years of active service, was transferred to the Retired Reserve, in recognition of honorable service and continued interest in the defense of our nation, Apr. 1, 1964. Died on Dec. 6, 1971, Hallettsville, TX; interred in St. Mary's Catholic Cemetery, Dec. 8, 1971, Hallettsville. American Legion accorded her full military honors. Submitted in loving memory by Mary R. Janak of Hallettsville, TX.

Janak, Melvin A., son of Aug and Agnes Pustka Janak, was born June 14, 1919, Weid, TX, near Hallettsville. Attended Weid Elementary School. Graduated Hallettsville High, 1937. Enlisted in U.S. Army Corps, June 15, 1942, San Antonio, Bexar Co., TX. Rank: Tech. Sgt. Theaters of Operation: African Campaign; Italian Campaign; Sicilian Campaign. Served in Africa, Algiers, and Casa Blanca during WWII. Battles: Sicilian Invasion, African Invasion, Italian

Invasion, Anzio Beachhead, Salerno, Fall of Naples Invasion, Cassino, Crossing of or Battle of Volturnio, Winter Line Campaign, May Offensive, Po Valley. Awards: Good Conduct, American Campaign, European African, five Battle Stars, Middle Eastern Campaign. Honorably discharged Sept. 27, 1945. Home of record: Moulton, TX.

Janausek, Walter, military service veteran. Home of record: Dallas, TX.

Janda, Andrew James, was born Nov. 5, 1946, to John B. and Albina Hromadka Janda. Attended La Grange Sacred Heart, Bishop Forest High School, and the University of Houston. Drafted into the Army Sept. 3, 1969 in the Fifth Div. Rank: E-5. Awards: National Defense Service, Viet Nam Service with BSS, Republic of Viet Nam Campaign, Purple Heart and Sharpshooter (Rifle M-14) Medals. Discharged July 7, 1971. Home of record: Houston, TX.

Janda, Anthony Leo was born on June 12, 1941, in Hostyn, TX, to John B. and Albina Hromadka Janda. Attended Sacred Heart in La Grange, St. John's Seminary in San Antonio, Blinn College in Brenham, and University of Texas. Enlisted in the Air Force at Kelly AFB, San Antonio, TX. Rank: A2C. Discharged July 31, 1963. Home of record: Houston, TX.

Janda, Frank, of Texas, served in the Seabees during WWII.

Janda, John Boniface, Jr., son of John Janda, Sr. and Albina Hromadka Janda, was born June 5, 1940, in Texas. Attended Sacred Heart, La Grange, TX, and La Grange, TX, High School, Blinn College in Brenham, and University of Texas in Austin. Entered the Army at Houston, TX. Rank: E-4. Discharged July 1969. Home of record: La Grange, TX.

Janda, John B., son of Josef F. and Ludmila Lidiak Janda, was born Nov. 7, 1915, in Hostyn, TX. Attended Moravian and Hostyn grade schools; graduated from La Grange High School in 1933. Drafted in the Navy in Nov. 1943 and stationed at Leyte Bay, Philippines, for eleven months. Rank: Electrician 3/C. Discharged Dec. 28, 1945. Home of record: La Grange, TX.

Janda, John H., was born Apr. 4, 1889. Served in U.S. Army Corps, WWI. Attained rank of Pvt. Died Sept. 17, 1965; buried in St. Mary's Cemetery, West, TX.

Janda, Frank Q., son of Mr. and Mrs. Joseph F. Janda, was born on Mar. 30, 1921, at Hostyn, TX. Attended Hostyn School, Radhost School, and graduated from La Grange High School. Enlisted in the Army June 10, 1942, at Ft. Sam Houston, TX. Trained at Camp Young, CA, and served in the 835th Aviation Engineers. Rank: Cpl. Served in Australia, India, Africa, and Italy. Awards: Good Conduct Medal, AP ET ribbon and five battle stars. Discharged Nov. 6, 1945.

Janda, George A., son of Cyril M. and Bessie Kallus Janda, was born Apr. 24, 1919, at La Grange, TX. Graduated from La Grange High School and the University of Texas. Entered military service on June 18, 1941, at Fort Sam Houston, TX, and served as Master Sergeant with the 222nd Infantry Regiment, 42nd Division in France, Germany, and Austria, including the Ardennes-Alsace, Rhineland, and Central Europe Campaigns and the Army of Occupation in Austria. Discharged on Dec. 22, 1945, at Camp Fannin, TX. Awards: BSS Medal, EAME Campaign Medal with two BSS,

American Theater Campaign Medal, American Defense Service Medal, Good Conduct Medal, and WWII Victory Medal. Home of record: Bellaire, TX.

Janda, Vaclav Louis, son of Aug J. and Theresa Kubala Janda, was born Jan. 15, 1915, Bluff, TX. Enlisted in U.S. Navy, Houston, TX, Apr. 20, 1942. Graduated from Radio Tech School, Corpus Christi, TX. Assigned as Radio Tech Instructor at Ward Island. Rank: ACETM (AA). Honorably discharged, Camp Wallace, Mar. 23, 1946. Settled in La Grange, TX. Operated the Janda Radio-TV Shop in La Grange for over 25 years. Died Aug. 13, 1986.

Janek, Albin F., was born May 23, 1910, West, TX. Served during WWII in U.S. Army Corps, attaining rank of Pvt. Died June 1, 1988; buried in St. Mary's Cemetery, West, TX.

Janek, Anton J., son of Mr. and Mrs. Janek, was born Dec. 12, 1919, West, TX. Inducted in 1941, into U.S. Army Air Corps, Duncan Field, San Antonio, TX. Stationed Duncan Field; Daniel Field, Augusta, GA; Bergstrom AFB, Austin, TX. Overseas Locations: CBI Theater, Dec. 1944. KILLED IN ACTION flying "The Hump" during WWII, Dec. 1944. Received Purple Heart. Attained rank of Tech/Sg. Buried National Cemetery at Chattanooga, TN. Submitted by Louis R. Janek.

Janek, Edward, entered the U.S. Armed Forces during WWI, 1918. Attained rank of Cpl.

Janek, Edward A. "Eddie," son of Mr. Janek and Carolyn Hykel Janek, was born Apr. 28, 1927, West, TX. Attended Alligator School, McClellan Co., TX. Enlisted at age 16 in U.S. Navy, Galveston, TX, Oct. 1943. Served in two different squadrons in Corpus Christi. Sent to the Amphibious Forces in 1944; went to Pacific the same year. Served on the USS *Bottineau* after WWII. At the Bikini Atom test in 1946. Served on the USS *Higbee* DD806 and the USS *Vicksburg* CL86, 1946-1947. Honorably discharged Sept. 1947. Employed by S.W. Bell, 1948. Recalled into U.S. Navy, Oct. 1950, during Korean Conflict. Honorably discharged Apr. 1952. Served on USS *Okanogan* APA 220, Korea and South China Sea. Stayed in the Reserves and retired in 1987, 40 years service, age 60. Awards: Presidential Unit Citation, Korean Presidential Unit Citation, GCM, American Theater/Asiatic Pacific Campaign with one BSS, China Service Medal, WWII Victory Medal, Navy Occupation Medal, United Nations Medal, Korean Service Medal w/2 BSS, National Defense Medal, Naval Reserve Meritorious Medal, Navy Expert Pistol Medal, Armed Forces Reserve Medal, Philippine Liberation Medal w/2 BSS, National Defense Medal, and Philippine Independence Medal. Married Doris Denke of Galveston, TX; three sons: Edward A. "Eddie" Jr., Craig (both of Galveston, TX), and Kyle Janek, M.D., of Houston, TX. All went to Texas A&M. Coached baseball in Galveston for 32 years. Now owns J and J Telecommunications, which is managed by Eddie, Jr., and Craig. Elected County Commissioner, Jan. 1, 1991. Home of record: Galveston, TX.

Janek, Harry, West, TX, WWII veteran, U.S. Army Air Corps.

Janek, Henry, of West, TX, served during WWII, U.S. Navy, in Pacific Area, Midway, Marshall, Gilbert Islands. Asiatic-Pacific Theater Ribbon. Attained rank of S 1/C.

Janek, Louis, Abbott, TX, WWII veteran, ETO.

Janek, Louis R., son of Mr. and Mrs. Janek, was born about 1916, West, TX, volunteered for U.S. Army Air Corps, July 31, 1934, Dallas, TX. Stationed: Randolph Field, San Antonio, TX; Love Field, Dallas, TX, 1945; Topeka, KS; West Palm Beach, FL; Mobile, AL; Kelly Field, San Antonio, TX; Brooks Field, San Antonio, TX, 1948; Hensley T., Grand Prairie, TX; James Connally Air Base, Waco, TX. Theater of Operations: America and EAME. North Africa Campaign, 1943; Sicily, 1943; England, 1943–1944; Natel, South America. Sept. 1945, came home; Asencion Island in Atlantic; Berlin Air Lift, Faeberg, Germany, 1948, Japan, 1956. Awards: EAME Campaign Ribbon, WWII; Presidential Citation;

BSS; Good Conduct Medal; WWII Victory Medal. Honorably discharged Nov. 1, 1967, James Connally AFB, Waco, TX. Attained rank of Master Sgt. Home of record: West, TX.

Janek, Wilma L., of West, TX. Graduate of King's Daughters Hospital in Temple, TX. Was a Flying Nurse during WWII. Medical Evacuation Service in England. Attained rank of Lt.

Janek, Wilson B., served in Army Air Corps, WWII, mechanic for Aircraft and Engines, attained rank of Sgt.

Janeska, Anton, served in U.S. Armed Forces during WWI. Member of SPJST Lodge 20, Granger, TX.

Janicek, John H., was born Aug. 28, 1895. Served in U.S. Armed Forces during WWI, 1917–1918. Member of SPJST Lodge 20, Granger, TX. Died May 11, 1955. Buried Calvary Catholic Cemetery, Granger, TX.

Janicek, Willie Victor, was born Dec. 23, 1921 in Terrell, to Joe and Katherine Jelinek Janicek. He completed 8th grade at Lone Star Community School. Entered the Army on Oct. 20, 1942 at Tyler, TX. Rank: Staff Sgt. Co. D, 166th Infantry in the Aleutian Islands. He was an Expert 37MM Anti-Tank Gunner and Expert Heavy Machine Gunner. Awards include American Theater Service, Asiatic-Pacific Service, Good Conduct and WWII Victory. Honorably discharged on Feb. 12, 1946, at Fort Lewis, WA. Married Ruby Trojacek on Nov. 9, 1948. Home of record is Terrell, TX.

Janish, Daniel Frank, son of Frank and Theresa Janish, was born Aug. 3, 1929, Fayetteville, TX. Education through 10th Grade. Enlisted in U.S. Armed Forces, Feb. 13, 1951, Ft. Sam Houston, San Antonio, TX. Theater of Operations: American. Served during Korean War. Was stationed in Alaska. Honorably discharged Jan. 22, 1953. Home of record: Houston, TX

Janish, Frank Joseph, son of Frank and Franciska Janish, was born Sept. 24, 1896, Frelsburg, TX. Educated through fifth grade. Enlisted in U.S. Army Corps during WWI, Columbus, TX. Attained rank of Pvt. Honorably discharged, Nov. 27, 1918. Died Jan. 23, 1979.

Janish, William F., son of Frank Janis and Frances Martinak, was born May 28, 1892, Frelsburg, Colorado Co., TX. Enlisted in U.S. Army Corps in Colorado Co., TX during WWI, Theater of Operations, Europe. Received WWI Victory Medal. Rank: Pfc. Assigned to 360th Infantry, 90th Division. Honorably discharged when the war was won. Died June 3, 1946; buried Fayetteville City Cemetery.

Janosek, Louis, was born about 1924, of Nueces Co., TX. Enlisted in the U.S. Army Corps during WWII. Assigned to ETO, 36th Infantry Division. KILLED IN ACTION during one of the battles in Italy. Submitted by Erwin E. Krejci of Corpus Christi, TX.

Janosky, Albert F., born Jan. 13, 1916, KILLED IN ACTION June 2, 1944, Biak Island. Buried Ft. McKinley, U.S. Cemetery, Manila, Philippine Islands. Marker in Holy Cross Catholic Cemetery, Granger, TX.

Janosky, Edward J., son of John J. and Antonia Baron Janosky, was born June 9, 1896, Nelsonville, TX. Education: Completed eighth grade, took bookkeeping course in business college. Enlisted in U.S. Army Corps during WWI at Camp Travis, San Antonio, TX. Served in American Theater of Operations. Rank: Pvt. Honorably discharged Mar. 25, 1919.

Died Mar. 19, 1965, Holland, TX. Submitted by son, Edward Janosky of Bryan, TX.

Janota, Alvin S., son of Mr. Janota and Mrs. Francis Janota of Taylor, TX. Enlisted in U.S. Army Corps, 1940, TX; basic training Ft. Sam Houston, TX; NCO Admn School, Camp Lee, VA. Theater of Operations: American and Asiatic-Pacific. Served in New Guinea and Philippines. Medals: Asiatic-Pacific Campaign Ribbon w/2 BSS; Philippine Liberation Ribbons. American Defense Medal; EAME Campaign Ribbon; WWII Victory Medal. Honorably discharged 1945.

Janota, Fred F., son of Mr. and Mrs. J. J. Janota, of Taylor, TX. Attended Hutto High School. Enlisted in U.S. Army Air Corps, 1941. Basic training: Brown Field and Eagle Pass Airfield. Theaters of Operation: American, Asiatic-Pacific. Campaigns in New Guinea, Biak, Leyte, Mindanao, Luzon, Okinawa, Japan. Medals: American Theater Medal, Asiatic-Pacific Ribbon w/4 BSS, Philippine Liberation Medal w/1 BSS, WWII Victory Medal, and Good Conduct Medal. Attained rank of S/Sgt before honorable discharge in 1945.

Janota, Johnnie J., son of Mr. and Mrs. J. J. Janota of Taylor, TX. Attended Hutto High School. Enlisted in U.S. Army Air Corps, 1941. Basic training: Sheppard Field, TX. Theater of Operations: American. Awarded American Defense Ribbon, WWII Victory, and Good Conduct Medals. Attained rank of Sgt. before honorable discharge in 1945.

Janota, Thomas W., son of Mr. and Mrs. J. J. Janota of Taylor TX. Graduated Thorndale High School. Enlisted U.S. Army Air Corps, 1942. Basic training: Brooksfield, LCNT School, Chanute Field, IL. Theater of Operations: American. Medals: Good Conduct Medal, WWII Victory Medal, and American Theater Campaign. Attained rank of Cpl. before honorable discharge in 1946.

Jansa, Arthur Melton, son of Mr. and Mrs. Frank Jansa of Taylor, TX. Attended the University of Texas. Enlisted U.S. Navy, 1944. Trained at University of Texas, Pre-Med. Served in V-12 for 16 months. Attained rank of V-12 before honorable discharge in 1945.

Jarma, Bennie A., son of Simon M. and Daller Ivicic Jarma, was born Nov. 6, 1922, Holland, TX. Graduated Holland High School; one semester, University of Texas; 11 years S.M.U. evening classes. Enlisted in U.S. Army Corps, Feb. 7, 1943, Dallas, TX. Boot Camp: Mineral Wells, TX, Camp Wolters. Theater of Operations: EAME. Battles: Normandy, Central France; Ardennes; Rhineland; Central Germany. Medals: American Theater Campaign Medal, AAME Campaign Medal w/5 BSS, Good Conduct, and Marksman Medal, WWII Victory Medal. Honorably discharged Dec. 8, 1945, Camp Fannin, Tyler, TX. Married Lillie Kutil, June 1, 1946; one son, one daughter-in-law, three granddaughters, ages 5, 7, 11. Employed with Sears, Dallas, TX. Retired after 35 years service (30 years as buyer); worked seven years with Watson's Food Service as salesman, retired 1989. Enjoying retirement!!! Member of SPJST and KJT Societies. Served 37 years on Dallas DSMA Softball Advisory Council. Hobbies: Watch football, baseball, basketball, golf, also enjoy fishing and hunting, and attending WWII Army reunions. Proud to have served country. Home of record: Dallas, TX.

Jarolik, Emil, Granger, TX, WWII veteran.

Jarosek, Allen, Granger, TX. WWII veteran. Member of American Legion Post No. 282, Granger, TX.

Jarosek, Daniel R., Sr., son of Joe V. and Hattie Polasek Jarosek, was born Sept. 3, 1925, Taylor, Williamson Co., TX. Education: St. Mary's Catholic School through sixth grade, Taylor, TX. Inducted into U.S. Army Corps, Ft. Sam Houston, TX, Dec. 17, 1941. Attained rank of Corporal. Theater of Operations: EAME. Battles: Battle of the Bulge, WOUNDED IN ACTION, taken PRISONER OF WAR in Germany. Medals: Purple Heart, BSS, EAME Theater Campaign Ribbon w/BSS, WWII Victory Ribbon. Honorably discharged Nov. 22, 1945. Married Lydia Fojtik on Jan. 26, 1948; three children: Daniel, Tom, Linda, six grandchildren. Home of record: Taylor, TX.

Jarosek, Daniel R., Jr., son of Daniel R. Sr. and Lydia Fojtik Jarosek, was born after 1948, Taylor, TX. Served in Viet Nam. Honorably discharged. Submitted by father, Daniel R. Jarosek, Sr., Taylor, TX.

Jarosek, Jeffery, of Granger, TX, is a Desert Storm U.S. Armed Forces veteran.

Jarosek, John F., son of Mr. and Mrs. Frank R. Jarosek of Hutto, TX. Attended Jonah School. Enlisted in U.S. Army Corps, 1940. Basic training at Ft. Sam Houston, TX. Further training Camp Wolters, TX; Camp Campbell, KY. Theater of Operations: European. Served in France, Germany and Belgium. Decorations: American Defense Medal, ETO Ribbon w/2 BSS, Infantry Badge, and Good Conduct Medal. Honorably discharged and reenlisted in Jan. 1946.

Jarosek, Stanley C., was born Nov. 25, 1917. Served in 25th Bomb Squad AAF during WWII. Rank: Sgt. Died Sept. 16, 1960. Buried Calvary Catholic Cemetery, Granger, TX.

Jarosek, Tom, son of Daniel R. Jarosek, Sr. and Lydia Fojtik, was born after 1948, Taylor, TX. Served in Viet Nam. Honorably discharged. Submitted by father, Daniel R. Jarosek, Sr., Taylor, TX.

Jaska, Albert H., son of John and Louise Jaska of West, TX. Attended Leggott School and Brk. Hill Co.. Entered U.S. Army Air Corps attached to Signal Corps. Received Medical Discharge, Nov. 4, 1944. Attained rank of Pfc. Married Albina Hejl.

Jaska, Edward V., son of Mr. and Mrs. Joseph Jaska, Ross, TX. Entered Army in 1942, attaining rank of T/5 during WWII. Served in USA. Awarded GCM, A.T. and Victory Ribbons. Discharged 1946.

Jaska, Ernest H., son of Joseph C. and Anastazie Hejl Jaska, was born Jan. 12, 1929, West, TX. Education: Ross Elementary, and West High School, B.S. Agricultural Engineering from Texas A&M, 1951. Commissioned 2nd Lt., U.S. Army, July 1951 at Texas A&M. Theater of Operations: Korea. Discharged 1st Lt., July 1953. Home of record: West, TX.

Jaska, Joe Walter, son of John and Louise Jaska, was born Sept. 13, 1917, West, TX. Attended Leggott School and in Hill Co. Entered the U.S. Armed Forces during WWII. Participated in the D-Day Landing in Europe. Awarded Purple Heart and other medals and ribbons. Attained rank of Pfc. prior to discharge in 1946. Married Mary Hejl. Buried in St. Joseph Cemetery at Penelope, TX.

Jaska, Louis B., son of Joseph F. Jaska and Anastazia, was born Nov. 5, 1917, Tokio (West), TX. Attended one-half year Texas A&M. Enlisted FSHT, Mar. 29, 1945. Rank: T5. Served at Camp Wolters, TX; Ft. Ord, CA; Angeles; Luzon; Philippine Islands; Finchhause, New Guinea; Ft. Hood, TX. Medals: Asiatic Pacific Ribbon; Victory Ribbon; Expert Rifleman; one overseas Bar. Honorably discharged July 29, 1946. General Merchandise Store Operator, 1946 to 1983. Farmer-rancher-operator, 1946 to 1993+, custom hay-baler and combiner, 1936 to 1993+. Home of record: Ross, TX.

Jaska, Michael Edward, son of Ernest H. and Virginia C. Muehlstein Jaska, was born Nov. 17, 1952, in Hillsboro, TX. Graduated in 1971 from Muenster, TX, High School, and Texas A&M University, College Station, TX, in 1975. Commissioned in the US Army, Special Forces, Aug. 15, 1975, in College Station, TX. Awards: Meritorious Service Medal (1st Oak Leaf Cluster), Army Commendation Medal (2nd Oak Leaf Cluster), Army Achievement Medal (2nd Oak Leaf Cluster), National Defense Service Medal, Humanitarian Service Medal, Army Service Ribbon, Overseas Service Ribbon (3rd Award), Ranger Tab, Special Forces Tab, Parachutist Badge. Served for Operation Proven Force, the air campaign in northern Iraq, operating in support of Operation Desert Storm from the Republic of Turkey. Still on active duty with rank of Major. Married Linda J. Shoupe; two children. Stationed at Ft Monroe, VA.

Jaska, Robert C., son of Joseph C. and Anastazie E. Hejl Jaska, was born Nov. 22, 1920, West, TX. Attended A&M, earning B.S. and M.S. degrees in Agricultural Engineering. Entered the armed services, College Station, TX, June 4, 1942. Served as Captain in the Ordnance Dept. in the China, Burma, India Theater. Awards: Asiatic Pacific Campaign Medal with two BSS; BSS Medal; American Theater Campaign Medal; Victory Medal. Honorably discharged Aug. 17, 1946.

Jecmenek, Leon Dean, son of Edward C. and Eleonora Jecmenek, was born Dec. 6, 1926, Ellinger, TX. Education: Ellinger, TX, Public School; La Grange, TX, High School; Blinn Junior College, Brenham, TX; Sam Houston State Teachers College, Huntsville, TX. Enlisted Apr. 10, 1945, in U.S. Army Corps, at Ft. Sam Houston, TX, during WWII. Served in American Theater of Operations. Medals: American Campaign Medal; WWII Victory Medal. Honorably Discharged, Oct. 9, 1946, Ft. Bragg, NC. Enlisted in AGD-U.S. Army Reserve, Ready Reserve, Dec. 15, 1949. Discharged as Tech Sgt. Mar. 14, 1953. Died Aug. 19, 1980. Submitted by Mrs. Evelyn V. Jecmenek, Ellinger, TX.

Jez, Alois Peter, son of Norbert Jez, Sr. and Aloisie Hickl, was born Aug. 22, 1920, Frydek, Austin Co., TX. Served four months in U.S. Army Corps during WWII. Married Wilhelmina Mlcak; six children: Margaret "Margie," Johnny (deceased), Sylvia M., Lorene J., Leslie Alois, Joseph. Died 1993; buried St. Mary's Catholic Cemetery, Frydek, Austin Co., TX.

Jez, Jarome L., son of Mr. and Mrs. Joe F. Jez of Taylor, TX. Enlisted in U.S. Army Corps, 1943; basic training at Ft. McClellan, OK. Theater of Operations: European. Served in Italy, France, Germany. Medals: ETO Campaign Ribbon w/3 BSS, Purple Heart (WOUNDED IN ACTION, 1944, France), Infantry Combat Badge, French Fourragere, Good Conduct Medal. Attained rank of T/4 before honorable discharge. Married Elsie Grieger.

Jez, Norbert J., served six years in U.S. Army Corps during WWII.

Jezek, Henry Lewis Smetana, son of Henry Joseph and Olga Smethana Jezek, was born Mar. 3, 1942 near Westphalia, Falls Co., TX. Graduated from A&M University in 1965 and United States Army War College, Carlisle Barracks, Pa. Entered the Army at Fort Hood in 1967 and was assigned to the 1st Armored Division. Served in combat as Infantry Platoon Leader and Company Commander, 2nd Battalion, 47th Infantry, 9th Infantry Division; returned to Fort Hood and was assigned to the 2nd Armored Division. Theater of operations: Southeast Asia, rank from 2nd Lieutenant to Colonel. Served 553 days as combat infantry officer in Viet Nam. Medals: Combat Infantryman's Badge, Silver Star, BSS with Valor Device with two Oak Leaf Clusters, Purple Heart, Meritorious Service Medal, Army Commendation Medal. Currently a Certified Public Accountant. Home of record: Temple, TX.

Jezek, Jerry, was born Dec. 28, 1912. Served in U.S. Army Corps during WWII; attained rank of Pfc. Died Dec. 13, 1986. Buried in St. Mary's Cemetery, West, TX.

Jezek, Vaclav Thomas, was born Aug. 2, 1892, of West, TX. Served in U.S. Armed Forced during WWI. Rank: Pvt., 5th Engrs., 7th Division. Died Nov. 24, 1945. Buried in St. Mary's Cemetery, West, TX.

Jezisek, Frank J., Granger, TX. WWII veteran. Member of American Legion Post No. 282, Granger, TX.

Jezisek, John C., Austin, TX. WWII veteran. Member of American Legion Post No. 282, Granger, TX.

Jousan, J. J., Haskell, TX. WWII veteran. Member of American Legion Post No. 282, Granger, TX.

Jurca, Albert Emil, son of Mr. and Mrs. Frank Jurca (of Needville, TX), was born July 23, 1917, Willow River, MN. Graduated from Richmond, TX, High School. Enlisted in the U.S. Navy, May 1936, San Diego, CA. Assigned to the battleship USS *New Mexico*. Received wings in 1941 at Aviation School in Pensacola, FL. Rank: Aviation Pilot First Class. On the plane with Ensign Donald Mason that sank a submarine. While on maneuvers from the base in Rhode Island on Aug. 30, 1942, was declared MISSING IN ACTION when the airplane, together with the six men aboard her, disappeared and was never heard from again.

Jurchak, Ronney Lynn, son of Mr. and Mrs. Sydney S. Jurchak, born Mar. 1, 1949, Houston,

Harris Co., TX. Graduated from Sam Houston High, Houston, TX. Attended Wharton College. Joined the military service in New Orleans, LA. Served as SP4 during the Viet Nam War. Awards: four BSS, National Defense Service Medal, Republic of Viet Nam Campaign Medal, Expert in Rifle Medal. Honorably discharged May 7, 1971.

Jurchak, Sydney Salby, son of Mr. and Mrs. John J. Jurchak, was born in Nelsonville, TX, on July 10, 1923. Attended Richmond High School. Enlisted in the Army in San Antonio, TX, on Oct. 28, 1942. Rank: Sgt. Served in the European Theater. Awards: EAME ribbon, two Bronze Battle Stars, Victory Medal, American Theater Ribbon, and Good Conduct Medal. Discharged Nov. 2, 1945.

Jurecka, Edward N., son of Mr. and Mrs. John H. Jurecka of Granger, TX. Attended Granger High School. Enlisted in U.S. Army Corps, 1941; basic training, Camp Polk, LA; further training, Ft. Knox, KY and in VA; Death Valley, CA. Theater of Operations: European. Served in England, Belgium, France, Germany. WOUNDED IN ACTION. Medals: BSS, Purple Heart, ETO Campaign Ribbon w/5 BSS, Good Conduct Medal. Attained rank of Sgt. before honorable discharge in 1945.

Jurecka, Ewald, Granger, TX, WWII veteran.

Jurek, Alphonse, served Mar. 1943–Jan. 1946, in U.S. Army Corps during WWII.

Jurek, Anton, served Oct, 1944–Jan, 1945, in U.S. Army Corps during WWII.

Jurek, Hubert Robert, son of Steve and Liddie Karasek Jurek of Fayette Co., TX, was born on Apr. 26, 1913 in Milam Co., TX. Attended school through the 8th grade. Inducted in the Army Apr. 15, 1941 at Ind. Sta., Houston, TX. Battles: Algeria French Morocco, Tunisia, Sicily, Naples-Foggia, Rome Arno, Southern France, Central Europe and Rhineland. Awards: EAME-Campaign Medal with eight BSS, and Good Conduct Medal. Discharged at Fort Sam Houston in San Antonio, TX. Married Alice Hejtmanek. Home of record: South Houston, TX.

Jurek, Vallie, served three and a half years, 1942–1946, in U.S. Army Air Corps during WWII.

Jurena, Alvin J., son of Mr. and Mrs. Jerome Jurena, Sr., was born on Jan. 22, 1923, in Schulenburg, TX. Enlisted in the service at Ft. Sam Houston, TX. Served in the Southwest Pacific, Philippine Islands, Okinawa and Japan. Battles: New Guinea, Southern Philippines and Luzon. Awarded: Asiatic-Pacific Campaign Medal with three BSS, Good Conduct, Philippine Liberation Ribbon, Victory Ribbon, one Service Stripe, two Overseas Service Bars. Served with the 4th Glider Section, Troop Carrier Squadron and the 375th troop carrier squadron with the U.S. Air Corps. Discharged Jan. 13, 1946.

Jurena, Jerome H., Jr., son of Jerome H. and Stacie Jurena, was born Sept. 21, 1933, Schulenburg, TX. Attended Schulenburg High. Graduated from A&I with a B.S. in physics. Enlisted in Armed Services Apr. 14, San Antonio, TX. Rank: Spec. 4/C. Served in Maryland during WWII in AntiAircraft Artillery. Received Good Conduct Medal. Honorably discharged Apr. 13, 1956.

Juricek, Joe J., Jr., son of Joseph L. Juricek, Sr. and Louise Spaniel Juricek, was born May 17, 1925, in Ennis, TX. Education: Ennis, Flowerton and La Parita, TX, elementary schools. Went into the service on June 12, 1944, at Fort Sam Houston, San Antonio, Bexar Co., TX. European

Theater of Operations. Rank: Pfc. Served in Ardennes (Battle of the Bulge), Rhineland. 36th Armored Infantry Regiment, 3rd Armored Div., Co. H. WOUNDED IN ACTION, Jan. 3, 1945. Medals: three Overseas Service Bars, EAME Campaign Medal w/2 BSS; Army of Occupation Medal, GCM; Purple Heart GO32 HQ; Combat Infantry Badge; WWII Victory Medal Marksman Badge; 3rd Armored Shoulder Patch. Honorably discharged July 31, 1946, Ft. Sam Houston, TX. Married Vlasta Bartosh, daughter of Raymond and Bessie Bartosh. Was very active in VFW No. 4853; liked to play bingo. Worked for the State Dept. of Public Transportation for 33 years, retiring Sept. 30, 1984. Member of SPJST, La Parita Lodge No. 161; KJT Lodge No. 87, all in Jourdanton, TX. Died on Oct. 10, 1988, of a heart attack; buried in St. Matthew's Catholic Cemetery, Jourdanton, TX. Submitted lovingly by his wife, Vlasta Juricek, in his memory. Home of record: Jourdanton, TX.

Juricek, Joseph L., son of Frank and Veronica Juricek, was born Nov. 16, 1894, Ennis, TX. Enlisted in the U.S. Army Corps, June 28, 1918, Ennis, TX. Rank: Pvt. 327th Co., MTC. Served in France. Medals: WWI Medal, Bronze Victory Badge, and Sharpshooter Medal. Honorably discharged Aug. 26, 1919, Camp Travis, TX. He was a farmer all of his life. While living in Ennis, TX, played bass horn in a Czech band. Also played the accordion. In 1933, moved into the Jourdanton, TX, area, where he lived the rest of his life. Member of SPJST La Parita Lodge No. 161, KJT No. 87, Jourdanton, TX. Married Louise Spaniel; four children: Joe Jr., Mary, Hattie, Georgia. Died Feb. 15, 1965, Jourdanton, TX; buried St. Matthew's Catholic Cemetery, Jourdanton, TX. Submitted in loving memory of her father-in-law by Vlasta Juricek of Jourdanton, TX.

Juroch, Jerry, S/Sgt., West, TX, WWII veteran.

Kabella, Frank J., was born Aug. 27, 1891, served in the U.S. Armed Forces during WWI. Rank: Pvt. 40 CO–CONV. Center. Died Jan. 29, 1967. Buried in St. Mary's Cemetery, West, TX.

Kachlir, Arnold, Granger, TX, WWII Veteran.

Kacir, George Sidney, son of August and Bettie Marie Lesikar Kacir, was born Apr. 21, 1930, Temple, TX. Education: BBA, MBA and JD, University of Texas at Austin, TX. Enlisted in U.S. Air Force, Wolters AFB, TX, Theater of Operations: Asia. Veteran of the Korean War. Earned pilot's wings from USAF. Graduated from Air War College, USAF; Combat Operations Officer; Forward Air Controller–South China Sea. Served over five years active duty (included service in Far East and S.E. Asia). Honorably discharged Jan. 17, 1958. Served in the Reserves, including service as a Liaison Officer at USAF Academy, Colorado Springs, CO. Now attorney-at-law. Married Dorothy Wood from Austin, TX; children: Donna Kacir Waskow (husband Doug); Linda Kacir Hopper (husband James) and Dan J. Kacir (wife Lauren); four grandchildren. Home of record: Temple, TX.

Kaderka, Adolph, served in U.S. Navy, Machinist Mate First Class. Hometown: Granger, TX. Deceased.

Kaderka, Anton L., son of Mr. and Mrs. Anton Kaderka of Granger, TX. Attended Granger High School. Enlisted U.S. Army Corps, 1944; basic training, Camp Wheeler, GA. Theater of Operations: EAME. Served in Italy and Europe. WOUNDED IN ACTION, 1944, Italy. Medals: Purple Heart/1 OLC; ETO Campaign Ribbon; WWII Victory Ribbon; EAME Ribbon w/2 BSS; Infantry Combat Badge; Good Conduct Medal. Attained rank of Pfc. before honorable discharge, 1946. Member of American Legion Post No. 282, Granger, TX.

Kaderka, August A., son of Mr. and Mrs. J. R. Kaderka of Granger, TX, was born June 16, 1918. Attended Granger High School. Enlisted U.S. Army Corps, 1941; basic training, Ft. Sill, OK; further training: TN; GA. Theater of Operations: EAME. Medals: American Defense Medal; WWII Victory Medal; Good Conduct Medal; EAME Campaign Ribbon w/4 BSS; American Theater Campaign Ribbon. Attained rank of Cpl. before discharge in 1945. Died June 18, 1983. Buried Holy Cross Catholic Cemetery, Granger, TX.

Kaderka, August John, son of Aug. A. and Vlasta H. Svehlak Kaderka, was born Sept. 17, 1947, Georgetown, Williamson Co., TX. Graduate of Granger High School, 1965; SWTSU, B.S., Aug. 1982. Enlisted in U.S. Army Corps, Georgetown, TX. Attained rank of Sgt. (E-6). Theater of Operations: Viet Nam. Military Occupation: Infantry. Engaged in War in Viet Nam in 1968 and 1969. Medals: BSS, Purple Heart, Army Commendation Medal, Viet Nam Campaign Medal, National Defense Medal, Combat Infantry Badge. WOUNDED IN ACTION. Honorably discharged Nov. 1973. Married Gladys Len Pekar; three children: Serena Gayle; Kelly Rae; Kylie Ann. Hobbies: Golf, fishing, hunting. Home of record: Mason, TX.

Kaderka, Daniel, Granger, TX, WWII veteran.

Kaderka, Donnie L., Granger, TX. Member of American Legion Post No. 282, Granger, TX. WWII veteran.

Kaderka, Emil J., Taylor, TX. WWII veteran. Member of American Legion Post No. 282, Granger, TX.

Kaderka, Jerry L., served in U.S. Navy: Sect. Navy Base # 15, Box 42, during WWII. Hometown: Granger, TX.

Kaderka, Joe, son of Mr. and Mrs. J. R. Kaderka of Granger, TX. Attended Granger High School. Enlisted in U.S. Navy, 1943; boot camp, Corpus Christi, TX. Assigned to USS *Moloy* DE 791. Theater of Operations: American. Served in U.S.

at Key West, FL. Attained rank of F 1/c before honorable discharge.

Kaderka, Joe B., son of Joseph Frank and Julia Tomecek Kaderka, was born Mar. 22, 1922. Graduate of Granger High School. Enlisted in the U.S Army Corps, at Ft. Sam Houston, TX, 1942; basic training, Camp Roberts, CA. Served in the European, African, and Middle Eastern Theater of Operations as a member of Company D, 386th Military Police Service Battalion, and 26th Field Artillery, 9th Division as an Ammunition Handler during WWII. Campaigns: Africa, Sicily, Normandy, France, Belgium, Germany, Central Europe, Ardennes: Alsace, Algeria-French Morocco. Medals: EAME Campaign Ribbon w/7 BSS, ETO Ribbon, Good Conduct Medal, WWII Victory Medal. Attained rank of Pfc. before honorable discharge, Ft. Bliss, TX, Oct. 23, 1945. Was a farmer and a carpenter. Married Margaret Jezisek; one daughter: Carolyn Kaderka Garrett. Grandparents were Fred Kaderka and Josephine Sustek Kaderka, Frank Tomecek and Julia Janosik Tomecek. Died June 20, 1992; interred at Holy Cross Cemetery in Granger, TX.

Kaderka, Louis, served in U.S. Armed Forces during WWI, 1917–1918. Member of SPJST Lodge 20, Granger, TX.

Kaderka, Louis, Sr., Granger, TX. Member of American Legion Post No 282, Granger, TX. WWII veteran.

Kaderka, Robert W., Round Rock, TX. Member of American Legion Post No 282, Granger, TX. WWII veteran.

Kaderka, Rudolph E., son of Mr. and Mrs. J. R. Kaderka of Granger, TX. Attended Macedonia School. Enlisted in U.S. Army Corps, 1938; basic training Ft. Sam Houston, TX. Theater of Operations: Asiatic-Pacific; American. Served in Hawaii, Pearl Harbor, ETO. Medals: American Theater Campaign Medal, Asiatic-Pacific Campaign Ribbon w/1 BSS, American Defense Ribbon w/1 BSS, Good Conduct Medal, WWII Victory Medal. Attained rank of T/Sgt. before honorable discharge in 1945. Reenlisted in 1945. Home of record: Granger, TX.

Kadlubar, Frank L., West, TX, military veteran.

Kadlubar, Joe V., son of Joe C. and Annie Domesle Kadlubar, was born Sept. 7, 1934, Mt. Calm, Hill Co., TX. Attended Leggott and St. Mary's Catholic School in West, TX, and TSTI in Waco, McLennan Co., TX. Enlisted in the U.S. Army Corps, Jan. 4, 1954, Dallas, TX. Basic training at Ft. Bliss, TX. Attended Food Service School at Ft. Hood, TX, before being transferred to Germany with the 11th Trans. Co. Helicopter. Rank: SP TRA. Medals: National Defense Service, AOM, Good Conduct. Honorably discharged Dec. 24, 1956, Ft. Chaffee, AR. Home of record: West, TX.

Kahanek, Frank J., was born Jan. 8, 1903. WWI veteran. Died May 5, 1954, Buried Calvary Catholic Cemetery, Granger, TX.

Kahanek, Frank M., son of Mr. and Mrs. Ignac Kahanek of Granger, TX. Attended Denison School. Enlisted in U.S. Army Corps, 1942; basic training, Ft. Sam Houston, TX, Love Field, TX, Camp Bowie, TX; CA; WA; KY. Served in Tinian Island and Saipan. Medals: American Theater Campaign Ribbon; Asiatic-Pacific Theater Ribbon; Good Conduct Medal; WWII Victory Medal. Theaters of Operation: Asiatic-Pacific; American. Attained rank of Pfc. before honorable discharge in 1946.

Kahanek, Leslie C., son of Charlie and Rozelie Duzi Kahanek, was born Oct. 9, 1917, Prague, OK. Attended elementary and high school in Prague, OK. Volunteered in U.S. Air Force, Sept. 13, 1940, Oklahoma City, OK. Entered Air Force at Brooks Field, San Antonio, TX. Locations of service: Elington Field, Houston, TX; Greenville, TX; Liberal Kansas AFB; Boeing Aircraft, Seattle, WA; Lowery Field, Denver, CO; Ft. Worth Air Field, Ft. Worth, TX; Kelly Field and Randolph Field, San Antonio, TX; Lincoln Air Force Field, Lincoln, NE. Attained rank of Pfc., promoted to T/Sgt. Sept. 1940 to June 1945; Commissioned Flight Officer June 2, 1945. Service included Aircraft

Maintenance and B-29 Flight Engineer. Citations and Medals: Carbine M-1 (sharpshooter); GCM; American Defense Service; Citation Certificate for Meritorious Service; A.F. Technician Badge. Honorably discharged Oct. 28, 1945. Home of record: Houston, TX.

Kahanek, Mildred M., daughter of Charles J. and Theresa Jaresh Kahanek, was born on May 13, 1917 at St. John, TX. She received her BA degree at U of H. Ms. Kahanek enlisted in the service at Houston, TX and served at US NAS Pensacola, Florida attaining the rank of Y2C. She received her discharge on Aug. 28, 1945. She resides in Yoakum, TX.

Kalenda, Charles, Jr., son of Charles Kalenda, Sr. and Veronika Ondruskova Kalenda, born Dec. 8, 1909, Temple, Bell Co., TX. Graduate of Ross Prairie School, Ratibor, TX (near Temple, TX), 1923. Enlisted U.S. Army Corps, 1942, San Antonio, TX. Achieved rank of Tech/Corporal. Quartermaster Corps, Theater of Operation, ETD. Fought in World War II. In Battle of the Bulge, St. Lo, France, Dec. 1944. Honorably discharged 1945. Civilian occupation was upholsterer. Home of record: Tutor Nursing Home, Temple, TX. Submitted by Joe Kalenda, Hallsville, TX.

Kalenda, Frank, son of Charles Kalenda, Sr. and Veronika Ondruskova Kalenda, was born July 8, 1911, Jaggerton, Haskell Co., TX. Education: Graduate of Ross Prairie School, Ratibor, TX (near Temple, TX), 1925. Enlisted U.S. Army Corps, June 1942, San Antonio, TX. Achieved rank of Cpl. Ordnance Support. Theater of Operation, ETO, England. Fought in WWII. Received Good Conduct Medal, Rifleman Medal (Sharpshooter), WWII Victory Medal. Honorable discharge Sept. 1945. Civilian occupation: carpenter. Retired Feb. 14, 1975. Married Olga Schiller Kalenda; one son: Frank James Kalenda. Hobby is fishing. Home of record: Temple, TX. Submitted by Joe Kalenda, Hallsville, TX.

Kalenda, Henry, son of Charles Kalenda, Sr. and Veronika Ondruskova Kalenda, was born Feb. 4, 1919, Temple, Bell, TX. Graduate of Ross Prairie School, Ratibor, TX (near Temple, TX), 1935. Enlisted U.S. Army Air Corps, 1943, San Antonio, TX. Gave Army Air Force Support. Theater of Operation: ETO, Occupation Army in Germany after WWII and during Korean Conflict. Honorably discharged. Civilian occupation: upholsterer-assembler, Bell Helicopter, Hurst, TX. Died Nov. 10, 1982; buried in Czech Cemetery, Seaton, Bell Co., TX. Married, one son: Steve Kalenda. Submitted by Joe Kalenda, Hallsville, TX.

Kalenda, Joe, son of Charles Kalenda, Sr. and Veronika Ondruskova Kalenda, was born May 8, 1930, Temple, Bell Co., TX. Education: Little Flock, Temple, TX, 1944; Temple High, 1947; University of Texas, Austin, TX, 1962. Enlisted Jan. 6, 1951, Dallas, TX, U.S. Navy, achieved rank of Eng. 1/C. Military occupation: diesel mechanic, hydraulic and refrigeration mechanic. Theater of Operations: Pacific: Subic Bay, Philippine Islands, Korea, Guam. Battles: Korean War. Medals: GCM, National Defense, Korean Service, United Nations. Honorably discharged Oct. 16, 1954. Civilian occupation: mechanical engineer. Retired Feb. 1, 1991. Married Florence V. Sturm Kalenda; four children: Carol, Terry, Karen, Lori. Hobbies: gardening, accordion music, charity volunteer work, study of Czech language and culture. Home of record: Hallsville, TX.

Kalenda, John, son of Charles Kalenda, Sr. and Veronika Ondruskova Kalenda, was born Dec. 2, 1932, Temple, Bell Co., TX. Education: Little Flock, Temple, TX, 1947; Temple High, 1950; Temple Junior College. Enlisted May 1950, Temple, TX. Military service: attained rank of ET-3, electronics technician. Theater of operations: Pacific, primarily Korea. Medals: GCM, National Defense, Korean Service, United Nations. Honorably discharged Dec. 1, 1953. Instrument technician. Hobby: study of Czech heritage. Married Beverly Kalenda; two children: Sharon and Sarah. Home of record: Newberg, OR. Submitted by Joe Kalenda, Hallsville, TX.

Kalich, Anton, attained rank of Sgt. serving in U.S. Army Corps, WWII. Hometown: Granger, TX.

Kalich, Gilbert Frank, son of Jim and Sophie Zrubek Kalich, was born Mar. 20, 1920, Granger, TX. Education: Catholic School, Granger, TX. Enlisted Jan. 9, 1945, Ft. Sam Houston, San Antonio, TX. Attained rank of Sgt. Theater of Operations: Pacific, Philippine Islands. Battles: World War II, Invasion of Lingayan Gulf on Northern Luzon, Clark Field, from Jan. 9, 1945

until Mar. 10, 1945, Mindanao, Philippine Islands, from May 12, 1945, until June 18, 1945. WOUNDED IN ACTION with shrapnel, "I almost got killed on my last day on the front line, from a mortar blast!" Medals: American Theater Campaign Medal, Asiatic-Pacific Campaign Medal with four BSS, Philippine Liberation Medal w/2 BSS, American Defense Service Medal, GCM, Purple Heart. Honorably discharged Aug. 14, 1945. Married Bessie E. Kalich; two children: Paul G. Kalich and Gloria Kalich Thrasher. After discharge, employed as mail carrier at the Dallas, TX, Post Office. Retired after 30 years in Aug. 1975. Home of record: Richardson, TX.

Kalich, Vinc J. "Jim," son of Valentine and Rosalie Kalich, was born July 19, 1895, Smithville, TX. Education: Kovar Bartons Creek Country School. Enlisted 1917, Ft. Crockett, Galveston, TX. Attained rank of Pfc. Btry F, 64 Arty CZC. Theater of Operation: Europe, American Expeditionary Force. Fought in battles in France. Honorably discharged Apr. 14, 1919. In May 1919, Granger, TX, married sweetheart, Sophie A. Zrubek; two children: Gilbert Frank Kalich and Lillian Kalich Campbell. Was a farmer all his life. Died on Nov. 11, 1955, Granger, TX; buried in Holy Cross Catholic Cemetery, Granger, TX. Submitted by son, Gilbert F. Kalich. Home of record: Richardson, TX.

Kalina, Jerry, Granger, TX, WWII veteran.

Kalina, Joe George, son of Frank and Mary Kalina, was born on Mar. 13, 1921 at Schulenburg, TX. Education included one year of college iat St. Phillips College, San Antonio, TX. Entered the service at Schulenburg, and served in Central Europe, Korea and Viet Nam. Rank: Sgt. Major. Participated in the Viet Nam Counteroffensive Phase III, TET Counteroffensive, Viet Nam Counteroffensive IV, Viet Nam Counteroffensive V, and Central Europe. Medals: Combat Infantry Badge, BSS Medal with Cluster, Viet Nam Campaign Medal, Central Europe Medal, Korea Service Medal, Good Conduct Medal with ten loops, National Service Medal, Victory Medal, Occupation Medal, Meritorious Service Medal with Cluster and Army Commendation Medal with Cluster. Discharged on Aug. 31, 1974, at San Antonio, TX. Home of record: San Antonio, TX.

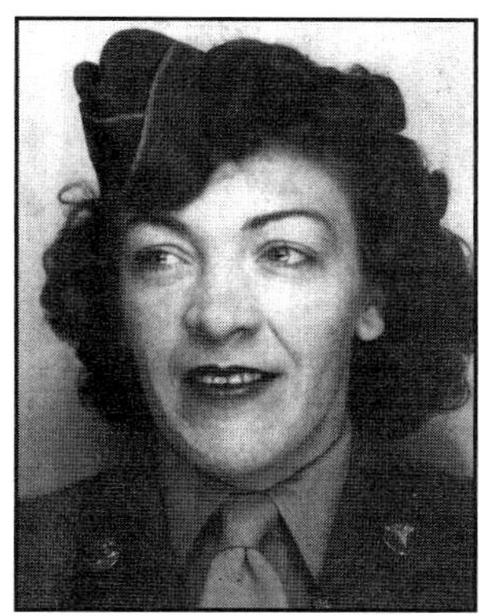

Kalisek, Henrietta A. Horak, daughter of Joe Horak and Lillie Cernoch Horak, was born Oct. 9, 1923, Penelope, TX. Attended Penelope High School in Penelope, TX. Entered the U.S. Air Force, May 18, 1944, Ft. Oglethorpe, GA. Rank: Pfc. Assigned to Connaly AFB, Waco, McLennan Co., TX, and Goodfellow Field, San Angelo, TX, as a Medical Technician (409). Received a Good Conduct Medal and an honorable discharge Jan. 30, 1946, Goodfellow Field, San Angelo, TX. Home of record: Portland, OR.

Kallus, Albin, West, TX, military veteran, U.S. Navy.

Kallus, Benjamin, son of Louis and Emilie Gerik Kallus, was born Nov. 1, 1916, West, TX. Education: Brooken, TX. Enlisted during WWII, Ft. Bliss, TX, attained rank of Pfc. Theater of operation: Europe. Battles: Tunisia, Sicily, Rome-Arno, South France, Rhineland. Medals: GCM, EAME Campaign Medal, eight BSS. Honorable discharge: Sept. 26, 1945, Ft. Sam Houston, TX. Died Sept. 21, 1970. Submitted by Jerome L. Kallus, Abbot, TX.

Kallus, Cyrill R., son of Robert F. Kallus and Cecilia Janda Kallus, was born on Feb. 3, 1916, at Hostyn, near La Grange, TX. Education: St. Rose High School in Schulenburg, TX, Tyler Commercial College in Tyler, TX, University of North Carolina in Chappel Hill, N.C., Pharmacy School at Fort Sam Houston, San Antonio, TX, and Blinn College at Brenham, TX. Entered the service at

Fort Sam Houston, San Antonio, on Feb. 3, 1941, and served in the European Theater. Rank: Staff Sgt. Medals: American Theater Campaign Medal, EAME Campaign Medal, Good Conduct Medal, one Service Stripe, and one Overseas Service Bar. Discharged Nov. 1, 1945, at Fort Sam Houston, TX. Home of record: La Grange, TX.

Kallus, Ernest, son of Richard J. Kallus and Frances Janda Kallus, was born Aug. 29, 1907, in Hostyn, TX, near La Grange, TX. Drafted into the Navy in Apr. 1946 in San Antonio, TX, Machinist Mate 1/c. Stationed at Naval Air Base, Corpus Christi, TX. Married Agnes Cernosek July 23, 1934. Died June 5, 1984, in La Grange, TX. Buried at Holy Rosary Catholic Cemetery in Hostyn, TX.

Kallus, Ernest A., son of Louis and Emilie Gerik Kallus, was born Sept. 12, 1914, West, TX. Education, Brooken, TX. Enlisted during WWII at Ft. Bliss, TX. Theater of Operation: Pacific. Honorable discharge 1945, San Antonio, TX. Died Apr. 25, 1979. Submitted by Jerome L. Kallus, Abbott, TX.

Kallus, Ernest Richard, son of Ernest and Agnes Cernosek Kallus, was born Sept. 11, 1940, in La Grange, TX. Commissioned as Ensign on June 6, 1962, upon graduation from the U.S. Navy Academy at Annapolis, Maryland. Designated a Naval Aviator and served in several maritime patrol squadrons including 531 and 60. Served in the Mediterranean, Cuba, Philippines, Viet Nam, and throughout the Pacific. Rank: Capt. Reported to duty on the staff of the Chief of Naval Operations in 1976, and concluded with an assignment as the Executive Assistant to the Chief of Naval Reserve. Upon retirement was Commanding Officer of Navy Air Reserve in Alameda, California. Decorations: Viet Nam Campaign, Viet Nam Service, National Defense Service and Air Medals, Battle Efficiency Ribbon, and Legion of Merit with one OLC. Home of record: Alameda, CA.

Kallus, Frank, was born Apr. 14, 1895. Served as a Pvt. in U.S. Army Corps during WWI. Buried in Lady Fatima Cemetery, Abbott, TX.

Kallus, Harry T., was born Mar. 7, 1923. Served as a Pvt., 80 Inf. Division, 3rd Army, U.S. Army Corps during WWII. KILLED IN ACTION Mar. 13, 1945. Buried in St. Mary's Cemetery, West, TX.

Kallus, Joe, West, TX, military veteran, Merchant Marine.

Kallus, John V., was born Feb. 13, 1926. Served in U.S. Army Corps during WWII as a Pfc. Died Oct. 4, 1990. Buried in St. Mary's Cemetery, West, TX.

Kallus, Raymond, West, TX, military veteran, USMC.

Kallus, Vaclav Thomas, son of Alois J. and Theresa Migl Kallus, was born Aug. 31, 1906, at Wied, TX. Graduated from Hallettsville High School, A&M University with a degree in agriculture, A&I University with a Master of Science degree in agriculture. Graduate work at Colorado State and A&M, where he obtained a permanent administrative certificate. Taught at Devine, Poteet, and Victoria public schools, and Victoria Junior College. Received numerous awards for his community, state, and church service. Inducted into the Army on Oct. 22, 1942 at Fort Sam Houston, TX. Served as a Staff Sgt. in the Pacific Theater to supervise the production of fresh fruit and vegetables for the servicemen on the Island of New Caledonia. Discharged on Oct. 1, 1945. Medals: Good Conduct Medal, and American Theater Campaign Medal. Married Helen Poimbeauf; two children: Marie and Tommy. Died Nov. 29, 1987. Buried in Resurrection Mausoleum, Victoria, TX.

Kaluza, Ernest, West, TX, WWII veteran, KILLED IN ACTION.

Kaluza, Ernest M., was born Nov. 1, 1894. Served in the U.S. Army Corps. Sgt. Co. G., 86th Infantry, during WWI. Died Apr. 7, 1959. Buried in St. Mary's Cemetery, West, TX.

Kana, Ivan A., son of Joe and Amalie Kristek Kana, was born Nov. 30, 1919, Holman, TX.

Education: grammar school, 9th grade, Pecan and Mid Field, two years. Enlisted Mar. 8, 1942, Ft. Sam Houston, TX. Rank attained: Tec 4. Theater of Operations: Asiatic-Pacific. Battle: New Guinea Go 105 WD 45 Campaign, member Medical Supplies. Medals: Asiatic-Pacific Campaign Medal w/1 BSS, GCM, WWII Victory Ribbon, one Service stripe, six Overseas Bars. Honorably discharged Dec. 26, 1945, Ft. Sam Houston, TX. Home of record: Bay City, TX.

Kapavik, Alois, son of Frank and Mary Kapavik, was born Dec. 2, 1891, in Frystak, Czechoslovakia. Received schooling in Frystak. During World War I, enlisted in the Armed Service at West, TX, and served in the Panama Canal Zone as a Pvt. Married Mary Retchel in 1920, at West, TX; two children: Willie Kapavik and Dorothy Kapavik Moore. Died June 16, 1955.

Kapavik, Louis, was born Dec. 2, 1890. Served as a Pvt. in the U.S. Army Corps, Infantry, during WWI. Died June 16, 1955. Buried in St. Mary's Cemetery, West, TX.

Kapavik, Willie, son of Mr. and Mrs. Louis Kapavik, West, TX. Attended schools in West, TX. Served as a Pfc. in the U.S. Army Corps during WWII.

Karkoska, Clement, Granger, TX. Member of American Legion Post No. 282, Granger, TX. WWII veteran.

Karkoska, John G., son of Mr. and Mrs. Karkoska, was born June 26, 1890. Served in U.S. Army Corps. Attained rank of Cpl. Military occupation: Band, Hq. Co. Field Arty., during WWI. Honorably discharged. Married Mary M. Straka. Died Feb. 4, 1954; buried Corn Hill, Williamson Co., TX.

Karlik, Albin C., son of Cyrill Karlick, of Frystak, Czechoslovakia, and Alzbeta Konvicka Karlik of Frenstat, Czechoslovakia, was born on Aug. 28, 1916, at West, TX. Education included 1,800 hours technical training and one year at Baylor University. Enlisted on Sept. 13, 1942, at Recruiting Station in Dallas, TX. Rank: T/Sgt. Served as Air Force Flight Engineer on a B-24 Bomber. Served in combat in the 716th Squadron, 449th Bomb Group, 15th Air Force. Flew 50 missions and participated in the Air Offensive in Europe, Northern France, Rome Arno, Southern France, Normandy, Rhineland, GO33 WD 45. Decorations included EAME Campaign Medal with six BSS, Distinguished Unit Badge, Distinguished Flying Cross, Good Conduct Medal, Air Medal with three OLC. After combat served as AAF Gun Instructor at Mt. Home, Idaho. Discharged at Fort Sam Houston, TX, on Sept. 21, 1945.

Karlik, Clement "Kelly," of West, TX, WWII veteran, U.S. Army Air Corps.

Karlik, Clement L., of West, TX. Entered AAC, 1942. Trained Sheppard Field and Camp Wolters, TX. Rank: Cpl.

Karlik, Edward William, was born Oct. 12, 1927. Served in the U.S. Army Corps during WWII. Died Nov. 1, 1990. Buried in St. Mary's Cemetery, West, TX.

Karlik, Frank, was born Oct. 2, 1894. Served in the U.S. Army Corps, WWI as a Pvt. Died Sept. 21, 1974. Buried in St. Mary's Cemetery, West, TX.

Karlik, Jerry J., of West, TX. Entered AAC, 1935. Served during WWII, in Philippines, as a S/Sgt. KILLED IN ACTION, Bataan. Awarded Purple Heart. Buried in St. Mary's Cemetery, West, TX.

Kasik, Bohus Charles, son of Charles and Frances Kovar Kasik, was born July 8, 1915/1925, Axtell, TX. Education: Alligator School. Enlisted during WWII, U.S. Army Corps, July 8, 1941, Ft. Sam Houston, TX. Rank attained: Sgt. Theater of Operation: Pacific; 37th Inf. Div. from the Aleutian Islands to Luzon in the Philippines. Received many medals and honors. Honorably discharged, July 8, 1945. Civilian occupation: farmer. Died June 1971. Submitted by John Ernest Kasik in memory of his brother. Home of record: Malone, TX.

Kasik, John Ernest, son of Charles and Frances Kovar Kasik, was born Apr. 20, 1926, West, TX. Education: through eighth grade, Alligator School and West High School. Enlisted in U.S.

Army Corps, Aug. 5, 1945, Dallas, TX. Theater of Operation: Korea, 6th Inf. Division. Honors: Rifleman Medal (sharpshooter); Victory Medal. Honorably discharged May 25, 1947. Civilian occupation: farmer and highway construction. Home of record: Malone, TX.

Kaska, Anton Leo, was born Jan. 13, 1926. Served in USNR during WWII as S/1. Died June 8, 1967. Buried in St. Mary's Cemetery, West, TX.

Kaska, George A., son of Mr. and Mrs. Joe Kaska, West, TX. Entered Army 1945. Served in U.S.A. during WWII with rank of T/5.

Kaska, Jerome Anton, was born Sept. 14, 1919. Served in U.S. Armed Forces during WWII. COC 853 ENGR AVN BN. Attained rank of Tec/5.

Kaska, John J., served in U.S. Army Corps, 142nd Infantry during WWII as a S/Sgt, in Germany, Italy and France. WOUNDED IN ACTION. Awarded BSS for heroic achievement.

Kasmiersky, Adolph J., son of Adolph S. and Marie Kasmiersky, was born Mar. 17, 1927, Fayetteville, TX. Attended Fayetteville school through eighth grade. Enlisted U.S. Air Force, La Grange and Ft. Sam Houston, TX, during WWII. Assigned to 8th Air Force, 501 Air Service Group. Theater of Operation: European. Medals: Army of Occupation w/German Clasp; WWII Victory Ribbon. Honorably discharged as a Cpl., Sept. 13, 1948, 10th Air Force Group M.P., Pope Air Force Base, NC. Home of record: Houston, TX.

Kasmiersky, Joe A., son of Adolph S. and Marie Kasmiersky, was born Mar. 22, 1923, Fayetteville, TX. High school graduate, Fayetteville, TX; Durham Business College, Houston, TX. Enlisted during WWII, U.S. Air Force, La Grange and Ft. Sam Houston, TX. Assigned to 8th Air Force, 306th Bombardment, Group H, attained rank of Staff Sgt. Theater of Operations: European. Medals: Gunners Wings, Air Medal, Silver Star w/three OLC, Purple Heart. KILLED IN ACTION, Oct. 22, 1944, over the North Sea.

Kaspar, Cyril D., son of Mr. and Mrs. Frank J. Kaspar of Taylor, TX. Attended St. Mary's Catholic School, Taylor, TX. Enlisted in U.S. Army Corps about 1942; basic training Camp Hale, CO. Theater of Operations: American. Medals: American Theater Campaign Ribbon; WWII Victory Medal, among others. Rank of Pvt. at time of honorable discharge, 1944.

Kaspar, Frank, served six years in U.S. Army Corps during WWII.

Kaspar, Joe B., son of Mr. and Mrs. Frank J. Kaspar of Taylor, TX. Education: St. Mary's Catholic School, Taylor, TX. Enlisted U.S. Army Air Corps, 1942; basic training Sheppard Field, TX; further training, Sparton School of Aeronautics, Tulsa, OK; GMC, Indianapolis. Theater of Operations: Asiatic-Pacific. Served in Biak, Netherlands, East Indies, Philippines. Awards: Good Conduct Medal, Philippine Liberation Medal, American Defense Ribbon, Asiatic-Pacific Theater Campaign Ribbon w/2 BSS, WWII Victory Ribbon. Achieved rank of Cpl. before honorable discharge, 1946. Married Maxine L. Key in Tulsa, OK.

Kaspar, Mathew R., son of Mr. and Mrs. Frank J. Kaspar, Taylor, TX. Education: St. Mary's Catholic School, Taylor, TX. Enlisted in U.S. Army Corps, 1943. Basic training, Camp Hale, CO. Theater of Operation: American. Medals: American Theater Campaign Ribbon, WWII Victory Ribbon, among others. Rank of Pvt. at honorable discharge, 1944.

Kaspar, Method R. "Mike," son of Frank I. Kaspar and Miss Urbanek Kaspar, was born June 6, 1922, Taylor, TX. Education: grade school, Taylor, TX, St. Mary's High School, Taylor, TX. Enlisted WWII, Ft. Sam Houston, TX. Attained rank of Pfc. Stationed at Camp Hale, CO, with 87th Mtn. Infantry, which was a ski troop unit. Received Good Conduct Medal. Honorably discharged Aug. 15, 1943, Camp Hale, CO. Home of record: Corpus Christi, TX.

Kaspar, Walter, served four years in U.S. Army Corps during WWII.

Kasparek, Albert D., son of Mr. and Mrs. Albert Kasparek, Taylor, TX. Attended Taylor High School. Enlisted U.S. Army Corps, 1943. Basic training, Ft. Sill, OK; further training, Camp Maxey, TX. Theater of Operations: Asiatic-Pacific. Served in Philippines at Manila w/165th FA Bn. Serr. Bty. Achieved rank of Sgt. before honorable discharge.

Kasper, Reubin J., son of John and Anne Kasper of Granger, TX. Enlisted in U.S. Army Corps, 1944; basic training, Camp Fannin, TX. Theater of Operations: EAME. Served in Germany. KILLED IN ACTION Mar. 1945 in Germany. Medals: Purple Heart, EAME Campaign Ribbon w/BSS, and others.

Katrola, Alvin, son of Mr. and Mrs. H. J. Katrola, Taylor, TX. Attended Granger High School, TX. Enlisted in U.S. Navy, 1942; boot camp, Norfolk, VA. Theater of Operations: Asiatic-Pacific. Served at Pearl Harbor. Medals: Asiatic-Pacific Campaign Ribbon, WWII Victory Medal. Achieved rank of Lt. (jg) before honorable discharge, 1945.

Katrola, Hubert, son of Mr. and Mrs. H. J. Katrola, Taylor, TX. Attended Granger High School, TX. Enlisted U.S. Navy; basic training at San Diego, CA. Served in Japan and Europe. Attained rank of CMM before honorable discharge.

Katrola, Johnnie, son of Mr. and Mrs. H. J. Katrola, Taylor, TX. Attended Granger High School, TX. Enlisted USMC, 1943; basic training San Diego, CA. Theater of Operations: Asiatic-Pacific. Medals: Asiatic-Pacific Theater Campaign Ribbon, WWII Victory Medal. Attained rank of Sgt. before honorable discharge, 1945.

Kazda, Walter J., son of Mr. and Mrs. Louis J. Kazda, was born Feb. 28, 1921, Waco, McClellan Co., TX. Four years of college. Commissioned in U.S. Navy, Dallas, TX. Attained rank of Lt. Cdr. Naval Carrier Fighter Pilot. Theater of Operations: Pacific Ocean, Pacific Islands, Okinawa, Japan. Awards: Air Medal, Pacific Theater of Operations and Invasion Coverage. Honorably discharged Dec. 1, 1945. Member of SPJST Lodge #6, Cottonwood. Home of record: Bellevue, WA.

Kebrle, John, military service veteran. Home of record: Dallas, TX.

Kelarek, John Joseph, son of Stepan Kelarek and Rosalie Vanek Kelarek, was born May 16, 1894, Hamburg, Germany, as his parents were en route to the United States from Ratibor, Moravia. Lived briefly in Nelsonville, TX, then moved near Taylor, Williamson Co., TX, before settling in Crosby, TX. Enlisted in the USMC, Houston, TX. Sworn in on Thanksgiving Day, Nov. 29, 1917, Paris Island, SC. Served in the 76th Company Infantry in France. Fought at St. Michael, Belleauwood, Argonne, where he was WOUNDED IN ACTION. Honorably discharged Aug. 13, 1919, Quantico, VA. Numerous medals including Sharpshooter, Purple Heart. Married Silvie Kostka, Jan. 21, 1922; two daughters: Jannie and Silvie. Died Jan. 8, 1948, Houston, TX.

Kercho, Alfred J., son of Tom and Agnes Miksik Kercho, was born Oct. 12, 1933, in Shiner, TX. Graduate of the University of TX at Arlington with a Bachelor of Business Administration degree. Enlisted in the Air Force June 11, 1952, at Lackland AFB, San Antonio, TX. Rank: Staff Sgt. Served as Pharmacy Technician in Air Force hospitals in Suwon, Korea, Carswell AFB, Fort Worth, and Tinker AFB, Oklahoma City, OK. Medals include Korean Service, Far East Operations, and Good Conduct. Discharged June 10, 1956, at Tinker AFB, Oklahoma City, OK. Employed in the accounting profession and for the past 20+ years has worked for the National Credit Union Administration as a Supervisory Examiner (Auditor). Home of record: Hurst, TX.

Kercho, Thomas Stephen, was born Dec. 7, 1891, in Rudenska, Moravia. Educated at Hallettsville, TX, High School. Enlisted in the Army at Camp Travis, San Antonio, on Sept. 19, 1917/18. Served in France and Germany with the American Expeditionary forces, 90th Division, 360th Infantry, Company K during

WWI. Awarded a Sharpshooter Medal. Participated in the St. Michael and Meuse-Argonne Campaigns, including battles at Villes-en-Haye and Puvenelle. Rank: Cpl. Discharged June 21, 1919, at Camp Travis, San Antonio, TX. Married Agnes Miksik, Nov. 4, 1919; four children: Annie (deceased in infancy), Viola Kercho Patek, Edwin and Alfred. Thomas died Nov. 27, 1961. Was a farmer in the Shiner area (Mount Olive and Boundary Line School neighborhoods) until 1952. Retired to Seguin, TX.

Kincl, Louis J., son of Mr. and Mrs. Joe Kincl, Taylor TX. Education: Texas A&M. Enlisted U.S. Army Air Corps, 1942; basic training at Santa Ana, CA; further training, AZ. Instructors training, Randolph Field, TX, received wings; instrument training, Bryan, TX. Theater of Operations: American. Served as instrument instructor at Lemore, Bakersfield, Mercedes, CA, and Marama, AZ. Medals: American Theater Campaign Ribbon, WWII Victory Medal. Rank: 1st Lt. at time of discharge, 1945. Married Gertrude Sladecek.

Klapuch, Edmund, son of Joseph and Marie Jurica Klapuch, was born Oct. 25, 1892, Novohrad Community, near Moulton, TX. Attended Velehrad School. Helped parents on farm, learned to do carpentry, and built houses which are still standing. Also built bridges. Volunteered when WWI was declared. Rank: Pvt. Company "C," 5th Texas Infantry. Mustered into Federal Service at La Grange, TX, Aug. 5, 1917, by President Wilson's Proclamation of July 3, 1917. Established camp at Camp Ehlers, south of La Grange, TX, on same date. Left for Camp Bowie, Ft. Worth, TX, Aug. 7, 1917. Company "C," 5th Texas Infantry, was composed of men who gladly and freely volunteered to serve their nation during the war with Germany. Transferred to Company "M," 143 Infantry, 36th Division, in the Argonne Forest in France. Fought in the final phase until Sedan was captured. Not wounded, but was gassed. Parents were notified that he was killed. Later, the War Dept. notified the family of the error. After the war, married Agnes Konvicka, at Moravia, TX; two children: Alvin and Helen Klapuch (Guion). Resided in Fayette Co. for two years. Moved to Taft, where he helped clear the land of mesquite trees. Bought a farm and began farming. Favorite pastime: reading about history and current events. Member of SPJST Lodge #23, Moravia, TX, and the American Legion. Died Nov. 25, 1965, Taft, TX. Buried in Ascension Catholic Cemetery, Moravia, TX, with full gravesite services.

Klaus, Bill, of West, TX, 36th Division, WWII veteran.

Klaus, Edward, of West, TX, military veteran, WWII.

Klaus, William J., son of Mr. and Mrs. Emil Klaus, West, TX. Enlisted Army, 1940. Served European Theater. Awarded ET with five Battle Stars, American Defense Ribbons, and Purple Heart. WOUNDED IN ACTION, Italy, 1944. Attained rank of T/5 prior to discharge, 1945.

Klecka, Rudolph, son of John and Carolina Toman Klecka, was born May 10, 1919 in East Bernard, TX. Attended school in East Bernard. Enlisted in the Armed Services on Feb. 24, 1942, at Houston, TX, during World War II. Served in the American and European, African, and Middle Eastern Theaters of Operations. Attained the rank of Technical Sgt. Awards and decorations: American Campaign Medal, European African Middle Eastern Campaign Medal, Good Conduct Medal, World War II Victory Medal, and Certificate of Merit. Discharged from the service on Oct. 3, 1945. Home of record: East Bernard, TX.

Klepac, Gene W., son of Mr. and Mrs. Tom Klepac, Sr., was born about 1943. Enlisted in USAF, June 28, 1963, San Antonio, TX. Air Police 4130 Combat Defense. Medals: GCM, Presidential Citation. Honorably discharged June 28, 1963. Married; three children. Home of record: Bay City, TX. Submitted by Mr. and Mrs. Jerry Fabrygel.

Klepac, Joseph F., was born Mar. 4, 1893. Enlisted in U.S. Army Corps in TX. Attained rank of Cpl. during WWI. Honorably discharged. Civilian occupation: Farmer. Married Annie L. Tschoerner; three children: Bill, Dorothy, and Frances. Died Dec. 24, 1975; buried Corn Hill, Williamson Co., TX. Submitted by Mr. and Mrs. Jerry Fabrygel.

Klepac, Raymond F., son of Paul and Angeline Tschoerner Klepac, was born June 13, 1925. Enlisted U.S. Army Corps about 1943, during WWII. Attained rank of Pfc. Died Mar. 31, 1989; buried Corn Hill, Williamson Co., TX. Submitted by Mr. and Mrs. Jerry Fabrygel.

Klepac, Thomas J., son of Mr. and Mrs. Tom Klepac, Jr., was born Oct. 21, 1945, Bay City, TX. Enlisted in U.S. Army, Dec. 7, 1965, Bay City, TX. Operations: Iron Triangle. Battles: S and D War Zone C, 6 months. Honorably discharged Sept. 22, 1967. Married; two children. Submitted by Mr. and Mrs. Jerry Fabrygel. Home of record: Richmond, TX.

Klepac, Tom, Jr., son of Mr. and Mrs. Tom Klepac, Sr. Enlisted in U.S. Army, Jan. 14, 1944. Honorable medical discharge Sept. 1944. Married; two children. Died Oct. 13, 1977. Hometown: Thrall, Williamson Co., TX. Submitted by Mr. and Mrs. Jerry Fabrygel. Home of record: Needville, TX.

Klima, Frank C., son of Frank and Annie Rybak Klima, was born Jan. 14, 1914, in Rosenberg, TX. Attended school in Moravia, TX, and Woodrow school in Damon, TX, through 1931. Attended electronic school in Damon. Prior to service was employed with the county AAA office in Richmond, TX, as a land surveyor. Enlisted Oct. 18, 1940, at Fort Sam Houston, San Antonio, TX, serving three years there. Rank: Sgt. Shipped overseas to England and landed in Normandy on D-Day. Captured three days later by the Germans and was a PRISONER OF WAR for one year in Germany, prior to liberation by the Russians. Received numerous medals and was discharged Oct. 6, 1945. Died June 12, 1972, age 58. Buried in Hungerford, TX.

Klimek, Charles, son of Joe F. Klimek, Sr. and Strdanel Klimek, was born Sept. 12, 1892, Live Oak Hill, TX. Education: Country Grade School. Enlisted during WWI. Rank: Pvt. Army Infantry. Served in Europe. Battles: France and other areas. Discharged about 1919. Was a farmer and lived near Frelsburg, TX, until his death on Aug. 25, 1978. Buried in Fayetteville Catholic Cemetery, Fayetteville, TX. Submitted by Louis J. Polansky, nephew, of Fayetteville, TX.

Klimek, John P., son of Joe F. Klimek, Sr. and Frances Sklar Klimek, was born Sept. 28, 1903, Frelsburg, TX. Education: grade school and barber school. Enlisted in U.S. Army Corps, TX during WWII. Assigned to Infantry, American Theater of Operations. Honorably discharged about 1945. Died June 19, 1962, buried in Fayetteville Catholic Cemetery, Fayetteville, TX.

Klimitchek, Fred Charles, son of Paul Louis and Millie Kallus Klimitchek, was born Mar. 6, 1927, West, McClellan, TX. Education: St. Mary's Catholic School and West High School, West, TX; Hillsboro Junior College and Baylor College. Inducted by local draft board in Hillsboro, TX, to report at Ft. Sam Houston, TX, May 24, 1945, into the U.S. Army Corps; Port of Embarkation, Brooklyn, NY. Made two trips to EAME and Asiatic-Pacific Theaters of Operation. Spent six months overseas, was clerk typist on ship. Served with the U.S. Army Transportation Corps, served aboard the USAT SS *Cape Neddick* and the USAT *Admiral Cuntz*. Basic training was at Ft. Lewis, WA. Medals and Decorations: American Campaign Theater Ribbon; Asiatic-Pacific Campaign Theater Ribbon; WWII Victory Medal; Good Conduct Medal. Honorable discharge at Camp Kilmer, NJ, Nov. 29, 1946, with the rank of T/5. Civilian occupation: farmer and rancher. Died Oct. 31, 1993.

Klimitchek, John R., son of Charles and Mary Neubert Klimitchek, was born May 11, 1911, Hallettsville, TX. His grandfather, Alois Klimitchek, was among the first Moravians from

Frenstat to come to Lavaca Co., TX, 1858. Attended Ezzell School, Hallettsville High School, Draughon's Business College, San Antonio, TX. Enlisted in the U.S. Army Corps, during WWII, Apr. 20, 1942. Rank: Cpl. Served 44 months, 17 of which were overseas. Served under General George Patton, 738th Field Artillery Battalion, Battles: Northern France, Rhine, Germany. Medals: BSS, received for meritorious service during the period of Aug. 23, 1944–May 9, 1945 in France and Germany. Served as Battalion Agent for a heavy Artillery Bn. and was required to make many arduous trips from higher HQ to his Battalion at all hours of day and night, through adverse weather conditions. Honorably discharged, Ft. Sam Houston, Dec. 5, 1945. Returned to ranching at home, Ezzell, TX. Apr. 16, 1955. Married Josephine Matula, daughter of John Matula and Frances Michna Matula. Two sons: Charles and Joseph. In 1947 was elected Lavaca County Commissioner, Precinct 4, an office held for nearly 30 years. Member of the American Legion, the VFW. Died September 3, 1976, and was accorded full military honors at his burial in the Sacred Heart Catholic Cemetery in Hallettsville, TX.

Klimitchek, Leo Albert, son of Paul and Millie Kallus Klimitchek, was born Nov. 21, 1924, in West, TX. Attended St. Mary's Catholic School and West High School in West, TX. Inducted into the U.S. Army at Dallas, TX on Mar. 17, 1943, during WWII. Basic training, Ft. Leonard Wood, MO. Served in the European, African, and Middle Eastern Theater of Operations as a member of Co. A, 318th Inf., 80th Div. with the rank of Pfc. Participated in the Northern France and the Ardennes:Alsace ("Battle of the Bulge") Campaigns. WOUNDED IN ACTION in the latter. Decorations include the Purple Heart, European African Middle Eastern Campaign Medal with two BSS, and the Combat Infantryman Badge. Discharged from the service at Borden General Hospital, Chickasha, OK, on July 27, 1945. Died Mar. 31, 1993. Buried St. Mary's Catholic Cemetery, West, TX. Submitted by daughter, Marie Klimitchek Dulak, West Columbia, TX.

Klimitchek, Paul Louis, son of Charles Klimitchek and Mary Neubert, was born June 21, 1893, Hallettsville, TX. Educated through 4th grade. Enlisted in U.S. Army Corps, July 23, 1917, at age of 24, in Cureo, TX, during WWI. Basic training at Camp Wolters. Served overseas in European Theater of Operations; fought in France and Germany. Battles: Champagne, Meuse, Argonne, from July 18, 1918–May 31, 1919. WOUNDED IN ACTION, gassed in France. Honorably discharged June 14, 1919. Farmer by occupation. Died May 7, 1956. Home of record: West, TX. Submitted by son, Fred Klimitchek of West, TX (now deceased).

Klimitchek, William Paul, son of Paul Louis and Millie Kallus, was born May 12, 1929, West, TX. Education through tenth grade at St. Mary's Catholic Elementary and West High Schools. Enlisted in U.S. Army Corps, 1952, Hillsboro, Hill Co., TX. Basic training at Ft. Sill, Lawton, Comanche, OK. Trained with the 31st Infantry Division, Headquarters Battery, 114 Field Artillery Battalion in Ft. Jackson, SC, Camp Atterbury, IN, Camp Gordon CA. In Korea, was assigned to communications and Patrol Duty. Fought in Ku-dong North Korea. KILLED IN ACTION Oct. 13, 1952. Took position in a foxhole that was mined when returning from ambush patrol. Medals: Purple Heart (posthumously), Korean Service Medal w/1 BSS, United Nations Medal, Combat Medal, Good Conduct Medal. Attained rank of Pfc. Civilian occupation was a farmer at West, TX. Buried in St. Mary's Cemetery, West, TX. Submitted by brother, Fred C. Klimitchek (now deceased).

Klinkacek, Francis, served as Assistant Pastor, Holy Family Church, Wharton, TX, and St. John's Catholic Church, Hungerford, 1940-42 when he was drafted into the U.S. Army as a Roman Catholic Chaplain. At one time served at Camp Callan, California, and several other camps during years as a chaplain. Returned to Galveston, Houston Diocese, TX, where he later died and is buried.

Klish, Raymond L., of West, TX. Entered Navy in 1945, attaining rank of S 1/C. Served aboard CASU 66. Awarded Amer. Def. and Victory Ribbons. Discharged 1946.

Knapek, Benjamin P., son of Paul and Ella Schwertner Knapek, was born Apr. 13, 1939, Penelope, TX. Attended Holy Trinity School and graduated high school at Jarrell, TX. Enlisted in the U.S. Air Force at San Antonio, TX, on Nov. 9, 1961. Assignments included MacDill Air Force Base, Tampa, FL; GA; and Naha Air Base, Okinawa, Japan. Separated from the service Nov. 8, 1965, in the rank of Sgt. Occupation: Farmer and rancher in Jarrell, TX, area.

Knapek, Ben J., son of Joe and Mary Hlavenka Knapek, was born Nov. 2, 1918, Penelope, TX. Attended Griffin School (rural school near Penelope, TX). Enlisted U.S. Army, 1944, Dallas, TX. Trained at Camp Hood, TX. Co. L 158th Inf. Regt, 8th Army. Theater of Operations: Asiatic-Pacific. Fought in Luzon. Medals: Combat Infantryman Badge, Asiatic-Pacific Campaign Ribbon w/1 BSS, Good Conduct Medal, Army of Occupation Ribbon, Japan Victory Ribbon, three overseas service bars. Honorably discharged, 1946. Married Lottie Grones; two sons. Home of record: Penelope, TX.

Knapek, Johnny A., Granger, TX. Member of American Legion Post No. 282, Granger, TX. WWII veteran.

Knapek, Raymond, West, TX, WWII veteran, U.S. Army Air Corps.

Kneitz, Joe, son of Joe and Mary Peter Kneitz, was born 1879, near Ammannsville, TX. Served in Spanish American War Foreign Service. Died about 1945; buried Corpus Christi, TX. Submitted by Evelyn Vecera, Bellaire, TX.

Kocian, Albin, son of Mr. and Mrs. Aug. Kocian, West, TX. Theater of Operations: Asiatic-Pacific. Rank: Pfc. Served in South Pacific, Okinawa, Hawaii, Saipan. WOUNDED IN ACTION. Awarded Purple Heart.

Kocian, Ernest William, son of William Charles and Antonia Macha Kocian, was born Aug. 14, 1924, West, TX. Graduated from West, TX, High School. Earned BBA degree at Baylor University, Waco, TX. Enlisted in the U.S. Army on July 17, 1943, at Mineral Wells, TX, during WWII. Theater of Operations: Asiatic-Pacific. 103rd Infantry, 43rd Div. Campaigns: New Guinea, Northern Solomons, Luzon, New Caledonia, New Zealand, New Guinea, Philippines, and Japan. Occupational force stationed in Yokohama, Japan. Medals: Silver Star, Asiatic-Pacific Campaign w/3 BSS, bronze arrowhead, Philippine Liberation Ribbon, Combat Infantryman Badge, two Purple Hearts. WOUNDED IN ACTION. Honorably discharged Nov. 9, 1945. Active in DAV; VFW, AARP, and past president of KJT Local Chapter. 4th Degree, Knights of Columbus. Eucharistic Minister and past president of Parish Council of Our Lady of Perpetual Help Catholic Church in Corpus Christi, TX. 37-year employee of Goodyear Tire and Rubber Company. Died Sept. 16, 1993; buried Seaside Memorial Cemetery in Corpus Christi. Survived by wife Rita Callaway Kocian, five children, and nine grandchildren. Home of record: Corpus Christi, TX. Submitted by his children.

Kocian, Frank Paul, was born Jan. 25, 1896. Served in the U.S. Army Corps as a Pvt. during WWI. Died Jan. 22, 1972. Buried in St. Mary's Cemetery, West, TX.

Kocian, William Charlie, son of August Kocian and Agnes Makovy Kocian, was born Mar. 23, 1896. Enlisted in the U.S. Army at Camp Travis, TX, on Aug. 17, 1918, during WWI. Co. C, 86th Div. Remained at Camp Travis until his discharge from the service on Feb. 13, 1919. Died May 12, 1964; interred at St. Mary's Cemetery in West, TX.

Kocian, William C., served as a Pvt. in the U.S. Army Corps Infantry during WWI. Discharged 1919.

Kocian, Willie A., West, TX, WWII veteran.

Kocurek, Albin Louis, son of Rudolph Joseph Kocurek and Julia Dubil, was born Nov. 12, 1924, Granger, TX. Attended Taylor High School. Enlisted and received basic training in 1944, U.S. Army Corps, and stationed at Camp Hood, now called Ft. Hood, in Killeen, TX. Assigned to the 98th Division Alliances, Iroquois Indians, Cavalry Recon. Further training: KY and AL. Theater of Operations: American, Asiatic-Pacific. Campaigns: Honolulu, Maui, Japan. Medals: American Theater Campaign Ribbon, Asiatic-Pacific Campaign Ribbon, WWII Victory Ribbon. Attained rank of Sgt. before being honorably discharged in 1946. Married Margaret Wilkerson; four married children and eleven grandchildren. Home of record: Houston, TX. Submitted by sister, Georgia Kocurek Chamberlain, of Austin, TX.

Kocurek, Jerry S., was born Dec. 26, 1923. Served in U.S. Army Corps during WWII as a Tec-5. Died Dec. 13, 1991. Buried in St. Mary's Cemetery, West, TX.

Kocurek, Marvin M., son of Willie A. (from Snook, TX) and Della M. Naivor Kocurek (from Ratabar, TX), was born Jan. 1932. Education: Graduated Rosenberg, TX, High, 1949. Enlisted Texas National Guard for two years, ten months, fifteen days. Rank: E-5. U.S. Army Corps, Jan. 1954 to Jan. 1956. Stationed at Ft. Holabird, MD, for two years. Married Esther Lopez; two sons: Eric and Omar, both graduated from university and working in construction in Alaska. Owned and operated Artic Faree in Anchorage, AK. Special interest: big game hunting and fishing; has many Boone and Crockett trophies. Home of record: Anchorage, AK. Submitted by brother William J. Kocurek, Richmond, TX.

Kocurek, Rudolph E., son of Steve and Agnes Spacek Kocurek, was born in 1912. Graduate of the University of Texas School of Business Administration. Served in clerical areas of the army during three years of active service in WWII.

Kocurek, Rudolph Joseph, son of Joseph and Frances Balusek Kocurek, was born Apr. 20, 1891, in a Circleville, TX, farmhouse near Taylor, TX. Served with the American Expeditionary Forces, U.S. Army Corps, Co. B, 142nd Inf. Reg., 36th Div. during WWI. Went to war zone by train from Canada to France. Arrived in USA from France on June 5, 1919, to Camp Merritt, NY. Married Julia Dubil, Jan. 1918; six children. First baby died of an influenza epidemic during war. Settled in Granger and took over business at a butcher shop in a partnership with his uncle, Louis Kocurek, located next to the Pruitt Hardware Store, which later was extended into a grocery store and Granger's first barbecue stand. Active in the Granger American Legion and is remembered for how proudly he always carried the American Flag in parades. Died Apr. 16, 1946; buried in Holy Cross Catholic Cemetery, Granger, TX.

Kocurek, Stephen R., son of Steve and Agnes Spacek Kocurek, was born in 1897. Joined WWI Army in Dec. 1917, and landed in Europe on April 28, 1918, as a Cpl. in Co. C, Third Div. Participated in Marne, St. Michael, Meuse-Argone offensives, and served in the army of occupation through Dec. 1918. Discharged June 1919.

Kocurek, William J., son of Willie A. (from Snook, TX) and Della M. Naivor Kocurek (from Ratabar, TX), was born Jan. 15, 1930. Graduated Rosenberg High School, 1947; Texas A&M College, 1951. Enlisted USAF, Dec. 1, 1951, Houston, TX. Served until Nov. 30, 1955. Served in Korea with 18th Fighter Bomber Wing, July 1952–July 1953 (75-P-51-Mustang Aircraft). Airman of the month for Apr. 1952 for his wing and the whole Fifth Air Force. Married Mary Jane Kubelka. Owned and operated Mustang Fence Co., Rosenberg, TX, 34 years. Special interests: Big game hunting and travelling around the world, including 10 trips to the Czech Republic in last 15 years, three times before 1989 when communists were ousted. Home of record: Richmond, TX.

Kocurek, Willie I., son of Steve and Agnes Spacek Kocurek, was born in 1910. Served in the Navy during WWII as a Lt. (jg), and was a full Lt. upon discharge. His tour of duty, after training in Hollywood Beach, FL, was aboard the USS *General Tasker H. Bliss*, as a deck officer. His ship crossed the Atlantic 26 times as the flagship of convoys of up to 100 ships from 1944 to 1946.

Koenig, Ivan, son of Hugo and Albina Holub Koenig, was born Sept. 24, 1925, in Fayette Co., TX. Enlisted in the U.S. Army at LaGrange, TX, in 1944 during WWII. Trained at Camp Hood, TX. Served in the Asiatic Pacific Theater of Operations with both the 86th and 36th Divisions. Participated in the Luzon Campaign. Awards and decorations include the Asiatic-Pacific Campaign Medal with campaign star, Army of Occupation Medal, Good Conduct Medal, Philippine Liberation Ribbon, Combat Infantryman Badge, and Distinguished Unit Citation. Discharged from the service in Nov. 1946. Home of record: Weimar, TX.

Kofnovec, John R., was born Dec. 10, 1923. Served during WWII in the U.S. Army Corps as a Pfc. Died March 14, 1993. Buried in St. Mary's Cemetery, West, TX.

Kofnovec, Robert G., son of Frank and Mary Kofnovec, Sr., was born on July 8, 1925, in Kaufman, TX. Completed two years of college at Southern Methodist University. Entered the service at Kaufman, and served with the U.S. Navy in the Pacific. Rank: Lt. Cmdr. Medals: Navy Commendation Medal, Viet Nam Service Medal with one BSS, National Defense Service Medal, Navy Unit Commendation, Asiatic-Pacific Area, American Area World War Victory Medal, Navy Good Conduct Medal (3rd award), American Defense Medal, and Battle Efficiency E. Discharged Nov. 1, 1968. Home of record: Valencia, CA.

Kofron, Charles, served in U.S. Armed Forces in France and Germany during WWI. Hometown: Nada, TX. Deceased.

Kohn, Frank, Jr., son of Mr. and Mrs. Frank Kohn, Sr., was born July 11, 1918, in Bardwell, TX. Attended Bardwell High School and joined the Navy on Mar. 29, 1944. Rank: Seaman 1C. Served in the Pacific Theater on board the Aircraft Carrier U.S.S. *Santee* during WWII. Participated in the Palau, Yap, Ulithi, Woleai Raid, Western New Guinea, Leyte Operation, Okinawa and Third Fleet Operation against Japan. The U.S.S. *Santee* received a Unit Citation from the president of the U.S. for service rendered in advanced areas of combat in the Pacific Theater. Discharged at Camp Wallace, on Dec. 20, 1945. Died on Nov. 10, 1981 and is buried at St. Joseph's Cemetery at Ennis, TX.

Kohn, Jerry A., son of Mr. and Mrs. Frank Kohn, Sr., was born Dec. 4, 1920, in Bardwell, TX. Member of the 2nd Signal Battalion, 19th Corp, during WWII. Rank: S/Sgt. Served in the European Theater at Normandy, Northern France, Ardennes, the Rhineland, and Central European Campaigns. Decorations: EAME Campaign with five BSS, Victory, Good Conduct, American Theater Campaign and Unit Citation, and three Overseas Service Bars. Discharged Nov. 25, 1945. Married, two children. Home of record: Dallas, TX.

Kohoutek, Charles J., son of Michael Kohoutek and Frances Bernard, was born Dec. 18, 1912. Enlisted about 1941/2, U.S. Army Corps, served during WWII. Married Otilie A. Kubacak. Died Nov. 29, 1982; buried Corn Hill, Williamson Co., TX.

Kohut, John Victor, son of John and Veronika Tomascik Kohut, was born July 15, 1886, in Milano, Milam Co., TX. Attended grade school and business administration. Enlisted in U.S. Army in Waco, TX. Assigned Quartermaster Corps. Rank: Cpl. Discharged Jan. 13, 1919. Married Millie Helble Green on Jan. 14, 1925; two children: Eleanor L. Kohut Rusnak and Lansing B. Kohut. Step-daughters are Alberta Green and Cleo Green Leibham. Was a merchant at Cyclone, TX, for 29 years. Died Sept. 9, 1977.

Kohut, Johnnie H., Sr., son of Joe F. and Frances Kohut, was born July 15, 1919, Midland, TX. Attended Cyclone High School through ninth grade. Drafted into the U.S. Army Corps, Apr. 4, 1940, San Antonio, Bexar Co., TX. Rank: S/Sgt. Theater of Operation: Europe. Battles: Tunisia, Naples, Foggia, Rome, Arno, Northern Apennines, Po

Valley. Medals: Good Conduct, American Defense Service, European African Middle Eastern Campaign w/5 BSS. Served overseas over three years. Honorable discharge Aug. 17, 1945, San Antonio, Bexar Co., TX. Home of record:Temple, TX.

Kohut, Lansing Benjamin, son of John V. and Millie L. Kohut, was born Jan. 13, 1931, in Cyclone, Bell Co., TX. Attended Temple High School and Administration Signal School. Enlisted Aug. 31, 1948, in Austin, TX. Rank: S/Sgt. Duty stations included Sheppard Field, Wichita Falls, TX; Camp Kilmer, NJ; 20th Communication Squadron Landsberg/Lech, Germany; Tyndall AFB, FL. Discharged Sept. 11, 1953, at Tyndall AFB. Medals: Occupation Medal (Germany), Medal for Humane Action, Berlin Air Lift Device. Home of record: Temple, TX.

Kohutek, Amil F., son of Rossie Kohutek, was born June 30, 1917, Walters, Cotton Co., OK. Attended schools in Devol, OK; Big Elm, Lone Star Elementary, Ada Henderson School, Cameron, TX. Enlisted in U.S. Army Corps during WWII. ETO: North Africa, Italy, South France, Eastern France, Germany, Austria, Naples Foggia, Rome Arno, Southern France, Central Europe, Rhineland. Decorations: EAME Campaign Medal w/5 BSS, one Bronze Arrowhead, American Defense Service Medal, GCM. Recommended for BSS, left service before it was presented, never caught up with him. Contracted malaria, yellow jaundice, pneumonia while on active duty. Honorably discharged Aug. 2, 1945, San Antonio, TX. Returned to San Angelo, TX, late 1945. Employed as a line driver, Sunset Motor Lines. Moved to Abilene, TX, 1960; continued driving freight truck. Moved to Irving, TX, 1963. Retired from East Texas Motor Lines in 1974, after 35 years and 3½ million miles driving commercial vehicles. Hobbies: self-taught welder, built some 400 barbecue grills in 35 years, gave most away. Presently involved in woodworking. Married Pauline Machann, from Rowena, TX; two daughters, Clara Kohutek Wiggins and Gladys Kohutek Cox (wife and daughters members of SPJST); four grandchildren. Elected president, 36th Division Assn., 1969. First elected official to travel outside the state—flew to Washington, DC, to present a plaque at the Tomb of the Unknown Soldier; Organized Battery C, 132nd Field Artillery Assn. Served as president, vice president, and as ex. secy. many times. Wrote several war stories for the *Texas T Patch Quarterly*. Home of record: Abilene, TX. Submitted by wife Pauline Kohutek of Abilene, TX.

Kokas, Frank J., son of John J. Kokas and Pauline Rose Glomb, was born Sept. 27, 1913, Kokernot, Gonzales Co., TX,. B.S. degree, Petroleum Engineering, University of Texas. Volunteered for U.S. Army Corps during WWII, May 14, 1942, Ft. Sam Houston, TX. Attained rank of T/3 from the Signal Corps. Served overseas in South Pacific at Fenschhafen, New Guinea; Philippines (near Clark Field); Kyoto, Japan, Occupation Troops. Medals and Awards: WWII Victory Medal, GCM, Rifle Marksman, American Theater of Operations Campaign Ribbon, Asiatic Pacific Theater Campaign Ribbon. Honorably discharged Feb. 7, 1946, Ft. Bliss, El Paso, TX. Submitted by Evelyn Vecera, Bellaire, TX.

Kokes, Louis A., Granger, TX, WWII veteran.

Kolacek, Clement F., was born Aug. 13, 1915. Cpl. in the USMC during WWII. Served Pacific area, Japan. Died June 11, 1973. Buried in St. Mary's Cemetery, West, TX.

Kolacek, Kake, West, TX, WWII veteran.

Kolacny, Jim Frank, son of Frank and Rosie Kolacny, was born Dec. 2, 1916, Shiner, TX. Education: Boundary Line School. Enlisted in U.S. Army Corps, Mar. 20, 1942, Ft. Sam Houston, TX, during WWII. Attached to 359th Co. E, 90th Division. Theater of Operation: ETO. KILLED IN

ACTION, June 12, 1944, Beach of Normandy. Submitted by Mrs. G. F. Butschek of Houston, TX.

Kolar, Adolph J., West, TX, WWII veteran.

Kolar, Frank, was born Nov. 16, 1892. Served in U.S. Army Corps during WWI as a Pvt. Died July 31, 1974. Buried in St. Mary's Cemetery, West, TX.

Kolar, Joe, son of Alois and Aloisia Oprsal Kolar (natives of Holomuc and Frenstat, Moravia, in the present day Czechoslovakia), was born Apr. 7, 1893, near West, McLennan Co., TX, oldest child and only son. Education: through third or fourth grade, West, TX. Moved to Shiner, Lavaca Co., TX. Enlisted in the U.S. Armed Forces Sept. 19, 1917, during WWI, at Camp Travis, San Antonio, Bexar Co., TX. Basic training at Camp Gordon, GA. Port of embarkation was Camp Upton, NY. Arrived in France May 7, 1918. Assigned to Co. A, 327 Inf., 82nd Div., American Expeditionary Forces. Rank: Pvt. Battles: Chateau-Thierry, St. Michiel. MORTALLY WOUNDED on Oct. 7, 1918, by the explosion of a shell near Hill 180, not far from the town of Cornay in the Argonne region, during the Argonne-Meuse offensive. Died soon after reaching the first aid station, and listed as KILLED IN ACTION. The commanding officer was Captain Roy A. Flynt from TN. Interred Sept. 11, 1921, in the Kolar family plot in the old Shiner Catholic Cemetery near the burial place of his friend, Frank Stanek. Is memorialized in the name of the American Legion Post in Shiner, Texas–Kolar-Stanek Post 201, as one of the two soldiers from Shiner killed in action in WWI. Submitted by niece Lois Jo Schindler of Victoria, TX.

Kolar, Milton Charles, was born June 10, 1923. Served in the U.S. Armed Forces during WWII as a Pfc. Died Oct. 14, 1982. Buried in Our Lady of Fatima Cemetery in Abbott, TX.

Kolar, Leo, West, TX, military veteran.

Kolenovsky, Albin, son of Mr. and Mrs. Frank Kolenovsky. Attended Taylor High School. Enlisted U.S. Army, 1944; basic training at Ft. Riley, KS. Theater of Operation: Asiatic-Pacific. Served in Philippines, Leyte, Luzon, Tokyo. Medals: Asiatic-Pacific Theater Campaign Ribbon w/2 BSS, Philippine Liberation Ribbon w/1 BSS, Infantry Combat Badge, Good Conduct Medal. Rank Pfc. Honorably discharged 1945.

Kolenovsky, Vladimir E., son of Emil and Albina Kolenovsky, was born Oct. 29, 1921, in Colorado Co., TX. Enlisted at Fort Sam Houston, TX, WWII. Served in the Invasion and received several medals. Home of record: Fayetteville, TX.

Kolinek, John Carl, son of Mr. and Mrs. Louis Kolinek. Entered U.S. Army Corps in 1944. Served E.T. Awarded EAME with one BSS, Victory Ribbons, two overseas Bars, Expert Carbine. Attained rank of T/5. Served during WWII. Discharged 1946.

Kollaja, Alvin A., son of John L. and Sophie Vasut Kollaja, was born Aug. 28, 1923, Fayetteville, TX. Education: Sts. Peter and Paul Catholic School, Plum, TX; St. John's Catholic School, Fayetteville, TX; Clarkwood, TX, Elementary School; Robstown and Corpus Christi High Schools; University of MN (CTD-USAA Corps), BS in Geology, SMU, Dallas, TX. Commissioned 1st Lt., U.S. Army Air Corps, San Antonio, TX. ETO, 8th Air Force, 457th Bomb Group, 748th Sqd., Glatton Air Base, near Peterborough, England. B-17 pilot. Flew 15 missions. Bombed several targets in Germany. Tour of duty cut short when war ended. "On one mission, made emergency landing on a bowling field, west of London, England, near Windsor Castle. RAF loaned us 500 gallons of 'petrol' so we could return to our base. There were no fatalities of our crew on our entire tour of duty. My ball turret gunner claims to have shot down an enemy jet fighter M.E. 262. In addition to training planes, also flew P-51 and A-26." Honorable discharge Sept. 10, 1947. Home of record: Midland, TX.

Kollaja, Edward Dan, son of John and Sofie Kollaja, was born Oct. 7, 1933 in Fayetteville, TX. He went to school at Roy Miller High School (1951) and Del Mar College, Corpus Christi, TX. Enlisted in Corpus Christi and served as a Pvt-2 in Thule, Greenland, and was discharged in Oct. 1955. Married, three children. Died Feb. 1992.

Kollaja, John L., son of Frank and Mary Divin Kolaja, was born Feb. 5, 1894, Fayetteville, TX. Attended grammar school, Park, TX. Enlisted in U.S. Army Corps Aug. 6, 1918, LaGrange, TX. ETO, France. "While marching to the battle front, messenger told Regiment the war was over." Member of American Expeditionary Force from Aug. 6, 1918 to July 16, 1919. Honorably discharged July 31, 1919, Camp Pike, AR. Married Sophie Vlasta. Died June 22, 1973. Submitted by son, Alvin A. Kollaja. Home of record: Midland, TX.

Kolos, Joseph, son of Mr. and Mrs. Vincent Kolos, was born June 13. 1892, in Rychaltice, Moravia, Austria. Attended Rychaltice public school. During WWI enlisted in the Czech-American Legionnaires, trained in Stanford, CT, on the farm of Gutzon Borglum, and served in France in the areas of Champagne, Aisne, Vouzieres, and Terron. Died Dec. 13, 1956.

Kolosova, Viola, daughter of Josef and Anezka Kolos, was born Apr. 18, 1921, Hallettsville, TX. Educated at St. Joseph's Catholic School, Yoakum, TX, and University of Texas in Austin. Enlisted in U.S. Army Corps, Ft. Sam Houston, San Antonio, TX, Aug. 5, 1943. Rank: Sgt. Stationed in Newport News, VA, a port of embarkation. General Patton left from this port with his Unit—such a well-kept secret that those not involved with the preparations didn't know until later. Honorably discharged Jan. 24, 1946. Married Harry L. Doenges. Home of record: Houston, TX.

Konarik, Johnnie W., served a half year in U.S. Navy during WWII.

Konarik, Peter S., served Mar. 1942–Apr. 1945, in U.S. Army Corps during WWII.

Konvicka, Ernest A., son of Anton and Agnes Konvicka, was born Aug. 3, 1931, Penelope, TX. Served in military service during the Korean War, attained the rank of S/Sgt. Theater of Operation: Korea. Medals earned: Korean Service Medal 2/w BBS, United Nations Service Medal, American Defense Service Medal. Honorably discharged Sept. 13, 1953. Home of record: Waco, TX.

Konvicka, Ignac, son of Frank and Agnes Indruch Konvicka. Born Mar. 25, 1892, in Dubina, Fayette Co., TX. Enlisted in the U.S. Army June 30, 1917, in Schulenburg and after training was sent to France. Assigned to the American Expeditionary Force on July 17, 1918. Battles: Champagne Bulge, and Meuse-Argonne. On Oct. 10, 1918, sustained a gunshot wound to left hand. Returned to the U.S. on Mar. 25th and was honorably discharged on Apr. 29, 1919. Made Houston his home and on July 3, 1922 married Emily Chaloupka; three children. Died July 20, 1977; interred in Angleton Cemetery. Submitted by Mary K. Scruggs.

Kopecky, Arnold Louis, son of Alois R. and Bertha Elizabeth Naiser Kopecky, was born Mar. 11, 1925, Granger, Williamson Co., TX. Education: Sts. Cyril & Methodius Catholic Elementary School, Granger, TX, High School. Served in U.S. Army Corps during WWII, 3rd Armored Div. Theater of Operations: EAME. WOUNDED IN ACTION. Medals: BSS, EAME Theater Campaign Medal w/7 BSS, Bronze Indian Arrowhead, Good Conduct Medal, Purple Heart, WWII Victory Medal. Honorably discharged. Married Marjorie Dodd; two children: Kathy and Janie. Civilian occupation: house painter. Died Apr. 27, 1988. Buried with military honors, Houston National Cemetery, Houston, TX. Submitted by Cecile K. Murph, Austin, TX.

Kopecky, Bernard Joseph, son of Alois R. and Bertha Elizabeth Naiser Kopecky, was born Mar. 18, 1920, Granger, Williamson Co., TX. Education: Sts. Cyril & Methodius Catholic Elementary School, Granger High School, Granger, TX. Served in U.S. Army Corps during WWII. Theater of Operations: EAME. WOUNDED IN ACTION. Served in North Africa; attained rank of Sgt. Medals: Purple Heart, EAME Theater Campaign Medal w/BSS, WWII Victory Medal. Honorably discharged. Married Helen Berry; three children: Martha Ann, Donna, and Howard. Civilian occupation: owned and operated jewelry store. Died Feb. 28, 1983; buried Rockdale, Milam Co., TX. Submitted by Cecile K. Murph, Austin, TX.

Kopecky, Daniel F., son of Mr. and Mrs. Frank Kopecky of Granger, TX. Graduated from Granger High School. Enlisted in U.S. Army Corps, 1942; basic training, Ft. Warren, WY; further training in Camp Butler, NC. Theater of Operations: Asiatic-Pacific. WOUNDED IN ACTION, Saipan, 1945. Fought in campaigns in Oahu, New Hebrides, Eniwetok, Saipan, Okinawa, Japan. Decorations: Asiatic-Pacific Campaign Theater Ribbon w/BSS, Infantry Combat Badge, Purple Heart. Rank: Sgt. Honorable discharge, 1945. Deceased.

Kopecky, Frank, served in U.S. Armed Forces during WWI, 1917–1918. Member of SPJST Lodge 20, Granger, TX.

Kopecky, Ivan Vincent, Sr., son of Vincent and Angela Skripka Kopecky, was born on Apr. 10, 1924, at Galveston, TX. Attended 1½ years at St. Edward's University, Austin, TX. Entered the service at Fort Sam Houston, San Antonio, TX, and served with the USAF in the European Theater of Operations. Fought in Europe, Africa, and the Middle East. Medals: European-African-Middle Eastern Campaign Medal with four BSS, Good Conduct Medal, Air Medal with three Oak Leaf Clusters, and the WWII Victory Medal. Discharged Oct. 7, 1945. Home of record: Texas City, TX.

Kopecky, Joe, served in U.S. Armed Forces during WWI, 1917–1918. Member of SPJST Lodge 20, Granger, TX.

Kopecky, Vincent (Jim), son of Joseph and Katherine Spalek Kopecky, was born on Aug. 27, 1897, at West Point. Fayette Co., TX. Entered the service on Sept. 7, 1917, at Fort Sam Houston, San Antonio, TX. Received the Bronze Victory Button. Discharged Mar. 26, 1919, at Fort Travis, TX. Died Nov. 18, 1973.

Korenek, Allen John, son of Leo Martin and Annie E. Janish Korenek, was born on Mar. 6, 1930, at Nada, Colorado Co., TX. Attended Nada Parochial School and Garwood High School. Entered the service at Columbus, TX. Rank: Cpl. Served in Korea with the USMC. Died Nov. 11, 1953.

Korenek, Joseph Albert, son of Leo Martin and Annie Janish Korenek. Born June 6, 1933 at their home in Nada, TX. Attended St Mary's School in Nada, Garwood High School, and El Campo High School. Entered the service at La Grange. Rank: Pfc. Served in the Korean Conflict. Received the Sharpshooter Medal. Discharged June 7, 1956, at Ft. Stewart, GA. Home of record: Garwood, TX.

Korenek, William Joseph, Sr., son of Joe Paul and Tressie F. Adamik Korenek, was born July 17, 1906, Elm Mott, McLennan Co., TX. Attained eighth grade education at Elk, TX. Self-educated through reading and study. Inducted into USMC, Feb. 28, 1944, Dallas, TX, during WWII. Basic training at Camp Pendleton, Oceanside, CA. Rank: Pvt. Battles: (HIA) WWII. Received Sharp Shooter Medal. Was a tank instructor during WWII at Camp Pendleton. Turned 38 in July of 1944; was discharged because of his age. Married Millie M. Houranek Sept. 15, 1934; two children: Rosemary Korenek Mynarcik and William Joseph "B.J." Korenek, Jr., four grandchildren, five great-grandchildren. Occupation: Union Carpenter. Member of Lodge 66 in Elm Mott, TX. Died Aug. 9, 1979; buried at St. Mary's Cemetery, West, TX. In December 1993, his wife Millie was 80 years of age, residing in Trent Rest Haven Nursing Home, Trent, TX. Submitted by daughter, Rosemary Korenek Mynarcik of Elm Mott, TX.

Kossa, Frank, son of John F. and Amalie Klecka Kossa, was born 1898, Ammannsville, TX. Was a runaway in 1914. An Army doctor added a few years to his age so he could enlist. Was transferred from his hometown of Schulenburg, TX, to Ft. Sam Houston in San Antonio, TX, where he drove vehicles in the motor transport division.

Worked with U.S. Bureau of Public Roads after WWI, and started a wholesale oil business in Jeffersonville, TX, while remaining in the U.S. Army Reserves. Worked as a field supervisor for public roads, building the first highway system at a time when there was nothing but dirt or gravel roads between Jeffersonville and Indianapolis. The materials to build the roads were from left-over WWI materials. Cars could travel at an unheard of 45 m.p.h. tops.

Ordered to Fort Knox at the outset of WWII, and assigned to the Army's petroleum bases in China, Burma and India. Supervised fueling planes. Director of Selective Service in 1948. Went to Washington, D.C. in 1957, to become Executive Director of the National Selective Service System under Gen. Lewis Hershey.

In WWI the military did not have modern equipment—a soldier was equipped with a gun—and there were few tanks. In WWII the armed forces were better equipped. In the Korean War it was hard to get supplies, but were able to fly them in after an airfield was built. Soldiers who didn't have good hospital facilities were transported by plane to other facilities. Had our own airfields and plenty of ammunition in the Viet Nam War, but it was a political war. You can't win wars with politics. You have to let the military win it, not the people sitting in the White House!

Retired as Col. in 1974, the only living veteran of four major American wars, having served 60 years in the military.

Chosen by Jeffersonville Mayor Richard Vissing to organize Clark County Civil Defense System in 1987. Married Grace Lindley who predeceased him. Married Jean Kossa in 1980. Home of record in 1987: Jeffersonville, TX.

Kostecka, Robert, was born June 6, 1930. Served as Cpl. in the USMC during Korean Conflict. Died Apr. 3, 1993; buried in St. Mary's Cemetery, West, TX.

Kostohryz, John J., was born July 2, 1899. Served in U.S. Army Corps, WWI, as a Pvt. Died Apr. 25, 1968; buried in St. Mary's Cemetery, West, TX.

Kosut, John Marial, was born Feb. 26,1921, in Houston, TX. Attained degree in engineering. Inducted into the U.S. Army Corps, June 1944. Sailed from Boston, MA, on the HMS *Aquitinia* to Glasgow, Dec. 22, 1944. Duty at Givet, France, Ft. Charlemont. Joined the 28th Div. Inf. at Fumay, France. WOUNDED IN ACTION Jan. 31, 1945, Obrey, France. Returned Mar. 27, 1945, on Hospital Ship *Acadia*. Medals: Purple Heart, Combat Infantry Badge, Bronze Star and Rhine-Danube Medal. Honorable discharge Oct. 7, 1947. Married Mary in El Paso, TX; four sons. Home of record: Katy, TX.

Kotrla, Edwin D., son of Joe and Albina Kovarek Kotrla, was born June 19, 1926, in Jonah, TX. Educated through the tenth grade. Enlisted at Ft. Sam Houston, TX, Feb. 1, 1945. Theater of Operations: Asiatic-Pacific. Medals: Asiatic-Pacific Campaign Ribbon, Good Conduct Medal, WWII Victory Ribbon, two overseas service bars. Witnessed a tidal wave on Oau Island. Honorably discharged Aug. 28, 1946. Married Mary Ann Faltesek; two sons. Home of record: Georgetown, TX.

Kott, Alfonse J., son of Frank J. and Frances M. Polach Kott, was born July 13, 1921, Theon, Williamson Co., TX. Education: Holy Trinity School, Corn Hill, TX, through sixth grade. Enlisted about 1941/2 in U.S. Army Corps, TX; basic training, Arkansas. Assigned to Infantry. Served on front line for almost one year in various locations. WOUNDED IN ACTION, WWII. Medals: EAME Campaign w/BSS, Purple Heart, WWII Victory Medal. Honorably discharged 1944. Civilian occupation: ginner and carpenter. Retired 1983. Hobby: Gardening. Home of record: Jarrell, TX.

Kott, Frank J., son of Martin and Agnes Chasak Kott, was born Oct. 8, 1891, in TX. Enlisted in U.S. Army Corps, WWI, honorably discharged.

Civilian occupation: ginner and carpenter. Married Frances M. Polach; two children: Alfonse J. and Emil William Kott. Died Sept. 1, 1964. Buried Corn Hill, Williamson Co., TX.

Kott, Joe, son of Martin and Agnes Chasak Kott, born about 1893, of Corn Hill, Williamson Co., TX. Enlisted in U.S. Army Corps, WWI, with American Expeditionary Forces. First Czech from Williamson Co., TX, to be KILLED IN ACTION. Killed in France about 1918(?). Submitted by Eileen Rosipal, Austin, TX.

Koudelka, Tony J., son of Antone F. and Barbara Ann Koudelka, was born Jan. 29, 1919, West, TX. Enlisted Feb. 3, 1942, Waco, McLennan Co., TX, during WWII. Theater of Operations: EAME. Battles: Ardennes; Rhineland; Central Europe; GO 33 WD 45. Medals: American Theater Campaign Medal, EAME Campaign Medal 2/3 BSS, Good Conduct Medal, WWII Victory Medal. Attained rank of Sgt. Honorably discharged Dec. 11, 1945. Retired from Waco *News Tribune*. Home of record: Waco, TX.

Kousal, Frank Richard, son of Mr. and Mrs. F. Kousal, was born Apr. 20, 1923, Waco, TX. Entered U.S. Army during WWII, assigned to 78th Div. Served in England, France, Belgium, Germany, Rhineland and Central Europe. Medals: A.T.O., ETO w/3 BSS, two overseas service bars, Expert Combat Badge, GCM and Victory Medal. Discharged Nov. 9, 1945 with rank of T/5.

Koutny, James "Jim," son of Joe Koutny and Albina Matejicek, was born Nov. 27, 1946. Education: Victoria High School; Victoria Jr. College; Weaver Airline School, TX. Enlisted U.S. Army Corps, Victoria, TX, Oct. 18, 1966. Attained rank of E-5. At Ft. Polk, LA, received Basic Training, Advanced Training, Special Training (Tigerland), and Armorer Training. At Ft. Bliss, TX, received Missile Training, Armorer and Supply Training, Quartermaster Training. Assigned to 36th Transportation Battalion (Infantry Support) in Viet Nam War, Mar. 1967–Mar. 1968. Medals: National Defense Service Medal, Viet Nam Service Medal w/4 BSS, Republic of Viet Nam Campaign Medal w/device, Good Conduct Medal, Marksman Rifle M-14, M-16 Badge. Honorable discharge Oct. 17, 1968. Hobbies: reading, painting, gardening, antique collecting. Married Louise Cooper, June 20, 1970; three children, daughter Karen Koutny Miller and son-in-law, Terry Miller; son Mark J. Koutny; son Jason P. Koutny. Civilian occupation: Central Power and Light (electric utility–16 years of service), Corpus Christi, TX. Past Boy Scout Leader, Member of VFW, Trinity Lutheran Church, Corpus Christi, TX.

Koval, Edwin, served in European Theater of Operations, as a S/Sgt. KILLED IN ACTION, England, during WWII.

Kovar, Francis Joseph, son of John D. and Frances Kovar, was born Jan. 29, 1909, Plum, TX. Education: State Teachers College, Huntsville, TX. Enlisted during WWII at Huntsville, TX, assigned to ETO, fought in the invasion of Italy and Salerno. Medals: Infantry Badge, BSS, Good Conduct Medal. Discharged Sept. 13, 1945 and again, Jan. 31, 1969. Home of record, Ft. Worth, TX.

Kovar, Gilbert Joe, son of Mr. and Mrs. John Kovar, Granger, TX, was born Aug. 27, 1917. Attended Granger School. Enlisted U.S. Army Corps, 1945, basic training, Ft. Lewis, WA. Pfc. Theater of Operations: Asiatic-Pacific. Medals: Asiatic-Pacific Theater Campaign Medal, Japan Occupation Medal, WWII Victory Medal. Served in Japan. Rank of Pvt. when honorably discharged. Died May 4, 1960; buried Holy Cross Catholic Cemetery, Granger TX.

Kovar, Jerome J., son of John P. and Matilda Kovar, was born Nov. 24, 1923, at Fayetteville, TX. Attended Fayetteville High School. Enlisted June 30, 1943, at San Antonio, TX. Served on six different ships in the South Central Pacific, in invasion of Saidan, Tinian, Iwo Jima and Okinawa. Attained the rank of

Coxswain. Medals: Pacific Theater of Operations, Saidan, Tinain, Iwo Jima, Okinawa, with three Battle Stars, Good Conduct Medal, Victory Medal. Discharged Mar. 4, 1946, at Galveston, TX. Home of record: New Ulm, TX.

Kovar, Joe K., son of Joe M. and Agnes Lazek Kovar, was born Mar. 18, 1915, Milam Co., TX. Enlisted in U.S. Army Corps, Apr. 21, 1941, San Antonio, TX. Served in Alaska and Attu Island. Attained rank of Tech Sgt. Honorably discharged Mar. 30, 1946. Married Milady Gelner; two children: Sandra and Jo Ann. Occupation: self employed as auto mechanic and gunsmith at Kovar Auto Service and Gun Repair. Home of record: Cameron, TX.

Kovar, John L., son of Mr. and Mrs. Anton T. Kovar, Taylor, TX. Attended schools in Williamson Co., TX. Enlisted U.S. Army Corps, 1941; basic training at Ft. Monmouth, NJ; further training, Claiborne, LA. Theater of Operations: American; Asiatic-Pacific. Served in Hawaii and Marianas. Medals: American Defense Medal, Asiatic-Pacific Theater Campaign w/1 BSS, Overseas Bars, Good Conduct Medal, WWII Victory Medal. Attained rank of T/5 when honorably discharged, 1945.

Kovar, Joseph J., was born Apr. 25, 1893, served in WWI, U.S. Army Corps. Married Feb. 18, 1919, Sophia S. Baca (born May 27, 1898, died Oct. 20, 1979), one child given: Edwin Kovar, possibly more? Died Mar. 10, 1977. Buried at St Mary's Catholic Cemetery, Frydek, Austin Co., TX.

Kovar, Kleofos Elios, son of John D. and Frances Kovar, enlisted during WWII, in the U.S. Army. Assigned to ETO. KILLED IN ACTION, Battle of the Bulge. Submitted in loving memory of his brother by Francis Joseph Kovar of Ft. Worth, TX.

Kovar, Raymond E., son of Mr. and Mrs. John Kovar, Granger, TX. Attended Granger High School. Enlisted U.S. Army Corps, 1941; basic training, Camp Roberts, CA; further training: Ft. Ord, CA; MO; NC. Theaters of Operation: European, Asiatic-Pacific. Campaigns: France, Belgium, Holland, Czechoslovakia, Marshalls, Philippines, Japan. Medals: ETO Campaign Ribbon w/2 BSS, American Defense Medal, Asiatic-Pacific Theater Campaign Ribbon, Pre-Pearl Harbor Ribbon, WWII Victory Medal, Good Conduct Medal. Attained rank of S/Sgt. prior to honorable discharge, 1946. Hometown: Little River, Williamson Co., TX.

Kovar, Willie E., son of Adolph and Rosie Kovar, was born Dec. 19, 1919, Ellinger, TX. Education: Completed eighth grade. Enlisted in U.S. Army Corps, Ft. Sam Houston, San Antonio, TX, Apr. 15, 1942. Theater of Operations: Pacific. Battles: Luzon. Decorations: American Defense Ribbon, Asiatic Pacific Theater Ribbon, Philippine Liberation Ribbon, Purple Heart, Silver Star Medal, WWII Victory Ribbon, GCM. WOUNDED IN ACTION by grenade on Apr. 25, 1945, at Battle of Luzon. Separation: Nov. 20, 1945, Ft. Bliss, El Paso, TX. Honorable discharge Nov. 19, 1948. Home of record: Ellinger, TX.

Kozuch, Felix Frank, Jr., son of Felix Frank Kozuch, Sr. and Agnes Spaniel Vrana Kozuch, was born Jan. 16, 1917, Wallis, Austin Co., TX, Education: Guardian Angel School, Wallis, TX, graduation, May 1934. Enlisted 1942 during WWII at Dodd Field, San Antonio, TX in U.S. Army Air Corps. Attained the rank of Tech. 5. Theater of Operations: EAME, England, France. Sent to France as Paratrooper. Served in Medical Corps, First Auxiliary Surgical Group; fought in Normandy Invasion, Battle of the Bulge. KILLED IN ACTION, Battle of the Bulge, Jan. 8, 1945. Interred in Ardennes American Cemetery and Memorial, Neuville-En-Condroz, Belgium, Plot B, Row 38, Grave 54. Received Purple Heart. Survived by his wife, Elizabeth "Betty" Nemec Kozuch (now deceased), whom he married in 1941, of Granger, TX, and three sisters, all of Houston, TX: Mrs. B. J. Arneaux, Tampa, FL, Mrs. E. T. Palmer, Houston, TX, and the submitter of this information, his sister, Sr. Julianna Kozuch at Our Lady of the Lake University, San Antonio, TX. Submitted lovingly in memory of our brother who gave his life, like so many others, that we can be free!

Kraitchar, Hubert Thomas, son of Thomas and Mary Kocurek Kraitchar, was born Jan. 17, 1895, in Caldwell, TX. Graduate of Caldwell, TX, High School. Enlisted in the U.S. Army on July 30, 1917, during WWI, at San Antonio, TX. Served with the American Expeditionary Forces in France as a member of Company F, 52nd Infantry, 6th Division. Rank: Cpl. Fought in the Geridemer Sector and Vosges Mountains and served in France from July 15, 1918 to June 12, 1919. Discharged from service at Camp Bowie, TX, on June 25, 1919. Died in Port Arthur, TX, on Jan. 29, 1982, at the age of 87. Birthplace and family home is now a museum in Caldwell, TX. (It should also be noted that "Kraitchar" is the American spelling of the Czech name "Krajca" and this family is the only one in TX, and perhaps the U.S., that uses the American spelling.)

Krajca, Frank Joe, son of Frank and Anna Krajca, was born Oct. 22, 1914, Yoakum, TX. Education: La Parita School, Jourdanton, TX. Enlisted in U.S. Army Corps, 1940, San Antonio, Bexar Co., TX. Theaters of Operation: America and EAME. Initially assigned to horse calvary; reassigned to Air Force in Tallahassee, FL, for approx. one year. Received training as munitions specialist. Tour of duty included Corsica and Salerno, Italy. Loaded ammunition and bombs on warplanes for bombing runs. Returned to Ft. Sam Houston, TX, end of WWII, 1945, received honorable discharge. Medals: American Theater of Operations Campaign Medal, EAME Campaign Medal, WWII Victory Medal. Married; one daughter: JoNell Krajca Heine, two granddaughters. Hobby: avid flea market enthusiast for past 25 years.

Krajca, Jerry John, son of Frank and Anna Krajca, was born Jan. 4, 1917, Yoakum, TX. Education: La Parita School, Jourdanton, TX. Enlisted in U.S. Army Corps, May 31, 1939, Ft. Sam Houston, TX. Theater of Operations: American. During WWII was assigned to famous Indian Head Division–Field Artillery, but injured knee on maneuvers at Camp Bullis. Placed on limited duty and assigned guard duty at German P.O.W. Camp at Brownwood, TX, and Italian P.O.W. Camp at Hereford, TX. Medals: American Theater of Operations Campaign Medal, American Defense Medal, Good Conduct Medal, Expert Carbine Badge, and WWII Victory Medal. Honorably discharged Nov. 11, 1945, Ft. Bliss, TX. Married Marie M.; four children: Marilyn Krajca Macklin; Dorothy Krajca Sims; William R. Krajca, and Jerry L. Krajca. Civilian occupation: tavern operator, service station operator, used car salesman. Died Jan. 12, 1969, San Antonio, TX.

Krajca, William Raymond, son of Jerry J. and Marie M. Krajca, was born Jan. 7, 1950, North Pleasanton, TX. Education: San Jose Mission, Harlandale High School, San Antonio, TX, S.W. Texas State College, San Marcos, TX. Enlisted in U.S. Air Force, Dec. 13, 1967, Lackland AFB, San Antonio, TX. Theater of Operations: American. Attended Electronics School, Keesler AFB, MS. Assigned to Heavy Ground Radar; stationed at Baron AFB, CA; Kotzebue AFS, AL; Calumet AFS, MI. Honorably discharged Dec. 12, 1971. Died July 8, 1992, San Antonio, Bexar Co., TX.

Kral, Alfons B., son of Mr. and Mrs. Frank Kral, entered U.S. Army Corps, 1945. Served in Korean Conflict as a Pfc.

Kramolis, Ramon F., son of Mr. and Mrs. Mike Kramolis, West, TX. Entered A.A.C., 1943. Served in Italy. Awarded ET with seven Battle Stars and Victory Ribbons. Discharged 1945 with rank of T/5. Died Aug. 9, 1988; buried in St. Mary's Cemetery, West, TX.

Kramolis, Walter R., son of Mr. and Mrs. Mike Kramolis, West, TX. Entered U.S. Army Corps, 1940. Served ET, 36th Div. Awarded EAME w/5 BSS and Med. Badge. Discharged 1945.

Krasucky, Joe V., Jr., son of Joe and Sophie Krasucky, was born on Sept. 26, 1948 at El Campo, TX. Graduated from Louise High School. Entered the service in Houston, TX, and received basic training at Fort Bliss, El Paso, TX, 1969. Served in Viet Nam with Co. C, 46th Eng. Battalion from May 1970 through Apr. 1971. Received Army Commendation Medal. Discharged Apr. 1, 1975. Home of record: Louise, TX.

Krauskopf, Emil, son of Jacob and Tereza Klekar Krauskopf, was born July 3, 1888, in Moravia, TX. Inducted into the Army Sept. 19, 1917. Rank: Pvt., Sqd. "A" Co. 327 Inf. Fought in WWI in 1918 with the A.E.F. at Toul, Marbachr, St. Michiel, and Meuse-Argonne. Received the Purple Heart. Discharged May 29, 1919. Died Jan. 19, 1977; buried at White Cemetery, Highlands, TX.

Krauskopf, Joe J., son of Emil and Mary Prasek Krauskopf, was born Mar. 15, 1920, in Deweyville, TX. Inducted into the Army Oct. 10, 1941. Rank: Tech 4, Bty. D97, Anti-Aircraft Artillery, Gun Bat. Received American Defense, Asiatic Pacific and Good Conduct Medals. Discharged Oct. 17, 1945 at Fort Bliss, TX. Home of record: Crosby, TX.

Krauskopf, Julius, son of Emil and Mary Prasek Krauskopf, was born Sept. 20, 1922 in Runge, TX. Inducted into the Army Nov. 10, 1942. Rank: Cpl., 3rd Army 99th Chemical Mortar Battalion. Theater of Operation: Central Europe. Fought in the battles at Rhineland and Rome-Arno. Received three BSS, Distinguished Unit and Good Conduct Medals. Discharged Nov. 15, 1945. Home of record: Harlingen, TX.

Krejci, Emil Archie, son of Emil Victor and Julia Helen Ermis Krejci, was born Oct. 2. 1930, Moulton, TX. Education: Dickson School, Moulton, TX, Sam and Will Moore Institute, Moulton, TX. Went into U.S. Navy about Sept. 1947, Houston, TX. Rank: Chief Petty Officer, Naval career man. Theater of Operations: Europe and Far East. Medals: National Defense Service Medal w/1 BSS, Armed Forces Expeditionary Medal, Korean Service Medal, Sixth Good Conduct Medal Award. Retired from the United States Navy Sept. 15, 1967. Home of record: San Diego, CA.

Krejci, Emil J., son of Emil and Anna Brandesky Krejci, was born Feb. 27, 1927, Corpus Christi, Nueces Co., TX. Education: Corpus Christi High School. Enlisted U.S. Army Corps, Apr. 30, 1945, Ft. Sam Houston, San Antonio, TX. Assigned to Asiatic-Pacific Theater of Operation, 382 Station Hospital. Medals: WWII Victory Medal, Asiatic Pacific Occupation Medal. Honorably discharged Nov. 2, 1946. Died July 30, 1990. Submitted by Erwin E. Krejci, Corpus Christi, TX.

Krejci, Erwin E., son of Emil and Anna Brandesky Krejci, was born Nov. 4, 1924, Corpus Christi, Nueces Co., TX. Graduate of Corpus Christi High School. Inducted into the U.S. Army Corps, Nov. 13, 1943, Ft. Sam Houston, San Antonio, TX. Basic training, Camp Blanding, FL. Assigned to European Theater of Operations, Co. G, 315th Infantry Regiment, 79th Div. Fought in Battles of Normandy, Northern France, Rhineland, Central Europe. Medals: EAME Campaign Medal W/4 BSS, WWII Victory Medal, GCM, Distinguished Unit Badge, Combat Infantryman Badge. In June 1945, Division was to move to Czechoslovakia, and the Sudetenland. 315th Regiment located at Marienead and the surrounding area. Regiment was involved in a parade in Pilsen, marking the return of President Benes to Czechoslovakia. Regiment received Croix De Guerre from French Government, Jan. 1949. Honorable discharge Feb. 8, 1946. Home of record: Corpus Christi, TX.

Krejci, Joseph J., son of Thomas and Catherine Bayer Krejci, was born Jan. 12, 1896, Shiner, TX. Education: Sunset, Lavaca Co., TX, Country School. Enlisted during WWI, Lavaca Co., TX. Assigned to ETO, with American Expeditionary Forces. Fought in Argonne Forest and St. Michiel. WOUNDED IN ACTION, hit by shrapnel in the right cheek at the jawbone in Nov. 1918. Some teeth were knocked out. Was in hospital in France the day the war ended, Nov. 11, 1918. Received Purple Heart, WWI Victory Medal. Honorably discharged 1919. Died Aug. 15, 1936. Submitted by Herman Bohuslav, Corpus Christi, TX.

Krejci, Victor Louis, son of Joe J. and Emily Krejci, was born Aug. 5, 1923, Moulton, TX. Earned B.S. from University of Texas in Austin, TX, Master of Education from S.W.T.S.U., San Marcos, TX, Post Graduate, Howard Payne University, Brownwood, TX. Enlisted in U.S. Navy, Houston, TX. Rank: Seaman 3/C. Assigned to North Pacific and

South Pacific Theater of Operations, WWII. Honorably discharged Nov. 10, 1945, Camp Wallace, TX. Home of record: Buda, TX. Submitted by Herman Bohuslav, Corpus Christi, TX.

Krenek, Charles, son of Charles Krenek and Mary Adamcik Krenek, was born Jan. 28, 1895, Colorado Co., TX. Educated through eighth grade. Enlisted Ft. Sam Houston, San Antonio, TX, Aug. 29, 1918, in U.S. Army Air Corps. Stationed at Kelly Field, San Antonio, TX. Honorably discharged Jan. 17, 1919, Ft. Sam Houston, TX. Married Emilia Peter (widow of Louis Vrana, one son, George Vrana to this union), Oct. 29, 1917, El Campo, TX. Five children: George (adopted by Charles), Jerome (died at age 5, diphtheria), Lorene, Margaret, Eugene, and Bernice. Died Nov. 6, 1979, at age of 84, in El Campo, TX, where Charles and Emilia had lived all their married life on a farm. Submitted by George L. Krenek of Wharton, TX.

Krenek, Frantisek, enlisted in the Confederate Army, Apr. 26, 1862, LaGrange, TX, by Lt. Welhausen. Became a Pvt. in Capt. Creuzbaur's Co. Texas Artillery. Among his tasks seems to have been herding horses according to his Company Muster Roll. Appeared on his final Muster Roll, April 1865.

Krenek, Henry, son of Joe M. and Marie Simek Krenek, was born Jan. 9, 1897, Ellinger, TX. Education: Ellinger School. In 1914, President Wilson ordered the U.S. Marines to take Veracruz in Mexico. The occupation of the Port continued for several months. War was averted only by mediation offered by the so-called ABC powers: Argentina, Brazil and Chile. Fighting continued until 1917. It was during this time that Henry Krenek served along the Mexican Border as a guard with the Border Patrol for about nine months. He saw many Mexicans shot and was appalled by the bloodshed. It is unknown whether he was discharged. Married Alma Fritsch. They raised one child: Nora Dell Fritsch. Henry died Jan. 17, 1969; buried at Live Oak Hill, near Ellinger, TX. Submitted by Liz McKinzie of Fayetteville, TX.

Krenek, Isadore L., son of Joseph and Josephine Maruna Krenek, was born May 6, 1915, Chriesman, TX. Enlisted in the U.S. Army Corps during WWII, Oct. 11, 1942. Attained rank of Pfc. Served in the EAME Theater of Operations. Assigned to Medical First Aid. Served as Quartermaster, 3113 Signal Corp Postal Clerk, 3160 Signal Corp Cable Patrol, 341 General Service Engineer Regiment. Received two BSS and a Good Conduct Medal. Honorably discharged Dec. 31, 1945. Married Lydia Shupak, Nov. 4, 1941, at Caldwell, TX; two children: Bernice and Stanley. Home of Record: College Station, TX. Submitted by Marie Neuman Gottfried of Brookshire, TX.

Krenek, Isidor, Sr., son of Frank and Annie Tomek Krenek, was born Apr. 24, 1894, Waller, TX. Education: Lone Pine. Enlisted in U.S. Army Corps, May 26, 1918, during WWI, Houston, Harris Co., TX. Attained rank of Pvt., Co. B, 64th Inf. Theater of Operations: France. Battles: Verdun, Front, No Man's Land (Muse). Left USA, 1918, returned Mar. 4, 1919. Was gassed and spent time in hospital during WWI. Honorably discharged Apr. 25, 1919. Married Mary Steffek. Died Sept. 23, 1975; buried Center Hill Cemetery, Lovelady, TX.

Krenek, Isidor, Jr., son of Isidor Krenek, Sr. and Mary Steffek Krenek, was born June 13, 1929, Houston Co., TX. Education: High School, Lovelady, TX. Enlisted in Lufkin, TX, Oct. 15, 1948. Theater of Operations: Far East. Medals: Korean Service Medal, Good Conduct Medal, United Nations Service Medal. Served two years overseas. Honorably discharged Aug. 12, 1952. Attained rank of Staff Sgt. Home of record: Lovelady, TX.

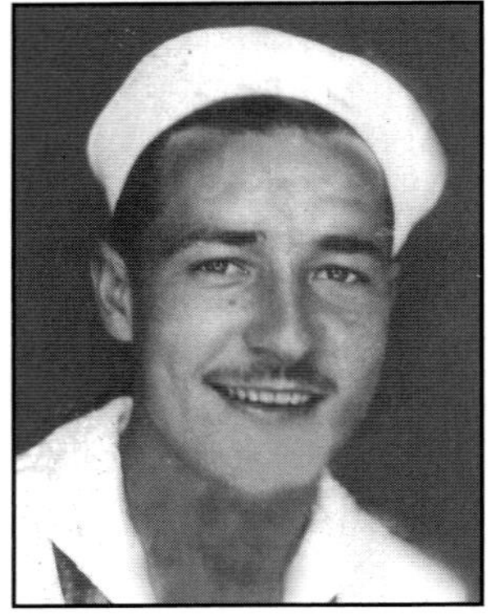

Krenek, James Brisco, son of Edward Isaac and Dora Mae Green Krenek, was born July 31, 1918, Lovelady, TX. Education: Kilgore, TX, High School. Enlisted in U.S. Navy, Feb. 13, 1942, Dallas, TX, during WWII. Attained rank of Y/3C. Theater of Operation: Combat activity 14th Naval Dist.; U.S. N.H. Peace Harbor. Honorable discharge, Feb. 19, 1943, San Diego, CA. Home of record: Crockett, TX.

Krenek, Jeff Charles, Sr., son of Isidor Krenek, Sr. and Mary Stefek Krenek, was born Sept. 27, 1926, Lovelady, TX. Education: Pearson Chapel, Lone Pine, Lovelady TX, through twelfth grade. Enlisted in U.S. Army Corps during WWII, Ft. Sam Houston, TX. Theater of Operation: European (Germany). Guarded prisoners of war for seven months, then served with 203rd AAA AW Bn driving a half-ton vehicle delivering official messages to other batteries. Honorably discharged Nov. 2, 1946, Ft. Sam Houston, TX. Medals: WWII Victory Ribbon, German Army of Occupation Medal. Married Cecilia Janak. Home of record: Crockett, TX.

Krenek, Jeff Charles, Jr., son of Jeff Charles Krenek, Sr. and Cecilia Janak Krenek, was born Apr. 8, 1942, Crockett, TX. Education: Lovelady High School; TSTI Waco, one year. Enlisted in U.S. Armed Forces, Oct. 25, 1972, Houston, TX. Support and Transportation Division. Medals: Marksmanship and several letters of outstanding performance. Served 18 months in Frankfurt, Germany, Co. B, 503rd S and T Bn. Honorably discharged Oct. 21, 1974, Ft. Jackson, SC. Home of record: Crockett, TX.

Krenek, Joe A., son of Joe and Josephine Maruna Krenek, was born Aug. 13, 1923, near Caldwell, TX. Enlisted at Fort Sam Houston, TX, on Jan. 28, 1943, and was a Cpl. in Battery C, 404th Field Artillery, 86th Division Blackhawk. Fought in Europe from Cologne, Germany to Austria. Was in the Battle of the Ruhr. While in Europe, was shot in the chest, but survived because bullet hit dog tag. After the war in Europe, sent to the South Pacific for cleanup and was also in the Philippines. Discharged Mar. 31, 1946. Medals: American Theater Medal, Purple Heart, European Campaign Medal with one BSS, Asiatic-Pacific Campaign Medal, Good Conduct Medal, and WWII Victory Medal. Married Henrietta Bobalik on Aug. 28, 1948, at Caldwell, TX; three children: Sally Laine Krenek Smith, Carla Jo Krenek, and Roger Alan Krenek. Resides in Pasadena, TX

Krenek, Joe A., Jr., son of Joe A. Krenek, Sr. and Sophie Mecha Krenek, was born Dec. 23, 1922, in Hungerford, TX. Entered the service Jan. 14, 1945, trained at Fort Sill, OK. Served in Japan and Philippines as a cook in the 13th Field Battalion. Discharged Nov. 19, 1946, at Fort Sam Houston, TX. Rank: Tech 4. Medals: Asiatic-Pacific Theater Ribbon, Philippines Liberation Campaign Ribbon, Army Occupation Medal (Japan), Japan Victory Ribbon with two Overseas Service Bars. Married Betty Janik; four children: Donnie Krenek, Ronnie Krenek, Bonnie Krenek Kocian, and Lonnie Krenek. Employed by Gulf Sulfur Company. Retired as shift foreman on July 7, 1984. Died Mar. 11, 1986, and is buried in St. John's Catholic Cemetery, Hungerford, TX. The family home of record: Wharton, TX.

Krenek, Joseph John, son of Joe M. and Marie Simek Krenek, was born Sept. 1, 1894, Ellinger, TX. Education: Ellinger School. Thought to have enlisted in U.S. Army Corps, Apr. or May of 1918. Pvt. w/Co B 56th, Engineers, WWI. A letter he wrote to a cousin is dated May 1918, while on a ship headed for France. WOUNDED IN ACTION, June 15, 1918. Stayed in a hospital in Paris, France, for 10 days. Died on June 25, 1918. Also had tuberculosis and spinal meningitis. Military funeral and was buried near Paris in a military cemetery. After the war, body brought home, buried in Live Oak Hill Cemetery at St. Mary's Catholic Church near Ellinger, TX. Family worked for one year to buy the tombstone that marks his grave. Today, it still stands as one of the tallest in the cemetery. Joseph Krenek never married. Submitted by Liz McKinzie of Fayetteville, TX.

Krenek, Troy, son of Adolph Joe and Lottie Knox Krenek, was born June 19, 1925, Houston Co., TX. Education: Lovelady High School; B.S., Sam Houston State; M.S., University of Houston. Enlisted in U.S. Navy during WWII, Houston Co., TX. Battles: WWII. Attained rank of Seaman First Class. Honorably discharged Dec. 20, 1945, Camp Wallace, TX. Taught school 36 years. Lifetime Member and Honorary Director of Houston Livestock Show and Rodeo. Home of record: Garwood, TX. Submitted by Anne C. Green, Houston, TX.

Krenek, Wilbur Joe, son of Ludwig Edward and Wima Sralla Krenek, was born Jan. 18, 1929, Crosby, TX. Education: Crosby Elementary and High School. Drafted by Selective Service, Houston, TX. Theater of Operations, Korea. Attained rank of Sgt. Honorably discharged Nov. 25, 1952. Married Edith Barker; one son: Richard Steven. Home of Record: Lake Jackson, TX.

Kresta, Anton, Jr., was born July 25, 1923, son of Anton Kresta, Sr. and Agnes Havel Kresta. Spent youth in the Komensky, TX, community. Enlisted March 1943 and completed basic training at Camp Wolters, Wichita Falls, TX. Overseas duty began in Dec. 1944 with the 145th Infantry Division Co. F. KILLED IN ACTION on Feb. 12, 1945, in Manila, Philippines.

Krhovjak, George J., son of Mr. and Mrs. Isidor Krhovjak, Taylor, TX. Graduate of St. Mary's Catholic High School. Enlisted U.S. Army Corps, 1944; basic training, Camp Hood, TX. Theater of Operations: Asiatic-Pacific. Medals: Purple Heart, Infantry Combat Badge, Asiatic-Pacific Theater Campaign Ribbon. Campaigns: Hawaii, Marianas, Okinawa. KILLED IN ACTION, May 1945, Okinawa.

Kriska, Bernard H., son of Joe and Mary Kubin Kriska, was born Jan. 4, 1927, in Ennis, TX. Attended St. John's School in Ennis, and Crozier Tech in Dallas, TX. Enlisted in the U.S. Army at Dallas, TX, during WWII. Served in the Asiatic-Pacific Theater of Operations. Decorations include the Asiatic-Pacific Campaign Medal, Good Conduct Medal, WWII Victory Medal, and the Philippine Independence Ribbon. Discharged at Camp Beale, CA, on Dec. 19, 1946. Home of record: Dallas, TX.

Kristynik, Bernard J., son of Josef and Martha Filip Kristynik, was born Sept. 6, 1928, Praha, TX. Seventh grade education. Enlisted La Grange, Fayette Co., TX, Oct. 7, 1952. Fought in Korean Conflict. Medals: Purple Heart, two BSS, United Nations Service Medal, National Defense Service Medal. WOUNDED IN ACTION. Honorably discharged July 16, 1954. Home of record: Garwood, TX.

Krivanek, Kenneth John, son of Victor John and Eva Cecilia Farney Krivanek, was born on Oct. 24, 1935, at Oklahoma City, OK. Attended Mustang High School, Central State College, East State University, and North State University. Called to active duty on Oct. 15, 1961, at Terrell, and served with the 49th Arm. Division at Fort Polk. Discharged Aug. 9, 1962, at Terrell, TX. Industrial Arts Teacher. Held offices in SPJST Lodge No. 92 and Lodge No. 180. Served as treasurer for the KJT Society No. 54, and as a Sales Representative for RVOS No. 144. Home of record: Fort Worth, TX.

Krizan, Billy Frank, was born Aug. 15, 1927. Served in U.S. Army Corps, WWII, as a Pvt. Died Oct. 25, 1991; buried in Bold Springs Cemetery, West, TX.

Krizan, A. Fred, West, TX, WWII veteran, KILLED IN ACTION.

Krizan, Fred A., served in the U.S. Armed Forces during WWII. WOUNDED IN ACTION, Italy, 1944. Served in Italy and France, N. Africa, Infantry, Third Division, rank S/Sgt. Received Purple Heart.

Krizan, Hermangel, served in the Regular Army, discharged 1955 as a Pvt. 2/C.

Krizan, Rudolf Robert, West, TX. Entered AAC, 1942. Served as a Sgt. in USA. Awarded AD and AT Ribbons. Discharged 1946.

Krnavek, Leroy G., son of Mr. and Mrs. Krnavek, born about 1923/4, in Nueces Co., TX. Enlisted U.S. Army Corps in TX, during WWII, and was assigned to European Theater of Operation. Received an honorable discharge. Died in the past few years. Submitted by Erwin E. Krejci, Corpus Christi, TX.

Krompota, George, Granger, TX, WWII veteran.

Kroschewsky, Julius R., son of Mr. and Mrs. Julius A. Kroschewsky, Taylor, TX. Education: University of Texas. Enlisted U.S. Army Air Corps, 1943; basic training, San Marcos, TX. Further training El Paso, TX. Theater of Operations: European. WOUNDED IN ACTION, 1945, Italy. Medals: ETO Campaign Ribbon w/4 BSS, Purple Heart, Air Medal w/2 OLC, Distinguished Flying Cross. Achieved rank of 1st Lt. prior to honorable discharge, 1945.

Kroulik, Alfred Raymond, Jr., son of Alfred Raymond Kroulik Sr. and Mildred McCoy Kroulik, was born May 8, 1948, Houston, Harris Co., TX. Education: Bachelor of Science, Stephen F. Austin State University, Nacogdoches, TX. Received commission as 2nd Lt. in the U.S. Army Corps, Aug. 19, 1972. Assigned to the Armor Branch. American Theater of Operations. Medals and Honors: Army Com. Medal, Army Reserve Achievement Medal, Armed Forces Reserve Medal, National Defense Service Medal, Order of Polonia Restituta 5th Class, Army Air Assault Badge. Honorable discharge Aug. 1982. Rank: Capt. Manager of automobile dealership in Houston, Harris Co., TX. Home of record: Houston, TX.

Kroulik, Alfred Raymond, Sr., son of Dr. John and Emily Lesikar Kroulik, was born Jan. 19, 1906, Austin Co., TX. Bachelor of Science, Texas A&M. Enlisted at Texas A&M College. Received commission during WWII. Attained rank of Lt. Col. in the U.S. Armed Forces. Theater of Operations: American. Medals: American Campaign Medal, and WWII Victory Medal. Retired from Reserves Feb. 1, 1966. Married Mildred McCoy; two children: Alfred Raymond Kroulik, Jr. and Karen Kroulik Bradbury. Died May 27, 1986. Information supplied by son, Capt. Alfred R. Kroulik, Jr. of Houston, TX.

Kroulik, John T., son of Dr. John and Emily Lesikar Kroulik, was born at Nelsonville, TX on May 20, 1910. B.A., M.A., and PhD degrees. Because of expertise in bacteriology, was commissioned on July 7, 1942 in the Sanitary Corps of the Army as a first Lt. Served as a bacteriologist in North Africa with the 4th Medical Laboratory for thirteen months. Served in Italy until the end of WWII with rank of Captain as a blood bank officer and as a bacteriologist with the 15th General Medical Laboratory. Took part in the Rome-Arno, Southern France, and North Apennines campaigns. Discharged Feb. 24, 1946. Remained in Reserves for a few years and was promoted to Major. Retired. Home of record: Houston, TX.

Krpec, Leo, son of Leopold and Agnes Orsak Krpec, was born July 19, 1918, Yoakum, Lavaca Co., TX. Education through eighth grade. Enlisted Nov. 1, 1939, Gonzales, Lavaca Co., TX, National Guard of Texas and the National Guard of the United States. Inducted into the U.S. Army Corp with Co. K 141st Infantry on Nov. 25, 1940. Military Occupational Specialty Chauffeur #345. Medals: EAME Campaign Ribbon w/4 BSS, American Defense Service Medal, GCM, Purple w/1 OLC, GO 49 Hq., 36th Div., Dec. 31, 1943, Distinguished Unit Badge. WOUNDED IN ACTION TWICE: Dec. 12, 1941, and Apr. 17, 1944. Served 1 year, 24 days in National Guard; served 2 years,

6 months, 1 day in Continental USA; overseas service, 2 years, 12 days. Honorable discharge from U.S. Army Corps on June 7, 1945, at Ft. Sam Houston, TX. Of Excellent Character Honorable Discharge from National Guard, July 6, 1945, Austin, TX. Civilian occupation: farmer, Shiner, TX, and Yoakum, TX. Died July 19, 1987. Submitted by John Sitka, Jr., of Rosharon, TX.

Krpec, Leon J., son of Michael and Vlasta Kahanek Krpec, was born May 15, 1938, El Campo, TX. High School education. Enlisted 1961, Houston, TX. Theater of Operations, U.S. and Korea. Served during peace time. Honorable discharge June 1963. Died May 18, 1993. Buried Hillje, TX.

Krumpock, Henry, Granger, TX, WWII veteran.

Krupa, Joe John, Jr., son of Joe John Krupa, Sr. and Lidie Mae Jurcak Krupa, was born Jan. 4, 1929, Caldwell, TX. Earned B.S., Mechanical Engineering, 1950, The University of Texas, Austin, TX. Received Commission as 1st Lt., 1950, U.S. Army Corps. Entered active service, Jan. 11, 1951, Houston, TX. Basic training, 28th Inf. Div., Camp Atterbury, IN. Theater of Operations: Far East Command. After graduation from OCS at Aberdeen Proving Ground, MD, assignment was to Tokyo Ordnance Depot in Japan. Medals: U.N. Service Medal, Korean Service Medal, National Defense Service Medal. Served during the "Korean Police action." Released from active duty on Oct. 24, 1953. Honorable discharge from U.S. Army Reserves Aug. 17, 1961. Civilian occupation: 31 years of employment with Moore Products Co. Retired in 1992. Married Alyce Brownlee in 1957; two children: son Dr. Joseph J. Krupa III, is an Oral and Maxillofacial Surgeon and Professor at the Medical College of Georgia, daughter Janet Krupa Jorrey lives in Garland, TX, with husband, Mark Jorrey, and three daughters. Home of record: Houston, TX.

Krupa, Joe John, Sr., son of Joseph Anton (immigrated to Texas in 1867 from Vsetin, Moravia at 18 years of age) and Frances Kocurek Krupa, was born Mar. 9, 1896, Dime Box, Lee, TX, in the area known as Hranice. Education: Tyler Commercial College, Tyler, TX. Enlisted in U.S. Army Corps, Apr. 28, 1918, Giddings, TX. Theater of Operations: American Expeditionary Forces, France. Assigned to Co. H, 360th Inf. Reg. "The Texas Brigade," 90th Div. Participated in Battle of St. Michiel (France) from Sept. 12, 1918, through Sept. 20, 1918. WOUNDED IN ACTION. Overseas service was in France from June 22, 1918, through Mar. 24, 1919. Honorably discharged Apr. 22, 1919, Camp Bowie, TX. Married Likie Mae Jurcak, Oct. 17, 1922. Lived remainder of life in the San Antonio Prairie Community of Burleson Co., near Caldwell, TX. One son: Joe John Krupa, Jr. Active in the American Legion and the DAV Posts. Died Sept. 27, 1964; buried in St. Mary's Catholic Cemetery, Caldwell, TX.

Kruppa, Henry, son of Richard and Martha Adamcik Kruppa, was born Feb. 3, 1922, Holman, TX. Education: Radhost and Hostyn, La Grange, TX. Enlisted in U.S. Army Corps during WWII at Ft. Sam Houston, TX. Theater of Operations: Asiatic-Pacific. Battles: Southern Philippines Liberation Ryukyus GO 105 WD 45. Awards: Asiatic-Pacific Campaign Medal w/2 BSS, Philippine Liberation Medal w/1 BSS, Good Conduct Medal, WWII Victory Ribbon w/2 overseas service bars. Honorably discharged Feb. 18, 1946, Ft. Sam Houston, TX. Rank: Cpl. Home of record: La Grange, TX.

Krutilek, Victor E., son of Joe Walter and Mary Pratka Krutilek, was born June 25, 1917, Taiton, TX. Education: Fayetteville, TX, High School. Enlisted in U.S. Armed Forces during WWII, Dec. 15, 1942, Ft. Sam Houston, San Antonio, Bexar Co., TX. Theater of Operations: EAME. Battles: Corsica, Italy, Southern France,

Germany. Decorations: EAME Campaign Ribbon w/4 battle stars, Good Conduct Medal, and a Unit Citation, WWII Victory Medal. Honorably discharged Nov. 16, 1945, Ft. Sam Houston, San Antonio, Bexar Co., TX. Never had a furlough during almost three years in service. Home of record: Houston, TX.

Kubacak, George C., son of Mr. and Mrs. F. A. Kubacak, West, TX. Entered AAF in 1942. Served in Pacific, le Shima and Okinawa, as a Pfc. Awarded AD, Victory, and AP Ribbons w/1 battle star. Discharged 1946.

Kubacak, John W., son of John C. and Anna Polansky Kubacak, was born on Apr. 14, 1911, at West, McLennan Co., TX. Attended West High School. Entered the service on Sept. 30, 1942, at Camp Wolters, and served with the 617th Air Service Squadron, 63rd. Air Depot Group. Rank: Sgt. Received the American Theater Campaign Ribbon, EAME Campaign Ribbon, Good Conduct Medal, Victory Ribbon, one Service Stripe, and one Overseas Service Bar. Discharged Mar. 4, 1946, Fort Sam Houston, TX. Died Sept. 29, 1978.

Kubacak, Raymond Joseph, son of Frank and Mary Smajstrla Kubacak, was born Apr. 6, 1920, at West, TX. Attended St. Mary's and West, TX, High School. Enlisted in the U.S. Army Air Corps at Camp Wolters, TX, on Jan. 5, 1943, during WWII. Served in the Asiatic Pacific Theater of Operations as a member of the 1874th Engineers and attained the grade of Cpl. (T/4). Campaigns: New Guinea, Philippine Islands, and Dutch East Indies. One of the first group of GIs to go into Japan after the atomic bomb was dropped on Hiroshima. Decorations include the Asiatic Pacific Campaign Medal with bronze arrowhead, Good Conduct Medal, WWII Victory Medal, and the Meritorious Unit Commendation. Discharged Jan. 13, 1946, at El Paso, TX. Home of record: West, TX.

Kubacak, Virgil Lee, son of George C. and Mary Ann Straten Kubacak, was born June 15, 1945. Graduate of West, TX, High School; Texas State Tech Inst., Waco, TX; Austin Com. College, Austin, TX; American Tech. Univ., Killeen, TX. Enlisted in USAF, 1963, San Antonio, TX. Theater of Operations: Southeast Asia (Thailand) during Viet Nam War. Medals: National Defense Service, Viet Nam Service, Viet Nam Campaign. Participated as support maintenance for Project "William Tell" at World Wide Weapons Meet, Tyndall AFB, FL, 1965. Attained rank of Airman First Class prior to honorable discharge Aug. 1967. Married Mary Ann Fridel; one child: Aaron K. Kubacak. Civilian occupation: quality engineer. Hobbies: building radio control model aircraft. Home of record: Round Rock, TX.

Kubala, Albert, was born in 1922. Served as a pilot in U.S. Army Air Corps in South Pacific during WWII. Rank: Lt. Died 1946; buried Holy Cross Catholic Cemetery, Granger, TX. Hometown: Granger, TX.

Kubala, Ben G. "Bennie," attained rank of Lt., U.S. Army Air Corps during WWII. Hometown: Granger, Williamson Co., TX.

Kubala, Eugene L., West, TX, WWII veteran.

Kubala, Ferdinand John, son of Benedikt A. and Martha A. Gallia Kubala, was born Sept. 24, 1934. Education: St. Edward's Catholic Grade School, 1948; Pleasant Grove High School, 1952, Dallas, TX; North Texas State College, BBA, 1956, Denton, TX. Commissioned an officer in the U.S. Air Force. 1st duty station: Tyndall AFB, FL; duty at various bases in USA, Canada, Viet Nam, Okinawa, Germany, and Saudi Arabia. Stationed at Da Nang (Monkey Mountain), Viet Nam, during the 1968 TET Offensive. Medals: BSS, Meritorious Service Medal w/OLC, Joint Services Commendation Medal, Air Force Commendation Medal, Air Force Outstanding Unit Award w/Valor Device and three OLC, Combat Readiness Medal, National Defense Medal, Viet Nam Service Medal w/3 OLC, Small Arms Expert Marksmanship Medal, Republic of Viet Nam Gallantry Cross w/Device, and Republic of Viet Nam Campaign Medal. Retired Nov. 30, 1984, after 28 years of service. Attained rank of Lt. Col. Principal participant in the ceremonies returning the Air Defense of Okinawa to the Japanese Self Defense Forces in 1972. During ceremony, a Japanese General asked him what John Wayne would think of him giving back the Islands without a fight. Married Peggy A. Miller of Tacoma, WA; eight children, nine grandchildren, and twin great-grandsons. Owner and operator of Fred's Vacuums, Electrolux Vacuum Cleaner Sales and Vacuum Cleaner Service. Home of record: Sumter, SC .

Kubala, Frank, Jr., son of Frank Kubala, Sr. and Hermina Rozacky, was born in Granger, TX, and served in the U.S. Army during WWII.

Kubala, George Joseph, Sr., son of Frank Kubala, Sr. and Hermina Rozacky Kubala, was born May 15, 1922, in Granger, TX. Attended school in Friendship, TX, and graduated from Robstown High School in 1940. Joined the Texas National Guard on Oct. 31, 1939. Enlisted in the U.S. Army on Nov. 25, 1940. During WWII, served in the European, African, and Middle Eastern Theaters of Operation in North Africa, Italy, and France. Participated in the Naples-Foggia, Rome-Arno, and Southern France Campaigns. Has vivid recollections of being trapped for 24 hours behind enemy lines in a wine cellar before being rescued. Decorations: European African Middle Eastern Campaign Medal with three campaign stars, American Defense Service Medal, Good Conduct Medal, and Combat Infantryman Badge. Separated from the service on May 20, 1945, with the rank of Staff Sgt. Employed as a tool and die man for General Motors until retirement on Jan. 1, 1988. Hobbies include fishing, hunting, gardening, and traveling. Married Elizabeth M. Hoag; two children: George Joseph Kubala, Jr., Angie Kubala Blanton. Home of record: Bancroft, MI.

Kubala, Henry August, son of John Frank and Anna Prihoda Kubala, was born Aug. 28, 1917, Granger, TX. Grade school education. Enlisted Sept. 27, 1943, U.S. Marine Corps, Whitesboro, TX. Theater of Operations: Asiatic-Pacific. Locations: Miramar Marine Base, San Diego, CA; Ewa Marie Camp, 3rd Marine Air Wing, Honolulu, Hawaii, Feb. 21, 1945, through Feb. 13, 1946. Non Combat Roll. Officers' Mess Cook Staff Sgt. Medals: WWII Victory Medal, American Campaign Medal, Sharpshooter Medal, Good Conduct Medal. Honorably discharged Mar. 13, 1946. Married Josephine Julia Oujesky; seven children. Member of Catholic Church. Hobbies: Taroky. Retired postal worker. Home of record: West, TX.

Kubala, Jessie J. Education: Holy Trinity School. Enlisted U.S. Army Corps, 1942; basic training, Camp Barkeley. Theater of Operations: EAME. Served in Normandy; France; Ardennes; Rhineland; Central Europe. Medals: Combat Infantry Badge, EAME Theater Campaign Ribbon w/5 BSS, one Bronze Arrowhead, Good Conduct Medal, WWII Victory Medal. Achieved rank of Pfc. prior to honorable discharge, 1945. Home of record: Jarrell, TX.

Kubala, Jos. J., served in U.S. Armed Forces during WWI, 1917–1918. Member of SPJST Lodge 20, Granger, TX.

Kubala, Julius, attained rank of Lt. U.S. Army Corps, WWII. Hometown: Granger, TX. Deceased.

Kubala, Kenneth Henry, Sr., son of Henry August and Josephine Julia Oujesky Kubala, was born Nov. 5, 1945, Pilot Point, TX. Received BS degree in Entomology from Texas A&M, Jan. 1968. Enlisted U.S. Army Medical Corps, Jan. 13, 1969, Ft. Sam Houston, TX. Basic training, Ft. Sam Houston, TX, Lyster Army Hospital, Ft. Rucker, AL, Republic of South Korea, Osani, Seoul, Pusan. Served in Korea during Viet Nam conflict, 44th Surgical Hospital Mobile Army (SHMA). Was last U.S. soldier to leave the compound at this place in summer of 1971 when U.S. Army downgraded force in Korea. The SHMA units were the offshoot of the "MASH" hospitals. Medals: two commendation medals for outstanding duty, Armed Forces Expeditionary Service Medal, National Defense Ribbon. Honorably discharged Dec. 23, 1971. Civilian occupation: city government employee, West, TX. Married Margaret Marie Hutyra; three daughters, one son. Home of record: West, TX.

Kubala, Lad J., son of John A. and Amalie Krenek Kubala, was born Feb. 6, 1895, Fayetteville, TX. Education: Granger, TX. Enlisted in U.S. Army during WWI, Austin, TX. Attained rank of Sgt. Assigned to Co. G. 9th U.S. Infantry, American Expeditionary Forces. Theater of Operations: European (France). Battles: Aisne, St. Michiel, Lisne-Marne, Meuse-Argonne, Defense Sector. Medals: US Gold Medal, "The Great War for Civilization" w/5 gold stars, Pistol and Rifle Sharpshooter Badge, WWI Victory Medal, Purple Heart. Was in Occupation of France. WOUNDED IN ACTION. Honorably discharged, 1919. Married Adella Cervenka; one child: Margie Elizabeth Kubala Foshee. Civilian occupation: Bookkeeper, retired 1951. Member of SPJST Lodge 20, Granger, TX. Died Apr. 7, 1956; buried in Granger, TX, Cemetery.

Kubala, Lowell Maurice, son of Paul Andrew and Anastatia "Stella Marie" Cernosek Kubala, was born June 20, 1931, Schulenburg, TX. Education: Texas A&M, College Station, TX. B.S. in Agricultural Education, May, 1953. Commissioned 2nd Lt., May 28, 1953, College Station, TX. Entered U.S. Army Corps, June 1953, Ft. Sill, Lawton, OK. Theater of Operations: Korea. Medals: National Defense Service Medal, United Nations Service Medal, Korean Service Medal, Army Commendation Medal, Army Reserve Medal, Meritorious Service Medal (twice). Status: Col., USAR retired (effective Aug. 29, 1985). Home of record: Weimar, TX.

Kubala, Victor, son of John F. and Anna Kubala, was born on June 18, 1919, at Granger, Williamson Co., TX. Entered service at Camp Wolters and served in the South Pacific at 17th Field Hospital, Fiji Islands. Pfc. Discharged in Jan. 1945. Member of SPJST Lodge 20, Granger, TX. Home of record: Pilot Point, TX.

Kubala, William J., died May 15, 1941, WWII veteran; Pvt., 12 Field Arty. Buried Holy Cross Catholic Cemetery, Granger, TX.

Kubala, Woodrow F., son of Mr. and Mrs. J. B. Kubala, Taylor TX. Education: Taylor High School. Enlisted U.S. Navy, 1942; boot camp San Diego, CA. Theater of Operations: Asiatic-Pacific. Medals: Presidential Unit Citation w/Star, Asiatic-Pacific Theater Campaign Ribbon w/15 BSS, American Defense Medal, and Philippine Liberation Ribbon w/2 BSS. Attained rank of BM 2/c prior to honorable discharge, 1945.

Kuban, John, served in U.S. Army Corps, WWI. Hometown Granger, TX. Deceased.

Kubena, Adolph V., son of Rudolph A. and Claudia Zdaril Kubena, was born Feb. 14, 1915, in Fayetteville, TX. Attended Fayetteville High School. Enlisted in the U.S. Army Air Corps on May 12, 1942, during WWII. Served in both the American and Asiatic Pacific Theaters of Operations. Sgt., aircraft maintenance technician, 555th Air Corps. Served in Alaska, Canada, and four CONUS installations. Decorations include the American Campaign Medal, Asiatic Pacific Campaign Medal, Good Conduct Medal, and WWII Victory Medal. Discharged Nov. 19, 1945. Home of record: Ellinger, TX.

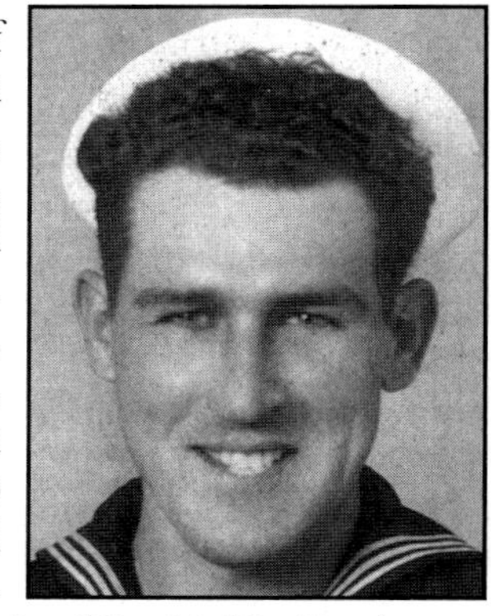

Kubena, Bohumir F., son of John and Katherine Tylich Kubena, was born July 22, 1917, Moulton, Lavaca Co., TX. Attended parochial and public schools in Moulton. Graduated from William A. Wood High School, Apr. 1937. Left the farm in Ganado, TX, in 1940, to attend welding school and received draft notice. Volunteered for the U.S. Navy, July 22, 1942. Basic training, San Diego, CA. Served on the Cargo Merchant Ship SS *John Howard Payne*, the Troop Transport Ship *President Monroe*, the Gasoline Tanker SS *Sacketts Harbor*, in the South Pacific area. Attained rank of Seaman First Class. Married Louise Sklenarik on Jan. 23, 1945, in Galveston, TX. Honorable medical discharge from the Navy June 1945, Corpus Christi, TX. Employed as truck driver in Ganado, TX, then by Alcoa in Point Comfort, TX, until Dec. 1977, when he took a medical retirement. Two sons: John E. and Frank A.. Member of the American Legion Post and Disabled American Veterans Organization. Home of record: Ganado, TX.

Kubena, Erwin J., son of John and Katherine "Katie" Tylich Kubena, born in Moulton, Lavaca Co., TX. Attended parochial and public schools in Moulton. Drafted July 16, 1941, into the peace time Army, before Pearl Harbor. Basic training at Dodd Field, San Antonio, Bexar Co., TX. Rank: Pfc., Co. K, 148th Inf, 37th Div., an Ohio Guard Division. Sailed for Suva, Fiji Island, for jungle warfare training on May 24, 1942. Battles included Guadalcanal, Russell Islands, New Georgia, Baiskora Trail, Bouganville Island. KILLED IN ACTION by a Japanese sniper at Manila, Philippine Island, Feb. 5, 1945. He had been overseas for 33 months at the time of his death, was unmarried, 30 years of age. Buried in Manila. At the request of family, body was exhumed and brought to Moulton, TX for reburial in the Catholic Cemetery beside his father and mother. Survived by brother, Bohumir F. Kubena, of Ganado, TX.

Kubena, Rudolph J., son of Rudolph A. and Claudia Zdaril Kubena, was born Feb. 6, 1912, at Fayetteville, TX. Attended Fayetteville High School. Served in the European, African, and Middle Eastern Theater of Operations as a member of the 357th Inf., 90th Div. Attained the rank of Staff Sgt. Participated in three military campaigns including Normandy. KILLED IN ACTION on July 7, 1944. Decorations include the Purple Heart, European African Middle Eastern Campaign Medal with three campaign stars, Good Conduct Medal, and the Combat Infantryman Badge. Interred in the Fayetteville, TX, Cemetery.

Kubicek, Benjamin, was born Dec. 31, 1918. Died Mar. 21, 1979; buried Holy Cross Catholic Cem., Granger, TX. WWII veteran.

Kubicek, Erwin J. "Jim, Jimmy," son of Oswald Anton and Hilda Ludmilla Bucek Kubicek, was born Jan. 20, 1918, Praha, Fayette Co., TX. Education: Velehrad School, Moravia High School, Hallettsville High School. 1936. Completed General Business Course, Draughon's Business College. Inducted into U.S. Army Air Corp, Ft. Sam Houston, TX, Apr. 21, 1943. Theater of Operations: Asiatic Pacific. Campaigns: Air Offensive Japan, China Defensive, Central Burma, India Burma, Air Combat Sumatra. Decorations: three Overseas Service Bars, BSS Medal, Distinguished Unit Badge, Good Conduct Medal, WWII Victory Ribbon, Asiatic Pacific Campaign Medal w/5 BSS, EAME Campaign Medal. Honorable Discharge as Staff Sgt., 468th Bombardment Group, Ft. Sam Houston, TX, Dec. 7, 1945. After discharge took course in Refrigeration and Air Conditioning. Home of record: San Antonio, TX.

Kubicek, Henry E., son of Mr. and Mrs. Kubicek, Taylor, TX. Graduate of St. Mary's Catholic High School. Enlisted U.S. Army Corps, 1940; basic training, Ft. Sam Houston, TX; further training, Randolph Field, TX. Theaters of Operation: CBI, American, Asiatic-Pacific. Medals: Asiatic-Pacific Theater Campaign Ribbon w/2 BSS, American Theater Campaign Ribbon, CBI Theater Campaign Medal, American Defense Medal, Good Conduct Medal, WWII Victory Medal. Achieved rank of Sgt. prior to honorable discharge, 1945.

Kubin, Edward W., son of Frank John Kubin, Sr. and Helen Kuder Kubin, was born Aug. 18, 1918, Bryan, TX. Education: Bowie Elementary School, Stephen F. Austin High, Bryan, TX, Texas A&M (3 Yrs). Enlisted Apr. 7, 1942, U.S. Army Air Corps (USAF), Dallas, TX. Graduated as Pilot and received Commission, 2nd Lt., Marfa Air Base, TX, March Air Base, CA, B-24 Combat Crew training. Embarked from USA, Oct. 1943 w/30th Bomber Group to Central Pacific on New B-24 "Come Close." Crew and plane remained a unit until completion of 30 missions. Sqdn 1st located Nanomea. Later staged from Tarawa and Makin; targets were in the Gilberts, Marshalls, Carolines.

Sqdn moved to Kwajalein after its capture by U.S. From here, targets were in Carolines (Truk), Panope. After completion of 1st tour, assigned as B-24 J Combat Pilot/crew instructor. In Aug, 1944, returned to 38 Bomb Sq 30th Bomb Gp, now located on Saipan, near Guam. Flew 12 additional combat missions for 112 hours as Asst Operations Officer. Back to USA for three years and assigned to Army of Occupation in Germany. Flew in Berlin Air Lift and returned to U.S. in 1949 for next 14 years. Viet Nam, 1955 (received and shipped eqpt loaned to French AF during their war w/N. Viet Nam—duty was not considered "wartime"), Germany and France, mostly as Base Supply and Staff Supply duties. Theater of Operations WWII: Asiatic Pacific w/3 BSS, Central Pacific, East Pacific, West Pacific. Decorations: Distinguished Flying Cross w/1 OLC, Air Medal w/3 OLC, Asiatic-Pacific Ribbon w/3 BSS, ATO Campaign Medal, Natl Defense Medal, Army of Occupation Medal w/Berlin Airlift Device, Air Force Longevity Ribbon, Air Force Commendation Medal w/1 OLC. Retired from active duty, Apr. 1, 1963. Lt. Col. Civilian Occupation: Federal Civil Service as Staff Civil Engineering Supply At SAC Hq and later w/San Antonio Real Property Maint. Agency. Married Leota B., one child. Home of record: Rt. 10, Box 39A57, New Braunfels, TX.

Kubricht, Charles Arnold, son of Dr. Theophilis and Rose Kubricht. Born June 16, 1917, in Wallis, TX. Enlisted in Bellville, Austin Co., TX. Education: H.S. diploma 1938, University of Houston, three years, Technical diploma in Science and Signal Corps Basic Training. Theater of Operations: Europe Signal Corps 3rd Armored Div., 146th Armored Signal Co. Battles: Normandy, Northern France Ardennes, Rhineland, Central Europe and Battle of the Bulge. Medals: one Service Stripe, four Overseas Service Bars, Good Conduct Medal GO 33 WD 45, Distinguished Unit Badge GO Hq VII Corps 24 Mar. 45, EAME Campaign Medal with five Bronze Stars, and the American Defense Service Medal. Attained rank of Technical, Fourth Grade. Discharged Oct. 21, 1945. Died Sept. 25, 1985. Submitted by Sherry Dieckmann, Houston, TX.

Kubricht, John Jacob, son of Dr. Theophilis and Rose Kubricht. Born July 24, 1907, at Taylor, TX. Attended Southwest Texas Teachers College. Enlisted in Houston, TX. Discharged Oct. 11, 1945. Died Oct. 27, 1981.

Kucera, Albin, of West, TX, WWII veteran.

Kucera, Antonyn Edgar, son of John and Veronica Steffek Kucera, was born Oct. 17, 1894, Ellinger, Fayette Co., TX. Was in the U.S. Army Corps during WWI. If the war had lasted three more weeks, would have been sent overseas. Honorable discharge, moved to Dallas, TX, 1920. Married Viola Kucera; daughter Kathleen Kucera Roderick/Miller, six grandchildren. Connected with cotton industry for over 50 years. Started as apprentice buyer with R. L. Dixon and Bro., in 1922. President of firm 1948-1966, until retirement. Past president of Dallas Cotton Exchange, Texas Cotton Assoc., and Dallas Cotton Shippers Assoc. Active member of NY and New Orleans Cotton Exchanges. Member of St. Michael, All Angels Episcopal Church, and the Dallas Country Club. Died June 10, 1970, Dallas, TX. Burial at Hillcrest Memorial Park, Dallas, TX.

Kucera, Charles E., son of Mr. and Mrs. Joe Kucera. Entered AAC in 1944. Awarded GCM and Victory Ribbon. Discharged 1946.

Kucera, Henry Payton, son of John and Veronica Steffek Kucera, was born Oct. 16, 1896, at Ellinger, TX. Attended elementary school at Ellinger. With no high school diploma, was examined and accepted at Sam Houston State Teachers College (Now Sam Houston University) at Huntsville, TX, and also at the University of Texas in Austin, earning BA and Law degrees in 1923. While in the service attended the University of Virginia and pursued courses in Military Government and the Italian language. Served in both WWI and II. During WWI served for ten months and attained the rank of Sgt. First Class. During WWII served in the European, African, and Middle Eastern Theater of Operations and attained the rank of Lt. Col. Participated in the Naples-Foggia, Rome-Arno, North Apennines, and Po Valley Campaigns. Served in Africa, Italy, the Balkans, and Trieste. Military Governor of Ravenna, Italy, and subsequently, of Trieste. Spoke Italian fluently, along with Czech, German, and

Spanish. Decorations: European-African-Middle Eastern Campaign Medal with four campaign stars, Meritorious Service Unit Plaque and Badge, and WWII Victory Medal. Separated from active service and into the Reserves on Feb. 10, 1945. Retired with rank of Col. on Sept. 18, 1955. Admitted to State Bar on Sept. 18, 1923. Moved to Dallas, TX, to practice law. In 1925, appointed Assistant City Attorney in Dallas, and in 1935 to City Attorney. Retired from public service in June 1965 after 40 years of distinguished service. Opened private practice as counsel to the firm of Hutchinson, Price, and Boyle, and later became a member of the firm. Retired in June 1980 to pursue his hobbies: reading, hunting, and fishing. Married Lucille Fears, July 12, 1928, Shreveport, LA; two daughters: Kathryn Kucera (deceased), and Karolyn Kucera Bowles, wife of Reverend Robert B. Bowles, Jr. Died on Sept. 25, 1983, and is interred in Grove Hill Cemetery in Dallas, TX.

Kucera, James D., son of Frank S. and Helen Kucera, was born Oct. 30, 1945, Sealy, TX. Graduated Sealy High School about 1963. Died in an auto accident, Austin Co., TX, Sept. 21, 1969. Buried St. Mary's Catholic Cemetery, Frydek, Austin, TX.

Kucera, John J., son of John and Rosie Caba Kucera, was born Nov. 7, 1909. Attended schools in Taylor and Wallis, TX. Enlisted in the U.S. Army at Edna, TX. Served in the European, African, and Middle Eastern Theater of Operations as a member of Co. G, 253rd Infantry. Participated in campaigns in North Africa, Sicily, Italy, and Germany during WWII. Decorations include the European-African-Middle Eastern Campaign Medal with four campaign stars. Separated from service Sept. 1945. Married Albina Kubicek; three daughters. Pioneered crop irrigation in the Knippa, TX, area in the mid 1950s. Died Oct. 13, 1958, at Brooke Army Hospital, Ft. Sam Houston, TX. Interred in St. Mary's Cemetery at Taylor, TX.

Kucera, Leon Stanley, son of Frank and Annie Kucera, was born Feb. 28, 1916, Ennis, TX. Education: Graduated Ennis High School and Navarro College. Rank of Captain. Enlisted in Ennis, TX. Theater of Operations: Europe. Fought in England, France, Belgium, Germany, Czechoslovakia. Honorably discharged Nov. 15, 1945. Married Emilie Loksa at Ennis, TX. Children: Lawrence and Martha. Home of record, Ennis, TX.

Kucera, Louis J., was born Apr. 24, 1923, served in AAF during WWII, 2543 Base Unit AAF. Died Oct. 10, 1962. Buried in St. Mary's Cemetery, West, TX.

Kucera, Mitchell J., was born Aug. 4, 1923, served in the U.S. Armed Forces during WWII–COD 385 Mil. Pol. Bn. Died May 12, 1972.

Kudelka, Edmund Leon, son of Adolph and Mary Skarpa Kudelka, was born Jan. 29, 1914, West, TX. Joined the National Guard, West, McLennan Co., TX. Rank: T/4. Served in the European Theater of Operation Fought in the battle at Salerno, Italy. Captured by the Germans and was a PRISONER OF WAR for 20 months in following camps: 7-A-Stalag, 2-B, 3-B, 3-A. Liberated on Apr. 16, 1945. Medals: Prisoner of War, WWII Victory, European Middle East Campaign. Honorably discharged Aug. 21, 1945, San Antonio, TX. Home of record: West, TX.

Kudelka, Ernest, of West, TX, 36th Division, WOUNDED IN ACTION. WWII veteran.

Kudelka, Henry, of West, TX, WWII veteran, U.S. Navy.

Kudelka, L., West, TX, WWII veteran, PRISONER OF WAR.

Kudelka, Raymond, of West, TX, 36th Division, WWII veteran.

Kudelka, Victor, son of Mr. and Mrs. W. E. Kudelka, Waco, TX. Attended Lee Jr. College. Entered AAC, 1941. Trained at Chanute Field, IL. Served in Pacific. Rank: T/Sgt. Awarded AP w/4 battle stars, GCM, AD, Pres. Cit. Discharged 1945.

Kulhanek, Arnold John, son of Theo. and Annie Honacek Kulhanek, was born on Friday, Dec. 12, 1947, La Grange, TX, Memorial Hospital. Attended St. John's Catholic School, Fayetteville, TX, nine years. Graduated from Fayetteville Public High School, May 29, 1966. Attended Blinn College in Brenham for two years. Inducted

into U.S. Army Corps at Brenham, TX, June 2, 1969, 2nd Battalion, 5th Cavalry (A.M.) 1st Cavalry Division (Airmobile). Shipped to Ft. Bliss, El Paso, TX, then Oakland, CA, for six weeks training. Shipped to Viet Nam and Cambodia on Oct. 27, 1969. WOUNDED IN ACTION when he accidentally set off trip flares and claymore mines which had been placed as a defense against the enemy at a "Landing Zone Ready" in Cambodia on May 29, 1970. Evacuated to 24th Evac. Hospital in Long Binh, Viet Nam. Died June 2, 1970, exactly one year from the date of enlistment. Submitted by Gold Star Mother.

Kulhanek, Charles, served in U.S. Armed Forces during WWI, 1917–1918. Member of SPJST Lodge 20, Granger, TX.

Kulhanek, Leonard M., son of Mr. and Mrs. Frank J. Kulhanek, Fayetteville, TX, was born Dec. 10, 1918, Pisek, TX. Graduate of Fayetteville High School, one year business college, Houston, TX. Enlisted U.S. Navy, June 29, 1940, Houston, TX. Served with U.S. Navy Recruiting Party in TX and LA, U.S. Naval Receiving Station, New Orleans, LA and San Francisco, CA, then served in Asiatic Pacific Theater of Operations on USS *Alchiba* (AKA). Battles: Solomon Islands, initial invasion on Bougainville and Emirau Island. Medals: American Campaign Medal, Asiatic Pacific Theater Medal, WWII Victory Medal, GCM, American Defense Ribbon, Merit Citation and three BSS. Honorable discharge Oct. 24, 1945.

Kunz, Delbert Joseph, son of Henry F. and Margaret Mary Mozisek Kunz, was born Dec. 14, 1950, Weimar, Colorado Co., TX. Graduate of Columbus, TX, High School. Enlisted in Houston, TX, during the Viet Nam Conflict, U.S. Army Corps. Theater of Operations: Viet Nam. Battles fought there. List of medals: National Defense Service Medal, Viet Nam Service Medal, Sharpshooter M-16 Medal, Army Commendation Medal, Viet Nam Campaign Medal. Achieved rank of SP4 by the date of honorable discharge at Ft. Dix, NJ, Aug. 25, 1971. Home of record: Magnolia, AR.

Kunz, Henry Fred, son of Joe and Lena Wanjura Kunz, was born Nov. 9, 1925, Schulenburg, Fayette Co., TX. Education, St. Michael's Catholic Grade School, Weimar, TX, High School, and Blinn College, Brenham, TX. Inducted into U.S. Army Corps, Jan. 31, 1944, Houston, TX. Assigned to South Pacific Theater of Operations, Battery A, 573rd Field Artillery Battalion. Fought in Battle of Luzon GO-105-WD-45-Philippines. Awards: American Theater Campaign Ribbon, Asiatic Pacific Campaign Ribbon w/1 BSS, Philippine Liberation Ribbon w/1 BSS, Good Conduct Medal, WWII Victory Ribbon, one Overseas Service Bar. Honorable discharge May 12, 1946, Ft. Sam Houston, TX. Home of record: Columbus, TX.

Kunz, James Harold, son of Henry F. and Margaret Mary Mozisek Kunz, was born Oct. 15, 1945, Houston, TX. Graduated from high school, Columbus, TX. Enlistment orders from Local Selective Service Board #44, La Grange, TX. Attained rank of SP/4, U.S. Army Corp. Theater of Operation: Germany. Took part in Path Finder Express in Spain, 1967. Honorably discharged Dec. 17, 1967, Ft. Dix, NJ. Home of record: Bryan, TX.

Kupcak, Louis, Jr., son of Mr. and Mrs. Louis Kupcak, was born Aug. 8, 1918, West, TX. Attended St. Mary's School, West, TX. Enlisted in U.S. Armed Forces, 1936. Served in Fort Francis, WY, E. Warren. Reenlisted. Served during WWII in Hawaii, Pearl Harbor, Philippines, Solomon Islands. Asiatic-Pacific Theater. Rank: Tech/Sgt. Awarded BSS and other medals and ribbons. Discharged 1945. Retired from the V.A. Medical Center, Waco, TX.

Kurtin, Anton W., was born Jan. 8, 1917. U.S. Army Corps. T. Sgt. Ninth Infantry Regt. BSM

PH. Died Mar. 31, 1971; buried Holy Cross Catholic Cemetery, Granger, TX. WWII veteran.

Kurtin, Laddie H., Granger, TX. Member American Legion Post No. 282, Granger, TX. WWII veteran.

Kusy, Edward E., son of Edward and Bozena Socha Kusy, was born July 31, 1926, Moravia, TX. Education, eight years grammar school, one year high school. Enlisted in U.S. Army Corps, Ft. Sam Houston, TX. Theater of Operations: American and Asiatic-Pacific Theater. Battles: Ryukyus. Medals: American Theater Ribbon, Asiatic Pacific Theater Ribbon, GCM, WWII Victory Medal. Received honorable discharge from U.S. Army Corps, Apr. 9, 1946. Reenlisted in USAF. Honorably discharged Feb. 4, 1950. Home of record: Schulenburg, TX.

Kutac, Herbert B., son of Robert and Welhelmina Knezek Kutac, was born Feb. 3, 1915, Praha, TX. Education, eighth grade, St. Mary's Catholic School, Praha, TX. Enlisted July 13, 1942, Ft. Sam Houston, TX, U.S. Army Corps, achieved rank of Cpl. Basic Training, Camp Roberts, CA. Assigned to 37th Div., 145th Inf., 3rd Bn.Theater of Operations: Asiatic-Pacific. Medical Aidman for 30 months and two days on Suva-Fiji Island. Battles: Northern Solomon Islands, Southern Philippine Islands, Luzon. Medals: Silver Star, two Purple Hearts, Asiatic Pacific Service Medal w/OLC, WWII Victory Medal. WOUNDED IN ACTION twice. Honorable discharge Sept. 27, 1945. Home of record, Hallettsville, TX.

Kutach, Casper J., son of Mike and Mary Kutach, was born Aug. 4, 1926, Shiner, TX. Graduate: Hallettsville High School, 1944, Southwest Teachers College, 1949, Kirksville College of Osteopathic Medicine and Surgery, 1965. Enlisted in U.S. Navy, Houston, TX, May, 1944. Assigned to Amph 5th Force. Theater of Operations: Asiatic-Pacific. Battles: Iwo Jima and Okinawa. Medals: WWII Victory Medal, Asiatic-Pacific Campaign Medal w/2 BSS, Navy and Air Force Commendation, Good Conduct Medal, Marksman Badge, American Defense Service Medal, American Campaign Medal, Occupation Medal. Honorably discharged, May, 1946, from U.S. Navy as BM2C. Enlisted Ft. Worth, TX, 1970, U.S. Air Force, Medical Sqdn. Served in the South Pacific with the Navy Amph. Force, WWII, also, Commander, Air Force Medical Squadron 406, Sheppard Air Force Base, TX. Honorably discharged Sept. 1974 from the USAF. Rank: Major. Married Ann Berkovsky, May 31, 1948; three sons: Bradley Allan Kutach, Michael A. Kutach, Dr. Brent L. Kutach, three grandchildren. Retired from medical practice, 1984. Homes of record:Rockport and Ft. Worth, TX.

Kutach, Dennis Otto, son of Julius and Agnes Strauss Kutach, was born Aug. 4, 1948, Shiner, TX. Education: high school. Enlisted USAF, during Viet Nam War, Lackland AFB, TX. Theater of Operations: American. Medals: American Theater Campaign Ribbon, Good Conduct Medal. Honorably discharged Oct, 1971, with rank of S/Sgt. President, 1st State Bank, Yoakum, TX. Married Georgia Darilek; four children. Active in community, Knights of Columbus, State Director of Independent Bankers of Texas. Home of record: Yoakum, TX.

Kutach, Edward L., son of Julius Kutach and Agnes Strauss, was born Jan. 24, 1941, Shiner, TX. Education: St. Ludmila's Academy, Shiner TX. Enlisted in USAF, Lackland AFB, TX. Attained rank of E-4 during Cuban Crisis. Medals: Good Conduct. Honorably discharged. Married Brenda Sassin; two sons: Edward L. "Eddie," Jr. and Michael. Civilian occupation: Buyer. Home of record: Stafford, TX.

Kutach, George Henry, son of Julius A. and Agnes Strauss Kutach, was born Aug. 18, 1944, Shiner, TX.. Education: St. Ludmila's Academy, Shiner TX, Sept. 1950 through May, 1962. Enlisted U.S. Army–ARNG, Austin, TX. Attained rank of E-6. Honorably discharged July 1, 1971. Civilian occupation: Systems Support Specialists, Texas Dept of Transportation. Married Erline Berckenhoff, Dec. 5, 1971; two children: Brian Paul and Dawn Marie. Hobbies: hunting, fishing,

dominoes, working crossword puzzles. Home of record: Shiner TX.

Kutni, Clara Mae, (see Shiller, Clara Mae).

Kutra, August John, son of Emil and Filomena Kutra, was born Apr. 15, 1916, Sealy (Frydek), Austin Co., TX. Inducted into U.S. Army Corps, Mar. 12, 1941, Houston, TX. Attained rank of Warrant Officer (jg). Served with 439th Signal Construction Battalion, Battles and Campaigns: European Theater, Algeria-French-Morocco, Sicily, Naples Foggia, Rome Arno, Rhineland, Southern and Northern France, Central Europe. Decorations: BSS, GCM, American Defense Service WWII, WWII Victory Medal, and European African Middle Eastern Campaign Medal w/9 BSS. Honorably discharged Feb. 7, 1946, Fannin, TX. Home of record: Houston, TX.

Kutra, Emil, served Apr, 1943–, in U.S. Army Corps during WWII.

Kutra, Louis S., son of Anton and Anna Kutra, was born Feb. 1, 1892. Enlisted in U.S. Army. Attained rank of Pvt. Served during WWI with American Expeditionary Forces. Died Feb. 10, 1980; buried St. Mary's Catholic Cemetery, Frydek, Austin Co., TX.

Kveton, Fred V., son of Jozef and Mary Kveton, was born Feb. 12, 1897, Valaske Mezrici, Moravia, Austria-Hungary. Education: Germany. Emigrated to USA from Port of Bremen, Germany, on Vessel *Chemnitz*. Last foreign residence, Mahr, Austria. Arrived Nov. 22, 1908. Applied for citizenship Sept. 12, 1914. Granted Certificate of Naturalization, age 21, U.S. Dist. Court, North Dist. of TX, Ft. Worth, June 22, 1918. Enlisted WWI, Natl. Guard, June 5, 1917. U.S. Army Corps, June 30, 1917, Wichita Falls, TX. Transferred to Co. K, 142nd Inf., 36th Div., July 1917. Trained one year, Camp Bowie, TX. Became Cpl., June 26, 1918. Went to France w/36th Div., July 1918. Trained over two months in France. To front line (several villages in France) on Oct. 8, 1918. WOUNDED IN ACTION, gun wound, steel plate in left thigh, Oct. 9, 1918. (In 21 days on the front, only 38 men survived out of 148 men in company.) Taken to hospital 48 hours after being wounded. Operated on night before Armistice signed. Released Dec. 15, 1918. He was proud that he was a barber on the sideline during his military service. He charged 25¢ for enlisted men and $1.00 for officers. Remained in France on light duty until discharge in June 17, 1919, Camp Bowie, TX. Battles: Meusse-Argonne, Champaign-St. Etienne. Received Purple Heart and Combat Medals. Received American Citizenship while in military service. Honorably discharged. Enlisted Sept. 9, 1919, Camp Travis, TX, Reserves. Discharged at Camp Normoyle Sept. 8, 1920. Married Mary Cervenka, Dec. 27, 1921. Lived at Electra, TX, on a farm one mile from Red River. 1st child born Aug. 1923. In 1924 purchased land, Abernathy, TX. Farmed at Electra until 1930. Three more children born. Spring of 1930, moved to West Texas, built a new home for his family and moved them. Two more children were born on the farm. Active in farming until 1960s. Lived on farm until Jan. 17, 1993, raising flowers, large gardens, and tending fruit orchard. Served on committees and farm boards. Active in SPJST and RVOS for years. Served on the board representing Dist. IV, when 1st retirement home was built in Taylor, TX. His wish was to live out his last days at the home, but it was too far from family. Moved to Hale Center's Hi Plains Nursing Home. Died there Nov. 15, 1993.

Kveton, Joe V., son of Vaclav and Frances Kveton, was born Mar. 29, 1908, in Granger, TX. Attended school in Granger. Served during WWII in the U.S. Army as a Medical Supplyman and attained the rank of Sgt. Served in the Asiatic Pacific Theater of Operations in the areas of China, Burma, and India. Awards and decorations include the Asiatic Pacific Campaign Medal and the WWII Victory Medal. Separated from the service in 1946. Owned and operated a grocery store. Active in Cub and Boy Scout activities. Enjoyed hunting and fishing. Married Gertrude Rizacky; one son, Russell Kveton. Died Mar. 9, 1971. Interred in the Taylor City Cemetery in Taylor, Williamson Co., TX.

Kyselka, Herman Raymond, son of Lee and Rosie W. Slovak Kyselka, was born Dec. 5, 1927, Elk, TX. Graduate of West High School, TX, 1947. Attended Troy State University, Ft. Rucker,

AL, 1975. Drafted into U.S. Army Corps, 1950, Ft. Sill, OK. Graduated from Officer Candidate School, Ft. Monmouth, NJ, 1952. Overseas assignments: Korea, 1953-54, 1955-56; Germany, 1959-60, 1967-69, 1970-72, 1975-77; Italy, 1964-66. Awards: Legion of Merit Medal, Meritorious Service Medal w/1 OLC, Army Commendation Medal w/1 OLC, Good Conduct Medal, National Defense Service Medal, Korean Service Medal w/2 BSS, United Nations Service Medal. Rank: Chief Warrant Officer CW-4, Missile Maintenance and Nuclear Weapons Technician. Retired Oct, 1980, Ft. Sill, OK. Home of record: Lawton, OK.

Kyselka, Joe Lewis, son of Lee and Rosie Slovak Kyselka, was born Feb. 2, 1926, Mart, TX. Education: elementary, Elk, TX; secondary, Axtell, TX. Enlisted in U.S. Army Corps, Camp Wolters, TX, during WWII. Basic training, Ft. Hood, TX. Rank: Pvt. Assigned to the Signal Corps, Pacific Theater of Operations. Battles: Luzon, Ryukyus, Saipan, Beach Head Okinawa. Medals: BSS, Combat Infantry Badge, Philippine Liberation Medal, GCM Medal. Was present at the raising of the U.S. Flag after the Battle of Okinawa. Honorably discharged May 31, 1946. Married Nellie Welch; two beautiful daughters: Linda Kyselka Gershack, Ft. Worth, TX, and Glenda Kyselka Johnston, Anchorage, AK. Member of VFW Post #9190, Haltom City, TX. Home of record: Ft. Worth, TX. Submitted by Christine Wyninger of West, TX.

L

Labaj, Emil (Emmett), son of Joe and Antonia Zapalak Labaj, was born Nov. 7, 1909. Attended Granger High School. Enlisted in Air Force at Ft. Sam Houston. Earned the Good Conduct Medal. Discharged Sept. 26, 1945 at Randolph Field, TX. Rank: Sgt. Member American Legion Post No. 282, Granger, TX. Died Aug. 11, 1986; buried in Granger's Brethren Cemetery.

Labaj, Frank, son of Joe and Anna Drizka Labaj, was born June 10, 1893, in Granger, TX. Education: Moravia Country School, south of Granger, TX. Enlisted Feb. 1 1918, at Ft. Sam Houston, TX, for the U.S. Army Cavalry. Served in France during WWI. Took care of mules which were used to transport supplies. Discharged July 15, 1919. Rank: Pvt. Member of SPJST Lodge 20, Granger, TX. Died Mar. 14, 1973; buried at Brethren Cemetery, Granger, TX.

Labaj, Lawrence F., son of Mr. and Mrs. J. A. Labaj, Granger, TX. Education: Moravia School. Enlisted, U.S. Navy, 1945; boot camp, San Diego, CA; further training, Fireman School and Repair Base, Camp Elliot. Theater of Operations: Asiatic-Pacific. Medals: Asiatic-Pacific Theater Campaign Ribbon, WWII Victory Medal.

Labaj, Mark Lee, son of Milton and Gladys Hejl Labaj, was born Feb. 3, 1952, in San Angelo, TX. Education: Reagan High School, Austin, TX, 1969; B.S., Aerospace Engineering, University of Texas, 1974, Master of Divinity, Moravian Technology Seminary, 1980; Doctor of Ministry, Austin Presbyterian Seminary, 1986. Attended AFROTC at UT. Served at Officer Training School, Lackland AFB, TX, 1975-1977. Scientific Research Assistant evaluating testing methods to screen pilot candidates. Discharged Jan. 26, 1977. Rank: Airman 1/C. Married Vernell Zak of Hallettsville in 1977; two children. Pastor, Temple Brethren Church. Resides in Temple, TX.

Labaj, Milton L., son of Frank and Louise Balusek Labaj, was born Nov. 3, 1926, in Granger, TX. Education: Granger High School, 1945, and Southern Graphics Arts Institute, Nashville, TN, 1948. Enlisted June 1, 1945, at Ft. Sam Houston, TX, in the U.S. Army Transportation Corps. Basic training at Camp Fannin, Tyler, TX. Theater of Operations: WWII, C&A, Hq. Depot Detachment, O.R.D., Ft Lawton, WA. Discharged Dec. 16, 1946, with rank of Pfc. Married Gladys Milady Hejl; one son: Rev. Mark Lee Labaj. Home of record: Austin, TX.

Labay, Allen, son of Mr. and Mrs. Frank Labay, Taylor, TX. Education: Texas A&M. Enlisted in U.S. Army Corps, 1943; basic training, Ft. Knox, KY. Transferred to U.S. Army Air Corps, became Aerial Gunner. Theater of Operations: European. Served in Italy. Medals: Air Medal w/OLC, ETO Campaign Ribbon w/5 BSS, WWII Victory Medal. Attained rank of Sgt. prior to honorable discharge, 1945.

Labay, Valentine C., son of Joseph Labay, Sr. and Anna Drlik Labay, was born July 24, 1917, Nada, TX. Attended St. Mary's Catholic School, Nada, TX. Enlisted U.S. Army Corps, June 3, 1942. Basic training, Camp Wallace. Advanced training, Camp Stewart, GA. Amphibiores, Camp Caravel, FL, Ft. Davis, SC, Camp Pickett, VA, Camp Patrick

Henry, VA. Staging Area: Newport News, VA; sailed for Oran, N. Africa, European Theater of Operation. Half Track Commander, Btry. C, 441-A.W.S.P. 15th Regt., 3rd Inf. Div. Battles: July 10, 1943, D-Day landing until completion and fall of Sicily, under Gen. George Patton Support Troops, 5th Army; D-4, at Salerno, Sept. 13, 1943, under Gen. Mark Clark; Casino, Italy, Dec. 27, 1943, D-Day Landing; Jan. 1, 1944, Anzio Beachhead until fall of Rome; Aug. 15, 1944 to Southern France, D-Day Landing at Southern France until St. Die in French Alps. Hospitalized at Dijon for trench or frozen feet. Transferred to hospital at Marseillaise, France. Dec. 13, 1944, loaded on USS *Mariposa*, landed at Boston, MA. Dec. 22, 1944, by train to Dewitt General Hospital, Auburn, CA; July 1945, transferred to Brooks Medical Hospital in San Antonio, TX. Honorably discharged Aug. 1945, certificate of disability. Five Major Battle Stars. Favorite sports: baseball, football, hunting, and fishing. Married Feb. 20, 1946, Leona Kubena; six daughters, three sons. Retired farmer and rancher. Home of record, Hallettsville, TX.

Lacik, Frank William, Jr., son of Frank William Lacik, Sr. and Mary Frances Patak, was born Nov. 30, 1924, near Garrett, Ellis County, TX. Attended St. John's Catholic School, Garrett, TX, and Ennis High School, Ennis, TX. Drafted from Ennis, TX, Nov. 3, 1943, into the U.S. Navy, Seaman First Class. Served on the USS *Dickens* APA 161, a Navy Troop Ship in the Pacific Theater of Operations. Landed troops in the Invasion of Iwo Jima and Okinawa. Medals: Asiatic Pacific, two Battle Stars, Philippine Liberation Medal. Honorably discharged Apr. 19, 1946. Home of record: Red Oak, TX.

Lacik, Frank William, Sr., son of John and Vlasta Bosecky Lacik, born Feb. 29, 1896, Garrett, TX. Attended Garrett School. Enlisted in the U.S. Army Corps, during WWI, in 1918. Assigned to the American Expeditionary Forces, Co. D, 359th Inf. Rank: Cpl. Battles: St. Michiel Offensive, Sept. 12–Sept. 16, 1918, Meuse Argonne Offensive, Oct. 22–Nov. 11, 1918, Villers en Hey Sector Aug. 24–Sept. 11, 1918, Puvenelle Sector, Sept. 17–Oct. 10, 1918, Preney Offensive Sept. 26, 1918. Honorably discharged June 24, 1919, Camp Bowie, TX. Became a farmer. Married Mary Frances Patak, Nov. 26, 1923; five children: Frank, J., Hattie, Mary, Helen, Evelyn. During WWII, worked at North American Aviation in Grand Prairie, TX. Died in the Veteran's Hospital, Dallas, TX, Apr. 4, 1973. Buried in Myrtle Cem., Ennis, TX.

Laeve, Raymond L., son of Otto and Rosie Mikes Laeve, was born Dec. 4, 1916, Granger, Williamson Co., TX. Education: Granger High School, Victoria Jr. Col., 1936, Texarkana Jr. Col., 1937, N.E. Center of LSU, 1938, East Texas State Univ., 1939-40, B.A. degree, 1941 (all on football scholarships). Commissioned Lt., U.S. Navy. Naval Patrol Plane Comdr. Enlisted at Grand Prairie, TX, as Naval Aviation Cadet, Jan. 1941. Operational training, Norfolk, VA; Banana River, FL; Corpus Christi, TX; Key West, FL (1942-43). Asiatic Pacific Theater of Operations. Battles: (Task Force 3, 5, & 7) VPB-202, flew the Zeng. Seaplane, Martin-Mariner PBM-3c/5D (2 torpedoes, 8-50 cal. machine guns; Tarawa, Kwajalien, Eniwetok, Truk, Saipan, Palau, Okinawa, and Japan-VPB-22. Honorable discharge Jan. 1946, Camp Wallace, TX. Retired. Married Helen Massey; four children, 12 grandchildren, one great-grandchild. Home of record: Georgetown, TX.

Lalla, Jerome T., WWII veteran. Member American Legion Post No. 282, Granger, TX.

Lalla, Robert J., WWII veteran. Member American Legion Post No. 282, Granger, TX.

Lalla, Walter H., son of Mr. and Mrs. Adolf Lalla, Granger, TX. Enlisted U.S. Army Corps; basic training, Ft. Riley, KS; additional training Camp Livingston, LA; Camp Hood, TX. Theater of Operations: EAME. Campaigns: Normandy, Rhineland, France, Central Europe. Medals: EAME Theater Campaign Ribbon, Service Ribbon w/4 BSS, Good Conduct Medal, WWII Victory Medal. Achieved rank of Sgt prior to honorable discharge, 1945.

Lalla, Walter I., WWII veteran. Member American Legion Post No. 282, Granger, TX.

Lalla, Walter T., Bartlett, TX. WWII veteran. Member American Legion Post No. 282, Granger, TX.

Lamer, Joe A., was born Dec. 24, 1921. Served in U.S. Army Corps during WWII, rank Pvt. Honorably discharged. Civilian occupation: Businessman, pub owner. Married Frances Martinka; four children: Mary Frances, Annie, Frances, Jodie. Died Apr. 6, 1991; buried Corn Hill, Williamson Co., TX.

Lamza, Leonard Joseph, son of Joseph Lamza and Amelia Kubos, was born Sept. 25, 1926, La

Grange, TX. Attended public schools in Hallettsville, TX. Enlisted in U.S. Army Corps, Feb. 12, 1945, TX. Rank: Pfc. Japanese Occupation, M.P., Co. B 800th M.P. Bn., Oct. 16, 1945, to Oct. 8, 1946. Medals: Asiatic-Pacific Campaign Ribbon, Good Conduct Medal, Army of Occupation Ribbon w/1 overseas bar. Theater of Operation: Asiatic-Pacific. Honorably discharged Dec. 1, 1946. Married Fannie P. Brezik, June 21, 1948; three daughters, five grandchildren. Retired salesman w/Sears Roebuck and Co., 39 years of service. Home of record: Houston, TX.

Landsfeld, Joe John, son of Joe Landsfeld and Mary Jakukik, was born Sept. 14, 1918, Ennis, TX. Attended schools in Ennis, TX. Enlisted in the U.S. Army Corps, Mineral Wells, TX. Rank: T-4. European Theater of Operation. Fought in the Battle of the Bulge. Medals: WWII Victory Medal, American Theater Service Medal, European Middle East Medal, GCM Medal. Honorable discharge, Ft. Sam Houston, San Antonio, TX, June 29, 1947. Home of record: Ennis, TX.

Lastovica, Henry, served three years in U.S. Navy during WWII.

Lastovica, Joseph, served six years in U.S. Army Corps during WWII.

Laza, Benny F., son of John and Francis Psencik Laza, was born Feb. 7, 1919, Rowena TX. Education: Eola School, Eola, TX. Enlisted Jan. 16, 1942, San Angelo, TX, Good Fellow Field in the Army Air Corps. Theater of Operations: Europe. Battles and campaigns: Rhineland GO 40 WD 45, Central Europe GO 48 WD 45. Decorations: EAME Ribbon, GCM, Air Medal. Served as a ball turret gunner in a B-17. Stationed in England. Honorably discharged Oct. 26, 1945. Died Apr. 15, 1988, Mereta, TX. Buried Mereta Cemetery, TX. Submitted by Milady Laza, San Angelo, TX.

Laza, John J. "Johnny," son of John W. and Carrie Bobalik Laza, was born Feb. 18, 1918, Ennis, TX. Enlisted in U.S. Army Corps, Mar. 15, 1941. Theater of Operations: Asiatic-Pacific. Assigned to Coast Artillery during WWII. Battles: the second wave on Okinawa, Philippine Liberation. Decorations: American Theater Ribbon, American Defense Ribbon, Good Conduct Medal, Asiatic-Pacific Theater Ribbon w/2 BSS, Philippine Liberation Ribbon w/1 BSS, two Overseas Service Bars, 1-3 year Service Stripe, WWII Victory Ribbon. Honorably discharged, Dec. 22, 1945. Home of record: Dallas, TX.

Laza, Willie F., son of John W. and Carrie Bobalik Laza, was born Aug. 4, 1925, in Ennis, Texas. Educated in Ennis. Enlisted in the Army in Ennis in 1943. Fought in Northern France and the Rhineland and Central Europe. WOUNDED IN ACTION at the Battle of the Bulge. Medals: Combat Infantry Medal, Purple Heart, Good Conduct Medal, Victory Ribbon with two BSS. Discharged 1946. Also served in the Korean War. Home of record: Ennis, TX.

Laznovsky, Alfred Wesley, son of Wesley Frank and Mary Kubin Laznovsky. Graduate of Ennis High School, University of Texas, Austin, TX. Enlisted U.S. Navy, Jan. 16, 1951, Dallas, TX. Received training at Pt. Lyautey, French Morocco. Served in Composite Sqdn. 9, at U.S. Naval Air Facility in Morocco. Medals: Good Conduct Medal and European Occupation Medal. Honorably discharged Dec. 2, 1954. Married Joan Burke of Austin, TX, on Sept. 30, 1955; four children. Retired from Montgomery Ward. Enjoy being grandparents of nine grandchildren. Home of record: Laguana Vista, TX, near South Padre Island. Submitted by Sylvia J. Laznovsky, Ennis, TX.

Laznovsky, Frankie George, son of Frank and Mary Trojacek Laznovsky, was born June 22, 1933, Ennis, TX. Education: Mote Elementary School,

one year Ennis High School, received high school diploma in service. Enlisted U.S. Air Force, Dec. 23, 1954. Basic training Jan. 4, 1955, Lackland AFB, TX. Received special training as an Intelligence Op. Tech. Served two tours in the United Kingdom, one tour in Germany and France and two tours in Thailand during the Viet Nam War. Saw Bob Hope USO Tour while in Thailand. Medals: Good Conduct Medal w/2 bar loops, AFLSA, AFGCM, AFOVA, AFGCM w/1 OLC. Received special recognition for voluntarily providing his expertise and time performing the combined mission of the 388th Tactical Fighter Wing and 56th Airborn Rescue and Recovery Squadron. Retired from service, Nov. 1, 1975, after serving 20 years, 10 months, 8 days. Rank: Staff Sgt. Approximately 11 years of this was overseas duty. Lived in Ennis, TX. Employed at Ennis Automotive. Died Nov. 27, 1986. Buried at Myrtle Cemetery, Ennis, TX.

Laznovsky, Jerry, son of Frank and Mary Trojacek Laznovsky, was born Sept. 4, 1914, Ennis, TX. Education: Mote Elementary School and graduated Ennis High School, 1931. Enlisted U.S. Army Air Corps, Mar. 4, 1942. Basic training at Sheppard Field, TX; special school at Lockheed in CA. Began overseas assignment, Jan. 1943, North Africa. Assigned to the Mediterranean Allied Force as an Air Force Maintenance and Flight Engineer. Served in French Morocco and participated in the Rome-Arno Campaign and Air Combat of the Balkans. Special assignment in Yugoslavia because of his knowledge of Czech language. Medals: Good Conduct Medal, EAME campaign ribbon, WWII Victory Medal, and other ribbons. Honorably discharged Nov. 8, 1945. Married Bessie Elleven in 1940; adopted two children, Gregson and Amy Lynn, making their home in Ennis, TX. Hobbies included Boy Scout Leadership, gardening, beekeeping, and activities in the Sokol Organization. Died Oct. 31, 1989; buried at Myrtle Cemetery, Ennis, TX.

Laznovsky, Jerry J. son of Charles and Matie Fraizal Laznovsky, was born on Jan. 15, 1917, in Ennis, Texas. Educated in Village Creek. Enlisted in Ennis on Feb. 11, 1941. Attained rank of Staff Sgt. Served in the North American Theater. Received the Good Conduct Medal and the North American Theater Medal. Discharged on Nov. 16, 1945, at Ellington A.F.B. Home of record: Ennis, TX.

Laznovsky, Johnny Joe, son of Edwin and Bessie Laznovsky, was born Jan. 17, 1950, in Ennis, TX. Graduated from St. John High School. Enlisted in the Army on Sept. 16, 1968, at Dallas, TX. Rank: SP5-E5. Theater of Operation: Viet Nam during the TET 69 Counter Offensive. Awards: National Defense Service, Viet Nam Service with one BSS, Viet Nam Campaign, and Rifle Expert. Discharged Sept. 15, 1971. Home of record: Ennis, TX.

Laznovsky, Milton Joe, son of Frank and Mary Trojacek Laznovsky, was born Feb. 23, 1927, Ennis, TX. Education: Mote Elementary School, and graduated Ennis High School, 1945. Drafted June 1945, Ennis, TX. Basic training at Camp Hood. Theaters of Operation: European and Viet Nam. Medals: Commendation w/1 silver star, Good Conduct w/5 BSS, European Theater; Army of Occupation; American Defense; American Viet Nam Action Force; Sharp Shooter. Retired from the U.S. Military, Jan. 1966, with rank of Sfc. E-7. Married Gilberte Chevassu of France; two children, one grandson. Employed in France, retiring in Jan. 1990. Enjoys gardening. Home of record: Bagneux, France.

Lebeda, Joe, son of Joe and Frances Kneitz Lebeda, was born 1900, Dubina, TX. Served in U.S. Army during WWI. Was to go overseas one day before Armistice. Honorably discharged. Died 1950; buried Dubina, TX.

Lednicky, Edward, served in U.S. Armed Forces

during WWI, 1917–1918. Member of SPJST Lodge 20, Granger, TX.

Lednickny, Edward F., son of Jerome J. Lednickny and Agnes G. Jaska, was born Sept. 8, 1937, West, TX. Education: St. Mary's Catholic School and West, TX, High School. Received B.S. and M.S. in Mechanical Engineering at Texas A&M. Attended Squadron Officer School and Armed Forces Staff College. Enlisted in the Air Force on July 5, 1959. Specialties included Navigator/Electronic Warfare Officer and Base Civil Engineer. Rank: Lt. Col. Assigned to Strategic Air Command, HQ Command, Tactical Air Command, and Military Airlift Command. Served at Osan Air Base, Korea, and a number of temporary duty assignments to Southeast Asia. Awards: Armed Forces Expeditionary Medal, Combat Readiness Medal, National Defense Service Medal, Viet Nam Service Medal with two Bronze OLC, Meritorious Service Medal, Commendation Medal w/2 Bronze OLC, and Outstanding Unit Award with one Bronze OLC. Retired as an Aerospace Engineer with Boeing, Ford and Loral Aerospace Companies at NASA Johnson Space Center, Houston, TX. Married to Catherine J. on May 7, 1960; four children: Thomas, Suzanne, James and John. Home of record: Houston, TX.

Lednicky, Jerome J., Jr., son of Jerome J. and Agnes G. Jaska Lednickny, was born May 22, 1936, West, TX. Education: St. Mary's Catholic School and West, TX, High School, Texas A&M. Commissioned 2nd Lt., May 24, 1957, U.S. Army Corps. Active duty 1/28/58–7/28/58. Attended Basic Inf. OFCR Course, Ft. Benning, GA. Assigned as Training Officer in Basic Training Bn., Ft. Smith, AR. Served in Army Reserve, 8/28/58–July 1967, in 345 MI Detachment LS1B in Waco, TX. Retired from Army Reserve, rank of Capt. Employed as an accountant by Cameron Iron Works, Houston, TX. Since Feb. 1961, has been a banker at State National Bank, West, TX. Married Lucille Agnes Gerik; four children: Kathleen L. Lednicky Horton; Ann Margaret Lednicky Melasky; Karen M. Lednicky McKenzie; Michael J. Lednicky. Home of record: West, TX.

Lednicky, Johnny, of West, TX, WWII veteran, U.S. Army Corps.

Lednicky, Rosalie, West, TX, WWII veteran, U.S. Army Nurse.

Lefler, James A., son of Mr. and Mrs. Frank Lefler, Taylor, TX. Education: Taylor High School. Enlisted U.S. Navy, 1942; basic training, San Diego, CA; additional training, Chicago IL; Miami, FL. Theater of Operations: Asiatic -Pacific. Medals: Good Conduct, American Defense, Asiatic-Pacific Theater Campaign Ribbon, WWII Victory.

Lefler, William, son of Mr. and Mrs. Tom Lefler, Taylor, TX. Education: Hutto schools. Enlisted U.S. Army Corps, 1944; basic training, Camp Crowder, MO; additional training, Camp Shelby, MS. Rank of Pvt. Honorable discharge, 1945. Married Lorene Schiller.

Lenart, Anton E., son of Mr. and Mrs. Anton Lenart. Entered U.S. Army Corps, 1944. Served in Manila, Luzon, Japan as a Pfc. Awarded GCM, Victory, Phil. Lib., Amer. Def. and AP Ribbon.

Lenart, Raymond E., son of Edd and Louise Jansky Lenart, was born May 19, 1924, West, TX. Education: St. Mary's Catholic School, West, TX. Enlisted in U.S. Army Corps, during WWII, Mar. 9, 1943, Waco, TX. Attained rank of Pfc. Theater of Operations: EAME. Served in Medical Detachment, 12th Inf. Reg. Medals: Good Conduct, Presidential Citation, EAME Campaign, European Theater Ribbon w/3 BSS. Honorably discharged Nov. 3, 1945. Civilian occupation: Farmer and Texas Dept. of Transportation. Home of record: V.A. Nursing Home, Waco, TX.

Leshikar, Hudson, son of Vilem Leshikar and Adela Chalupa, was born on Oct. 31, 1925, in Taylor, TX. Educated in Taylor. Enlisted at Fort Sam Houston on Dec. 31, 1943, Co. D, 255th Inf. 63rd Inf. Div. Campaigns: Rhineland, Central Europe. Assisted to load, aim, fire, clean, and maintain heavy machine guns to provide fire in support for tactical units and in defense of enemy aircraft and counter attack. Awards: Combat Infantryman Badge, EAME Theater Ribbon with three BSS, Good Conduct Medal, Army of Occupation Ribbon, Purple Heart, Overseas Service Bars. WOUNDED IN ACTION. Honorable discharge May 10, 1946. Home of record: Taylor, Texas.

Leshikar, Marvin James, son of Frank S. and Johanna Supdlenak Leshikar, was born June 5, 1921. Taylor High School, 1938; University of Texas, Austin, TX, 1938–1940 and 1946, Pharmacy degree; University of Texas Medical School, Galveston, TX, 1947–1951, Doctor of Medicine. Enlisted in the Army Air Corps Sept. 11, 1940, Taylor, TX. Reported for duty at Brooks Field, San Antonio, TX. Discharged as a Tech Sgt. Jan. 19, 1943, to enter officer ranks. Served in European Theatre of Operations as Aircraft Maintenance Officer. Discharged with rank of Capt. Feb. 9, 1946. Married Barbara Jean Rosendahl, five children, six grandchildren.

Leshikar, T'Odon Charles, Jr., son of T'Odon Charles Leshikar, Sr. and Angel Dexter Leshikar, was born Jan. 10, 1946, Austin, Travis Co., TX. Received BBA in Accounting from University of Texas at Austin, MBA in Accounting from St. Edwards University. Received commission at University of Texas at Austin, TX. Inducted into U.S. Army at San Antonio, TX. Rank: Capt. Theater of Operations: Viet Nam. Medals: Silver Star; BSS w/V and two OLC; Soldier's Medal; Air Medal; Army Commendation Medal; Purple Heart; Good Conduct Medal; National Defense Medal; Viet Nam Service Medal; Viet Namese Cross of Gallantry w/Silver Star and Palm Leaf; Viet Nam Combat Medal; Combat Infantryman's Badge; Parachute Wings. WOUNDED IN ACTION in Viet Nam. Honorably discharged July 13, 1969. Home of record: Lockhart, TX.

Lesikar, A. J., son of A.T. and Albina Macek Lesikar, was born about 1923, Seaton, TX. Attended Seaton High School. Entered Seabees in 1942, trained in Norfolk, VA. Carpenters Mate 1/C, 9th Con. Bn. Served in Iceland, Hawaii, Tinian, and Okinawa. Awards: EAME Campaign, Asiatic-Pacific Campaign with one BSS for the Okinawa Op., Good Conduct, and Expert Rifleman. Discharged 1945. Married Anita Jecmenek. Died Apr. 1974; buried in Seaton Cemetery, Seaton, TX. Submitted by son, Jeffrey Lesikar, Duncanville, TX.

Lesikar, Charlie J., son of Carl C. and Rosa Brushart Lesikar, was born on Mar. 10, 1916, in New Ulm, TX. Attended New Bremen Elementary School. Received GED through Blinn College. Decorations: American Theater Campaign Medal, EAME Campaign Medal with three BSS, Good Conduct Medal, two Overseas Bars. Rank: T5. Honorably discharged Oct. 31, 1945, at Ft. Sam Houston. Died Mar. 6, 1982 in Bellville, TX. Information submitted by his sister, Rosalie Lesikar, of New Ulm, TX.

Lev, Joe, son of Emil and Mary Veselka Lev, was born Aug. 12, 1918, in Praha, TX. Attended Praha School and then was engaged in farming. Joined the Army in May 1942. Received training at Camp Hood. KILLED IN ACTION on July 24, 1944, on Luzon Island by New Guinea.

Lezak, August, served Mar. 1941–Oct. 1945, in U.S. Army Corps during WWII.

Lichnovsky, Harry Dominic, son of Frank and Annie Hutyra Lichnovsky, was born Oct. 26, 1915, West, TX. Attended schools in West and Kemp, TX; business course at 4-C College, Waco, TX. Worked in family grocery store until Aug. 1943. Enlisted in the U.S. Navy on Aug. 30, 1943, Dallas, TX, during WWII. Training and tours at the Naval Air Station in Corpus Christi, TX, where he worked in Commissary. Theater of Operations: Asiatic-Pacific. Seaman 1/C aboard the battleship USS *New Jersey*; Marshall Islands, Japan. Back was injured during naval operations at Okinawa. Discharged Dec. 21, 1945, at Camp Wallace, TX. Home of record: West, TX.

Lichnovsky, Henry, Capt. in U.S. Army Corps, WWII. Was a dentist. Hometown: Schulenburg, TX. Deceased.

Lichnovsky, Joe, Capt. in U.S. Army Corps, WWII. Was a veterinarian. Hometown, Nada, TX. Deceased.

Lichnovsky, Richard, attained rank of Capt. in U.S. Army Corps, WWII. Was a dentist. Hometown, Nada, TX. Deceased.

Licka, Emil M., was born July 22, 1907. Cpl. U.S. Army, WWII. Died May 5, 1969; buried Holy Cross Catholic Cemetery, Granger, TX.

Lidiak, Leon Paul, son of Paul and Emma Dolezal Lidiak, was born Aug. 29, 1931, at La Grange, TX. Attended Sacred Heart School and La Grange High School. Enlisted in the U.S. Navy at Houston, TX, during the Korean Conflict. Participated in naval operations at Inchon and Hungnam. Decorations include the Navy Commendation Medal with Combat A Device, Good Conduct Medal, Korean Service Medal with four campaign stars, and the National Defense Service Medal. Discharged May 20, 1953. Home of record: Houston, TX.

Lindemann, Edward Otto, son of August Clark and Annie Ernestine Jeschke Lindemann, Granger, TX. Education: Granger High School. Married Otylice A. Tallas. Enlisted U.S. Army Corps, 1943; basic training, Camp Claiborne, LA; further training, Camp Sutton, NC. Theater of Operations: Asiatic-Pacific. Served in Guadalcanal; Solomon Islands. Medals: Asiatic-Pacific Theater Campaign Ribbon; Good Conduct Medal; WWII Victory Medal. Honorably discharged, 1946. Attained rank of Sgt. Home of record: Granger, TX.

Lindemann, James William, son of August Clark and Annie Ernestine Jeschke Lindemann, was born Aug. 18, 1919, Wharton Co., TX. Education: Moravia Elementary School and Granger High School, Williamson Co., TX. Enlisted in U.S. Navy, Jan. 18, 1945; boot camp, San Diego, CA. Theater of Operations: Asiatic-Pacific. Medals: Asiatic-Pacific Theater Campaign Medal w/BSS and Ribbon, Good Conduct Medal, WWII Victory Medal. Served in Hawaii and Guam. PC 1244 ran into a mine in the South Pacific in 1945. Achieved rank of MoMM 3/c prior to honorable discharge, Apr. 13, 1946. Married Viola; children: James Earl and Jo Ann. Rancher. Retired Feb. 1990. Hobbies: hunting and fishing. Home of record: Mason, TX. Submitted by daughter, JoAnn Lindemann, Mason, TX.

Lindemann, Woodrow A., son of Mr. and Mrs. August C. Lindemann, Granger, TX. Enlisted U.S. Army Corps, 1940; basic training Ft. Sam Houston, TX; additional training, Camp Harahan, LA; Camp Stoneman, CA. Theater of Operations: Asiatic-Pacific. Served in South Pacific, Luzon, Northern Solomons. Medals: Asiatic-Pacific Theater Campaign Ribbon w/2 BSS, Philippine Liberation Ribbon, one BSS, American Defense Ribbon, WWII Victory Ribbon. Attained rank of S/Sgt. Married Helen Cervenka. Home of record: Granger, TX.

Liska, Bob, military service veteran. Home of record: Dallas, TX.

Loeve, Clarence Henry, son of Henry V. and Mary Martinets Loeve, Granger, TX. Graduate of Granger High School. Enlisted U.S. Navy, 1943; basic training, San Diego, CA. Theater of Operations: Asiatic-Pacific. Assigned to Comp. Sqd. 42, USS *Guadalcanal*; Fighting Sqd. 34, USS *Kula Gulf*. Medals: Asiatic-Pacific Theater Campaign Ribbon w/BSS; WWII Victory Medal. Attained rank of S 1/c before honorable discharge, 1945. Member American Legion Post No. 282, Granger, TX.

Loeve, Edward Jerome, son of Henry V. and Mary Martinets Loeve. Graduated from Granger, TX, High School, 1951. Enlisted in the U.S. Navy during the Korean Conflict, and served aboard an aircraft carrier. Participated in naval operations off the shores of Korea. Assigned aircraft carrier was the first to go around the Cape of Good Horn and the first aircraft carrier whose planes engaged enemy jet aircraft in aerial combat. Decorations: Korean Service Medal, Korean Campaign Medal, United Nations Service Medal, and Good Conduct Medal. Separated from service on Dec. 20, 1955. Retired from his civilian occupation in Sept. 1993. Married Rosemary Lee Zoella; four children: three girls and one boy. Home of record: Austin, TX.

Loeve, Leonard B., son of Mr. and Mrs. Henry

Loeve, Granger, TX. Education: Granger High School. Enlisted U.S. Navy, 1943; basic training San Diego, CA. Theater of Operations: Asiatic-Pacific. Assigned USS *Portland* in Marshall. Served in raids on New Guinea, Carolines, Leyte, Luzon, Okinawa. Medals: Asiatic-Pacific Theater Campaign Ribbon w/9 BSS, WWII Victory Medal, among others. Achieved rank of S 1/c before being honorably discharged.

Loeve, Oswald Arthur, son of Otto and Rose Mikes Loeve, born Sept. 21, 1914. Education: Moravian School, Granger, TX, finished 8th grade 1929, Granger High School, graduated 1932, California College of Commerce, graduated 1962. Enlisted in U.S. Navy, June 15, 1934, in Houston, TX. Served as Chief Quartermaster in the ETO. Battles: Sicily, Anzio, Elba-Pianoso Landings, and Southern France. Decorations include: American Theater, American Defense, European-Middle Eastern, Pacific Theater, China Service, WWII Victory, Good Conduct, National Defense, United Nations, Korean Service, and Occupation. In 1938 was aboard USS *Boise* on its shakedown cruise. Discharged Feb. 2, 1959. Home of record: Long Beach, CA.

Loika, Gilbert W., son of Louis F. and Julia Barina Loika, born May 20, 1922, Ballinger, Runnels Co., TX. Attended Ballinger High School, received Associates Degree, San Angelo, TX. Enlisted in U.S. Army Air Corps, San Antonio, TX. Assigned to American Theater of Operations. Medals: GCM; Rifle Marksman. "I was Crew Chief on five ATIIs and loaded these planes with lots of bombs!" Honorably discharged Jan. 14, 1944, San Antonio, TX. Home of record: San Angelo, TX.

Lovecky, John S., son of Mr. and Mrs. Anton Lovecky, was born Oct. 23, 1919, Abbott, TX. Attended West, TX, schools. Entered U.S. Army Corps, 1941. Trained at Ft. Sam Houston. Served European Theater as Pfc. WOUNDED IN ACTION, Germany, 1944. Awarded Purple Heart, GCM, BSS, Pres. Cit., and Belgian Fouriagere. Discharged, 1945. Married Juanita Smith. Died Jan. 14, 1988. Buried in Waco Memorial Park Cemetery, Waco, TX.

Lovecky, Louis, son of Mr. and Mrs. Anton Lovecky, Abbott, TX. Served in U.S. Armed Forces during WWII. Married Mary Simicek. Buried in military cemetery in California.

Lovecky, Steve R., son of Mr. and Mrs. Anton Lovecky, born Sept. 7, 1921, Abbott, TX. Served in U.S. Army Air Corps as Sgt. during WWII. Married Anna Ruth Foit. Died Sept. 26, 1989; buried in West Brethren Cemetery, West, TX.

Loykasek, Calvin, WWII veteran of Granger, TX.

Loykasek, Daniel H., son of Frank and Ida Sheila Loykasek, was born Nov. 5, 1915, Port Lavaca, TX. Attended Lane View School, Ennis, TX. Entered the U.S. Army Corps, Ft. Sam Houston, San Antonio, TX. Theater of Operation: Asiatic Pacific. Rank: Pfc. Medals: Asiatic Pacific Campaign Ribbon, Army Occupation Japan, WWII Victory, GCM Medal, two overseas service bars. Honorable discharge Aug. 31, 1946, San Antonio, TX. Home of record: Dallas, TX.

Lucien, Robert, was raised in the Tours and West, TX, area. Entered U.S. Navy, 1941; trained San Diego, CA. Served in S.W. Pacific as PO 1/C. Awarded Pre Pearl Harbor, ATAP Ribbons, two Battle Stars, GCM.

Lucien, William F., son of Mr. and Mrs. Frank Lucian, entered U.S. Navy, 1943, served in Okinawa and China as ARM 2/C. Awarded GCM, AT, AP, and Victory Ribbons. Discharged 1946.

Luksa, Louis I., son of Jan. and Emily Luksa, Enlisted at Ft. Sam Houston, TX; Theater of Operation: EAME. KILLED IN ACTION, 1943, Italy. Medals: Purple Heart, BSS. Submitted by Edwin L. Hlavaty, Caldwell, TX.

M

McNatt, Wiley, Jr., son of Wiley McNatt, Sr. and Frances Pavlicek McNatt (daughter of Vinc Pavlicek [descendant of Ignac Pavlicek and Veronica Miculka, immigrants from Palkovice, Moravia, 1860, on the "Jeverland"] and Agnes Broz), was born about 1917, Texas. Wiley was KILLED IN ACTION, 1945, when plane was shot down over Holland.

Macalik, Tonie Zhanel, daughter of Anton and Mary Zhanel, Macalik was born Apr. 19, 1922, in Ennis, TX. Attended Central High School and Metropolitan Business College. Enlisted in the Army on Aug. 5, 1943, at Dallas, TX. Rank: Tech. 4/C. Medals include American Theater Campaign, Good Conduct, Victory, and WAAC. Discharged Jan. 11, 1946. Died Mar. 26, 1961.

Mach, Adolph, Jr., son of Adolph Mach, Sr. and Cathryn Sana Mach, was born Nov. 6, 1914 in Waco, TX. During World War II, enlisted in the U.S. Army at Ft. Sam Houston, TX. Served in the European, African, and Middle Eastern Theater of Operations as a member of the U.S. Army Signal Corps and attained the rank of Technical Sgt. Participated in the Normandy, Northern France, Rhineland, Ardennes: Alsace, and Central Europe Campaigns. Awards and decorations include the BSS Medal, European-African-Middle Eastern Campaign Medal with five campaign stars, Good Conduct Medal, and the Meritorious Unit Citation Badge. Discharged July 7, 1945 at Ft. Sam Houston, TX. Was a mechanic prior to his death on Nov. 4, 1985. Interred in the Chapel Hill Cemetery at Chapel Hill, TX.

Mach, Edd, son of Adolph and Cathryn Sana Mach, born May 4, 1924, Elk, TX. Attended Elk Elementary School and La Vega High School in Bellmead, McLennan Co., TX. Joined the U.S. Marine Corps Jan. 31, 1942, Dallas, TX. Served in the Pacific Theater during WWII. Paratrooper with the 1st Marine Paratroop Regiment and 22nd Marine Regiment. Attached to the 1st, 2nd, 4th and 5th Marine Divisions. Fought in Solomon Islands, Marshall Islands (Saipan), Iwo Jima. Participated in the Occupation of Japan. Awards: Pacific Asiatic Campaign Ribbon; American Campaign Ribbon; Occupation; WWII; GCM. Attained rank of Cpl. Honorable discharge Feb. 6, 1946, Corpus Christi, TX.

Mach, Fred J., son of Adolph Mach, Sr. and Cathryn Sana Mach, was born Apr. 10, 1919, in Elk, TX, and attended high school at Elk. Enlisted in the U.S. Army at Dallas, TX, during WWII, and served in the European, African, and Middle Eastern Theater of Operations, attaining the rank of Pfc. Participated in the Naples-Foggia, Rome-Arno, Southern France, Rhineland, and Central Europe Campaigns. Awards and decorations include the European-African-Middle Eastern Campaign Medal with five campaign stars and a bronze arrowhead, American Campaign Medal, and Good Conduct Medal. Discharged at Ft. Sam Houston, TX, on Aug. 14, 1945. Married Margaret Navara; one son. Building contractor in the Waco, TX area. Died June 5, 1982; interred in the SPJST Pavelka Cemetery in Elk, McLennan Co., TX.

Mach, Joe G., of West, TX, served in the U.S. Armed Forces during WWII as a Pvt. Asiatic-Pacific Theater of Operations. Rifleman with Field Artillery, 41st Div. KILLED IN ACTION on Mindanao, Philippine Islands, Mar. 10, 1945.

Mach, Leslie T., military service veteran. Home of record: Ennis, TX.

Mach, Raymond T., military service veteran. Home of record: Dallas, TX.

Mach, Wesley Frank, son of Frank and Josephine Honza Mach, was born Dec. 11, 1931, Ennis, TX. Attended St. John's High School, Ennis, TX.

Enlisted in U.S. Navy, Dallas, TX; served in Korean War on USS *Boxer* CV21. Awards: Korean Presidential Unit Medal, Korean Service Medal, United Nations Service Medal, National Defense Medal, China Service Medal, GCM Medal. Honorably discharged July 19, 1955, Kingsville Naval Base.

Mach, William T., son of John T. and Mary Vrana Mach, was born July 14, 1921, in Ennis, TX. Attended Lane View Grade School. Enlisted in the U.S. Army Corps in Ennis, TX, July 1942. Stationed at Camp Gruber, OK, Camp Roberts, CA, Camp McCoy, WI, Camp Picket, VA, as T/4 Sgt., Medical Detachment, 264th Engineer, Combat Battalion in England, France, Germany (served in Rhineland, Central Europe during WWII) and Australia. Medals: American Theater Campaign with three BSS, EAME Campaign Medal with two BSS, Good Conduct and WWII Victory Medal. Discharged Mar. 2, 1946, Camp Fannin, TX. Married Annie Pekar; one daughter, three sons. Worked for Ford Motor Co. in Dallas and Louisville, KY, and retired after 32 years of service. Home of record: Mesquite, TX.

Macha, Edith Martha, daughter of Victor H. and Albina Bartos Macha, was born Aug. 27, 1917 in Brownsfield, TX. Education: University of Colorado, Boulder, CO, and the University of St. John's, New York, earning a Nursing degree and becoming a Registered Nurse. Began military career during World War II at Corpus Christi, TX, in the U.S. Navy Medical Corps. Served in the Asiatic-Pacific Theater of Operations. Served in WWII, the Korean Conflict, and the Viet Nam Conflict. Retired with the rank of Cmdr., U.S. Navy in May 1971. Home of record:Lubbock, TX.

Macha, Ernest Joe, son of Joe and Edna Horecka Macha, was born Dec. 31, 1945, in Wharton, TX. Attended Holy Family Catholic Grammar School and Hungerford schools, graduating from East Bernard High School in 1964. Attended Wharton Co. Junior College and Sam Houston State University, Huntsville, TX, in 1970, earning a B.A. in Business. Drafted into the U.S. Army during the Viet Nam War in Nov. 1970 at Wharton, TX. Basic and advanced training at army clerk school at Fort Leonardwood, MO. Rank: SP5. Honorably discharged in May 1971 at Fort Sam Houston, San Antonio, TX. Home: Wharton, TX.

Macha, Leroy W., son of Frank J. Macha, Jr. and Annie Klimek Macha, was born on Dec. 19, 1922, in Hungerford, TX. Attended Hungerford and Wharton Schools. Graduated from A&M University in 1947. Entered the Army while attending A&M by enlisting in Reserve Corps. Activated in Mar. 1942 to Camp Beauregard, LA. Basic training at Camp Roberts, Santa Rosa, CA. Army Spec. training at University of California, Berkeley, CA. Served at Camp Bowie, Brownwood, TX, then enlisted in the Air Force at Sheppard Field, Wichita Falls, TX; Keesler Field, Biloxi, MS; Biggs Field, El Paso, TX. Discharged Nov. 30, 1945 at Ft. Bliss, TX. Married Ann Kovar at East Bernard, TX, June 11, 1947; three children: Larry L. Macha, Gene A. Macha, and Judy Macha Brown. Operated Macha Grocery in Hungerford, TX, from July 1947 to Aug. 1974. Elected Wharton County Commissioner, Precinct 2, and served from 1975 to 1983. Home of record: Hungerford, TX.

Machac, Ben G., son of Paul and Josephine Machac, was born in St. John, TX, Mar. 21, 1917. Enlisted in U.S. Army Corps, Mar. 17, 1942, Ft. Sam Houston, TX. Served as Rifleman Instructor 745 in WWII. Rank: T/Sgt. Fought in the Battle of Normandy (GO 33 WD 45); fought 33 days on the front lines before being captured; PRISONER OF WAR in Germany 10 months. Escaped Apr. 8, 1944. Earned the Combat Infantryman Badge, EAME Campaign Medal w/1 BSS. Honorably discharged Nov. 5, 1945. Had five brothers in WWII. Mother received a Pin for having six sons in the military service.

Machac, Delphine Charles, son of Mr. and Mrs. Julius Machac, was born Nov. 24, 1929, in Glen Flora, TX. Graduated from Blessing High School.

Drafted into the Army at Fort Sam Houston, TX, on Feb. 4, 1951. Rank: Pfc. Served two years, including five months in Goose Bay Labrador during construction of the Air Base. Discharged Feb. 5, 1953, at Fort Lee, VA. Moved to Victoria, TX, with wife and family in 1962. Employed by Mrs. Baird's Bakery as a route supervisor.

Machac, Fred A., son of Paul Machac, Sr. and Josephine Krenek Machac, was born in Novohrad, Lavaca Co., TX. Entered military service at Ft. Sam Houston, San Antonio, TX. Served during WWII. Rank: Sgt. Awards: European African Middle Eastern Medal; GCM Medal; five overseas Service Bars. Honorable discharge Oct. 12, 1945 at AAF Separation Base, Randolph, TX.

Machacek, Bill Cyril, son of Frank and Mary Nemec Machacek, was born June 8, 1929, in Holland, Bell Co., TX. Attended schools in Holland, Jarrell and Granger. Enlisted in the Army in San Antonio, TX. Served as a truck driver for an infantry division. Discharged Nov. 30, 1952 at the rank of Pfc. Married Mary Lee Polasek; five children. Home of record: Houston, TX.

Machacek, Charles A., Sr., son of John W. and Frantiska Nemec Machacek, was born Mar. 2, 1922, Granger, TX. Education: Moravian Public School, Granger, TX; Sts. Cyril & Methodius Catholic School, Granger, TX; Granger Public School, Granger, TX; University of Alabama, Ext. in Mobile, AL. Enlisted in U.S. Army Corps, Jan. 10, 1941, San Antonio, TX. Theater of Operations: American. Honorable discharge as a S/Sgt., Dec. 5, 1945. Enlisted U.S. Air Force, Apr. 23, 1951, Mobile, AL. Theater of Operations: Korea; dodged bombs in Korea. Honorable discharge, as a T/Sgt., Oct. 14, 1952. Married Alice D. Machacek; three children: Laura M. Machacek Stephens; Mary M. Machacek Horn; Charles A. Machacek, Jr. Retired from USAF. Civil Service as Senior Industrial Engineer. Father and three brothers all served in military. Unable to locate list of medals. Home of record:San Antonio, TX.

Machacek, Clement W., son of John W. and Frantiska Nemec Machacek, served from enlistment in 1952, for over 20 years in U.S. Air Force and U.S. Army. Retired at rank of Capt. Theater of Operations: Far East, Europe, Viet Nam, and Saudi Arabia Desert Storm. Submitted by brother, Charles A. Machacek, Sr.

Machacek, Frankie S., son of Mr. and Mrs. Frank Machacek, Granger, TX. Education: Jarrell High School. Enlisted U.S. Army Corps, 1944; basic training, Camp Hood, TX; further training, Camp Rucker, AL. Theaters of Operation: American; European. Served in England, France, Austria. Medals: Combat Infantry Badge; BSS, American Campaign Theater Ribbon, ETO Campaign Medal, WWII Victory Medal. Attained rank of Pfc. before honorable discharge.

Machacek, John F., son of John W. and Frantiska Nemec Machacek, enlisted in 1944, served for over 20 years in U.S. Army and U.S. Marine Corps. Served in Far East and Europe. Retired at rank of T/Sgt. Submitted by brother, Charles A. Machacek, Sr.

Machacek, John W., son of Mr. and Mrs. Machacek, born in Praha, Czechoslovakia, enlisted in U.S. Army Corps during WWI, served with American Expeditionary Forces, in the ETO, France and Germany, over four years. Honorably discharged with rank of Cpl. Submitted by son Charles A. Machacek, Sr.

Machacek, Wesley E., son of John W. and Frantiska Nemec Machacek, enlisted in U.S. Marine Corps, 1952, served for over six years in Far East and Europe. Honorably discharged as Sgt. Submitted by brother, Charles A. Machacek, Sr.

Machala, Jack Alois, son of Joe Emil and Vivian Francis Janczak Machala, was born Aug. 16, 1946, Houston, Harris Co., TX. Graduated 1964, Sealy High School, TX; Graduated 1970, Blinn Jr. College, Brenham. Enlisted Sept. 27, 1965, U.S. Navy. Military Occupation: Aerographers Mate. Stationed aboard USS *Wright* (CC-2). Theater of Operations Viet Viet Nam. Honorable discharge

Sept. 27, 1971. Married Sharon Kay Prihoda; three children: Carrie Lynn; Robin Marie; Mindy Noelle. Hobbies: water skiing; snow skiing; tennis; softball. Civilian occupation: Design Engineer, Southwestern Bell. Home of record: Sealy, TX.

Machala, Jerry, served Mar. 1941–Oct. 1945, in U.S. Army Corps during WWII.

Machala, Louis Raymond, son of Mr. Machala and Bertha Mary Tobolka, was born Aug. 15, 1924, Granger, TX. Attended Granger Catholic School, Forney, TX, Forney High School, and Southern Methodist University. Enlisted in the U.S. Marine Corps in Dallas, TX, Jan. 28, 1944 and achieved the Rank of Corporal. Served in the Pacific during WWII and fought battles on Iwo Jima as #1 Machine Gunner, 3rd Marine Division. 9th Regiment, 2nd Battalion, Fox Co. (called the Fighting Fox). Honorable discharge Apr. 16, 1946.

Machan, Henry John, son of John J. and Frances Sefcik Machan, was born Sept. 25, 1912 in Caldwell, TX. Attended public schools through 9th grade in Burleson Co., vocational school in Milwaukee, WI, and college at the University of Houston, TX. Entered the Army at Houston, TX and was in the Infantry, 3rd Army. Fought at the Battle of the Bulge in WWII. Medals include Sharp Shooter, Good Conduct and Purple Heart. KILLED IN ACTION at the Battlefield in France Nov. 11, 1944. Buried at New Tabor Cemetery in Burleson Co., TX.

Machan, Joseph John, son of Tom and Helen Fitzgerald Machan, was born Dec. 21, 1913, in Caldwell, TX. Attended schools through 9th grade in Burleson Co., TX, Lee College and San Jacinto Jr. College. Enlisted in the Army in Cameron, Milam Co., TX. Rank: Sgt. 71st AA Radar in Washington, DC, Light Pontoon Engineering in KY and Scottfield, IL. Received American Theater, Good Conduct and WWII Victory Medals. Discharged Dec. 4, 1945. Home of record: Pasadena, TX.

Machann, Edward Henry, son of John J. and Lydia Ann Hovorak Machan, was born July 9, 1925, Burleson Co., TX, the 6th of 11 children. Two older brothers, Frank Tom and Johnnie W. also served in U.S. Military. Education: Caldwell, TX. Enlisted in U.S. Army Corps, Jan. 17, 1945, Somerville, Burleson Co., TX. Trained at Ft. Bliss, TX. Theater of Operations: Asiatic-Pacific. Medals: Good Conduct Medal; WWII Victory Medal, Asiatic-Pacific Theater Ribbon. Honorably discharged at Ft. Sam Houston, TX, Dec. 4, 1946. Employed by and retired from General Tire and Rubber Company, Waco, TX. Married Lucille Virginia Glenn, June 30, 1950; two children: Janice Lucille Machan Nelson and Glen Edward Machan. Had many interests and activities: Deacon and Sunday School teacher at Bellmead 1st Baptist Church, member of Bellmead Masonic Lodge #1329, AF & AM of Texas. Enjoyed outdoors, especially hunting and boating. Seldom missed an opportunity to return to hometown and help his family with farming responsibilities. Died Oct. 27, 1986 at home in Waco, McLennan Co., TX. Buried at Chapel Hill Cemetery, Waco, TX. Submitted by daughter, Janice Machan Nelson, Waco, TX.

Machann, Frank Tom, son of John J. and Lydia Ann Hovorak Machann, was born prior to 1925, Burleson Co., TX, served during WWII in U.S. Armed Forces. Submitted by niece, Janice Machan Nelson, Waco, TX.

Machann, Johnnie W., son of John J. and Lydia Ann Hovorak Machann, was born prior to 1925, Burleson Co., TX. Served during WWII in U.S. Armed Forces. Submitted by niece, Janice Machan Nelson, Waco, TX.

Machart, August A., son of John F. and Mary J. Vesely Machart, was born Aug. 29, 1921, at Shiner, TX. Completed three years of high school prior to enlistment into the U.S. Army at Ft. Sam Houston, TX, during WWII. Served in the European, African, and Middle Eastern Theater of Operations and attained the rank of Pfc. Participated in the Naples-Foggia, Rome-Arno, Po Valley, and Northern Apennines Campaigns. Decorations include the European African Middle Eastern Campaign Medal with four campaign stars, and Good Conduct Medal. Discharged Oct. 22, 1945. Home of record:Yoakum, TX.

Machart, John Frank, son of Vaclav and Maria Riha Machart, was born Dec. 14, 1895, in Praha, TX. Enlisted in the U.S. Navy at Houston, TX, during WWI. Served with the American Expeditionary Forces in Europe, specifically in Scotland and England, as a Seaman 2/C. Duties included mine laying operations in the English Channel. Discharged July 23, 1919. Married Mary J. Vesely. Died in Nov. 1976.

Machscek, Charles, WWII veteran of Granger, TX.

Machu, Frank Raymond, son of John T. and Vera Pokarny Machu, was born Mar. 10, 1895, Granger, TX. Education: Moravia School, Granger, TX. Enlisted in U.S. Army Corps during WWI. With the American Expeditionary Forces Overseas. Medals: WWI Victory Medal, and others. Honorably discharged late 1918. Married Annie Korenek. Hobbies: fishing and swimming. Died Apr. 23, 1937; buried in Machu Cemetery, near Granger, TX.

Machu, Johnny Daniel, son of John Ludwik and Frances Emilie Kopecky Machu, was born Sept. 16, 1925, in Granger, Williamson Co., TX. Attended Moravia School and Granger and Taylor High Schools. Inducted into U.S. Navy, Nov. 27, 1943, in San Antonio, TX. In charge of maintenance of motor vehicles. Received the American Area Victory Medal. Discharged Feb. 17, 1946, as Motor Machinist Mate 2/C. Married Dolores Angeline Cervenka; three children. Died Oct. 4, 1986; buried in Machu Cemetery, Granger, TX.

Machu, Johnnie Leonard, son of Johnnie Daniel and Delores Cervenka Machu, was born Aug. 8, 1951, in Taylor, Williamson Co., TX. Attended Taylor public schools and was a honor graduate in May 1969. Enlisted in the Naval Reserves May 26, 1970, and went active in Austin, TX, Aug. 8, 1971. Served as an engine mechanic. Discharged Apr. 18, 1973, as Engineman-3. Married Marilyn Urbanek. Home of record: Taylor, TX.

Macik, Albin Ladislav, son of Joseph and Mary Krcma Macik, was born June 27, 1915, West, TX. Attended St. Mary's School in West, TX, and West High School. Entered military service in Dallas, TX. Served in Company F, 124th Infantry, New Guinea and Southern Philippines, WWII. Rank: S/Sgt. Awards: WWII Victory Medal, one Service Stripe, three overseas Service Bars, American Theater Campaign Medal, Asiatic-Pacific Campaign Medal w/2 BSS, Philippine Liberation Medal w/1 BSS, GCM Medal. Honorable discharge, Ft. Sam Houston, TX, Dec. 25, 1945.

Macik, Alois "Lewis," son of Joseph and Marie Krcma Macik, was born Jan. 23, 1909, Tours, TX. Education: St. Mary's Catholic School, West, TX. Enlisted in U.S. Army Corps during WWII, 1942, Camp Wolters, TX. Rank: Pfc. Assigned to 2009th Ord. Maint. Co. A.F., Capt. O.R.D. Dept. Theater of Operations, Europe. Medals: EAME, WWII Victory, and others. Sailed home from Marseille, France, on U.S.S. *John Ericsson*. Honorably discharged Sept. 1, 1945. Died Oct. 25, 1986. Submitted by nephew, Arnold Dobecka, of Ennis, TX.

Macik, Stanislav, Penelope, TX, WWII veteran, U.S. Army Corps, PRISONER OF WAR.

Macik, Stanislav John, son of Mr. and Marie Krcma Macik, was born in West, TX, Nov. 23,

1918. Attended St. Mary's Catholic School, West, TX, and Penelope High School. Entered military service Oct. 24, 1942, Abilene, TX. Rank: Cpl. Served in North Africa with Co. A, 766th Military Police Bn. during WWII. Awards: American Campaign Medal, Asiatic Pacific Campaign Medal, WWII Victory Medal, one service stripe, one overseas service bar, GCM Medal. Honorably discharged Jan. 30, 1946. Died Sept. 5, 1981.

Majek, Charlie M., son of Leopold and Rosie Majek, was born Nov. 7, 1923, at Cameron, TX. Enlisted in the U.S. Army at San Antonio, TX during WWII. Trained as a driver, tank driver, and mechanic, and served in the Asiatic Pacific Theater of Operations, attaining the rank of T/Sgt. Participated in the Leyte and Southern Philippines Campaigns, serving at Okinawa, Leyte, and Ruykyus. Decorations include the Asiatic Pacific Campaign Medal with two campaign stars and bronze arrowhead, Good Conduct Medal, WWII Victory Medal, and Philippine Liberation Ribbon with two BSS. Discharged Dec. 28, 1945. Home of record: Corpus Christi, TX.

Makovy, Albina J., of West, TX, WWII veteran.

Makovy, Charles F., son of Mr. and Mrs. J. H. Makovy, Ross, TX. Entered Navy, 1942. Attended Tokyo School. Served in Asiatic-Pacific Theater, during WWII, aboard USS *Sirius*. Awarded A.P. Ribbon and GCM. Attained rank of Csf. prior to discharge, 1945.

Malcik, Wilson John, son of John and Rose Bubela Malcik, was born in Rosebud, Falls Co., TX, Nov. 1, 1918. Attended Rosebud High School, North Texas State Teachers College, and the Aeronautical University, Chicago, IL. Joined the U.S. Air Force, Sept. 17, 1940, Barksdale Field, LA. During WWII served in Papua, New Guinea, East India, and Bismarck Archipelago, as an airplane maintenance technician. Rank: M/Sgt. Awards: Presidential Citation, Airplane Mechanic Technician Badge, Asiatic Pacific Theater Medal w/4 BSS; American Defense Service Medal, and GCM Medal. Treated for service connected mental fatigue in Dec. 1944, and was honorably discharged, Apr. 2, 1945, having served his country for five and a half years. Died June 17, 1993.

Malina, Benjamin H., Sr., son of Mr. and Mrs. Frank J. Malina, was born Dec. 30, 1914, Hochheim, TX. Attended school through ninth grade. Enlisted in U.S. Army Corps, Feb. 13, 1937, Ft. Sam Houston, TX. Served in the 2nd Div., 23rd Inf., D Co. Medals: Expert 30 Caliber Machine Gun and Sharpshooter w/50 Caliber Machine Gun Medals, also GCM Medal. Honorably discharged Feb. 11, 1940. Reenlisted Feb. 2, 1942, Foster Field, Victoria, TX. Rank: T/Sgt. Served in the India and China, American Theater Asiatic Pacific. Honorably discharged Mar. 14, 1946, Ft. Bliss, TX.

Malina, William J., son of Tom and Anna M. Elsik Malina, was born in Shiner, TX, Jan. 1, 1933. Graduated from Shiner H.S. Inducted into the U.S. Army Corps, May 1, 1953, Ft. Sam Houston, TX. Basic training, Ft. Bliss, El Paso, TX. Attended Gunner School Ft. Bliss, TX; served in Headquarters Bty., 56th AAA Missile Bn., Ft. Monroe, VA. Corp. Rank: E-4. Awards: National Defense Service Medal, Good Conduct Medal. Honorably discharged Apr. 29, 1955, Ft. Monroe, VA.

Malish, Theodore E., son of Mr. and Mrs. Paul Malish, Georgetown, TX. Enlisted U.S. Army Air Corps,1940; basic training Denver, CO; further training: TX, NV, UT, WA, CA. Theaters of Operations: American, European. Served in England on five missions. Awards: Air Medal, Purple Heart, Presidential Citation Medal, American Theater Campaign Ribbon, ETO Campaign Ribbon w/5 BSS. Achieved rank of S/Sgt before being KILLED IN ACTION, in France, June 1943.

Malota, Jerome John, Sr., son of John Valentine and Julia Maria Tichavsky Malota, was born Jan.

19, 1922, Fayetteville, TX. Education: Willow Springs School in Fayette Co., TX; New Bremen School, Austin Co., TX. Drafted into U.S. Army Corps, Austin Co. Court House, Bellville, TX. Active duty Nov. 21, 1942, Camp Wolters, TX. Moved to Camp Wallace, TX. Theater of Operations: Europe. Assigned 534th Triple A Bn. (Anti Aircraft Artillery), Bty. C, 3rd Army (joined together with 5th and 7th Armies while in battle). Battles: Naples-Foggia, Rome-Arno, Southern France, Rhineland, Central Europe. Medals: North African Campaign Bar, ETO Ribbon w/5 battle stars, one bronze arrowhead, Good Conduct Medal, four Overseas Service Bars. Got credit for shooting down three German planes. Special event was when company turned in guns and artillery Aug. 2, 1945, ending the war for him. Honorably discharged Oct. 25, 1945. Married Rosie Mathilda Kollaja; three children: Margie Ann Malota Stockman; Jerome John Malota, Jr., and Kenneth Ray Malota. Enjoys working on farm in Fayetteville, TX, that has been in the family for five generations, and enjoys helping his family. Retired from Houston Poster, and Foster and Kleiser Advertising Companies as a billboard sign hanger. Home of record: Houston, TX.

Maly, Bessie, daughter of Frank and Maria Musha Maly, was born June 14, 1917, Shiner, TX. Education: 6th grade, Sunset School. Enlisted in WAAC, Dallas, TX. Assigned to WAAC Detachment Hospital, Feb. 14, 1943 through Jan. 15, 1946. Medals: American Theater Campaign Medal, Good Conduct Medal, WWII Victory Ribbon, WAAC Ribbon. Honorably discharged Jan. 15, 1946, Ft. Sam Houston, San Antonio, TX. Married Mr. Prochaska. Home of record: Ft. Worth, TX.

Maly, Bohus J., son of Frank and Maria Musha Maly, was born June 22, 1914, Shiner, TX. Education: St. Ludmilla Catholic School, Sunset Public School, Shiner, TX. Enlisted Ft. Worth, Tarrant, TX, U.S. Army Corps, about 1942. Theater of Operations: EAME. Assigned to Cannoneer Co., 350th Inf. Battles: Gun Crewman, Light Artillery 844th Combat Infantryman; Rome-Arno; No. Apennines GO 33 WD 45. Decorations: American Theater Campaign Medal, Good Conduct Medal, Combat Ribbon, EAME Campaign Medal w/2 BSS, WWII Victory Medal. Honorably discharged Nov. 30, 1945, Camp Fannin, TX. Home of record: Roanoke, TX.

Maly, Jerry J., son of Paul and Ruzena Karban Maly, was born Oct. 26, 1913, in Garber, OK. Graduated from Garber High School and attended Oklahoma State University at Stillwater, OK, B.S. in General Engineering. Inducted into the U.S. Army at Enid, OK, on July 20, 1942, during WWII. Attained the rank of Cpl. before being commissioned as a Second Lt. upon graduation from OCS in Feb. 1943. Served in the European, African, and Middle Eastern Theaters of Operations with the U.S. Army Medical Corps, attaining the rank of First Lt. before discharge on Jan. 19, 1946. Married; five children. Resided in Texarkana, TX, and had been Chief, Depot Facilities, at the Red River Army Depot at Texarkana, TX, for some 25 years. Died Apr. 22, 1987.

Maly, Ladik, son of Paul and Ruzena Karban Maly, was born Dec. 13, 1916, in Garber, OK. Graduated from Garber High School and Oklahoma A&M College at Stillwater, OK. Was in the V7 program at Notre Dame, where he enlisted on Mar. 4, 1944. Commissioned as a Lt. (jg). Served in the South Pacific as a skipper of LCT 684 which carried support troops around the island of Moratai during the fighting and occupation. His LCT also carried troops from ship to shore during the initial occupation of Japan at Wakayama. His ship and one other were the only ones to go all the way to Tokyo Bay. Separated from service on May 28, 1946, in Memphis, TN. Honorable discharged on Jan. 21, 1954. Resides in Azle, TX.

Marak, Arthur, of West, TX, WWI veteran.

Marak, Bedrich Joe, was born June 9, 1926, Corn

Hill, Williamson Co., TX. Enlisted U.S. Army Corp, about 1944, during WWII. Pfc., Trp D8 Cavalry. Died Jan. 24, 1969; buried Corn Hill, Williamson Co., TX.

Marak, Jerome Rudolph, son of August and Mary Kohut Marak, was born in Bomarton, TX, Nov. 2, 1911. Attended Bomarton School. Served in the Infantry in Germany under General Patton during WWII. Rank: Sgt. WOUNDED IN ACTION. Received injuries to feet. Awarded the Purple Heart and several medals. Honorably discharged Feb. 11, 1946, Ft. Sam Houston, TX. Died May 22, 1981.

Marchak, Alvin William, son of Mr. and Mrs. W. E. Marchak, was born in Deanville, TX, Apr. 16, 1916. Earned a B.A. at the University of Texas and Master of Education, University of Houston. Entered military service at Dodd Field, San Antonio, TX. Served during WWII in ATC North Africa TO and ATC China Burma India TO. Rank: S/Sgt. Awarded the Air Medal w/2 Clusters and the Distinguished Flying Cross. Honorable discharge Oct. 17, 1945.

Marek, Albert Joseph, son of Joseph L. Marek and Catherine Ann Mudrick, was born May 8, 1926, West, TX. Education: West High School, TX; Texas A&M University, B.S. E.E., College Station, TX. Enlisted 1944, Dallas, TX, U.S. Navy, during WWII. Rank: Petty Officer 3rd Class (EM). Theater of Operations: EAME; American; Asiatic-Pacific. Served North Atlantic, Convoy Escort Duty, USS *Edsall* (DE129); South Pacific, USS *Edsall* (DE 129). USS *Mattanikan* (CVE101). Medals: WWII Victory Medal, American Campaign Medal, Asiatic-Pacific Campaign Medal, EAME Campaign Medal, Navy Occupation Service Medal (Asia), China Service Medal. Honorable discharge 1946. Married Theresa M. Marince; five children: Michael, Christopher, Mark, Sharon, Robert. Technical Project Manager, LTV Aerospace Co., Retired. Member of S.W. Watercolor Society, honorary member of Knights of Columbus, Member of North Dallas Tennis League, Catholic Church, Republican Party. Hobbies: Golf, tennis, bowling, dancing, travel, watercolor painting, yard work. Home of record: Dallas, TX.

Marek, Alfonse D., son of Joe and Millie Marek, was born in Abbott, TX, Apr. 30, 1919. Attended Abbott School through eighth grade. Joined the military service, Dallas, TX, May 18, 1942. Rank: Sgt. Served in the European Theater of Operations during WWII. Battles: June 6, 1944, Invasion at Normandy, Northern France, Ardenne, Rhineland, and Central Europe. Honorable discharge Sept. 10, 1945.

Marek, Alfred J., son of Joseph L. and Catherine Ann Mudrick Marek. Born May 8, 1926 in West, TX, twin of Albert J. Education: West High School and Texas A&M University, B.S. E.E., College Station, TX. Enlisted in U.S. Navy in Dallas, TX. Served on the USS *Matanikan* (CUE 101) in the South Pacific. Medals: WWII Victory, American Campaign, Asiatic-Pacific, Navy Occupation Service (Asia) and China Service. Discharged in 1946 as Petty Officer 3/C(EM). Married Mary Louise Giesen; three children. Home of record: Dallas, TX.

Marek, Andrew E., son of Mr. and Mrs. V. L. Marek, Granger, TX. Education: Granger, TX, schools. Enlisted U.S. Army Corps, 1941; basic training, Ft. Knox, KY. Theater of Operations: EAME. Served in Ireland, England, North Africa, French-Morocco, Italy. Medals: EAME Theater Campaign Ribbon w/4 BSS, American Defense Medal, Good Conduct Medal, Combat Infantry Badge;,WWII Victory Medal. Attained rank of Sgt. before honorable discharge, 1945. Married Sue Cervenka.

Marek, Benjamin C., son of Mr. and Mrs. Joe Marek. Entered Army, 1941. Served in Canada. Awards: A.D., A.T., G.C.M., E.A.M.E. Ribbon. Rank of Cpl. prior to discharge, 1945.

Marek, Benjamin Louis, son of Louis and Lydia Mikeska Marek, was born Jan. 11, 1931, Tunis, Burleson Co., TX. Education: finished three yrs college. Enlisted U.S. Army Corps, Mar. 12, 1951, Ft. Sam Houston, TX. Theater of Operations: Korea. Assigned to 307th Military Police Bn., Co. C Training Cadre and Post Duty at Ft. Sam Houston, Railroad Escort Duty Albuquerque, NM, to Kansas City and Dallas. Medals: Korean War Medal, Good Conduct Medal. Home of record: Houston, TX.

Marek, Clifton Patrick, son of Vince L. and Isabelle Rosipal Marek, was born Aug. 12, 1949, in Taylor, Williamson Co., TX. Attended school in Friendship, TX, and graduated from Granger High School in 1967. He also attended Temple Junior College, Temple, TX. Enlisted in the U.S. Navy at Austin, TX, during the Viet Nam Conflict. Served in the Viet Nam waters as a Gunner's Mate aboard the USS *Camberra* (CA-70). Participated in the "Battle of Hue" and "Operation Sea Dragon" in Viet Nam. His ship also experienced an explosion in the gunpowder room which resulted in the serious injury of four personnel. Awards and decorations: National Defense Service Medal, Viet Nam Service Medal with campaign star, Republic of Viet Nam Service Medal, and Meritorious Unit Commendation Ribbon. Separated from service on Jan. 18, 1969. Works for the U.S. Postal Service as a Postmaster. Married Janis Elaine Rathke; two sons: Chad Christopher and Blake Anthony. Home of record: Granger, TX. Member American Legion Post No. 282, Granger, TX.

Marek, Daniel J., son of John and Mary Marek, was born June 9, 1923, Snook, Burleson Co., TX. Education: B.A. from Moravian College, Bethlehem, PA; Bachelor of Divinity from Austin Presbyterian Seminary, Austin, TX. Enlisted in U.S. Army about 1942, Houston, TX. Theater of Operations: Europe. Medals: American Theater Campaign Medal, EAME Campaign Medal w/1 BSS, GCM, and WWII Victory Medal. Honorably discharged Feb. 12, 1946. Married. Home of record: Taylor, TX.

Marek, Edmund F., son of Mr. and Mrs. Frank Marek, West, TX. Entered Army 1944, during WWII. Served as T/5 in Hawaii, Marshalls, Caroline, Iwo Jima, Okinawa and Korea. Discharged 1945.

Marek, Edward J., son of Vaclav and Mary Marek, was born Sept. 23, 1917, in Engle, TX. Attended school in Engle and farmed before entering the Army during WWII. Was in the 81st Infantry Wildcat Division which landed on Peleliu, Philippines, on Sept. 24, 1944. KILLED IN ACTION that same day. WWII Military Veteran of Granger, TX.

Marek, Edward J., of West, TX, WWII veteran. Theater of Operations: Asiatic- Pacific. Served in South Pacific.

Marek, Edward John, son of Mr. and Mrs. Joe R. Marek, West, TX. Entered Navy 1942. Theater of Operations: Asiatic-Pacific. Served in South Pacific with rank of SC 1/C during WWII.

Marek, Edwin Albert, son of Edwin John and Mabel Jakubik Marek, was born May 28, 1947, Bryan, TX. Completed high school and interior communications electrician training. Enlisted U.S. Naval Reserve, Houston, TX. Theater of Operations: Mediterranean, U.S. Naval Reserve 6th Fleet. Assigned to USS *Independence*, CVA62. Honorably discharged July 12, 1972. Home of record: Anderson, TX. Submitted by Benjamin L. Marek, Houston, TX.

Marek, Edwin John, son of Louis Marek and Lydia Mikeska, was born Nov. 25, 1920, Tunis, Burleson Co., TX. Education: finished 7th grade, finished Bob Boyle Aircraft Bldg. Tech. School, Dallas, TX., Military Policeman school, telephone switchboard operator school. Enlisted at Caldwell TX, U.S. Army Corps. Theater of Operations: EAME. Battles: Battle of the Bulge, Megte France, Liberate Dachau Concentration Camp. Served in England, France, Germany, Belgium, Luxembourg, Austria and Czechoslovakia. Served under Gen. George Patton in U.S. 3rd Army, Bty. B, 547th AAA AW Bn. Medals: WWII Ribbon, Good Conduct Medal, EAME Campaign Ribbon w/2 BSS, WWII Victory Medal. Honorably discharged Apr. 30, 1946. Died Nov. 17, 1973. Submitted by Benjamin L. Marek, Houston, TX.

Marek, Engelbert L., son of Mr. and Mrs. V. K. Marek, Granger, TX. Education: Granger schools. Enlisted U.S. Army Corps, 1937. Basic training, Ft. McIntosh, TX. Theater of Operation: EAME. Served in Australia, New Guinea and Philippines. Medals: Asiatic-Pacific Theater Campaign Ribbon w/3 BSS, American Defense Ribbon, Good Conduct Medal, Unit Citation Medal, Combat Medic Badge, WWII Victory Medal. Attained rank of Pfc. before honorable discharge, 1945.

Marek, Engelbert T., son of Vince L. and Millie Virginia Janak Marek, was born Aug. 22, 1919 in Granger, TX. Attended elementary and high school in Granger. Enlisted in the U.S. Army on Jan. 10, 1938. Served in the Asiatic Pacific Theater of Operations during WWII, and participated in campaigns at New Guinea, Papua, and Luzon. Decorations include the American Defense Service Medal, Asiatic-Pacific Campaign Medal with three campaign stars, Philippine Liberation Ribbon with one BSS, Good Conduct Medal, and Distinguished Unit Badge. Married Janelle Guthrie; three children: Nelwyn Persky, Kirk, and Glenn Marek. Engelbert died Mar. 10, 1966, and is interred at Taylor, TX.

Marek, Frank Irvin, son of Mr. and Mrs. A. C. Marek, Thrall, TX. Education: Laurence Chapel School. Enlisted U.S. Navy, 1944, basic training, San Diego, CA. Theater of Operations: Asiatic-Pacific. Medals: Asiatic-Pacific Theater Campaign Ribbon w/2 BSS, WWII Victory Medal. Attained rank of S 1/c before honorable discharge, 1946.

Marek, Frank Joseph, son of Joe J. and Albina Ermis Marek, was born in Buckholts, TX, Nov. 28, 1927. Attended school in Buckholts, TX. Entered military service in Austin, Travis, TX. Boot camp in San Diego, CA, 1945. Served in the Pacific and in Europe during WWII, and in the Korean War, participated in the Korean Coast evacuation. Assigned to the USS *Rendova* CVE 114, USS *Antitam* CV 36, USS *Acullia* AO 56, USS *Mercury* AKS 20, and went around the world twice. Rank: MMI. Awards: WWII Victory Medal, Philippine Ind., National Defense, Navy Occupation A&E Korea, United Nations, China Service, GCM w/1 BSS. Honorably discharged May, 1955.

Marek, John, son of John J. and Rozina Matus Marek, was born June 3 or 7, 1897, West, TX. Education: Liberty Grove Grammar School. Enlisted during WWI, Sept. 5, 1918, West, TX. Attained rank of Pvt. Theater of Operations: American. 33rd Co. 165 Depot Brig. Honorably discharged Jan. 6, 1919. Married Antonie Smajstrla. Died Jan. 26, 1969, West, TX. Buried: St. Mary's Catholic Cemetery, West, TX.

Marek, Louis, son of John and Frances Supak Marek, was born Apr. 10, 1894, Tunis, Burleson Co., TX. Education through seventh grade. Enlisted June 28, 1918, Caldwell, TX, during WWI. Trained at Camp Travis, TX, and Camp Grant, IL. Theater of Operations: Europe. WWI. American Expeditionary Forces in France Nov. 12, 1918–July 5, 1919. Medals: WWI Victory Medal, European Campaign Medal, Good Conduct Medal, among others. Honorable discharge July 14, 1919, Camp Bowie, TX. Died July 31, 1955. Submitted by son, Benjamin L. Marek, Houston, TX.

Marek, Milton Joseph, son of Louis and Lydia Mikeska Marek, was born Oct. 15, 1922, Tunis, Burleson Co., TX. Completed seventh grade. Completed Bob Boyle Aircraft Bldg. Technical

School, Dallas, TX, and Coast Artillery Cannoneer and Gun School. Enlisted in U.S. Army Corps, Oct. 29, 1943, Ft. Sam Houston, TX. Basic training, Ft. Morgan, AL. Theater of Operations: Asia-Pacific. Saipan and Iwo Jima ground combat. Medals: Asia-Pacific Campaign Medal w/2 bronze battle stars, Good Conduct Medal, WWII Victory Medal. Coast Artillery Cannoneer and Gun Crewman, 155-MM Cannon. Attained rank of Cpl. Honorably discharged Jan. 21, 1946, Camp Fannin, TX. Died May 5, 1962. Submitted by Benjamin L. Marek, Houston, TX.

Marek, Raymond Joseph, son of John and Antonie Smajstrla Marek, was born Aug. 15, 1921, West, TX. Education: Cottonwood grammar school; West, TX, High School; Southern Methodist University, B.S. in Mechanical Engineering. Enlisted in U.S. Navy, Oct. 12, 1942, San Francisco, CA, during WWII. Rank: Machinist Mate 1/C. Theater of Operations: Asiatic-Pacific. Battles: Gilbert Islands, Nov. 29–Dec. 3, 1943; Marshall Islands, including Occupation of Kwajalein and Majure Atolls, Jan. 31–Feb. 8, 1944; Occupation of Entiwetok Atoll, Feb. 17–25, 1944; Marianas Occupation, capture and occupation of Guam, July 21–25, 1944; assault and occupation of Iwo Jima, Mar. 9-16, 1945. Medals: American Campaign, Asiatic Pacific Campaign w/4 Battle Stars, Navy Occupation Service, Philippine Liberation. Honorably discharged Sept. 27, 1945. Married Mary L. Gerik. Home of record: West, TX.

Marek, Richard, WWII veteran of Granger, TX.

Marek, Robert R., son of Henry J. and Anna Haisler Marek, was born July 27, 1917, Providence, TX. Attended public schools in Alief Addicks ISD, and Draughon's Business College, Houston, TX. Entered the U.S. Army Corps, Oct. 22, 1942, Ellington Field, TX. During WWII was stationed with the 482nd AAF Base Unit, Keister Field, MS, also in Espsilante, MI, Laredo, TX, Herrington, KS, Chico, CA, Merced, CA, serving as an airplane and engine mechanic. Rank: Sgt. Honorable discharge Feb. 25, 1946.

Marek, Ronald David, son of Raymond J. and Irene Marek, was born May 26, 1949, Caldwell, TX. Education: high school. Enlisted in U.S. Air Force, FL. Attained rank of T/Sgt. Theater of Operations: American-Viet Nam. Medals: Air Force Long Tour Ribbon, National Defense Service Medal, Good Conduct Medal, Viet Nam Service Medal w/3 BSS. Served 20 years as Jet Engine Technician. Retired after 20 years service at Like AFB, AZ. Home of record: Caldwell, TX. Submitted by Edwin L. Hlavaty.

Marek, Sheridan Baily "Buck," son of Mr. and Mrs. Frank V. Marek, Temple, TX. Graduate of Granger High School, TX. Enlisted U.S. Army Air Corps, 1942, basic training, Sheppard Field, TX; further training, Santa Ana, CA, Tulare CA, Mercedes, CA. Commissioned 2nd Lt. and received wings at Douglas, AZ, May, 1944. KILLED IN SERVICE OF COUNTRY in plane crash at Yuma, AZ, June 1944. WWII veteran of Granger, TX.

Marek, Vince L., Jr., son of Mr. and Mrs. Vince L. Marek, Sr., Granger, TX. Education: Granger High School. Enlisted U.S. Army Corps, 1945. Basic training at Ft. Belvoir, VA. Attained rank of Pvt. before being honorably discharged, 1945. Member American Legion Post No. 282, Granger, TX. WWII veteran.

Maresh, Frank Louis, son of Joe V. and Mary Supak Maresh, was born June 26, 1944, in Granger, TX. Attended Sts. Cyril & Methodius School, Granger High School, and Temple Junior College, Temple, TX. Enlisted in the U.S. Army at San Antonio, TX, on July 19, 1965, during the Viet Nam Conflict. Served in Viet Nam as a Construction Engineer and attained the rank of Specialist 4/C. Decorations: National Defense Service Medal, Viet Nam Service Medal with one campaign star, and the Republic of Viet Nam Campaign Medal. Separated from the service on July 11, 1967. Employed as Service Technician for IBM. Hobbies: hunting, camping, fishing, and camping. Married

Christine A. Maresh. Home of record: Granger, TX.

Maresh, Jerry H., son of Joseph V. and Annie Kalas Maresh. Born Feb. 5, 1919 in Hungerford, Wharton Co., TX. Enlisted Jan. 7, 1942 in San Antonio, TX in the US Army, 127th Infantry. Served as a Rifleman in the Asiatic-Pacific Theater. Battles included: New Guinea and the Southern Philippines. Decorations: Asiatic-Pacific Campaign Medal with three bronze stars, Distinguished Unit Badge, Philippine Liberation Medal with BSS, and Good Conduct Medal. Discharged as a Pfc. July 13, 1945. Married Marie Pavelka; five children. Member American Legion Post No. 282, Granger, TX. WWII military veteran. Died Jan. 8, 1989; buried in Holy Cross Cemetery, Granger, TX.

Maresh, Ladislav Henry "L.H.," son of Joseph V. and Anna Kalas Maresh, born July 15, 1925, Granger, TX, attended Sts. Cyril & Methodius Catholic School in Granger, Temple Jr. College. WWII, U.S. Army. EAME Theater of Operations. Rank: Cpl. Battles: Algeria-French Morocco, Central Europe, and Ardennes: Alsace "Battle of the Bulge" Campaigns. WOUNDED IN ACTION three times. Awards: BSS Medal, Purple Heart w/ two OLC, EAME Campaign Medal w/3 BSS, Good Conduct Medal, and Distinguished Unit Citation. Discharged Jan. 13, 1946. Married Martha Otillie Naizer Nov. 17, 1947; one child: Martha Bridget Maresh Knight. Active in Granger community, Sts. Cyril & Methodius Catholic Church, Boy Scouts, Red Cross, Salvation Army, member Granger City Council 10 years, and board member Williamson and Burnet Co. OEO Program, six years. 1959, Printer and foreman of Nasinec Publishing Co., Inc., 1959; Business Mgr. and Editor, 1971. Died July 2, 1975. At the time of death was President, State Council Catholic Workman and Catholic Workman Supreme Trustee, member KJT Soc. # 28, Volunteer Fire Dept., American Legion, VFW, Interred at Holy Cross Catholic Cemetery at Granger, TX.

Maresh, Timothy, a native of Granger, TX. Education: Granger High School, University of St. Thomas in Houston, and degree from University of Texas School of Law. Active duty in the USMC from 1951–1953. Attained the rank of First Lt. Remained in the Marine Corps Reserve until 1977. Retired with rank of Lt. Col. Assignments: Senior Air Director in Air Defense Control, Squadron Operations Officer, Commander of Squadron, and Intelligence Officer of Marine Air Group 41.

Marik, Albert A., son of Ignac and Anna Kubez, was born Feb. 21, 1908, East Bernard, TX. Education: East Bernard High School. Enlisted Feb. 24, 1942, Ft. Sam Houston, TX. Basic training, Camp Haan, CA; further training, Ft. Ord, CA. Honorable discharge Nov. 28, 1944, Ft. Sam Houston, TX. Rank: Pfc. Awarded Good Conduct Medal. Owner of A.A. Marik Road Gravel and Red Clay, East Bernard, TX. Home of record: East Bernard, TX.

Marik, C. Frank, son of John I. and Josephine Spacek Marik, was born June 11, 1932 in East Bernard, TX. Education: Holy Cross Catholic School, East Bernard High School, St. Edwards University, Austin, TX, B.A. in Economics from St. Thomas University in Houston, TX. Served in Air Force Cadet Training in Harlingen, TX. Died Feb. 27, 1986. Submitted by Clarice Simpson (sister).

Marik, William Frank, son of Ignac and Helen Marik, was born June 25, 1942, in East Bernard, TX. Joined the U.S. Army, and assigned to Co. B, 51st Signal Bn. Served in Korea. Discharged with rank of SP4 E-4 on May 14, 1969. Residence of record: East Bernard, TX.

Markos, Jerry T., son of Mr. and Mrs. Frank Markos, West, TX. Entered Army, 1944. Served E.T. as a Pfc. Awarded GCM, ET w/2 battle stars, and Combat Infantry Badge.

Markos, Willie T., son of Mr. and Mrs. Frank Markos, West, TX. Entered Army 1942. Served w/rank of T/4 in Philippines, Ryukyus and Okinawa. Awarded Combat Infantry Badge, GCM, Purple Heart, AP w/2 battle stars, one Bronze Arrowhead and PL Ribbon. WOUNDED IN ACTION, 1944, Leyte. Discharged 1946.

Maroul, Eugene Garland, son of Henry Joseph and Vlasta Kovar Maroul, was born Mar. 8, 1940, West, TX. Education: West Columbia, TX, high school, 1958; Univ. of Sam Houston, BBA, 1966 and MBA, 1969. Enlisted U.S. Army Corps, Apr. 1962, Angleton, TX. Basic training, Ft. Chaffee AR; AIT, Ft. Knox, KY. Overseas duty, 11th AC-Landshut, Germany. Honorable discharge Jan. 1964, Brooklyn Army Terminal, NY. Accounting Teacher, McLennan Community College, Waco, TX. Married Kay Rogers; two children: James Matthew, Louis Christopher. Home of record: Abbott, TX.

Maroul, Henry Joseph, son of Jan and Kristina Svejdar Maroul, was born Jan. 18, 1912, Damon, TX. Served his country 1931–1934, Citizen Military Training Camps-War Dept. of the U.S. Stationed at Camp Bullis, TX. Married Vlasta Kovar; three sons, Henry Joseph, Jr., Eugene Garland, Jimmy Patrick. Died Oct. 6, 1968. Submitted by son, Eugene of Abbot, TX.

Maroul, James Matthew "Matt," son of Eugene Garland and Kay Rogers Maroul, was born May 20, 1967, Texas City, TX. Education: public school, Abbot, TX, McLennan Community College, Waco, TX, Texas A&M, College Station, TX. Enlisted U.S. Army Corps, Houston, TX, Rank: E-4. Radio Communications Specialist, Ft. Sill, OK, following completion of Airborne Course, Ft Benning, GA. Assigned to 11th ACR in Fulda, Germany, sent to S.W. Asia for three months during that tour, following tour in Germany, spent 15 months w/319th AFAR of 82nd Airborne in Ft. Bragg, NC. Theater of Operations: Southwest Asia. Battles: Desert Shield. Medals: Army Commendation Medal, Good Conduct Medal, five Army Achievement Medals, S.W. Asia Medal, National Defense Ribbon. Honorably discharged Feb. 25, 1994. Attended Texas A&M University, accounting and finance degrees, Aug. 1996. Home of record: Abbott, TX.

Martinec, Anton, Jr., son of Anton Martinec, Sr. and Olga Martinec, was born about 1928, Rogers, TX. Graduated Rogers High School, 1943. Entered U.S. Army Corps, Sept. 1943. Basic training, Camp Gruber, OK, before going overseas. Served four months with 79th Division. Participated in Battle of Cherbourg. KILLED IN ACTION, July 12, 1944. Buried St. Joseph's Catholic Cemetery, Cyclone, Bell, TX. Was only child; parents both buried beside son.

Martinek, Albert E., son of Charlie Joe and Theresa A. Mikeska Martinek, was born Mar. 17, 1917, in Temple, TX. Attended grade school before entering the Army at Fort Sam Houston, San Antonio, TX. Fought in Central Europe, Ardennes, Normandy, Northern France and Rhineland in WWII. Rank: Cpl. Medals: Good Conduct, American Defense Service, EAME Campaign with five BSS, and Meritorious Service Plaque. Discharged Oct. 3, 1945. Home of record: Temple, TX.

Martinek, Albin C., Jr., son of Albin C. Martinek, Sr. and Annie Repka Martinek, was born Nov. 9, 1918, Red Ranger, Bell Co., TX. Education in Red Ranger School. Enlisted during WWII, U.S. Army Air Corps, ETO, assigned to 131st Sqdn., 452nd Bomb Group. Bomber shot down while flying on a mission over Trier, Germany. First reported missing, later reported KILLED IN ACTION on Jan. 2, 1945. Received Purple Heart posthumously.

Martinek, Charlie Joe, son of Charlie Joe and Theresa A. Mikeska Martinek, was born Feb. 10, 1922, in Temple, TX. Attended grade school and entered the Army at Fort Sam Houston, San Antonio, TX. Rank: Sgt. Fought in Central Europe, Ardennes, Normandy, Northern France, and Rhineland in WWII. Awards: Good

Conduct Medal, ETO Ribbon with five Battle Stars, and the American Defense, and Combat Badge. Discharged Nov. 26, 1945. Died Jan. 16, 1973.

Martinek, Joseph, son of Charles Joseph and Betty A. Martinek, was born in Ft. Worth, Tarrant Co., TX, Aug. 24, 1919. High school diploma, Ft. Worth, TX. Two years of technical school (machine shop). Enlisted, Dallas, TX. Served in Naples-Foggia Europe. Battles: Rome-Aero, Southern France, and Rhineland, Central Europe. Awards: EAME Campaign Medal w/5 BSS, and one Bronze Arrowhead, American Defense Service Medal, Good Conduct Medal. Honorable discharge Aug. 8, 1945.

Martinets, F. E., Jr., U.S. Navy: S.S. Mission, Santa Clara. Served in U.S. Armed Forces during WWI, 1917–1918. Member of SPJST Lodge 20, Granger, TX.

Martinets, F. E., Sr., served in U.S. Armed Forces during WWI, 1917–1918. Member of SPJST Lodge 20, Granger, TX.

Martinka, Anton H., son of Anton J. and Catherine Krchnak Martinka, was born in Granger, TX, Oct. 23, 1923. Attended Sts. Cyril & Methodius Catholic School. Entered U.S. Army Corps, 1943, Ft. Sam Houston, San Antonio, TX. Basic training, Camp J. T. Robinson, AZ. Theater of Operations: Asiatic-Pacific. Served in the South Pacific during WWII. Battles: Luzon, Bouganville, Solomons, Philippines. Assigned to Infantry, 37th Division. Medals: Combat Infantry Badge, Philippine Liberation Ribbon w/Beachhead Arrow, Asiatic-Pacific Theater Campaign Ribbon w/2 BSS, Good Conduct Medal, WWII Victory Medal. Attained rank of Pfc. before honorable discharge, 1945.

Martinka, Bill A., Granger, TX. WWII veteran. Member American Legion Post No. 282, Granger, TX. Deceased.

Martinka, Charlie P., was born Nov. 2, 1908. WWII veteran. Pfc., US Army. Died Mar. 14, 1974. Buried Holy Cross Catholic Cem., Granger, TX.

Martinka, Cyril, WWII veteran of Granger, TX.

Martinka, Henry Alfonse, son of John S. and Annie Straka Martinka, was born July 15, 1922, in Granger, TX. Attended Sts. Cyril & Methodius School in Granger. Enlisted in the U.S. Army on Dec. 4, 1942. Rank: Sgt. Decorations include the Rifle Qualifications Badge and the Good Conduct Medal. Separated from the service on Nov. 20, 1964. Home of record: Florence, TX.

Martinka, Jerome, son of Joe and Albina Martinka, was born in the Hillje, TX area. Served in the Asiatic Pacific Theater of Operations as a member of the U.S. Marine Corps, during WWII. MORTALLY WOUNDED and KILLED IN ACTION at Okinawa.

Martinka, Johnny P., son of Mr. and Mrs. Anton Martinka, Granger, TX. Education: Granger High School. Enlisted U.S. Army Corps, 1944; basic training, Camp Hood, TX; further training, Camp Rucker, AL. Theater of Operations: Asiatic-Pacific. Served in Manila, Philippines as Engineer. Medals: Expert Combat Infantry Badge, Asiatic-Pacific Theater Campaign Medal, WWII Victory Medal. Rank, Pvt., when honorably discharged. Member American Legion Post No. 282, Granger, TX.

Martinka, Laddie J., Bartlett, TX. WWII veteran. Member American Legion Post No. 282, Granger, TX.

Martinka, Larry, Granger, TX. WWII veteran. Member American Legion Post No. 282, Granger, TX.

Martinka, Pete, WWII veteran of Granger, TX.

Maruska, Gary Wayne, son of George Edwin and Dorothy Mae Pavelka Maruska, was born Oct. 27, 1946, Austin, TX. Education: Taylor High School, TX (1960-64), Blinn Jr. College, Brenham, TX, 1966, Texas A&M, 1969. Received commission as officer, Nov. 1968, College Station, TX, U.S. Air

Force. Military Occupation: Aircraft Maint. Officer in Air Training command. Attained rank of Capt. Medals: Distinguished Graduate OTS, Dist. Graduate Aircraft Maint. Off. Course, Sqdn. Commander T-37, T-38, Aerospace Systems. Honorable discharge, Oct. 21, 1973. Self-employed Owner/Operator of Aladdin Carpets. Married Annette Jane Veselka; children: Yvette P., Matthew C. Hobbies: hunting, baseball, outdoors. Home of record: Taylor, TX.

Maruska, George, served in U.S. Navy, WWII. Hometown: Granger, TX. Deceased.

Maruska, Henry, served in USMC, during WWII. Hometown: Granger, TX. Deceased.

Masar, Frank, served in U.S. Armed Forces during WWI, 1917–1918. Member of SPJST Lodge 20, Granger, TX,

Masarik, Clifford, served a half year in U.S. Army Corps during WWII.

Masek, Hattie Dorothy, daughter of Frank A. and Aurelia Branecky Masek, was born Oct. 16, 1923, Flatonia, TX. Education: East Bernard High School and St. Joseph School of Nursing, Houston, TX. Enlisted in the U.S. Navy Nurse Corps at Corpus Christi Naval Station, TX during WWII. Rank: Lt. Served in Naval hospitals in Corpus Christi, TX, San Diego, CA, Oakland, CA. WWII Victory Medal. Honorably discharged Mar. 18, 1954, total service, nine years, five days. Married Joseph Henry Hlavinka; one son: Don. Home of record: Kerrville, TX.

Masek, Joe S., son of Frank A. and Aurelia Branecky Masek, was born Jan. 25, 1933, at Praha, TX Graduated Orchard, TX, High. Attended the University of Texas, Austin. During the Korean Conflict, Enlisted in the USMC at Houston, TX, June 9, 1951, during Korean Conflict. Served in Korea Apr. 10, 1953–May 2, 1953. Participated in three military campaigns, and attained the rank of Cpl. Decorations include the Korean Service Medal with three campaign stars, United Nations service Medal, National Defense Service Medal, and Good Conduct Medal. Discharged June 8, 1954. Home of record: Wharton, TX.

Mashek, Ed, of West, TX, WWII veteran.

Matcek, James Cy, son of Frank and Emily Kroboth Matcek, was born in Garwood, TX, July 4, 1928. Attended Garwood High School, U.S. Army Signal Corps Radio Operator School, University of Houston. Entered military service at Ft. Sam Houston, San Antonio, TX. Served during WWII in the European Theater, and the U.S. Occupation of Germany, as an International Morse Code Operator. Honorably discharged May 27, 1949.

Mateja, Frank, Jr., son of Frank and Martha Mateja, was born Nov. 29, 1945, Sealy, TX. Graduated Sealy High School. Enlisted in U.S. Army, attaining rank of Pfc. Lived in San Felipe, Austin Co., TX. Died May 28, 1977. Buried St. Mary's Catholic Cem., Frydek, TX.

Matejka, Frank Marek, son of Frank J. and Rosalie Marek Matejka, was born Feb. 2, 1928, Tunis, Burleson Co., TX. Education: Caldwell High School, two years. Enlisted in U.S. Army Corps, May 1, 1946, Ft. Sam Houston, TX. Theater of Operations: Asiatic-Pacific. Stationed at Yokohama, Japan, attained rank of Pfc.. Honorable discharge, June 4, 1947, Camp Stoneman, CA. Deceased Oct. 27, 1992. Submitted by Rosalie Matejka, Houston, TX.

Matejka, Jaroslav (Jerry) V., son of Frank and Alvina Matejka, was born Aug. 18, 1894, in Nelsonville, TX. Received a B.S. degree in Electrical Engineering from the University of Texas. Commissioned into the Army on July 10, 1917 as 2nd Lt. in the Coast Artillery and Signal Corps. Served in the Army for 38 years. Theater of Operations were the Panama Canal Zone, British Isles, Philippines and Japan. Served as Commander of Fort Monmouth, N.J., Chief Signal Officer of the European Command, Director of Production of the Munitions Board and Deputy Chief of Staff for Logistics, Allied Forces Central Europe in France. Decorations include the Legion of Merit with two

OLC, the French Legion of Honor, and the Croix de Guerre with Palm. Retired on Oct. 31, 1955. Rank: Gen. Named Assistant to the Director for Telecommunications Office of Defense Mobilization. Married Myrtle E. O'Reilly; two daughters: Katherine and Gardina. Died May 22, 1980, and was interred in Arlington National Cemetery.

Matejka, Ladimir K., Sr., oldest son of Frank and Alvina Matejka, was born Feb. 17, 1891, in Temple, TX. Completed education in Caldwell, Burleson Co. Enlisted in the Army on May 22, 1917, at Ft. Sam Houston, TX, at age 26. Assigned to the Flying School Detachment Air Service (A) in San Antonio where he remained for more than 20 months. Appointed Sgt. First Class Jan. 10, 1918. Honorably discharged on Jan. 27, 1919, at Kelly Field, TX. Married Ruth C. Thomas; one son: Ladimir K. Matejka, Jr. Died on Mar. 2, 1980. Buried at Buena Vista Cemetery in Brownsville, TX.

Matejowsky, Edwin P. Education: Taylor High School. Enlisted U.S. Navy, 1943; basic training, Corpus Christi, TX. Stationed at San Diego, CA. Theater of Operations: American. Medals: American Theater Campaign Medal, WWII Victory Medal. Attained rank of S 1/C prior to honorable discharge, 1946.

Matlock, Anton J., WWII veteran of Granger, TX.

Matocha, John F., son of John J. and Anna Korenek Matocha (both born in Hovezi), was born July 22, 1894, Plum, TX. Enlisted Oct. 9, 1917, La Grange, TX, U.S. Army Corps. Served with American Expeditionary Force in France, left May 9, 1918. Theater of Operations: Europe. WWI Victory Medal. Honorably discharged July 14, 1919. John's sister, Antonia Matocha, was the 1st Czech child to be born in Plum, TX, Dec. 28, 1890. Died June 1, 1925; buried Plum, TX, Cemetery.

Matous, Wilbur Gene, son of William J. and Henrietta Cabla Matous, was born Aug. 16, 1943, Temple, TX. Education: Seaton, TX, Elementary, Rogers, TX, High School. Enlisted U.S. Army, Nov. 18, 1976, St. Louis, MO. Enlisted in Army at age 33. Rank: Staff Sgt. Tank Commander with 1st Cavalry Div. at Ft. Hood, TX. Theater of Operations: Southwest Asia. Battles: Desert Shield/Desert Storm, Aug. 7, 1990 through Feb. 28, 1991. Medals: Army Commendation, Good Conduct, South West Asia Service, Liberation of Kuwait from Saudi Arabia. Still on active duty. Lives near Ft. Hood, TX, with wife, Irene and three sons, one step-son, two step-daughters, and seven grandchildren. Home of record: Kempner, TX

Matula, Edward E., Sr., son of Joe E. and Emilie Konecny Matula, was born Dec. 11, 1922, Granger, TX. Served with the CCC at Camp Wood, TX, 1939–1940. Enlisted in the U.S. Army Corps, 1941. Basic training at Ft. Sam Houston. Served with Hq 23rd Inf. Regt. through May 1945. Trained at Ft. Sam Houston, Wisconsin and England before the invasion of Normandy, June 6, 1944. WOUNDED IN ACTION, hit at St. Lo by mortar shell shrapnel. Hospitalized in France, later transferred to USA and honorably discharged on disability from combat wounds received during battle, July 1945. Medals: American Defense, European Liberation, WWII Victory, Infantry Combat Badge, Purple Heart, BSS. Submitted by his brother, Emil E. Matula of San Antonio, TX.

Matula, Emil E., son of Joe E. and Emilie Konecny Matula, was born Apr. 4, 1918, Granger, TX. Enlisted in U.S. Army Corps, Jan. 3, 1937, Dodd Field, TX. Assigned to Co. M, 9th Inf., as Pvt. Reenlisted Jan. 3, 1940, assigned to Co. D, 35th Inf. Rgt, Schofield Barracks, HI. Promotions: Pfc. Apr. 1940, Cpl. Dec. 1940, Sgt. Oct. 16, 1941, 1st Sgt. Apr. 24, 1942, and commissioned Mar. 1,

1945, on battlefield as 2nd Lt. Led 2nd Platoon of Co. G, 35th Inf. until June 22, 1945. Battles: Pearl Harbor, Dec. 7, 1941, Guadalcanal, Dec. 16, 1942–Feb. 12, 1943, invaded Vella Lavella Island, New Georgia Island and spent 145 days in combat w/35th Inf., 25th Inf. on Luzon, Philippines, where he was WOUNDED IN ACTION three times. Rotated stateside, after five and a half years of foreign service and combat duty w/35th Infantry Regt. of the 25th Infantry Div. Decorations: Good Conduct Medal, American Defense Medal w/BSS, Combat Infantry Badge, Asiatic-Pacific Campaign Ribbon w/4 BSS, Philippine Liberation Ribbon and Medal w/1 BSS, Purple Heart w/2 OLC and BSS w/1 OLC, awarded for Bravery/Unit Citation. Participated in Regimental football w/9th Infantry, football and basketball for 35th Infantry Reg. Honorably discharged, 1945. Married Evelyn. Served as President, V.P., Secy. with KJT 102 and Dist. Secy. and President of Dist. 11 KJT, Secy., V.P. and Pres. of Dist. 7 SPJST and Lodge #133, Chairman of KJT Convention 1970, Chairman of 1980 SPJST Convention, V.P. of SVPS and Secy. Treas. of Chapter 11 Slavonic Mutual Fire Ins. Assoc. Delegate to five conventions KJT and SPJST, on publication committee of Vestnik, SPJST, eight years. Pres. and Secy. of Alamo Chapter 2, San Antonio Pearl Harbor Survivors Assoc. and Secy. and Pres. of Mens Club at Holy Name Parish, Conv. Chairman and 2nd V.P. of 25th Inf. Div. Assoc. Conv. for past 10 years. Active w/Battle Field Commissioned Assoc., w/Convention in San Antonio in 1987. Home of record: San Antonio, TX.

Matula, Eugene G., son of Julius C. Matula, Sr. and Cecelia Sulak Matula, was born Mar. 5, 1925, at Burr, Wharton Co., TX. Attended Hungerford schools and entered the Marine Corps in San Antonio, TX, on Jan. 17, 1945. Trained at Paris Island, SC, and served at Camp Pendleton, CA, Honolulu, HI, and Guam. Discharged Nov. 1, 1946, at Great Lakes, IL. Married Helen Marie Dobias at East Bernard, on Nov. 25, 1947; three children: Thomas Gene, Richard Carlton, and Elizabeth Ann. Employed at Gulf Sulfur Company, New Gulf, TX. Retired as Asst. Maintenance Foreman in Nov. 1982. Home of record: Wharton, TX.

Matula, Frank J., son of Valentin George Matula, Sr. and Emily Matula, was born Oct. 29, 1918, Shiner, Gonzales Co., TX. Education: Sacred Heart Catholic School, finished 8th grade, Hallettsville Public School. Enlisted in U.S. Army Corps, Ft. Sam Houston, San Antonio, TX, Feb. 1941. Served in WWII in the European Theater of Operations. Fought in two D-Day Landings and seven Campaigns in Africa, Italy, France, Germany, Austria. Medals: WWII Victory, Good Conduct, EAME w/5 BSS. Honorable discharge Oct. 1945. Retired from plumbing and electrical business. Lives on a farm, Hallettsville, TX.

Matula, Frank J., Jr., son of Frank J. Matula, Sr. and Mary Bartosh Matula, was born in Hallettsville, TX, Nov. 28 1917. Attended grade school in Hallettsville. Joined the U.S. Army Corps, Ft. Sam Houston, TX, Jan. 16, 1942. Served in Pacific during WWII, 5-16-42–8-17-44. Rank: Pfc. Medals: Asiatic Pacific Service and GCM AR 600-68. Honorably discharged Oct. 20, 1945.

Matula, Frank J., Sr., son of Joseph and Mary Kapuan Matula, was born Aug. 21, 1889. Enlisted in the U.S. Army Corps, Hallettsville, TX. Served in Europe during WWI. Battles: Sazerias Hage Puvenelle Sec. Demonst Meuse-Argonne, St. Michiel Aff., Meuse-Argonne and Army of Occupation. Honorably discharged June 28, 1919. Died July 5, 1960.

Matula, Frank L., Taylor, TX. WWII veteran. Member American Legion Post No. 282, Granger, TX.

Matula, Fred A., son of Mr. and Mrs. Emil Matula, West, TX. Entered Army, 1944. Served w/rank of Sgt. in Philippines. Awarded GCM, P.L., Victory and AP Ribbon w/1 Battle Star.

Matula, Henry, son of Joe E. and Emilie Konecny Matula, was born Granger, TX. Enlisted in U.S. Marine Corps, 1950. Honorably discharged 1955.

Matula, Joe, son of Joe E. and Emilie Konecny. Matula, was born Granger, TX. Enlisted in U.S. Air Force, 1955. Honorably discharged 1957.

Matula, Joe J., son of John I. and Frances Michna Matula, was born Aug. 29, 1927, Hallettsville, Lavaca Co., TX. (3 of his grandparents immigrated from Moravia, Czechoslovakia: John

Matula from Kozlovice, Frances Jalufka from Vetrkovice, John Michna from Rychaltice). Education: elementary school, Ezzell. Graduated from St. Joseph's Catholic School in Yoakum, TX, May, 1944. Drafted into U.S. Army Corps, Jan. 10, 1946, Ft. Sam Houston, TX. Some of 18-yr-old classmates were drafted before graduation. Assigned as truck driver at Borden General Hospital in Chickasaw, OK. Sent to Ft. Lewis, WA, then assigned to William Beaumont General Hospital, El Paso, TX, where he served as mail clerk, until honorable discharge, Apr. 9, 1947, with the rank of Pvt. Medals: WWII Victory, Rifle Expert, and GCM. Returned to parents' homestead at Ezzell, TX, to continue farming and ranching. Retired from Alcoa, Point Comfort, 1983, after 17 years. Since that time, has continued farming and ranching on the Matula homestead, where he resides with his 92-year-old mother. Enjoys reading, carpentry, and working outdoors. Home of record: Ezzell, TX. Submitted by sister, Frances Matula Holley of Hallettsville, TX.

Matula, John I., son of Mr. and Mrs. John Matula, was born Apr. 4, 1895, Hallettsville, TX. Father, John, along with a brother and sister, and his grandfather, Ondrej Matula, immigrated to Lavaca Co., TX, from Czechoslovakia in 1869 and were among the first Czechs to settle in that area. Education: Ezzell School through sixth grade. Drafted into U.S. Army Corps, June 25, 1918, TX, stationed in WV and AR, as a hospital aide. Honorably discharged Oct. 25, 1919, Camp Pike, AR. Returned to family farm after discharge. Married Frances Michna, Nov. 20, 1923; three sons, three daughters. Farmer and rancher, an avid sports enthusiast, esp. baseball. True patriot in every sense of the word. Believed in his country and felt it was an honor to be able to serve in the military. Member of VFW. Lived on Matula homestead until he became ill. Died on Jan. 16, 1987, age 91. Buried with full military honors at Koerth Catholic Cemetery, near Hallettsville, TX. Submitted by daughter, Frances Matula Holley of Hallettsville, TX.

Matula, Julius Martin, son of Martin Willie and Mary Catherine Stockbauer Matula, was born Jan. 9, 1932, Inez, Victoria Co., TX. Graduated from Patti Welder High School, Victoria, TX, in 1949. Enlisted in the USAF Mar. 29, 1951 at Corpus Christi, TX. Basic training at Lackland AFB, San Antonio, TX on May 26, 1951, further training: Technical School, F. E. Warren AFB, Cheyenne, WY, Sr. Auto/Truck Mechanic, June 1951–Sept. 1951. Foreign service time was 2 years, 4 months, 23 days. Served with OCCUPATION FORCES at Johnson AFB, Japan, located 30 miles from Tokyo. Worked side by side with Japanese civilians as a mechanic in the automotive mechanic shops on the base from 1951–1954. AN INTERESTING TIDBIT: While on a three day pass, climbed to the top of Mt. Fuji and looked down into the crater! Promoted to S/Sgt. Dec. 1, 1953. Awards: Korean Service Medal, United Nations Medal, National Defense Service Medal, Good Conduct Medal and Japan Occupation Medal. Honorably discharged, Sheppard AFB, Wichita Falls, TX, on Mar. 28, 1955. Married Marjorie Mican; two sons: Alan and David, one granddaughter: Mary Jacqueline, and one step granddaughter, Jennifer Redding. Member of VFW Post 4146 in Victoria since 1955. Retired Process Operator from DuPont Plant in 1990. Worked for DuPont for 27 years. Prior to that time, worked in a local garage as an auto mechanic, for over seven years. Home of record: Victoria, TX.

Matula, Laddie A., Sr., son of Mr. and Mrs. Adolph J. Matula, was born Nov. 5, 1929, Granger, TX. Graduated from Granger High School, Business School of Accounting and attended the University of Texas. Entered the U.S. Army Corps, Aug. 27, 1948, Austin, TX. Served in the European Theater for 44 months. Remaining term of enlistment was served at Ft. Hood, TX, and Austin, TX, with civilian component duty. Honorably discharged Aug. 26, 1954. Entered the U.S. Army Reserve in Aug. 1955 and served 14 years. Rank: Master Sgt. Retired in Sept. 1969 with 20 years combined active and reserve military service.

Matula, Louis, Jr., son of Louis Matula, Sr. and Emelie Pazderny Matula, was born June 12, 1912, Hallettsville, Lavaca Co., TX. Graduate Hallettsville, TX, High School. Enlisted in U.S. Air Force, 1941. Attained rank of Sgt. Supplies Clerk. Theater of Operations: EAME. Stationed in Italy overseas. Medals: WWII Victory Medal, and EAME Campaign Medal. Honorably discharged 1945. Married Ann Marek. Owned and operated grocery store. Died Nov. 22, 1988, Hallettsville, TX. Buried Sacred Heart Catholic Cemetery, Hallettsville, TX. Submitted by Margaret Franta Bures of El Campo, TX.

Matula, Louis A., son of John I. and Frances Michna Matula, was born Jan. 14, 1934, Hallettsville, TX. (three of his grandparents immigrated from Moravia, Czechoslovakia: John Matula from Kozlovice, Frances Jalufka from Vetrkovice, John Michna from Rychaltice). Education: elementary school at Ezzell, TX, in late '30s and '40s. Drafted into U.S. Army Corps, June 13, 1956, Ft. Sam Houston, TX. Received basic training, Camp Chaffee, AR, Rank: Pfc. Assigned to 25th Lightning Division, whose purpose was to be on alert for any warlike activity anywhere in the world. Spent last 16 months at Scofield Barracks in Hawaii, where he served as truck driver. Medals: Expert Rifle Medal, Driver w/badge, GCM. Honorable discharge, May 14, 1958. Married Lorene Chilek, Jan. 5, 1974; two sons: Jeffrey and Darren. Employed at Alcoa, Point Comfort, TX. Enjoys sports and hunting. Resides with his family at Ezzell, TX on the Matula homestead. Submitted by sister, Frances Matula Holley, Hallettsville, TX.

Matula, Raymond E., son of Rudolph L. and Lillian B. Cervanka, was born June 17, 1940, Taylor, TX. Attended Sts. Cyril & Methodius School, Granger High, graduated from Texas A&M College. Received Commission in the USAF May 26, 1962. KC-135A Instructor Pilot and EC-135C Pilot. Flew 252 combat missions in SE Asia during 1967-1974, during the Viet Nam Conflict. His combat refueling operations are credited with numerous aircraft saves in SE Asia. Following Robert. Kennedy's assassination in 1968 he ferried Kennedy family members and campaign entourage including John Glenn, from Los Angeles, CA, to Washington, DC. Decorations include Distinguished Flying Cross, Air Medal (5th Award), Air Force Commendation Medal w/OLC, and Meritorious Service Medal. Raymond retired from the Air Force on Oct. 1, 1982 in the grade of Major. Home of record: Bossier City, LA.

Matula, Robert F., son of Mr. and Mrs. Emil Matula, West, TX. Entered Navy, 1942. Served w/rank of M 1/C in Aleutians, Gilberts, Marshalls and Marianas during WWII. Awarded GCM, three ribbons w/4 Stars. Discharged, 1945.

Matula, Theo, son of Joe E. and Emilie Konecny Matula, was born Granger, TX, enlisted in U.S. Air Force, 1957, honorably discharged 1959.

Matula, Tobias J., was born on Mar. 3, 1926, served in U.S. Army Air Corps, WWII, as a Sgt. Died Oct. 3, 1989. Buried in St. Mary's Cemetery, West, TX.

Matula, Valentin George, Jr., son of Valentin George Matula, Sr. and Emily Matula, was born Oct. 5, 1923, Hallettsville, TX. Educated in Hallettsville, TX. Entered the U.S. Navy in 1941, later was appointed to the U.S. Naval Academy. Graduated in 1946. Rank: Cmdr. Assumed the Command of RVAH-1 in Apr. 1965. Squadron deployed aboard the USS *Independence* May 1965. Commanding Officer of Reconnaissance Attack Squadron One. Was one of two Sanford, FL, Navy fliers who died as a result of an aircraft accident July 20, 1965, on board the carrier, USS *Independence* in the South China Sea off the coast of Viet Nam. Wife Ann and two children. Burial with full military honors were held Aug. 2, 1965, at the Arlington National Cemetery, Arlington, VA.

Matula, William J., son of Joe E. and Emilie Konecny Matula, was born Jan. 5, 1927, Granger, TX. Education: Granger schools. Drafted on Feb. 5, 1945, U.S. Navy. Basic training, San Diego, CA. Assigned to USS *Commencement Bay*. Theater of Operations: Asiatic-Pacific. Served in South Pacific

until Jan. 1946. WOUNDED IN ACTION. Honorably discharged from the U.S. Navy with 100% disability due to wounds received aboard the USS *Commencement Bay*. Medals: American Defense Medal, WWII Victory Medal, South Pacific Medal, Asiatic-Pacific Theater Campaign Medal w/BSS, Purple Heart. Resides in VA Nursing Home in Lake Charles, LA. Submitted in honor to him by his oldest brother, Emil E. Matula, Sr. of San Antonio, TX.

Matus, Albin J., son of Mr. and Mrs. John Matus, Elm Mott, TX. Entered AAC in 1942. Served A.P. w/rank of Cpl. Awarded AT, AP w/3 BSS, GCM, Service Stripe and one overseas bar. Discharged 1945.

Matus, Ben A., was born Oct. 4, 1927. Served in U.S. Army Corps with rank of Pfc. during WWII. Died Aug. 5, 1980. Buried in St. Mary's Cemetery, West, TX.

Matus, Emil, was born Nov. 2, 1895, served in U.S. Army Corps, Co. M, 141st Inf., 36th Div., during WWI, with rank of Pvt. Died Mar. 19, 1962. Buried in St. Mary's Cemetery, West, TX.

Matus, Ernest J., of West, TX. WWII veteran.

Matus, Frank W., West, TX. WWII veteran, U.S. Army Air Corps, Yuma, AZ.

Matus, Joe W., was born Jan. 28, 1903. Served during WWII in U.S. Army Corps with rank of Pvt. Died Oct. 23, 1983. Buried in St. Mary's Catholic Cemetery, West, TX.

Matus, Louis J., son of Mr. and Mrs. F. M. Matus, of West, TX. Attended Leggott School. Entered Navy in 1945. Served in San Diego, CA. Repair BOS. Awarded A.T. Victory Ribbons. Rank: Pfc. prior to discharge, 1946. Married Mary Hanak.

Matus, Robert J., son of Joe F. and Ludmila Trilica Matus, was born Oct. 19, 1935, in West, TX. Attended Texas A&M University, B.S., 1958, and Hardin-Simmons University, M.A., 1969. Enlisted in the Air Force in San Antonio and was commissioned as a Second Lt. with advancement later to Lt. Col. After completing navigator training, assigned as a navigator in the KC-97 aircraft with assignments in FL, NJ, Canada, and Europe. Then was assigned to the KC-135 aircraft with tours of duty in CA, TX, AK, Europe, and Southeast Asia. Service also included duty as Professor of Aerospace Studies at San Francisco State University. Medals: Distinguished Flying Cross, Air Medal with 5 OLC, Meritorious Service Medal, Air Force Commendation with 2 OLC, Combat Readiness with 2 OLC, Viet Nam Service Medal, Republic of Viet Nam Campaign Medal, Air Force Expeditionary Medal, Air Force Outstanding Unit Award, Small Arms Expert Marksmanship Ribbon, Air Force Longevity Service Ribbon with 4 OLC. Retired from the Air Force in 1980 and started a second career at General Dynamics in Fort Worth. Married to the former Nance Webb; one son.

Matus, Rudolph W., West, TX. WWII veteran, U.S. Army Corps, assigned to Infantry, served overseas in Holland.

Matus, Rudolph W., son of Mr. and Mrs. John Matus, Elm Mott, TX. Entered Army during WWII, in 1943, rank of Pvt. Served in France and Holland. Awarded GCM. KILLED IN ACTION, Holland, 1944.

Matusek, Bennie J., son of A. L. (Louis) and Mary B. Kubena Matusek, was born Jan. 24, 1930, Hungerford, Wharton Co., TX. Graduated Wharton High School, Wharton Co. Junior College, Texas A&M University. Commissioned 1st Lt. Enlisted Ft. Sam Houston, TX. Basic training, Ft. Riley, KS. OCS, Infantry School, Ft. Benning, GA. Assigned to Ft. Bliss, El Paso, TX. 2nd Assignment: 75th Maneuver Area Command (Reserves Unit) Houston, TX. Theater of Operations: USA. Honorably discharged Feb. 10, 1954, Ft. Bliss, El Paso, TX. Married Barbara Dill; five children, three grandchildren. Employed by Shell Oil Company for 37 years as an Industrial Hygiene Technician in Health and Safety. Retired in 1991. Home of record: Deer Park, TX.

Matusek, Julius M., son of A. L. and Mary Kubena Matusek, was born in Hungerford, TX, July 4, 1917. Enlisted in Oct. 19, 1942, Houston, TX. Served in the South Philippine Islands, Okinawa, Leyte during WWII. Medals: American Theater Campaign, Asiatic Pacific Campaign with two BSS, one Bronze Arrowhead, Philippine Liberation Ribbon with one BSS, WWII Victory Medal and Good Conduct Medal. Honorably discharged Jan. 15, 1946.

Matusek, Laddie A., son of Adolph J. and Justina Janak Matusek, was born Oct. 15, 1925, Weid, TX. Graduated from Hallettsville High, Baldwin Business College in Accounting, U.S. Navy School in Communications under a U.S. Naval Program at Texas A&M, attended University of Houston, Victoria, TX. Entered military service at Ft. Sam Houston, TX. Served most of the time in the South Pacific during WWII on the USS LST 597, USS LCT (6) Gr. 70, USS LCT (6) Gr. 66 LCT 1259 and USS LCT (L) 619. Discharged honorably, Camp Wallace, TX, Feb. 27, 1946.

Matusek, Leo B., son of Louis A. and Mary A. Kubena Matusek, was born Feb. 3, 1921, Wharton Co., TX. Graduate: elementary and high school and University of Houston. Enlisted with orders at Ft. Sam Houston, TX, July 1, 1942. Education in U.S. Army Air Corps: Radio Technician Communication Specialist, Airplane Mechanic Specialist, Airplane Instrument Specialist. Rank: Cpl. (assigned Sgt. duty). Theater of Operation: EAME. Battles: WWII, Europe Air Offensive, Normandy, Northern France, Ardennes, Rhineland, Central Europe. Medals and Awards: Overseas Service Medal w/6 BSS, Good Conduct Medal, Purple Heart (150th U.S. Hospital, Mar. 19, 1945), Distinguished Unit Badge, May, 1944-56th Air Fighter Group, Marksman "Pistol" Left Hand Badge. WOUNDED IN ACTION two times. Was with 358th Fighter Group. Honorable discharge Oct. 22, 1945. Was overseas undercover agent. Home of record: Pearland, TX 77581.

Matusek, Louis Edward, son of Louis A. and Mary A. Kubena Matusek, was born in 1918, Hungerford, TX. Volunteered for the Air Force on Dec. 12, 1941. Served with the Engineering Squadron loading bombs and ammo on board planes. Theater of Operation: England, France, Belgium, Holzkirhen and Germany. Rank: T-5. Discharged in 1945. Married Georgia Olsovsky in 1948; five children. Retired from the air conditioning and heating business. Home of record: Houston, TX.

Matusek, Marcus M., served in U.S. Marine Corp Aug. 16, 1950–May 25, 1951, in Korea. Participated in the assault and seizure of Inchon Korea, capture and securing of Seoul, Korea, the Wonson Hungnam Chosin Campaign. Participated in operations in South and Central Korea. Rank: Pfc. Awards: one year Cofg Authority ALNAV 7501, Purple Heart, BSS Medal, Presidential Unit Citation w/1 BSS, Korean Service Medal w/2 BSS, China Service Medal, and GCM Medal.

Matusik, Frank L., son of Mr. and Mrs. Frank Matusik, was born Nov. 6, 1913, West, TX. Entered Navy, 1943 as Chaplain during WWII. Rank: Lt. Served in U.S.A., Pearl Harbor, Eniwetok. Discharged 1945. Died Apr. 18, 1951; buried in St. Mary's Cemetery, West, TX.

Matusik, Harry J., son of Mr. and Mrs. Frank Matusik, West, TX. Entered Navy 1942. Served in S. Pacific. Awarded AP and Victory Ribbons. Discharged 1945 with rank of TM 1/c.

Matusik, Joseph A., son of Mr. and Mrs. Frank Matusik, West, TX. Entered Navy, 1944 during WWII. Served on USS Kretchin in AP. Awarded Victory AP and AT Ribbons. Discharged with rank of CM 3/C in 1946.

Matustik, Raymond E., of Texas, WWII veteran, 36th Inf. Div., U.S. Army Corps. Served overseas in Germany.

Matysek, Charlie L., was born Jan. 2, 1923. Served in U.S. Navy during WWII. Enlisted June 15, 1943. Served on a ship in Pacific. Theater of Operations: Asiatic-Pacific. Achieved rank of Coxswain before being honorably discharged, Feb. 13, 1946. Died May 29, 1953; buried Calvary Catholic Cemetery, Granger, TX. Hometown: Granger, TX.

Matysek, Edwin E., Served in the U.S. Air Force, 1956–1960. Achieved rank of Airman 1/C. Stationed in Africa. Hometown: Granger, TX.

Matysek, Henry C., son of Mr. and Mrs. Joe J. Matysek, Granger, TX. Education: Granger High School. Enlisted U.S. Army during WWII, 1941. Basic training, Ft. Leonard Wood, MO. Theater of Operations: EAME. Served in French-Morocco, Africa, Tunisia, Sicily, Italy, Austria. Medals: Silver Star, Arrowhead, EAME Theater Campaign Ribbon w/6 BSS, American Defense Ribbon, Good Conduct Medal. Rank: T/Sgt. prior to honorable discharge, 1945. Sheriff of Williamson Co., TX, at the time of his death.

Matysek, Jerry A., military service veteran. Home of record: Irving, TX.

Mayer, Ladik, was born May 19, 1923. WWII veteran. T/5, U.S. Army. Died June 9, 1976; buried Holy Cross Catholic Cemetery, Granger, TX.

Mazac, Albert A., son of Mr. and Mrs. Mazac, Taylor, TX. Education: Granger High School. Enlisted U.S. Army Corps, 1941. Basic training Camp Wallace, further training, Ft. Bliss. Theater of Operations: EAME. Served in Normandy, France, Ardennes, Central Europe. Medals: American Defense Medal, EAME Theater Campaign Ribbon w/5 stars, WWII Victory Medal. Achieved rank of S/Sgt prior to honorable discharge, 1945.

Mazac, Gerald, son of Mr. and Mrs. Joe Mazac, Taylor, TX. Education: Granger High School. Enlisted U.S. Army Corps, 1942, basic training Ft. Lewis, WA, further training, CA. Theater of Operations: Asiatic-Pacific. Medals: Asiatic-Pacific Theater Campaign w/BSS, Philippine Liberation Ribbon, Good Conduct Medal, WWII Victory Medal. Rank: Pfc. prior to honorable discharge, 1945. Married Mary Valis.

Mazac, Jerry J., son of Joseph John and Louise E. Kaspar Mazac, was born Sept. 25, 1927, Rosenberg, Ft. Bend Co., TX, Education: Rosenberg, Frydek, USN GED. Enlisted in U.S. Navy, July 1, 1948. Served in Military Occupation of Japan. Theater of Operations: Marianas Islands. Served in Korean War, aboard USS *Bon Homme Richard* (CV31). Medals: Good Conduct, Korean, Japan Occupation. Honorable discharge July 1952. Served July 1, 1948–July 1952, in U.S. Navy, but not during WWII. Married Mary G. Rabel; four children: Susan Marie, Rebecca Ann, Jerome Charles, Allen. Owner of Western Auto in Sealy, TX. Retired 1989. Hobbies: hunting, fishing, golf, travel. Home of record: Sealy, TX.

Mazoch, Alphonse D., was born Sept. 4, 1913. WWII veteran. S/Sgt., 331 Bomb. Group, AAF. Died Feb. 16, 1963; buried Holy Cross Catholic Cemetery, Granger, TX.

Mazoch, Edwin John, son of Steve and Louise Stasny Mazoch, was born June 22, 1922, Granger, TX. Attended Granger Elementary and High School. Enlisted in the U.S. Navy during WWII. Served in all three WWII Theaters of Operations: American, Asiatic-Pacific, and European, African, and Middle Eastern, attaining rank of Yeoman First Class. Served on Destroyer USS *Charles F. Ausburne* commanded by Commodore Arleigh "31 Knot" Burke, who later became Chief, Naval Operations, Tenders, USS *St. George* (A.V. 16) and USS *Hamlin*. Participated in numerous naval operations, including New Guinea, Rabual, Bougainville, Okinawa, and The Slot. Was in operations at Empress Auga Bay in Nov. 1943, night engagement off Cape St. George, 1st bombardment of Kavieng, occupation of Japan, aboard the Destroyer *Charles F. Ausburne* when it was hit by a Kamikaze suicide plane. Edited and created artwork for the Destroyer Squadron 16 newspaper, "Sweet 16." Decorations: Asiatic-Pacific Campaign Medal with six campaign stars, American Campaign Medal, European African Middle Eastern Campaign Medal, WWII Victory Medal, Good Conduct Medal, and Presidential Unit Citation. Discharged on Mar. 4, 1946. Married Theresa Hyzak, of Granger, June 23, 1947; three children: James, Kenneth, and Kathryn. Began civil service

career starting out as GS3 Clerk Typist and retiring Feb. 1978, Corpus Christi, TX as a GS11. Died Oct. 17, 1982; interred Seaside Memorial Park at Corpus Christi, TX.

Mazoch, Jerome Michael, son of Cyril Joseph and Anna Vacek Mazoch, was born in La Grange, (Holman), TX, Sept. 29, 1926. Attended Holman Public School, Weimar ISD, La Grange P.S. Graduated from Blinn Jr. College, Brenham, TX. Entered military service in San Diego, CA. Served in the Asiatic Pacific Theater of Operations. Participated in the Battle of Okinawa during WWII. Awards: Asiatic Pacific Medal, Okinawa Campaign Medal, WWII Victory Medal, GCM Medal. Honorably discharged on July 2, 1946 (WWII), Dec. 14, 1951 (Korean War), July 2, 1954 (Inactive Reserves).

Mazoch, William C. "Willie," son of Steve Mazoch and Louise S. Stasne Mazoch, was born Feb. 5, 1913, Granger, Williamson Co., TX. Education: Granger, TX. College–was a Victory and Shreveport, LA, Centenary. Enlisted in Williamson Co., TX, U.S. Army Corps. Painted airplanes in San Antonio, TX. WWII veteran. Rank: S/Sgt. Honorably discharged. Married Minnie Zbranek; two children: Linda Mazoch Dlouhy and Larry Mazoch. Hobbies: fishing. Died Oct. 4, 1968; buried Holy Cross Catholic Cemetery, Granger, TX. Hometown: Granger, TX.

Mechel, Emil, West, TX, WWII veteran. Theater of Operations: Asiatic-Pacific. Served overseas on Mariana Islands.

Mechell, Emil, was born May 3, 1919, served in WWII in U.S. Navy as Petty Officer 3/C, Amphibious Forces. Served Pacific Theater, Hawaiian Islands, and Marianas. Boatsman Mate 2/C, U.S. Navy, WWII. Died Aug. 2, 1974. Buried in St. Mary's Cemetery, West, TX.

Mehevec, Jerry Leroy, son of Jerry and Mary Lesikar Mehevec, was born Aug. 31, 1940, Thrall, Williamson Co., TX. Graduate of Thrall ISD. Enlisted in U.S. Air Force, Lackland AFB, TX. Rank: E-4. DET II Thailand, 1962, Military Advisor. Medals: Good Conduct. Stood watch and stayed on alert during Cuban Crisis in Okinawa. Honorably discharged Dec. 21, 1962. County Commissioner, Williamson Co., TX. Married Anne Louise Buenger; Adam and Stacy. Home of record: Taylor, TX.

Meiske, Leonard, son of Mr. and Mrs. Theo Meiske, Taylor TX. Education: Waterloo School. Married Alma Hehman. Enlisted U.S. Army Corps, 1945, basic training, Ft. Bliss, TX. Served in Yokohama, Japan. Medals: WWII Victory Medal, Asiatic-Pacific Theater Campaign Medal. After WWII, served in Occupation of Japan.

Meiske, Richard F., son of Mr. and Mrs. Theo Meiske, Taylor, TX. Education: Waterloo School. Enlisted U.S. Army Air Corps, 1942. Basic training Gulfport, MS, further training: MS, MI, CA. Theater of Operations: Asiatic-Pacific. Served in New Guinea, Leyte, Australia, Luzon. Medals: Air Medal w/3 OLC, Good Conduct Medal, WWII Victory Medal, Asiatic-Pacific Theater Campaign Ribbon w/BSS. KILLED IN ACTION on Luzon, 1945.

Mekolik, John J., son of John and Annie Griger Mekolik, was born Apr. 7, 1920, Taylor, Williamson Co., TX. Education: Thrall High School. Enlisted U.S. Army Corps, Feb. 4, 1941, Ft. Sam Houston, TX, prior to WWII. Assigned to 36th Div., 143 Inf., Co. I. Theater of Operations: EAME. Served in Europe. Jan. 22, 1944, WOUNDED IN ACTION and taken PRISONER OF WAR, at Rapido River. Orders were to hold at all cost. All men were killed or wounded, taken POW. Medals: Purple Heart, BSS, Combat Infantry Badge, EAME Theater Campaign Medal w/2 BSS, POW Medal, four Overseas Bars, Good Conduct Medal. Honorably discharged Sept. 10, 1945. Civilian occupation: farmer. Married Vlasta E. Bohac; seven children: Jimmy, John, Angeline, Monica, Robert, Katherine, Patrick. Hobbies: hunting, fishing, skiing. Home of record: Taylor, TX.

Merka, Daniel Gabriel, son of Charles and Rosie Orsak, was born May 3, 1917. Attended Moravia School. Enlisted in the Army Infantry Sept. 29, 1941, at Ft. Sam Houston, TX. Served as a rifleman and cook in the Aleutian Islands. Medals: American Defense Service Medal, Asiatic-Pacific Campaign Medal, and Good Conduct Medal. Discharged from Camp Cooke, CA, Oct. 19, 1945, as a Pfc. Married Mary Martinka; four children. Member, American Legion Post No. 282, Granger,

TX. Died Oct. 26, 1978; buried in Holy Cross Cemetery, Granger, TX.

Merta, Jerome Fred, son of Vaclav and Ludmila Katyza Merta (both immigrated to U.S.A. from Zamberk, Czechoslovakia to Taiton, TX), was born Sept. 25, 1921, Taiton, TX. Education: elementary, Taiton, TX, high school, El Campo, TX. Inducted into U.S. Army Corps, Aug. 12, 1942, Houston, TX. Entered into active service, Aug. 26, 1942. Theater of Operations: America and EAME. Battles: Rhineland, Central Europe GO105 WD 45. Marksman Rifle. Medals: American Theater Campaign Ribbon, EAME Campaign Ribbon w/2 BSS, Good Conduct Medal, WWII Victory Ribbon w/1 service stripe and one overseas service bar. Overseas Mar. 1, 1945–Feb. 28, 1946 (11 months, 28 days). Transferred to 69th Inf. Div., 271st Bn. L Co. Landed in Liverpool, England, then to combat through the European Theater. Discharged from Ft. Sam Houston, TX, Jan. 27, 1946. Stayed on father's farm for three years, then was with U.S. Dept. of Agriculture for 27 years and retired. Married Mary Jo Bilicek, Nov. 5, 1949; four boys and one girl, seven grandchildren. Spent most of lifetime in El Campo, Wharton Co., TX, which is home of record.

Merta, Joseph Henry, son of Vaclav and Ludmila Katyza Merta (both immigrated to U.S.A. from Zamberk, Czechoslovakia to Taiton, TX), was born Feb. 11, 1914, Taiton, TX. Education: Jones Creek Country School. Inducted into U.S. Army Corps, Jan. 29, 1942, Ft. Sam Houston, TX, during WWII. Assigned to Tank Destroyer Unit in Okinawa. Theater of Operations: America and Asiatic-Pacific. Rank: T/5. Medals: American Theater Campaign Medal, Asiatic-Pacific Campaign Medal, Good Conduct Medal, WWII Victory Ribbon, one service stripe, two overseas service bars. Served overseas, 1 year, 2 months, 22 days. After four years was honorably discharged Jan. 27, 1946. Married July 20, 1946, Annie Labay; two sons (both preceded him in death). Spent lifetime in El Campo as a carpenter in construction field. He and three brothers served in WWII (13 children in family, seven boys, six girls). Submitted by brother, Jerome Merta, of El Campo, TX.

Mertz, Allen Joe, was born July 21, 1948. Served in U.S. Armed Forces after WWII. Sp. 4, 146 Signal Co. Died Apr. 24, 1969. Buried Holy Cross Cemetery, Granger, Williamson Co., TX.

Michal, Emil Jaroslav, son of J. J. and Emma Pechacek Michal, was born Sept. 20, 1911, in Fayette Co., TX. Graduated high school, Texas A&M at College Station, B.S., Chemical Engineering, 1932. Attending the University of Houston when called to active duty. Reported to Camp Roberts, CA, Mar. 1942. Attended the U.S. Army Field Artillery School at Ft. Sill, OK, Intelligence School, London, England, and took specialized courses at Paris College in Paris, France. Trained in artillery but was transferred to a tank destroyer unit when these units were first formed in 1942. Attained the rank of Capt. and was Company Commander of different units in the battalion. His unit, the 818th Tank Destroyer Bn., was sent to the European, African, Middle Eastern Theater of Operations, initially to Northern Ireland and England for training and preparation for invasion of the Continent. The 818th served first with the 1st Army but later was one of the original units in General Patton's 3rd Army when it was formed in France. Participated in the Normandy, Northern France, Rhineland, Ardennes:Alsace, and Central Europe Campaigns and was WOUNDED IN ACTION near Chartres, France. Decorations include the Purple Heart, European-African-Middle Eastern Campaign Medal with five campaign stars, Distinguished Unit Citation. Foreign awards: Order of Day of Belgium and Citation from Luxembourg. Spent 27 months overseas, 11 of which were in combat. At one time headquartered in Pesak, Czechoslovakia, the area from where grandmother Pechacek had immigrated. Released from the service and placed on inactive reserve duty in Mar. 1946. Home of record: Flatonia, TX.

Michalcik, Daniel Leroy, son of Joseph Frank and Elizabeth Hohensee Michalcik, was born in Moulton, TX, Jan. 17, 1930. Education: eighth grade. Entered military service on Feb. 2, 1951, in El Campo, TX. Served in the Korean War and was stationed on Okinawa. Served: AUS-Army Feb. 5, 1951–Apr. 27,

1954, Wheel Vehicle Mechanic, Pfc.-E3; ARNG-Army Sept. 29, 1955–Sept. 28, 1958, Cook; Senior Tract Vehicle Mechanic, Sept. 1958-Sept. 1961. Aualified as Marksman-U.S. Rifle CA, 30 M1. Honorably discharged Sept. 28, 1961, with rank of Sp 4-E4.

Michalek, Anton V., was born Jan. 6, 1918. WWII veteran. S/Sgt U.S. Army. Died June 24, 1975; buried Holy Cross Catholic Cemetery, Granger, TX.

Michalek, Joe J., was born Feb. 27, 1920. Served in U.S. Army during WWII. Died June 29, 1975; buried Holy Cross Catholic Cemetery, Granger, TX.

Michalek, Raymond B., Penelope, TX. WWII veteran. Member, American Legion Post No. 282, Granger, TX.

Michalik, Daniel John, son of Anton and Emilie Jansa Michalik, was born Aug. 9, 1931, Holland, TX. Graduate of San Angelo, TX, High School, Oklahoma A&M, Stillwater, OK. Enlisted in Abilene, TX, about 1951, USAF. Theater of Operations: European. Medals: National Defense Service, Good Conduct, Army Occupation of Germany. Honorable discharge Dec. 12, 1955, Manhattan Beach AF Stn., Brooklyn, NY, with rank of Airman 1/C. Retired from civil service, Sept. 1, 1986, with a total of 34 years of service. Home of record: San Angelo, TX.

Michalik, Edmond Anton, son of Anton and Emilie Jansa Michalik, was born Apr. 18, 1920, Taylor, TX. Attended school through ninth grade, Byersville and Holland, TX. Entered Army Air Corps about 1942, Ft. Sam Houston, TX. European Theater of Operations: Rome Arno 15th Air Force, 87th Depot Repair Sqdn. during WWII. Rank: Cpl. Awards: American Defense, EAME Theater Ribbon w/1 BSS, WWII Victory Medal and GCM, WWII Victory Medal. Honorably discharged Jan. 14, 1946, Lackland AFB, San Antonio, TX. Married Agnes Milian; two sons, one daughter. Truck driver for freight company, retired after 30 years. Home of record: San Angelo, TX.

Michalik, Ruben Daniel, son of Anton and Emilie Jansa Michalik, was born Dec. 19, 1921, Taylor, TX. Education: Columbia School, Byersville School, Holland, TX. Enlisted in U.S. Army Corps, Ft. Sam Houston, TX, about 1942. Rank: Sgt. Theater of Operations: EAME. P.T. Boats. Decorations: EAME Campaign Medal, WWII Victory Medal, Good Conduct Medal, among others. Honorably discharged Aug. 27, 1945, Ft. Thomas, KY. Married Dorothy Carnitz of Burbank, IL; two daughters: Diane Michalik Klecka of Addison, IL, Carol Michalik Steinbrenner of Villa Park, IL. Died Nov. 5, 1988; interred at Bethania, IL. Submitted in honor of her brother, by Georgia Michalik Simcik of San Angelo, TX.

Michalsky, Alfred Cyril, son of Peter Valentine and Frances Krenek Michalsky, was born Nov. 19, 1927, Fayetteville, TX. Education: Ellinger School and St. John's Catholic School in Fayetteville, TX. Enlisted in U.S. Army, Mar. 19, 1946. Rank: Cpl. Sent to Ft. Sam Houston, TX. Rifle M-1 Marksman. Received WWII Victory Medal. Discharged Dec. 20, 1946. Recalled Sept. 29, 1950, for Korean Conflict. Sent to Camp Carson, CO, then to Anchorage, AL, to Ft. Richardson. Never went overseas. Honorably discharged Aug. 9, 1952. Married Irene; two children, four grandchildren. Retired after working 35 years with Texas Highway Dept. Likes to work outside, tinkers with old vehicles and tractors, and enjoys raising cattle. Home of record: La Grange, TX.

Michalsky, Bernard Jacob, son of Peter Valentine and Frances Krenek Michalsky, was born July 25, 1934, Fayetteville, TX. Education: St. John's Catholic School, Fayetteville, TX. Enlisted in U.S. Army, Apr. 6, 1954, La Grange, TX. Basic training Ft. Bliss, TX. Sent to Fairbanks, AK. Trained in artillery. Never sent overseas. Received National Defense Medal and Good Conduct Medal. Honorably discharged Mar. 21, 1956. Married Jeanette; six children, two step-grandchildren. Retired after 17 years working at gravel pits as welder and mechanic. Home of record: Ellinger, TX.

Michalsky, Eugene Henry, son of Peter Valentine and Frances Krenek Michalsky, was born Jan. 24, 1931, Fayetteville, TX. Education: St. John's Catholic School, Fayetteville, TX. Drafted into U.S. Army, Aug. 6, 1952, La Grange, TX. Basic training at Camp Roberts, CA. Advanced training Camp Haugen, Japan. Learned to ski. Sent to Korea. Served in 24th Div., Co. C, 19th Inf. Reg. as cook. Served 12 months on the 38th Parallel. While serving there, the U.S. would fire heavy artillery overhead to let the enemy know they were around. Used to watch the planes drop bombs. Had to be on the alert 24 hours a day. Served six months as prisoner guard, guarding prisoners at Camp No. 6, Nonsan, Korea. PRISONER OF WAR (hostage) for 30 days in Nonsan, one of 77 men held by South Korean soldiers. Medals: Good Conduct Medal and POW Medal. Honorably discharged Aug. 17, 1954. Married Margaret; five children, six grandchildren, and one step grandchild. Retired after 37 years as a meat processor. Enjoys playing dominoes, shooting pool, traveling, and meeting people. Home of record: Fayetteville, TX.

Michan, Roman A., was born Aug. 26, 1896. WWI veteran. Died Nov. 25, 1972; buried Calvary Catholic Cemetery, Granger, TX.

Michna, Roman, served in U.S. Armed Forces during WWI, 1917–1918. Member of SPJST Lodge 20, Granger, TX,

Michulka, August Edward, son of Josef and Frances Shula Michulka, was born in East Bernard, TX, Apr. 11, 1922. Education: high school equivalency. Entered military service in Houston, TX, Mar. 17, 1943. Served in the Asiatic Pacific Theater of Operations for 2½ years, CBI–China, Burma, India, during WWII. Worked as a rigger and gearman. Earned the WWII Victory Medal, Sharpshooter Rifle Badge, and GCM Medal. Honorably discharged Feb. 21, 1946.

Miculka, Vladik E., son of Anton and Mary Pavlicek Miculka, was born Nov. 28, 1904, Houston, Harris Co., TX. Education in Houston, TX. Enlisted in U.S. Army Corps, 1941, Houston, TX. Rank: Sgt. before honorable discharge May 5, 1945. Died June 2, 1991, TX.

Migel, George T., son of Mr. and Mrs. Migel, was born in Flatonia, TX, Mar. 16, 1919. Entered military service at Ft. Sam Houston, TX, and served in Germany during WWII with the 84th Div., 335th Inf. A.T. Co. Fought in the Battle of the Bulge. WOUNDED IN ACTION. Awarded the Purple Heart. Was a heavy weight boxer for the 84th Div. Discharged at Camp Fannin, TX. Rank: T/Sgt.

Mikel, Bob L., son of Joseph and Ann Zobojnik Mikel, was born Jan. 21, 1921, Ennis, TX. One of four Mikel brothers. Education: Ennis schools and University of Houston School of Technology. Inducted into U.S. Army Corps, WWII, July 25, 1942, Ennis, TX. European and Asiatic Pacific Theaters of Operations and Aleutians. WOUNDED IN ACTION, May 11, 1945, while serving with the 387th Inf., Co. M, in Europe. Medals: Purple Heart, Aleutian Campaign Medal/1 BSS, EAME Theater Campaign Medal/1 BSS, Asiatic-Pacific Theater Campaign Medal/1 BSS, Good Conduct Medal. While in Czechoslovakia at end of WWII, received permission and a jeep to visit Czech grandparents he had never met. Was turned back, however, at the Russian sector and was unable to complete trip. It was a disappointment he never forgot! Mustered out Dec. 21, 1945, San Antonio,

TX. Married Helen Pavlacka, July 1, 1946; five children, 11 grandchildren. Made Houston, TX, permanent home. Died Mar. 14, 1988. Submitted by widow, Helen Pavlacka Mikel, Houston, TX.

Mikel, Fred Louis, son of Joe and Anna Mikel, was born Oct. 5, 1922, Ennis, TX. Graduated Central High School, Ennis, TX. Enlisted in U.S. Army Corps, Dallas, TX. Theater of Operation: Asiatic-Pacific, American. Battles: New Guinea, Southern Philippines Liberation, Invasion of New Guinea, Finschha Fen and Holladia, Leyte, Mindoho, Mindhao, WWII. Medals: American Theater Campaign Medal, Asiatic-Pacific Campaign Medal w/2 BSS, GCM, WWII Victory Ribbon, one Service Stripe, four Overseas Service Bars. Honorably discharged Jan. 23, 1946. Home of record: Ennis, TX.

Mikes, Alphons J., son of James/Vaclav and Mary Kokas Mikes, was born in Shiner, Lavaca Co., TX, Aug. 19, 1917. Attended Green School, St. Ludmila Academy, Shiner and Southern Methodist University, Dallas, TX. Entered the military service at Ft. Sam Houston, TX, Mar. 20, 1942. Ranks: Aviation Cadet, Sept. 12, 1942; graduated Flight Training, Pilot, July 28, 1943, Capt. Served in the European Mediterranean Theater. Battles: Air Offensive Europe, Naples Foggia, Western Europe and Rome-Arno Campaigns. Medals: Distinguished Flying Cross, Air Medal W/7 OLC, EAME Campaign W/4 BSS, Letter of Commendation from Commanding General, 15th Air Force, group awarded three Presidential Unit Citations, one of which was for dive bombing Ploesti Refiners. With 82nd Fighter GP, Foggia, Italy, flew P-38 Lightning Twin Engine Fighters on 56 long range high altitude missions, escorting B-17 and B-24 Bombers and strafing, dive bombing over Italy, Germany, Austria, Hungary, the Balkan countries. Credited with one Me 109 destroyed and two damaged in the air, and numerous planes, convoys, trains, other targets destroyed on the ground. Separated from the service Aug. 12, 1945. Resides with wife Anita at their home of record: Shiner, TX.

Mikeska, Adolph, son of Frank D. and Kristina Stastny Mikeska, born Apr. 18, 1909, Bell Co., TX. Educated at Seaton School. Raised by stepmother Anna Divoky Mikeska, as mother died when he was quite small. Enlisted at San Antonio, TX, U.S. Army Corps, during WWII. Very sick with meningitis while stationed at San Antonio. Fought in Northern France and Rhineland. Medals: EAME Campaign Medal, two BSS, GCM, WWII Victory Medal, Rifle Marksman Medal. Honorably discharged Feb. 17, 1946, rank of Pfc. Died Apr. 17, 1972; buried in Seaton Cemetery, Bell Co., TX.

Mikeska, Eddie, son of Mr. and Mrs. Frank Mikeska, Abbott, TX. Entered Army, 1942. Rank: Pvt. Trained in Hammer Field, CA, and Hamilton Field, CA. Discharged 1943.

Mikeska, Frank M., son of Frank and Lydia Klecka Mikeska, was born Sept. 14, 1920, Wallis, TX. Enlisted U.S. Army Air Corps, Oct. 14, 1942. Stationed in England during WWII. Married an English girl. Honorably discharged Oct. 28, 1945. Died July 12, 1987.

Mikeska, George, of Abbott, TX. Entered Army in 1942. Rank: Cpl. Served in France and Germany. Awarded Victory and ET Ribbons w/2 Battle Stars. Discharged as Cpl. in 1946.

Mikeska, George Lad, son of Joe P. and Lillian Ann Marek Mikeska, born Mar. 31, 1921, Six Mile Port, Lavaca Co., TX. Education: Placedo, TX, schools, Patti Welder High School, Victoria, TX. Enlisted San Antonio, TX, June 24, 1944. Theater of Operations: Asiatic-Pacific. Assigned to South Pacific, 2nd Marine Div. Before entering service, he worked at the Glen Martin Airplane Factory, Baltimore, MD, as an Airplane Assembler 610. Discharged Mar. 1946. Worked various jobs in Victoria, Houston, Waco, TX. Retired in Alvin, TX. Died Sept. 9, 1990, Alvin, TX. Submitted by sister Marjorie Mikeska Johnston, Victoria, TX.

Mikeska, Henry A., West, TX. WWII veteran, KILLED IN ACTION.

Mikeska, Joe L., Jr., son of Joe L. and Frances Belicek Mikeska, Sr., Taylor, TX. Education: Bartlett School. Enlisted U.S. Army Air Corps, 1942. Basic training, Miami Beach, FL, further training, NJ. Theater of Operations: EAME. Served in Africa, Italy, Tunisia, Po Valley. Medals: EAME Theater Campaign Ribbon w/4 BSS, Good Conduct Medal, WWII Victory Medal, one service stripe, five overseas bars. Rank: Cpl. prior to honorable discharge, 1945.

Mikeska, Joseph Arnold, son of Joe P. and Lillian Ann Marek Mikeska, was born June 16, 1923, Six Mile Port, Lavaca Co., TX. Education: Placedo, TX, schools, Patti Welder High, Victoria, TX. Before entering the service, worked at the Glen L. Martin Airplane Factory, Baltimore, MD, Airplane Assembler 610. Also worked construction, Victoria and Houston, TX. Enlisted Ft. Sam Houston, TX, Aug. 24, 1944, U.S. Army Corps. Theater of Operations: EAME. Campaigns: Rhineland and Central Europe. WOUNDED IN ACTION. Medals: Combat Infantry Badge, Purple Heart Medal, EAME Theater Ribbon/3 BSS, GCM, Rhineland Campaign Ribbon, EAME Campaign Medal, WWII Victory Medal. Died in a hospital in Houston, Harris Co., TX, July 43, 1984. Buried at Memorial Park Cemetery, Victoria, TX. Submitted by his sister, Marjorie Mikeska Johnson, Victoria, TX.

Mikeska, Nelson Frank, son of Frank and Mary Surovik Mikeska, was born in Welcome, TX, Feb. 19, 1922. Attended Austin public schools and Pasadena High School. Joined the military service at Camp Wolters, Mineral Wells, TX. Served in the South Pacific during WWII. Battles: Leyte and Okinawa. At the end of WWII, served six months in the Army of Occupation of Korea. Rank: Buck Sgt. Awarded two Battle Stars, Sharp Shooter (Rifle), and GCM Medals. Caught in a typhoon, enroute to Korea; 350 men and three ships were lost. Honorably discharged in San Antonio, TX, 1946.

Mikeska, Willie W., son of Joe L., Sr., and Frances Belicek Mikeska, Taylor, TX. Married Elizabeth Blad. Enlisted U.S. Navy, 1943, basic training, San Diego, CA. Assigned to USS *Indianapolis*. Theater of Operations: Asiatic-Pacific. Served in Marshalls, Gilberts, Carolines, Marianas. Medals: Asiatic-Pacific Theater Campaign Medal w/9 BSS, Purple Heart, WWII Victory Medal. RANK: S 2/C. WOUNDED IN ACTION on USS *Indianapolis* when Jap kamikaze suicide plane crashed on ship in Mar. 1945. USS *Indianapolis* was returning to USA, after unloading atomic bomb. KILLED IN ACTION, when USS *Indianapolis* was sunk off Leyte.

Miksik, Wesley Jim, son of Jim S. and Emilie Roznovsky Miksik, was born in DeWitt, TX, Sept. 28, 1930. Attended Caranwahug Elementary School, Plainview Elementary School, El Campo and Louise, TX, High Schools. Entered military service in Houston, TX, Sept. 6, 1950. Honorably discharged Sept. 12, 1953.

Mikulec, Alfred Hubert, son of Frank V. and Emilie Balusek Mikulec, was born in Marak, Milam Co., TX, Jan. 1, 1928, ninth child of ten. Attended Marak Sts. Cyril & Methodius Catholic School and Marak Public School. Entered military service Ft. Sam Houston, TX, Apr. 14, 1946. Served as Medical Aide, MAV. 657. Also, served with the Occupation of Japan Forces. Rank: Pfc. Received the WWII Victory Medal and the Army of Occupation Medal, Japan. Honorable discharge Sept. 26, 1947 at Ft. Sill, Lawton, Comanche, OK. Occupation: farmer. Never married. Died Feb. 10, 1988. Buried at Sts. Cyril & Methodius Catholic Cemetery, Marak, TX. Submitted by Lillian B. Mikulec, Buckholts, TX.

Mikulec, Alphonse E., son of Frank V. and Emily Balusek Mikulec, was born Sept. 16, 1914, Marak, Milam Co., TX, 3rd of 10 children. Education: Sts. Cyril & Methodius Catholic School and Cameron School. Volunteered for U.S. Army on Mar. 17, 1941, Ft. Sam Houston, San Antonio, TX. Trained in TX, LA, WI. Served in Ireland, Wales, England, France, Belgium and Czechoslovakia. Medals: ETO Ribbon w/5 BSS, American Defense Medal, Good Conduct Medal, and WWII Victory Medal. Arrived back in USA, July 13, 1945; discharged in 1945. Married Marcella Janicek, 1945; two children, two grandchildren. Member of Majek Orchestra for many years. Owner and operator of National Hall and Cafe before retirement in Cameron, TX. Died Mar. 1993, Olin Teague Medical Center, Temple, TX. Buried St. Monica Catholic Cemetery, Cameron, TX. Submitted by Lillian B. Mikulec, Buckholts, TX. Picture shows Alphonse giving speech in Czech in Pilsen, Czechoslovakia during celebration upon liberation of Pilsen.

Mikulec, Frank Paul, Jr., son of Frank V. and Emily Balusek Mikulec, Dec. 3, 1916, Marak, Milam Co., TX, 4th child of ten. Education: School Sts. Cyril & Methodius Catholic Parish, Marak. Farmer before military service. Enlisted in U.S. Army Corps, Ft. Sam Houston, San Antonio, TX, Nov. 20, 1940, prior to WWII. Assigned Co. G, 38th Inf. Second (Indian Head) Div. Rank: Pfc. Received extensive training as Infantryman, Ranger, and Ski Trooper in TX, LA, Camp McCoy, WI. Arrived in Ireland, 1943, for more training. Entered battle June 6, 1944, France Invasion, Normandy Beach. WOUNDED IN ACTION June 16, 1944, St Lo, France. Honorable discharge, Aug. 5, 1945. Medals: Purple Heart, ETO Ribbon, American Defense Ribbon, Pre-Pearl Harbor Ribbon, Expert Rifleman and Bayonet Medal, GCM, Combat Infantry Badge and BSS Medal. Married Lillian Mikulec, Aug. 5, 1947; four children, six grandchildren. Occupation: farmer, rancher, merchant. Died July 29, 1987; buried at Sts. Cyril & Methodius Catholic Cemetery, Marak, TX. Submitted by Lillian B. Mikulec, Buckholts, TX.

Mikulec, Norbert J., son of Frank V. and Emily Bolusek Mikulec, was born May 18, 1930, Marak, Milam Co., TX, tenth child of ten. Education: Sts. Cyril & Methodius Catholic School, Marak, TX and Cameron, TX, High School. Drafted into U.S. Army, Feb. 1952. Basic Training with the 10th Inf. Div., Fort Riley, KS, Co. C, 87th Inf. Rank: Cpl. Served in Copenhagen, Germany with the 28th Div. Artillery Hqs HQ Battery. Honorably discharged Feb. 1954, Ft. Chaffee, AR. Worked for Coca Cola Co. for six years before and after service. Married Flora Pawelko in Cameron, TX, Aug. 4, 1956; two children, two grandchildren. Moved to Dallas, TX, 1958, attended Barber College. Owns and operates 5-chair barber shop, University Park, Dallas, TX. Home of record: Dallas, TX. Submitted by Lillian B. Mikulec, Buckholts, TX.

Mikulec, Theodore E., son of Frank V. and Emily Balusek Mikulec, was born Dec. 30, 1918, Marak, Milam, TX, 5th child of ten. Education: Attended Sts. Cyril & Methodius Catholic School, Marak, TX. Inducted into U.S. Army, July 17, 1943, Ft. Sam Houston, San Antonio, TX. Trained at Camp Wallace, TX, and Camp Claiborne, LA. Served in England, France, Belgium, Holland, and Germany in the 335th Inf., Anti-Tank Company. Medals: WWII Victory Medal, American Theater Medal, EAME Campaign Medal w/3 BSS, and GCM. Honorably discharged Dec. 22, 1945, Camp Fannin, TX, Rank: Pfc. Married Rita Hertenberger; three children, six grandchildren. Retired farmer. Home of record: Buckholts, TX. Submitted by Lillian B. Mikulec, Buckholts, TX.

Mikulencak, Albert F., son of Frank J. Mikulencak, Sr. and Frances Kofron Mikulencak, was born Aug. 21, 1916, Nada, Colorado Co., TX.

Enlisted July 1945, Ft. Sam Houston, TX, U.S. Army. Received Good Conduct Medal. Rank: Pvt. Assigned Army Hdq. Co. Honorable discharge Dec. 12, 1945. Married Ann Hajda; four children: Dr. Albert F. Mikulencak, Jr., Dorothy Mikulencak Montz, Alice Mikulencak Pawelek, Barbara Mikulencak Garrett. Civilian occupation: Merchant, retired 1978. Hobby: traveling to visit grandchildren. Home of record: Elgin, TX.

Mikulencak, Arthur Edward, son of Charlie and Annie Pokorny Mikulencak, was born Feb. 7, 1923, Taylor, Williamson Co., TX. Education: San Gabriel School through seventh grade. Inducted Feb. 5, 1943, Ft. Sam Houston, TX, U.S. Army Air Corps, 399th Signal Company Aviation T/5. Theater of Operation: EAME. Battles: Northern France, Rhineland GO, 33 WD, 45. Medals: EAME Campaign Medal w/2 BSS, Good Conduct Medal, Meritorious Unit Award, WWII Victory Medal, Marksman Rifle Badge. Honorable discharge, Jan. 18, 1946, Camp Fannin, TX. Married Lillie Mae Mikeska; three children, eight grandchildren, four great-grandchildren. Was a farmer all of life; loved his wife and family and had great family values. Built a three bedroom house, could fix anything that broke, was a welder and mechanic. Died June 21, 1990; buried, Taylor City Cemetery, Taylor, TX. Submitted by his widow, Lillie Mae Mikulencak.

Mikulencak, Bernard Joseph Francis, son of Frank John and Frances Antonia Kofron Mikulencak, was born Feb. 6, 1926, in Granger, TX. Attended Sts. Cyril & Methodius School, Granger High School, and the University of TX, B.A. degree. Enlisted in the U.S. Navy in Jan. 1944 at Austin, TX, during WWII. Attended Boot Camp at Camp Wallace, TX, and served in the Asiatic-Pacific Theater of Operations in the Naval Carrier Aircraft Service as an AM 3-C. Served in the Pacific areas of Saipan, Tinian, and Guam in the Marianna Islands. Decorations: Asiatic-Pacific Campaign Medal, WWII Victory Medal, and Good Conduct Medal. Separated from service on June 26, 1946. Married Lillian Zurovetz. Retail merchant. Retired May 1977. Enjoys fishing, hiking, and craftwork. Home of record: Granger, TX.

Mikulencak, Edward Anton, son of Anton and Marie Rosipal Mikulencak, was born Feb. 21, 1923, in Granger, TX. Graduated from Granger High School in 1941. Enlisted in the U.S. Navy at San Antonio, TX, during WWII. Served in the Asiatic-Pacific Theater of Operations aboard the USS *Kittson* (APA 123) and the USS *Lycoming* (APA 155). Participated in naval operations in the liberation of the Philippine Islands and in the invasion of Okinawa. Separated from service on Oct. 26, 1945. Retired from the Corpus Christi Fire Department in Mar. 1980. Home of record: Granger, TX.

Mikulencak, Emil R., Dallas, TX. WWII veteran. Member, American Legion Post No. 282, Granger, TX. Deceased.

Mikulencak, Frank John, Jr., son of Frank John, Sr., and Frances Antonia Kofron Mikulencak, was born Nov. 21, 1922, in Nada, TX. Attended Sts. Cyril & Methodius School, Granger High School, and the University of Texas at Austin. Enlisted in the U.S. Navy on Sept. 3, 1942, at Austin, TX, during WWII. Rank: Yeoman First Class. Served in the Asiatic Pacific Theater of Operations in the Pacific areas of the Philippine Islands and China. Also served in Panama and at U.S. bases. Sailed through the Bermuda Triangle and also survived treacherous typhoons at sea. Decorations include the Good Conduct Medal, Asiatic-Pacific Campaign Medal, WWII Victory Medal, American Campaign Medal, and Philippine Liberation Ribbon. Honorable discharge on Mar. 23, 1946. Married Georgia Vlasta; three children: David J. Mikulencak, Diana C. Mikulencak Bosshard, Lucy J. Mikulencak Hamilton. Owned and managed a general merchandise retail business in Granger before retiring in Nov. 1984. Hobbies are bowling, fishing, and gardening. Home of record: Granger, TX. Member, American Legion Post No. 282, Granger, TX.

Mikulencak, Joe M., served in U.S. Armed Forces during WWI, 1917–1918. Member of SPJST Lodge 20, Granger, TX,

Mikulencak, Josef Frank, son of Anton and Marie Rosipal Mikulencak, was born Oct. 1, 1921, in Granger, TX. Attended Sts. Cyril & Methodius School and Granger High School. Enlisted in the U.S. Navy, Aug. 5, 1941, Houston, TX, during WWII. Served in the South Pacific as a Gunman aboard the USS *San Francisco*. Battles: Salve, Solomon Islands. Participated in naval operations at Guadalcanal, Bougainville, Cape Esperance, and Salamau. Only one of his 16 man gun crew to survive when area was hit while the USS *San Francisco* was engaged in one of its many encounters in the Pacific. Although WOUNDED IN ACTION, rendered aid to others and was awarded a Medal of Commendation. Witnessed the sinking of the ship on which the five Sullivan brothers lost their lives. Decorations: Purple Heart, Presidential Unit Citation, Navy Commendation Medal, American Campaign Medal, and the Asiatic-Pacific Campaign Medal with four campaign stars. Separated from service Nov. 29, 1945, with rank of Coxswain, V-6. Worked for the U. S Postal Service until retirement in 1978. Married Loretta Skrovan; three children: Paul, Mandy Mikulencak Dougherty, and Tesse Mikulencak Knox. Hobbies included fishing, horse racing, cattle, and carpentry. Died Mar. 19, 1984; interred in the Holy Cross Catholic Cemetery at Granger, TX.

Mikulik, Adolph Joseph, son of Joseph and Barbara Blahuta Mikulik, was born Oct. 27, 1894, in Praha, near Flatonia, TX. Attended Komensky Elementary in Lavaca Co., TX. Enlisted in the Army on June 25, 1918 at Hallettsville, TX. Rank: Pfc. Assigned to American Expeditionary Force in France for 11 months. Awarded the Bronze Victory Medal. Discharged Aug. 5, 1919, at Camp Travis, TX. Married Cecelia L. Jemelka; three daughters, two sons. Farmed near Moulton, until WWII, and then worked at the Corpus Christi Naval Base as an Aircraft Mechanic until retirement. Died Jan. 6, 1970, in Corpus Christi, TX.

Mikulik, Eugene A., Sr., son of John and Rosie Krenek Mikulik, was born in Schulenburg, TX, Feb. 10, 1925. Attended school in Engle, TX. Entered military service at Ft. Sam Houston, San Antonio, TX. Served during WWII in Rhineland Central Europe. Rank: Pfc. Awards: Combat Infantryman Badge, two Service Bars, EAME Campaign Ribbon w/2 BSS, Army Occupation Ribbon, Germany, GCM Medal. Served with 508th Parachute, 82nd ABD and Infantry. Honorably discharged June 7, 1946.

Mikulik, Wallace Adolph, son of Adolph J. and Cecilia Jemelka Mikulik, was born Nov. 5, 1932, Moulton, TX. Education: Komensky Elementary, Moulton, TX, Corpus Christi, TX, College-Academy, Delmar College, Corpus Christi, TX. Enlisted about 1951, Ft. Sam Houston, TX, USAF. Basic training, Ft. Bliss, El Paso, TX, Anti-Aircraft Artillery Field Training, Grand Island, NY, Computer Training, Camp Welfleet, Cape Cod, MS. Served a half year, 56th Operations and Specialist Detachment, Ft. Niagara, NY. Theater of Operations: USA (American). Assigned 56th Anti Aircraft Artillery Operations and Intelligence Specialist Detachment, Ft. Niagara, NY. Medals: National Defense Service Medal, GCM. American Theater Campaign Ribbon. Rank: Spec. 4–Cpl. Honorably discharged Feb. 4, 1955. Home of record: Corpus Christi, TX.

Mikus, James Edward, son of Edward J. Mikus, Sr. and Bessie Cernosek Mikus, was born in Inez, TX. Enlisted at San Antonio, in Aug. 1942. Rank: T/4. Served in the Asiatic Pacific Theater of Operations. Fought in New Guinea and Southern Philippines Liberation. Discharged Dec. 10, 1945, at Fort Sam Houston, TX. Medals: Asiatic Pacific Theater Campaign Ribbon with two BSS, Good Conduct Medal, Philippine Liberation Ribbon with one BSS, Victory Ribbon, one Service Stripe, five Overseas Service Bars, one Bronze Arrowhead to AP Campaign Medal. Married

LaVerne Jeanette Eismann on July 2, 1947, at Grand Prairie, TX. Career Civil Service employee, retiring from NASA Johnson Space Center, Houston, on Dec. 31, 1974. Died Mar. 24, 1992, at Memorial City Rehab Hospital in Houston and is buried in the Shelby Cemetery, Shelby, TX.

Mikus, John Konstant, son of John Frederick and Mary Herminia (Urbanovsky) Mikus, was born Dec. 12, 1919, Fayetteville, TX. Graduated from University of CA with a B.S. in Science, General Agriculture, June 16, 1949. Enlisted in the U.S. Navy, Jan. 8, 1942, Houston, TX. Boot camp in San Diego, CA, Sec Base, San Francisco, CA. Served at Armed Guard Center (Pacific), Treasure Island, San Francisco, CA, during WWII. Also served on the USS *Ocelot* (1 x 110) Korean Area, USS *Jason*, sea duty. Rank: Chief Yeoman (T). Citation from the Commander of the U.S. Naval Training and Distribution Center, San Francisco, CA, Commodore R. W. Cary, USN, reads "for meritorious duty performed as Operations Yeoman at the Armed Guard Center (Pacific) from June 1942 until Nov. 1944. His outstanding leadership and efficiency in organizing the files of some 2,400 vessels and some 47,000 personnel when there was no available precedent and his orderly administration of the unique tabulation system originated by himself resulted in considerable benefit to this Command and to the U.S. Naval Service." Honorably discharged Jan. 10, 1946, Camp Wallace, TX. Married Helen Emma Trnovsky; three children: John William, David Paul, and Eileen Marie. Died July 2, 1972; buried at St. John's Catholic Cemetery, Fayetteville, TX.

Milberger, William, West, TX, WWII veteran.

Milder, Anton Louis, son of Ignac J. and Josefa C. Milder, was born June 10, 1926, Corn Hill, Williamson Co., TX. Enlisted in U.S. Army Corps during WWII, about 1944, Williamson Co., TX. Rank Pvt., 9136 Tech SVC Unit. Honorably Discharged. Married Meta. Died Jan. 1, 1968. Buried Corn Hill, TX.

Milder, Joseph Frank, son of Ignac J. and Josefa C. Milder, was born Apr. 30, 1912, Corn Hill, Williamson Co., TX. Enlisted in U.S. Army Corps, about 1940. Served during WWII, attaining rank of Sgt., Co. A, 26 Sig Trng Bn. Honorably discharged. Married Bessie Kristen. Died Jan. 23, 1960, buried Corn Hill, TX.

Miller, Eugene Ernest, son of Frank Stephen and Philomena Pavlicek Miller, was born July 26, 1946, Waco, McLellan Co., TX, fourth of five children. Education: St. Mary's Parochial School, Reicher High School, Waco, TX, Hill Junior College, Hillsboro, TX, DeVry Institute of Technology, Dallas, TX, Texas State Technical College, Waco, TX. Enlisted Mar. 1966, Waco, TX, U.S. Naval Reserves, Rank: HM2. Dec. 1, 1966, completed training as Hospital Corpsman in San Diego, CA. Assigned to the U.S. Naval Hospital, Charleston, SC. Dec. 1967, received orders for Viet Nam. Theater of Operations: U.S. Naval Hospital, Charleston, SC, 2nd Bn., 1st Marine Div., Viet Nam. WOUNDED IN ACTION, May 8, 1968. Medals: BSS, Purple Heart, National Defense Service, Viet Nam Campaign, Viet Nam Service, Viet Nam Cross for Gallantry. Honorable discharge Mar. 1, 1972. Married Deborah Lynn Phelps, Jan. 4, 1969; four children: Eugene Ernest, Jr., Michael Joseph, Timothy Wayne, Joseph Stephen. Lived in Carrollton, TX. Worked for Otis Engineering Corp, an oil field service and manufacturing company. In Apr. 1994, Gene was laid off from Haliburton (formerly Otis), after 23½ years of service. Presently working toward degree in Laser Electro-Optics at Texas State Technical College, Waco, TX. Enjoys photography, softball, running, and out of doors. Home of record: Abbott, TX. Submitted by brother, Rev. Msgr. Frank S. Miller, Abbott, TX.

Miller, Henry A., son of Jerry R. and Lillie A. Cernosek Miller, was born May 26, 1926, in Megargel, TX. Enlisted in the Navy in Dallas, TX, and served in the Pacific. Rank: ENDFN. Medals: Good Conduct, II Victory, and Asia Pacific American Theater. Honorably discharged on July 9, 1946. Recalled during the Korean War and discharged for the second time on July 9, 1954. Home of record: Dallas, TX.

Miller, Jerry Frank, son of Jerry R. and Lillie A. Cernosek Miller, was born Aug. 25, 1922, in Megargel, TX. Enlisted in the Army at Archer City. Sent to Camp Wolters, TX. Served in the Pacific in the 96th Inf. Div., Co. B, 382nd WF. Fought in the Leyete A-Day and Okinawa L-Day battles. Rank: Pfc. Received two Purple Hearts, Infantry Badge, Pacific-Theater, and Good Conduct medals. Two wounds. Discharged Nov. 23, 1945. Home of record: Megargel, TX.

Miller, Jerry Robert, son of Mr. and Mrs. Anton Miller, was born Apr. 3, 1895 in Burleson, TX. Inducted in the Army June 24, 1918, in Weatherford, TX. Stationed at Camp Johnson, FL, the 362nd Field Remount Sqdn. Discharged Jan. 2, 1919, at Camp Bowie, TX. Died Apr. 18, 1987, in Megargel, TX.

Miller, Leslie Daniel, son of John Lambert and Matilda Kocurek Miller, was born July 10, 1943, Dallas, TX. Education: graduated McCollum High School, TX. Enlisted in National Guard, 1961. Rank: E-4, Spec. 4. Maintenance-OJT Motor Pool–Helicopter Maint. Theater of Operations: Texas (America). Sharp Shooter Badge. Honorable discharge, 1970. Married Gabriele Mae Rosipal; two children: Jennifer and Brian Joseph. Central Feight Lines truck driver. Hobby: Music. Home of record: Round Rock, TX.

Minarcik, Alvin, son of Julia and John Minarcik, Jr., was born Feb. 12, 1921, at Fayetteville, TX. Attended several schools due to moving conditions. Last school attended was Willow Springs. Entered the service at Fort Sam Houston, TX, on Nov. 4, 1942. Served in the Medical Supply Unit, 119th Station Hospital, of which 26 months was combat in New Guinea, attaining the rank of Sgt. T/4. Medals: American Theater Campaign Medal, Asiatic-Pacific Campaign Medal with one BSS, Good Conduct Medal, WWII Victory Medal. Discharged Jan. 16, 1946, at Camp Fannin, TX. Died Nov. 1, 1980.

Mitchon, August Adolph, son of Cyril Mican and Agnes Matula Mitchon, was born Jan. 29, 1893, in Moravia, TX. Attended school at Rocky Creek for six years. Worked on farm until he enlisted at Hallettsville, on Oct. 8, 1917, as a Pvt., in Co. G, 104th Inf. Theater of Operations: St. Agnant and Bois de Brigade elis Marines. WOUNDED IN ACTION July 22, 1918, by machine gun bullet. Received the Purple Heart and Silver Victory Medal. Honorably discharged May 10, 1920, at Fort McPherson, Georgia. Opened a shoe repair shop in Schulenburg in 1924, and worked there until retirement in 1963. Married Anna Kallus on July 6, 1920, in St. John, TX. Died July 11, 1977, and was given a military burial at St. Rose Catholic Cemetery in Schulenburg, TX.

Mitchon, August Joseph, son of August Adolph and Anna Kallus Mitchon, was born Mar. 1, 1923, in San Antonio, TX. Graduated from Schulenburg High School in 1940, and was employed at the Employment Commission. Married Earline Ruth Grasshoff on Oct. 26, 1942. Drafted into the Army Feb. 16, 1943, at Fort Sam Houston, TX. Assigned to Co. A, 785th Tank Bn., Fort Knox, KY, and later transferred to 2510th AAF BU, Brooks Field, as Supply Clerk. Awarded the American Theater Ribbon, Victory Medal and Good Conduct Medal. Discharged on Nov. 29, 1945, at Randolph Field, and returned to the Employment Commission until his retirement on Aug. 31, 1982. Home of record: Austin, TX.

Mlcak, Albert, son of Anton W. Mlcak, Jr. and Kristina Kutra, was born Jan. 1, 1925, Sealy, Austin Co., TX. Enlisted in U.S. Naval Reserve, Jan. 4, 1941, Houston, TX. Served a half month in U.S. Navy during WWII. Honorably discharged Feb. 16, 1945, San Diego, CA. Married Mary Alice Finch, Nov. 25, 1958; two children: Lynette M.

Mlcak Waldrep, Laura A. Mlcak. Died Apr. 3, 1992. Widow's home of record: Houston, TX.

Mlcak, Albin, Sr., son of August Simon and Johanna Belunek Mlcak, was born Mar. 1, 1919, Sealy, Austin Co., TX. Education: St. Mary's Catholic School, Frydek, Austin, TX. Enlisted in U.S. Army Corps, Apr. 23, 1943, Houston, TX. Assigned to Co. F, 393rd Eng. Special Service Reg, Camp Claiborne, LA. Served Apr. 1943–Dec. 1943, U.S. Army Corps, during WWII.Honorably discharged because father died and he was needed on the farm. Married Annie Petrash, Aug. 30, 1941, Galveston, TX; three children: Albin, Jr., Ronald, Randy. Shop foreman in Galveston, TX. Retired Apr. 1984. Hobbies: fishing, ,and travel. Home of record: San Felipe, TX.

Mlcak, Dennis James, son of John and Lillie Machala Mlcak, was born Dec. 11, 1935, Sealy, Austin Co., TX. Education: U.S. Army Engr. School, July 1958–Oct. 1958, Ft. Belvoir, VA. Enlisted in U.S. Army Corps, Apr. 20, 1958, Houston, TX. Surveyor/Construction. Theater of Operations: American. Assigned to Ft. Belvoir, VA, Army Reserves for five years, four months. Married Edith L. Pavlicek, Nov. 9, 1958; three children: Deanna Maria Mlcak Arnold, Roxane G. Mlcak, DDS, Audrey L. Mlcak Rossi. Civil Engineer, Texas Highway Dept. Home of record: Houston, TX.

Mlcak, Edward C. "Eddie," son of Joseph and Josephine Pavlicek Mlcak, was born July 18, 1922, Frydek, Austin Co., TX. Commissioned a 1st Lt., U.S. Army Air Corps, during WWII, First Pilot (Aircraft Comdr) B-24. Was in heavy bombardment and MISSING IN ACTION for a few days. Name is on monument erected by St. Mary's Catholic Church, in thanksgiving for the return of 75 parishioners who served in WWII, 1941-1945. Married Gwendolyn E. Graff, Sept. 8, 1947; adopted Mark Stanton Mlcak. Civilian occupation: Area Supt. Home of record: Gordonville, TX.

Mlcak, Fred August, son of Frank Joe and Antonia Belunek Mlcak, was born July 1921, Frydek, Austin Co., TX. Education: St. Mary's Catholic and Frydek Public Schools, Frydek, TX. Enlisted in U.S. Army Corps, Sept. 29, 1942, Houston, TX, Rank: Sgt. Automotive Mechanic and Driver. Theater of Operations: CBI during WWII. Medals: American Theater Campaign Medal, Asiatic-Pacific Campaign Medal w/3 BSS, CBI Campaign Medal, WWII Victory Ribbon. Honorably discharged Jan. 3, 1946. Civilian Occupation: Farmer, and Owner of Fairbanks Tractor and Eqpt. Co. Married Florence Mlcak June 27, 1953; two children: Kenneth Mlcak and Jeanne Mlcak Netardus. Died June 8, 1988; buried St. Mary's Catholic Cemetery, Frydek, Austin, TX. Widow's home of record: Houston, TX.

Mlcak, Henry Richard, son of August Simon and Johanna Belunek Mlcak, was born Dec. 30, 1915, Frydek, Austin Co., TX. Great grandparents, Augin Mlcak and Frantiska Tomanek Mlcak of Rosteni, Moravia, Czechoslovakia, were one of the first families to settle in the San Felipe-Frydek area in May 1871. Education: Frydek High School, TX. Enlisted in U.S. Army Air Corps, Jan. 25, 1943, Houston, TX. Rank: Cpl. Theater of Operations: American. Served with 1383rd Army Air Corps Base Unit in Goosebay, Labrador, Canada. Medals: American Theater Campaign Ribbon, Good Conduct Medal, WWII Victory Ribbon, Service Stripe and Overseas Service Bar. Discharged Mar. 8, 1946. Civilian occupation: Farmer, Auto Mechanic, and machinist at Cameron Iron Works. Retired Jan. 1980. Married Albina A. Bogar; children: Patricia Ann Mlcak Bagwell, Marie Lynn Mlcak Speight, Henry August Mlcak. Hobbies: fishing and traveling. Died Oct. 5, 1993. Buried at St. Mary's Cemetery, Frydek, TX. Widow's home of record: Sealy, TX. Submitted by daughter, Patricia A. Mlcak Bagwell of Round Rock, TX. (She has submitted practically all of the Frydek, Austin Co., TX, veterans' information).

Mocek, Jerry E., son of Anton and Christine Parma Mocek, was born in Seymour, TX, Oct. 24, 1920. Entered the military service, Dallas, TX. Served in the China, Burma, India (CBI) Theater,

with the Air Transport Command during WWII as airplane maintenance chief and flight engineer. Rank: S/Sgt. Awards: Distinguished Unit Badge, WWII Victory Medal, Air Medal, Asiatic Pacific Theater Campaign Medal w/2 BSS, GCM Medal. Honorable discharge at Camp Fannin, TX, Dec. 10, 1945.

Mohel, Daniel John, son of Emil and Hattie Halvzan Mohel, was born July 1, 1943. Attended Granger H.S., Temple Junior College, and Austin Community College. Enlisted in the U.S. Navy , Austin, TX, during the Viet Nam Conflict. Sworn into the service at his home in Granger, TX. Trained at the U.S. Naval Training Center in San Diego, CA. Served aboard the USS *Yorktown* (CVA-10), USS *Marsh,* and USS *Barton* (DD-722) as a Torpedoman's Mate, 3rd Class Petty Officer. Received National Defense Service Medal. Separated from service on July 20, 1966. Salesman with the Frito Lay Corporation. Married Carolyn Davis; one daughter: Dana. Home of record: Taylor, TX.

Mohel, Jimmie, son of Mr. and Mrs. J. P. Mohel, Taylor TX. Education: Taylor High School. Enlisted in U.S. Army Corps, 1944. Basic training, Ft. Monmouth. Theater of Operations: Asiatic-Pacific. Served in Hawaii and Marianas Island w/Signal Construction Co. Medals: American Defense Medal and Ribbon, Asiatic-Pacific Theater Campaign Medal and Ribbon w/1 BSS, Good Conduct Medal, WWII Victory Medal. Rank: S/Sgt. prior to honorable discharge, 1945. Married Dolly Zimmer.

Mohel, Robert Lee, son of Emil and Hattie Halvzan Mohel, was born Oct. 11, 1938. Attended high school at Granger, TX. Enlisted in the U.S. Army at Ft. Sam Houston in San Antonio, TX. Served during the Cuban and Berlin Crises in the Signal Corps. Separated from service in 1968, and is a truck driver.

Married Leta Nichols; two children: Cindy and Sandra. Home of record: San Antonio, TX.

Mokry, Jerry Joe, son of Mr. and Mrs. George Mokry, Granger, TX. Education: Granger High School. Enlisted U.S. Navy, 1945. Boot camp, San Diego, CA, further training, Camp Elliott. Theater of Operation: American. Medals: American Theater Campaign Medal, American Defense Medal, WWII Victory Medal. Rank: S 2/c prior to honorable discharge.

Mokry, Lillian, daughter of Mr. and Mrs. George Mokry, Granger, TX. Education: Granger High School. Enlisted U.S. Army Cadet Nursing Corps, 1943, training, Seton's Hospital, Austin, TX.

Mokry, Raymond M., was born Jan. 6, 1918, died July 9, 1984, buried Calvary Catholic Cem., Granger, TX. WWII veteran.

Mokry, Ronald J., U.S. Navy: USS *Lawrence* APA 153. WWII veteran. Granger, TX.

Mokry, Willie V., WWII veteran of Granger, TX.

Molloy, Danelo A. W. E. "Bill," son of Alexander Raymond "Pat" and Frances Evelyn Wenglar Molloy, was born Nov. 17, 1931, Los Angeles, CA. Education: Moravia School, grades 1–7, J. L. Long, Woodrow Wilson, Highland Park, TX, grades 8–12. Univ. of Texas, Austin, one year. Enlisted U.S. Air Force, Jan. 15, 1951, Dallas, TX. Basic training: Lackland AFB, TX. Medical Field Service School, Ft. Sam Houston, TX, USAF Hospital, Sheppard AFB, Wichita, TX. American Theater of Operations. Medals: National Defense Service, Good Conduct. Honorably discharged Jan. 15, 1955. Rank: Airman 1/C. Married Mary K. Bird; two children: Michael and Melissa. Retired from U.S. Postal Service after 33½ years; currently realtor. Home of record: Rowlett, TX.

Moravec, Daniel John, son of Henry and Elsie Moravec of Ross, TX. Education: Ross School, West High School, Tarleton University. Entered service, 1944, U.S. Navy, E5, EN2, Viet Nam, Carol Teinert Campaign. Received GCM w/3 stars and medals, Viet Nam Ribbon. Discharged June 1968.

Morris, Alphonse Nick, son of Joseph Nick and Albina Berkovsky Morris, was born July 16, 1915, Sweet Home, TX. Education: Sweet Home School and College at Corpus Christi, TX, engineering degree. Enlisted U.S. Army Corps, Corpus Christi, TX. Assigned to U.S. Army Corp of Engineers, H&S Co., 1268th Engr., C Bn. Theater of Operations: EAME. KILLED IN ACTION Sept. 29, 1945, Luzon, Philippine Islands. 12 men were swept into the raging, treacherous waters of the Ibulao River in the jungles of Luzon near Habian. No bodies were recovered. Medals received: Purple Heart, EAME Campaign Medal, WWII Victory Medal. Submitted by Virginia M. Brenek, Houston, TX.

Motal, Adolf Eugene, son of Adolf Andrew and Konstantina Octavia Kocian Motal, was born in Hallettsville, TX. Attended the University of Houston. Entered military service in Hallettsville, TX. Rank: Cpl. Served during WWII in the Pacific, aboard USAT *General E. T. Collins*. Trained as laboratory, dental and x-ray technician and pharmacist. Awards: Pacific, WWII Victory, and Good Conduct Medals. Had three brothers also serving in the Pacific.

Motal, Anton, Jr., son of Anton Motal, Sr. and Agnes Zahradnik Motal, was born Oct. 26, 1908, at Pierce, TX. Served during WWII and attained the rank of Sgt. Separated from service on May 11, 1946. Died Oct. 31, 1981.

Motal, Frank, son of Frank and Agnes Motal, was born Oct. 10, 1893, in Moravia, TX. Served with U.S. Army Corps, Infantry, A.E.F. in France diromg WWI as a Pvt. in the 139th Unit. By the time he got to France, the war ended. Died Aug. 3, 1932.

Motis, Willie, was born Jan. 15, 1899. Served in U.S. Navy, C13 MUS. Died Nov. 22, 1983; buried Bold Spring Cemetery, West, TX.

Motl, Louis L., son of Bernard and Amalie Svadja Motl, was born June 5, 1923 in Wallis, TX. Went to Guardian Angel School and Wallis High School. Enlisted in Houston, TX, and served in the European Theater as a T/4. Medals: American Theater Campaign Medal, EAME Campaign Medal with three BSS, WWII Victory Medal. Discharged Dec. 30, 1945. Home of record: Santa Fe, TX.

Motloch, Anton Joe, was born Mar. 18, 1914. WWII veteran. Sgt., US Army. Died July 18, 1989; buried Holy Cross Catholic Cem., Granger, TX.

Motloch, Louis W., was born 1915. WWII veteran. T/5 US Army. Died 1975; buried Holy Cross Catholic Cem., Granger, TX.

Moudry, Charles Ray, son of Joe L. and Bessie Fisher Moudry, was born July 20, 1946, Bellville, Austin, TX. Education: Bellville Jr. High, Furr Jr. and Sr. High. Vocational welding. Enlisted in U.S. Army Corps, Apr. 1966, Houston, TX. Theater of Operations: Viet Nam. Basic training, Ft. Riley KS. Assigned to 3rd Bn. 39th Inf. of the 9th Inf. Div. Embarked for Viet Nam Dec. 9, 1966. In an exceptionally heavy mortar attack by the Communists, was KILLED IN ACTION on Mar. 8, 1967. Medals: National Defense Service, Marksmanship Rifle M-1 Badge, Viet Nam Campaign, Combat Infantry Badge, Viet Nam Service, Purple Heart, Viet Nam Mint, Viet Nam Gallantry Cross w/Palm. Member of Sts. Peter and Paul Catholic Church of Bellville, TX, and the Nelsonville SPJST Lodge.

Moudry, Edwin, son of Joe L. and Bessie Fisher Moudry, was born Aug. 12, 1934, Bellville, TX. Education: Bellville High School. Enlisted June 6, 1957, La Grange, TX. Theater of Operations: America and EAME. Basic training, Fort Chaffee, AR, Ft. Carson, CO, Ft. Ord, CA. Special training Class Room Henry

Kaserne, Munich, Germany 18 months. Served as Tech inspector for vehicles. Medals: Overseas Duty Medal, Marksmanship Rifle M-1, Badge. Discharged honorably into reserves, May 23, 1959. Permanent honorable discharge June 5, 1963. Married Johnelle Thoede; five children. Self-employed 34 years, Braesmain Texaco/ Moudry Motors, Houston, TX. Home of record: Houston, TX. Submitted by wife, Johnelle Moudry of Houston, TX.

Mozisek, John J., son of John and Mary Janca Mozisek, was born Apr. 18, 1883. Fought in WWI as a Pvt., Co. L, 154 Inf. Died Aug. 19, 1954.

Mraz, Mills Milan Method, son of Louis and Julia Gallia Mraz (grandson of Karel Gallia and Agnes Hermes, great-grandson of Andrej Gallia and Marianna Kladivo, who immigrated on the *Jeverland* in 1860), was born July 15, 1915, Lavaca Co., TX. Served in U.S. Armed Forces during WWII. KILLED IN ACTION, 1942. Married Matilda Slansky about 1940; one son: Mills Mraz, Jr., born about 1943.

Mrkos, Frank, was born Feb. 2, 1894, of West, TX. Served in U.S. Army Corps as Pvt. during WWI. Died Mar. 17, 1969. Buried in the West Brethren Cemetery, West, TX.

Mrkos, Willie T., was born Aug. 15, 1922. Served in U.S. Army as T/4 during WWII. Died Dec. 28, 1985. Buried in the West Brethren Cemetery, West, TX.

Mucha, Edwin H., son of Mr. and Mrs. Joe Mucha, Taylor, TX. Education: Taylor High School. Enlisted U.S. Army Corps, 1942, basic training, VA, further training: MO, OR, CA. Theater of Operations: European. Served in Scotland, England, France, Holland, Germany. Medals: ETO Campaign Medal w/5 BSS, Good Conduct Medal, American Defense Medal w/4 Overseas Bars, WWII Victory Medal, Ribbons. Rank of Pvt. at honorable discharge, 1946.

Mucha, Joe J., son of John and Julie Mucha, was born Oct. 23, 1901, Burleson Co., TX. Enlisted in U.S. Army Corps, served in National Expeditionary Force, WWI. Theater of Operation: Europe. Battles: Austria. Medals: WWI Victory Medal. Honorably discharged 1919. Submitted by Edwin L. Hlavaty.

Mucha, Milton, U.S. Navy. USS *Nassau*. WWII veteran. Granger, TX.

Muehlstein, Frankie, Jr., son of Frankie Muehlstein, Sr. and Eleanor Machovsky Muehlstein, was born Nov. 21, 1945 at Stamford, TX. Attended high school in Abbott, Hillsboro Junior College, and North Texas State University at Denton. Enlisted in the USAF at Hillsboro, TX. Served in Viet Nam and attained the rank of Staff Sgt. Was involved in a plane crash in Alaska on Nov. 27, 1970, while enroute to Viet Nam. Decorations include the Viet Nam Service Medal and the National Defense Service Medal. Discharged from service at Malstrom Air Force Base, Great Falls, MT. Home of record: China Springs, TX.

Mundkowsky, Norbert P., son of Mr. and Mrs. Oscar Mundkowsky, Taylor, TX. Education: San Antonio Tech. High School. Enlisted U.S. Army, 1940, basic training, Ft. Sam Houston, TX, further training, Camp Swift, Camp Maxey and Ft. Dix, NJ. Theater of Operations: American and European. WOUNDED IN ACTION, Germany, 1945. Medals: ETO Campaign Medal w/2 BSS, American Theater Campaign Medal, American Defense Medal, Good Conduct Medal, BSS, Silver Star, Ribbons, WWII Victory Medal. Rank: Sgt. before honorable discharge. Married Mildred Lucille Helgren.

Mundkowsky, Roy T., son of Mr. and Mrs. Oscar Mundkowsky, Taylor, TX. Education: Graduate of Thrall High School. Enlisted U.S. Army Corps, 1942, basic training, Camp Howze, LA, further training, NJ. Theater of Operations: European. WOUNDED IN ACTION, Germany, 1944. Medals: Good Conduct, ETO Campaign Medal w/1 BSS, Combat Infantry Badge, Ribbons. Rank: S/Sgt. prior to honorable discharge, 1945.

Muras, Charles Joseph, son of Charles and Ann Muras, was born May 6, 1914, La Grange, TX. Finished sixth grade in Rutersville, TX. Enlisted in U.S. Navy, Houston, TX, Apr. 8, 1941, prior to WWII. Basic training: San Diego, CA. Rank: Boatswain's Mate First Class. Served on USS *Maryland* (SURVIVOR OF THE JAPANESE BOMBING OF PEARL HARBOR, Dec. 7, 1941), Floating Dry Dock

Training Center, Tiburon, CA, USS ABSD-7, USS LCI(L)1060. Medals: Asiatic-Pacific Theater Campaign Medal w/4 BSS, American Theater Campaign Medal, American Defense Medal w/1 BSS, Good Conduct Medal, WWII Victory Medal. Honorably discharged Dec. 16, 1946. Married Agnes Prazak; three sons: Charles Patrick, Larry Joseph, Allan Raymond. Retired from Armco Steel, Inc. Hobbies include gardening, taking care of house and neighbors. Home of record: Houston, TX.

Muras, Jerome, Waco, TX, WWII veteran, U.S. Army Corps.

Muras, Jerome W., son of Frank Muras, Sr., and Marie Petarek Muras, was born in Fayette Co., TX. Joined the U.S. Army Corps, Ft. Sam Houston, San Antonio, TX, Oct. 31, 1940. Rank: S/Sgt. Served in the European Theater during WWII. Battles: Rhineland G0 40/ND45 and Central Europe G0 48 WD45. Served with Field Artillery in France, Belgium, Holland, Germany, Czechoslovakia, Austria. Awards: American Defense Service Ribbon, EAMF Service Ribbon, two BSS, GCM Medal. Honorably discharged Oct. 22, 1945. Died Jan. 24, 1994; buried in St. Martin's Cemetery, Tours, TX.

Murphy, Alvin, served in U.S. Army Corps, WWII. Hometown, Granger, TX.

Musil, Emory B., son of Frank J and Ettie Slovacek Musil, was born in Stamford, TX, Aug. 27, 1922. Earned a B.S. degree in Education at Midwestern State University, Wichita Falls, TX. Entered military service, Dec. 21, 1941, Abilene, TX. Rank: Sgt. Served in the Asiatic Pacific during WWII. Fought in Air Offensive Japan and Truk Island. Medals: Asiatic Pacific Theater Campaign, GCM, American Theater Campaign, WWII Victory. Honorable discharge, Dec. 22, 1945. Home of record: Wichita Falls, TX.

Frank M. Musil, son of Frank J. and Ettie Slovacek Musil, was born May 26, 1920, Stamford, TX. Education included U.S. Air Force Airplane Mechanics, Technical School, Montana State University, Military Science. Entered military service at Dodd Field, San Antonio, TX. Rank: S/Sgt. Awards: WWII Victory Medal, A.F. GCM Medal, American Defense Service Medal, American Campaign Medal, Air Crew Engineer Silver Wings. Honorable discharge Dec. 5, 1945.

Musil, Joseph Stephen, son of Frank Joseph and Ettie Slovacek Musil, was born Nov. 21, 1917, at Stamford, TX. Education: Stamford, TX, elementary and high school, University of Texas at Austin for three years. Inducted into the U.S. Army Air Corps, Mar. 10, 1941, Ft. Bliss, TX. Stationed there until May 23, 1943. Served in 62nd Field Artillery Hq. Battery, 1st Calvary Div., Fort Bliss. Transferred to Air Corp for pilot training at Garner Field, Uvalde, and Randolph Field, San Antonio, TX. Commissioned and received wings May 24, 1943, at Moore Field, Mission, TX. Stationed there until Dec. 27, 1945. Assigned to Central Training Command as a pilot for Bombardier Training School at San Angelo Army Air Base. Received Aircraft Commander Training in B-24s at Fort Worth Army Air Field and crew training at Gowden Air Force Base, ID. Assigned to 492nd Bomb Squadron, 10th Air Force China-Burma-India. 7th Bomb Group, 10th Air Force, as B-2 Commander. Made 48 trips over the "Hump" in CBI transporting aviation fuel to 14th Air Force in China. Responsible for five-man crew. Decorations: American Defense Service, Asiatic Pacific Campaign w/1 BSS, CBI Campaign Medal w/BSS, American Theater Campaign Medal, and WWII Victory. Theater of Operations: CBI, Asiatic-Pacific, and American. Discharged from active duty Dec. 27, 1945, and from reserves May 16, 1955. Home of record: Hempstead, TX. Died Nov. 28, 1988; buried at Waller Cemetery, Waller, TX. Submitted by Mrs. Alice F. Musil, Hempstead, TX.

Mussil, Mabrey L., son of Dr. and Mrs. A. C. Mussil, Granger, TX. Education: Graduate, Thrall High School. Enlisted U.S. Army Corps. Basic training, Camp Hood. Asiatic-Pacific Theater of Operations. Medals: A-P Theater Campaign Medal, WWII Victory Medal, ribbons. Served in Japan. Rank: Pfc. prior to honorable discharge.

Mussil, Theodore Frank, son of Dr. and Mrs. A. C. Mussil, Granger, TX. Education: Granger High School. Enlisted U.S. Navy, 1940. Boot camp, San Diego, CA. Theater of Operations: Asiatic-Pacific. Served in Hawaii, Philippines and S.W. Pacific. WOUNDED IN ACTION, 1941. Rank: S 2/c prior to honorable medical discharge, 1942. Medals: Asiatic-Pacific Theater Campaign Medal w/BSS, Purple Heart, and others.

Muzny, John, served in U.S. Armed Forces during WWI, 1917–1918. Member of SPJST Lodge 20, Granger, TX,

Mynar, Edward Joseph, son of Edward V. and Mary Lou Kessler Mynar, was born in Waco, TX, Aug. 15, 1951. Attended St. Mary's School and West High School in West, TX. Entered military service, Ft. Gordon, GA, May 11, 1971. Rank: Pfc. Served with the Military Police NO-PONF-EF in Korea 95B10 Military. Awards: National Defense Service Medal, Army Expairition Medal-Korea, Marksman Badge M16 Cal-45. Honorably discharged Feb. 14, 1973. Died June 19, 1982.

Mynar, Edward Vince, son of Joseph and Mary Marek Mynar, was born in West, TX, July 2, 1922. Attended St. Mary's School in West, TX. Entered military service in Dallas, TX. Served in the South Pacific, Ryukyus G033, WD45 during WWII. Rank: Cpl. Battles: Asiatic Pacific, Philippines, Okinawa. Awards: South Pacific Campaign Medal w/2 BSS and one Bronze Arrowhead, Philippine Liberation Ribbon W/1 BSS, WWII Victory Medal and GCM Medal. Honorably discharged Jan. 14, 1946.

Mynar, Emil Ignac, son of Ignac and Johanna Pavel Mynar, was born Aug. 21, 1889, Fayette Co., TX. Enlisted in U.S. Army Corps in Fayette Co., TX, during WWI. Assignment: Cook. Theater of Operations: Europe. Received WWI Victory Medal. Honorably discharged at end of war. Died Dec. 13, 1978; buried Wharton City Cemetery, TX. Submitted by Emil F. Petter, Wharton, TX.

Mynar, John J., son of Joe and Mary Marek Mynar, was born in West, TX, Oct. 26, 1914. Attended school at Liberty Grove and St. Joseph's School, near West, TX. Enlisted in the U.S. Army Corps Oct. 14, 1942, Camp Wolters, Mineral Wells, TX. Rank: Cpl. Served in the 103rd Infantry Div. during WWII in Europe: France, Germany, Switzerland, Austria and Italy. WOUNDED IN ACTION in France, Nov. 17, 1944. Awarded the Purple Heart. Honorably discharged Jan. 9, 1946, San Antonio, TX. Died Apr. 22, 1989.

Mynar, Joseph J., son of Joseph and Mary Marek Mynar, was born in West, TX, May 16, 1920. Attended St. Mary's School in West, TX. Inducted into the U.S. Army Corps during WWII. Assigned to Infantry on Aug. 18, 1944, Co. L, 184th Inf. Div. Rank: Pfc. Theater of Operations: Asiatic-Pacific. KILLED IN ACTION, June 5, 1945, Ryuku Islands, Okinawa. Posthumously awarded the Purple Heart and the Good Conduct Medal.

Mynar, Martha (see Prasifka, Martha Mynar).

Mynar, Rudolph, son of Ignac and Johanna Pavel Mynar, was born May 3, 1896, Fayette Co., TX. Enlisted in U.S. Army Corps during WWI. Rank: Pfc. Theater of Operations: Europe. Received

WWI Victory Medal. Honorably discharged after war was won. Died Jan. 29, 1973, Fayette Co., TX; buried in Fayetteville Cemetery, TX. Submitted by Emil F. Petter, Wharton, TX.

Mynarcik, Daniel Alois, son of Joseph J. and Otillie Macicek Mynarcik, was born June 8, 1928, at West, TX. Earned Certificate of High School Equivalency at Austin, TX, after having attended grade and high school in Ross, TX. Attended Texas State Technical College, Waco, TX. Enlisted in the U.S. Army Corps, Mar. 17, 1955, at Waco, TX. Basic training at Ft. Ord, CA, other training at Ft. Leonard Wood, MO. Served during the Viet Nam Conflict, attaining the rank of Staff Sgt. Medals: Good Conduct and Rifle Marksman. Discharged Sept. 17, 1963. Served two years in U.S. Army, six years in U.S. Army Reserve, after Korean War. Married Rosemary Korenek; two children: David Paul and Daniel Alois, Jr. Home of record: Elm Mott, TX.

Mynarcik, Edward Frank, son of Frank and Janie Kocian Mynarcik, was born Nov. 25, 1927, in West, TX. Attended West High School, West, TX. Enlisted in Dallas, TX, and was a M/Sgt in the USMC. Fought in the Chinese Spring Offensive, 1951, Advance to Punchbowl Battle, Battle for Hill 854. Discharged Feb. 28, 1952, in San Diego, CA. Medal: PUC with two Stars, Marine Corps Good Conduct, China Medal, American Theater, Asiatic-Pacific, WWII Victory, Japanese Occupation, National Defense, Korean Theater with four Stars, United Nations Medal, Korean PUC. Died Mar. 13, 1986; buried in St. Mary's Cemetery, West, TX.

Mynarcik, Joseph J., son of Mr. and Mrs. Joe Mynarcik of West, TX. Entered Army 1942. Served as a Cpl. in U.S.A. Awarded GCM and A.T. Ribbon. Discharged 1945.

Mynarcik, Louis, son of Mr. and Mrs. Joe Mynarcik, West, TX. Entered Army 1944. Served as S/Sgt. in CBI Theater (China, Burma, India). Awarded GCM and three Battle Stars. Discharged 1946.

Mynarcik, Louis Albert, son of Joe J. and Otillie Macicek, was born Apr. 20, 1926, at West, TX. Attended schools at both Ross and West, TX. Enlisted in the Army Corps, Dallas, TX, during WWII. Served as Sgt. in CBI Theater. Awarded GCM, CBI Campaign Ribbon w/3 Battle Stars. Participated in numerous military campaigns before discharge from service on May 22, 1946. Home of record: West, TX.

N

Naidl, George Edward, son of Charles Edward and Violet Fay Hoffman Naidl, was born Mar. 22, 1940, Racine, WI. Education: Miami Jackson High School, Miami, FL; University of FL, Gainesville, FL; University of MD, Spangdahlem, Germany, B.A.; Arizona State University, Tempe, AZ, M.S. Enlisted: Jan. 18, 1963, Miami, FL. Rank: Capt. Theater of Operations: Viet Nam, 1965-1967. Medals: Distinguished Flying Cross w/1 OLC; Air Medal w/11 OLC; Meritorious Service Medal; Air Force Commendation Medal; Air Force Good Conduct Medal w/1 OLC; Air Force Longevity Service Ribbon w/4 OLC; Small Arms Expert Marksmanship Ribbon w/1 Bronze Service Star; Air Force Presidential Unit Citation; Air Force Outstanding Unit Award w/2 OLC; National Defense Service Medal; Viet Nam Service Medal w/4 BSS; Republic of Viet Nam Gallantry Cross w/Palm; Republic of Viet Nam Campaign Medal. Assigned as a Navigator-Bombardier to the 8th Bomb Squadron (Yellowbirds), Clark Air Base, Philippines. Flew 222 combat missions (42 out-of-country) in B-57 aircraft, operating from Danang Air Base (Oct. '65-July '66) and Phan Rang Air Base (Oct. '66–Mar. '67). Later assigned to Davis-Monthan Air Force Base, AZ, as an F-4 Weapons Systems Officer and Intelligence Officer training pilots and navigators bound for Southeast Asia. Retired from service, Jan. 31, 1983. Home of record: Plano, TX.

Naizer, Anton Cyril, son of Johann and Johanna Janak Neusser/Naizer, was born July 5, 1895, Granger, William, TX. Education: Granger Catholic School. Enlisted in U.S. Army Corps, San Antonio, Bexar, TX, during WWI. Took basic training in Georgia. Embarked from New York, on ship *Harrisburg*, to Brest, France, was assigned to Co. C, 307th Infantry, 77th Division, went from Brest to Weiheim; upon arrival, was nine miles from battle front lines when peace was announced. Honorably discharged 1918. Married Sophia Span. Civilian occupation was farming. At retirement was custodian for American Legion, where he was a member, in Taylor, TX. Served as Legion Honor Guard. Member of SPJST Lodge 20, Granger, TX. Died Oct. 9, 1969, Taylor, TX; buried St. Mary's Catholic Cemetery, Taylor, TX.

Naizer, Bernard B., son of John and Marcela Bartosh Naizer, was born about 1926, Granger, TX. Education: Catholic elementary school, graduated Granger High School. Enlisted in U.S. Navy, 1944, TX. Basic training in San Diego, San Francisco and Treasure Island. Theater of Operations: Asia-Pacific. Served in the Pacific and India. Rank: Seaman 2/C, USS *Horace Greeley*, a cargo ship. Traveled to Pearl Harbor in 1945. Was on a tanker, USS *Crater Lake*. Then went to India and Iran. Stayed on ocean the whole time. Honorable discharge June 1946 at Camp Wallace, Galveston, TX. Medals: American Theater of Operations Campaign, EAME Campaign, and APO Ribbon w/1 BSS. Returned home to Granger, TX, June 1946. Retired farmer. Home of record: Granger, TX.

Naizer, Daniel Louis, son of John R. and Marcella Bartosh Naizer, Granger, TX. Education: Granger High School. Enlisted U.S. Navy, 1945; boot camp, San Diego; further training: Shoemaker, CA, and OR. Theater of Operations: Asiatic-Pacific. Served on Guam and Okinawa. Medals: Asiatic-Pacific Campaign, WWII Victory.

Naizer, Joe J., son of Adolf and Mary Cervenka Naizer, was born Mar. 12, 1916. Graduated from high school in Granger, TX, in 1938. Served in

U.S. Army Air Corps during WWII. Attained rank of Technical Sgt. Served in the European, African, and Middle Eastern Theater of Operations. Participated in campaigns in Normandy and Utah Beach. Decorations: European African Middle Eastern Campaign Medal with two campaign stars, and others. Separated from service in Nov. 1945. Married Rosie Naizer; eight children: four boys, four girls. Home of record: Granger, TX. Member, American Legion Post No. 282, Granger, TX.

Naizer, John H. "Johnny," son of Mr. and Mrs. John R. Naizer, Granger, TX, was born Nov. 3, 1922. Education: Granger High School. Enlisted U.S. Army Air Corps, 1942; basic training, San Diego, CA; further training, KS. Theater of Operations: American. Medals: AAF Tech. Badge w/ A.P. Mech. Bar, American Theater Campaign, Good Conduct, WWII Victory. Attained rank of S/Sgt prior to honorable discharge, 1945. Died June 10, 1982. Buried Calvary Catholic Cem., Granger, TX. Member, American Legion Post No. 282, Granger, TX. Deceased.

Naizer, John Rudolph, son of John and Marcella Bartosh Naizer, was born about 1924, Granger, TX. Education: Catholic Elementary School, Granger High School. Called into the Army Air Corps, 1942; trained in San Diego and Kansas. Theater of Operations: American. Medals: AAF Tech. Badge 2/AP Mech Bar, ATO, Good Conduct, WWII Victory Ribbon. July 16, 1942, was transferred to Wendover, Utah; July 29, 1942, transferred to Salt Lake City, UT, Sept. 14, 1942, Ft. George Wright, Spokane, WA; Dec. 20, 1942, transferred from Sq. A to Prov. Sqdn. M Bks. as Messenger. Dec. 30, 1942, Pierre SD to Bomb Group. Worked as Mechanic on the big bombers. Was first Granger soldier to be stationed in Washington. Honorably discharged in 1945. Married Georgia Gaida; two children: John Joe and Betty Jane, five grandchildren. Civilian occupation: Naizer Hardware Store and farmer. Died May 1993.

Naizer, Raymond William, WWII veteran of Granger, TX.

Naplava, Dan Stanley, son of John and Annie Naplava, Sr., was born Dec. 26, 1923, Houston, TX. Education: St. Paul Lutheran School, Houston, seven years; John Marshall Jr. High, Houston, TX, one year; Jefferson Davis Sr. High, Houston, TX, 3 years. Enlisted U.S. Air Force, Houston, TX. Assigned to 101st Airborne Division (Parachute Badge, Glider Badge, Combat Med. Badge). Theater of Operations: EAME. Battles: Ardennes, Rhineland and Central Europe. Medals: American Theater Campaign, EAME Campaign w/3 BSS, Good Conduct, WWII Victory. Honorably discharged, Jan. 1, 1946. Home of record: Houston, TX.

Naplava, John W., Jr., son of John W., Sr. and Annie Ademek Naplava, was born May 22, 1916, Houston, Harris County, TX. Education: Houston, TX, grammar school, and John Marshall Junior High, one year Jefferson Davis High. 1930 Depression forced him out of school to go to work. After many varied jobs, went to work for the Continental Can Company, Houston, TX, until enlisting in U.S. Army Air Corps, Sept. 20, 1942, entering active service, Sept. 28, 1942. Served with 373rd Bombardment Sqdn., Pacific Theater of Operations, Bismarck Archipelago, New Guinea, Southern Philippine Liberation, and Luzon. Medals: American Theater Campaign, Asiatic Pacific Theater Campaign w/4 BSS, Philippine Liberation Ribbon w/2 BSS, Good Conduct, WWII Victory Ribbon, one service stripe, three overseas Service Bars, Marksman Rifle Badge. Honorably discharged Jan. 13, 1946, Ft. Sam Houston, TX. Returned to Continental Can Company until retirement Apr. 24, 1970, at age 54. Married Iona Havens, Houston, TX, Dec. 30, 1937. Is a hard working Czech, always honest, and proud to serve country in WWII. Home of record: Palacios, TX.

Narovec, Henry, son of Joe Narovec and Rose Marak, was born on May 17, 1913, in Waco, TX. Attended Dean Highland Elementary School, Waco High School, and Baylor University. Enlisted at Camp Wolters during WWII and served at Camp Lee, VA, in the Quartermaster Demonstration Battalion. Decorations include the Good Conduct Medal and Qualification Badge. Separated from the service on Aug. 11, 1945, at the 1326th SCU, ASF Regional Hospital, Camp Lee, Virginia. Died in July 1987.

Nastoupil, Carl J., Jr., son of Carl J. Nastoupil, Sr. and Mary Kallus, was born July 25, 1920, Sealy, TX. Graduated from Sealy schools, 1937, Massey Business College, Houston, TX, 1939. Commissioned in U.S. Army Air Corps, Sept. 24, 1942, San Antonio, TX. Attained rank of Lt. Col. Military Occupation: Airplane Pilot. Theaters of Operation: EAME, Korea, Viet Nam. Battles: WWII, Korea, Viet Nam. Awards: Distinguished Flying Cross, Air Medal w/3 OLC, Air Force Longevity Service Medal w/4 OLC, American Campaign Medal, EAME Campaign w/5 BSS, WWII Victory Medal, Army of Occupation-Germany Medal, National Defense Service Medal, Viet Nam Service Medal, Armed Forces Medal, Purple Heart. WOUNDED IN ACTION. Retired May 31, 1967. Civilian Occupation: Veterans Service Officer, retired July 1985. Married Doris M. Felcman; two children: Carl J. III and David W. Received Minuteman Award from State of Minnesota for Advisory Service to MN Air National Guard. Hobbies: golf, bowling, automobile tinkering. Home of record: Sealy, TX.

Navara, Adolph, son of Vince Navera and Rozina Holubec, was born Mar. 22, 1894, at Burlington, TX, in Milam County and attended the Hallsburg School near Waco. Inducted into the Armed Services at West, TX on June 25, 1918, during WWI. Served with the American Expeditionary Forces in France as a Sgt. in the Gas Detachment, Demolition Group from Sept. 23, 1918 to Oct. 28, 1919. Honorably discharged Nov. 7, 1919, at Camp Pike, AR. Decorations include the Armed Services Commendation. Married Millie Pechacek; three daughters: Edna, Emma, and Marguerite. Engaged in farming in the Elk Community near Axtell, TX. Died on Dec. 25, 1971, in the Veterans Administration Hospital's Nursing Care Unit in Waco, TX.

Navratil, Luddie, daughter of Frank and Sophie Navratil, West, TX. Graduated Providence Hospital School of Nursing as Registered Nurse. Served in U.S. Navy as Lt. Three years in European Theater of Operations. Home of record: West, TX.

Navratil, Robert John, was born Oct. 2, 1915. Served in U.S. Navy as Pharm. 3/C during WWII. Theater of Operations: Asiatic-Pacific. Died Nov. 12, 1987. Buried in St. Mary's Cemetery, West, TX.

Neal, Charles Anton, was born June 3, 1933. Served in U.S. Armed Forces since WWII. Died Jan. 28, 1968. Buried Holy Cross Cemetery, Granger, Williamson Co., TX.

Neckar, Ben John, was born Aug. 29, 1918. Served in U.S. Army Corps as Sgt. during WWII. Died Nov. 10, 1981; buried in St. Mary's Cemetery, West, TX.

Necker, Estelle Ann Wachsman, daughter of John Nechar and Agnes (deceased), was born Dec. 15, 1913, three miles east of West, TX. Education: 42 more hours and would have B.S. degree. Enlisted Oct. 15, 1942, Shreveport, LA. Served during WWII as nurse. Commissioned as 1st Lt. Assigned to the Asiatic Pacific Theater of Operations. Served in Australia, New Guinea, and the Philippine Islands. Received extensive training in dermatology. Medals: Asiatic Pacific Campaign w/2 BSS, Philippine Liberation Ribbon, WWII Victory.

Battles: invasions of Luzon, Philippine Islands, and Okinawa. Last stationed in the Philippine Islands (eight months). Honorably discharged Mar. 9, 1946. Civilian occupation: Registered Nurse at McCloskey VA Hospital, Temple, TX; Private Duty Nurse, Waco, TX. Married Mr. Wachsmann. Home of record: Lott, TX.

Nemec, Adolph Louis, was born June 17, 1924. WWII veteran. Died May 18, 1987; buried Holy Cross Catholic Cemetery, Granger, TX.

Nemec, Frank J., West, TX. WWII veteran, Theater of Operations: Asiatic-Pacific.

Nemec, Pete, WWII veteran of Granger, TX.

Nemec, Stan, served in U.S. Armed Forces during WWI, 1917–1918. Member of SPJST Lodge 20, Granger, TX.

Nemec, Valentine, served in U.S. Armed Forces during WWI, 1917–1918. Member of SPJST Lodge 20, Granger, TX.

Nemec, William Frank, son of Frank Joseph Nemec and Mary Velma Kucera, was born Dec. 29, 1932, Bryan, TX. Graduate, Stephen F. Austin High School, 1950, Bryan, TX. Enlisted in U.S. Air Force, Aug. 26, 1952, Houston, TX. Theater of Operations: Northeast Air Command–Iceland. Received Good Conduct Medal. Honorably discharged Aug. 25, 1956. Married childhood sweetheart, Mary Holler, Aug. 28, 1954; three children: William Frank Nemec, Jr.; Kathleen Sue Nemec Jones; David Leland Nemec, two grandsons: Kyle William Nemec and Aaron David Nemec. All are KJT members. Have been active as member and officer in Local KJT Society #14, Bryan, TX. Have been involved in dairy industry–all phases, before and after military service, up to and including present time. Home of record: Bryan, TX.

Nemecek, Alfred R., son of Mr. and Mrs. Rudolph Nemecek, West, TX. Attended West High School. Married Virginia Moucka. Entered Army in 1942. Trained Camp Wolters, TX. Served in Alaska. Discharged 1945.

Nemecek, Edward M., son of Ernest Nemecek and Francis Karlik, was born June 12, 1915, in Waco, TX. Attended St. Mary's School at West, Allen Military Academy at Bryan, and Hillsboro Junior College. Enlisted in the U.S. Army Air Corps at Camp Wolters, TX, during WWII. Served in the Asiatic Pacific Theater of Operations and attained the rank of Sgt. Decorations include the Asiatic Pacific Campaign Medal, Good Conduct Medal, and WWII Victory Medal. Discharged on Mar. 11, 1946. Home of record: West, TX.

Nemecek, Joseph H., son of Mr. and Mrs. Rudolph Nemecek, West, TX. Entered AAC in 1942, during WWII. Served w/rank of Pfc. in Australia, Guadalcanal, Bismarck, Orch. New Guinea, and Solomons. Awarded A.P. Ribbon w/4 Battle Stars, and GCM. Discharged1945.

Nemecek, Raymond, West, TX. WWII veteran, Asiatic-Pacific Theater of Operations.

Nemic, Albert L., son of Cyril M. Nemic and Annie Juricek, was born on Apr. 6, 1906, in Gainesville, TX. Attended Crosby High School and North TX State University. Enlisted in the U.S. Army at Houston, TX (142nd Infantry Band, 36th Infantry Division.) in 1926. Also attended the U.S. Army Signal School and Engineer School. Served in the European, African, and Middle Eastern Theater of Operations during WWII. Participated in campaigns in Italy, France, and Germany, including Salerno D-Day operations, Rapido, Anzio, and Southern France D-Day operations. Served in numerous Signal Corps related assignments to include that of Post Signal Officer, Ft. Hood, TX, during the period, Sept. 10, 1945–Jan. 14, 1947. In 1947 transferred to Ready Reserves; retired in 1960. Rank: Lt Col. Home of record: Dallas TX.

Netardus, John J., son of John J. Netardus and Elizabeth Kallus, was born July 7, 1926. Enlisted in the Armed Services on Nov. 14, 1944, at Ft. Sam Houston, TX, during WWII. Served in the Asiatic Pacific Theater of Operations and participated in campaigns in the Philippine

Islands (Visayan). Also participated in the occupation of Korea. Separated from the service on Nov. 16, 1946. Home of record: Slidell, Louisiana.

Netek, Dominic F., Jr., son of Dominic F., Sr. and Marie Netek, was born in San Antonio, Bexar County, TX. Enlisted U.S. Navy, July 1966. Served on USS *Sacramento* AOE-1, Largest supply ship in the Navy. Served all his time in combat, Viet Nam. Medals: Achievement Navy (with Combat V), AFEM-Korean, entitled to wear Korean Service Medal, Viet Nam Campaign, Viet Nam Service, Victory. Sailed to Hong Kong, China, Japan, Australia, Philippines. Honorably discharged July 1969. Married Clara; three children. Employed as foreman at Shell Refinery, Deer Park, TX. Home of record: Pasadena, TX. Submitted by Dominic Netek, Sr.

Netek, Dominic F., Sr., son of Leo Netek and Mary Kernavek, was born Jan. 28, 1922, Corpus Christi, TX. Education: attended Kostoryz Public School, Corpus Christi; attained high school diploma in Army schools. Enlisted in the U.S. Army on Feb. 16, 1940, Ft. Sam Houston, TX. Served in the EAME Theater of Operations during WWII. Attained rank Staff Sgt. 23rd Infantry, 2nd Division. Landed in France, D-Day, Normandy Invasion on June 6, 1944. WOUNDED IN ACTION, Normandy, on Aug. 29, 1944. Returned to duty in time to participate in the Battle of the Bulge in Belgium in Nov. 1944. WOUNDED IN ACTION a second time in Germany on the Elsenborn Ridge and hospitalized in England. WOUNDED IN ACTION a third time! Battles: Northern France, Central Europe, Normandy, Ardennes, Rhineland. Transferred from England to the Torney General Hospital at Palm Springs, CA. Honorable medical discharge on Nov. 7, 1945. Decorations include the Silver Star for bravery, BSS for valor, Purple Heart w/2 OLC, Presidential Unit Citation, Distinguished Unit Badge, Good Conduct Medal, EAME Campaign Medal, American Defense Service Medal, American Campaign Medal, WWII Victory Medal, Bayonet Expert, Sharpshooter w/rifle. Married in June 1943 to Marie Spacek; three children: Dominic F. Netek, Jr., Eileen Netek Heath and Michael Netek, and eight grandchildren. Celebrated 50th wedding anniversary on June 19, 1993. Employed at Kelly Air Force Base, San Antonio, as a production supervisor, now retired. Enjoys retirement and has made four trips to Europe. Life member of American Legion, and DAV, and Order of the Purple Heart. Home of record: San Antonio, TX.

Netek, Michael R., son of Dominic, Sr., and Marie Netek, was born in San Antonio, TX. Enlisted in U.S. Army Corps, Aug. 1972, Ft. Sam Houston, TX. Assigned to 321st Civil Affairs Group, Ft. Sam Houston, TX for two years; transferred to Houston, TX. Attained the rank of Specialist 4. Married Debbie; two children. Employed with Goodrich Chemical Company, Deer Park, TX. Home of record: Deer Park, TX. Submitted by father Dominic Netek, Sr.

Nevlud, Joseph A., son of Frantisek and Aloisia Klecka Nevlud, was born Oct. 20, 1892, in Frycovice, Moravia. Attended Vysehrad School in Hallettseville, TX. Enlisted at Camp Bullis, TX, Sept. 17, 1917, and served as Sgt., Headquarter Co. 360th Inf., 180th Bn., 90th Div. during WWI. Blew in with the 'Draft.' Played the B-flat clarinet with Co. M, 360th Band, Nov. 26, 1918, in Marville, Germany. 1st Concert was played Sept. 12, 1917, w/20 men. Discharged at Camp Travis June 21, 1919. Organized and was bandmaster of popular Wied's Nevlud Brass Band, 1919. Played for dances, weddings, and celebrations, including laying of cornerstone for new Catholic Church at Shiner, TX. Helped start the Worthing Brass Band; played with Worthing Band until his 70s. Married Marie (Mary) Smolik, Nov. 10, 1919; children: two boys, Jaro Nevlud, Ladislav Nevlud (died in infancy), three girls, Ludmilla Nevlud and Justina Nevlud (both died in infancy), Marie Nevlud Stryk. Retired from farming at Mont, TX, and moved to Pearland, TX, at age 81. Died May 10, 1980, in Pearland, TX.

Nors, George William, Sr., son of Edward A. Nors and Frances E. Kubacak, was born June 6, 1945, Grant Bowie Hospital, Hillsboro, TX. Education: Graduated Abbott, TX, schools, May 1963. Enlisted Oct. 24, 1965, 3rd Recruit Training Bn., San Diego, CA, USMC. Attained rank of L/Cpl-E3. Sent overseas to Support Battalion, Forced Troops, Fleet Marine Force, Pacific from CA, Apr. 2, 1966–Oct. 1, 1966. Assigned 11th Motor Transport Battalion, Camp Pendleton, Oct. 2, 1966, then sent to Viet Nam, Dec. 3, 1966–Oct. 8, 1967. Returned stateside, 3rd Marine Air Wing, El Toro, CA, Oct. 9, 1967. Honorably discharged, Oct. 24, 1967. Medals: Meritorious Mast. Viet Nam, June 20, 1967. Married May 30, 1970, Fran E. Polansky: children: Rita Jane; Julia Ann, George William, Jr. Work for City of West as Water and Sewer Supt. Home of record: West, TX.

Nors, Joe E., son of Henry Nors and Antonia Hejl, was born Mar. 4, 1926, in Hill, TX. Enlisted in the Army on June 20, 1944, during WWII. Served in the European, African, and Middle Eastern, and Asiatic-Pacific Theaters of Operations, attaining rank of Pfc. Separated from service Apr. 14, 1946. Home of record: West, TX. Died Dec. 13, 1989; buried in St. Mary's Cemetery, West, TX.

Nors, Joe J., of West, TX, U.S. Army Corps, WWII veteran.

Nors, John H., was born Aug. 26, 1919. Served during WWII in U.S. Army Air Corps. Attained rank of Pfc. Died Oct. 9, 1989; buried in St. Mary's Cemetery, West, TX.

Nors, Louis T., was born Sept. 12, 1918. Served in U.S. Army Corps during WWI. Died Aug. 11, 1988; buried in St. Mary's Cemetery, West, TX.

Nors, Peter P., served in the European, African, Middle Eastern Theater of Operations during WWII as a member of the 7th Depot Replacement Squadron during 1943-1945. Attained the rank of Staff Sgt. Home of record: Mount Calm, TX.

Novacek, Bernard Otto, son of Albert Novacek and Barbara Kodet, was born May 24, 1930, Verdiqre, NE. Education: graduated high school, Verdiqre, NE. Employed at the Emil A. Jerman International Harvester Implement Store until enlistment in the USAF, Oct. 19, 1951, Induction Center, Omaha, NE. Basic training, Lackland AFB, TX. Attained rank of Pfc. Transferred to Sheppard AFB, TX. Attended the A&E Mechanic School, promoted to Airman 2/C, permanently assigned to SAFB, TX. Attended the Tech Instructor Course, instructed young airmen in recip. engin. (R2800 engines). Attained the rank of Staff Sgt. Honorably discharged Oct. 18, 1955. Medals: National Defense Service, Good Conduct, Master Instructor Badge, many Instructor Performance Certificate Awards. Worked for Civil Service until retirement. Married Wanda; four children. Home of record: Burkburnett, TX.

Novak, David S., was born Oct. 26, 1906. Served in USAF during WWII and Korean Conflict. Rank: M/Sgt. Retired. Died Feb. 14, 1974; buried in St. Mary's Cemetery, West, TX.

Novosad, Jerry J., son of John F. Novosad (8/26/1893–11/6/1977) and Rosie Kutra (3/5/1897–5/26/1973), was born Dec. 24, 1928, Frydek, Austin, TX. Enlisted in U.S. Army Corps during Korean War. Served a half year. Civilian occupation: Machinist, retired 1980. Married Opal McCleskey, Aug. 12, 1963. Info by Frydek CYO, Lawrence Sodolak.

Novosad, Joe John, son of Joseph Novosad and Louise Kutra, was born Sept. 12, 1928, Sealy, Austin County, TX. Education: Frydek Catholic and Public Schools, Frydek, TX, 1934-44; Sealy High School graduate, 1946; Univ. of Houston, School of Technology, Houston, TX, 1954-55. Enlisted Apr. 8, 1952, Houston, TX, in USMC. Attained rank of Sgt. Electronics Instructor. Bootcamp, Marine Corps Depot, San Diego, CA; Aircraft Familiarization School, Naval Air station, Jacksonville, FL; Electronics Technician School,

Naval Air Station, Millington, TN; Instructors' Training School, Naval Air Station, Millington, TN; remained as Electronics instructor rest of active duty. Received National Defense Medal. Honorably discharged from active duty on Apr. 7, 1954; from Reserves on Apr. 7, 1960. Married high school sweetheart, Helen Remmert, Feb. 17, 1947, Sealy, TX, where he was employed in residential construction until drafted. Civilian Occupation: Radio-TV Repairman, 20 years, and Radio-TV Repair Instructor in Houston Community College, Houston, TX. Retired 1990. Moved into home built by themselves in Texas Hill Country between Buchanan and Inks Lake, 60 miles NW of Austin, TX. Hobbies: genealogy, travel. Compiled Kutra and Vesely family history books. Also taught at the Harris County Rehab Center for several years. Home of record: Burnet, TX.

Novosad, Joe W., son of John F. Novosad and Rosie Anna Kutra, was born on July 18, 1918, in Sealy, Austin County, TX. Education: GED; Baking and Cooking School, 2 months. Enlisted into the U.S. Army on June 24, 1941 at Houston, TX. Attained rank of Cpl. Basic Training Horse Cavalry. Cooked 12 months–France. During WWII served in the European, African, and Middle Eastern Theater of Operations as member of Troop C, 17th Cavalry Recon Squadron. Participated in the Normandy, Southern France, and Northern France campaigns. Captured on Aug. 3, 1944, near St. Malo, France, and was a PRISONER OF WAR for nine months on Jersey Island until his release in May 1945. Medals: American Theater of Operations Campaign, EAME Campaign, WWII Victory, Good Conduct, and American Defense Service. Honorably discharged, Ft. Sam Houston, TX, Nov. 28, 1945. Married Lillian B. Bond, Sept. 19, 1970. Civilian Occupation: retired from Exxon, 1983. Home of record: Sealy, TX.

Novosad, Joseph W., served 5 years, 5 months in U.S. Army Air Corps during WWII.

Novosad, Lillie Frantiska (Ruhmann), daughter of Mr. and Mrs. Paul F. Novosad, was born Mar. 19, 1924, Fayetteville, TX. Attended Fayetteville High School and IBM school in NY. Enlisted in the Armed Services at Houston, TX, on Apr. 22, 1944, during WWII. Served in the American Theater of Operations in assignments at Palm Beach, FL, New York, NY, and New Orleans, LA. Decorations include the American Campaign Medal and the Good Conduct Medal. Home of record: Houston, TX.

Novosad, Tom, son of Henry Novosad and Mary Erbanec, born 1918, East Bernard, TX. Education: East Bernard schools, University of Texas School of Engineering, Austin, TX. Military service, WWII. Married Mary Janis; four children. Home of record: Houston, TX.

Novotny, Jerry E., was born Dec. 9, 1909. Served in U.S. Army Corps during WWII w/rank of Pvt. Died Nov. 8, 1968; buried in Lady Fatima Cemetery, Abbott, TX.

O

Okruhlik, Charlie Martin, son of Charles and Hermina Okruhlik, was born Sept. 6, 1918, Praha, TX. Education: Praha Catholic School and Hungerford Public School. Enlisted Camp Wolters, TX, during WWII, U.S. Army Corps. Theater of Operations: Pacific. Assigned to Co. L, 17th Inf., 7th Army Div. Battles: "I made beach head first wave at Attu Aleutian Islands, Marshall Islands, Leyte-Philippines and Okinawa." Medals: Purple Heart, BSS. WOUNDED IN ACTION in the face. Honorable discharge Oct. 3, 1945. Married Clara, whom he met on Thanksgiving Day, 1942, at her parents' home in Arroyo Grande, CA. Barber in Rosenberg, TX, for 47 years. Plays organ in Holy Rosary Church. Home of record: Rosenberg, TX.

Olexy, John, served in U.S. Armed Forces during WWI, 1917–1918. Member of SPJST Lodge 20, Granger, TX.

Olsovsky, Albert L., of Elm Mott, TX. Entered U.S. Army Corps during WWII, 1942. Served w/rank of T/5 in Pacific. Awarded AP w/2 BSS, Victory, and Philippine Lib. Ribbons w/1 BSS. Discharged 1945.

Olsovsky, Frank G., son of John Olsovsky and Mary Dusek of Praha, TX, was born in 1895. Served in the Army from 1917–1919, Pfc., Quartermaster, Supply Sector, in France. Married Sophie Jasek; seven children. Farmed in the Wallis and Praha areas. Died in 1973.

Ondreas, Albert, son of John Ondreas and Rosie Zapalac, was born Oct. 8, 1930, in Buckholts, Milam County, TX. Attended Woodrow School near Damon, TX. Enlisted in the U.S. Army at Ft. Sam Houston, TX, during the Korean Conflict. Served as a Tank Gunner and attained the rank of Cpl. prior to separation from service on Jan. 23, 1954. Now retired. Enjoys doing woodwork. Married Bernice Hrachovy. Home of record: Brazoria, TX.

Ondreas, John, Jr., son of John Ondreas, Sr. and Rosie Zapalac, was born June 26, 1927, in Cameron, TX. Attended school in Buckholts, TX, and the Woodrow School near Damon, TX. Enlisted in the U.S. Army on Mar. 14, 1946, at Ft. Sam Houston, TX. Served as a Rifleman in units at Camp Robinson, AR, and Ft. Hood, TX. Separated from service on Sept. 16, 1947. Retired from Alcoa in Aug. 1980, where he had been a crane operator. Married Margie V. Hrachovy; two children: Robert Wayne and Kenneth James. Hobbies are shrimping, hunting, fishing, and gardening. Home of record: Van Vleck, TX.

Ondrej, August, was born Aug. 17, 1894. Served in U.S. Army during WWI, attaining rank of Pfc. Died Mar. 16, 1978; buried in St. Mary's Cemetery, West, TX.

Ondrusek, George J., son of John and Theresa Ondrusek, was born Sept. 6, 1916, Shiner, TX. Education: St. Ludmilla's Catholic School, Shiner, TX. Enlisted in U.S. Army Air Corps, Shiner, TX, Oct. 15, 1942. Rank: T/Sgt. Theater of Operations: Europe, WWII. Radio Man and Gunner, B-17 Flying Fortress, 23 missions. KILLED IN ACTION over France, Feb. 4, 1944. Medals: Purple Heart, Good Conduct. Buried in Shiner Catholic Cemetery, TX. Submitted by his brother, William Ondrusek, San Antonio, TX.

Ondrusek, William, son of John and Theresa Ondrusek, was born Oct. 5, 1914, Shiner, TX. Education: St. Ludmilla's Catholic School, Shiner, TX. Enlisted at Victoria, TX, Feb. 4, 1942, U.S. Army Air Corps. Theater of Operations: American. Airplane Maintenance Technician. Medals: GCM, American Theater Ribbon, WWII Victory Ribbon. Honorably discharged, Dec. 21, 1945. Home of record: San Antonio, TX.

Opella, Ilean I., West, TX, WWII veteran.

Orsak, Jerry J., Sr., son of Charlie J. and Frances Horak Orsak, was born Oct. 30, 1925, in Hochheim, TX. Education: San Angelo High School and Jr. College. Enlisted Jan. 27, 1945, at Ft. Sam Houston, TX. Served in the European Theater. Awards: Army Occupation Medal, WWII Victory Medal. Discharged Dec. 1, 1948. Rank: Staff Sgt. Enlisted in A.F. Reserve July 1, 1949; discharged Feb. 28, 1970, at the rank of Master Sgt. Home of record: San Angelo, TX

Orsak, Joseph Charles "Joe," son of Joseph Orsak and Mary Lidiak, was born Jan. 3, 1950, Houston, Harris Co., TX. Education: St. John's Catholic School, Fayetteville, TX, Fayetteville High School, Blinn College, Brenham, TX. Enlisted in U.S. Navy, La Grange, TX. Theater of Operation: Viet Nam. Stationed NTS, for boot camp and Radioman School, San Diego, CA; assigned to South Pacific, Mediterranean, and Panama on the AOR-2 USS *Milwaukee* for 16 months, which was a support oiler ship during the Viet Nam War. Medals: GCM, Viet Nam Service Medal w/1 BSS. Honorably discharged Apr. 9, 1975. Rank: E-4. Married Debra; three children. Home of record: Brenham, TX. Submitted by wife, Debra Orsak.

Orsak, Julius Joe, son of Ernest J. Orsak and Agnes Konarik, was born Dec. 7, 1904, Fayetteville, TX. Education: Sealy, TX, Public School through third grade. Enlisted in U.S. Coast Guard, Galveston, TX, Sept. 2, 1930. Theater of Operations: American and Asiatic-Pacific. Battles: South Pacific, WWII. Medals: American Campaign, American Defense, Asiatic Pacific Campaign, National Defense, WWII Victory, FIDELITY ZEAL OBEDIENCE, U.S. Coast Guard Medal. Retired Oct. 1, 1954, Lake Worth Inlet Lifeboat Station, Riviera Beach, FL. Rank: ENLC. Home of record: Richmond, TX. Submitted lovingly in his honor by Robert E. Spacek of Richmond, TX.

Oslick, Alfonse, son of Francis and Ann Oslick, was born Jan. 8, 1895, Koberice, Moravia, Austria. Enlisted in U.S. Army Corps, May 14, 1917, Austin, TX. Rank, Pvt. Theater of Operations: European. Medals: EOT Campaign, WWI Victory. Honorably discharged Mar. 7, 1919. Civilian Occupation: Farmer, watchmaker. Married Lestie Mary Holubec; two children: Chester A. and Theodore J. Member of SPJST Lodge 20, Granger, TX. Died Oct. 22, 1967; buried Taylor City Cemetery, Taylor, TX. Submitted by son, Theodore J. Oslick, Taylor, TX.

Oslick, Chester Alphonse, son of Alphonse and Lestie Holubeck Oslick, was born May 27, 1922, in San Antonio, TX. Graduated from San Gabriel High School in 1940. Enlisted Nov. 16, 1942, San Antonio. Stationed in U.S., England, and France, attaining the rank of Tech Sgt. Overseas duty Mar. 21, 1944–July 19, 1945. Participated in the Normandy, Rome Arno, Northern France, Southern France, Ardennes, Central Europe and the Rhineland Campaigns. Served as a Crew-Chief of a C-47 transport. Member of the 436th Troop Carrier Group, 80th Troop Carrier Squadron, dropped paratroopers, towed gliders and re-supplied by air drops. Plane was hit by gun fire several times but no one ever got wounded. Decorations: EAME Campaign Medal with seven Bronze Stars, Air Medal with three OLC, Distinguished Unit Badge, and Good Conduct Medal. Married Gussie Rieger, Jan. 24, 1947; two sons: Douglas Lynn and Gary Ross. Home of record: Thorndale, TX.

Oslick, James G., son of Theodore James and Annie Jean Burkhart Oslick, was born May 7, 1951, in Taylor, Williamson Co., TX. Attended San Gabriel and Thorndale Elementary School, Rockdale High School, and Texas A&M University. Commissioned as a 2nd Lt. at graduation

from Texas A&M, May 4, 1973. Undergraduate pilot training at Craig AFB, Selma, AL. Active Duty 11th and 73rd (reserves) Aeromedical Airlift Sq., Scott AFB, IL. Reserve squadron was activated for Desert Storm. Decorations include: Air Force Commendation Medal, A.F. Outstanding Unit Award, Combat Readiness Medal, National Defense Service Medal, Small Arms Expert Marksmanship Ribbon, A.F. Longevity Service Award, Armed Forces Reserve Medal, Air Force Training Ribbon, and Humanitarian Award. Still in the Air Force Reserve. Married Margaret Bonaros in 1978 when she was assigned to the 57th Aeromedical Evacuation Sq. as a flight nurse. Both achieved the rank of Lt. Col. They have two children: Matthew James and Laura Michelle. Home of record: O'Fallon, IL.

Oslick, Theodore J., son of Alphonse and Lastie Mary Holubec Oslick, was born Dec. 19, 1923, in San Antonio, TX. Educated in San Gabriel public schools. Enlisted in the Army Infantry Sept. 9, 1944, at Ft. Sam Houston in San Antonio, TX. Served in the Pacific Theater in WWII. Battles: liberation of Luzon, Philippines. WOUNDED IN ACTION. Decorations: Asiatic-Pacific Campaign Ribbon with one Bronze Star, Philippine Liberation Ribbon with one Bronze Star, Philippine Independence Ribbon, Purple Heart, Good Conduct Medal, and Meritorious Unit Award. Discharged at rank of Pfc. Nov. 24, 1946. Married Annie Jean Burkhart; one son: James. Home of record: Taylor, TX.

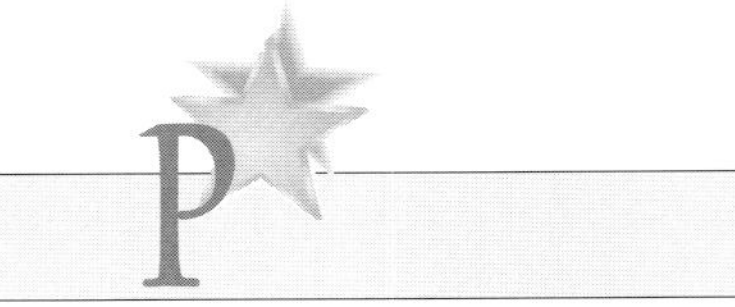

Pacha, Bill I., was born Feb. 14, 1914. WWII veteran. Sgt. 1908 Svc Comd Unit. Died Oct. 16, 1964; buried Holy Cross Catholic Cem., Granger, TX.

Palousek, Frank J., son of Frank and Rozina Palousek, was born Oct. 2, 1896, Corn Hill, Williamson Co., TX. Enlisted during WWI, U.S. Army, rank Pvt. Served in Btry. F, 133 Field Artillery. Honorably discharged after WWI. Married Marcella Schrahak; children: Victor, Bill, Margie, Louis. Civilian Occupation: Farmer. Died Sept. 16, 1957. Buried Corn Hill, Williamson Co., TX.

Palousek, Victor F., son of Frank and Marcella Schrahak, was born Aug. 22, 1921, Corn Hill, Williamson Co., TX. Education: Holy Trinity Catholic School, Jarrell High School, and graduate of Bastrop High School, TX. Enlisted in U.S. Army Corps about 1941, Ft. Sam Houston, TX. Attained rank of Staff Sgt. Assigned to Signal Corps. Medals: WWII Victory Medal, several others. Honorably discharged Dec. 1946. Civilian occupations: farmer; plant manager, barber, realtor. Married Louise Zrubek; three children: Susan, Constance, Victor F., Jr. Hobbies: fishing, arts and crafts. Died July 4, 1972; buried Corn Hill, Williamson Co., TX.

Parma, Edward J., Sr., son of Ignace J. Parma and Annie Nesrsta, was born Dec. 5, 1919, at Temple, TX. Attended St.John's Parochial School in Ennis and graduated from Ennis High School. Member of the Catholic Sokols until drafted into the service during World War II on Oct. 17, 1941. Transferred to flight training on Apr. 6, 1943, and received pilot wings on Aug. 4, 1944. Later received flight officer and radar observer wings on Feb. 10, 1945. Served in both the American and Asiatic-Pacific Theaters of Operations. Flew 15 missions from Tinian, in the Marianas, to Japan as a radar operator. Medals: Air Medal with clusters, American and Asiatic-Pacific Campaigns, World War II Victory, and the Presidential Unit Citation. Released from active service on Mar. 25, 1946, as a Second Lt. Remained in the Air Force Reserves until Feb. 7, 1963. Discharged as a Capt. Married Adail R. Kubin on Nov. 23, 1948; three daughters and two sons. Pursued career in the grocery business from 1946 to 1978. Employed with Leggett and Platt, Inc. from 1978 until retirement in 1987. Active in the American Sokol, KJT, and St.John's Parish in Ennis, TX. Home of record: Ennis, TX.

Parma, Edwin G., son of Frank Parma and Mary Frances, was born May 12, 1913, Waco, TX. Education: two years SMU and NTAC, Arlington, TX. Commissioned 1st Lt. in U.S. Army Corps. Volunteered Oct. 1942, U.S. Army Corps, Dallas, TX. Theater of Operations: Asiatic-Pacific. Battles: Philippines and Okinawa. Medals: Asiatic-Pacific Theater Campaign w/2 BSS. Honorably discharged Mar. 1946. Home of record: Dallas, TX.

Parma, John F., West, TX, WWII veteran. Theater of Operations: Asiatic-Pacific.

Patek, Charles, son of Jim Patek and Albina Husinseky, was born Jan. 19, 1920, at Shiner, TX. Attended St. Ludmila's Academy in Shiner. Enlisted in the U.S. Army Air Corps at San Antonio, TX, during WWII. Served in the Asiatic Pacific Theater of Operations as a member of Headquarters Squadron, V Fighter Command in Japan and attained the rank of Pvt. Discharged June 10, 1946. Home of record: Seguin, TX.

Patek, Jim, Sr., son of John Patek and Vera Mauric, was born in Sept. 1896, at Shiner, TX. Attended school in the Boundary Line community near Shiner. Served as a member of the U.S. Army Depot Brigade during WWI. Died Apr. 19, 1955.

Pausewang, Joseph, U.S. Navy, of Granger, TX, is a Desert Storm U.S. Armed Forces veteran.

Pavas, Elmer J., son of Louis and Mary Pavas, was born May 3, 1938, at Praha, TX. Attended Novohrad Elementary School and Moulton High School. Enlisted in the U.S. Army in San Antonio,

TX, on Sept. 13, 1957. Served in Berlin, Germany, for 18½ months as a member of the 3rd Battle Group, 6th Inf. and attained the rank of Specialist 4/C. Decorations include the Berlin Freedom Award. Discharged on Sept. 10, 1959, at Ft. Sheridan, Illinois. Home of record: Boerne, TX.

Pavelka, Albin F., son of Mr. and Mrs. V. J. Pavelka, Mart, TX. Entered Army in 1944, during WWII. Attained rank of Cpl. Served in ET. Awarded EAME, GCM, and Victory Ribbons. Discharged 1946.

Pavelka, Anton J., son of Mr. and Mrs. V. J. Pavelka, Mart, TX. Entered Army in 1943, during WWII. Served in Pacific. Awarded AT, GCM, and Victory Ribbon. Discharged 1946.

Pavelka, Charles W., son of Mr. and Mrs. Willie Pavelka, was born Dec. 7, 1921, in Mart, TX. Attended Hallsburg School. Entered the Army in July 1942, and trained at Camp Wolters and in MD. Rank: Sgt. Served in Tunis, Sicily, Naples, and Rome, Italy. Medals: EAME with four Stars, Combat Infantry Badge, five Overseas Bars and one Service Stripe, GCM. Home of record: Mart, TX.

Pavelka, Edwin J., son of Mr. and Mrs. Willie Pavelka, was born Sept. 10, 1923, in Mart, TX. Attended Riesel High School. Entered AAC in 1942. Rank: S/Sgt. Served in the European Theater. Discharged in 1945, reenlisted and served 20 years, retiring on Jan. 1, 1968. Medals: Victory Ribbon, Air Medal, ET, AT, GCM, Korean Service Medal, WWII Victory Medal, United Nation Medal, EAME Service Medal, ND Medal, AF Longevity Award. Home of record: Waco, TX.

Pavelka, Joe, was born in 1898. Enlisted in the U.S. Army on Jan. 10, 1918, during WWI, at the age of 20. Served in France as a member of the American Expeditionary Forces and participated in combat in the Argonne Forest along the French-German border. One of six WWI veterans who were honored for their service in 1993 at a Veterans Day Service at the Olin E. Teague Hospital in Temple. Received a specially-inscribed WWI Victory Medal commemorating the 75th anniversary of the end of WWI. Also received a Meritorious Commander's Award from the 13th Corps Support Command at Ft. Hood along with a Proclamation from the Temple Mayor and a Certificate of Citation from State Representative Dianne Delis. The ceremony included his three daughters: Irene Pavelka Beard, Dorothy Pavelka Newsman, and Joyce Pavelka Simians, along with two grandsons, a granddaughter, and a great-grandson. Resident in the VA home in Temple, TX.

Pavelka, John Joe, son of John Peter Pavelka and Marie Eva Schlezinger, was born Apr. 12, 1919, in Corn Hill, Williamson County, TX. Attended Holy Trinity Catholic School in Corn Hill. Enlisted in the U.S. Army at Ft. Sam Houston, TX, during WWII. Served as an Artilleryman and attained the rank of Pfc. Farms in the Bartlett area. Married Valeria Dorothy Holubec; five children: Joseph Henry, John Gerard, Dorothy Katherine Pavelka Stefek, Martha Jane, and Timothy Louis. Home of record: Bartlett, TX.

Pavelka, Miro Arthur, son of Jim and Mary Pavelka, was born June 12, 1915, Dallas, TX. Moved to Ennis TX, 1916. Graduate of Ennis H.S., 1932; Mechanical Engineering, Texas A&M. Enlisted U.S. Navy, Mar. 20, 1942, Dallas, TX. Assigned to 65th Construction Bn., Davisville, RI. After a period of stateside duty, was transferred to Guam, Asiatic-Pacific Theater of Operations, with this unit for duration of WWII. Honorably discharged

Nov. 1, 1945. Rank: Machinist's Mate 1/C. Retired from U.S. Postal Service in 1980. Died Mar. 13, 1985; interred at Myrtle Cemetery, Ennis, TX. Submitted by Dr. Miro A. Pavelka, Dallas, TX.

Pavelka, Robert W., son of Mr. and Mrs. Willie Pavelka, was born July 26, 1933, in Mart, TX. Attended Mart High School. Enlisted June 10, 1953. Trained at El Paso, TX. Rank: S/Sgt. Served in Korea. Discharged June 10, 1956. Medals: GCM, Korean Ribbon, Sharpshooter Medal. Home of record: Abbott, TX.

Pavlas, Alfred J., of West, TX, WWII veteran. Theater of Operations: Asiatic-Pacific.

Pavlas, Bernard Alfred "Bennie," son of Rudolf Pavlas and Mary Pavlicek, was born Dec. 22, 1926, Engle, Fayette County, TX. Schooled at Pine Springs, Engle, and Flatonia, TX. Enlisted U.S. Army Corps, Apr. 10, 1945, Ft. Sam Houston, TX. Theater of Operations: EAME. Stationed in Munich, Germany, 10 months w/Battery C, 390th Anti-Aircraft Artillery Automatic Weapons Bn. as a cook, under General Patton. Medals: Army of Occupation Ribbon (Germany), WWII Victory Ribbon, Overseas Service Bar. Honorably discharged Oct. 29, 1946. Married Margaret; two sons, one daughter, two grandsons, and one granddaughter. Owned Gulf service station, Schulenburg, TX, 25 years. Semi-retired. Hobbies: fishing and gardening. Home of record: Schulenburg, TX.

Pavlas, Emmerick Joe, was born Oct. 28, 1915. Served in the U.S. Armed Forces during WWII, 138 Base Unit AAF. Rank: T/Sgt. Married Victoria Sutter. Died Aug. 3, 1966. Buried in Lady Fatima Cemetery, Abbott, TX.

Pavlas, George, son of Willie J. Pavlas and Albina Darilek, was born Oct. 1, 1919. Education: through 11th grade, Komensky High School, TX. Enlisted Mar. 24, 1942, Ft. Sam Houston, TX, U.S. Army Corps. Theater of Operations: EAME. 5th Army, 102nd QM Bakery Co. Battles: Africa, Sicily, Rome-Arno, Italy. Medals: American Theater Campaign, EAME Campaign w/2 BSS, Good Conduct, WWII Victory, one service stripe, three overseas service bars, ribbons. Honorably discharged Nov. 11, 1945. Home of record: Moulton, TX.

Pavlasek, Richard Bernard, son of John Pavlasek and Anna Kopecky, was born Aug. 15, 1933, in Corpus Christi, TX. Graduated from Robstown H.S., and Federal Aviation Academy. Served from Feb. 1954 to Feb. 1956 in U.S. Army, Corps of Engineers. Stationed in U.S. and France. Medals: NDSM, Good Conduct. Honorably discharged. Rank: Specialist 4/C. Married Velma; five children. Meteorologist. Past dist. president of K.J.T., one of the founding and charter members of the Czech Heritage Society of South Texas, and also of the Travis-Williamson Co. Czech Heritage Society in Austin. Home of record: Austin, TX.

Pavlicek, Billy, served Oct. 14, 1948, in U.S. Army Corps during WWII. Name is on monument erected by St. Mary's Catholic Church, Frydek, TX, in thanksgiving for the return of 75 parishioners who served in WWII, 1941-1945.

Pavlicek, Clarence L., son of Mr. and Mrs. Ignac Pavlicek, Taylor TX. Education: Rice's Crossing School. Enlisted U.S. Army Corps, 1942; basic training, Camp Barkeley; further training: OR; MS. Theater of Operations: European. Medals: ETO Campaign Medal and Ribbon w/1 BSS, Combat Infantry Badge, Good Conduct Medal, Purple Heart Medal, Ribbons, WWII Victory Medal. Served in Germany. WOUNDED IN ACTION, 1945, Germany. Attained rank of S/Sgt prior to honorable discharge. Married Fay Honeycutt.

Pavlicek, Edward J., served Oct, 1942–Oct. 1944, U.S. Navy, during WWII.

Pavlicek, Frank, Tours, TX, military veteran.

Pavlicek, George D., son of Frank K. Pavlicek and

Julia Geiptner, was born Sept. 13, 1916. Education: St. Ludmila's Academy, Shiner, TX, Komensky, 1937. Entered service on Mar. 29, 1942, 90th Div., Co. D, 357th Inf. Stationed at Camp Berkeley, CA, and Fort Dix before going to England on Apr. 9, 1944. Sent to France, June 1944. WOUNDED IN ACTION July 7, 1944, and died as a result. Awarded Purple Heart, and others. Buried in Praha on May 4, 1948.

Pavlicek, James, West, TX. Military veteran. Served in Australia.

Pavlicek, Joe, served in U.S. Army Corps, after WWII. Info by Frydek CYO, Lawrence Sodolak.

Pavlicek, Joe F., was born Nov. 26, 1893. Served in the U.S. Military during WWI. Married Amalie (9/27/1897–5/1/1985). Died Dec. 22, 1952. Buried St. Mary's Catholic Cemetery, Frydek, TX.

Pavlicek, Julius I., son of Mr. and Mrs. I. J. Pavlicek, Taylor, TX. Enlisted U.S. Army Air Corps, 1942; basic training, Brooks Field. Medals: American Theater Campaign and Ribbon, WWII Victory and Ribbon. Attained rank of Sgt. prior to honorable discharge, 1945.

Pavlicek, Leo S., West, TX, Korean War veteran. KILLED IN ACTION.

Pavlicek, Willie, served in U.S. Army Corps, after WWII. Info by Frydek CYO, Lawrence Sodolak.

Pavlik, Stanley J., son of Mr. and Mrs. John Pavlik, Taylor, TX. Education: St. Mary's Catholic School. Enlisted U.S. Army Corps, 1940; basic training, Ft. Sam Houston, TX; further training, Camp Bowie, TX. Theater of Operation: Asiatic-Pacific. Served in Australia, New Guinea, Netherlands, East Indies, Philippines, Okinawa. Medals: A-P Theater Campaign w/4 BSS, Philippine Liberation, American Defense, Good Conduct, ribbons. Attained rank of S/Sgt. prior to honorable discharge, 1945.

Pavliska, Ed, WWII veteran of Granger, TX.

Pavliska, Eddie Joe, son of Raymond Pavliska and Henrietta Ermis, was born Apr. 2, 1947, Seymour, TX. Education: University of Tucson, AZ, El Toro, CA, May 14, 1969. Enlisted USMC, Mar. 1972, Camp Pendleton, CA. Rank: E-5, Mess Sgt. (Cook). Served in Da Nang, Viet Nam. Honorably discharged. Employed with Texas A&M Experiment Station, Eagle Lake, TX. Home of record: Eagle Lake, TX.

Pavliska, John, Jr., son of John Pavliska, Sr. and Cecelia M., was born Oct. 12, 1909, Taylor, Williamson County, TX. During WWII, enlisted in U.S. Army Corps, Mar. 22, 1942, Ft. Sam Houston, TX. Attained rank of Sgt. in U.S. Infantry. Theater of Operations: EAME. KILLED IN ACTION, July 26, 1944, invasion of France. Medals: Purple Heart, among others. Buried in France. Submitted in loving memory by relative, Geraldine T. Heisch, Round Rock, TX.

Pavliska, Raymond Victor, son of Bohoslav Pavliska and Frances Zak, was born Oct. 24, 1920, Floresville, TX. Enlisted about 1942, NRS, San Antonio, TX, U.S. Navy. Boot Camp, Great Lakes, IL. USD Base (SC) San Diego, CA. Assigned to USS *Block Island*; went thru Panama Canal to New York City; two trips to Belfast, Ireland (on one of these trips, stopped at Newfoundland). Made two trips searching for U-Boats. On 2nd trip, Escort Carrier CVE 21 USS *Block Island*, was sunk, May 23, 1943. On another trip, picked up some German prisoners of war and delivered to Casa Blanca. Sent back stateside for 30 day leave; before 30 days were up, sent to Bremerton, WA, to Escort Carrier 106. Traveled to San Francisco, CA, went under Golden Gate Bridge, back to San Diego, CA. Then to Camp Wallace, TX, for discharge. Places served were the USDD Base (SC) San Diego, CA; USS *Block Island* 21 and 106 CASU 5 Fighting Squad 98. Honorable discharge, Camp Wallace, TX, Jan. 19, 1946. Home of record: Seymour, TX.

Pavliska, Willie, WWII veteran of Granger, TX.

Pecena, Alvin Edward, son of Thomas J. Pecena and Julia Mrnustik, was born July 23, 1923, Wheelock, TX. Education: Franklin High School, TX. Enlisted during WWII, U.S. Naval Air Force, Apr. 14, 1944, San Antonio, TX. Rank: Aviation Machinist's Mate, 2/C. Honorable discharge June 3, 1946, Camp Wallace, TX. Died

Nov. 27, 1978; buried Resthaven Cemetery, Oklahoma City, OK. Submitted by Elise Pecena, Houston, TX.

Pecena, Ben J., son of Thomas J. Pecena and Julia Mrnustik, was born Dec. 28, 1915, Shiner, TX. Education: Franklin High School, TX; Texas A&M, 1939. U.S. Army Corps, Houston, TX. Theater of Operation: American. Stationed Ft. Sam Houston, TX. HDS Detachment. Medals: American Theater Campaign, Good Conduct, WWII Victory, one service stripe. Honorable discharge. Rank: Sgt., Jan. 26, 1946. Died Mar. 28, 1983. Buried Concord Cemetery, Concord, TX. Submitted by Elsie Pecena, Houston, TX.

Pecena, Thomas Frank, son of Thomas J. Pecena and Julia Mrnustik, was born May 10, 1919, Dime Box, TX. Graduated Franklin, TX, H.S., 1932; Brantley Draughon Business College, Ft. Worth, TX. Enlisted Feb. 8, 1940, Ft. Worth, TX. Boot camp, San Diego, CA. Theater of Operations: Asiatic-Pacific; American. Assigned to USS *Houston*. Battles: Southwest Pacific, Java Sea, from Dec. 7, 1941–Feb. 28, 1942. Rank: Radioman 3/C. KILLED IN ACTION Feb. 28, 1942, when ship was sunk. Medals: Purple Heart, American Campaign, Asiatic-Pacific Campaign w/BSS, Good Conduct, American Defense Service, WWII Victory, Ribbon Bar w/star. Presidential Unit Citation awarded the USS *Houston* for outstanding performance against enemy forces. Submitted by Elsie Pecena, Houston, TX.

Pecena, William Linhard, son of Thomas J. and Julia Mrnustik Pecena, was born June 18, 1927, in Wheelock, TX. Education: Franklin, TX, High School. Enlisted in the Navy Oct. 1944. Served in the Pacific. Discharged 1946. Died May 2, 1984; buried in Grove Hill Memorial Park Cemetery, Dallas, TX.

Pechacek, Ivan Joe, son of Mr. Pechacek and Angelina Mlandenka, was born Jan. 5, 1924, Elk, TX. Attended school at Elk and LaVega at Bellmead. Enlisted Jan. 25, 943, in the U.S. Army, Ft. Sam Houston, TX. Theater of Operations: European, African, Middle Eastern. Rank: Cpl. (T/4). Campaigns: Normandy, Northern France, Rhineland, Central Europe, and Ardennes:Alsace. Medals: European African Middle Eastern Campaign w/5 stars, Good Conduct, and the Distinguished Unit Citation Badge. Discharged Oct. 17, 1945, Camp Swift, TX. Home of record: Axtell, TX.

Pechal, Joseph, fought in Spanish American War of 1898 (Cuba). Lived at 600 East Milam St., Ennis TX. Was a special officer for the Southern Pacific Railroad, between Dallas, TX, and Houston, TX. Buried in St. Joseph Cemetery. Submitted by George C. Valek, Dallas, TX.

Pechal, Joseph, Jr., son of Joseph Pechal, Sr. and Mary Valek, was born July 13, 1913, at Ennis, TX. Graduated from Ennis High School and enlisted at Randolph Field, TX, as a Pvt. Discharged at Randolph Field in late 1936 or early 1937. Buried at St. Joseph Cemetery at Ennis, TX.

Pechanec, Charles "Charlie," served May 1942–Oct. 1944, U.S. Army Corps, during WWII. Served in the Medical Corp, Military Police.

Pechanec, Emil, enlisted in 1943, TX. Served 14 months, U.S. Army Air Corps.

Pechanec, Frank, served two years, 1941–1943, Infantry, U.S. Army Corps, during WWII.

Pechanec, Willie, son of Mr. and Mrs. Pechanec, enlisted in U.S. Army Corps, 1943, TX. Honorably discharged 1947. Submitted by Annie Polasek, Houston, TX.

Pekar, Andrew B., son of Mr. and Mrs. Joe Pekar. Education: Graduate, Granger High School. Enlisted U.S. Army Corps, 1941; basic training in TX. Further training, CO, NC, TN, VA. Theaters of Operation: American; European. Served in Germany, France and Central Europe. Medals: Good Conduct, American Defense, ETO Campaign Medal w/3 BSS, ATO Campaign Medal, WWII Victory Medal, Ribbons. Commissioned Capt. prior to honorable discharge, 1945.

Pekar, Frank Louis, son of Joseph Alois Pekar and Hermina Agnes Janak, was born Aug. 8, 1924, in Granger, TX. Graduated from Granger High School in 1943 and attended the University of Houston. Enlisted in the U.S. Navy on June 15, 1943, at Ft. Sam Houston, TX, during WWII. Basic training, San Diego, CA. Served in the Asiatic-Pacific Theater of Operations in the Midway Islands and at Pearl Harbor as a Storekeeper Second Class. Awards and decorations: Asiatic Pacific Theater Campaign Medal, American Campaign Medal, Good Conduct Medal, and WWII Victory Medal, American Defense Medal. Attained rank of SK 2/C prior to being separated from the service Dec. 29, 1946, at San Francisco, CA. Supervisor for the U.S. Postal Service at the time of retirement on Dec. 29, 1979. Married Evelyn Sladecek; two children: Cecilia and Gregory. Home of record: Granger, TX.

Pekar, Gregory Francis, son of Frank Louis and Evelyn C. Sladecek Pekar, was born Aug. 18, 1957, in Houston, TX. Commissioned at Texas A&M University, June 30, 1981, in College Station, TX. Theater of Operations: VA, TX, Germany, Saudi Arabia and MO. Rank: Maj. in the U.S. Army Engineers. Served in Desert Shield and Desert Storm with the 3rd Armored Div. Decorations: Southwest Asia Service Ribbon with three campaign stars, Bronze Star Medal, Army Commendation Medal w/ four OLC, Army Achievement Metal w/ four OLC. Still on active duty. Qualified as Ranger and Paratrooper. Home of record: Wayneville, MO.

Pekar, Jerry P., son of Vinc Pekar and Emma Prihoda, was born Feb. 4, 1917, Rosenberg, TX. Enlisted U.S. Army Corps, Sept. 29, 1941, Houston, TX. Attained rank of Tech 5th grade, Component AVS, Sevice T.C.; 174 Port Company Transportation Corps. Assigned to Base Command, Iceland. Theater of Operations: EAME. Medals: EAME Campaign Medal and American Defense Service Medal, WWII Victory Medal, Lapel Button issued ASR Score. Honorably discharged Oct. 19, 1945, Camp Fannin, TX. Married Frances Gritzman; three children. Died Sept. 17, 1978. Services held in Sts. Cyril & Methodius Catholic Church. Burial in church cemetery. Submitted by Evelyn Vecera of Bellaire, TX.

Pekar, Joe, Jr., son of Mr. and Mrs. Joe Pekar, Sr. WWII veteran of Granger, TX.

Pekar, John C., son of James and Annie Pekar, was born May 27, 1916, Sweet Home, TX. Earned high school GED. Enlisted in U.S. Army Corps, July 17, 1934, during WWII, Ft. Sam Houston, TX. Theater of Operations: European. Medals:

Combat Infantry Badge, BSS, WWII Victory Medal. Attained rank of Senior Master Sgt. Retired from service. D.O.D. June 1, 1966, HDQ, UAAF Bolling AFB, Washington, D.C., 1129th Special Activity. Home of record: San Antonio, TX.

Pekar, Joseph B., son of Joseph Alois Pekar and Hermina Agnes Janak, was born Aug. 5, 1915, at Granger, TX. Attended Sts. Cyril & Methodius School. Graduated from Granger H.S., 1934. Enlisted U.S. Army Air Corps, Mar. 5, 1940, Ft. Sam Houston, TX; basic training, Sheppard Field, TX. During WWII assigned to the Graduate Airplane Mechanic School, Air Corps Training Command at Sheppard Field in Wichita Falls, TX. Medals: ATO Campaign, Good Conduct, WWII Victory, ribbons. Separated from service Sept. 29, 1945. Rank: Staff Sgt. Married Judith Mae Spacek; three sons, one daughter. Worked for 32 years until retirement on July 5, 1979. Hobbies: all sports and gardening. Home of record: Granger, TX.

Pekar, Louis J., was born Nov. 5, 1921. Served in US Army. WWII veteran. Member, American Legion Post No. 282, Granger, TX. Died Oct. 23, 1983; buried Holy Cross Catholic Cemetery, Granger, TX.

Pekar, Richard J., was born Apr. 16, 1895. Military veteran, WWI. Died Sept. 29, 1919; buried Holy Cross Catholic Cemetery, Granger, TX.

Pekar, Theodore A., son of Albert J. and Augustina Cervenka Pekar, Granger, TX. Graduate, Granger High School. Enlisted U.S. Army Corps, 1942; basic training, Ft. Lewis, WA; further training Camp Clipper, CA. Served in Hawaii, Phoenix Islands, Philippines. Medals: Asiatic-Pacific Theater Campaign w/1 BSS, Philippine Liberation w/2 BSS, Purple Heart w/OLC, Combat Infantry Badge, Bronze Arrowhead. WOUNDED IN ACTION in the Philippines. Attained rank of S/Sgt. prior to honorable discharge, 1945.

Perchacek, Frank Fred, Jr., son of Frank Fred Perchacek and Emma Hajek, was born Apr. 5, 1922, in Flatonia, TX. Graduated high school; attended University of Texas at Austin for 3½ years. Enlisted in U.S. Army Air Corps, San Antonio, TX, during WWII, as an air cadet on Sept. 25, 1942. Called to active duty on Feb. 11, 1943. Commissioned as 2nd Lt., U.S. Army Air Corps, Sept. 24, 1944. Served in the European, African, and Middle Eastern Theater of Operations as a member of the 2nd Div., 8th Air Force operating out of England. As the lead navigator or "Mickey Man" of his unit ("Mickey Man" and "Deputy" were nicknames given to lead navigators and their alternates, because they used latest technology, radar, to guide aircraft to and from targets.), he was responsible for insuring that over 400 aircraft arrived at and returned from their targets. Participated in numerous flight operations including bombing raids on Berlin and bombing missions in the Ardennes in support of the Battle of the Bulge. One of the most memorable missions was a return flight from a night bombing raid in which his aircraft got separated from the rest of the squadron. As the aircraft left the mainland and approached its base in England, on mandated radio silence, he began receiving a guiding signal from the base. However, the signal was not coming from where he had calculated it should be. Even though the aircraft was low on fuel, he managed to convince the crew members that the signal was false and that his calculations were correct. It was later learned that the signals were coming from a German submarine off the coast of England which was trying to lure Allied aircraft to the North Sea. After release from active duty, he became a member of the 433rd Troop Carrier Wing, a reserve unit, located at Kelley AFB at San Antonio, TX. Remained in the Air Force Reserves until retirement as a Maj. on Apr. 6, 1966. Home of record: Austin, TX.

Pertl, Clarence Stanley, born Apr. 21, 1925, in the Caldwell community of Burleson Co., Texas. Parents, Stanislav Otto Pertl and Annie Rose Sebesta Pertl, were also born in Caldwell community. Inducted into the United States Navy on Apr. 30, 1944. Rank: Seaman 1/C. Served on USS *Napa* in the Pacific. Amphibious Force. Landed on Iwo Jima on Feb. 19, 1945 (D-Day) with the

Marines. WOUNDED IN ACTION on Iwo Jima and received the Purple Heart. Visited ports in Seattle, Hawaii, Saipan, Guam, Okinawa, Manila, Yokohama, Japan, and Tsingtao, China. Honorable discharge Mar. 5, 1946.

Pertl, Stanislav Otto, son of Vincent Pertl (born Nov. 1854 in Austria (Czech lands) and died Mar. 11, 1911), and Emily Hejl. Enlisted in the United States Army on July 11, 1917. Served in the Champagne Front AGF from July 17, 1918 to May 8, 1919. Honorably discharged on May 22, 1919, with the Bronze Victory Button.

Pesek, Adolf, of Shiner, TX, served in U.S. Armed Forces, WWI. Deceased.

Pesek, Benedict, of Shiner, TX, served in U.S. Armed Forces during WWII.

Pesek, Bohdan, of Shiner, TX, served in U.S. Armed Forces during WWII.

Pesek, Dennis, son of Ernest J. Pesek and Vlasta Pivonka, served in U.S. Marine Corps, Viet Nam. Hometown: LaMarque, TX.

Pesek, Edwin, son of Mr. and Mrs. John Pesek, Taylor, TX. Enlisted USMC, 1942. Boot camp, San Diego, CA. Additional training, Camp Pendleton. Theater of Operations: Asiatic-Pacific. Served in New Zealand, Guadalcanal, New Hegrides, Bougainville. Medals: Asiatic-Pacific Theater Campaign Medal and Ribbon w/BSS, Purple Heart. Attained rank of Pfc., prior to being KILLED IN ACTION, Bougainville, 1943.

Pesek, Ernest J., son of Tom Pesek and Lillie Kallus. Volunteered for U.S. Army Corps, Dodd Field, TX, just prior to WWII, Mar. 21, 1941. Served with M.P. unit at Brownwood, TX. Entered Officer's School at Ft. Benning GA. Received commission 2nd Lt. Assigned to 79th Inf. Div. Theater of Operations: EAME. Battles included D-Day invasion. Retired from active duty as Infantry Major, June 30, 1947. Medals: Infantry Combat Medal, BSS. Served in U.S. Army Reserve as Officer 1947 through 1952. Married Vlasta Pivonka, Jourdanton, TX, Jan. 12, 1946; eight children. Retired from Union Carbide, Texas City, TX, 1983, 36½ yrs service. Member of KJT, K of C, Queen of Peace Men's Club, Czech Heritage Singers (past president and vice-pres.). Active RVOS Sales Representative. Home of record: LaMarque, TX.

Pesek, Ernest, of Shiner, TX, served in U.S. Armed Forces during WWII.

Pesek, Jaro, of Shiner, TX, served in U.S. Armed Forces during WWII. Deceased.

Pesek, John Thomas, Jr., son of John Thomas Pesek, Sr. and Elizabeth G. Kallus, was born Nov. 15, 1921, Shiner, Texas. Education: BS, 1943, MS, 1947, PhD, 1950. Enlisted Jan. 1943, Houston, TX, U.S. Army Air Corps. Theater of Operations: European. Assigned to 15th Air Force as Navigator-Radar. Served in WWII, Battle of Europe. Medals: Distinguished Flying Cross, Air Medal w/3 OLC, ETO Campaign Medal w/BSS. Honorably discharged Dec. 1945, Randolph Field, TX.

Pesek, John Thomas, Sr., served in U.S. Armed Forces, WWI. Married Elizabeth G. Kallus.

Pesek, Martin, son of Ernest J. Pesek and Vlasta Pivonka, presently in USAF, Colorado Springs, CO. Hometown, LaMarque, TX.

Pesek, Richard, son of Ernest J. Pesek and Vlasta Pivonka, served in U.S. Marine Corps, Viet Nam. Hometown: LaMarque, TX.

Pesek, Tommy, of Shiner, TX, served in U.S. Armed Forces, Viet Nam. KILLED IN ACTION.

Peter, Emil, son of Joseph Peter, Jr. and Barbara Vrana, was born Oct. 1, 1878, in Dubina, TX. Attended Capital Business College and St. Edward's College at Austin. Enlisted in the Texas National Guard in 1904 at Brenham and during WWI was a Cornetist in the Army Band, Texas National Guard. Died Oct. 27, 1963.

Peter, James V., son of Mr. and Mrs. Valentin Peter, born Sept. 28, 1914, Floresville, TX. Enlisted in U.S. Army Corps, Dec. 1941. Theater of Operations: EAME; Asiatic-Pacific. Member of a combat division, famous for its role in the St. Michiel and Argonne battles of last war, been in England for five months. KILLED IN ACTION, June 12, 1944, Normandy.

Peter, Julius, son of Joseph Peter, Jr. and Barbara Vrana, was born July 4, 1889, in Dubina, TX. Enlisted into the 36th Division Calvary in 1915 and during WWI served with this unit in France as a member of the American Expeditionary Forces. Discharged from the service in 1918. Died Oct. 16, 1966.

Peter, Victor A., son of Leo Peter and Dorothea Hoffmann, was born Dec. 8, 1918, Hillje (El Campo), Wharton County, TX. Attended Adams #1 Rural School, then El Campo schools, later the University of Houston, Houston, TX. Enlisted U.S. Army Corps, Feb. 24, 1942, Ft. Sam Houston, San Antonio, Bexar Co., TX, during WWII. Assigned to Co. D, 160th Inf., 40th Div. Spent three years in South Pacific, ending on Luzon and Negroes, Philippine Islands, on detached service in Communication Section of 1st Bn. HDQ. Promoted to Staff Sgt. just a few days before discharge. Honorable discharge Aug. 6, 1945, Ft. Sam Houston, San Antonio, TX. Employed as Director of Sales, Plumbing and Hardware Wholesale. Married Lillia Mae Mills of Hungerford, TX; two stepchildren: George Shotwell and Heather Shotwell Chandler. Vice President of Harris County Chapter Czech Heritage Society (one of the founding fathers). On Board of Trustees for the Texas Czech Heritage Society, Director of Czech Educational Foundation of Texas. Home of record: Pasadena, TX. Our good friend died Mar. 9, 1996, leaving wonderful memories and many to miss him.

Peters, Gene, son of Charlie Peters and Esther, was born May 8, 1941, Beeville, TX. Education: high school. Enlisted in U.S. Armed Forces. Medals: Sharpshooter, Expert Badge. Honorable discharge Nov. 20, 1965. Home of record: Beeville, TX. Submitted by Esther Peters, Beeville, TX

Petr, Charlie, military service veteran. Home of record: Ennis, TX.

Petr, Edwin, military service veteran. Home of record: Ennis, TX.

Petr, Emil, military service veteran. Home of record: Ennis, TX.

Petr, Frank, military service veteran. Home of record: Ennis, TX.

Petr, William, military service veteran. Home of record: Ennis, TX.

Petrusek, Benjamin John, son of Frank and Jane Sabrsula Petrusek, Wallis, TX, was born Aug. 27, 1921 in Sealy, Austin Co., TX. Education: Wallis High School, University of Texas at Austin, B.A. in Geology; USNR Midshipman School, Notre Dame University; 1943 commissioned as Ensign in U.S. Navy. Theatres of Operation: WWII American, European (Mediterranean), Asiatic Pacific. Battles: Communications Officer USS LST 263 Amphibious Force in air raid off Oran, N. Africa; 14 shuttle trips into Anzio beachhead; Invasion of Southern France. In Pacific, duty as Executive Officer USS LST 718. Shuttle trips in Philippines, Okinawa, Korea and Japan. Medals: American Theatre, European Theatre (two Battle Stars), Asiatic Pacific, Philippine Liberation, Victory Medal, Naval Reserve Medal, and the Armed Forces Reserve Medal. Events on active duty: Air raids in Mediterranean, transported U.S. Army troops and equipment into beachheads, transported enemy POWs, In Pacific, at sea, caught in fierce typhoon off Okinawa, in Yokahoma, Japan, in harbor on day armistice signed with Japan. Married Minnie (Hermina) Mokry, daughter of Charles and Hedwiga Mokry, in 1943; two children. Released from active duty Feb. 11, 1946. Continued in active Naval Reserve; retired in 1975 with present rank of Capt. Home of record: Metairie, LA.

Petruy, Willie G., son of John Petruy and Christine Skopik, was born Apr. 8, 1932, Ennis, TX. Graduate, Ennis public schools, 1950. Enlisted in U.S. Navy, Dallas, TX, Jan. 9, 1951. Boot Camp, San Diego, CA. Served on USS *George*

Clymer APA-27, homeport San Diego, during Korean Conflict. Served on USS LST-1141, home port San Diego; USS *H. W. Gilmore* AS-16, home port Key West, FL; USS *Bugara* SS-331, home port San Diego; USS *Swordfish* SSN-579, home port Pearl Harbor, HI; USS *Simon Bolivar* SSBN-641, home port Charleston, SC; USS *Halibut* SSN-T87, home port Pearl Harbor, HI; USS *Remora* SS-487, home port Charleston, SC; USS *Holland* AS-32, home port Charleston, SC. Shore duty tours included recruiting duty, Vallejo, CA. Instructor duty, Fleet Ballistic Missile Submarine Training Center Charleston, SC. Instructor duty, Propulsion Engineering School, Engineman "C" School, Great Lakes, IL. Last tour of duty was as "Command Master Chief" at U.S. Naval Air Station, Corpus Christi, TX. Retired w/30 years service as Master Chief Engineman (Submarines) Feb. 28, 1981. Home of record: Alexandria VA.

Petter, Alphonse F., son of Mr. and Mrs. Frank Petter, West, TX. Entered Army in 1942 during WWII. Served in Africa and Italy. KILLED IN ACTION in Mt. Vista, Italy, 1944. Awarded Purple Heart.

Petter, Anton J., son of Mikolos Peter/Petr and Anna Blahuta, was born Sept. 28, 1891, in Moravia, Lavaca County, TX. Attended school at Moravia Elementary. Enlisted in the Army on Apr. 26, 1918 in Wharton, TX. Rank: Pvt. Stationed in France and fought in the battles of St. Michael, Tront, and Verdun. WOUNDED IN ACTION from a mustard gas attack. Discharged Jan. 25, 1919 at Camp Pike, AR. Married Adella Mozisek on Nov. 19, 1919; two children: Walter and Jeanette. Worked in a rice mill until retirement. Died July 18, 1972, in El Campo, TX.

Petter, Arnold Edward, son of Frank M. Petter and Marcella, was born Apr. 21, 1910, in Wallis, TX. Education: Wallis Catholic School, Wallis, TX; Rosenberg High School, 1929; University of Texas, Austin, B.S. in Elementary Education, 1933. Commissioned July 21, 1942. Completed Navy Service Indoctrination at Naval Training School, Harvard University; Radar School, MIT; Special Aviation Radio, Croft Laboratories, Cambridge, MA. qualified as Radar Officer. Attained rank of Lt. Commdr-S(A)T USNR. Medals: American Theater of Operations Campaign Medal, WWII Victory Medal. Honorably discharged June 6, 1946, U.S. Naval Air Station, Jacksonville, FL. Married Dec. 26, 1942, Velasta L. Mussil, Granger, TX. Died Mar. 31, 1972, Houston, TX. Buried Greenlawn Memorial Park, Rosenberg, TX. Submitted by Mrs. Velasta Miller, Rosenberg, TX.

Petter, Benjamin J., son of Mr. and Mrs. Frank Petter, West, TX. Entered Army in 1940, served during WWII, w/rank of Cpl. in Africa and Italy. WOUNDED IN ACTION, Alta Villa, Italy. Died in Italy Sept. 22, 1943. Awarded GCM, Pre-Pearl Harbor, Purple Heart.

Petter, Emil F., son of William Petter and Mary Mynar, was born Apr. 26, 1918, Park, Fayette Co., TX. Graduate of Fayetteville, TX, High School, 1937. Drafted Feb. 7, 1941, U.S. Army Corps in La Grange, TX. Stationed at Ft. Sam Houston, TX, in Medical Corp. Nov. 30, 1942, shipped on *Queen Mary* to European Theater of Operations. Stationed in England for two years, then for one year in France. Discharged Oct. 25, 1945. Home of record: Wharton, TX.

Petter, Henry J., Jr., was born Feb. 21, 1926, West, TX. Served in U.S. Navy during WWII. Died Apr. 19, 1975; buried in West Brethren Cemetery, West, TX.

Petter, Jim John, son of Jim Petter and Clara Waligura, was born July 17, 1944, El Campo, Wharton County, TX. Education: St. Philips Catholic Elementary, El Campo High, Wharton Jr. College, Lamar Tec. Voc. College, Altus, OK, Jr. College. Enlisted in USAF Aug. 8, 1966, Wharton, TX. Assigned to 4th Mobile Communications Group, Altus AFB, OK. Military Occupation: Teletype Maintenance 36330. Medals: Marksmanship, Good Conduct. Honorably discharged Aug.

20, 1970, having attained rank of E-4. Married Frances Lucille Lehnert; two children: Amy Marie and Gregory James. Hobbies: hunting, fishing, woodworking. Civilian Occupation: Machinist. Home of record: Pflugerville, TX.

Picha, Anton J., was born May 17, 1911. Served in U.S. Army Corps during WWII. Attained rank of Pfc. Died Sept. 2, 1974. Buried in St. Mary's Cemetery, West, TX.

Picha, Frank F., son of Cyrill Picha and Mary Rejcek, was born Nov. 18, 1913, West, McLennan Co., TX. Education: through 7th Grade, Alligator School, McLennan County, TX. Enlisted Hill County, TX. Attained rank of Cpl. Theater of Operations: Asiatic-Pacific. Medals: Asiatic-Pacific Campaign Medal w/1 BSS, Good Conduct Medal, WWII Victory Medal, two service stripes, Overseas Bars, Ribbons. Honorable discharge Jan. 31, 1946. Home of record: Ft. Worth, TX.

Pinter, Raymond J., son of Mr. and Mrs. Tom Pinter, Abbott, Hillsboro, TX. Entered Army during WWII, in 1943. Served European Theater, attaining rank of Pfc. Awarded EAME w/2 BSS and GCM. Discharged 1945.

Pinter, Sam, son of Joe and Rosie Pinter, West, TX. Attended West High School, West, TX. Served in U.S. Air Force, 1952–1956, Korean War. Marshall Island, Eniwetok Island. Pacific Testing Atomic Bomb–Air Force tested Hydrogen Bombs Aircraft. Atomic Research and Development Command. Attained rank of Airman F/C prior to discharge, Dec. 1956. Married Joyce Hill.

Piter, Frank, son of Joseph Piter and Mary Louise Bartodej, was born Nov. 20, 1895, in Lavaca Co., TX. Enlisted in the Army at Chandler, Oklahoma. Theater of Operation: France, serving in the Med. Dept., CAS. Det. 11th Rec. BU162 DB. Discharged Nov. 30, 1918. Died May 18, 1934.

Pivonka, Ernest R., son of Vince and Leona Pivonka, was born June 25, 1942, in La Parita, TX. Educated at La Parita, graduated from Jourdanton, TX, High School. Attended San Antonio College, graduated from A&I University, Kingsville, TX. Enlisted in the USMC, Aug. 22, 1960, in San Francisco, CA. Rank: Cpl. Served as a guard at the U.S. Embassy in Rome, Italy. Received Good Conduct Medal, among others. Honorably discharged Aug. 21, 1964, Brooklyn, NY. Works as an accountant, Chevy Chase, MD. Married Barbara Brizz. Home of record: Fairfax, Virginia. Submitted by his aunt Vlasta Juricek, Jourdanton, TX.

Pivonka, Herbert D., son of Ludwig Pivonka and Frances Hruska, was born Jan. 21, 1920, Caldwell, TX. Education: Through 8th grade at High Prairie School. Enlisted U.S. Army Corps, 1942, Ft. Sam Houston, TX. Theater of Operations: European. Basic training, Camp Roberts, CA; additional training: Camp Butner, NC; Camp Gordon, GA; Ft. Dix, NJ; FL. Served on campaigns in England, France, Belgium, Germany. Medals: ETO Campaign Medal w/4 BSS, CBI Medal, Purple Heart w/1 OLC, BSS, Combat Infantry Badge. WOUNDED IN ACTION twice, France, 1944, Germany, 1944. Honorably discharged 1945, Ft. Sam Houston, TX. Home of record: Caldwell, TX.

Piwetz, Florian W., "Pete," son of William Emil Piwetz and Ludmilla Marek "Millie," was born Feb. 27, 1922, Fayetteville, TX. Graduated Fayetteville High School, University of Houston, B.S., 1950. Enlisted in the U.S. Army Air Corps during WWII on Mar. 30, 1942. After basic training, attended Flight Maintenance and Mechanics School at Biloxi, MS, and Air Gunnery School at Kingman, AZ. Flight Crew Training in the B-26 Martin Marauder Bomber at Barksdale Field, LA. Assigned to duty in the European, African, Middle Eastern Theater of Operations. Ferried a new B-26 from Atlanta, GA, through Miami, Puerto Rico, British Columbia, Brazil, Ascension Island, West Africa, and England to Northern Ireland and became a member of the 599th Bomber Squadron, 397th Bomber Group, 9th Air Force. Participated in air campaigns in Central Europe, Rhineland, Northern France, Normandy, and Ardennes:Alsace. Participated in 65 combat bombing missions as Flight Engineer/Gunner, attacking bridges, ammunition storage, and railroad yards in throughout Occupied France, Normandy, Germany, and Belgium. He made two combat flights on D-Day attacking fortifications near the Normandy beach landings. Awards and decorations: Air Medal w/OLC, EAME Campaign Medal with five BSS, GCM. Discharged June 23, 1945 as a Technical Sgt. Married Effie Ann Jasek, five children: Jackie Piwetz Lemoine, Jan Piwetz Esenwein, Michael J. Piwetz, Mark A. Piwetz, Martin M. Piwetz. Home of record: Houston, TX.

Piwetz, Frank Fred, son of William Emil Piwetz and Ludmilla "Millie" Marek (grandparents: Josef and Agnes Piwetz, Jan and Rosara Marek), was born Feb. 27, 1922, Fayetteville, TX. Graduated Fayetteville High School. Enlisted U.S. Navy, Houston, TX, USAAF, Ft. MacArthur, CA. Theater of Operations: America. Sgt. U.S. Navy Aviation Cadet V5. Medals: American Campaign Medal, GCM, WWII Victory Medal. Honorably discharged Feb. 15, 1946. U.S. Navy-fighter Flight Training (Pilot) June 1942 to Aug. 1943. Flight Training Instructor, USAAF (Pilot) Aug. 1943 to May 1944, USAAF, B-29 Air Crew Gunner, May 1944 to Feb. 1946. Home of record: Fayetteville, TX. Submitted by brother F. W. Piwetz, Houston, TX.

Piwetz, Steven Ludwig, son of William Emil Piwetz and Ludmilla Marek, grandson of Josef and Agnes Piwetz and Jan and Rosara Marek. Education: Graduated Fayetteville High School. Enlisted 1936, TX. Boot camp, San Diego, CA. Chief Petty Officer, Aviation Ordnance. Theater of Operations: WWII, Asiatic Pacific Theater, Korean War. Battles: Midway and Coral Sea, numerous other actions throughout the war. Served in Scouting Sqdn. 3, Fighting Sqdn. 3, Fighting Sqdn. 6 and Carrier Group 5. Served at various times, aboard aircraft carriers USS *Ranger*, USS *Essex*, USS *Valley Forge*, USS *Hancox*, USS *Lexington*, and USS *Saratoga*. Medals: American Defense, Asiatic Pacific w/9 BSS, Navy Unit Commendation, Japanese Occupation, China Service, Korean Service, Presidential Citation, and others. Retired in 1956, after 20 years of service. Died of leukemia, Jan. 20, 1958; buried Fayetteville Catholic Cemetery, TX. Submitted by brother, F. W. Piwetz, Houston, TX.

Plachy, Jerry, served in U.S. Army Corps, WWII. Hometown: Buckholts, Milam Co., TX.

Plachy, Pavel J., was born Jan. 5, 1897, Zarosicich, Moravia. WWI veteran. Died Sept. 3, 1921; buried Holy Cross Catholic Cemetery, Granger, TX.

Plasek, W. W., West, TX. Entered Navy 1944, during WWII. Served in Hawaii. Attained rank of Lt. Discharged 1946.

Plsek, Bennie, of West, TX. WWII veteran.

Plsek, Edward A., West, TX. Entered Army 1941. Attained rank of T/5. Served in Aleutians and Germany. WOUNDED IN ACTION, Germany, 1945. Awarded GCM, Combat Inf. Badge, Purple Heart, AP Ribbon w/1 BSS, ET Ribbon w/2 BSS. Discharged 1945. Buried in St. Mary's Cemetery, West, TX.

Plsek, Robert W., West, TX. Entered AAC, 1940. Served in Australia and N. Guinea. Awarded GCM and AP w/4 Battle Stars. Discharged 1945.

Pochyla, Benjamin H., Waco, TX. Entered Army 1929. Served in Australia, Japan, Korea. Attained rank of Cpl. Awarded DSM, Legion of Merit, AD, AT, AP w/5 Battle Stars, P.L. w/2 Battle Stars, Victory Ribbon.

Pochyla, Fredrick L., Waco, TX. Attained rank of 2nd Lt. in U.S. Armed Forces. Served in Philippine and Japan. Awarded GCM, AT, AP w/1 Battle Star, P.L. w/1 Battle Star, and Victory Ribbon.

Pochyla, Herbert William, son of Mr. and Mrs. H. F. Pochyla. Entered Army 1941. Attained rank of Capt. Served in U.S.A. Discharged 1946.

Podhrasky, Julius, military service veteran. Home of record: Dallas, TX.

Podsednik, Edward A., son of Mr. and Mrs. Joe Podsednik, West, TX. Entered Army 1940. Served in France, England, Belgium, Czechoslovakia. WOUNDED IN ACTION, Belgium. Awarded GCM, Purple Heart, Pres. Cit., six Battle Stars.

Podsednik, Edward Francis, son of Anton J. Podsednik and Annie Vrba, was born Oct. 13, 1919, Tours, TX. Education: Tours, TX, Elementary, West, TX, High School. Enlisted Ft. Sam Houston, TX, U.S. Armed Forces. Attained rank of Staff Sgt, 53rd Bn. Theater of Operations: EAME. Battles: Algeria-French Morocco, Tunisia, Sicily, Rome-Arno, Naples-Foggia. Medals: EAME Campaign Medal w/5 BSS, American Defense Medal, Good Conduct Medal, Purple Heart, WWII Victory Medal, Ribbons. WOUNDED IN ACTION. Honorably discharged Sept. 28, 1945, Ft. Sam Houston, TX. Home of record: West, TX.

Podsednik, Erwin J., Tours, TX. Entered Army in 1940. Served in Philippines and Japan. Awarded AT, AP w/1 BSS, PL w/1 BSS, Victory, and GCM. Attained rank of Pfc. prior to discharge, 1945.

Podsednik, Frank Anton, son of Anton J. and Annie Vrba Podsednik, was born Oct. 7, 1926, at Tours, TX. Attended West High School in West, TX. Enlisted in the Navy in Waco, TX, Oct. 23, 1943. After training in San Digeo, CA, was stationed aboard the USS *Pres. Hayes* (APA#20). Served at Iowa Jima, Okinowa, Guam, Leyte Islands, and New Guinea. Medals: Philippine Liberation Ribbon w/ two stars, Victory Ribbon and Medal, Asiatic Pacific Area with three stars, American Theater Medal, Good Conduct Medal, Campaign Medal, and four Bronze Battle Stars. Was hurt aboard the ship connecting mine cutters to cut enemy mines. Discharged Apr. 19, 1946, in New Orleans, LA. Address of record: Elm Mott, TX.

Podsednik, Johnnie Frank, son of Mr and Mrs Louis C. Podsednik. Born July 8, 1927, in Leroy, TX. Education: four years of college. Enlisted July 1945, in Waco, TX. Served in San Diego, CA, and Long Beach Naval Base, Long Beach, CA. Discharged Jan. 22, 1947, at the rank of PHM 2/C. Home of record: Houston, TX.

Podsednik, Richard A., entered AAC, 1942. Trained in UT, AZ, and DE. Awarded AT, GCM, and Victory Ribbons. Discharged 1945. Rank at time of discharge was Pfc.

Podsednik, Robert August, West, TX. Entered Navy 1945. Served in China, Japan, Pearl Harbor, and San Francisco. Attained rank of S 2/C. Discharged 1946.

Podsednik, Victor, entered Army 1943. Served in Okinawa. Attained rank of T/5. Awarded AT, AP, GCM, and Victory Ribbons.

Podsednik, William, trained in UT, CO, KS. Served during WWII in India, Mariannas. Attained rank of Cpl. Awarded A.T., A.P. w/1 Silver Star, GCM, Dist Unit Badge, Victory Ribbons. Discharged 1946.

Pokladnik, Joann Marie, daughter of Robert Jerry Pokladnik and Helen Ruth Baleja, was born Feb. 19, 1958, Dallas, TX. Graduate: Lake Highlands High School, 1977, Dallas, TX, UTA, TSTI. Enlisted in U.S. Navy, May 9, 1983, Dallas, TX. Assigned to 6th Fleet, Mediterranean Sea. Member of multi-national peacekeeping force with 6th Fleet, Beirut, Lebanon, 1983. Received Navy Expeditionary Medal. Honorably discharged July 15, 1986. Home of record: Dallas, TX.

Pokladnik, Robert Jerry, son of Emil Matt and Marie Lillian Kopecky, was born Mar. 17, 1928, Dallas, TX. Graduate of North Dallas High School, 1946. Enlisted in U.S. Army Corps, Oct. 2, 1950, Dallas, TX. Theater of Operations: Far East Command (Japan and Korea). 40th Infantry Division. Battles: North of 38th Parallel. Medals: Army Occupation Medal (Japan), United Nations Service Medal, Combat Infantry Badge, Korean Service Medal w/1 BSS. Honorably discharged Sept. 19, 1952. Home of record: Dallas, TX.

Pokladnik, Robert Jerry, son of Cyril F. Pokladnik

and Anna Kartous, was born Dec. 24, 1920, Foley, MN. Education: Foley Public Schools, University of MN (1 yr., Foley, MN). Graduated Southern Methodist University, Dallas, TX. Enlisted U.S. Army Reserves, Sept. 7, 1942, San Antonio, TX. Called to active service, Jan. 25, 1943. Assigned to Signal Corps, attached to Air Force. Theater of Operations: EAME. Battles: Normandy, Northern France, Ardennes, Rhineland, Central Europe. Medals: American Defense Service Medal, EAME Campaign Medal w/5 BSS, Good Conduct Medal, Meritorious Unit Award, WWII Victory Medal. Honorable discharged Nov. 10, 1945, Camp Fannin, TX. Home of record: Dallas, TX.

Pokorney, Joe Raymond, son of Mr. and Mrs. Joe A. Pokoroney, Taylor, TX. Education: Taylor High School. Enlisted U.S. Army Corps, 1943. Basic training, Ft. Bragg, NC. Theater of Operations: European. Served in Italy. Medals: ETO Campaign Medal w/4 BSS and ribbon, WWII Victory Medal and ribbon. Attained rank of Cpl. prior to honorable discharge, 1945.

Pokorny, Paul, Jr., son of Paul Pokorny, Sr. and Sophie Steinbach, was born May 4, 1934, Circleville, TX. Education: Circleville, Tyler, Coupland and Taylor TX through 8th grade, finished high school in U.S. Army Corps. Drafted Nov. 8, 1956, Ft. Sam Houston, TX. Rank: Quarter Master, Spec 4. Stationed at Paris, France, in the Communication Zone (COMZ) for approx. 19 months, 1957–1958. Medals: Good Conduct, American Defense, Sharp Shooter. Honorably discharged Nov. 13, 1958. Occupation: construction material supplier. Hobbies: fishing, hunting, golf. Married Bernice Keepac. Home of record: Taylor, TX.

Polansky, Ado Henry, son of Ado E. Polansky and Mary Krajca, was born Nov. 18, 1940. Education: Jourdanton High School, Jourdanton, TX. Enlisted in U.S. Army Corps, Feb. 27, 1962, San Antonio, Bexar, TX. Theater of Operations: CONUS and South Korea. Served with the HHS Battery 1st Bn. 73d Artillery 1st Armored Div., 4th U.S. Army. Assigned to Ft. Leonard Wood, MO, for basic and motor pool mechanic training. Stationed at Camp Pehlman near Munsan-ni, (north of Seoul), Korea, from the summer of 1962 to the summer of 1963. Reassigned to Ft. Hood, TX, until honorably discharged Feb. 26, 1965. Medals: Sharp Shooter (Rifle), Sharp Shooter (M-14). Married Katharyn; two children: Lisa Polansky Bustamente and Robert Polansky, and two grandchildren. Home of record: Jourdanton, TX.

Polansky, Alphonse V., son of Mr. and Mrs. F. Polansky, West, TX. Entered Navy 1945, attained rank of S 2/C. Served in U.S.A. Awarded Victory and A.P. Ribbons.

Polansky, George R., son of Frank C. Polansky and Victoria Snokhous, was born Apr. 8, 1921, West, TX. Attended St. Mary's Catholic School, West, TX. Enlisted in U.S. Army Corps, June 29, 1942, Camp Wolters, TX. Basic training, Camp Carson, CO. Theater of Operations: European. Served in France, Germany, Belgium, Holland and Czechoslovakia, with Co. C, 314th Inf., 79th Div. Decorations: WWII Victory Medal, European Theater Campaign Ribbon W/4 BSS, Combat Infantry Badge. Honorable discharge Nov. 1945. Achieved the rank of T/5. Civilian occupation: cotton gin employee and farmer. Home of record: West, TX.

Polansky, Henry Lee, son of Henry and Mathilda Polansky, was born Aug. 5, 1924, Jourdanton, TX. Education: Sacred Heart Catholic School, Floresville, TX, Pleasanton High School, Pleasanton, TX. Enlisted in U.S. Army Air Corps, 1942, San Antonio, TX. Theater of Operations: America and EAME. Received commission as 2nd Lt. and his wings at Lubbock, TX, Apr. 15, 1944. Then stationed Emporia, KS, prior to overseas duty. Married Laura Louise; one son: Carl Henry Polansky (born 10/13/45, died 10/15/45). Battles: 1st Pilot on a B-24 Liberator Bomber, in action three months, on 8th mission, when plane was damaged over Germany, later crashing in Scotland. KILLED IN ACTION Mar. 31, 1945; buried in American Armed Forces Cemetery, England. Reinterred in Ft. Leavenworth National Cemetery, KS, Aug. 3, 1948. In letters from him written two days before his death, he spoke of victory and returning home.

Polansky, James Frank, son of Ado E. Polansky and Mary Krajca, was born Apr. 22, 1947, Jourdanton, TX. Education: Jourdanton High

School. Enlisted in U.S. Air Force, Nov. 21, 1967, Lackland AFB, San Antonio, TX. Theater of Operations: CONUS and S.E. Asia. Weapons Mechanic, 42nd Munitions Maintenance Sqdn., 4252 Strategic Wing (SAC). Assigned to Lowrey AFB and Carswell AFB prior to assignment in S.E. Asia. Stationed at Kadena AFB, Okinawa, from Dec. 1968 to June 1970. Reassigned to Dyess AFB until honorable discharge, Nov. 19, 1971. Received Air Force Commendation Medal. Home of record: Jourdanton, TX.

Polansky, Louis J., Sr., son of Alois J. Polansky and Johanna Chovanec, was born Mar. 15, 1891, Fayetteville, TX. Education: Fayetteville Chromcik Academy, Hill's Business College, Waco, TX, 1916, Mechanic School, 1917. Physically rejected by the draft board–classed 4D. Enlisted Dec. 13, 1917, in U.S. Aviation Corps. Airplane mechanic during WWI, Love Field, Dallas, TX. Considered a top mechanic. After the war, worked as a mechanic for Smith Ford Motor Company, Taylor, TX. Attained rank of Sgt. Probably discharged about 1919. Died Jan. 13, 1969; buried Fayetteville Catholic Cemetery, Fayetteville, TX. Submitted by son, Louis J. Polansky, Jr. of Fayetteville, TX.

Polansky, Raymond F., son of Mr. and Mrs. Fred Polansky, Mart, TX. Entered Army in 1942. Served European Theater. Awarded seven BSS, Dist. Unit Badge w/2 OLC. Attained rank of S/Sgt. Discharged 1945.

Polasek, Dominic F., WWII veteran. Member, American Legion Post No. 282, Granger, TX.

Polasek, Joe, West, TX, military veteran.

Polasek, John F., was born Aug. 15, 1892, of Corn Hill, Williamson County, TX. Enlisted in U.S. Army Corps, about 1918, from TX. Served in WWI. Civilian occupation: Farmer. Married Frances Lefner; five children: John, Emil, Genevieve, Georgia, Mary. Died Feb. 19, 1970; buried Corn Hill, TX.

Polasek, Johnnie Joe, son of Arnold C. Polasek and Otillia Havran, was born Oct. 24, 1935, La Grange, Fayette, TX. Graduate- La Grange High School, 1954; attended University of Hawaii, Durham's Business School, Austin, TX. Enlisted in USMC at U.S. Naval Center, Austin, TX. Attained rank of Sgt. Meritoriously promoted twice, receipt of letter of Commendation from USMC Division Commander. Theater of Operations: Asiatic-Pacific. Medals: Meritorious Service, Good Conduct. Honorably discharged Sept. 1959. Civilian Occupation: Sales rep for heating and air conditioning wholesale distributor. Married Lorenda Anne Jetter; two sons: Stephen Charles and Edward Gene. Top salesman in U.S. for nationwide wholesale corporation in 1977 and 1978. Home of record: Austin, TX.

Polasek, Johnny, enlisted during WWII, 1941. Assigned to Infantry. Honorably discharged 1943. Submitted by Annie Polasek.

Polk, Henry Thomas, son of Leroy James Polk and Vlasta Shumbera, was born Jan. 27, 1945, Hallettsville, TX. Education: St. Michael Catholic School, Weimar, TX; Bishop Forest High School, Schulenburg, TX; Texas A&M, College Station, TX, B.S., Mechanical Engineering; Oklahoma State University, Stillwater, OK, M.S., Mechanical Engineering; graduate work in Computer Science, one semester at University of Houston, TX. Enlisted Mar. 4, 1969, U.S. Army Corps, La Grange, TX. Theater of Operations: U.S.A. First U.S. Army, Cold Regions Research and Engineering Laboratory. Medals: National Defense Service Medal, Good Conduct Medal, M.M. Badge, M-14. Honorably discharged Mar. 3, 1971. Occupation: Software Development Engineer. Married Mary Catherine Repal; one son: George. Home of record: Houston, TX. Submitted by Vlasta Polk, Weimar, TX.

Polk, Leroy James, son of Adolph Polk and Mary Rainosek, was born Jan. 22, 1918, in the Weimar

area, Colorado Co., TX. Attended St. Michael School in Weimar (GED in 1946), and Blinn Junior College in Brenham, TX. Received orders at Weimar and was inducted at Houston Reception Center, July 9, 1942. As a Tec. 5 served with Co. A Signal Aircraft Warning Bn., Motor Vehicle Mechanic, New Guinea and Luzon (Philippine Islands). Discharged Dec. 25, 1945, Fort Sam Houston, San Antonio, TX. Medals: Carbine Sharpshooter, American Theater Campaign Medal, Good Conduct Medal, Asiatic-Pacific Campaign Medal with two BSS, Philippine Liberation Ribbon, Victory Ribbon, one Service Stripe, three Overseas Service Bars. Married Vlasta Shumbera; two sons. Employed as motor vehicle mechanic, and in 1953 went to work for a gas refinery. Retired in 1980 for health reasons. Hobbies: cattle ranching, welding, and woodworking. Home of record: Weimar, TX.

Pomykal, Jerry, was born 1895, served in U.S. Army during WWI. Died 1983; buried in West Brethren Cemetery, West, TX.

Pomykal, Woodrow Amos, son of Adolph John Pomykal and Anna Malcik, was born Apr. 13, 1918, at Rosebud, TX. Graduated from Rosebud High School and attended Texas A&M College at College Station. Enlisted in the U.S. Army Air Corps at Los Angeles, CA, during WWII. Served in both the American and the European, African, and Middle Eastern Theaters of Operations as a member of the 306th Bomber Group. Attained the rank of Technical Sgt. Participated in air campaigns in Central Europe, Rhineland, Normandy, Northern France, and Ardennes:Alsace. Decorations include the Air Medal, American Campaign Medal, European African Middle Eastern Campaign Medal with five campaign stars, Good Conduct Medal, and WWII Victory Medal. Discharged Nov. 19, 1945, at Ft. MacArthur, CA. Home of record: Ft. Worth, TX.

Poncik, Anton, Jr., son of Anton Poncik, Sr. and Josephine Kopecky, was born July 25, 1916, Muldoon, TX. Education: Gobble Creek School, Wharton County, TX. Inducted May 18, 1942, Houston, TX. Assigned to 147th Armored Signal Bn., U.S. Army Corps, Truck Driver Light, Messenger Dispatcher. Battles: Normandy, France, Belgium, Holland, Germany. Theaters of Operation: American, EAME. Medals: American Theater Campaign Medal, EAME Campaign Medal w/5 BSS, Good Conduct Medal, WWII Victory Medal, one Service Stripe, two Overseas Stripes, Lapel Button, Ribbons. Honorably discharged Dec. 3, 1945, Ft. Sam Houston, TX. Died June 17, 1981, El Campo, TX. Submitted by daughter Bernice Poncik Kocian of Wharton, TX.

Poncik, Daniel, son of Joseph Poncik and Albina Sula, was born Oct. 13, 1932, Frydek, Austin, TX. Enlisted in U.S. Army Corps, attaining rank of Pfc. Battles: Korea. Died Sept. 28, 1983; buried St. Mary's Catholic Cemetery, Frydek, TX.

Poncik, Frank Alvin, son of Anton J. Poncik and Josephine Kopecky, (7th child of 10) was born Moravia, TX, Mar. 19, 1911. Education: finished 7th grade. Drafted, Feb. 1942. Basic training, San Francisco, CA. 7th Div., Com 184th Inf. Theater of Operations: Asiatic-Pacific. Campaigns: South Pacific, Kwajalein, Leyte, Paro, Ponsun, Okinawa. WOUNDED IN ACTION. Medals: Purple Heart, Asiatic-Pacific Campaign Medal w/BSS, WWII Victory Medal, and others. Honorable discharge Oct. 1945. Moved to Houston, TX, to work. Married Laura Naclarik; two children. Owned business as a landscape artist. Home of record: Houston, TX.

Poncik, John P., son of Peter and Vinnie Poncik, was born Sept. 15, 1929, Ellinger, TX. Earned GED certificate, July 1952; Sam Houston State University, BBA degree, 1958. Enlisted Jan. 4, 1950, Houston, TX, USMC. Served in Korea from Sept. 1950–Nov. 1951 with First Marine Air Wing. Landed at Inchon, Korea, and was stationed at Kimpo Airfield. Later, participated in amphibious landing at Wonsan and in operations at Hamhung and Hungnam, North Korea. Medals: Korean Service Medal, Presidential Unit Citation Medal, Army Distinguished Unit Citation, National Defense Service Medal, Korean Presidential Unit Citation Medal, United Nations Service Medal,

Good Conduct Medal. Honorably discharged with rank of Staff Sgt., Jan. 3, 1955, at Marine Corps Air Station at Cherry Point, NC. Married Ruth. Home of record: Galveston, TX.

Poncik, Victor J., son of Lewis Poncik and Emma Lednicky, was born Feb. 6, 1917, near Granger, Williamson Co., TX. Graduated from high school and attended Hillsboro Junior College. Attended the U.S. Air Force Institute of Technology. Enlisted in the U.S. Army Air Corps during WWII. Served in the Asiatic Pacific Theater of Operations. Assignments encompassed Java, Australia, New Guinea, and other parts of the Far East. On active duty during the Korean and Viet Nam Conflicts. Flew B-17s, B-24s, B-25s, and B-29s, and was also qualified in jet aircraft. Decorations include the Silver Star Medal with OLC, Distinguished Flying Cross, Air Medal, and Distinguished Unit Citation with three OLC. Retired from the U.S. Air Force on Feb. 1, 1968, at Scott AFB, IL with the rank of Lt. Col. Home of record: Carrollton, TX.

Popp, Albert Edward, son of Adolph J. Popp and Vincie Horsak, was born Oct. 9, 1922, West, TX. High school education. Enlisted in U.S. Navy, Dec. 7, 1942, during WWII, San Antonio, TX; sworn in at Houston, TX. Basic training, Great Lakes Naval Training Center. Theater of Operations: Asiatic-Pacific. Stationed on heavy cruiser, the USS *Chester*. Battles: Iwo Jima, Betio Island, Tarawa Atoll, Gilbert Islands, Saipan, Guadalcanal, Marianas, Truk, Palou, Yip, Ulithi, Bonins, Kurile Island, Moleai, West Carolines, Philippine Islands, Leyte, Luzon, Marshall, and others. Medals: WWII Victory Medal, American Campaign Medal, Asiatic-Pacific Campaign Medal, GCM, Ribbons, others. Honorable discharge Nov. 8, 1945. Two children: Christine and Michael. Died Apr. 17, 1960; buried in Ft. Sam Houston National Cemetery, San Antonio, TX, with full military honors. Submitted by Mary Popp, San Antonio, TX.

Popp, Billy Adolf, son of Adolf R. Popp and Mattie Turek, was born Aug. 11, 1926, Abbott, TX. Graduate, 1943, Abbott High School, Four C Business College, 1947. Enlisted Abbott, TX, WWII. U.S. Army Corps. Attained rank of Technical Sgt. Theater of Operations: Asiatic-Pacific. Battles: Philippine Liberation. Medals: Philippine Liberation, Asiatic-Pacific Campaign w/BSS, WWII Victory, Rifle Expert, Good Conduct. Honorably discharged Nov. 30, 1946. Died of heart attack, Aug. 30, 1977. Buried at Ridge Park Cemetery, Hillsboro, Hill, TX. Submitted by Mrs. Bernice Popp, Whitney, TX.

Popp, Charles A., son of Albin E. Popp and Mary Novotny, was born Nov. 14, 1943, San Antonio, TX. Graduated high school and one year of college. Enlisted in U.S. Navy, Nov. 14, 1962, San Antonio, TX. Boot camp, San Diego, CA. Sent to Naval Air Technical Training Center, Memphis, TN. Served two years as Aviation Electronics Technician, Petty Officer 2/C, Aircraft Carrier, USS *Bon Homme Richard*, off the coast of Viet Nam with the VA 192 world famous Golden Dragons. (Attack Squadron of the A-4 Skyhawk) Decorations: Expeditionary Service Medal, National Defense Service Medal, Good Conduct Medal. Honorably discharged Oct. 15, 1966. Home of record: San Antonio, TX.

Popp, Edmund L., Abbott, TX. Entered Army, 1940. Served in EAME Theater. Attained rank of S/Sgt. WOUNDED IN ACTION, Italy, 1943. Awarded GCM, EAME Ribbon w/4 Battle Stars, Purple Heart. Discharged 1945.

Popp, Ernest F., West, TX. Entered Army 1940, attained rank of T/Sgt. Served N. Africa and Italy. Awarded GCM and ET Ribbon w/3 Battle Stars. Discharged 1945.

Popp, Ernest W., son of Adolph J. Popp and Vincie Horsak, was born Mar. 25, 1916, West, TX. Graduated high school. Inducted into U.S. Army Corps, Jan. 28, 1941, Ft. Sam Houston, TX. Theater of Operations: European, 75th Inf. Div. Participated in the Battle of the Ardennes (Battle of the Bulge), the Rhineland and Central Europe. Decorations: American Defense Service Ribbon, American Theater Campaign Ribbon, EAME Campaign Ribbon w/3 BSS, GCM, WWII Victory Ribbon and Combat Infantry Badge, one Service Bar and two Overseas Stripes. Returned to USA, Nov. 1945. Honorably discharged Dec. 1945. Home of record: San Antonio, TX.

Popp, Gordon Franklin, son of Joe L. Popp and Betty Valek, was born Apr. 2, 1933, at West, TX. Attended St. John's High School in Ennis, TX. Enlisted in the USMC in Dallas, TX, and served in the Korea and Viet Nam Theater of Operations as a M/Sgt. Fought in battles in the CCF Winter Offensive 1950 and the CCF Spring Offensive 1951, Khe-San-Hvc-Chu Bai. Discharged Sept. 1, 1958, at Cherry Point, NC. Medals: PUC with three Stars, Marine Corps Good Conduct with five Stars, National Defense, Korea Medal with two Stars, United Nations Medal, Korean PUC with two Stars, Viet Nam Medal with three Stars, Letter of Commendation. Retired from the Marine Corps with 20 years service. Home of record: Crozet, VA.

Popp, Henry John, was born June 12, 1937, served in U.S. Coast Guard, attaining rank of EN2. Died Jan. 29, 1991. Buried in West Brethren Cemetery, West, TX.

Popp, Joseph Lloyd, son of Frank Popp and Emma Hessel, was born Oct. 1, 1906, in West, TX. Graduated from West High School and enlisted in the Air Corps in West, TX. Served as a Cpl. in the Invasion of France, Battle of Bulge, Battle of St. Lo. WOUNDED IN ACTION two times. Discharged on Oct. 12, 1945, at the AAF Regional Hospital, San Antonio, TX. Medals: Good Conduct, European Theater with three Stars, Purple Heart with one Star, American Theater.

Popp, Kenneth Joe, son of Joe L. Popp and Betty Valek, was born Feb. 18, 1930, in West, TX. Graduated from St. John High, Ennis, TX, and attended Baylor University for three years. Enlisted in Dallas, TX, and was a M/Sgt in the USMCR. Fought in the Invasion of Inchon, Battle for Seoul, Chosin Reservoir, CCF Spring Offensive, 1951. WOUNDED IN ACTION twice. Discharged Aug. 1, 1977, Waco, TX. Medals: Purple Heart with one Star, PUC with three Stars, Marine Corp Good Conduct, Marine Corp Reserve with four Stars, National Defense, Navy Occupation (Japan), Victory Medal American Theater, Korean medal with four Stars, United Nations, Korean PUC with two Stars. Retired from Marine Corp with 30 years service. Home of record: Waco, TX.

Pospisil, John Anton, son of Karel Pospisil and Anezka Janosec, was born Jan. 22, 1922, Corn Hill, Williamson Co., TX. Enlisted in U.S. Army Corps, during WWII. Attained rank of Sgt. Served in Co. L, 87th Inf. Served in WWII, BSM. Honorably discharged. Employed by Plastic Laminate Manufacturer. Married Margaret J.; one son: John. Died Apr. 7, 1962, Corn Hill, TX.

Pospistil, Charlie F., son of Mr. and Mrs. Karel J. Pospistil, Granger, TX. Education: Holy Trinity School. Enlisted U.S. Army Corps, 1941; basic training, Camp Bowie, TX. Theater of Operations: EAME. Served in Africa, Italy, France, Germany, Austria. Medals: EAME Theater Campaign Medal w/BSS, Pre-Pearl Harbor Medal and Ribbon, Good Conduct Medal, Silver Star, WWII Victory Medal, Ribbons. Attained rank of Pfc. prior to honorable discharge, 1945.

Pospistil, John A., son of Mr. and Mrs. Karel J. Pospistil. Education: Holy Trinity School. Enlisted U.S. Army Corps, 1942; basic training, Camp Hale, CO. Theater of Operations: Asiatic-Pacific, American, EAME. Served in Kiska, Italy, and other places. Medals: American Theater Campaign Medal, EAME Theater Campaign Medal, Asiatic-Pacific Theater Campaign Medal, Good Conduct Medal, Infantry Combat Badge, Ribbons. Attained rank of Sgt. prior to honorable discharge, 1945.

Post/Pustejovsky, Melvin J., son of Albert and Cecelia Pustejovsky, was born Dec. 12, 1916, in Moulton, TX. Graduated from Moulton High School. On Mar. 21, 1942, enlisted at Fort Sam Houston, in the U.S. Army Air Corps, 493rd Bomb Sqdn., and served in Burma and India for 30 months. Discharged Jan. 6, 1946. Medals: Distinguished Unit Badge, American Theater, Good Conduct Medal, Asiatic Pacific Theater, Victory Medal. Home of record: Houston, TX.

Powell, Richard Arlan, son of Pete Powell and Wilhelimina Kilnar, was born May 14, 1942, Wharton, TX. BBA Degree, Southwest Texas University. Enlisted Mar. 1965, U.S. Army Corps, Houston, TX, during Viet Nam War. Served in U.S. Army, U.S. Army of the Pacific, U.S. Army of Hawaii. Honorably discharged Apr. 1967. Home of record: Wharton, TX.

Prachyl, Wesley, son of William A. Prachyl and Mary Vrana, was born Sept. 14, 1930, Ennis, TX. Graduate of St. John Catholic High School, Ennis, TX. Drafted Feb. 11, 1952, USMC; sworn in, Dallas, TX. Basic training, San Diego, CA. Stationed: Camp Pendleton, CA, Tank Driver, 3rd Marine Div., 7th Tank Bn. Assigned to Korea, Mar. 1953. With First Marine Div. along Imjin River. Armored amphibious vehicles were set up as artillery. In combat until ceasefire. Remained tuntil discharge. WOUNDED IN ACTION, eye injury while on training maneuver in Korea. Taken by helicopter to Hospital Ship, USS *Consolation*. Stayed on hospital ship one month. Medals: Sharpshooter Award, United Nations Service Medal, National Defense Service Medal, Korean Service Medal w/2 BSS. Attained rank of Cpl. Honorably discharged Feb. 4, 1954, Treasure Island, San Francisco, CA. Married Nov. 20, 1951, Dorothy Vavra; three children: Michael, Cathy, and Stephen. Retired from Ennis Business Forms after 32 years service, Linotype operator. Home of record: Ennis, TX.

Prasifka, Joseph, was born May 30, 1921. Served in U.S. Navy during WWII, attained rank of MM2. Died Aug. 28, 1990. Buried in St. Mary's Cemetery, West, TX.

Prasifka, Martha Mynar, Texas WWII veteran, U.S. Women's Army Corps. See Mynar, Martha Prasifka.

Prasifka, Method Henry, West, TX. Entered Navy 1942. Attained rank of Coxswain. Served China. Awards: Philippine Liberation w/1 BSS, and Victory Ribbon. Discharged 1946. Died Dec. 9, 1972; buried in St. Mary's Cemetery, West, TX.

Prasifka, Robert W., West, TX. Entered Navy, 1944. Served in Japan, China and Pacific, attaining rank of S 1/C. Awards: AT, AP, Philippine Liberation and Victory Ribbons. Discharged1946.

Pratka, Allen J., son of Joe T. Pratka and Frances H., was born June 19, 1930, Ganado, TX. Education: B.S., Aero Engineering, University of WY. Enlisted Houston, TX, Jan. 16, 1951, U.S. Air Force. Awarded wings and officer commission, Oct. 25, 1952. Rank: Maj. Flew combat in Korea 1953, and Viet Nam 1967. Married Dorothy L.; five children, six grandchildren. Retired. Home of record: Pleasanton, TX.

Prause, Glen A., son of Mr. and Mrs. Glen J. Prause, was born June 15, 1928, La Grange, TX. Graduated La Grange High School. Enlisted in U.S. Army Corps, Ft. Sam Houston, TX, 1948. Attained rank of Master Sgt. Theater of Operations: Japan and Korea. Honorably discharged in 1950 and reenlisted in 1950, Occupation Army in Japan. Honorably discharged Oct. 18, 1952. Battles: Korea. Decorations: Korean Service Medal w/1 Bronze Service Star, United Nations Service Medal, Army Occupation Medal (Japan). Home of record: La Grange, TX.

Prcin, Anton, WWII veteran of Granger, TX.

Prcin, Aug J., son of Joseph Frank Prcin and Millie Volcik, was born Jan. 9, 1924, Williamson Co., TX. Education: Hare and Friendship schools. Enlisted Mar. 15, 1943, U.S. Army Corps, Ft. Sam Houston, TX. Assigned to 37th Div., L Co., 145th Inf. Attained rank of S/Sgt. Served during WWII, WOUNDED IN ACTION. Theater of Operations: Asiatic-Pacific. Battles: Northern Solomons, Luzon. Medals: BSS Medal, Purple Heart, Asiatic Pacific Campaign Medal w/2 BSS, Philippine Liberation Medal w/1 BSS, Good Conduct Medal, WWII Victory Ribbon, four overseas service stripes. Honorably discharged Dec. 23, 1945. Married Willadeen Wernl; two children, four grandchildren. Retired TV electrician, May 1, 1986. Home of record: Taylor, TX.

Prihoda, Frank J., son of Joseph and Julia Prihoda, was born Jan. 22, 1913, Flatonia, TX. Enlisted U.S. Army Corps, Ft. Sam Houston, TX. Theater of Operations: EAME. Assigned to 5th Armored Div., Co. A, 22 Armored Engineers. Battles: Normandy, Northern France, Ardennes, Rhineland, Central Europe. Medals: EAME Campaign Medal w/5 BSS, Good Conduct Medal, WWII Victory Medal, Ribbons. Honorable discharge Oct. 10, 1945. Died June 1, 1983. Submitted by widow, Mrs. Frank Prihoda, Flatonia, TX.

Prihoda, Frank John, son of Martin and Rosalie Prihoda, was born Oct. 27, 1918, West Point, Fayette Co., TX. Education: Kirtley, TX, through 6th grade. Enlisted in U.S. Army Corps, May 12, 1942, Ft. Sam Houston, TX. Theater of Operations: EAME. Battles: WWII, Central Europe, Tunisia, Sicily, Normandy. Medals: EAME Campaign Medal w/8 BSS and Bronze Arrowhead, Good Conduct Medal, Purple Heart (Dec. 1, 1944), BSS (July 9, 1945). WOUNDED IN ACTION June 20, 1944, EAME. Assigned to Anti-Tank Co., 60th Inf., H1 9th Inf. Div. Overseas from Oct. 23, 1942–Sept. 9, 1945. Honorable discharge Sept. 17, 1945, Ft. Sam Houston, TX, at the rank of Tech. Sgt. Married Edith Srubar, Apr. 15, 1947; two daughters: Barbara Ann Prihoda Kneupper and Patricia Jean Prihoda Schmedding. Died Apr. 24, 1982, Santa Rosa Hospital, San Antonio, TX. Buried Apr. 28, 1982, Ft. Sam Houston National Cemetery, TX. Submitted lovingly in his memory by Edith Prihoda.

Prikyl, Robert W., son of Mr. and Mrs. Frank Prikyl, West, TX. Entered Army 1941. Served during WWII in Pacific, attaining rank of Pfc. Awards: AP w/3 Battle Stars, AD, Victory Ribbons, Unit Cit. Bar. Discharged 1945.

Prikryl, Ignatius R. "Ike," son of Rufus W. Prikryl and Amalia Jasek. Education: St. Cyril's Catholic School, Granger High School. Married Gertye Maye Pekar. Enlisted U.S. Army Corps, 1942, San Antonio, TX. Basic training, Camp Robinson, AZ; further training, FL. Theater of Operations: EAME. Served with 37th General Hospital in Africa and Italy. Medals: EAME Theater Campaign Medal w/2 BSS and ribbon, Good Conduct Medal and ribbon, WWII Victory Medal and ribbon. Attained rank of T/5 prior to honorable discharge, 1946.

Prikryl, John William, son of Rufus W. Prikryl and Amalia Jasek, was born Nov. 24, 1921, Granger, Williamson Co., TX. Education: St. Cyril's Catholic School, Granger, TX, High School, 1940. Enlisted in U.S. Army Corps, Oct. 21, 1942, San Antonio, TX. Basic training, Camp Rucker, AL; further training, Camp Pickett, VA. Theater of Operations: ETO. Tank Driver. Fought in Battle of the Bulge, France, Omaha Beach. WOUNDED IN ACTION July 11, 1944, Battle of the Bulge. Sent to England to recover; rejoined Tank Bn., 1944. Medals: ETO Campaign Medal w/4 BSS, WWII Victory Medal, Purple Heart, Bronze Arrowhead, Presidential Citation (among others), together with Ribbons. Attained rank of T/4 (Sgt.) prior to being honorably discharged Nov. 1, 1945. Civilian Occupation: farmer, cafe owner, and operator, rural mail carrier. Retired Nov. 1987. Married Marilyn Emily Sturm; three children: Daniel, James, and Joyce. All District Guard in high school. Hobbies: fishing, baseball, football. Home of record: Taylor, TX.

Prikryl, Rudolph L., son of Andrew Prikryl and Albina Blahuta, was born Apr. 23, 1920, Penelope, TX. Education: Penelope School, TX. Inducted in U.S. Army Corps, July 10, 1944. Assigned to Co. I, 21st Inf. Regt. Basic training, Camp Wolters, TX. Overseas, Dec. 31, 1944 to Southern Philippines, Mindanao, occupied Japan. Theater of Operations: Asiatic-Pacific. Medals: Asiatic-Pacific Campaign Medal w/1 BSS, Good Conduct Medal, two overseas service bars, WWII Victory Ribbon, Philippine Liberation Ribbon w/1 BSS. Honorably discharged Feb. 3, 1946. Died Oct. 14, 1982; buried Moore Memorial Gardens, Arlington, TX. Submitted by C. M. Prikryl, West, TX.

Prikryl, Rufus Raymond, Sr., son of Rufus William Prikryl and Amalia Jasek, was born Aug. 12, 1916, Granger, TX. Graduated Granger High School, 1936. Enlisted in U.S. Army Corps, Mar. 19, 1942, Ft. Sam Houston, TX. 57MM Gunner, EAME Theater of Operations. Battles: WWII, Normandy, Northern France, Rhineland. Decorations: EAME Campaign Medal, Central Europe w/4 BSS, Purple Heart, WWII Victory Medal. WOUNDED IN ACTION, EAME, Dec. 18, 1944. Honorably discharged Oct. 23, 1945. Farmer until retirement on Oct. 28, 1982. Likes hunting and fishing. Married Mary H. Mikeska; two children: Rufus Raymond Prikryl, Jr., Rebecca Barbara Prikryl Beck. Home of record: Granger, TX.

Prnka, Frank, West, TX, military veteran.

Prnka, George, of West, TX. WWII veteran, U.S. Army Air Corps. Theater of Operations: EAME. Fought in Africa.

Prochaska, Bessie Maly, see Maly, Bessie.

Prokop, Henry, served June 1945–Sept. 1946, USMC, during WWII. Name is on monument erected by St. Mary's Catholic Church, Frydek, Tx, in thanksgiving for the return of 75 parishioners who served in WWII, 1941-1945.

Provasnik, Cyril, WWII veteran of Granger, TX.

Provazek, Jim F., attained the rank of Pfc. and served in the U.S. Army Corps during WWII. Submitted by Evelyn Vecera, Bellaire, TX.

Provazek, Joe D., son of Charlie and Anna Provazek, was born May 15, 1931, in Cameron, TX. Attended school in Cameron and Seaton and two years at M.C.C. College, Waco, and Barber College, Dallas. Enlisted in Temple, and served in Frankfurt, Germany, receiving several medals. While in Germany was stationed near the Czech border. Discharged Apr. 1956. A barber for 37 years, retiring in 1986. Hobbies: fishing and hunting. Married to Ethel Provazek; one daughter. Home of record: China Springs, TX.

Provaznik, Cyril M., son of Mr. and Mrs. John Provaznik, Granger, TX, was born July 6, 1914. Education: Granger High School. Enlisted U.S. Army Corps, 1945; basic training, Ft. Sam Houston, TX. Rank: Sgt. Theater of Operations: Asiatic-Pacific. Served in Philippines. Japanese PRISONER OF WAR, four years. Medals: Philippine Defense Ribbon, Pres. Citation w/2 OLC, Purple Heart, Combat Infantry Badge, Asiatic-Pacific Theater Campaign Medal w/1 BSS, Philippine Liberation Medal, and Good Conduct Medal. WOUNDED IN ACTION, 1942, Bataan. Died Sept. 6, 1975. Buried Holy Cross Catholic Cemetery, Granger, TX.

Provaznik, Joe, son of Mr. and Mrs. John Provaznik, Granger, TX. Education: Granger High School. Enlisted U.S. Army Corps, 1944; basic training, Camp Roberts, CA. Theater of Operations: Asiatic-Pacific. Served in Manila, Kure Naval Base, Japan. Medals: Asiatic- Pacific Theater Campaign Medal, WWII Victory Medal.

Pustejovsky, Albin J., Jr., son of Albin J. Pustejovsky, Sr. and Leona Hykel, was born Feb. 6, 1948, at Waco, TX. Enlisted in the Armed Services at Key West, Florida, during the Viet Nam Conflict. Discharged in 1969 in CA. Home of record: Dallas, TX.

Pustejovsky, Alois R., son of Joe Pustejovsky and Julia Peterek, was born June 20, 1916, TX. Enlisted in U.S. Army Corps, Apr. 4, 1945. Theater of Operations: Asiatic-Pacific. Army of Occupation, Japan. Medals: Asiatic-Pacific Campaign Ribbon, Army Occupation Ribbon, Japan, WWII Victory Ribbon, Overseas Service Bar. Honorable discharge Aug. 12, 1946. Married Bertha Machala; two daughters. Lifetime member of VFW. Died May 20, 1984, Houston, TX. Family's home of record: Houston, TX. Submitted by Joe Ann Fabrygel, Needville, TX.

Pustejovsky, Bernard R., son of Mr. and Mrs. Julius Pustejovsky of Abbott, TX. Entered Army 1944; attained rank of Pfc. Awards: Victory, and AT Ribbon. Discharged 1946.

Pustejovsky, Daniel, son of Joe D. Pustejovsky and Mary Kolar, was born on Aug. 28, 1926, in Abbott, TX. Graduated from Abbott High School, attended North Texas Agricultural College in Arlington, TX, and Texas A&M University at College Station, TX. Enlisted in U.S. Navy in Mar. 1944 at Dallas, TX, during WWII. Aviation Cadet at North Texas Agricultural College, Arlington, TX, Naval Air Station, Grand Prairie, TX, and at

Pre-Flight School, St.Mary's College, Orinda, CA. Separated from active service on Oct. 25, 1945, and from the reserves in Aug. 1949. Married Flo Marie Thompson; ten children: five sons and five daughters, twenty grandchildren. Semi-retired farmer who grew cotton, grain, and cattle. Home of record: Hillsboro, Hill Co., TX.

Pustejovsky, Frank Joe, Jr., son of Frank Joe Pustejovsky, Sr. and Josephine Chasak, was born Mar. 28, 1946, in Cameron, TX. Attended school at Holland, TX. Enlisted in U.S. Army on Apr. 16, 1968. Served in Viet Nam in 1967-1968 as a Rifleman in the 7th Cavalry, 2nd Bn., 1st Cavalry Div. (Airmobile). Decorations: Air Medal, Good Conduct Medal, Viet Nam Service Medal, Republic of Viet Nam Campaign Medal, National Defense Service Medal, Combat Infantryman Badge, Viet Nam Gallantry Cross w/Palm, and other weapon qualification badges. Separated from service on Apr. 16, 1970. Married Mary Jane Maresh. Employed by IBM. Enjoys street rodding (building hot rods). Home of record: Pflugerville, TX.

Pustejovsky, Jerry H., son of Aug. Pustejovsky and Stevie Snokhus, was born July 15, 1922, Penelope, TX. Education: through 10th grade at Penelope High School. Enlisted U.S. Army Air Corps, Waco, TX. Assigned to 1304th AA Base Unit, Bengal Wing, India. Theater of Operations: CBI. Attained rank of Cpl. before honorable discharge. Awards: WWII Victory Ribbon, American Theater Campaign Ribbon, Asiatic-Pacific Theater Campaign Ribbon w/2 BSS and Medal, District Unit Badge. Died Sept. 19, 1972.

Pustejovsky, John P., was born June 25, 1893. Served in U.S. Armed Forces during WWI, 1917–1918, attaining rank of S/Sgt. in Co. A, 111th Engrs., 36th Div. Member of SPJST Lodge 20, Granger, TX. Died July 19, 1972; buried in Lady Fatima Cemetery, Abbott, TX.

Pustejovsky, Leonard Alois, son of Joseph Pustejovsky and Julia Peterek, was born Apr. 22, 1925, Wallis, TX. Enlisted in U.S. Army Corps, Mar. 10, 1944. Theater of Operations: Asiatic-Pacific. Battles: Battle of Luzon, WWII. Medals: BSS, WWII Victory Medal, Sharpshooter Medal, Squad Leader Medal, Good Conduct Medal, and Combat Infantry Badge. Rank: Staff Sgt. Squad leader for Infantry Unit. Was in combat for 654 days–from Australia to Japan. Supervised squad of 12 men in Technical Employment to destroy enemy personnel and to assist in the capture and holding of enemy installations. Honorable discharge May 1, 1946. Married Mildred Fabrygel; three children. Member of Holy Family Catholic Church, Bay City, TX, and VFW. Home of record: Bay City, TX.

Pustejovsky, Raymond Charlie, son of Aug Pustejovsky and Stevie Snokhus, was born June 4, 1925, Penelope, TX. Education: through tenth grade, Penelope High School. Enlisted in U.S. Army Corps, Muskogee, OK, 1943. Attained rank of Pfc. Assigned to Co. C, 359th Inf. Reg., 90th Div. Fought in battle at Billinger, Germany. KILLED IN ACTION Dec. 10, 1944. Awards: Purple Heart, European Theater w/2 Battle Stars, Good Conduct Medal, Infantry Badge. Buried in St. Mary's Cemetery, West, TX.

Pustejovsky, Raymond P., son of Raymond A. and Rosa Pustejovsky, was born Aug. 15, 1946, El Campo, TX. Graduate of Louise School, W.C. Junior College, 2 years. Enlisted in Wharton, TX, W.S. Army Reserve. Attained rank of SP/5. Stationed USARERU Medical Laboratory, Landstuhl, Germany. Medals: National Defense Service Medal, M-14 Marksman Medal, Ribbons. Honorable discharge Feb. 28, 1971. Home of record: Louise, TX.

Pustejovsky, Richard R., son of Mr. and Mrs. Ray W. Pustejovsky, Granger, TX. Education: Granger High School. Enlisted in U.S. Navy, 1943; basic training, San Diego, CA, during WWII. Medals: WWII Victory Medal, and others. Attained rank of S 1/C prior to honorable discharge, 1945.

Rab, Adolph E., son of John Rab and Agnes Barta, was born June 13, 1910, in Praha, TX. Attended Novohrad School. Participated in battles of Anzio, Cassino, and Rome. KILLED IN ACTION Dec. 27, 1944, in Northern Italy. Serving as cannoneer when an enemy shell landed in nearby foxhole. Posthumously received a Purple Heart. Rank: Pfc. Buried in a military cemetery in Italy.

Rabel, Henry, of Granger, TX. Served in U.S. Navy.

Rabel, Jerry, of Granger, TX. Served in U.S. Armed Forces.

Rabel, Joe, of Granger, TX. Served in U.S. Navy.

Rainosek, Daniel Lawrence, son of A. C. Rainosek and Elizabeth Svrcek. Education: La Grange High School, TX, 1950–1952. Served two years Army Reserve Corps of Engineers. Enlisted Sept. 9, 1952, San Antonio, TX, U.S. Air Force. Served at Bergstrom AFB, Austin, TX. Honorably discharged Oct. 1953. Home of record: Austin, TX.

Rainosek, Edward A., Sr., son of Anton Rainosek, Sr. and Filomena Steffek, was born Sept. 24, 1910, La Grange, TX. Education: La Grange High School. Enlisted Feb. 23, 1937, Ft. Sam Houston, TX, U.S. Army Corps. Served at Ft. D. A. Russell, Randolph Field, Lowery Field, CO, Barksdale, LA, Ellington AFB, TX. Medals: Expert Gunner, American Defense, American Theater, GCM, WWII Victory, Korean Service, United Nations Service, National Defense, NCO Leadership Academy, GCM. Attained rank of Master Sgt. Died Oct. 22, 1987. Buried Forest Park Cemetery, Houston, TX. Submitted by Evelyn Vecera, Bellaire, TX.

Rainosek, Ivan, son of Anton Rainosek, Sr. and Filomena Steffek, was born Aug. 14, 1914, and reared in La Grange, TX. Attended La Grange High School. Enlisted in Army, 1942. Trained at Camp Shelby, MS, AZ, and NY. Served in Africa and Italy. Awards: GCM, European Theater w/3 BSS, Com. Infantry Badge and Purple Heart. MISSING IN ACTION Oct. 23, 1944. Official death recorded Oct. 24, 1945. KILLED IN ACTION, near Poianoro, Italy. Assigned to Co. B, 339th Inf. 38, 157, 843. Attained rank of Sgt. Submitted by Evelyn Vecera, Bellaire, TX.

Recek, Anton H., son of John Recek and Adela Kubala, was born Dec. 4, 1921, in La Grange, TX. Attended the Hostyn School. Enlisted in the U.S. Army on Sept. 28, 1942, during WWII. Served in the Asiatic-Pacific Theater of Operations and participated in operations in China, Burma, and India. Awards and decorations include the BSS, American Campaign Medal, Asiatic Pacific Campaign Medal with campaign star, Good Conduct Medal, Distinguished Unit Badge, and WWII Victory Medal. Separated from the service on Nov. 27, 1945, at Camp Fannin, TX. Home of record: La Grange, TX.

Recek, Peter, son of John Recek and Magdalene Krahulik, was born Apr. 22, 1896, St. Mary's (near Hallettsville), Lavaca Co., TX. Education: Vysehrad School near Hallettsville, TX. Enlisted during WWI in U.S. Army Corps; assigned to 517 Motor Truck Co. Theater of Operation: European. Rank: Pvt. Medals: ETO Campaign Medal, American Expeditionary Medal, WWI Victory Medal. Honorably discharged. Died May 8, 1920 of ruptured appendix. Buried St. Mary's Cemetery near Hallettsville, TX. There is a photo of him on his tombstone. Submitted by Shirley Drexler Moczygemba, Yorktown, TX.

Recek, Raymond, of West, TX, WWII veteran.

Regmund, Jerry, son of Henry Regmund and Barbara Kosarek, was born Jan. 26, 1915, Bryan, TX. Education: Corpus Christi, TX, High School, Texas A&M, 1938, Commanding General Staff School, Ft. Leavenworth, KS, and Ft. Monroe, VA. Enlisted in Army Reserves, called to active duty Aug. 1, 1940. Theater of Operations: U.S.A. Attained rank of Col. before honorable discharge on Feb. 6, 1946. Died July 14, 1973. Home of record for widow, Mrs. Jerry Regmund: Corpus Christi, TX. Submitted by Erwin E. Krejci, brother-in-law, Corpus Christi, TX.

Regmund, John W., Jr., son of John W. Regmund, Sr. and Frances Marek, was born Corpus Christi, Nueces Co., TX. Education: Corpus Christi High School and University of Cincinnati. Commissioned as Lt. in USAF, Ft. Sam Houston, TX. Bombardier on a B-26 in the European Theater of Operations. KILLED IN ACTION, Mar. 1945; interred in France. Submitted by cousin, Erwin E. Krejci, Corpus Christi, TX.

Reisner, Louis, was born Mar. 26, 1920. WWII veteran. Pfc., U.S. Army. Died Sept. 21, 1970; buried Holy Cross Catholic Cem., Granger, TX.

Reisner, Ottis, WWII veteran of Granger, TX.

Rejcek, Albert B., was born Jan. 24, 1928. Served in U.S. Army in Korea. Attained rank of Pfc. Died Nov. 29, 1980; buried in St. Mary's Cemetery, West, TX.

Rejcek, Anton V., son of Anton and Mary Rejcek, was born on June 16, in West, McLennan Co., TX. Attended schools in the West area before enlisting into the U.S. Army on Sept. 26, 1940, at Camp Bowie, Brownwood, TX. Served initially in the 143rd Inf., 36th Div. for three years and then in Headquarters, 12th Army Group for two years. During WWII he served in the European, African, and Middle Eastern Theater of Operations and participated in the Normandy, Northern France, Central Europe, Ardennes: Alsace, and Rhineland Campaigns. Decorations include the European-African-Middle Eastern Campaign Medal with five campaign stars, American Defense Service Medal, and the Good Conduct Medal. Separated from the service at Ft. Sam Houston, TX on July 26, 1945. Semi-retired from farming. Home of record: West, TX.

Rejcek, Edmund J., Sr., was born Oct. 20, 1941. Served in the U.S. Army in Viet Nam, attaining rank of Pfc. Died Aug. 13, 1988; buried in St. Mary's Cemetery, West, TX.

Rejcek, Raymond John, son of John Frank Rejcek and Agnes Elizabeth Kohut, was born Feb. 26, 1919, West, McClennan Co., TX. Education: grammar school and other courses. Enlisted in U.S. Army Corps. Attained rank of Staff Sgt., 3203rd Engineer Water Supply Company, Mineral Wells, TX. Basic training and on to Ft. Leonardwood, MO, for further training. Theaters of Operation: EAME, Asiatic-Pacific. Fought in nine battles throughout the EAME and Asiatic-Pacific Theaters. Worked as an automotive chief mechanic in charge of a 7-man crew in both Theaters. Also repaired and overhauled truck and tractor motors, replaced damaged parts with materials salvaged from wrecked vehicles and serviced stationary engines and machinery, made repairs on heavy artillery, running gear and carriages under fire. Medals: Legion of Merit for services in Italy, EAME Campaign Medal w/4 BSS, American Theater Campaign Medal w/1 BSS, Italian Cross from Italian Government, Asiatic-Pacific Campaign Medal, United Nations Service Medal, American Defense Service Medal w/1 BSS, Korean President Unit Citation Emblem w/2 BSS, Good Conduct Medal three and a half years. Embarked from U.S.A. to Oran, Africa, all the way through to Burzerdie, Africa, to Sicily, Italy, into Salerno to Naples on through Burma Pass. From here went to Pacific Theater and landed in Kiska to the Philippine Islands. During this trip, crossed the Equator, went to Suez Canal, had to turn around and go back to the Panama Canal to get to Kiska. From Philippines, came back home to U.S.A. Honorably discharged Dec. 3, 1945. Married Mertie Fay Bradley, June 21, 1947; four children, three grandchildren, one great-grandchild, as of 1993. Life member of the VFW, member of American Legion, member of Slavonic Benevolent Order of State of Texas, Lodge #84, Dallas, TX. Home of record: Dallas, TX.

Rek, Joe John, Jr., son of Joe John Rek, Sr. and Emily Kucera, was born Oct. 16, 1924, at Wallis, TX. Attended Slovan (Bordovice) Elementary School located near Rek Hill, and graduated from Fayetteville High School in 1942. Enlisted in the U.S. Navy during WWII. Served in the American Theater of Operations aboard ships in the South Atlantic (Brazil). Also served in the Asiatic-Pacific Theater of Operations and participated in naval operations at Okinawa. Discharged from the Navy in Apr. 1946. In Apr. 1947 joined the U.S. Coast Guard and served on various ships and at locations in the U.S. Retired from the U.S. Coast Guard in Mar. 1964 at the rank of Chief Warrant Officer. Awards and decorations include American and Asiatic Pacific Campaign Medals, Navy and Coast Guard Good Conduct Medals, WWII Victory Medal, National Defense Service Medal, and Naval Occupational Medal. Home of record: Bryan, TX.

Rek, Lad Joe, son of Joe Rek and Ruzina Wiesner, was born Jan. 6, 1920, Fayetteville, TX, on Rek Hill. Mother died when he was less than one year old. Enlisted in the U.S. Navy before WWII, served aboard ship in the Pacific Theater, before and after the attack on Pearl Harbor. Ship departed Pearl Harbor Dec. 4, 1941, three days before the attack. Details of service are not available. Married to Lillian Jurecka. Died Aug. 5, 1978. Submitted by half-brother, Joe John Rek, Jr., Bryan, TX.

Rektorik, Archie Joe, son of Jaro and Agnes Rektorik, was born Mar. 19, 1926, Robstown, TX. Education: Robstown, TX, 12 years. Enlisted Ft. Sam Houston, TX, abt 1944. Attained rank of Tech Sgt. Theater of Operations: Pacific. Battles: Okinawa. WOUNDED IN ACTION, Okinawa. Awards: Asiatic-Pacific Ribbon w/1 BSS, Good Conduct, WWII Victory Ribbon, Korean Occupation Ribbon, three Overseas Service Bars, Purple Heart. Honorably discharged Nov. 1, 1946. Married Alice Marie Tousek of Moulton, TX, May, 1948; two married daughters, four grandsons. Retired from farming and construction work. Enjoy dancing, go as often as possible. Home of record: Robstown, TX.

Repa, Arnold Frank, son of Paul Repa and Frances Pekar, was born 1926, Granger, TX. Attended Sts. Cyril & Methodius School in Granger. Enlisted in the U.S. Army during WWII at Ft. Sam Houston, TX on Aug. 3, 1944. Served in the European African and Middle Eastern Theater of Operations as a member of Company G, 114th Inf. Reg., 44th Div. Participated in the Rhineland and Central Europe Campaigns as a front line Command Post Messenger. Awards and decorations include the European African Middle Eastern Campaign Medal with two campaign stars, American Campaign Medal, Good Conduct Medal, Army of Occupation Medal, and WWII Victory Medal. Separated from the service on July 4, 1946. Civilian occupations were farmer and carpenter. Enjoys reading and gardening. Married Helen Nemec; three children: Bernadette (Boni), Moerbe, and Dennis Ray. Member of American Legion Post No. 282, Granger, TX. Died 1987; buried Holy Cross Catholic Cem., Granger, TX.

Repa, Edwin A., Sr., son of Paul Repa and Frances Pekar, was born on Jan. 14, 1925. Attended Sts. Cyril & Methodius School in Granger. Enlisted in the U.S. Army in 1943 at Ft. Sam Houston, TX, during WWII. Assigned to Camp Wolters for 3 months and subsequently assigned to the 289th Inf. Div.. Served with the Division in Hawaii and Oraha, Japan and attained the rank of Sgt. Decorations include the Expert Infantryman Badge, Good Conduct Medal, WWII Victory Medal, and three Overseas Service Bars. Separated from the service on Feb. 27, 1946. Married Marie Hajda on Apr. 20, 1948; six children. Retired at age 62 as a homebuilder and owner of Edwin Repa Construction Company. Was also a former

Granger City Councilman and Bank Director of Granger National Bank. Member of American Legion Post No. 282, Granger, TX. Died on Feb. 24, 1990, at the age of 65 in Granger, TX. Buried Holy Cross Catholic Cem., Granger, TX. Stone states date of death Feb. 14, 1990.

Repka, Albert, son of Vilem "Willie" Repka and Annie Galetka, was born Apr. 23, 1913, Hallettsville, Lavaca Co., TX. Enlisted in U.S. Army Corps, Feb. 10, 1940, Recruiting Station, Ft. Sam Houston, TX. Theater of Operations: EAME. Campaigns: Normandy, Northern France, Rhineland, Ardennes, and Central Europe. WOUNDED IN ACTION twice, Sept. 17, 1944, and Dec. 18, 1944, EAME Theater of Operations. Medals: Purple Heart w/1 OLC, Distinguished Unit Badge w/1 OLC, EAME Campaign Medal w/5 BSS, American Defense Service Medal, Good Conduct Medal, WWII Victory Medal. Honorably discharged July 1, 1945, Ft. Sam Houston, TX. Civilian Occupation: Oil Field Worker (Texas Oilfields), Bachelor. Died Mar. 24, 1962; buried in Vsetin Czech Moravian Brethren Cemetery, Vsetin, TX (Hallettsville, TX). Submitted by nephew, Henry J. Repka of Houston, TX.

Repka, Alvin W. "Shorty," son of Vilem "Willie" Repka and Annie Galetka, was born July 1, 1926, Hallettsville, Lavaca Co., TX. Education: Stacy School, Lavaca Co., TX. Enlisted in U.S. Army Corps, Dec. 8, 1945, Ft. Bliss, TX. Attained rank of Pfc. Medals: Army of Occupation, WWII Victory Medal. Assigned to Co. A, 1st Bn., 16th Inf. Honorably discharged July 24, 1947, Camp Kilmer, NJ. Oilfield worker, cement contractor, Albuquerque, NM. Died Nov. 15, 1986; buried Mt. Calvary Cemetery, Albuquerque, NM. Submitted by nephew, Henry J. Repka of Houston, TX.

Repka, Herman, son of Vilem "Willie" Repka and Annie Galetka, was born Jan. 26, 1916, Hallettsville, Lavaca Co., TX. Education: Boethel School, Lavaca Co., TX. Enlisted in U.S. Army Corps, Feb. 10, 1940, Ft. Sam Houston, TX. Theater of Operations: EAME. Battles: Normandy, Northern France, and Germany Campaigns. WOUNDED IN ACTION June 8, 1944. Served as a rifleman with 23rd Inf. in France and Belgium, truck driver–2nd Quartermaster Co. Medals: American Defense Service, Meritorious Service Unit Emblem, EAME Campaign, Good Conduct, Combat Infantryman Badge, Lapel Button, WWII Victory. Honorably discharged, May 26, 1945, Brooke Convalescent Hospital, Ft. Sam Houston, TX. Service station operator and Serviceman Trucking Company, Hallettsville, TX. Died Nov. 17, 1978; buried in Sacred Heart Catholic Cemetery, Hallettsville, TX. Submitted by stepson, Henry J. Repka of Houston, TX.

Repka, Julius, son of Joseph Repka and Mary Blaha, was born on Dec. 5, 1896, in Hallettsville, Lavaca Co., TX. Attended the Radhost School in Hallettsville. Inducted into the U.S. Army on June 23, 1918, at Victoria, TX, during WWI. Served in France with the American Expeditionary Forces as a member of Co. F, 55th Inf., 7th Div. Participated in the defense of the Purnenelh Sector west of Mosell from Oct. 10–Nov. 9, 1918, and in the offense of the Sector from Nov. 9–Nov. 11, 1918. Separated from the service on July 2, 1919, at Camp Bowie, TX. Was a farmer in the Inez, TX, area. Married Angelina Koutny; two sons: Eugene J. and Ernest J. Died Apr. 25, 1957 (Angelina on Feb. 4, 1988). Both are interred in the Resurrection Catholic Cemetery at Victoria, TX.

Repka, Lee Paul, son of William Repka and Francis Matocha, was born Aug. 14, 1923, TX. Enlisted in military service, Jan. 14, 1942. Theater of Operations: EAME. Chief for Hospital in Europe. Was in Europe, France, England, Belgium. Honorably discharged Nov. 18, 1945. Married Rosalie M. Majeski; one child. Home of record: Houston, TX. Submitted by Joe Ann Fabrygel, Needville, TX.

Reznicek, Frank J., son of Mr. and Mrs. Frank Reznicek, West, TX. Entered AAC in 1943. Served

in N. Africa as a Pvt. KILLED IN ACTION, Mediterranean Area, 1943, during WWII. Awarded the Purple Heart.

Reznicek, Robert W., son of Karel Reznicek and Anna Krutova, was born Dec. 8, 1910, in Tours, McLennan Co., TX. Attended the Brigman Elementary School at Penelope, TX. Enlisted in the service on Sept. 19, 1942, at Hill, TX, during WWII. Served in the Asiatic-Pacific Theater of Operations and participated in campaigns at Guam and Okinawa. Decorations include the Asiatic-Pacific Campaign Medal with campaign star, Good Conduct Medal, and World War Victory Medal. Separated from the service on Jan. 13, 1946 at Camp Fanning, TX. Farmer, carpenter, and building construction before retirement. Home of record: Ft. Worth, TX.

Rippel, Joseph Adolph, son of Charles Rippel and Agnes Steffek, was born Apr. 24, 1895, Freyburg, Fayette Co., TX. Moved to La Grange, TX about 1899. Educated in La Grange, TX. Inducted into the National Army on Apr. 28, 1918, La Grange, TX, during WWI. Sent to Camp Travis, TX, for training. Assigned to Co. L, 360th Inf., part of the famous Texas Brigade of the 90th Div. Sent overseas June 14, 1918. Served in France with this brigade as Cpl. until June 17, 1919. Received six weeks of concentrated training in France–at Aignay-le-Duc, a village near Dijon. Moved to vicinity of Toul, where preparations for the St. Michiel drive had already begun. Participated in heavy battles in the Verdun sector and other areas across France until the Armistice. Part of the Army of Occupation in Germany. Arrived home safely without any wounds, but the metal helmet he wore has a deep dent in it where it was hit by a bullet or shrapnel. Honorably discharged on June 21, 1919. Married Mary Porter; three daughters. Agent for Sinclair Oil Company in La Grange, TX, and later a farmer near Raymondville in the Rio Grande Valley. Died on Mar. 27, 1965; buried in Raymondville Cemetery in the Valley. Submitted lovingly in her father's memory by Jody Rippel Feldtman Wright of San Antonio, TX.

Ripple, Henry E., son of Jerry F. Ripple and Francis Polak, was born Aug. 21, 1918, Rowena, TX. Education: Eola, TX, Grammar School, Groenwald Grammar School, Rowena, TX, Ballinger, TX, High School, Paint Rock, TX, High School. Graduated May 19, 1938. Enlisted June 16, 1944, U.S. Army, Ft. Sam Houston, TX. Assigned to 22nd Inf., Co. L. Attained rank of Pfc. Theater of Operations, European Theater. Battles: Rhineland, Central Europe. Medals: American Theater Campaign, EAME Campaign w/2 BSS, GCM, WWII Victory. "The most memorable event that happened was on the front lines in Europe. My very close buddy and I were digging a foxhole together at night. When a barrage of enemy screaming meemies started coming over a hill, I jumped into the foxhole, but he sat on the surface level of the ground, with only his feet in the foxhole, to eat his K-rations. One of the meemies hit and exploded right next to our foxhole. Shrapnel went through his helmet and into his head. He died instantly. It was very difficult for me to write to his wife and children to tell them what happened to their loved one, that my buddy had been killed in action. I was WOUNDED IN ACTION on barbed wire." Honorably discharged Jan. 22, 1946. Married Ann Lydia Dusek; two children: Henry E. Ripple, Jr. and Sharon Ann Ripple Barker. Retired Mar. 31, 1990. Hobbies: arts and crafts, gardening, and keyboard playing. Home of record: Taylor, TX.

Ripple, Larry M., son of Louis Ripple and Lillian Petter, was born Apr. 19, 1913, El Campo, TX. Education: El Campo High School; B.B.A. at University of Houston, TX; M.S. at Shippensburg College, PA; Air Command and Staff College, Maxwell AFB, AL; Army War College, Carlisle Barracks, PA. Induction: 1954, Houston, TX. Attained rank of Col., Theater of Operations: S.E. Asia. Battles: Viet Nam (1965-66 and 1972). Medals: Legion of Merit w/OLC, BSS, Meritorious Service Medal,

Air Medal (awarded twice), Joint Service Commendation Medal, Army Commendation Medal, National Defense Service Medal w/Silver Service Star, Viet Nam Cross of Gallantry w/Silver Star, Viet Nam Staff Service Medal, Staff Service Medal, Viet Nam Armed Forces Honor Medal, Viet Nam Campaign Medal, authorized to wear the Joint Chief's of Staff ID Badge, and Aircraft Crewman's Badge. Retired from active duty, July 31, 1984, 30 years service. Home of record: Hampton, VA.

Rochen, Albin Francis, son of Eddie Charles Rochen and Rosa Krenek, was born on Dec. 30, 1920, near Waller, TX. Graduated from Waller High School and enlisted into the U.S. Navy at Houston, TX, in May 1942. Part of a volunteer replacement group sworn in to replace the lost crew of the original USS *Houston*. Served in both the Asiatic-Pacific and the European, African, and Middle Eastern Theaters of Operations. Participated in naval operations at Sicily, Gilbert Islands, Guam, Philippine Islands, and Japan. Decorations include the European-African-Middle Eastern Campaign Medal and the Asiatic-Pacific Campaign Medal. Separated from service on Jan. 5, 1946. Married Winona Sisa at Hempstead, TX; two sons: Robert David and Harold Gene. Died in 1991 at Waller, TX, and is interred in the Catholic Cemetery at Waller.

Rochen, Henry Frederick, son of John Rochen and Marie Hajek, was born on May 30, 1893, at Ammannsville, TX. Family settled south of the city of Waller in the 1890s. Inducted into the U.S. Army on Sept. 5, 1917, at Hempstead, TX. Served in France with the American Expeditionary Forces as a Pfc. in Co. K, 360th Inf., 90th Div. Arrived in France on June 21. Participated in campaigns at Vilbison from Aug. 24–Sept. 11, St. Michael from Sept. 12–16, Lunewells from Sept. 17–Oct. 10, and Meuse-Argonne from Oct. 22–Nov. 11, when the war ended. Separated from service on June 21, 1919, at Camp Travis, TX. Married Pauline Bessie Lamza on Jan. 8, 1924, Poth, TX; two children: Richard Rochen and Georgie Mae Rochen Bertoesch. Died Apr. 1, 1973; wife on Jan. 17, 1953. Both are interred in the Poth Catholic Cemetery.

Rochen, Joe Peter, son of John Rochen and Marie Hajek, was born on Aug. 1, 1889, in the Hostyn area near Ellinger, TX. Moved to the Czech community south of the city of Waller in the 1890s. Inducted into the U.S. Army on June 27, 1918, at Hempstead, TX. Served in Germany and France in WWI with American Expeditionary Forces as a Pvt. in the Wagon C., #302-2 MC. Arrived in Europe on Sept. 20, 1918, and his sister, Cecelia Rochen nee Hajek, recalls that he spent his time in Germany and worked in kitchens. Separated from service at Camp Travis, TX, on Sept. 27, 1919. Decorations include the WWI Victory Medal. Married Vlasta Sabrsula on Nov. 30, 1920; six children: Annie Mary Rochen Parenica, Clarence Charlie Rochen, Rosa Rochen Dolik, Ruby Rochen Ellerman, and Deloris Rochen Matej. Deceased.

Rochen, Walter W., son of Eddie Charles Rochen and Rosa Krenek, was born Dec. 16, 1930, near Waller, TX. Enlisted in USMC on Feb. 27, 1952. Served in Korea. Received his separation from active duty on Feb. 19, 1952, and was discharged from the USMC Reserve on Feb. 26, 1960. Medals: National Defense Service, Korean Service with one Star, and United Nations Service. Earned an Associate in Arts degree in business from Blinn Junior College, Brenham, TX after the war. Married Bessie Lenora Gaidousek on Sept. 13, 1958, in Houston, TX; six children: Diane Rose Rochen, Michele Lenora Rochen Gubbels, Michael Edward Rochen, Sharon Renee Rochen, Andrew John Rochen, and Mark Walter Rochen. Walter is employed with the State Highway Department. Home of record: Rosenberg, TX.

Rod, Gilbert Frank, son of J. J. Rod and Anna Hubenak, was born Oct. 17, 1926, Pierce, Wharton Co., TX. Education: El Campo High

School, 1943; Wharton County Junior College, degree 1948; University of Texas, B.B.A., 1950. Enlisted in U.S. Army, TX, Mar. 29, 1945. Assigned to Asiatic-Pacific Theater of Operations for one year as clerk-typist and classified correspondent in Adjutant General's office, Records Branch, General Hq., Armed Forces Pacific, Manila, Philippine Islands. Honorably discharged Dec. 5, 1946, Ft. Sam Houston, TX. Married Gladys Musil; four daughters, three sons. Manager of Hardware and Implement Company, past president of El Campo Lions Club, Past Grand Knight, Knights of Columbus, played and coached baseball, inducted into South Central Texas Semi-Pro Baseball Hall of Fame. Died Mar. 10, 1989; interred in Holy Cross Memorial Park, El Campo, TX. Submitted lovingly in his memory by widow, Gladys Musil Rod. Home of record: El Campo, TX.

Roeder, Edmund L., son of Louis M. Roeder and Mary Hucek, was born Nov. 13, 1917, Shiner, TX. Education: Bunjes and St. Ludmila's Academy, Shiner, TX, and St. John's Seminary, San Antonio, TX. Inducted into U.S. Army Corps about 1942, Ft. Sam Houston, TX. Assigned to Co. L, 358th Inf. Regt, 90th Inf. Div., Camp Barkeley, TX, until the war ended in Europe. Duties were administrative (clerk), squad leader, and platoon sgt. Theater of Operations: EAME. Battles: Normandy, Northern France, Rhineland, Ardennes, Central Europe. WOUNDED IN ACTION four times. Medals: Silver Star, BSS, Purple Heart w/3 OLC, Good Conduct Medal, EAME Campaign Medal w/5 BSS, WWII Victory Medal, Army Reserve Medal, Combat Infantryman's Badge. Discharged June 1945. Enrolled at Landig College of Mortuary Science, Houston, TX. Earned license as an embalmer and funeral director in the State of Texas. Pursued this profession over 48 years. In June 1949, enlisted in U.S. Army Reserves. Accepted an appointment as 2nd Lt. in Oct. 1950. Assignments and duties were numerous. Attended several schools. Graduate of the U.S. Army Quartermaster Officer Career Course and the U.S. Army Command and Staff College. Retired with rank of Maj., Dec. 1977. Married Jo Eileen Strauss of Hallettsville, TX, Jan. 1943; two sons, two daughters, five grandchildren and one great-grandchild. One son is veteran of Viet Nam War. Home of record: Hallettsville, TX.

Rokyta, Frank Alfons, son of Frank Joe Rokyta and Delfie Holy, was born Mar. 22, 1921, at Port Lavaca, Calhoun Co., TX. Enlisted in the U.S. Army at Ft. Sam Houston, TX, during WWII. Served in both the American and European, African, and Middle Eastern Theaters of Operations. Decorations include the American Campaign Medal, European African Middle Eastern Campaign Medal with two campaign stars, and Good Conduct Medal. Separated from service on Mar. 5, 1946, at Camp Fannin, TX. Home of record: Victoria, TX.

Rosipal, Charlie, U.S. Navy: CASU 44 Div. 9. WWII veteran of Granger, TX.

Rosipal, Cyril Charles, son of Joseph F. Rosipal and Agnes Marie Mokry, was born July 21, 1941, Tynan, Bee Co., TX. Education: Sts. Cyril & Methodius Catholic School, Granger, TX, eight years, graduated May 1960. Enlisted U.S. Army Reserves, about 1959, San Antonio, TX. Combat Engineer. Theater of Operations: American. Earned Sharp Shooter Badge. Married Eileen Rose Sladecek; two children: Christopher Edward and Charles E. "Chuck." Civilian occupation: sales representative. Home of record: Austin, TX.

Rosipal, Herbert Frank, son of Joseph F. Rosipal and Agnes Marie Mokry, was born Dec. 10, 1938, Skidmore, Williamson Co., TX. Education: Sts. Cyril & Methodius Elementary School, Granger, TX. Graduate of Granger High School. Enlisted about 1956, U.S. Army Corps, San Antonio, TX. Attained rank of E-5. Armored Maintenance Spec. Theater of Operations: American. Decorations: Top Maint. Spclst. Honorably discharged Feb. 1964. Civilian occupation: electrical technician. Married Adele M. Spaniel; four children: Melissa, Patrick, Sharon, Eric. Hobbies: fishing, hunting, sports. Home of record: Taylor, TX.

Rosipal, John, son of Joseph Rosipal and Agnes Mokry, was born July 12, 1945, Tynan, Bee Co., TX. Education: Sts. Cyril & Methodius Catholic School, Granger, TX, Granger High School, 1963, two years college, CCAF. Enlisted Oct. 12, 1965, USAF, Lackland AFB, TX. Air Transportation and Logistics Management. Theater of Operations: Pacific Theater. Okinawa, Japan, Viet Nam, Philippines, Thailand. Battles: Viet Nam, 1967-

68, TET Offensive, 1968. Was in on closedown of Thailand Bases, 1975-76. Eyewitness to release of PRISONERS OF WAR from Viet Nam at Clark AFB, Philippines, 1973. Medals: Meritorious Service, Viet Nam Campaign, Outstanding Unit Citation, Presidential Unit Citation. Attained rank of E-8 prior to retirement Nov. 1, 1985. Civilian occupation: Materials Planning Manager. Married Mazie L. Baxley; four children: Susan D. Rosipal Daniel, Gilbert L. Rosipal, Kathy E. Rosipal Hannah, Barbara J. Rosipal. Hobbies: fishing, gardening, and watching football. Home of record: Austin, TX.

Rotor/Rotrekl, Jerry J., son of Anton Rotrekl and Frances Stepnek, was born on Apr. 27, 1910, in Slavkov U Brno, Czechoslovakia. Immigrated to the U.S. in 1912 with parents and sister Rosa, landing at Galveston, TX. Graduated from Forest Avenue High School, Galveston, 1928, and attended Texas A&M College, earning B.A. (Accounting and Statistics) in 1932. Entered the U.S. Army as a 2nd Lt. in the 473rd AntiAircraft (AA) Bn. during WWII. Assigned to the European, African, and Middle Eastern Theater of Operations, departing from New York for Scotland in 1943 aboard troop ship, *Ile de France*. Unit initially provided antiaircraft defense in England against enemy aircraft and "Buzz Bombs." Landed at Utah Beach, Normandy, France, on July 10, 1944. Participated in combat at Jorges, St. Lo, and in the hedgerows through Avaranches, Countance, and La Haye de Priest. The 473rd AA Bn. participated in campaigns in Normandy, Northern France, Rhineland, and Central Europe (France, Belgium, Holland, Luxembourg, Germany, and Czechoslovakia). At one time or another the battalion was attached to and supported the I Army commanded by General Hodges, III Army commanded General Patton, IX Army commanded by General Simpson, II Army commanded by General Montgomery (British) in Holland, and several Infantry and Airborne Divisions. Unit had been assigned to the 2nd Armored Division as artillery and ground support and on VE Day in May 1945, the division spearhead reached Klatony, Czechoslovakia, near Pilsen. Did not get the opportunity to visit home town as it was in the Russian sector. After serving in Munich, Germany, as part of the Occupation Army, returned to the U.S. and was separated from service on Dec. 31, 1952. Decorations include the Purple Heart for wounds received on Aug. 4, 1944, near Rennes, France, and the European-African-Middle Eastern Campaign Medal with five campaign stars. WOUNDED IN ACTION. Worked for the Dallas Water Utilities Accounts Division for 43 years and retired in 1975.

Rozacky, Alvin Rudolph, son of Rudolph Rozacky and Albina Machu, was born Aug. 13, 1915, in Granger, TX. Attended Friendship and Granger schools and also Moravia Country School. Enlisted into the U.S. Army, 2nd Inf. Div., in Oct. 1939, at Ft. Sam Houston, TX. Served in the European, African, and Middle Eastern Theater of Operations with the 897th Field Artillery, 75th Inf. Div. during WWII. Attained the rank of Sgt. Participated in campaigns in Belgium, France, Holland and Germany, specifically in the Battle of the Bulge in the Ardennes, Colmar Rhur Bulge, Colmar Pocket, and Battle of Rhur. Was a Jeep driver and radio operator for the Division Commander. Lost one Jeep to a mine explosion and another was blown up by a German Tiger tank. Decorations include the BSS, European African Middle Eastern Campaign Medal with three campaign stars, and Good Conduct Medal. Separated from service on Nov. 13, 1945. Was a farmer and worked in the grocery business until retirement in Mar. 1982. Married Beatrice Bucek; three children: James Naizer, stepson, Barbara Jean Naizer Limmer, stepdaughter, and Adolph Naizer. Hobbies: hunting, fishing, and traveling. Home of record: Taylor, TX.

Rozacky, Clifton Joe, son of Henry Rozacky, Sr. and Rosie Machu, was born May 26, 1929, in Granger, TX. Graduated from Granger High School in 1948. Enlisted in the U.S. Army on Feb. 13, 1951, at Ft. Sam Houston, TX, during the Korean War. Served as an Instructor in the U.S. Army Signal Corps and attained the rank of Cpl. Decorations include the Army of Occupation Medal. Separated from service on Jan. 19, 1953. Worked at Alcoa as an Electrical Maintenance Supervisor until retirement in Jan. 1984. Married Dorothy Marie Matula; three children: Michael, Larry, and David. Hobbies: hunting, fishing, cooking, and gardening. Member of American Legion Post No. 282, Granger, TX. Died Apr. 6, 1993, and is interred at Granger, TX.

Rozacky, Edward John, son of Frank Raymond Rozacky, Jr. and Mathilda Gorubec, was born Dec.

22, 1940. Attended Sts. Cyril & Methodius School in Granger and graduated from Granger High School in 1959. Enlisted in the U.S. Army at San Antonio, TX, and attended basic training at Ft. Polk, LA, and advance training at Ft. Ord, CA. Served in Viet Nam and participated in "Operation Paul Revere." On one occasion was unable to get to company due to Viet Cong action and had to eat bananas and wild pineapples for 28 days. On another occasion was captured (PRISONER OF WAR) and managed to escape the same day. Capture took place about 60 miles north of Plieku on the Ho Chi Minh Trail. Also suffered a wound to his right hand. (WOUNDED IN ACTION) Decorations include the Viet Nam Service Medal with one campaign star, Republic of Viet Nam Campaign Medal, National Defense Service Medal, and Sharpshooter Badges, along with other citations. Separated from service on Dec. 22, 1967. Before going into the service, worked as manager of an auto parts store; now is a machinist at Trepan Tools Company. Married Amalie Gola; two children: Jason Wayne and Laura Lynn. Enjoys being with family, and also hunting and fishing. Home of record: Brenham, TX.

Rozacky, Henry Charles, Jr., son of Henry Charles Rozacky, Sr. and Rosie/Rosa J. Machu, was born Nov. 25, 1922, in Friendship, Williamson Co., TX. Graduated from Friendship High School in 1940. Enlisted in the U.S. Navy on Dec. 2, 1942, during WWII. Basic training, Los Angeles, CA; further training, San Diego, CA. Served in the Asiatic-Pacific Theater of Operations for 28 months. Served on NTS, San Diego, LCS (PAC), USS LCI (g.) 345, and USS *Flager*. Decorations include the Asiatic-Pacific Theater of Operations Medal with three campaign stars. Separated from service on Jan. 26, 1946, having attained rank of MoMM 1/c. Civilian occupation was that of a farmer and carpenter. Married Louise Marie Shirocky; two children: Kimberly Rozacky Raymond and Karilynn Marie Rozacky Kallus. Hobbies: gardening, woodworking, fishing, and hunting. Member of American Legion Post No. 282, Granger, TX. Died Feb. 2, 1982, and is interred in Holy Cross Cemetery at Granger, TX.

Rozacky, John Edwin, son of Henry Charles Rozacky, Sr. and Rosie/Rosa J. Machu, was born June 25, 1918, in Granger, TX. Attended Friendship Public School and graduated in 1936. Enlisted in the U.S. Navy on Mar. 2, 1945, at Taylor, TX, during WWII. Basic training, San Diego, CA, further training, Basic Engineering School, Gulfport, MS. Served in the American Theater of Operations at Roosevelt Base, Treasure Island, San Diego, CA, Naval Repair Base. Separated from service on Apr. 3, 1946. Was a farmer until retirement in June 1983. Married Gladys Maureen Ray. Member, American Legion Post No. 282, Granger, TX. Home of record: Thorndale, TX.

Rozacky, Lawrence, son of Henry Charles Rozacky, Sr. and Rosie/Rosa J. Machu, was born Aug. 25, 1933, in Granger, TX. Attended Friendship grade school and graduated from Granger High School in 1951. Served in the U.S. Navy from June 27, 1952–June 22, 1956, as a Storekeeper aboard the USS *Essex,* during the Korean Conflict. Attained the rank of 2nd Class Petty Officer. Employed by chemical plant. Retired June 1993. Married Dorothy H. Repa; four children: Deborah, Ronnie, Randall, and Russell. Hobbies include fishing and hunting. Home of record: Alvin, TX.

Rozacky, Rudolf "Rudy," served in U.S. Armed Forces, Granger, TX.

Rozacky, William, son of Frank Rozacky and Frances Kalpec, was born Feb. 21, 1913, in Granger, TX, and attended schools in Granger. Enlisted in U.S. Army Corps, 1942, during WWII. Basic training, Camp Swift, TX; further training, Camp Young, CA, Camp Van Dorn, MS. Theater of Operations: Asiatic-Pacific. Participated in the Ryukyus Campaign at Okinawa. Medals: Asiatic-Pacific Theater Campaign w/1 BSS. Attained the rank of T/5, Tech Sgt. Honorably discharged 1946. Employed by Williamson County Road District. Died Feb. 3, 1973; interred in the Holy Cross Cemetery at Granger, TX.

Roznovak, C. L., Sr., son of Mr and Mrs C. F. Rosnovak, was born on July 11, 1926, in El Campo, TX. Completed high school and attended college for a year. Enlisted in the U.S. Army at Houston, TX, in Dec. 1944, during WWII. Served in the Asiatic-Pacific Theater of Operation as a member of the 25th Inf. Div. Participated in the Luzon Campaign. Decorations include the Good Conduct Medal, Asiatic-Pacific Campaign Medal, Philippine Liberation Ribbon, and Rifleman Badge. Separated from service on Nov. 26, 1946. Home of record: Pasadena, TX.

Roznovak, John L., son of Josef and Annie Roznovak, was born Apr. 29, 1894, Granger, Williamson Co., TX. Education: grade school. Enlisted Ft. Sam Houston, TX, U.S. Army Corps. Attained rank of Cpl.; assigned 395 Motor Transport Group. Received WWI Victory Medal. Honorably discharged May 1919. Married Agnes Hurta; two sons: Marvin and Reynold. Died Apr. 1986; buried Taylor, TX, City Cemetery.

Roznovak, Marvin G., son of John L. Roznovak and Agnes Hurta, was born Dec. 11, 1920, Taylor, Williamson Co., TX. Graduate, Taylor, TX, High School, 1938. Enlisted during WWII, U.S. Army Corps, Ft. Sam Houston, TX. Assigned to Armored Inf. Attained rank of Staff Sgt. Theater of Operations: EAME. Fought in Central Europe: Munich, Germany, Pilsen, Czechoslovakia. Medals: EAME Theater Campaign w/1 BSS. The service company of the 69th Armored Inf. spearheaded an attack in Sudaten Land near and in Pilsen, Czechoslovakia, where they encountered German SS Troops. Interpreted for the Company Commander so the Czech people could tell us where the enemy was hiding (which was mostly in church towers). Honorably discharged Nov. 10, 1945. Retired farmer. Married Artie B. Preuss; one daughter: Kathy Roznovak Woodward. Hobbies: deer hunt, and visit with other retirees and veterans. Home of record: Taylor, TX.

Roznovak, Reynold T., son of John L. Roznovak and Agnes Hurta, was born Mar. 4, 1923, Taylor, Williamson Co., TX. Graduate, Taylor High School, 1942; attended Arlington College for a short time. Very active in FFA and wanted to raise registered cattle. Enlisted U.S. Army Corps, Ft. Sam Houston, TX, during WWII. Attained rank of Pfc., assigned to 137 Inf. Div. Theater of Operations: Asiatic-Pacific. Fought in Philippine Islands, Guadalcanal, Bouganville, Manila, Luzon. Lost his glasses in one landing, needed these very much. KILLED IN ACTION, May 13, 1945, by Japanese mortar fire, Luzon, Manila. Initial burial in the cemetery, Luzon, Manila, in 1948; brought home to Taylor, Williamson Co., TX, City Cemetery for final burial.

Roznovsky, Anton A., was born May 20, 1907. Served in U.S. Army during WWII. Died June 26, 1987; buried in St. Mary's Cemetery, West, TX.

Roznovsky, Aug V., son of Mr. and Mrs. Vinc Roznovsky, Granger, TX. Enlisted U.S. Army Air Corps, 1939; basic training, Randolph Field, TX. Additional training, Keesler Field, MS, Ellington Field, TX. Theater of Operation: American, Asiatic-Pacific. WOUNDED IN ACTION, Tarawa, 1945. Medals: American Theater Campaign, Asiatic-Pacific Theater Campaign w/5 BSS, Air Medal w/5 OLC, Purple Heart, Silver Star, American Defense, Good Conduct, WWII Victory, Ribbons. Attained rank of S/Sgt. prior to honorable discharge, 1945.

Roznovsky, Frank, son of Frank Roznovsky and Bessie Stepan, was born Nov. 5, 1921, in Gonzales, TX. Graduated from high school and during WWII enlisted in the Armed Service at Ft. Sam Houston, TX. Served in the Asiatic-Pacific Theater of Operations. Decorations include the Good Conduct Medal and Sharpshooter Badge. Separated from service on Dec. 2, 1942. Home of record: Houston, TX.

Roznovsky, Joe J., Jr., son of Mr. and Mrs. Joe J. Roznovsky, Sr., Granger, TX. Education: Macedonia School. Enlisted in U.S. Army Corps, 1942; basic training, Ft. Sam Houston, TX; additional training, CA, AL. Theaters of Operation: American, Asiatic-Pacific. Served in the Philippines. Awards: American Theater Campaign Medal, A-P Theater Campaign Medal w/1 BSS, Good Conduct Medal, WWII Victory Medal, Ribbons. Attained rank of T/5 (Tech Sgt.) prior to honorable discharge, 1946.

Roznovsky, Joe John, Sr., son of Mr. and Mrs. Vinc Roznovsky, Granger, TX, was born Apr. 8, 1902. Graduate, Friendship High School. Enlisted U.S. Army Air Corps, 1942; basic training, Brooks Field, TX. Theater of Operations: American. Served in 1st and 4th Air Forces, Langley Field,

VA, Mitchell Field, NY, Salinas, CA. Sg 483 Base Unit. Attained rank of Sgt. prior to honorable discharge 1945. Died Sept. 17, 1958; buried Holy Cross Catholic Cemetery, Granger, TX.

Roznovsky, John E., son of Mr. and Mrs. Vinc Roznovsky, Granger, TX. Education: Friendship High School. Enlisted U.S. Army Corps, 1939; basic training, Brooks Field, TX; further training at U.S. Army Air Field, Midland, TX. Medals: Good Conduct Medal, Pre-Pearl Harbor Medal, Ribbons, WWII Victory Medal. Attained rank of M/Sgt. prior to honorable discharge 1945.

Roznovsky, Ladis F., was born Aug. 12, 1915. WWII veteran. T. Sgt. US Army. Died Dec. 10, 1988; buried Holy Cross Catholic Cem., Granger, TX.

Roznovsky, Landis, son of Mr. and Mrs. Vinc Roznovsky, Granger, TX. Education: Friendship High School. Enlisted U.S. Army Corps, 1940; basic training, Ft. Sam Houston, TX. Theater of Operations: Europe. Served in Italy. Medals: ETO Campaign Medal w/2 BSS, American Defense Medal, Rifleman's Badge, Good Conduct Medal, WWII Victory Medal. Attained rank of Sgt. prior to honorable discharge 1945.

Roznovsky, Louis, son of Mr. and Mrs. Vinc Roznovsky, Granger, TX. Education: Friendship High School. Married Elsie Sebek. Enlisted U.S. Army Air Corps, 1940, basic training, Brooks Field, TX, additional training, CO, FL. Theater of Operations: American, Asiatic-Pacific. Served in Philippines and Japan, later, U.S.A. Awards: Good Conduct Medal, American Defense Medal, American Theater Campaign Medal, Asiatic-Pacific Theater Campaign Medal w/BSS, Philippine Liberation Medal, and WWII Victory Medal. Attained rank of Sgt. prior to honorable discharge.

Roznovsky, Vincence, was born Sept. 22, 1874, Buchachech, Moravia. WWI veteran. Died Sept. 8, 1924; buried Holy Cross Catholic Cemetery, Granger, TX.

Rusnak, Ervin Steve, Sr., son of Steve A. Rusnak and Frances Havel, was born Dec. 10, 1920, in Cooks Point, Burleson Co., TX. Education included high school and Anderson Airplane School. Enlisted in the Air Force Aug. 21, 1942, in San Antonio, TX. Served at Sheppard Field, Wichita Falls,TX, Lincoln Army Air Field, Lincoln, NE, and Alamogordo Army Air Field, Alamogordo, NM, where he was an airplane and engine mechanic on B-29 aircraft. Rank: Sgt. Discharged Feb. 1, 1946, in San Antonio, TX. Medals: American Theater Ribbon, WWII Victory Ribbon. Married Eleanor L. Kohut; two children: Ervin Steve Rusnak, Jr., and Sharon Ann Rusnak Sulak. Retired from Braniff Airlines. Home of record: Irving, TX.

Ruzicka, Henry, son of John and Mary Ruzicka, was born on Feb. 14, 1895, at Ad Hall, Milam Co., TX. Served in France during WWI with the American Expeditionary Forces as an infantryman. Decorations include the WWI Victory Medal and Red Chevron Stripe. Separated from service in 1918. Died Feb. 26, 1960.

Ruzicka, Josephine Chilson, daughter of Henry and Albina Ruzicka, was born Feb. 2, 1922, at Ft. Worth, Tarrant Co., TX. Graduated high school and attended college for a year. Enlisted into the U.S. Navy during WWII on Nov. 26, 1942, at Washington, DC, and served in the American Theater of Operations attaining the rank of Yeoman First Class. Decorations include the American Campaign Medal and WWII Victory Medal. Discharged on Oct. 27, 1945. Married Mr. Chilson. Home of record: Hampton, VA.

Ruzicka, Leo, Abbott, TX, WWII veteran, U.S. Army Air Corps.

Ruzicka, Leopold Martin, son of Leopold Ruzicka and Josefa Popp, was born Aug. 26, 1890, Lipnik n/b (Moravia), Czechoslovakia. Immigrated to USA and settled in Abbott, Hill Co., TX, at the outbreak of WWI. Enlisted in U.S. Army Corps, and was stationed in San Antonio, TX. Honorably discharged shortly after the end of the war. Received WWI Victory Medal, among others. Married Frances Marek; five children: Mollie Ruzika Beseda, Leopold Martin Ruzicka, Jr., Eveline Ruzicka Greener, Frances Ruzicka Lewis, Jerry Ruzicka. Moved to Morton, TX, in 1946. Owned cotton gins in both areas. Had the first "air

blast" gin in the Abbott area. Died Oct. 31, 1969, Morton, TX. Interred at Resthaven Cemetery, Lubbock, TX. Submitted by Doris Beseda, Lubbock, TX.

Ruzicka, Marcel B., son of Mr. Ruzicka and Mrs. Julia S. Ruzicka, Taylor, TX. Enlisted U.S. Army Corps, 1942; basic training, Ft. Belvoir, VA. Theater of Operations: European. Served in North Africa, Italy, France, Germany. Medals: ETO Campaign Medal w/5 BSS, Good Conduct Medal, WWII Victory Medal. Attained rank of T/4 Sgt. prior to honorable discharge 1945. Married Libbie Stovacek.

Rybak, Ernest V., son of Ernest J. and Annie Rybak, was born Aug. 16, 1923, in Moravia, TX. Attended Woodrow Grade School, Damon, TX, and Richmond High School through 1938. Attended arc welding school, Houston, TX. Prior to service, was employed by Houston Ship Building Corporation as a first class welder. Volunteer of the National Guard, Rosenberg, TX. Enlisted at RCTG Station, Houston, TX, and served at Ellington Field, TX, and McCook, NE, as a Cpl. Discharged Feb. 18, 1946, at Camp Fannin, TX. Medals: American Theater Campaign, Good Conduct, WWII Victory. Died Apr. 1, 1972, age 49, and was buried in Garden of Gethsemane Cemetery, Rosenberg, TX.

Ryza, James Edward, son of Rudolph John Ryza and Erlene J. Horecka, was born Nov. 19, 1948, La Grange, TX. Graduated East Bernard High School. Drafted in Wharton, TX, Aug. 7, 1969. Attained Rank of Specialist 4/C. Medals: GCM, National Defense Service Medal, Viet Nam Service Medal and Viet Nam Campaign Medal, one O/S Bar. Honorably discharged June 25, 1971, Ft. Myer VA. Home of record: East Bernard, TX.

Ryza, Rudolph John, son of Frank Ryza (born Czechoslovakia) and Frances Matocha (born Rutersville, TX), was born Jan. 5, 1924, La Grange, TX. Education: through 5th grade, Hostyn, TX. Inducted Apr. 20, 1943, Los Angeles, CA. Theater of Operations: America. Medals: American Theater Campaign Medal, Good Conduct Medal, WWII Victory Ribbon. Known for his musical ability. Played saxophone and clarinet in the Army Stage Band and trombone in the Army Marching Band. The reason he was drafted in California, was that he left home at a young age to pursue his wish to perform in big bands, and went to the west coast. Served in 338th Army Services Band and 338th Army Dance Band, Ft. Sam Houston, TX. Farming and music were his main desires. Honorably discharged Feb. 27 1946, Ft. Sam Houston, TX. Married Erlene J. Horecka; one son: James Edward. Died Oct. 24, 1989. Information furnished by son, James E. Ryza of East Bernard, TX.

Sacky, June, daughter of Richard Sacky and Frances Sykora, was born June 23, 1966, Houston, Harris Co., TX. Pvt. Sacky entered the U.S. Army, Jun, 1990, Fort Gorden, GA. Now stationed in Saudi Arabia.

Saha, Eddie, served four years, U.S. Army Corps, during WWII.

Saha, Emil Louis, son of John Saha and Teresie Novosad, was born Aug. 4, 1919, Frydek, Austin Co., TX. Education, 1st through 8th Grade, Frydek, Austin Co., TX. Enlisted in U.S. Army Corps, Mar. 12, 1941, Houston, Harris Co., TX. Attained rank of Cpl. Assigned as Tank Commander, 753rd Tank Bn. Theater of Operations: Sicily, Central Europe (France, Italy, Belgium, Germany), Rome-Arno, Naples Foggia, Rhineland, North Africa. Medals: seven Distinguished Unit Badges, American Defense Service Medal, BSS, Purple with three OLC, EAME Campaign Medal with six BSS, Good Conduct Medal, Croix de la Guerre with Silver Star. WOUNDED IN ACTION four times, Oct. 29, 1944, Jan. 24, 1945, Mar. 22, 1945, Apr. 19, 1945. Cited as best tank gunner in his battalion. Before enlistment, Cpl. Saha worked with Austin Company, during early days of Dow Construction. Maj. Gen. John E. Dahlquist is quoted in awarding him BSS "for meritorious service in direct support of combat operations from July 10, 1943 to Oct. 31, 1944, in Sicily, Italy, and France ... Cpl. Saha, demonstrated extraordinary skill in the use of all tank weapons ... knocked out a large number of enemy vehicles ... completely disrupted hostile traffic retreating to north ... destroyed 17 enemy vehicles, one anti-tank gun and large number of hostile soldiers." Children: Suzanne Saha Kucera, Garry Ray Saha, Anne Saha Gilbert, Kathleen Saha Boyett, Marvin James Saha, Michael John Saha, Cynthia Saha Heard. Served U.S. Army Corps, during WWII. Died Mar. 29, 1972; buried St. Peter's Catholic Cemetery, Blessing, Matagorda, TX, with full military honors. Lovingly submitted in his memory by his widow, Lena Saha of Palacios, TX.

Saha, Paul, served U.S. Army Corps, during WWII.

Samek, John, son of John Samek and Vincencie Lorence, was born on May 24, 1897, in Borove Policka, Austria, Hungary. The family embarked from the Port of Bremen, Germany, on June 12, 1907, on the ship *Cassel*. Arrived in Galveston on July 2, 1907, where they settled. Attended country schools in Cook Co. Became a naturalized citizen on Sept. 12, 1918, upon registration for the draft. Filed a declaration of intent to become a citizen of the U.S., and renounced all loyalty to Charles, Emperor of Austria, and the Apostolic King of Hungary on Mar. 5, 1917. Enlisted on May 20, 1917, at Fort Sam Houston in San Antonio, TX. Stationed at Camp Wilson, San Antonio, Camp Logan, Houston, Leon Springs, Brownsville, Camp Pike, AR, and Fort Sam Houston in San Antonio. Earned Sharpshooter medal. Discharged June 1919 at Camp Pike. Married Julia Myrtle Morris on Nov. 16, 1924. Died Oct. 4, 1984 in Denton, TX.

Sassin, Louis F., son of Frank and Mary Sassin, was born Nov. 20, 1927, Hallettsville, Lavaca Co., TX. Attended school at Komensky, Stacey, TX. Enlisted Apr. 11, 1946, Ft. Sam Houston, TX. Honorably discharged Apr. 5, 1947; reenlisted Feb. 5, 1951, honorably discharged Jan. 22, 1953. Married Evelyn T. Galetka, Nov. 1, 1959; two sons: David and Larry. Occupation: barber. Home of record: Freeport, TX.

Sbrusch, Eddie, son of Mr. and Mrs. Joe Sbrusch, volunteered for service in July 1941 and was sent to the Philippines. Rank: Pvt. In June 1944 local relatives were notified that he was a PRISONER OF WAR of the Japanese. KILLED SERVING COUNTRY on Sept. 7, 1944, when an American submarine sent a torpedo into a Japanese convoy ship on which he was a prisoner.

Scasta, Ed W., son of Mr. and Mrs. Scasta, was born in Brazos Co., TX. Served honorably in military service during WWI. Married Stella Blazek.

Scasta, Louis A., son of Ed W. Scasta and Stella Blazek, was born Nov. 15, 1920, Wheelock, Brazos Co., TX. Graduate of Franklin High School, TX, and S.W. Business University, Houston, TX. Inducted Nov. 2, 1944, Ft. Sam Houston, TX. Basic training, Ft. Hood, TX. Left for Asiatic-Pacific Theater of Operations. Served w/43rd Inf. Div., Philippines, during the Luzon Campaign. Reassigned during Occupation of Japan to G-2 Section, 8th Army Hq, stationed in Yokohama. Medals: Asiatic-Pacific Theater Campaign Ribbon w/1 BSS, Philippine Liberation Campaign Ribbon w/1 BSS, Army of Occupation Ribbon (Japan), WWII Victory Ribbon w/2 overseas Service Bars and the Good Conduct Medal. Honorably discharged Oct. 28, 1946. Member of 1st Presbyterian Church, Bryan, TX. Retired Accountant of Texas A&M University and The Texas A&M University System. Married Laurie Harlan. Home of record: Franklin, TX.

Schattel, Albert Francis, son of William Edward Schattel and Caroline Morris, was born Oct. 3, 1907 in East Bernard, TX. Served in the Asiatic-Pacific Theater of Operations in the Philippine Islands, during World War II. PRISONER OF WAR, captured by Japanese at Corregidor. He was aboard the Japanese transport ship that was torpedoed by U.S. Forces in 1942 as it was transporting U.S. POWs to the Japanese mainland. KILLED SERVING HIS COUNTRY.

Schiller, Alden L., son of Joe Schiller and Frances Pomykal, was born on Feb. 4, 1915, at Oscar, Bell Co., TX. Attended Casey School through the 8th grade. Enlisted in the U.S. Army at Ft. Sam Houston, and served with 111th Combat Engineer Bn., 36th Inf. Div. in Europe, attaining the rank of Tech 5. Fought in the battles at Naples-Foggia, Rome-Arno, Southern France, Rhineland, Germany and Central Europe. Received the EAME Campaign Medal with five bronze battle stars and one arrowhead, the American Defense Service Medal and the Good Conduct Medal. Not wounded by the enemy, but sustained a broken ankle while running to take cover during an attack and was hospitalized for a couple of weeks. Discharged on Aug. 22, 1945, at Ft. Sam Houston, TX. Home of record: Temple, TX. Married Martha Sula; two children and two grandchildren.

Schiller, Edwin E., son of Vince Schiller and Bertha Wetzel, was born Nov. 28, 1920, Ocker, Bell Co., TX. Education took place at Cyclone School, Bell Co., TX. Enlisted at Temple, TX, U.S. Army Air Corps, 1945. Honorably discharged, date and places of service unknown. Died July 8, 1980; interred in Forest Park Cemetery, Houston, TX. Submitted by Ella S. Provazek, Dallas, TX.

Schiller, Joe Lee/see Bravenec, son of Edwin and Vlasta Schiller, was born Jan. 6, 1923, Bell Co., TX. Educated at Cyclone and Meeks schools and Little Elm School at Oscar, TX, east of Temple, TX. Enlisted first in National Guard, Temple, TX, later enlisted in U.S. Army Corps. Assigned to 36th Div. Was in Salerno Invasion, almost to Naples, Italy. Achieved rank of Cpl. KILLED IN ACTION during this invasion, Oct. 4, 1943. Received Purple Heart Medal and Certificate posthumously. Final resting place, Hillcrest Cemetery, Temple, TX. Submitted by Ella S. Provazek, Dallas, TX.

Schiller, Robert A., son of Vince Schiller and Bertha Wetzel, was born July 29, 1917, at Rosebud, Falls Co., TX. Attended high school at Cyclone, TX. Inducted into the U.S. Army on Jan. 2, 1942, Temple, TX, during World War II, then sent to San Antonio, TX. Rank: Cpl. Served in the European, African, and Middle Eastern Theater of Operations as a member of the 2nd Inf. Div. Participated in the Normandy (D Day landings), Northern France, and Ardennes: Alsace (Battle of the Bulge) Campaigns, Belgium and Czechoslovakia. WOUNDED IN ACTION. Family did not hear from him for 11 weeks, however, they heard through the grapevine that he was hospitalized. Received the Purple Heart Medal. Discharged from service on Aug. 6, 1945. Married Anna Marie Looka; four children. Retired. Home of record: Spring, TX. One of the submitters is Ella S. Provazek, Dallas, TX.

Schimcek, Alvin A., son of Charles Schimcek and Clara Seim, was born Nov. 29, 1918, in Floresville, TX. Went to Webbville Elementary School in Wilson Co., TX. Enlisted at Dodd Field, Fort Sam Houston, on Jan. 6, 1942, and was in the Asiatic Pacific Theater of Operations as a Cpl., serving in

the Philippine Liberation and Okinawa Campaign. Stationed at Pearl Harbor during the Battle of Midway in 1942. In Leyte, Philippine Islands, in Mar. 1945, Okinawa in Apr., May, June, and July 1945. Discharged Oct. 1, 1945. Medals: Good Conduct, Asiatic-Pacific Campaign, Philippine Liberation with BSS, Okinawa Campaign with BSS, six Overseas Chevrons, one hash mark, PCA Shoulder Patch Insignia. Worked at Pearl Brewery in San Antonio for over 35 years. Retired as a ground maintenance supervisor in 1980. Active in fraternal organizations, plays dominoes, dances, gardens and travels. Married Frances Schimcek; one son and one daughter. Home of record: San Antonio, TX.

Schmidt, Anton Thomas, was born May 10, 1894. WWI veteran. Pvt., 133 Field Arty., 36 Div. Died Aug. 1, 1952; buried Holy Cross Catholic Cem., Granger, TX.

Schulte, Norman D., son of Carl A. Schulte and Stephanie Janik, was born Nov. 4, 1946, in Houston, TX. Graduated from Reagan High School in May 1968, and enlisted in Houston on June 3, 1968. Left for action Nov. 8, 1968, in the Republic of Viet Nam as a SP4 E4 in Co. C, 1st Bn., 20th Inf., 11th Inf. Brigade, holding defensive position near the village of An Thach near Quang Ngai City, South Viet Nam when he was mortally wounded (KILLED IN ACTION) in a sniper fire. Medals: BSS, Purple Heart, Good Conduct, National Defense Service, Viet Nam Service Medal with one Bronze Service Star, Viet Nam Campaign Ribbon, Combat Infantryman Badge, Military Merit Medal, Gallantry Cross with Palm. Buried Aug. 22, 1969, at Forest Park Cemetery Westheimer in Houston, TX.

Schutza, Julius A., son of Mr. and Mrs. A. J. Schutza, Waco, TX. Entered Ground Forces Army in 1944 during WWII. Served as a Pvt. in Luzon. KILLED IN ACTION, Luzon, 1945. Awards: Good Conduct Medal, Purple Heart.

Schutza, Lawrence, son of Mr. amd Mrs. Alfred Schutza, West, TX. Entered Army, 1943, during WWII. Served in France and Germany with rank of Pfc. WOUNDED IN ACTION, Germany, 1944. Awards: Good Conduct Medal, Victory ET w/2 BSS, Purple Heart, AT Ribbon. Discharged 1944.

Schwertner, Darwin R., son of Mr. and Mrs. H. W. Schwertner. Education: Texas A&M College. Married Marjorie Franks. Enlisted U.S. Navy, 1943. Basic training, San Diego, CA. Attended Naval Storekeepers School. Theater of Operations: Asiatic-Pacific. Served in South Pacific, Marshalls, Gilberts. Medals: Asiatic-Pacific Theater Campaign Medal w/2 BSS, Purple Heart, Ribbons. WOUNDED IN ACTION, Jan. 1944. Achieved rank of S 2/c, prior to honorable discharge, 1945.

Schwertner, Eugene J., son of Mr. and Mrs. H. W. Schwertner. Education: Texas A&M College. Enlisted in Seabees, 1942, basic training, Norfolk, VA, additional training Port Hueneme, CA. Theater of Operation: Asiatic-Pacific. Served in Guadalcanal, Okinawa, Pacific Area. Medals: Navy Commendation Medal w/2 BSS, Good Conduct Medal, Asiatic-Pacific Theater Campaign Medal, WWII Victory Medal, ribbons. Attained rank of BM 1/c prior to honorable discharge, 1946.

Schwertner, Herman W., Jr., son of Mr. and Mrs. Herman W. Schwertner, Sr., Schwertner, TX. Education: Texas A&M College. Married Laurine Weeler. Enlisted, U.S. Army Air Corps, 1942, basic training, Foster Field, TX. Served in Belgium and Germany. Theater of Operations: European. Medals: two Good Conduct Medals, ETO Campaign Medal, two Unit Citations. Attained rank S/Sgt. prior to honorable discharge.

Sebesta, Lawrence W., Jr., son of Lawrence W. Sebesta, Sr., and Mildred Mikeska, was born Sept. 2, 1944 in Dodge City, KS. Graduated from Lamar High School in Rosenberg, and entered the Army in Rosenberg. Rank: Specialist 4/C. Served in the Army Medical Corp in Augsburg, Germany. Received National Defense Service and Marksman Medals. Discharged Nov. 1, 1968. Married Vickie; three sons. Home of record: Houston, TX.

Sebesta, Lawrence W., Sr., son of William A. Sebesta and Rosie Esterak, was born Feb. 11,

1923, in Fairchilds, Ft. Bend Co., TX. Graduated from Snook, TX, High School. Enlisted in the Army Air Force in Houston, TX. Rank: Cpl. Served during WWII. Awards include Aircraft Crew Member, Flying Engineer Wings, Good Conduct Medal and Marksman Award. Discharged Dec. 17, 1945. Married Mildred Mikeska; two children: Lawrence W., Jr. and Judy, and five grandchildren. Home of record: Rosenberg, TX.

Sebesta, William Adolph, son of Joe Sebesta and Mary Mikeska, was born Dec. 2, 1895 in Merle, Burleson Co., TX. Education went through the third grade. Enlisted in the Army at Richmond, TX. Rank: Pvt. Theater of Operation: France. Fought in World War I where he was WOUNDED IN ACTION (exposed to chlorine gas). Discharged May 19, 1919. Married Rosie Esterak; four children: Ivan, Laurence, Dorothy and Jo Ann, and nine grandchildren. Died June 12, 1960, and is buried at Greenlawn Memorial Cemetery in Rosenberg, TX.

Sebestik, Frank M., son of Augin Sebestik and Maria Smeja, was born July 3, 1908, Strizovice, Czechoslovakia. Graduated high school and three and a half years of Machinist Trade School. Enlisted in U.S. Army Corps, Mar. 24, 1941, Dallas, TX. Served in the 177th Signal Corps, Ft. Monmouth, NJ, Camp Claiborne, LA, and 123rd Army Air Corps, Dayton, OH. Attended Army Military Government School, Boston, MA, studied languages, customs, economics and types of government in foreign countries. Served 15 months overseas, Theater of Operations: EAME, in Army Air Corps: Rome-Arno (Italy), Medals: EAME Service Medal w/1 Bronze Battle Star, WWII Victory Medal. Honorably discharged Oct. 3, 1945, Sheppard Field, Wichita, TX. Attained rank of Staff Sgt. Died July 6, 1985, at age 77. Burial, Restland Memorial Park, Dallas, TX. Submitted by his widow, Mrs. Frank Sebestik of Dallas, TX.

Sebik, Anton, of West, TX, at Camp Barkley, military veteran.

Sebik, Joe J., was born Mar. 12, 1907, served during WWII with rank of Pfc in U.S. Army Corps. Died Feb. 4, 1977. Buried in St. Mary's Cemetery, West, TX.

Sefcak, Roland H., son of Mr. and Mrs. E. B. Sefcak, Taylor, TX. Education: Taylor Schools. Married Bertha Rozacky. Enlisted U.S. Army, 1945, basic training, Ft. Lewis, WA. Served in New Caledonia. Rank of Pvt. when honorably discharged.

Sefcik, Edmund, son of Mr. Sefcik and Mrs. Rose Sefcik, Taylor, TX. Graduate, Taylor High School. Enlisted U.S. Army Corps, 1943, basic training, Ft. Knox, KY, additional, Camp Bowie, TX. Theater of Operations: European, American. Served in Germany and U.S.A. WOUNDED IN ACTION, Germany, 1945. Medals: ETO Campaign Medal w/2 BSS, Combat Inf. Badge, Purple Heart, Good Conduct Medal, ATO Campaign Medal, WWII Victory Medal, Ribbons. Attained rank of Pfc. prior to honorable discharge.

Sefcik, John D., Sr., son of John J. Sefcik and Annie Chaloupka, was born Jan. 21, 1921, Seaton, Bell Co., TX. Education: high school, Jr. college, Temple, TX, Brewster College, Chicago, IL, and SMU, Dallas, TX. Enlisted in U.S. Army Corps 1940, Ft. Sam Houston, TX. Theater of Operations: American, EAME. Ardennes and Central Europe. Medals: Legion of Merit, BSS, Meritorious Service Medal, Army Achievement Medal, Reserve Armed Forces Medal w/2 HG Devices, Occupation of Germany Medal, WWII Victory Medal, EAME w/2 BSS, American Campaign Medal, National Defense Medal. With the 102d Inf. Div., was assigned as Admn. Asst. (Chief W.O.) to the Chief of Staff, Div. HQ. Div. hit Siegfried Line on the German Border, next to Holland, Oct. 1944, continued under the U.S. 9th Army to Roer River, and held the line until conclusion of the Battle of the Bulge. Fought its way to Krefeld, Rhine River.

The 102d Inf. Div. crossed Rhine River at Wesel and fought its way through central Germany to the Elbe River, where they met the Russian Army soldiers on May 7, 1945. Occupation Germany until Oct. 1945, USA Nov. 1945. Direct commission, 2nd Lt., U.S. Army Reserves, 1948. Active in the USAR until mandatory retirement in 1978, w/rank of Col. Graduated from Command and General Staff College and Civil Defense Staff College. Married Norma Kuzel; two children: John D., Jr., and Camille. After 43 years, John, Sr. and Norma were divorced. Married Christine Gajdica Goodlett. Home of record: Dallas, TX.

Sefcik, Raymond J., son of Mr. and Mrs. John A. Sefcik, Taylor, TX. Enlisted in U.S. Army Corps, 1943, basic training, Camp Wolters. Theater of Operations: European. Served in England and France. Medals: ETO Campaign Medal w/BSS, Purple Heart, WWII Victory Medal, Ribbons. KILLED IN ACTION, France, 1945.

Sefcik, Rudolph, son of Joseph Sefcik and Theresa Mastena, was born Oct. 29, 1915, Eastgate, Liberty Co., TX. Education: Wolf Island School District and Dayton High School. Enlisted in U.S. Army Corps, Ft. Sam Houston, TX, Apr. 7, 1941, prior to WWII. Theaters of Operation: European and Asiatic-Pacific. Germany and Philippines. Attained rank of Master Sgt. Medals: American Defense Ribbon, American Theater Ribbon, GCM, ETO Medal, Asiatic Pacific Theater of Operations Medal, Meritorious Service Medal, WWII Victory Medal. Honorably discharged Dec. 31, 1945, Ft. Bliss, El Paso, TX. Died July 13, 1993. Buried, St. Mary's Catholic Cemetery, West, TX. Submitted by widow, Maxine Sefcik. Home of record: West, TX.

Sefcik, Victor J., U.S. Navy: USS *Moffett*. WWII veteran of Granger, TX.

Seith, Englebert J., son of Mr. and Mrs. Joe Seith, West, TX. Entered Army 1944, during WWII. Trained at Camp Wolters, Ft. Sam Houston. Attained rank of Pfc. Awards: Sharp Shooter Medal and Good Conduct Medal.

Selensky, Edward G., son of Joseph Pete Selensky and Celestina Martin, was born July 7, 1927, in Houston, TX. Graduated from high school. Drafted into the Army during WWII at Houston, TX. Discharged Aug. 17, 1946. Home of record: Crosby, TX.

Selucky, Edward Daniel, son of Joe Selucky, Jr. and Margie Pauline Strmiska, was born Sept. 14, 1947 in Granger, TX. Attended Sts. Cyril & Methodius School in Granger, and graduated from Granger High School in 1966. Enlisted in the U.S. Army on Mar. 24, 1968 at Ft. Polk Louisiana, during the Viet Nam Conflict. Served with the Artillery as Section Chief and Gunner and attained the rank of Sgt. Separated from service on Mar. 24, 1970. Works as a plumbing superintendent and is an avid fisherman, hunting. Married Aleene May Volek; two children: Lisa and Michael. Member, American Legion Post No. 282, Granger, TX. Home of record: Granger, TX.

Selucky, Jerry J., son of Joe Selucky, Jr. and Margie Pauline Strmiska, was born June 1, 1945, in Taylor, TX. Attended Sts. Cyril & Methodius School in Granger, and Granger Independent School District. Enlisted in the U.S. Army on May 16, 1968 at Ft. Sam Houston, TX, during the Viet Nam Conflict. Served with Engineer Construction units and attained the rank of Sgt. Separated from service on May 16, 1970. Works as a plumbing supervisor. Has three children: Jerry, Jr, Patricia, and Janis. Home of record: Georgetown, TX.

Selucky, Joe, Jr., son of Joe Selucky, Sr. and Mary Kolacek, was born Feb. 21, 1914, in Granger, TX. Attended school at Friendship, TX. Enlisted in the U.S. Army on Nov. 25, 1942, at Camp Wolters, TX, during World War II. Discharged on Jan. 23, 1943. Married Margie Pauline Strmiska; five children: Jerry J. Selucky, Edward Selucky, Mildred Selucky Menscher, Clarence Selucky, and Carolyn Selucky Johnson. Was a farmer until his retirement in July 1956. Enjoyed hunting and playing dominoes. Member, American Legion Post No. 282, Granger, TX. Died Aug. 11, 1980, and is interred in Holy Cross Cemetery at Granger, TX.

Selucky, Steve, was born Apr. 4, 1904. Pvt., US Army. WWII veteran. Member, American Legion Post No. 282, Granger, TX. Died Oct. 15, 1983; buried Holy Cross Catholic Cemetery, Granger, TX.

Sembera, Frank A., was born July 3, 1907, West, TX. WWII veteran. Theater of Operations: EAME. Fought in North Africa, Mediterranean. Served in U.S. Army Corps. Attained rank of Pfc. Died Oct. 27, 1985. Buried in St. Mary's Cemetery, West, TX.

Sevcak, Roland Hugo, son of Emitt Sevcak and Justine Balusek, was born July 16, 1914, in Gainesville, TX. Attended West End School and Taylor Middle and High Schools. Enlisted, during WWII, in the U.S. Army on Apr. 15, 1945, at Ft. Sam Houston, TX. Served in the Asiatic Pacific Theater of Operations at New Caledonia as a truck driver and attained the rank of Cpl. Awards: include the Asiatic Pacific Campaign Medal with one campaign star. Separated from service on Aug. 10, 1946. Was a sign painter and a sketch artist. Retired Aug. 1981. Hobbies: drawing cartoons and working crossword puzzles. Married Bertha Rozacky; two children: Nancy Sevcak Kunze and Dixie Sevcak Rhoads. Home of record: Taylor, TX.

Sevcik, Anton Charles, attained rank of Pfc. Assigned to MG CO, 360th Inf., U.S. Army Corps, with American Expeditionary Forces during WWI. Eeceived WWI Victory Medal. Submitted by Evelyn Vecera, Bellaire, TX.

Sevcik, Anton Matej, son of Matej Sevcik and Filomena Tomek, was born Mar. 6, 1919, near Buckholts, TX. Attended school in Buckholts and Cameron, TX, graduating in 1937. Entered the Army at Dodd Field, San Antonio in Nov. 1940 and then departed for Fort Ringold. Promoted several times and was there until 1942. Attended Office Cadet School at Fort Benning, GA, and was commissioned 2nd Lt. Served in the 323rd Inf. at camps in AZ and CA. Overseas duty to Hawaii, Guadalcanal, Peleliu, Philippines, Japan, and other islands in the western Pacific. Was also in Co. B, 63rd Inf., 6th Div. Went through Fort Bliss Separation Center and then home to Buckholts. Relieved from active duty on Feb. 5, 1946. Medals: Asiatic Pacific Theater Ribbon w/2 BSS, Philippine Liberation Ribbon w/1 BSS, WWII Victory Medal, American Theater Ribbon, American Defense Ribbon, and Combat Infantryman Badge. Earned master's degree from A&M University in 1951, taught school in El Campo, TX, retiring in 1981. Married Emilie Eva David in 1947; three children. Hometown: El Campo, TX.

Seward, Wid Wright, Jr., son of Wid Wright Seward, Sr. and Louise Imelda Zernicek, was born Sept. 13, 1949, in El Campo, TX. Attended school in Lincoln, AR, and the University of Arkansas. Entered the Marines Jan. 1, 1968, in Little Rock, AR. Rank: Cpl. Theater of Operations was I Corp in Viet Nam with Mike Co. 3rd Bn., 9th Marine Reg., 3rd Marine Div. FMF. Served in Viet Nam, where he was WOUNDED IN ACTION, as a member of the 3rd Bn., 9th Marine Reg., 3rd Marine Div. from June 1968–Feb. 1969. Attained the rank of Lance Cpl. Awards: Purple Heart, National Defense Service Medal, Viet Nam Service Medal, Viet Nam Campaign Medal, and others. Discharged June 2, 1969, at Portsmouth, VA. Home of record: Lincoln, AR.

Shiller, Clara Mae, daughter of Mr. and Mrs. E. M. Shiller. Entered Navy Nurse Corps, 1943, during WWII. Served in Hawaii. Attained rank of Lt./jg. Awards: American Defense Ribbon, Asiatic-Pacific Ribbon, WWII Victory Ribbon. Discharged 1946. Married John Kutni, Waco, TX. Died in 1993. Buried in Oak Wood Cemetery, Waco, TX.

Shiller, Edward V., son of Mr. and Mrs. E. M. Shiller, Waco, TX. Entered Army, 1943. Served EAME during WWII, attaining rank of T/Sgt. Awards: GCM, American Defense, WWII Victory and ET Ribbons. Discharged 1946.

Shimek, Alfons Joe, son of Emil and Elizabeth Shimek, was born on Apr. 8, 1926, at Schulenburg, TX. Graduated from Schulenburg High School in 1944. Inducted on Oct. 10, 1944, at Fort Sam Houston, TX. Served in Japan and the Philippines in WWII and fought in the battle at Luzon GO 105 WD 45.

Received the Asiatic Pacific Theater Campaign Ribbon w/1 Bronze Battle Star, Good Conduct Medal, Philippine Liberation Ribbon with one Bronze Battle Star, Army of Occupation Ribbon (Japan), Victory Ribbon, and two Overseas Service Bars. Discharged on Nov. 23, 1946. Died on Mar. 21, 1987, and is buried at Schulenburg, TX.

Shimek, Joe L., son of Joe J. Shimek and Julia Franton, was born July 7, 1922, in Fayetteville, TX. Attended school through the 8th grade. Entered the Army at Houston, TX. Discharged Dec. 5, 1942. Died Sept. 23, 1985.

Shimek, Johnnie, Jr., son of John Shimek and Annie Sternadel, was born Feb. 28, 1919, Schulenburg, Fayette Co., TX. Attended St. Rose of Lima Catholic School. Enlisted in U.S. Army Corps, Oct. 16, 1941, Ind. Station, Ft. Sam Houston, TX. Theater of Operation: North Africa, Sicily, Italy, Salerno to Cassino, to the Alps w/91st Cavalry RCN Alert Sqdn, was attached w/Fifth U.S. Army and 10th Mountain Div. WOUNDED IN ACTION, Oct. 1944, Italy. Hospitalized for two months in 33rd General Hospital, Leghorn, Italy. Medals: American Defense Service, EAME Campaign w/6 BSS, Good Conduct, Silver Star, Purple Heart, WWII Victory. Honorably discharged Sept. 17, 1945, Ft. Sam Houston, TX, with rank of Tech 4/Sgt. Died Apr. 22, 1987; buried St. Rose of Lima Catholic Cemetery, Schulenburg, TX. Submitted by Evelyn Vecera, Bellaire, TX.

Shimek, Lee Roy, son of Joe Shimek and Julia Franton, was born Aug. 31, 1927, in Crosby, TX. Attended school through the ninth grade. Entered the Army at Houston, TX. Stationed in China during WWII, and discharged in Oct. of 1946. Died July 4, 1985.

Shimek, Otto L., son of Joe Shimek and Julia Franton, was born Feb. 19, 1917 in Fayetteville, TX. Attended school through the eighth grade. Entered the Army at Houston, TX, was discharged Nov. 10, 1943. Died Sept. 3, 1959.

Shirocky, Alvin Roy, son of Louis Shirocky and Mary Gaida, was born in Granger, TX, on Sept. 15, 1922. Graduated from high school in Friendship, TX. Served, during WWII, in the U.S. Army Air Corps as a mechanic until his separation in Dec. 1945. Rank: Sgt., 4144 Base Unit AAF. Died Aug. 14, 1956, and is interred in Holy Cross Catholic Cemetery, Granger, TX.

Shirocky, Joe Daniel, son of Louis Shirocky and Mary Gaida, was born in Granger, TX, on Mar. 12, 1928. Graduated from Granger High School in 1946. Enlisted in the U.S. Army in Oct. 1950 at Ft. Sam Houston, TX. Served in Japan and in Korea as a Medic, during the Korean Conflict. Awards include the Army of Occupation Medal, Korean Service Medal, with one campaign star, United Nations Service Medal, one Overseas Bar, and Combat Medic Badge. Separated from service on Oct. 11, 1952 with the rank of Sgt. Was a farmer. Retired Jan. 1993. Married Betty Jean Rozacky; six children: Mitchell, Lorna Shirocky Warnke, Gregory, Alan, Dean, and Shelly. Member, American Legion Post No. 282, Granger, TX. Home of record: Granger, TX.

Shirpig, Oscar, served in U.S. Armed Forces during WWI, 1917–1918. Member of SPJST Lodge 20, Granger, TX.

Shumbera, August L., Jr., son of August L. Shumbera, Sr. and Vlasta Kroboth, was born July 23, 1932, Weimar, Colorado Co., TX. Education: Weimar High School, TX; Texas A&M, College Station, TX, B.S. in Agricultural Engineering; Penn State University, University Park, PA, B.S. in Meterology; Texas A&M, College Station, TX,

Master of Science in Meterology. Received commission, enlisted in USAF, Parks AFB, CA, Mar. 11, 1954. Attained rank of Lt. Col. Theater of Operations: Far East. Medals: Commendation Medals in 1967, 1969 and 1973, Good Conduct Medal w/1 OLC. Retired from military service Sept. 30, 1976, after 22 years. Occupation: National Physical Scientist, Climatic Data Center and Director of World Data Center A for Meteorology. Married Patricia Ann Butzin; three children. Home of record: Black Mountain, NC. Submitted by sister, Vlasta Shumbera Polk of Weimar, TX.

Shumbera, August, Sr., son of Anton Shumbera and Anna Tumis, was born Nov. 27, 1888, in Ammannsville, Fayette Co., TX. Attended Ammannsville grade school through the fourth grade. Inducted July 25, 1918, in Columbus, TX. Left from New York City for overseas duty in France on Oct. 13, 1918. Discharged Feb. 16, 1919, at Camp Travis, TX. Married to Vlasta Kroboth; five children and eight grandchildren. Farmer and rancher. Enjoyed hunting. Died Apr. 24, 1965, in the V.A. Hospital in Houston, and was buried in the Masonic cemetery in Weimar, TX.

Siegel, Jerry G., son of Mr. and Mrs. Bill Siegel, was born Feb. 5, 1943, in Shiner, TX. Graduated from St. Ludmila's Academy in Shiner and had 56 hours of college with the Community College of the Air Force. Enlisted in Victoria, and served in the Viet Nam Conflict. Was involved in B-52 bomber air raids, maintaining inflight refueling and inflight radio relay operations. Medals: Viet Nam Service Medal, Republic of Viet Nam Campaign Medal, Small Arms Expert Marksmanship Medal, USAF NCO PME Graduate Ribbon, National Defense Service Ribbon, Army and Air Force Good Conduct Ribbon with four OLC. Retired Sept. 1, 1983. Home of record: San Antonio, TX.

Siegel, Severine Louis, son of Rudolph Siegel and Elizabeth Marek, was born Aug. 27, 1917, in Shiner, TX. Schooling was in Shiner. Enlisted in the Army at Fort Sam Houston, in Feb. 1940. Rank: Sgt. Fought in battles in New Guinea, Dutch New Guinea, Morati, Biak, Leyete, and North Luzon, Philippines. Medals: American Defense Service Medal, American Theater Campaign Medal w/1 BSS, five Overseas Service Bars, Good Conduct Medal, Victory Ribbon w/1 Service Stripe, Asiatic-Pacific Campaign Medal w/3 BSS, Philippine Liberation Medal. WOUNDED IN ACTION when blown up by a mine, causing severe burns and other injuries. Discharged at Fort Sam Houston on Nov. 24, 1945. Married in Brisbane, Australia in 1944 to Marjorie L. Scott; four sons and one daughter. Three sons were in the service: one in the Air Force in Viet Nam Conflict, one in the Air Force in Guam, and one in the Navy in the Mediterranean. Home of record: Victoria, TX.

Sikora, Simon A., son of Adolph Sikora and Mary Brandl, was born Aug. 2, 1911, in East Bernard, Wharton Co., TX. Attended Hungerford schools and entered the Army in June 1940, training at Camp Wolters, Mineral Wells, TX. Discharged in Oct. 1941 and reenlisted Jan. 28, 1942. Served at Ft. Lewis, Washington. Married Mary in Australia on Sept. 28, 1944; three sons: Garion, Dale, and Simon A., Jr. Retired Farmer. Home: Wharton, TX.

Simcik, Albert, son of Joe P. Simcik and Adela Hejl, was born 1918 in Taylor, TX. Attended various schools in Taylor and graduated from Taylor High School in 1936. Enlisted in San Antonio and served overseas during WWII. Discharged in 1945 in San Antonio. Member, American Legion Post No. 282, Granger, TX. Died Nov. 17, 1983.

Simcik, Clifton Alvin, son of Joe Simcik and Agnes Repa, was born Apr. 7, 1922, Granger, TX. Education: San Angelo, TX, High School, VA Ag School, San Angelo College. Enlisted about 1942, Dallas, TX, U.S. Navy. Basic training, NTS, San Diego, CA, NATTC 87th and St. Anthony, Chicago, IL, VR 3 USNAS, Olathe, KS, Air Trans Sqdn. 5, PSC USNB Bremerton, WA. Theater of Operations:

America and Asiatic Pacific. Medals: Asiatic-Pacific Area Campaign Medal, American Area Campaign Medal, Good Conduct Medal, WWII Victory Medal. Honorably discharged Feb. 5, 1946. Home of record: San Angelo, TX.

Simcik, Ernest Richard, son of Mr. and Mrs. John Simcik, Waco, TX. Entered Army 1944. Served in Belgium and Germany, attaining rank of T/4. Awarded Good Conduct Medal.

Simcik, Joe, son of Frank Simcik and Rosie Krause, was born in Valasske Mezirici, Moravia, Czechoslovakia, immigrated to Williamson Co., TX, as a small child. Some elementary school in Czechoslovakia, through 2nd grade, Moravia School in Williamson Co., TX. Enlisted in U.S. Army Corps, Sept. 19, 1917, Taylor, TX. Assigned to Co. I, 360 Inf. Theater of Operations: Europe. American Expeditionary Forces, Apr. 25, 1918–May 6, 1919. Battles: Toul Sr July 14, 1918, Aug. 4, 1918, Aug. 8, 1918, Marbough Sr Aug. 17, Sept. 19, 1918, St. Michiel, Sept. 12-16, 1918, Meuse-Argonne Sept. 26, Nov. 1, 1918. WOUNDED IN ACTION (poison gas) Oct. 25, 1918, at Meuse- Argonne. In Co. A, 320 MG B Apr. 2, 1918–May 21, 1919. Described on honorable discharge issued May 21, 1919, as being 5' 3", brown eyes, black hair, and of a red complexion. Member of SPJST Lodge 20, Granger, TX. Civilian occupation: farmer. Died June 19, 1980.

Simcik, John Cecil, son of John Simcik, immigrant from Valasske Mezirici, Moravia, Czechoslovakia, and Mary Hanak from Cestovice Hana, Moravia, Czechoslovakia, was born Feb. 4, 1921, Waco, McLellan Co., TX. Enlisted in U.S. Army Corps, Mar. 25, 1942, Camp Wolters, TX. Basic training, Ft. Leonard Wood, MO. Commissioned Oct. 14, 1942, Ft. Belvior, VA. Assigned 9th Armored Engr. Bn., Ft. Riley, KS. Received Desert training at Camp Isis, CA. Reassigned with B Co. of 9th Armored Engrs. to 133rd Engr. Combat Bn. to the 3rd Army Sent overseas Feb. 1944, Belfast, Ireland, then to Camp Carrick Blacker. Mar. 1944, Sent to Ensham Parks, England. Entered France and combat June 1944. Temporarily assigned to 1st Army, 15 Corps. Rejoined 3rd Army, 8 Corps when 3rd Army became active. Worked with 4th Armored Div., 5th and 6th Armored Div. Captured by the Africa Corps of the German Army, Aug. 28, 1944. Sent to Stalag Limburg, Germany, Oflag 64 Shubin Poland. Walked from Shubin, Poland Jan. 21, 1945, to Parcom, Germany. Entrained Parcom Mar. 6, 1945. Arrived Oflag BB, Hamburg, Germany, Mar. 9, 1945. Liberated by Combat Team 4th Armored Div., Mar. 27, 1945. Recaptured Mar. 29, 1945, and sent to Nuernberg, Germany. Bombed by U.S. Air Corps on a raid in Nuernberg Rail Yards. Marched to Moosburg, Stamlager VIIA. Arrived Apr. 20, 1945. Liberated by 14 Armored Div., Apr. 30, 1945. Arrived Waco, TX, June 17, 1945. Assigned Army Reserve. Discharged with rank of Ltc. Engrs., Feb. 4, 1981. Married Mary Lee Marak of West, TX, May 14, 1946; five children: three boys, two girls. WOUNDED IN ACTION, Hammelburg, Germany. Medals: Purple Heart, European Theater Ribbon, two BSS, American Theater Ribbon. Home of record: Waco, TX.

Simcik, Wilford J., son of Joseph Simcik and Agnes Repa, was born Oct. 30, 1923, Granger, TX. Education: high school and junior college, San Angelo, TX. Enlisted in USAF, Induction Station, Abilene, TX. Theater of Operation: EAME. Battles: Rhineland, Normandy, Ardennes, Northern France. Medals: Air Crew Badge, Good Conduct Medal, Distinguished Unit Badge, Co. 11, HQ, 9th Air Force, Jan. 15, 1945, Air Medal w/6 OLC, EAME Campaign w/4 BSS, WWII Victory Ribbon. Military Schools: Aviation Mechanic, Aerial Gunnery. 39 Missions: 10 in B-17 Flying Fortress, High Altitude, 8th Air Force, 29 in B-26 Marauder, Medium Altitude, 9th Air Force. Top Turret Position–Flight Engineer. Honorably discharged Aug. 31, 1945. Married Georgia Michalik; four daughters. Retired from sales. Home of record: San Angelo, TX.

Simecek, Charles J., son of Charles P. Simecek and Agelina R. Gelner, was born Feb. 6, 1947, in Cameron, TX. Education: St. Pius V School, Southmore Junior High, Sam Rayburn High School, and Durham Business College. Enlisted at

Fork Polk, Louisiana, and fought in Viet Nam, Iron Triangle, Mekong Delta, TET Offensive. Attained the rank of Sgt. Medals: National Defense Service, Good Conduct, Marksman, Viet Nam Service, Viet Nam Commendation, three Overseas Bars. Home of record: Pasadena, TX.

Simek, Anton L., son of Mr. and Mrs. A. A. Simek of Jarrell, TX. Education: Holy Trinity School. Enlisted U.S. Army Corps, 1938; basic training, Ft. Sam Houston, TX. Reenlisted, U.S. Army Air Corps, 1941, reenlisted in A.A.F., 1945. Theater of Operations: American. Medals: American Defense Medal, American Theater Campaign Medals, Good Conduct Medal, WWII Victory Medal, Ribbons. Attained rank of S/Sgt before honorable discharge. Married Angeline Zurovetz.

Simek, Johnnie J., son of Joe A. Simek and Mary Sladecek, was born Dec. 16, 1935, Corn Hill, Williamson Co., TX. Education: Holy Trinity Catholic Elementary, Corn Hill, TX; Jarrell High School, TX, through 9th grade. Enlisted in U.S. Army Reserve, May 1956, Ft. Chaffee, AR. Attained rank of Sgt. Assigned to Inf. Sent to Ft. Jackson, SC. Honorable discharge May 30, 1964. Married Alice Albina Lefner; two children: Monica Rose, Mark. Employed as heavy eqpt. operator. Hobby: carpentry. Church organist for many years, including time spent in military. Home of record: Jarrell, TX.

Simpson, Joseph Earl, son of Thomas B. Simpson and Anna C. Kurtin, was born Apr. 27, 1923, Houston, Harris Co., TX. Education: St. Thomas High School, University of Texas, B.B.A. Enlisted Feb. 15, 1943, Ft. Sam Houston, San Antonio, TX, U.S. Army Corps. Served in European Theater of Operations, Ruhr Valley Campaign. Decorations: BSS and Purple Heart. WOUNDED IN ACTION, Jan. 28, 1945. Honorably discharged Sept. 28, 1945. Home of record: Houston, TX. Submitted by Evelyn Vecera, Bellaire, TX.

Sinkule, Jerry A., son of Mr. and Mrs. Mat Sinkule, West, TX. Entered Army 1940, trained and sent to European Theater, attaining rank of Sgt. Awards: EAME w/5 BSS, GCM, American Defense, Dist. Unit Badge w/BSS. Discharged in 1945.

Sinkule, Johnnie A., son of Mr. and Mrs. Max Sinkule, West, TX. Entered AAC in 1942, during WWII. Served in Italy, attained rank of Pfc. Awards: six BSS, EAME, AT Ribbon, GCM. Discharged 1945.

Siska, Ferdinand F. "Fred," son of Ferdinand Siska (born Cervna 4, 1876; died Dubna 29, 1945) and Anna (born Prosinc 8, 1890; died Cervna 23, 1978). Enlisted in U.S. Navy, during WWII, attaining rank of S-1. Served Nov. 1942–May 1945. Owned store and baled hay. Married Apr. 24, 1946, Olga V. Zboril (deceased May 2, 1981); four children: Julia Siska Kuhn, Dorothy Siska Rainosek, Fred Siska, Jr., Larry Siska. Died Nov. 25, 1980; buried St. Mary's Catholic Church, Frydek, TX.

Sitka, Henry J., son of Joe Sitka, Jr. and Clara Munsch, was born Sept. 28, 1930. Enlisted in the Army on Oct. 29, 1948, at Camp Chaffee, AR. Rank: Sgt. At the Occupation of Japan and fought in the Korean War. Received Good Conduct, Sharp Shooter and Occupational Medals. Discharged July 25, 1952. Home of record: Hallettsville, TX.

Sitka, John, son of John Sitka and Agnes Orsak, was born May 17, 1929, in Shiner, TX. Attended St. Joseph's School in Yoakum and Brazosport College in Lake Jackson. Inducted Feb. 5, 1951, at Fort Sam Houston in San Antonio. Assigned to 102nd Q.M. Bakery Co. and served 14 months overseas in Europe. Discharged Dec. 31, 1952, from active duty and from the reserves on Mar. 28 1956.

Sitka, John J., son of John Emil Sitka and Albina Steffek, was born Dec. 4, 1914, in Hallettsville, TX. Attended Saint Mary's Convent School and Brown School. Enlisted May 3, 1942, at Dodd Field, San Antonio, TX, with training at Camp Shelby, MS, Camp Coxcomb, LA, Camp Young, CA, and Fort Dix, NJ, attaining rank of Cpl. Landed in Africa Jan. 13, 1944, and fought in the

North African area, then to Sicily, and on Mar. 12, 1944, in Terracina at the Gustav line. Received the Purple Heart for his bravery and SACRIFICING HIS LIFE for our country. Buried in the U.S. Military Cemetery in Carano, Italy, and in 1948 the family received his body from overseas. Now interred in Saint Mary's Catholic Cemetery, Hallettsville, TX.

Sitka, Julius F., son of Joe Sitka, Jr. and Clara Munsch, was born Sept. 11, 1921. Entered the Army on Oct. 9, 1942, at Fort Sam Houston, San Antonio, TX. Theater of Operation was Central Europe. Rank: Pfc. Fought at Ardennes, Rhineland and Central Europe in WWII. Medals: EAME Theater with three BSS, American Theater, Good Conduct, and Victory. Discharged Dec. 3, 1945. Home of record: Shiner, TX.

Sitka, Louis A., son of John Emil Sitka and Albina Steffek, was born June 10, 1922, in Hallettsville, TX. Attended Brown School. Enlisted Oct. 13, 1944, at Fort Sam Houston, San Antonio, TX. Served in Luzon, Philippines, and Tokyo, Japan, attaining the rank of Staff Sgt. Medals: Asiatic-Pacific Theater Ribbon, Philippine Liberation Ribbon, Army of Occupation Ribbon, Japan Victory Ribbon, Good Conduct Medal, and two Overseas Service Bars. Discharged Oct. 25, 1946. Home of record: Hallettsville, TX.

Sitka, Robert L., son of Joe Sitka, Jr. and Clara Munsch, was born Oct. 24, 1918. Enlisted in the Army on Mar. 21, 1942 at San Antonio, TX. Fought in WWII, D-Day, Normandy Beach Head, June 6, 1944, as a Machine Gunner with Reg. 90th Inf. Div., Co. H, 359th Inf. Rank: Sgt. KILLED IN ACTION at St. Lo., France, on July 26, 1944, just 20 days after landing at the beach. Received the Purple Heart and EAME Medal.

Sitka, Ronald J., son of Henry J. Sitka and Martha Stryk, was born Aug. 3, 1953. Entered the Army on Aug. 3, 1972, at Fort Sam Houston, San Antonio, TX. Rank: Sgt. Theater of Operation: Germany, during the Viet Nam Conflict. Medals: Commendation for Meritorious Service, Good Conduct, and Expert M-16 Rifle. Discharged Aug. 17, 1974. Home of record, Victoria, TX.

Skala, Henry Edward, Sr., son of Frank Skala, Sr. and Lottie Koslosky, was born Apr. 18, 1930, Clarkson, TX. Education: Clarkson Grade School, Cameron High School, TX. Enlisted Ft. Sam Houston, U.S. Army Corps. Sent to Camp Chaffee, AR, Ft. Knox KY, Ft. Hood, TX, Korea (13 months). Fought in Korean War. Decorations: (C1B) Combat Inf. Badge, Good Conduct Medal. Honorable Discharge Dec. 9, 1953. Farmer. Married Shirley Ann Meier; three sons: Henry Edward, Jr., Ronnie, Rayland (died at 22 years in 1986). Home of record: Temple, TX.

Skerik, E., West, TX, WWII veteran. KILLED IN ACTION.

Skerik, Frank, son of Mr. and Mrs. Joe Skerik, West, TX. Entered AAC in 1942, during WWII. Trained in NY, TX. Attained rank of Cpl. Awards: GCM, Victory, and Amer. Def. Ribbon. Discharged 1946.

Skerik, Henry R., son of Mr. and Mrs. Joe Skerik, West, TX. Entered AAC in 1942, during WWII. Served in England, France, and Germany, attaining rank of Cpl. Awards: GCM, Victory, EAME w/3 BSS, and AT Ribbon. Discharged 1945.

Skerik, Joe, son of Mr. and Mrs. Joe Skerik, West, TX. Entered service in 1940. Served in Africa, Italy, and France, attaining rank of Pfc. KILLED IN ACTION, France, 1944. Awards: GCM, Victory, ET w/4 BSS, Purple Heart, BSS, and Oak Leaf Cluster.

Skerik, Willie A., son of Mr. and Mrs. Joe Skerik, West, TX. Entered Army 1945. Served as Pvt. Trained at Camp Hood, TX. Discharged 1945.

Sklenarik, Ladislav, born June 14, 1894. Enlisted during WWI; assigned to Texas Brigade Depot, Co. 165. Rank: Pvt. Married Louise. Died Apr. 24, 1961; buried St. Mary's Catholic Cemetery, Frydek, Austin Co., TX.

Sklenarik, Otto, son of Edward and Anna Sklenarik, was born Sept. 21, 1927, in Sealy, Austin Co., TX. Family moved to Ganado in 1929/1930, and engaged in farming. Attended White Hall School in Ganado, TX. Inducted into the U.S. Army at Ft. Sam Houston, TX, on Jan. 10, 1946. Transferred to Fort Monmouth, NJ; trained as Radio Operator for 12 weeks, and assigned to 63rd Inf. Reg., at Kunson, Korea. Was in a Rifle Company, pulled guard duty, and received training through field problems and was familiar with pistol, carbine and rifle. Honorably discharged Aug. 4, 1947, at Camp Stoneman, CA. Medals: WWII Victory, and Army of Occupation, Japan. Died May 8, 1976, and is buried in the Catholic Cemetery in El Campo, TX. Married Evelyn; four sons: Clarence, Lawrence, Melvin, and Michael, and daughter Theresa.

Skrabanek, Raymond W., son of Frank and Frances Skranbanek, was born Feb. 21, 1912, in Holliday, Wichita Co., TX. Completed high school and later enlisted in Houston, TX, June 21, 1939, serving two years in the U.S. Army Corps as S/Sgt at Ft. Sam Houston, TX. Assigned to 9th Inf., K Co., 2nd Div., in Mortar Squad. On June 26, 1941, transferred to the Air Force Training Command, U.S. Army Air Corps, as Master Sgt. at Kelly Field. Served in the 5th Air Force in the Southwest Pacific as Line Chief in the South Philippine Liberation, Luzon and Western Pacific Campaigns. Medals: American Defense Service Medal, Asiatic-Pacific Service Medal w/3 BBS. Discharged Oct. 26, 1945, with a Good Conduct Medal for a total of six years service. Married Ruby Parker; six children: Raymond W., Jr., Larry, Shirley Skrabanek Kober, Mary, Sandra, Martha, nine grandchildren, three great-grandchildren. Lived in Jacinto City, TX. Retired from U.S. Postal Service. Involved in many activities: Presbyterian Church and Czech activities. Died Dec. 13, 1994; burial in San Jacinto Memorial Park Cemetery.

Skrabanek, Robert L., son of John T. Skrabanek and Frances Bravanec, was born on Nov. 18, 1918, in Snook, TX. Received B.S. and M.S. from A&M University and a PhD from Louisiana State University. Enlisted in the U.S. Navy at College Station, TX, on Jan. 26, 1942. Served in the Pacific and Atlantic Ocean, attaining the rank of U.S. Navy Senior Grade Lt. Participated in battle while serving on U.S.S. *Lassen*, *Mazama*, *Wilcat*, and *Yorktown*. Received the Asiatic-Pacific and Philippine Liberation Medals. Discharged Mar. 23, 1946. Married Kathryn Kohler; one son and one daughter. Emeritus Professor, A&M University. Has published writings about Czechs in journals, magazines, and books, and is the author of *We're Czechs* published in 1988. Home of record: College Station, TX.

Skrasek, Joe, son of John Skrasek and Frances Polasek, was born on Dec. 15, 1919, at Fort Worth, TX. Education at Diamond Hill High School. Enlisted in Fort Worth, and was inducted in the Army at Camp Wolters, TX. Attained the rank of Staff Sgt. and served in Africa, Sicily and Italy. Medals: EAME Campaign w/5 Battle Stars in Africa, Sicily, and Italy, EAME Campaign Medal w/5 Battle Stars, and the Good Conduct Medal. Battles: Tunisia, Sicily, Naples, Foggia, Rome, Arno, North Apennines. Discharged at San Antonio on Oct. 3, 1945. Played football in high school. Started an automobile dealership in 1940, which he owned until retirement in Dec. 1983. Married Helen Sonka of Ennis, on Nov. 4, 1945; two sons: Ronald Joe and Gary Steven, and five grandchildren. Moved to Ennis, TX, in Jan. 1985. Among hobbies was a love of dancing. Died Feb. 22, 1987.

Skrhak, Adolph, WWII veteran of Granger, TX.

Skrhak, John, served in U.S. Armed Forces during WWI, 1917–1918. Member of SPJST Lodge 20, Granger, TX.

Skrhak, Rudy, Rogers, TX. WWII veteran. Member, American Legion Post No. 282, Granger, TX. Deceased.

Skrivanek, Jesse E., son of John Skrivanek and Elizabeth, was born Mar. 15, 1916, Ennis, Ellis Co., TX. Education: B.A. and M.A., University of Texas in Austin. Drafted June 12, 1941, in U.S. Army Corps, Dallas, TX. After basic training, promoted to Sgt. Four months later, enrolled in Class No. 4, Officer Training School. Commissioned 2nd Lt., Went overseas, Feb. 1943; served as supply officer and later as company commander for 18 months. Theater of Operations: EAME. Battles: Sicily, Naples-Foggia and Rome-Arno. Medals: EAME Campaign w/3 BSS, American Campaign, WWII Victory. Honorably discharged from active duty Mar. 25, 1946, as Capt. Remained in Reserves for next 20 years, finally attaining rank of Lt. Col. Home of record: Austin, TX.

Skrla, Steve, Jr., son of Steve Skrla, Sr. and Blanche Baletka, was born Aug. 16, 1920, in Crosby, TX. Inducted into the Army Jan. 25, 1945, at Houston, TX. Rank: Tech 5. Served in Battery C, 545th Field Artillery Bn. and 63rd Field Artillery. Served in WWII in the Philippines and received WWII Victory, Army of Occupation and Asiatic-Pacific Medals. Discharged Dec. 12, 1946, at Camp Beale, CA. Home of record: Crosby, TX.

Skrla, Steve, Sr., son of Jan. Skrla and Marie Lastovica, was born Mar. 29, 1892, at Driskova, Czechoslovakia. Came to America, May 16, 1913, at age 21. Inducted into the Army Sept. 4, 1918, at Houston, TX, during WWI. Rank: Pvt., 29th Co. 8 Fr BW 165 DB, 53rd Field Artillery and Util. Det 2 MC. Discharged Apr. 4, 1919, at Camp Travis, TX. Died Feb. 26, 1935, and is buried at SPJST Cemetery in Crosby, TX.

Skruhak, A. J., son of Mr. and Mrs. Frank Skruhak, Granger, TX. Education: Granger High School. Enlisted U.S. Army Air Corps, 1941. Basic training, Lowery Field, CO, additional training, NE, TX. Theater of Operations: Asiatic-Pacific, American. Served in Pacific. Medals: Air Medal w/OLC, Unit Citation Medal w/3 OLC, Asiatic-Pacific Theater Campaign Medal w/1 BSS, American Theater Campaign Medal, American Defense Medal, Air Battle over Japan Medal, Good Conduct Medal, WWII Victory Medal, ribbons. Attained rank of Flight Officer prior to honorable discharge, 1945. Married Florence Hartmann.

Skurka, Johnnie W., son of Mr. and Mrs. John P. Skurka, Jarrell, TX. Education: Jarrell school. Enlisted U.S. Army Air Corps, 1942. Basic training, Kearns, UT, additional training, TX, WY. Theater of Operations: CBI. Military Occupation: B-24 Gunner. WOUNDED IN ACTION, China, 1944. MISSING IN ACTION, Feb. 1945, from over French Indo-China. Attained rank of S/Sgt. prior to that time. From Jarrell, Williamson Co., TX.

Sladecek, Albert J., son of Joseph F. Sladecek and Emilie David, was born Jan. 24, 1916, Granger, Williamson Co., TX. Educated probably through sixth grade. Enlisted in U.S. Army Corps, about 1934, Williamson Co., TX. Mess Sgt. (cook)/Staff Sgt. Served in WWII. Received several medals and citations. Honorably discharged 1945. Farmer. Died July 20, 1978, Corn Hill, Williamson Co., TX. Member, American Legion Post No. 282, Granger, TX.

Sladecek, Anton C., son of Anton A. Sladecek and Frances Janosec, was born on Nov. 23, 1930, in Holland, Bell Co., TX. Graduated from Holland High School in 1949. Enlisted in the U.S. Army at Ft. Sill, OK, and served in Europe (France) as a welder. Awards: Army of Occupation Medal, Good Conduct Medal, and others. Separated from service on Oct. 10, 1956. Retired. Married Dolores Schindler; five children: Mike, Donald, Steven, James, and Susan. Hobbies are hunting and fishing. Home of record: Holland, TX.

Sladecek, Edward, Jr., son of Mr. and Mrs. Edward Sladecek, Sr. of Granger, Williamson Co., TX. WWII veteran of Granger, TX.

Sladecek, Edward John, son of Edward Charles Sladecek and Regina Piela, was born on Apr. 10, 1920, in Granger, TX and attended Granger High School. Enlisted in the U.S. Army Air Corps on Jan. 8, 1942, during WWII. Served in the European, African, and Middle Eastern Theater of Operations as a Motor Sgt. in the 10th Fighter Squadron. Participated in air offensive operations in Central Europe, Northern France, Normandy, and the Rhineland. Awards: European African Middle Eastern Campaign Medal with five campaign stars, Good Conduct Medal, and Distinguished Unit Badge, and others. Separated from service on Sept. 15, 1945. Rank: Staff Sgt. Automotive Technician. Retired in 1982. Hobbies are hunting and fishing. Married Angeline Cmerek. Member, American Legion Post No. 282, Granger, TX. Home of record: Granger, TX.

Sladecek, Joe R., Taylor, TX. WWII veteran. Member, American Legion Post No. 282, Granger, TX.

Sladecek, John T., Corn Hill, TX. WWII veteran. Member, American Legion Post No. 282, Granger, TX.

Sladecek, Louis J., son of Bedrick R. Sladecek and Emilie S. Stojanik, was born Mar. 30, 1916, Corn Hill, Williamson Co., TX. Enlisted in U.S. Army about 1942, during WWII. Rank: Pvt. Member, American Legion Post No. 282, Granger, TX. Died Nov. 22, 1968. Buried Corn Hill, TX.

Sladecek, Richard Joseph, son of Willie Joseph Sladeck and Mary Jo Kajs, was born Jan. 17, 1946, Georgetown, Williamson Co., TX. Education: Jarrell High School and Austin School of Electronics, Elkins Institute. Enlisted Nov. 1965, Ft. Polk, LA. Served in the Viet Nam Conflict, TET Offensive as a Sgt. E-5. Military Occupation: Quad-50/Tanks. Medals: KDSM, 1-O/F Bar, GCMDL, VSM, VCM, OCMDL. While stationed in El Paso, TX, he and twin brother Robert, became celebrities when the local paper ran an article about "seeing double" and the identical lives they had lived up to that point. Discharged at Fort Lewis, WA, on Nov. 6, 1968. Joined the National Guard, Feb. 1975. Currently has rank of Sfc. Married Mary Evelyn Stefek; five children: Michael Joseph, Richard Joseph, Jr., Mary Theresa, Robert Anthony, Ryan Matthew (deceased at 11 days). Civilian occupation: Communications Superintendent. Hobbies: baseball and working with electronics. Home of record: Austin, TX.

Sladecek, Robert Willie, son of Willie Sladecek and Mary Jo Kajs, was born Jan. 17, 1946, in Georgetown, Williamson Co., TX. Education: Jarrell High School and Austin School of Electronics, Elkins Institute. Enlisted Nov. 1965, Ft. Polk, LA. Served in the Viet Nam Conflict, TET Offensive as a Sgt E-5. While stationed in El Paso, TX, he and twin brother, Richard, became celebrities when the local paper ran an article about "seeing double" and the identical lives they had lived up to that point. Stationed in Viet Nam, approx. 30 miles from his brother, was the first time they had ever been separated. Both had several dangerous encounters and both became ill with malaria while in Viet Nam. Medals: KDSM 1–O/F Bar, OCMDL, VSM, VCM, Army Commendation Medal. Honorably discharged, Ft. Lewis, WA, Nov. 6, 1968. Electronic Technician. Hobbies: baseball and electronics. Died Jan. 28, 1973; buried Corn Hill, Williamson Co., TX.

Sladecek, Rudolph. WWII veteran of Granger, TX. Attained rank of Sgt. prior to honorable discharge.

Sladecek, Victor Henry, son of Edward Charles Sladecek and Regina Piela, was born on July 15, 1914 in Corn Hill, Williamson Co., TX. Graduated from Granger High School in 1933. Enlisted into the U.S. Army Air Corps on Apr. 1, 1942, during WWII. Rank: T/Sgt. Served in both the American and Asiatic-Pacific Theaters of Operations as a Radio Mechanic. Participated in campaigns in China, Burma, and India. Decorations: American Campaign Medal, Asiatic Campaign Medal, Good Conduct Medal, WWII Victory Medal, and Distinguished Unit Badge. Separated from service on Jan. 7, 1946 at Ft. Bliss, TX with the rank of Technical Sgt. Auto mechanic. Hobby: ham radio operator. Died on June 10, 1973; interred in Holy Cross Catholic Cemetery at Granger, TX. Marker states date of birth as July 11, 1914.

Sladek, Erwin Arnold, Jr. "Bugger," son of Erwin Arnold "E.A." Sladek, Sr. and Frances Venticek, was born Aug. 17, 1948, Bryan, Brazos Co., TX. Education: La Grange High School, TX, Blinn College, Brenham, TX, Texas A&M, College Station, TX. Bachelor of Science, Education (Biology, Physical Education, and Health), University of Houston, Victoria, TX, M.S., Educational Administration. Entered U.S. Army Corps June 15, 1971, Ft. Leonard Wood, MO. Drafted as teacher in Victoria ISD, TX. Assigned 284th Military Police Co., 18th MP Brigade, Viet Nam, American Theater: 52nd Military Police Co., 5th U.S. Army, Ft. Sam Houston, San Antonio, TX. Specialization: 95B20 Military Policeman. Battles: Viet Nam. Decorations: National Defense Service Medal, Viet Nam Service Medal, Republic of Viet Nam Campaign Medal with 60 Device, U.S. Army Commendation Medal (Viet Nam), GCM, Marksman Badge (M-16 Rifle and .45 caliber Pistol). Separated from service at Ft. Sam Houston, TX, Apr. 25, 1973. Rank: Spec 4/Acting Sgt. Married Bonnie Koether. Teacher, Assistant Principal, High School Principal, Assistant Superintendent, La Grange ISD. Home of record: La Grange, TX.

Sladek, Erwin Arnold, Sr., son of Arnold J. Sladek and Ada Koehl, was born July 27, 1924, in Fayetteville, TX. Attended St. John's School, Fayetteville High School and A&M University with a B.S. in Animal Husbandry, Jan. 1950. Enlisted May 18, 1943 at Fort Sam Houston, and served during WWII in the Northern Solomons and Southern Philippines as a S/Sgt in Co. H, 132nd Inf., Motor Gunner (Heavy). Medals: Victory Ribbon, four Overseas Bars, Asiatic-Pacific Campaign Ribbon with two BSS and one Bronze Arrowhead, Philippine Liberation Ribbon with one BSS, Good Conduct Medal. Discharged at Fort Sam Houston, on Dec. 5, 1945. Married Frances A. Ventricek; 4 children: Erwin A. Sladek, Jr,. Dr. Jim Sladek, Patricia Sladek Korenek, and Shirley Sladek Norsworthy. Real Estate salesman. Home of record: La Grange, Fayette, TX. Submitted by son, Erwin A. Sladek, Jr., La Grange, TX.

Sladek, Erwin Arnold, Jr., son of Erwin A. Sladek, Sr. and Frances Ventricek, was born on Aug. 17, 1948 in Bryan, TX. Attended St. John's School, Fayetteville, Sacred Heart, La Grange, Blinn Junior College, Brenham, Texas A&M University, College Station, B.S., Education, and the University of Houston, Master of Education. Enlisted into the U.S. Army on June 15, 1971, during the Viet Nam Conflict, at Houston, TX. Served in Viet Nam as a Military Policeman in the 284th MP Co., 18th Military Brigade and in the 52nd MP Co. at Ft. Sam Houston, TX. Awards: National Defense Service Medal, Viet Nam Service Medal, Republic of Viet Nam Campaign Medal, Army Commendation Medal, and Good Conduct Medal. Separated from service at Ft. Sam Houston, TX, on Apr. 25, 1973. High school principal. Home of record: La Grange, TX.

Sladek, Eugene A., son of Mr. and Mrs. Albert Sladek, Thrall, TX. Graduate of Thrall High School. Enlisted U.S. Army Corps, 1944; basic training, Ft. Custer, MI; additional training, IL, OK. Theater of Operations: Asiatic-Pacific. Served in Leyte and Mindanao. Medals: A-P Theater Campaign Medal, WWII Victory Medal. Attained rank of T/5 prior to honorable discharge.

Sladek, Theodore W., son of Mr. Sladek and Mrs. Mary Sladek, Taylor, TX. Enlisted, 1945, U.S. Army Corps; basic training, Camp Crowder, MO. Theater of Operations: American. Served at Walter Reed Army Hospital, Washington, DC. Medals: American Theater Campaign Medal, WWII Victory Medal, Ribbons. Rank of Pvt. when honorably discharged. Married to Anna Tucek.

Slansky, Peter, son of Anton L. Slansky and Sophie Chovanec, was born Oct. 4, 1928, Fayetteville, Fayette Co., TX. Education: Mixville and Frydek, TX. Enlisted U.S. Army Corps May

16, 1946, Bellville, Austin Co., TX. Military occupation was cook. Attained rank of Cpl. Completed 18-month-term Oct. 1949 and returned to the home of his parents for 90 days. Served May 1946-Oct. 1948, U.S. Army Corps, during WWII. Name is on monument erected by St. Mary's Catholic Church, in thanksgiving for the return of 75 parishioners who served in WWII, 1941-1945. Again entered the service for a three year period to end Jan. 1951. Sent to Japan in Oct. 1949, and left for Korea in June 1950. KILLED IN ACTION in Malsanni, Korea, in Aug. 1950. Buried there the following day in an American cemetery. The remains were later shipped to Sealy for a funeral mass said by Fr. Lad Klimicek at St. Mary's Catholic Church at Frydek. Rev. Alois Nesvadba delivered the sermon in Czech and English. Peter was buried with full military honors.

Slavik, Frank, military service veteran. Home of record: Cameron, TX

Slavik, Frank, Sr., son of Alois Slavik and Mary Konopka, was born Feb. 9, 1885, Kromeric, Moravia, Czechoslovakia. Immigrated to USA with parents in Apr. 1904. Attended A&M College and Business College in St. Louis, MO. Street car conductor, St. Louis, MO, before enlistment, Apr. 16, 1918, during WWI. Rank: Musician 2/C. Sailed overseas with American Expeditionary Force, June 28, 1918. WOUNDED IN ACTION, France. Honorable discharge with excellent character, June 16, 1919. Married Henrietta Zavodny, Sept. 24, 1935; three children, seven grandchildren. Preceded in death by one child. Died Jan. 31, 1973. Buried at Sts. Cyril & Methodius Catholic Cemetery, Marak, Milam Co., TX. Submitted by Lillian B. Mikulec, Buckholts, TX.

Slavik, Frank E., son of Frank Slavik and Henrietta Zavodny, was born Jan. 12, 1938, in Cameron, TX. Attended Cameron, TX, schools. Entered the U.S. Army July 1955 at age 17. Served two years at Fort Ord, GA, Fort Bliss, TX, and Grand Island, NY. Discharged at Camp Chaffee, AR, in July 1957 with SP4 rating. Reenlisted in 1960 and remained at Fort Hood, TX. Sent to Offset Printing School at Fort Belvior, VA, with SP5 rating. Given High Security Clearance, and went to work at the Pentagon, Washington, DC for the Atomic Energy Commission for more than three years. Next assignment was with Supreme Headquarters Allied Powers Europe in Paris, France. After duty in France, was assigned to Hunter Army Air Field, GA, and promoted to Staff Sgt. In 1968 sent to 7th Siop Group, Far East. In 1970 to 1975 assigned duty in the Joint Chiefs of Staff, Pentagon Washington, DC. In 1975 to 1979 assigned to 30th Eng. Bn., Fort Belvior, VA with duties as Platoon Sgt. and 1st Sgt. Received many decorations during service to country. Retired in 1979. Married Betty Driscoll; five children, five grandchildren. Family traveled to all his tours of duty except the Far East. Home of record: Hewitt, TX.

Slavik, John, son of Joseph Slavik and Agnes Kostroun, was born May 17, 1925, Buckholts, Milam Co., TX. Education: Sts. Cyril & Methodius Catholic School; Marak, Yoe High School, Cameron TX. Enlisted: NRS, San Antonio, TX. Attained rank of Radioman 2/C. Attended NT School (Radio) University of Colorado, Boulder CO. NTSch (Comm) Los Angeles, CA. All Theaters of Operation. Battles: involved with aircraft and submarine attacks. Sailed around the world on first assignment. Honorably discharged Mar. 20, 1946. Home of record: Buckholts, TX.

Slay, Isidor Hohn, son of Frank Slay and Barbara Holub, was born Dec. 18, 1917, Decatur, TX. Education: St. Mary's Catholic School, West, TX. Enlisted at Camp Wolters, TX. Rank: Pvt. Fought in Normandy and Northern France. WOUNDED IN ACTION in the service of his country. Medals: EAME Campaign Medal w/2 BSS, Purple Heart, Good Conduct Medal. Honorably discharged Oct. 11 1945, Baxter GH, Spokane, WA. Died Sept. 1, 1978.

Slivensky, Walton E., son of Mr. and Mrs. H. O. Slivensky, Taylor, TX. Education: Taylor High

School. Enlisted U.S. Army Corps, 1943; basic training, Ft. Francis E. Warren, WY. Theater of Operations: Asiatic-Pacific. Served in New Caledonia, Leyte, Aomori, Honshu, Japan. Medals: Asiatic-Pacific Theater Campaign Medal, Philippine Liberation Medal, Good Conduct Medal, WWII Victory Medal, Ribbons. Attained rank of S/Sgt. prior to honorable discharge, 1946.

Slovacek, Alois, Jr., son of Mr. and Mrs. Alois Slovacek. Entered National Guard in 1941, during WWII. Attended Baylor. Trained in Brownwood, TX. Attained rank of Sgt. Discharged in 1946.

Slovak, Eugene H., son of Henry J. Slovak and Teresie Dvorak, was born on Aug. 23, 1933, in Rose, TX. Earned GED plus fifty college semester hours. Enlisted in the U.S. Army on Apr. 15, 1953 at Waco, TX, during the Korean Conflict. Stationed at Ft. Hood, TX, Camp Chaffee, Ft. Smith, AR, and Ft. Knox, KY. Wheel and track vehicle mechanic. Earned carbine and rifle Marksmanship Badges. Separated from service on Apr. 14, 1961. Military service included six years in the Reserves. Home of record: West, TX.

Slovak, Frank J., son of John Slovak and Angeline Janek, was born June 23, 1921, in Dallas, TX. Attended John Henry Brown Elementary School in Dallas, West High School, and Forest Avenue High School in Dallas. Enlisted, during WWII, in the U.S. Coast Guard at Ft. Worth, TX. Served in the American Theater of Operations and attained the rank of MoMM 3/C. Served on vessels in Atlantic conducting anti-submarine and air-sea rescue operations. Also served on vessels out of Key West, FL, which conducted mine sweeping operations. Awards: Good Conduct Medal, American Campaign Medal, and WWII Victory Medal. Separated from service on Feb. 14, 1946. Home of record: Houston, TX.

Slovak, Henry J., son of Frank G. Slovak and Veronica Janda, was born on Apr. 13, 1907, in Waco, TX. Completed education through the 10th grade. Enlisted, during WWII, in the U.S. Army Air Corps at Waco, TX, on Sept. 18, 1942. Served as a mechanic at Sheppard Field, Wichita Falls, TX, Blackland AFB, Waco, TX, and Laughlin Field, Del Rio, TX. Separated from service on Oct. 17, 1945. Died on Dec. 14, 1971, and is interred in St. Mary Cemetery at West, TX.

Slovak, John, son of Anton and Johana Slovak, was born Feb. 7, 1894, at West, TX. Attended West Elementary School. Enlisted, during WWI, in the U.S. Army on Dec. 13, 1917. Served with the American Expeditionary Forces in France as a member of the 248th Aero Squadron at Libourne, France. Discharged Mar. 1919. Marble cutter. Helped Joseph Lastelick construct the 20 foot in diameter Seal of Texas that hangs on the back wall of the Hall of State which is located at the Texas State Fair Grounds in Dallas. Married Angelina Janek. Member of SPJST Lodge 84 in Dallas. Died in 1984, and is interred at Grove Hill Memorial Park in Dallas, TX.

Slovak, Walter Louis, son of Joe Slovak and Louise Jurik, was born on Sept. 27 in Ennis, TX. Attended elementary school in Ennis and Bardwell, TX. Inducted at Camp Wolters, TX. Served overseas for eleven months in France, Germany, and Austria, with 265th Engineers, 65th Div., as a wire chief. Supervised the installation, testing, repair, and general maintenance of a central office and other telephone equipment in a military communications system. Oversaw the installation of switchboards, telephones, and auxiliary equipment. Fought in the Rhineland, Central Europe GO 33 WD 45. Medals: Good Conduct, American Theater Campaign, EAME Campaign, w/2 BSS, Soldiers Medal GO 37 Hq 65th Inf. 30 May 45, WWII Victory. Discharged Jan. 1, 1946, at Camp Fannin, TX. Died July 22, 1985.

Smahlik, Ignac A., son of Joseph and Mary Jurach Smahlik, was born on Oct. 28, 1920 at Yoakum, Lavaca Co., TX. Enlisted Sept. 17, 1942, San Francisco, CA. Attained the rank of Pfc. and

served in the European Theater of Operations, participating in the battles at Rhineland and Central Europe. Medals: Sharp Shooter Rifle, American Theater Campaign, E.A.M.E. Campaign w/2 BBS, Good Conduct, and WWII Victory Medal. Discharged on Feb. 28, 1946, at Camp Fannin, TX.

Smaistrla, Frank Henry, son of Frank and Marie Smaistrla, was born June 19, 1921, East Bernard, TX. Enlisted in U.S. Army, about 1942, Houston, TX. Attained rank of Cpl. Theater of Operations: Asiatic Pacific. Battles: New Guinea and Luzon. Medals: Asiatic Pacific Campaign, Philippine Liberation Campaign, Good Conduct. Honorable discharge, Nov. 12, 1945. Farmer and rancher. Died Apr. 22, 1992, East Bernard, TX. Buried Holy Cross Catholic Cemetery, East Bernard, TX.

Smajstrla, Edward Henry, son of Mr. and Mrs. Ed Smajstrla, West, TX. Entered Navy, 1944, during WWII. Attained rank of MS. Trained in San Diego, CA. Discharged, 1944. Married Tracie Kallus.

Smajstrla, Geoge X., son of Mr. and Mrs. Ed Smajstrla, West, TX. Attended West High School, West, TX, and Tyler Junior College, Tyler, TX. Attended Naval Merchant Marine Academy. Attained rank of Cadet Midshipman, Reserve USNR. Served in U.S.A., Pacific Theater, North Sea, Atlantic, Gulf of Mexico during WWII. Discharged 1946. Married Lillie Pavlas.

Smajstrla, John J., West, TX. Entered Army in 1941. Served during WWII, in ETO. Attained rank of Sgt. Awards: Inf. Badge, ET w/6 BSS, American Def. Ribbon. Discharged 1945.

Smajstrla, Raynold, son of Mr. and Mrs. John Smajstrla, Elk, TX, was born Feb. 21, 1916. Attended Elk School. Entered Army Air Corps, Apr. 1942, during WWII. Instructor, Engine Repair in Wichita Falls, TX. Flew with the Man Power Air Force Training Command, attaining rank of Sgt. Awards: Instructor Badge, GCM, Engineer Wings, other awards. Discharged 1944.

Smesny, Albert Louis, son of Ludvik and Frances Skarpa Smesny, was born in Eastgate/Dayton, Liberty Co., TX, Nov. 4, 1931. Lived on a farm and attended school in Dayton. Enlisted in the U.S. Army on Dec. 7, 1948. Spent time in Japan, North Korea, and South Korea. Fought on the front lines with the Third Inf. Div., 15th Reg., Third Bn. WOUNDED IN ACTION by a mortar fragment in South Korea on Jan. 31, 1951. Awards: Purple Heart, Combat Inf. Badge, Good Conduct Medal, Occupation Medal (Japan), Korean Service Medal, Bronze Service Star, U.N. Occupation Service Medal (Korea), and the Korean Presidential Unit Citation. Honorably discharged with rank of Cpl. on Dec. 6, 1951. Married Georgia Baca Smesny, Houston, TX; three grown children, and three grandchildren. Retired from Armco Steel.

Smesny, Edwin, son of Ludvik and Frances Skarpa Smesny, was born Sept. 1, 1927, in Dayton, TX. Attended school in Dayton, TX. Enlisted in U.S. Army Corps, Liberty Co. during WWII, assigned with the 388th Military Police Service Bn. Served in the European Theater. Performed duties of Train Board riding military supply trains to guard against pilferage. Medals: WWII Victory Medal, Army of Occupation Medal. Discharged Mar. 2, 1947, Ft. Dix, NJ, rank Pfc. Employed by Armco Steel, Houston, TX, 1949–1984. Retired. married June Ann Stasney, Nov. 5, 1949, Crosby, TX; three children: Edwin Charlie, Jr., Kathleen Ann, Charlene June. Home of record: Houston, TX.

Smesny, Emil Steve, son of Joe V. and Mary Rachunek Smesny, was born Jan. 25, 1929, Eastgate, Liberty Co., TX. Enlisted Feb. 6, 1951, Ft. Sam Houston, TX. Theater of Operations: Korea. Assigned to Co. B, 74th Engr Bn. Medals: Korean Service Medal w/2 BSS, United Nations

Service Medal, National Defense Service Medal. Honorably discharged attaining rank of Cpl. Married Nancy Lee McWhirter; three daughters: Karen Smesny Rabel, Mary Nell Smesny Frizzell, Sheryl Smesny. Home of record: Dayton, TX.

Smetak, Marcell A., son of Mr. and Mrs. A. A. Smetak. Entered Merchant Marines, 1944, during WWII. Served in South Pacific. Discharge, 1944.

Smidovec, Arthur, served three months, 1948, U.S. Army Corps.

Smidovec, Frank L., was born Apr. 9, 1925. Served three years, U.S. Navy. Attained rank of S2, during WWII. Died Apr. 27, 1987, St. Mary's Catholic Cem., Frydek, Austin Co., TX.

Smilek, Frank, son of Mr. and Mrs. Paul Smilek, Sr., was born in Czechoslovakia. Served in the U.S. Coast Guard during WWII.

Smilek, Jerry, son of Mr. and Mrs. Paul Smilek, Sr., was born on Jan. 30, 1920, in Sealy, TX. Graduated from Sealy High School in 1938 and attended business school in Houston, TX, where he was later employed. Enlisted on Oct. 13, 1941, in Houston, TX. Rank: Sgt. Departed from Ft. Dix, NJ, aboard the USS *Crystobal* on Jan. 13, 1943, and arrived in Oran, French North Africa, Jan. 26, 1943. WOUNDED IN ACTION Aug. 18, 1943, and died Aug. 31, 1943. Body was returned to the U.S. five years later and reinterred in Sealy Cemetery.

Smilek, Paul, son of Mr. and Mrs. Paul Smilek, Sr., was born in Czechoslovakia. Served three years in the U.S. Army in San Antonio, TX, and three years in the U.S. Coast Guard off Galveston, TX, in the 1930s.

Smilek, Rudolph, son of Mr. and Mrs. Paul Smilek, Sr., was born in Czechoslovakia. Served in the Merchant Marines during WWII.

Snapka, George W., was born Apr. 24, 1914. Served in U.S. Army during WWII, attaining rank of S/Sgt. Died Nov. 23, 1985. Buried in St. Mary's Cemetery, West, TX.

Snapka, Method, of West, TX, WWII veteran.

Snapka, Rudolph, West, TX, WWII veteran, U.S.Navy.

Snokhous, George, West, TX, 36th Div., European Theater of Operations. Military veteran, WWII.

Snokhous, Henry A., son of Mr. and Mrs. Joe Snokhous, West, TX. Entered Army 1945. Trained at Camp Hood, TX. Attained rank of Pfc. Served in Japan.

Snokhous, Jimmie A., son of Ludvik Josef (Louis) and Sidonia Devorsky Snokhous, was born Jan. 17, 1926, West, TX. Education: St. Mary's Catholic School and West High School, West, TX, B.A. and M.S. at Baylor University. Enlisted in U.S. Marines in Dallas, TX. Attained rank of Cpl. Theater of Operations: South Pacific. Battles: Mindanao. WOUNDED IN ACTION at Mindanao. Medals: Purple Heart, Good Conduct, 1st Battle Star, So. Pacific Campaign Medal, WWII Victory Medal. Honorably discharged June 1, 1946. Married Betty; two children: Michael Daniels and Joanne Daniels. Retired. Enjoys hobbies of bridge, traveling, land development. Home of record: Guatemala City, Guatemala C.A., Zone 14. Submitted by brother, Raymond Joseph Snokhous.

Snokhous, Paul J., was born Oct. 1, 1903, West, TX. Served in the U.S. Armed Forces during WWII, 328th HARCFT CO TC. Died Feb. 6, 1964. Buried in St. Mary's Cemetery, West, TX.

Snokhous, Raymond Joseph, son of Ludvik Josef (Louis) and Sidonia Devorsky Snokhous, was born Aug. 18, 1929, West, TX. Education: St. Mary's Catholic School and West High School, West, TX; University of Houston, Houston, TX, B.A., 1951, M.B.A., 1952; South Texas College of Law, Houston, TX, Juris Doctor, 1962. Enlisted in U.S. Army Corps, Ft. Sam Houston, San Antonio, TX, 1952. Theater of Operations: Korea. 101st Airborne Inf., 1952–1954, Camp Breckenridge, KY. Stationed at Ft. Knox, KY, 1954. Medals: Good Conduct Medal, American Theater of Operations Medal. Honorable discharge Nov. 23, 1954. Married Jolene; two children: Mark E. Snokhous and Karen Snokhous Nunnely. (Karen was born at Camp Breckenridge, for total cost of $6.75!) Occupation: Sr. Vice President, Government and Regulatory Affairs, for Houston Industries Inc. Hobbies include restoring his father's blacksmith shop and old farm machinery. Home of record: Houston, TX.

Snokhous, Willie E., son of Mr. and Mrs. Joe Snokhous, was born July 27, 1925, West, TX. Entered Marines in 1943 during WWII. Served in Philippines and China, attaining rank of Sgt. Awards: P.L. Ribbon, China Occupation Ribbon, Asiatic-Pacific Ribbon, and WWII Victory Ribbon. Discharged 1946. Died Nov. 11, 1988. Buried in St. Mary's Cemetery, West, TX.

Snykal, Louis, military service veteran. Home of record: Austin, TX.

Sobotik, Benedict Blaze, son of Louis and Frances Sitka Sobotik, was born Feb. 4, 1932, in Hallettsville, TX. Graduate of University of Texas School of Dentistry. Entered the service Mar. 15, 1951. Boatswain's Mate First Class, USN-1. Served USNTC, San Diego, CA. Medals: National Defense Service Medal, United Nations Service Medal, China Service Medal, Korean Service Medal w/4 Stars, Good Conduct Medal. Dr. Ben Sobotik and his wife Lorene, sons Chris and Kel, were all killed in an automobile accident, Oct. 21, 1983. Funeral services were held at St. Mary's Catholic Church in Taylor, TX.

Sobotik, Jesse Frank, son of Frank Joe and Marie Ann Matus Sobotik, was born on June 6, 1926, at Rosenberg, TX. Valedictorian of El Campo High School, 1943. Received B.S. in Naval Science from Rice University, Houston, in 1946, B.B.A. in Accounting in 1949, and an M.P.A. in Accounting in 1952 from University of Texas in Austin. Enlisted in the Navy at Dallas, in Jan. 1944. Trained at Mississippi College, Louisiana Tech, Rice University, and U.S. Navy Supply Corps School. Served as Supply and Disbursing Officer in the Atlantic Fleet, in WWII, and attained the rank of Lt. Discharged Sept. 11, 1947, at U.S. Naval Station, Brooklyn, NY. Home of record: Houston, TX.

Sobotik, Louis P., son of Louis and Frances Sitka Sobotik, was born Jan. 25, 1923, in Hallettsville, TX. Inducted into the Army Jan. 13, 1943, at Fort Sam Houston, TX. Rank: Tech/Sgt. Airplane Maintenance Technician with 4142nd AAF Base Unit. Served in Naples-Foggia Rome-Arno. Separated from service on Oct. 9, 1945, at Patterson Field, Ohio. Medals: European-African-Middle Eastern Ribbon with two BSS, AAF Tech Badge with Airplane Mechanic Bar, Carbine Ss, Rifle Ss. Home of record: Baytown, TX.

Sobotik, Stanley Alvin, son of Frank Sobotik and Marie Matus, was born Aug. 16, 1924, Caldwell, TX. Education: El Campo H.S., TX, S.W. Business University, Houston, TX. Enlisted Houston, TX. Theater of Operation: Europe. Assigned to European 407th Bomb Sqdn., 92nd Bomb Group (H). Graduated with honors in 1942. Finished business course May 11, 1943, volunteered for U.S. Army Air Corps, May 13, 1943, Houston, TX. Shipped to Sheppard Field, Wichita, TX, for basic training on May 29, 1943. Finished 10 hour flying course at Hastings College, NE. Was classified as navigator at Santa Ana, CA. Had preflight classes at Ellington Field, TX. Commissioned as 2nd Lt. at San Marcos Air Field at the age of 19, in Apr. 1944. Additional training at Lincoln, NE, and Alexandria, LA. Departed from Kearney, NE, for England, Aug. 15, 1944. KILLED IN ACTION, Sept. 11, 1944, during second mission over Merseburg, Germany. Submitted by Blanche Stibora, Stafford, TX.

Sodolak, Charles F., was born Sept. 28, 1896. Served in U.S. Army Corps during WWI. Attained rank of Pvt. Married Mary. Mayor of Frydek, TX, and wrote newspaper articles in the *Sealy News*. Died May 6, 1981; buried at St. Mary's Catholic Cem., Frydek, Austin Co., TX.

Sodolak, Eddie A., son of Louis C. and Annie J. Mlcak Sodolak, was born Feb. 28, 1922, Frydek, Austin Co., TX. Graduated Sealy High School, 1941; one year University of Texas, 1942, B.C.S. from University of Benjamin Franklin in 1950, three and a half years of Russian, Univ. of MD, 1955. Enlisted in Army Air Corps during WWII, Nov. 5, 1943, Houston, TX. Attained rank of Pfc. Student entire time of military service. Theater of

Operations: American. Medals: American Theater Campaign Medal, Good Conduct Medal, WWII Victory Medal. Honorably discharged Mar. 18, 1946. Name is on monument erected by St. Mary's Catholic Church, in thanksgiving for the return of 75 parishioners who served in WWII, 1941-1945. Served Nov. 1942–May 1945, U.S. Navy, during WWII. Worked as Airplane Electrical Mechanic, managed a non-commissioned officers club. Married Virginia Mordecai, Apr. 3, 1946; two children: Patricia Ann and Michael Edward. Special Agent, FBI, retired Feb. 25, 1977. Municipal Court Judge, San Felipe, TX, retired 1978. Hobbies: care of home, plant trees, scouting, help law enforcement. Honors: Scouting Bronze Pelican Emblem, Member of Order of the Arrow. Home of record: Sealy, TX.

Sodolak, Jerry, served Nov. 1945–June 1947, U.S. Army Corps, during WWII.

Sodolak, Louis John, Jr., son of Louis Charles Sodolak, Sr. and Annie Josephine Mlcak Sodolak, served a half month, U.S. Navy, during WWII. Married Margaret Sula, Nov. 25, 1947; five children: David James Sodolak, Geraldine Ann Sodolak Adams, Frances M. Sodolak, Louis F. Sodolak, Kenneth P. Sodolak. Died Apr. 8, 1979; buried St. Roch's Catholic Cem., Mentz, TX. Widow's home of record: Cat Spring, TX.

Sodolak, Ludwig J., served Nov. 1943–1945, U.S. Army Corps, during WWII.

Sodolak, William Frank "Willie," son of Louis Charles and Annie Johanna Mlcak Sodolak, was born Jan. 6, 1921, Sealy, Austin Co., TX. Education: Mixville and Frydek Public Schools. Enlisted Nov. 7, 1942, Houston, TX. Served Nov. 1942–1946, U.S. Army Air Corps. Automotive Equipment Operator. AAF345. Medals: American Theater of Operations Campaign, Good Conduct, WWII Victory. Honorable discharge Feb. 27, 1946. Married Gladys Irene Ernstes; four children: Rosemary Sodolak Ermis, Margaret Sodolak Sanford, Kathryn Sodolak Paul, William Frank Sodolak, Jr. Owned and operated Riverside Service Station and Cafe. Hobbies: woodwork, making homemade wine, pickles, and sauerkraut, enjoying family, playing tarok, raising trees. Elected Alderman of San Felipe, TX, Church Council and Church Bldg. Committeeman. Died Jan. 8, 19--; buried St. Mary's Catholic Cem., Frydek, Austin Co., TX. Submitted by widow, Gladys Sodolak, whose home of record is Sealy, TX.

Soukup, Benjamin, of West, TX, WWII veteran.

Soukup, Bennie R., son of Mr. and Mrs. Charlie Soukup, Waco, TX. Attended Waco High. Entered Coast Guard during WWII, 1943. Served in San Juan, Puerto Rico, Hawaii, attaining rank of RM 2/C. Awards: AT, AP, and WWII Victory Ribbons. Discharged 1946.

Soukup, Emil, of West, TX, WWII veteran.

Soukup, George J., son of Mr. and Mrs. Joe Soukup, West, TX. Entered Army during WWII, 1944. Served on Luzon, attained rank of Pfc. Awards: Combat Inf. Badge, AP w/1 BSS, Phil. Lib. w/1 BSS, WWII Victory Ribbon. Discharged 1946.

Soukup, Henry, Waco, TX,. Entered Coast Guard, during WWII, 1943. Served in San Juan, Puerto Rico and Hawaii, attaining rank of RM 2/C. Awards: AT, AP, and WWII Victory Ribbons. Discharged 1946.

Soukup, Joseph, son of Mr. and Mrs. Frank Soukup, West, TX. Entered Navy during WWII, 1944. Served in S.W. Pacific and Japan, attaining rank of WT 3/C. WOUNDED IN ACTION, Okinawa. Awards: Purple Heart, Amer. Def., AP w/2 Battle Stars, Phil. Lib. Ribbon. Discharged 1946.

Soukup, Louis H., was born June 4, 1915, served in U.S. Army during WWII, attained rank of TEC/5. Died Aug. 20, 1975, West, TX. Buried in St. Mary's Cemetery, West, TX.

Soukup, Louis J., was born Sept. 23, 1917. Served in U.S. Army, WWII, attaining rank of TEC/4. Died Dec. 19, 1989. Buried in St. Mary's Cemetery, West, TX.

Soukup, Walter R., West, TX, WWII veteran, Theater of Operations: European.

Soukup, Wenceslav, was born Aug. 12, 1911. Served in U.S. Army during WWII, attaining rank of T/Sgt. Died Nov. 10, 1992. Buried in St. Mary's Cemetery, West, TX.

Sowa, Boniface, served four years. Reenlisted, U.S. Army Corps, during WWII.

Spacek, Alois J., son of Edmund and Veronica Spacek, was born about 1929, TX, served in U.S. Army Corps, Korean Conflict, assigned to 4th Eng. Bn, Inf. Div. Education: St. Mary's University, San Antonio, TX, B.A. degree. Attended Engineer School, Ft. Velvoer, VA. After two years military service, had own electrical shop, Jourdanton, TX. He and son Vernon lost their lives in a car wreck. Survived by widow, Ann Spacek and daughter JoAnn of Jourdanton, TX. Submitted by Dominic Netek, San Antonio, TX.

Spacek, Anton, II, son of Anton Spacek I and Mary Zapalac, was born on Aug. 9, 1923 in Bellville, TX. Attended Pecan School in Holman. Enlisted at Fort Sam Houston and served at the Post of Corozal Canal Zone. Discharged on Nov. 16, 1946, at Fort Sam Houston, TX.

Spacek, Egnac John, was born Sept. 24, 1897, served in U.S. Navy during WWI, attaining rank of E-2. Honorably discharged. Died Oct. 28, 1970; buried St. Mary's Catholic Cemetery, Frydek, Austin Co., TX.

Spacek, Frank, served in U.S. Armed Forces during WWI, 1917–1918. Member of SPJST Lodge 20, Granger, TX.

Spacek, Frank Louis, Jr., son of Frank Louis Spacek, Sr. and Evelyn Foyt Spacek, was born Jan. 1, 1952, Bellville, TX. Graduated from North Side High School, Ft. Worth, TX, 1970. Enlisted in USMC, July 28, 1970, Ft. Worth, TX. Theater of Operations: Viet Nam. Battles: Viet Nam Conflict in Da Nang, South Viet Nam, 1971. Attended Marine Corp Boot Camp, Sept. 1970, San Diego, CA. Stationed at MCAS, Yuma, AZ. Planned to retire, Sept. 30, 1990, after 20 years of service. Promoted to Master Sgt. Medals: Navy Achievement w/Gold Star, Good Conduct W/Silver Str, Viet Nam Campaign Medal, Viet Nam Service Medal, National Defense Medal, Presidential Unit Citation, Meritorious Unit Citation. Home of record: Watauga, TX. "*Semper Fi.*"

Spacek, Frank Louis, Sr., son of Anton and Mary Zapalac Spacek, was born Feb. 24, 1921, Sealy, TX. Education: Sealy School, Sealy TX. Enlisted U.S. Naval Reserve, Dallas, TX, July 14, 1942. Battles: WWII. Medals: National Defense, Good Conduct, WWII Victory. Attached to the Navy Seabees, construction worker, and was on Mt. Surabachi when the Marines raised the American Flag in Iwo Jima, when the Japanese surrendered during WWII. Honorably discharged Jan. 31, 1946, Camp Wallace, TX. Submitted lovingly, in his memory, by Evelyn Spacek, widow, of Watauga, TX.

Spacek, Jerome A., son of Anton Spacek I and Mary Zapalac Spacek, was born Sept. 21, 1928, in Bellville, TX. Educated at the high school in La Grange. Enlisted in Houston, TX, going to San Diego, CA, Aug. 14, 1950. Rank: AM3 in the 7th Fleet. Assigned to a torpedo bomber squadron (VS-892) N.A.S. North Island, San Diego, CA. In Hawaii for three months, then to Atsugi, Japan. Stopped over at Okinawa, patrolled the Formosa waters, returned to the States, later transferred to a seaplane squadron which went to the Philippines, then returned to Treasure Island for separation June 2, 1954. Received the Good Conduct Medal and other medals. Home of record: Houston, TX.

Spacek, Joe T., son of Edmund J. and Veronica Netardus Spacek, was born Jan. 18, 1921, Jourdanton, TX. Enlisted at Naval Recruiting Station, San Antonio, TX, July 1942, in U.S. Navy during WWII. Served on board USS *James O'Hara* APA-90, "Attack troop transport." Campaign Ribbon, Atlantic Ocean, Mediterranean Sea and Pacific Ocean. EAME Theater: Invasion of Sicily,

Salerno, Asiatic-Pacific Theater: Invasion of Saipan, Anguor, Leyte, Lingayen Gulf, Iwo Jima. American Campaign: Good Conduct Ribbon. Philippine government: Manila, Lusson. Unloading Texas National Guard, 36th Inf. Div., Instrumental in making Flag Pole to raise the American Flag on Mt. Surabaci on Iwo Jima. Honorably discharged with rank of Chief Petty Officer, Oct. 5, 1945 at Naval Recruiting Station, Camp Wallace, Houston, TX. Retired U.S. Government. Married Viola Klein; three sons, five grandchildren, two great-grandchildren. Hobbies: fishing and traveling. Home of record: San Antonio, TX.

Spacek, Joseph A., son of John P. and Rosie Orsak Spacek, was born Aug. 6, 1895, Fayetteville, TX. Education: Lovelady and Crockett Schools in Houston Co., TX, also, Ross and Abbott Schools in Hill Co., TX. Enlisted Sept. 19, 1917, Richmond, TX, National Army, sent to Camp Travis, TX, assigned to Machine Gun, 360th Inf., 90th Div., Famous Texas Brigade! Sent overseas. Theater of Operations: Europe. Battles: Villers on Haye, St. Michiel, Ruvenelle, Muese-Argonn. Medals: WWI Victory Medal, Purple Heart, among others. WOUNDED IN ACTION, shrapnel, gassed, shell shock, refused to seek help when wounded. Honorable discharge June 20, 1919, Camp Travis, TX. Died Aug. 22, 1969; buried at Forest Park Catholic Cemetery, Houston, Harris Co., TX. Submitted lovingly in his honor and memory by Robert E. Spacek of Richmond, TX.

Spacek, Richard Michael, son of Jerome Albert and Shirley Ann Meyers Spacek, was born June 17, 1958, in Hillsboro, TX. Attended Alief Hastings High School. Enlisted in Houston, and was sent to San Diego, CA as an E5 in the 7th Fleet; assigned to Launch and Recovery of Aircraft (Catapults and Arresting Gear). Medals: Naval Reserve Meritorious, Navy Expeditionary, Sea Service Deployment Ribbon. Served from Nov. 1977 to Apr. 1985, and was serving on the USS. *Ranger* at N.A.S. Le Morre, CA, when discharged. Home of record: Houston, TX.

Spencer, William, Jr., son of Mr. and Mrs. William Spencer, Sr., enlisted in U.S. Navy, Corpus Christi, TX, WWII. Submitted by Agnes Elzner Burge, Kerrville, TX.

Spinn, Elroy C., son of Mr. and Mrs. Charlie Spinn, Granger, TX. Education: Alligator School. Enlisted U.S. Army Corps, 1943; basic training, Camp Wolters, TX; additional training, Ft. Meade, MD. Theater of Operations: American, EAME. Served in campaigns in France and Germany. WOUNDED IN ACTION at Brest, 1944. Medals: American Theater Campaign Ribbon, EAME Theater Campaign, Purple Heart, Silver Star, BSS, WWII Victory, Ribbons. Attained rank of Sgt. prior to honorable discharge, 1945.

Spinn, Elton W., Granger, TX. WWII veteran. Member, American Legion Post No. 282, Granger, TX.

Sramek, Joe, II, son of Joe and Gustava Lat Sramek, was born on Nov. 29, 1919, in Ennis, TX. Attended Ennis High School and enlisted into the U.S. Army Air Corps at Dallas, TX, on Nov. 17, 1941. Served in the American Theater of Operations in assignments in the U.S., Panama Canal Zone, Guatemala, and Puerto Rico, during WWII. Awards: American Campaign Medal, American Defense Service Medal, and WWII Victory Medal. Separated from service on Nov. 6, 1945. Home of record: Ennis, TX.

Srba, Ed H., son of Mr. and Mrs. Anton Srba, Granger, TX. Enlisted U.S. Army Corps, 1938; basic training, Ft. McIntosh, TX. Theater of Operations: Asiatic-Pacific. Served during WWII in Australia, New Guinea, Admiralties, Leyte, Luzon. WOUNDED IN ACTION, Luzon, 1945. Medals: Purple Heart, Asiatic-Pacific Theater Campaign w/4 BSS, WWII Victory, ribbons. Attained rank of T/5 prior to honorable discharge, 1945. Married Frances Volek.

Sruba, Frank, West, TX, WWII veteran.

Stach, David Leroy, son of Frank and Stephania Hatla Stach, was born Mar. 6, 1919, Buckholts, TX. Graduated from Yoe High School, Cameron, TX. Enlisted in the service during WWII. Rank: Tech Sgt. KILLED IN ACTION Aug. 3, 1943. Buried at Cameron, TX. A memorial marker is located in Cameron, TX, listing names of men from Milam Co., TX, losing their lives during WWII. You will find the names of two brothers: David and Paul Stach. Submitted by Evelyn Vecera, Bellaire, TX.

Stach, Paul, son of Frank and Stephania Hatla Stach, was born Dec. 14, 1917, Buckholts, Milam Co., TX. Graduated from Yoe High School, Cameron, TX. Attended Texas A&M, receiving degree in Agricultural Administration and Marketing and Finance in May 1940. Commissioned a Major in the U.S. Army Air Corps during WWII. Was a Bomber Pilot stationed in England. Had over 50 bombing missions over Germany. On D-Day, June 6, 1944, was shot down by enemy fire and KILLED IN ACTION over Normandy, France. Buried at Ft. Sam Houston National Cemetery, San Antonio, TX. His name is listed on a Memorial in Cameron, TX, of men killed in WWII. Submitted by Evelyn Vecera, Bellaire, TX.

Stach, Stanfield A., son of Frank and Stephania Hatla Stach (Frank and Stephania were born in Moravia, Czechoslovakia, and came to USA by boat, entering the Port of Galveston. They married in Texas.), was born May 25, 1911, Buckholts, Milam Co., TX. Attended Yoe High School, Cameron, TX. Studied at Allen Academy, then Texas A&M. Played football at both schools. Received degree from A&M in Agricultural Administration and in Marketing and Finance in May, 1936. Commissioned Capt. in U.S. Army Corps. Commanded Co. A, 1st Bn., 501st Parachute Inf. Reg., which was a part of the 101st Airborne Div. Company was composed of three officers and around 140 enlisted men. Invaded Holland by parachute on Sept. 17, 1944. Will always be proud of the men in his company who fought bravely and fearlessly in both Holland and in Bastogne, Belgium, now known as the Battle of the Bulge. WOUNDED IN ACTION in the right ankle by a German mortar shell at Bastogne, Belgium in Jan. 1944. Was pulled from battle and sent to a hospital in England. After recuperation, was sent back to the USA. Decorated with the Silver Star, BSS, and Purple Heart for his part in the battles of Holland and Belgium. He is proud to be of Czech descent and to have had the opportunity to defend his country. Submitted by Evelyn Vecera, Bellaire, TX.

Stalmach, Bungess C., son of Mr. and Mrs. C. J. Stalmach, Taylor, TX. Education: Taylor High School. Enlisted U.S. Army Air Corps, 1938; basic training, Randolph Field; additional training, Mather Field, CA. Served during WWII. Honorable discharge, 1943.

Stalmach, Donald Daniel, son of Mr. and Mrs. C.J. Stalmach, Taylor, TX. Education: Taylor High School. Enlisted U.S. Navy, 1942; basic training, San Diego CA; additional training, WA. Served aboard the *Nassau,* an air craft carrier and the *Santa Fe,* a light cruiser, in WA during WWII. Attained rank of GC 3/c prior to honorable discharge.

Stanek, Frank, son of Joseph and Tresia Dolezal Stanek (both natives of present day Czechoslovakia), was born May 2, 1896, near Shiner, Lavaca Co., TX. Attended Green and St. Ludmila's Schools in Shiner, TX. Enlisted Sept. 19, 1917, Camp Travis, San Antonio, TX, went to Camp Gordon, GA, for basic training, then to port of embarkation, Camp Upton, NY. Arrived in France on May 7, 1918, Co. A, 327 Inf., 82nd Div. w/American Expeditionary Forces. Rank: Pvt. Fought at Chateau-Thierry and Battle of St. Michiel. KILLED IN ACTION on the battlefield in the Argonne Forest on Oct. 8, 1918. Buried on the Stanek family plot in the old Shiner Catholic cemetery near the burial place of his friend, Pvt. Joe Kolar. Pvt. Frank Stanek, one of two soldiers from Shiner killed in action in WWI, is memorialized in the name of the American Legion Post in Shiner, TX: Kolar–Stanek Post 201. Submitted by Lois Jo Schindler, Victoria, TX.

Stanislav, Alfred, son of Mr. and Mrs. Joe Stanislav, West, TX. Entered Army, 1941. Served in EAME Theater, attaining rank of S/Sgt. WOUNDED IN ACTION, Italy. Awards: GCM, ET Ribbon w/7 Battle Stars. Discharged 1945.

Stanislav, Frank J., son of Jan. E. Stanislav, Jr. and Mary Ann Marak, was born Nov. 16, 1886, McLennan Co., TX. Education: St. Basil's College, Waco, TX, St. Louis University, St. Louis, MO, graduated degree in medicine. Interned Providence Hospital, Waco, TX. Enlisted in the U.S. Army Corps, July 1, 1918, Waco, McLennan Co., TX. Attained

rank of 1st Lt., Medical Corps. Assigned to Base Hospital No. 123 at Hospital Center No. 20, France, Evacuation Hospital No. 22, Coblenz, Germany. Was overseas, Aug. 11, 1918 through Apr. 10, 1919, in France and Germany, with the American Expeditionary Forces, Aug. 11, 1918 through Apr. 10, 1919. Honorably discharged May 10, 1919. Married Meta Loesch, July 19, 1917; one child: Helen. Practiced medicine and surgery in Waco, TX, for over 38 years. Served on Medical Staff at Providence Hospital and Hillcrest Hospital in Waco. Lecturer and teacher at Nurses' Training School of Providence Hospital. Active member of the County and State Medical Association, St. Mary's Catholic Church, Knights of Columbus, and VFW. Died 1961, Waco, TX.

Stanislav, Joe R., son of Mr. and Mrs. Joe Stanislav, West, TX. Entered Navy 1943 during WWII. Served in Guam, attained rank of PHM 2/C. Discharged 1946.

Stanislav, John E. (J.E.) III, son of Jan. E. Jr. and Mary Ann Marak Stanislav, was born Mar. 8, 1883, near West in McLennan Co., TX. Education: Denton Country School. Inducted in the Army Sept. 6, 1918, in West, TX, at the age of 35. Rank: Pvt. Assigned to the 1st Training Bn., Camp Travis, San Antonio, TX. Honorably discharged Jan. 1, 1919. Owned and operated a farm before entering the Army and after discharge. Owned and operated a cotton gin with his brother in Abbott, TX, in the 1920s. Active member of the Church of the Assumption, Parish trustee, Knights of Columbus, RVOS, and KJT. Married Agnes Rose Kallus Nov. 16, 1909. Died July 23, 1952; buried in St Mary's Catholic Cemetery, West, TX.

Stanislav, Leonard R., son of Rudolph and Agnes Cernosek Stanislav, was born Feb. 11, 1929, at West, McLennan Co., TX. Education: grade and high school, West, TX; B.S., Texas A&M University; M.A. University of Texas; Post Graduate, Southern Methodist University and University of Texas in Dallas. Service: 386 Armored Eng. Bn., 49th Armored Div., Texas National Guard, 1948-1949. Unit Command Section 3750 USAF Hospital, Sheppard AFB, Wichita Falls, TX, 1950-1953. Honorable discharge. Married Anita Louise Nitschke, Dec. 31, 1954; children: Terry Joe, Mark, Paul, Monica and Chad. Residence of record: Parker, Collin Co., TX.

Stanislav, Norbert Eugene, son of Rudolph A. Stanislav and Agnes Cernosek, was born Nov. 7, 1938, West, McLennan Co., TX. Education: Texas A&M and University of North Texas, B.S. Psychology, Texas Christian University, Ranch Management. Attained rank of Capt. in USMC, in OCS at Quantico, VA, Mar. 1962 through May 1962. Assigned to Camp Lejeune, NC, Dec. 1962 through Feb. 1963. In Marine Corps Reserve Forces–June 1965 through Sept. 1971. Honorably discharged Sept. 1971. Married Barbara Ann Staton; two children: Deborah Lynn, born Dec. 1961, and Richard Craig, born Apr. 1963. With Neiman Marcus Fort Worth since June 1965, as Vice President/General Manager. Ranching part time. On board of directors of following organizations: Fort Worth Zoo, Boy Scouts of America, Better Business Bureau. President of University of North Texas Alumni Association, Trustee of University of North Texas. Hobbies: snow skiing, gardening, horse training. Home of record: Fort Worth, Tarrant Co., TX.

Stanislav, Robert, son of Joe and Martha Stanislav, was born Jan. 26, 1933, Abbott, TX. Graduated from West High School. Inducted into U.S. Navy, Dallas, TX. Served in Pacific and Korean Conflict. Received China Service Medal, National Defense Service Medal, Korean Service Medal (3) and the United Nations Service Medal. Served on Destroyer USS *Nicholas* DDE 449 and the USS *Mackensie* DD 836. Boiler Operator 2nd Class. Honorably discharged July 22, 1955.

Stanislav, Rudolph Alious "Rud," son of Jan. E. Stanislav, Jr. and Mariama "Mary Ann" Marek, was born Jan. 17, 1893, West, McLennan Co., TX. Education: Bold Springs, TX, Grade School. Enlisted in the U.S. Army Corps, June 25, 1918, West, TX. Attained rank of Pfc. Marksman and Horseman not mounted. Assigned to Field Remount SQ 323, American First Army. Overseas

Sept. 8, 1918, through June 28, 1919, France and Germany. Battles: Saint Michiel and Meuse-Argonne. Honorably discharged July 8, 1919. Farmer, owner and operator of grocery store, West School Board Trustee, City Commissioner and Mayor Pro-tem of West, TX (1935-1947), Director of National Bank of West, First National Bank of West, and West Bank and Trust. Active member of the Church of the Assumption, Knights of Columbus, RVOS, and VFW. Married Agnes Cernosek; Nov. 22, 1927; children: Leonard Rudolph, Rudolph John, Norbert Eugene, (twins) Johana "Joanie" and Mary Jane. Died Mar. 16, 1965, West, TX.

Stanislav, Rudolph John, son of Rudolph A. Stanislav and Agnes Cernosek, was born Feb. 10, 1932, West, McLennan Co., TX. Education: St. Mary's Catholic Elementary School, West High School, Texas A&M University. Theater of Operation: Europe (Italy, France, Germany), Pacific (Okinawa, Viet Nam, Thailand). Battles: Cuban Missile Crises, India and China Border Dispute, Berlin Airlift, Tet Offensive and Khe Sanh. Enlisted Oct. 1948, at College Station, TX, in U.S. Air Force as a Pvt. in HQ Co 143d. Discharged Jan. 1950. Graduated Texas A&M, Jan. 1954. Commissioned 2nd Lt., USAF. Served as Flight Instructor, Missile Launch Officer, Navigator Troop Carrier, Director MWR, Director Quality Assurance. Flying experience: Master Navigator with over 4700 flying hours and 973 combat hours in Viet Nam. Aircraft–C130-A&E, C-47, T-29, B-25 and F-89. Attended Squadron Officer School, Command and Staff College, Armed Forces Staff College and Industrial War College. Medals: Legion of Merit, Air Force Distinguished Flying Cross, Air Medal w/ four OLC, Meritorious Service Medal w/ one OLC, Air Force Commendation Medal w/20 OLC, Presidential Unit Citation, Air Force Outstanding Unit Award w/ four OLC, Armed Forces Expeditionary Medal w/1 BSS, Viet Nam Service Medal w/1 OLC, Combat Readiness Medal. Married Mavis Aycock of Montgomery, AL; two children: Lisa and Christopher. Retired Mar. 31, 1984, HQ AAFES, Dallas, TX, as a Colonel. Home of record: DeSoto, TX.

Stanislav, Terrance J., Capt., USAF. 1979-1980: Vance AF Base Enid, OK, Flight 71 Pilot Training. 1980-1983: Pilot instructor, 25th Flight Training Sq., T-38. 1983-1985: Branch Chief, Flight Screening Program, Officer Training School, T-41, Lackland AFB, San Antonio, TX.

Starek, John, son of Frank Starek and Emily Kakac, was born Apr. 25, 1919, Scurry, TX. Education: Telico Elementary, Alamo Elementary, Ennis, TX, Elementary, Ennis High School through grade nine. Enlisted in U.S. Army Corps, July 8, 1941, Dallas, TX. Boot camp: Ft. Sill, OK. Theater of Operation: EAME, WWII. Battles: Sent with 15 Army Hospital Center, on detached service at Port Weymouth, England, to get ready for D-Day. Loaded troops for invasion, then detached to Air Force, Newberry, England, to evacuate wounded soldiers into England. Medals: Good Conduct, European Ribbons, Hash Marks. Honorably discharged Oct. 3, 1945, Ft. Sam Houston, San Antonio, TX. Home of record: Dallas, TX.

Stark, A. M., son of Mr. and Mrs. Stark, made his home with Mr. and Mrs. Dave Sloan, Taylor, TX. Enlisted U.S. Army Corps, 1940; basic training, Camp Bowie, TX; additional training: Camp Blanding, FL, Camp Edwards, MS. Theater of Operations: European. Served in Africa and Italy. German PRISONER OF WAR eight months. Medals: EOT Campaign Medal w/BSS, WWII Victory Medal, POW Medal, and others Honorably discharged 1945.

Stasney, Chester J., son of Frank and Vera Stasney, was born Oct. 6, 1929, Crosby, TX. Education: Crosby High School and Lee College. Enlisted U.S. Armed Forces, Jan. 4, 1951, Baytown, TX. Theater of Operations: Korea War. Honorably discharged Dec. 18, 1952. Current place of residence, Highlands, TX.

Stasney, Edwin Lee, son of Ed and Philipine Stasney, was born May 28, 1922, Praha, TX.

Graduated Beasley, TX, High School. Enlisted in U.S. Army Air Force, Sept. 10, 1942, Kelly Air Force Base, San Antonio, TX. Battles: Rome-Arno Northern Appenines, Po Valley Southern France, Rhineland, and Air Combat Balkans. Decorations: Distinguished Unit Badge, EAME Campaign Medal w/7 BSS, Good Conduct Medal. Attained rank of Staff Sgt. in 1108th Army Air Force Base Unit. Honorable discharge Oct. 12, 1945. Married Sophie. Home of record: Needville, TX.

Stasney, Frankie August, son of Edwin Lee and Sophie Stasney, was born May 22, 1950, Alvin, TX. Graduated from Needville, TX, High School. Attended Wharton Co. Junior College, and Texas A&M University. Enlisted in the USMC, Oct. 3, 1968. Decorations: National Defense Service Medal and Good Conduct Medal. Honorable discharge Aug. 18, 1970. Rank: Sgt. Home of record: Beasley, TX.

Stasney, James Edward, Jr., son of James Edward Stasney, Sr. and Mary Lou Stasney, was born June 18, 1947, Liberty, TX. High school education. Enlisted in the U.S. Army Corps during the Viet Nam War at Ft. Ord, CA. Basic training, Ft. Ord, CA, AIT, Ft. Rucker, AL. Theater of Operations: Viet Nam. Battles: Viet Nam, TET Operation. Medals: Sharp Shooter Medal, Viet Nam Ribbons. Honorably discharged Oct. 13, 1969. Current place of residence: Highlands, TX.

Stasney, James Edward, Sr., son of Frank W. and Vera Stasney, was born Feb. 1, 1925, Crosby, TX. Education through ninth grade, Crosby, TX. Enlisted during WWII, Houston, Harris Co., TX. Theater of Operations: American, Asiatic-Pacific. Battles: Luzon and New Guinea. Served in New Caledonia, New Zealand, Luzon and New Guinea, First Scout. Medals: American Campaign Medal, Asiatic-Pacific Campaign Ribbon w/3 BSS, Philippine Liberation Ribbon w/1 BSS, Good Conduct Medal, WWII Victory Medal, Rifleman 745 Combat Inf. Badge (Rifle 22 Expert), Purple Heart. WOUNDED IN ACTION, Jan. 16, 1945, Luzon. Honorably discharged Nov. 13, 1945. Married Mary Lou Stasney; five children: James Edward, Jr., Ronald E., Dale R., Richard J., Robert W. Retired from Exxon. Home: Highlands, TX.

Stasney, Kenneth Edwin, son of Edwin Lee and Sophie Stasney, was born July 2, 1952, La Marque TX. Graduated Needville, TX, High School. Attended Wharton Co. Jr. College, and Lamar University. Enlisted USMC, Sept. 21, 1972. Decorations: National Defense Service Medal, Good Conduct Medal, Sharpshooter Badge. Honorable discharge Sept. 20, 1974. Rank: Cpl. Home of record: East Bernard, TX.

Stasney, Ronald E., son of James Edward, Sr. and Mary Lou Stasney, was born Aug. 15, 1949, Baytown, Harris, TX. Completed two years of college. Enlisted at Ft. Polk, LA, in U.S. Army Corps, during Viet Nam War. Basic training at Ft. Polk, LA, AIT at Ft. Sill, OK. Theater of Operations: Koutem, Viet Nam. Medals: Sharpshooter. Honorably discharged Sept. 3, 1971. Home: Highlands, TX.

Stasny, John, Jr., son of Mr. and Mrs. John Stasny, Sr., was born 1900; died 1940; buried Calvary Catholic Cem., Granger, TX. WWI veteran.

Stastny, Arnold, served Feb. 1944–May. 1946, U.S. Navy, during WWII.

Stastny, Cyril Method, Sr., son of John Peter Stastny and Tereze Brhel, was born June 10, 1920, Frydek, TX. Completed seventh grade at Frydek

Public School. Was oldest in family, had to farm cotton. Enlisted in U.S. Army Corps, May 1942, TX. Assigned as Surgical Technician, Ft. Sam Houston, TX. Theater of Operations: EAME, stationed overseas at Tauton Summerset, England. Received Good Conduct Medal. Honorably discharged Nov. 11, 1945. Worked in a 52-patient ward with only one doctor and one nurse. At the Invasion of France, gliders flew above like geese and 600 wounded soldiers were brought in that evening. Served May 1942–Oct. 1945, U.S. Army Corps, during WWII. Retired from work force in 1983. Married Marie Surovcak, Nov. 12, 1946; four children: Jeanette Stastny Klekar, Lorine Stastny Rogers, Cyril Method Stastny, Jr., Rose Stastny. Used to enjoy collecting and restoring cars, farming and cattle, and polka dancing. Now enjoys fishing, dominoes and listening to good Czech polka music. Home of record: Sealy, TX. Submitted in honor of her father by Rose Stastny of Austin, TX.

Stastny, Edwin, son of Frank J. Stastny and Annie Baca, was born near Fayetteville, TX. Education: elementary and high school in Crosby and Fayetteville, TX. Inducted into U.S. Army Corps prior to June 1944, Ft. Sam Houston, San Antonio, TX, during WWII.

Stastny, Frank James, son of Mr. and Mrs. Stastny, was born Feb. 3, 1928. Served Apr. 1946–Mar. 1948, U.S. Army Corps, during WWII. Married Frances J.; two daughters: Patsy Stastny and Donna Stastny Mieth (may have other children who were not listed). Died Nov. 14, 1988; buried St. Mary's Catholic Cem., Frydek, Austin Co., TX.

Stastny, Frank L., son of Frank J. Stastny and Annie Baca, was born Nov. 15, 1917, Fayetteville, TX. Education: St. John's Catholic Elementary in Fayetteville and High School in Crosby, TX. Inducted into U.S. Army Corps on Jan. 9, 1942, Ft. Sam Houston, San Antonio, TX, during WWII. Honorably discharged Oct. 6, 1945, Ft. Sam Houston, TX. Served three years, eight months, 28 days. Theater of Operations: EAME. Battles: Africa, Casablanca, French Morocco, Europe. Medals: EAME Battle Campaign w/5 BSS for Sicily, Rome-Arno, Southern France, Rhineland, and Central Europe, Good Conduct Medal, WWII Victory Medal. Home of record: Fayetteville, TX.

Stastny, Joe A., West, TX. Entered U.S. Armed Forces in 1943, during WWII. Served in New Guinea, Philippines, Japan, attained rank of T/5. Awards: AP w/2 BSS, Phil. Lib. w/1 BSS, WWII Victory Ribbon w/4 overseas bars, one service stripe. Discharged 1946.

Stastny, Joe S., West, TX, Military Veteran.

Stastny, Johnnie J., son of Frank J. Stastny and Annie Baca, was born July, 1924 near Fayetteville, TX. Education: elementary and high school in Crosby and Fayetteville, TX. Inducted into U.S. Army Corps on June 1944, Ft. Sam Houston, San Antonio, TX, during WWII. Basic training at Camp Joseph T. Robinson, Little Rock, AR, then assigned to 5th Reg., 1st Cavalry Div., Asiatic-Pacific Theater of Operations. Participated in the Philippine Liberation and the occupation of Japan. Entered Japan through Tokyo Bay, to Yokohama, and Tokyo on the day of the signing of the Japanese surrender in Tokyo Bay by General Douglas MacArthur, Sept. 2, 1945. Honorably discharged May 1946. Rank: Tech Sgt. (T-4). Married Angeline Kubala; two sons and a daughter (all married). Resided in Houston, Harris Co., TX. Attended the University of Houston, then worked in management and accounting until retirement.

Stastny, Steve J., Jr. son of Steve J. Stastny, Sr. and Rosie Stastny, was born about 1914, Kaufman, TX. Education: grammar school. Enlisted about 1941, Dallas, TX. Served as Rifleman Instructor, Tech 5, India, Central Burma. Medals: American Service, GCM, three Overseas Service Bars, Asiatic Pacific Service w/2 BSS, and the Distinguished Unit Badge. Honorably discharged Sept. 21, 1942. Died July 19, 1964.

Stavinaha, Leonard, WWII veteran of Granger, TX.

Stavinoha, Daniel John, son of Edwin L. Stavinoha and Annie Zabransky, was born Nov. 15, 1926, Engle, Fayette Co., TX. Education: St. Mary's Catholic School, Praha, TX, Engle High School. Enlisted in U.S. Navy, Oct. 20, 1944, Houston, TX. Boot camp, San Diego, CA. Served in A.P. in Okinawa on USS *Haywood* and USS *Kerchow* transport ships. Medals: A.P., AM-Dif., and WWII Victory Ribbon. Honorably discharged Mar. 23, 1946, San Francisco, CA. Home of record: Schulenburg, TX. Submitted by Maxine Sefcik, West, TX.

Stavinoha, Edwin Eugene, son of Edwin L. Stavinoha and Annie Zabransky, was born July 24, 1930, Engle, Fayette Co., TX. Education: Engle Junior High and Schulenburg, TX, High School. Enlisted July 8, 1951. Attained rank of Sgt. in USMC. Theater of Operations: Asiatic Pacific Theater. Served on the *Bon Homme Richard* and the *Antietam* aircraft carriers. Received GCM Medal. Relieved from active duty in 1953 before discharge. Home of record: Katy, TX.

Stavinoha, Eugene Frederick, son of Edwin L. Stavinoha and Annie Zabransky, was born Oct. 6, 1920, Engle, Fayette Co., TX. Education: Engle School, TX, St. Mary's Catholic School, Praha, TX. Enlisted in U.S. Navy, Nov. 29, 1940, Houston, TX. Boot camp, San Diego, CA. Theater of Operation: American Theater, Asiatic-Pacific Theater. Battles: Dutch Harbor, AK, Okinawa, New Hebrides, Guadalcanal, Munda, Bouganville. Medals: American Theater, Good Conduct, American Defense, WWII Victory Medal, Asiatic-Pacific Campaign Ribbon. Honorably discharged Dec. 24, 1946, San Francisco, CA. Home of record: Glen Burnie, MD.

Stavinoha, Henry John, son of Henry Joseph Stavinoha and Mary Wichita, was born Jan. 10, 1918, Temple, TX. Finished two years Temple Junior College, got flying license at Temple Millar and Darwin Airport. Inducted at Dodd Field, San Antonio, TX, into U.S. Army Air Corps. Sent to Kerns, UT, for basic training, then to Lincoln, NE, Army Air Corps, as instructor in Air Craft Maintenance. Also was sent to specialist schools in Chicago, IL, Amarillo, TX, for B-29, Yuma, AZ for B-17 and AT6 for Crew Chief. Married soon after WWII started, before enlisting in Army Air Corps. Daughter born in Lincoln, NE. Lost our son at birth, daughter born in Temple, TX, when war was over. Honorably discharged Dec. 5, 1945. Received American Campaign Medal, Good Conduct Medal, WWII Victory Medal. Achieved rank of Sgt. Occupations: grocery store, Curtis Candy Co. route salesman, power plant operator at Scott-White Hospital, Temple, TX, until went to work at V.A. Hospital, Waco, TX. Still on the job each week day at the pharmacy. Home of record: Waco, TX.

Stavinoha, Wilbur A., son of Edwin L. Stavinoha and Annie Zabransky, was born Apr. 24, 1933, Engle, Fayette Co., TX. Education: Engle School and Schulenburg High School. Enlisted at Houston, Harris Co., TX, Sept. 3, 1952, U.S. Navy. Theaters of Operation: CIB, Asiatic-Pacific, Viet Nam, Korea. Boot camp, San Diego, CA. Served on USS *Andromeda* AKA-15 (two and a half years), USS *Pender Co.* 1080 (6 mo.), USS *Romulus* ARL-22 (1 yr.), remainder of four years on Pacific Coast. Medals: United Nations Defense, National Defense, Korean Ribbon, Good Conduct. Honorably discharged Aug. 30, 1956, Bremerton, WA. Home of record: Highlands, TX. Submitted by Maxine Sefcik, West, TX.

Stefek, Danny, USMC, of Granger, TX, is a Desert Storm U.S. Armed Forces Veteran.

Stefek, Joe E., was born Feb. 9, 1924, Georgetown, Williamson Co., TX. Enlisted in U.S. Army Corps, Mar. 15, 1943. Assigned to Inf. Rank: Cpl. Trained at Ft. Leonard Wood, MO. Theater of Operations: EAME, American. Fought in England, France, Belgium, Germany, Austria. In France, 1944, was WOUNDED IN ACTION, PRISONER

OF WAR of Germans for nine months. Medals: Good Conduct, Distinguished Unit Badge, two overseas service bars, American Campaign, WWII Victory, Purple Heart, EAME Theater Campaign w/2 BSS. Married Martha David; four children. Farmer and rancher. Member, American Legion Post No. 282, Granger, TX. Home of record: Georgetown, TX.

Stefek, Louis, Jarrell, TX. WWII veteran. Member, American Legion Post No. 282, Granger, TX.

Stefek, Willie Frank "Bill," son of Josef John Stefek and Mary Ann Knapek, was born Apr. 16, 1930, Granger, Williamson Co., TX. Education: Moravia, Granger, VA, H.S. diploma, self study human behavior, management, resources developer. Enlisted in U.S. Army Corps, Aug. 25, 1948, Austin, TX. Attained rank of T-Sgt. Supply and Maintenance Technician, Recreation Specialist. Theater of Operations: Pacific, Okinawa, Ryukyu Islands, Yokohama, Honshu Island, Japan. Served with Filipino Scouts, 44th Inf. Reg., Okinawa. Developed and furnished 320 dayrooms for soldiers, Ft. Hood, TX. Organized and developed the U.S. Army Outdoor Recreation Program for soldiers and families at Ft. Hood and world wide. Medals: Good Conduct, Army Occupation Japan, Expert Marksman. Honorably discharged June 23, 1952. Married Margaret Dorothy Sladecek; four children: William Wayne Stefek, Marilyn Rose Stefek Wortham, Carol Jean Stefek Daude, Robert Gene Stefek, seven grandkids. Employed 37 years as director of U.S. Army Outdoor Recreation. Retired July 31, 1987. Hobbies: farming, plant nursery, exploring wilderness. District manager Catholic Union of Texas, KJT, Director West Bell Co. Water Supply Corporation, Killeen, TX, 1969-1991. Home of record: Killeen, TX.

Steffek, Albin W., son of Mr. and Mrs. Joe Steffek, Granger, TX, was born Mar. 23, 1924. Education: St. Cyril Catholic School. Enlisted USMC, 1943. Basic training, San Diego, CA; additional training: Goleta, CA, Santa Barbara, CA. Theater of Operations: Asiatic-Pacific. Served in Marianas, Philippines, Guam, Japan. Medals: Asiatic-Pacific Theater Campaign w/BSS, WWII Victory. Attained rank of Pfc., prior to honorable discharge. Married Lillian. Died Mar. 30, 1986. Buried Holy Cross Catholic Cem., Granger, TX.

Steffek, Ignac D. "Ike," was born Nov. 17, 1930. Married Florence. Died Apr. 8, 1990; buried Holy Cross Catholic Cem., Granger, TX.

Steffek, Joe E., son of Mr. and Mrs. Joe J. Steffek, Granger, TX. Enlisted U.S. Army Corps, 1943. Basic training, Ft. Leonard Wood, MO. Theater of Operations: European. Served campaigns in England, France, Belgium, Germany, Austria. German PRISONER OF WAR nine months. Medals: District Unit Badge, Purple Heart, Good Conduct, EOT Campaign w/BSS, WWII Victory, ribbons. WOUNDED IN ACTION, France, 1944. Attained rank of Cpl. prior to honorable discharge, 1945. Married Martha David.

Steffek, Joseph F., son of Joseph Steffek and Annie Ezzell, was born June 12, 1913, Hallettsville, TX. Educated through sixth grade. Went into U.S. Army Corps during WWII at San Antonio, TX. Theater of Operations: Europe. Battles: France, Belgium, Luxembourg, Germany. Medals: WWII Victory, EAME Campaign w/5 battle stars. Honorably discharged Oct. 20, 1945. Married Elsie A.; three children. Farmed, ranched and gathered pecans. Hobbies: fishing, squirrel hunting, gardening and raising fruit trees. Home of record: Hallettsville, TX.

Steffek, Linhart Marion, son of Emil and Adela Steffek, was born Aug. 16, 1928, Needville, TX. Education: Needville High School, Richmond High School. Enlisted in U.S. Coast Guard, Nov. 26, 1948, Houston, TX. Petty Officer, 2/C. Served on CGC *Cherokee*, CGC *Chinook*, CGC *Winnebago*. Patrolled in the North Atlantic, East, South, Centra, and North Pacific. Home Ports: Norfolk, VA, Baltimore, MD, Honolulu, HI. Theater of Operations: American and Pacific. Received Good Conduct Medal. Honorably discharged May 26, 1952, New Orleans, LA. Home of record: Missouri City, TX.

Steffek, Louis, WWII veteran of Granger, TX.

Steffek, Rhonda, U.S. Navy, of Granger, TX, is a Desert Storm U.S. Armed Forces veteran.

Steffek, Richard James, son of Joseph Adolph Steffek and Lucy Cecilia Beyer, was born Mar. 25, 1948, Taylor, Williamson, TX. Education: Sts.

Cyril & Methodius Catholic School, Granger High School, 1966. Enlisted in U.S. Naval Reserve, Nov. 10, 1966, Austin, TX. Military occupation: Gunner's Mate. Served aboard USS *William V. Pratt*–DLG-13 in search and rescue operations off coast of North Viet Nam. Decorations: National Defense Medal, Viet Nam Campaign Medal. Rescued several pilots who were shot down over North Viet Nam. Honorably discharged Nov. 9, 1972. Married Susan Marie Brosch; children: Richard Joseph, Aaron Matthew, Ashlee Marie. Civilian occupation: Cable Splicing Tech. Hobbies: Hunting, fishing, woodworking. Served eight years on Granger City Council, two years as Mayor of Granger. Home of record: Granger, TX.

Steffek, Ronald Edward, son of Joseph Adolph Steffek and Lucy Cecilia Beyer, was born June 6, 1946, in Taylor, TX. Attended Sts. Cyril & Methodius School at Granger and graduated from Granger High School in 1964. Enlisted in the U.S. Navy at Austin, TX, Nov. 10, 1966, during the Viet Nam Conflict. Served in the Viet Nam area aboard the USS *William Pratt* (DLG-13) as a Gunner's Mate. Participated in naval operations in the Gulf of Thonkin. Separated from service on Nov. 9, 1971. Employed by Alcoa as a rodding operator. Married Peggy Ann Simcik; three children: Rhonda (served in the Navy, honorable discharge, Nov. 1993), Rebecca Steffek Skrhak, and Ronnie. Hobbies: playing the accordion, gardening, and fishing. Home of record: Granger, TX.

Stegient, Lige Ernest, son of Pete Stegient and Anna Rose Tomascik, was born Jan. 12, 1915, Cameron, TX. Enlisted in U.S. Army Corps, Camp Bowie, TX. Assigned to Co. A, 36th Armored Inf. Reg. Theater of Operations: EAME. WOUNDED IN ACTION, France, Battle of the Bulge, WWII. Medals: Purple Heart, EAME Campaign, WWII Victory. Attained rank of Sgt. Prior to military service, worked in Civilian Conservation Corps, honorably discharged Apr. 17, 1935. Died Nov. 19, 1976, TX. Submitted by Verna Shook of Athens, TX.

Stepan, Fred Rudolph, son of Peter Stepan and Alzabetha (Elizabeth) Kahanek, was born on Mar. 6, 1896, in Vlcovice, Moravia #70, in the Czech Lands, the eldest of nine children. Immigrated with his parents at 18 months of age. Attended Brownson School (Hillje, TX), six weeks in El Campo, TX. Enlisted June 25, 1918, Wharton, TX, during WWI. Stationed in San Antonio, TX. Theater of Operations: American. Rank: Pvt., Battery 54th Field Artillery. Medals: WWI Victory, Good Conduct, American Theater of Operations Campaign Ribbon, among other awards. Honorably discharged Feb. 24, 1919, El Campo, TX. Married Annie Dluhos in Oct. 1924 (age 28); four daughters: Viola, Albina, Alice Mae, and Jeraldine. Died Feb. 24, 1989, El Campo, TX. Submitted by Jerri Stepan Gruber, Houston, TX.

Stepan, Joe, West, TX, WWII veteran. Theater of Operations: Asiatic-Pacific.

Stepan, Joe R., of West, TX, U.S. Army Corps, WWII veteran.

Stepan, John Lee, West, TX, WWII veteran, USMC.

Stepan, Raymond J., son of William Stepan and Marie Bedrich, was born Jan. 29, 1922, in Bleiberville, TX. Enlisted Nov. 21, 1942 in Bellville, and served in Sicily, Normandy, Northern France, Ardennes, Rhineland, Central Europe as Tech 5 (Medical Technician). WOUNDED IN ACTION. Medals: EAME Campaign w/6 BSS and one Bronze Arrowhead, Purple Heart, BSS, Good Conduct, four Overseas Bars. Discharged Oct. 17, 1945. Home of record: Hempstead, TX.

Sternadel, Walter F., son of Frank Sternadel and Rosalie, was born Feb. 9, 1920, West, TX. Educa-

tion: St. Mary's Catholic School (elementary) West High School (equiv.), Sawyer School of Business, Southern Cal University, Stanford University. Enlisted Santa Monica, CA, U.S. Army Corps, 65th Inf. Div. Theater of Operations: EAME. Battles: German Campaign, Central Europe Campaign, Southern France Campaign. WOUNDED IN ACTION. Medals: Purple Heart, WWII Victory, Silver Star, EAME Ribbon w/3 BSS, Combat Inf. Badge, BSS, Expert Combat Inf. Badge, Good Conduct Ribbon, American Theater Ribbon. Attained rank of T/Sgt. prior to honorable discharge, May 31, 1946. Home of record: Redding CA. Submitted by Martha Monthei, Abbot, TX.

Stiba, Benjamin F., son of Mr. and Mrs. Frank Stiba, Taylor, TX. Education: San Marcos State Teachers College. Enlisted U.S. Army Air Corps, 1945; basic training Keesler Field, MS; additional training, Tyndall Field, FL, TX. Theater of Operations: American. Medals: American Theater Campaign, WWII Victory, ribbons, among other medals. Attained rank of Pfc. prior to honorable discharge.

Stiba, Ernest A., son of Mr. and Mrs. John J. Stiba, Taylor, TX. Education: Coupland High School. Enlisted U.S. Navy, 1944; basic training, San Diego, CA. Theaters of Operation: Asiatic-Pacific, American. Served in Ulithe and U.S.A. Attained rank of S 1/C prior to honorable discharge. Medals: Asiatic-Pacific Theater Campaign, AOT Campaign, WWII Victory, ribbons.

Stiba, John E., son of Mr. and Mrs. John J. Stiba, Taylor, TX. Education: University of Texas. Enlisted in U.S. Navy and trained at Columbia University. Theaters of Operation: European, Asiatic-Pacific, American. Commissioned Lt. (jg). Medals: EOT Campaign w/4 BSS, Asiatic-Pacific Theater Campaign, AOT Campaign, WWII Victory, American Defense.

Stiba, Robert Lee, son of Tom H. Stiba and Nannie A. Hanson, was born Oct. 4, 1939. Graduated from Taylor High School in 1959. Earned A.A. from Temple Junior College in 1961, and B.S. from Southwest State University in 1961. Enlisted in the U.S. Army at San Antonio, TX; Basic training at Ft. Polk, LA. Underwent Advance Individual Training at Ft. Gordon, GA. Served overseas in Germany as a Military Policeman. Awards: National Defense Service Medal, Marksmanship Medal, and others. Separated from service on Aug. 31, 1967. Archaeologist and house painter. Numerous hobbies include fishing, camping, photography, flint kneading, gardening, and growing old time roses. Home of record: Taylor, TX.

Stibora, Joseph John, son of Joseph Stibora and Adela Cook, was born Aug. 26, 1930, in Ellinger, Fayette Co., TX. Attended Southwestern Business University and University of Houston, TX. Enlisted on Mar. 15, 1951, in Houston. Basic training at Fort Sam Houston and advanced basic training at Fort Bliss, TX. Assigned to Headquarters Unit, 1st Guarded Missile Group, Fort Bliss, TX. Discharged Mar. 14, 1953, at Fort Bliss, TX. Home of record: Stafford, TX.

Stiborik, Cecelia Anne, daughter of Antonin Stiborik and Cecelia Capak-Najvar, was born in Taylor, Texas. Educated at Barnard College and Columbia College. Received PhD from the University of Michigan. Enlisted at Fort Sam Houston, TX, on Oct. 21, 1942, with sister Mary. Theaters of Operation: U.S., 8th Air Force HQ, High Wycombe, England, and France. Discharged at Fort Sam Houston, TX, Nov. 1945. Married Mr. Dreyfuss. Resides in Ann Arbor, MI.

Stiborik, Joseph A., was a native of Taylor, TX. Family moved to Rockdale, TX. Employed at Industrial Generating Co. Was part of the 509th Composite Group, elite men especially chosen and given months of intensive training in Wendover, UT, before being sent to Tinian. One of the crew (the radio man) on the *Enola Gay* that dropped the atomic bomb on Hiroshima, Aug. 6, 1945. Awarded the Flying Cross and a Battle Star. Married Helen Stiborik who preceded him in death in 1981; two daughters: Stephanie Stiborik Reeves of Rockdale, TX, and Melanie Stiborik Graves of Houston, TX. Died July 1984, and was buried in Rockdale, TX, with military honors–taps were played, guns saluted, and daughters were presented with an American flag.

Stiborik, Mary Therese, daughter of Anton Stiborik and Cecilia Capak, was born in Taylor, TX. Attended St. Mary's Parochial School and Taylor High School, graduating in 1936. Enlisted at Fort Sam Houston, TX, Oct. 21, 1942, serving at Fort De Moines, IA, Fort Custer, MI, and Fort Sheridan, IL. Served in the European Theater of Operations at Supreme HQ Allied Expeditionary Forces in Mar. 1944, Kingston, England, Versailles, and Reims, France, and Frankfurt, Germany. Medals: EAME Campaign with one BSS, WAAC Service Ribbon, Good Conduct, three Overseas Service Stripes. Discharged at Fort Sam Houston, TX, in 1945. Married Mr. Burke. Home of record: Taylor, TX.

Stojanik, Alfred, WWII veteran of Granger, TX.

Stojanik, Edwin D., Sr., son of John Stojanik and Frances Blinka, was born Nov. 14, 1923, Granger, TX. Education: Palacky School, Granger, TX. Enlisted in U.S. Navy during WWII, about 1942. Stationed aboard USS *Langley*. Served in South Pacific. Medals: WWII Victory, Asiatic-Pacific Campaign, and others. Honorably discharged Dec. 29, 1945, Camp Wallace, Galveston, TX. Retired from Alcoa, Rockdale TX, 1975. Married Alice Machu in 1948; four children: Edwin Jr., Robert, Larry, Melody, five grandchildren. Hobbies: fishing and hunting. Home of record: Thrall, TX.

Stojanik, Howard J., Granger, TX. WWII veteran. Member, American Legion Post No. 282, Granger, TX.

Stojanik, Jessie Lee, son of John Stojanik and Frances Schirpik, was born Nov. 13, 1921, in Walburg, Williamson Co., TX. Attended Palacky School. Enlisted in U.S. Army on Nov. 16, 1940. Served in the European, African, and Middle Eastern Theater of Operations as Military Policeman, during WWII. Participated in campaigns in North Africa and Europe. WOUNDED IN ACTION, in combat, left for dead, later found alive. Awards: Purple Heart, American Defense Service Medal, European-African-Middle Eastern Campaign Medal, WWII Victory Medal, and others. Separated from service on Mar. 26, 1946, and began farming. Married Agnes L. Michalek; three children: Sharon Grimes, Donna Reid, and Jessica Meier. Enjoyed hunting and playing dominoes. Member, American Legion Post No. 282, Granger, TX. Died May 19, 1983, and is interred in Holy Cross Cemetery at Granger, TX.

Stojanik, John, was born June 9, 1816. Military veteran. Died Mar. 19, 1908. Buried Calvary Catholic Cem., Granger, TX.

Stojanik, Robert James, son of Edwin D. Stojanik, Sr. and Alice Machu, was born Aug. 19, 1954, Thrall, TX. Education: Thrall Public School. Enlisted in military service, 1971, TX. Assigned to Co. C, 3rd Bn., 20AJT Bde, 1st Plt., Ft. Ord, CA. Honorably discharged 1974. Employed at Westinghouse, Round Rock, TX. Married Connie Lucio; one daughter: Destinee Stojanik. Home of record: Round Rock, TX.

Stojanik, William John "Willie," son of John Stojanik and Anna Palousek, was born Jan. 25, 1917, near Granger, TX. Education: Macedonia and Palacky, near Granger. Enlisted in the U.S. Army during WWII at Ft. Sam Houston, TX. Attained rank of Pfc. Assigned to the famous 36th "Texas" Div. in France, and as a member of the 132nd Field Artillery Bn., of the 7th Army. First landed in North Africa, then Bloody Salerno, Naples, Rome, battles at Cassino, San Pietro and Velletri (on the Anzio Beachhead). Fought in the strategic battles of Montelimar where German 19th Army was destroyed and the Vosges Mountains, key to Alsaice and southern Rhine. Men of 132nd have been awarded Silver Stars, BSS Medals, Legion of Merits, Air Medals, Div. Citations and Purple Hearts. (Willie, mercifully, was not wounded). Honorable discharge Aug. 13, 1945, Ft. Sam Houston, TX. Married Sybil Machu at the Brethren Church in Taylor, TX; two sons: William John Jr. and Don Wayne. Hobbies: gardening, carpentry repairs, and dancing. Enjoyed visiting with family. Loved grandchildren! Employed by University of Texas Air Conditioning Dept. for 23 years. Died

July 6, 1991, in Houston, TX. Buried in Machu Cemetery, Granger, TX. Home of record: Austin, TX, where family has lived for 44 years.

Stojnik, Will, WWII veteran of Granger, TX.

Stluka, Ernest B., son of Ben J. Stluka and Louise Kolar, was born Dec. 6, 1921, Shiner, Lavaca Co., TX, the eldest son. Attended school in Knox Co., TX, St. Ludmila's Academy, Shiner, TX, graduated Shiner High School, 1939. Enlisted in the U.S. Army Air Corps, July 31, 1942. Received basic training at Sheppard Field, Wichita, TX, transferred to Englewood, CA. Received diploma as an Aerial Engineer. Completed gunnery training at Lyndall Field, FL. After staying at Columbia, SC, went to Brazil, England, then to India, to the China, Burma, India Theater of Operations. Rank: S/Sgt. MISSING IN ACTION, July 11, 1943. One year later, U.S. Government reported that he and six other crew members were KILLED IN ACTION when their B-25 went down over the mountains in the vicinity of Lamping, China. The bodies were not recovered until Nov. 1948, because the mountains were impassable by any vehicle. Reburial rites for the crew were held in the Jefferson National Cemetery, St. Louis, MO, Aug. 20, 1949. Submitted by Lois Jo Schindler, Victoria, TX.

Strauss, Ben J., son of Otto Strauss and Agnes Netardus, was born in Shiner, TX, Aug. 4, 1917. Attended high school and business school. Enlisted at Fort Sam Houston on Nov. 18, 1941, and served in Southern France, Rhineland, North Apennines, Po Valley, Algeria French Morocco, Tunisia, Naples Foggia, Rome Arno. Rank: Tech Sgt. Medals: Distinguished Unit Badge 12th A.F., EAME Campaign w/9 BSS, American Defense Service, American Theater Campaign, Good Conduct. Had several audiences with Pope Pius XII when stationed in Italy. Discharged Sept. 19, 1945, at Fort Sam Houston, TX. Home of record: Houston, TX.

Strmiska, James, USMC, of Granger, TX, is a Desert Storm U.S. Armed Forces Veteran.

Strnadel, Charlie J., son of John Strnadel and Josephine Orsak, was born Jan. 22, 1894, in Ellinger, Fayette Co., TX. Attended grade school in Ellinger. Enlisted in the Army at Wharton, on Apr. 9, 1918, and served as a Pvt. in the Medical Corps in France and Germany. Awarded the Good Conduct Medal and was discharged Sept. 10, 1919. Died Dec. 18, 1978.

Struhall, Louis, served in U.S. Armed Forces during WWI, 1917–1918. Member of SPJST Lodge 20, Granger, TX.

Stryk, Joe L., son of John and Stazie Stryk, was born on Feb. 14, 1922, at Praha, TX. Completed the eighth grade. Enlisted at Fort Sam Houston, and served in the American and Asiatic Pacific Theater of Operations. Attained the rank of S/Sgt. Fought in New Guinea and Southern Philippines. WOUNDED IN ACTION three times: Oct. 1944, May 1945, and June 1945. Received the American Theater Campaign Medal, Asiatic Pacific Campaign w/2 Battle Stars, Philippine Liberation w/2 Battle Stars, Good Conduct, and Purple Heart w/2 OLC. Honorably discharged on Nov. 30, 1945. Home of record: San Antonio, TX.

Stryk, Joe Louis, Jr., son of Joseph Stryk and Rosalie Kupcak, was born Feb. 12, 1918, Praha, TX, the 5th of 6th children. Education: eight years in Praha, TX, Catholic school. Inducted into U.S. Army Corps June 1942; basic training, Ft. Sam Houston, TX. Rank: Pfc. Shipped to St. Petersburg, FL. Assigned to U.S. Army Air Corps Radio School. Shipped to Sioux Falls, SD, Sept. 1942, for Radio Tech Training. Attached to 811th Tech Sch Sqdn, AAFTTC. Feb. 1943. Contracted measles and pneumonia. After two months in Army Hospital, was given an Honorable Medical Discharge, Apr. 3, 1943. Moved to Rosenberg, TX, May 1943. Employed by Western Auto Store until 1947. Bought Texaco Service Station dealership, operated it for 25 years. Purchased a liquor store, 1968, owned for eight years. Worked for HiLo Auto Parts until retirement in 1986. Married

Wilma Matocha, Feb. 16, 1942, Catholic Church, Cistern, TX; four children: Michael, Patrick, Mark, JoAnn, ten grandchildren. One son served in the U.S. Army Corps, completed tour of duty in Viet Nam. One grandson is a career Navy seaman who participated in the Gulf War. Home of record: Rosenberg, TX.

Stryk, Larry L., son of Joe and Annie Stryk, was born on June 28, 1948, at La Grange, TX. Graduated from high school and enlisted at San Antonio, TX. Participated in two cruises to the West Pacific, including four tours to Viet Nam. Medals: National Defense Service, Viet Nam Service, Good Conduct, Viet Nam Campaign, and others. Honorably discharged May 1970 at the rank of E-4. Home of record: San Antonio, TX.

Strzinek, William G., son of William Strzinek and Emelia, was born Aug. 10, 1926, Cameron, TX. Education: Yoe High School, Cameron, TX; management courses at Western Michigan University in Kalamazoo; SMU, Dallas, TX; Hillsdale College, Hillsdale, MI. Enlisted about 1944, San Antonio, TX, U.S. Army Corps. Theater of Operations: Asiatic-Pacific–Guam. Medals: Asiatic-Pacific Campaign Ribbon, Good Conduct, WWII Victory Ribbon. Attained rank of Sgt. prior to honorable discharge, Feb. 1947. Married Kathryn. Sales manager for Kraft Foods Co., Kansas area, 41 years. Hobbies: fishing and golf. Home of record: Conroe, TX.

Stuchlik, Jerry F., son of Mr. and Mrs. F. J. Stuchlik, Weir, TX. Graduate of Weir High School. Enlisted U.S. Army Corps, 1940. Basic training, Ft. Bliss, TX. Additional training, Laredo, TX, Ft. McIntosh, TX. Theater of Operations: Asiatic-Pacific. Served in New Guinea, Luzon, Philippines, Bismarck Archipelago. Medals: Asiatic-Pacific Theater Campaign w/4 BSS, American Defense, Philippine Liberation w/1 BSS, Inf. Combat Badge, Good Conduct, ribbons, WWII Victory. Attained rank of S/Sgt prior to honorable discharge, 1945.

Stuchly, Elwin A., Axtell, TX, U.S. Army Corps, stationed Amarillo, TX, Army Base, WWII veteran.

Suchomel, Anton, son of Stanislav Suchomel and Mary Naviratil, was born Jan. 17, 1921, Granger, Williamson Co., TX. Education: Sts. Cyril & Methodius Catholic School and Alligator High School, three years. Enlisted U.S. Army Corps, Jan. 20, 1942. Basic training, San Antonio, TX, additional training, Jackson, MS. Attained rank of Tech 4/C in 451st Ordnance Heavy Auto Maintenance Company. Prepared food using a daily menu as a guide. Set up and operated field ranges of all varieties, cleaned all machinery and equipment and assigned duty soldiers to various tasks concerning the preparation of food and cleaning the kitchen. Requisitioned supplies and maintained record of supplies used. Served overseas for six months in this capacity in the European Theater of Operations. Medals: EAME Theater Campaign, American Theater Campaign, Good Conduct, WWII Victory, Ribbons. Attained rank of Sgt. prior to honorable discharge, Jan. 6, 1946. Married Ann Jansky; two children: Steven Suchomel and Cathy Suchomel Kostroun. Semi retired in 1986 as farmer. Home of record: Taylor, TX.

Suchomel, Stanislav J., son of Stanislav Suchomel and Mary Naviratil, was born May 11, 1919, Granger, TX. Education: Sts. Cyril & Methodius Catholic School and Alligator High School, one year. Enlisted U.S. Army Corps, Mar. 19, 1942. Basic training, Camp Barkeley, LA; additional training, CA, NJ, NY. Theater of Operations: European. Served in Normandy GO 33 WD 45, N. France GO 33 WD 45, Rhineland GO WD 45, Central Europe GO 40 WD 45. Medals: EAME Campaign w/4 BSS, Good Conduct, Bronze Arrowhead, Purple Heart, WWII Victory. WOUNDED IN ACTION, France, 1944. Served in Service Bty. 395 Armd. Field Artillery Bn. Served in Europe for 18 months as cannoneer, ammunition, power charges, loaded and fired gun. Attained rank of Pfc. prior to honorable discharge, Oct. 20, 1945. Married Dorothy Machu. Retired from Taylor Bedding, Taylor, TX, 1965. Died Mar. 21, 1992, Granger, TX. Buried Holy Cross Catholic Cemetery, Granger, Williamson Co., TX.

Sugarek, Edwin M., son of Charles Sugarek (born Kuncice, Moravia, immigrated 1856, Galveston, died 10/22/32, Beeville) and Amalia "Molly" Horak (born 4/9/1856, Catspring, TX, died

8/21/51, Bee Co., TX), was born Dec. 22, 1891, in Bee Co., TX. Enlisted, during WWI, in the U.S. Army in Sept. 1917, and trained at Camp Travis, TX. Served with the American Expeditionary Forces in France as a member of Co. A, 327th Inf., 90th Div. KILLED IN ACTION Oct. 16, 1918. Family received news of death in Dec. 1918, a month after the WWI Armistice went into effect. Family had received a letter from him in Nov. dated Oct. 2, 1918. However, it was after Oct. 2 that the 90th Div. engaged in sustained combat and suffered heavy casualties. Accordingly, his death came as shock to family members and friends. He is remembered as a true patriot who gave his life for his country.

Sugarek, L. E., son of Charles Sugarek and Amalia "Molly" Horak, was born about 1889, Beeville, TX. Enlisted in the U.S. Army Air Corps during WWI and was stationed at Kelly Field No. 2, San Antonio, TX at the time the news came that his brother, Edwin M., was KILLED IN ACTION. The news was received by the family in Dec., 1918.

Sugarek, Loren David, son of Rudolph Stanley Sugarek and Viola Annie Holubec, was born Oct. 7, 1945, at Hebbronville, TX. Attended Mathis, TX, High School, Blinn Junior College at Brenham. Received B.B.A. from Sam Houston State University at Huntsville. Enlisted in the U.S. Army at Houston, TX, during the Viet Nam Conflict. Served in Viet Nam as a member of the 101st Airborne Div. and attained the rank of Spec 5/C. Awards: BSS Medal, Army Commendation Medal, National Defense Service Medal and Viet Nam Service Medal. Discharged June 5, 1970. Died May 23, 1977, and is interred in Veterans Cemetery in Houston, TX.

Sula, Clarence J., son of George Sula and Bessie Sodek, was born on Nov. 22, 1920, at Temple, Bell Co., TX. Attended grade school, high school, and business college. Enlisted at Fort Sam Houston, TX, Aug. 21, 1942. Attained the rank of Staff Sgt., serving in the American Theater of Operations. Military Police Escort Guard, Medical Corp, Inf. Replacement Training Command and Armored Inf. Discharged Feb. 13, 1946. Home of record: Burlington, TX.

Sula, George E., son of Josef Sula and Anna Sivek, was born on Dec. 28, 1890, in Austria. Attended grade school. Enlisted in the U.S. Army at San Antonio, TX. Served in France and Germany as Pfc., Co. B, 315th M.P., 90th Inf. Div. Honorable discharge June 25, 1919. Died Feb. 18, 1935.

Sula, James C., son of Clarence J. Sula and Wanona Schneider, was born on Mar. 10, 1947, at Rosebud, TX, May 25, 1966. Served in Viet Nam as SP 5. Discharged May 23, 1969. Home of record: Temple, TX.

Sulak, Aug, West, TX, WWII veteran, U.S. Army Air Corps. Theater of operations: CBI.

Sulak, Bernard was born Apr. 24, 1910, in West, TX, to John Alois Sulak and Mary Kulhanek. Attended West High School and Texas A&M College, earning a Bachelor of Petroleum Engineering. Enlisted at Camp Wallace. Served 33 months in Europe, Africa, and the Middle East. Received the European African Middle Eastern Campaign Medal, two BSS for Rome Arno and Naples Foggia Campaigns, American Defense Service Medal, American Campaign Medal, and WWII Victory Medal. Discharged Nov. 26, 1945. Died Oct. 18 1985.

Sulak, Charles James, was born Jan. 12, 1917. Served in U.S. Navy, WWII. Attained rank of AM-3. Died Feb. 17, 1961. Buried in St. Mary's Cemetery, West, TX.

Sulak, Edward G., son of John Alois Sulak and Mary Kulhanek, was born Jan. 29, 1916, at West, TX. Attended high school and trade schools.

Enlisted in West, in the Medical Det. 143 Inf., 36th Div., and fought in battles as a Sgt. in Naples Foggia and Rome Arno. WOUNDED IN ACTION Nov. 23, 1943. Medals: European African Middle Eastern w/2 Stars, Good Conduct, Purple Heart, American Defense Service Medal. Discharged Sept. 30, 1945, at Camp Edwards, MA. Home of record: West, TX.

Sulak, Eugene Adolph, son of C. Y. and Anna Sulak, was born Feb. 11, 1922, West, TX. Enlisted in the Navy on Dec. 7, 1944, in Waco, TX. Served in WWII on the USS *Tweedy* Destroyer Escort as Seaman 2/C. Home of record: West, TX.

Sulak, Jerome A., son of Mr. and Mrs. Daniel Sulak, Penelope, TX. Entered Army, 1942, during WWII. Served in China, India and Marianas, attaining rank of S/Sgt. Awards: GCM, AP w/5 Battle Stars, Air Medal w/2 Clusters, DFC, and PL Ribbon. Discharged 1945.

Sulak, Joe, West, TX. WWII veteran. PRISONER OF WAR.

Sulak, Joe C., of West, TX. U.S. Army Corps, WWII veteran.

Sulak, John, was born Aug. 18, 1870, West, TX. Served in U.S. Army during WWI. Died Jan. 24, 1979. Buried in St. Mary's Cemetery, West, TX.

Sulak, John Louis, son of Louis John Sulak and Emilie Hanzelka, was born Nov. 18, 1907, in West, TX. Attended La Grange High School and graduated Magna Cum Laude from St. Edward's University in Austin, with a major in Journalism. Enlisted in the Navy May 18, 1937, in Houston, TX. Served as a Radarman aboard the tanker USS *Monongahela* in the South Pacific. Rank: Radarman 1/C. Decorations: Navy Commendation with one Battle Star, American Campaign, Asiatic Pacific Campaign w/4 Battle Stars and Philippine Liberation w/1 Battle Star. Discharged Sept. 14, 1945, at Camp Wallace, TX. Married Lillie Kallus, May 18, 1937. Died July 14, 1960, and is buried at La Grange City Cemetery.

Sulak, Sylvester, of West, TX. WWII veteran, USMC.

Sulak, Valerian Albert, son of Mr. and Mrs. V. J. Sulak. Entered Navy during WWII, 1944. Served in Philippines, Okinawa, Japan. Attained rank of COX. Awards: AT, WWII Victory, AP, PL Ribbons, and two Battle Ribbons. Discharged 1946.

Sulak, Walter George, was born May 17, 1948. Served in U.S. Navy in Viet Nam. Died Nov. 25, 1989, West, TX. Buried in St. Mary's Cemetery, West, TX.

Sulak, Wesley, was born Sept. 12, 1930. Served in U.S. Air Force in Korea. Died Feb. 20, 1993, West, TX. Buried in St. Mary's Cemetery, West, TX.

Sulak, William J., was born Oct. 23, 1892. Served in the U.S. Army Corps, Mech Co. M, 141st Inf, Died Jan. 26, 1963, West, TX. Buried in St. Mary's Cemetery, West, TX.

Sumbera, Jerome H., son of Anton Sumbera and Andela Fiser, was born June 18, 1909, La Grange, TX. Completed fifth grade, Radhost School. Enlisted in U.S. Armed Forces during WWII, June 15, 1942, Ft. Sam Houston, San Antonio, TX. Theater of Operations: American and Asiatic-Pacific. Battles: New Guinea, Luzon, Philippines. Medals: American Theater Campaign, Asiatic-Pacific Theater Campaign w/2 BSS, Philippine Liberation Ribbon w/1 BSS, WWII Victory Ribbon, Service Stripe, four overseas service bars. Honorably discharged Nov. 11, 1945. Married Mary Dusek; three sons: John, Daniel, James. Farmer and blacksmith. Died July 1, 1980, Buried at Granger, TX. Submitted by niece, Carolyn Meiners, of La Grange, TX.

Sumbera, John George, son of Anton Sumbera and Andela Fiser, was born Oct. 12, 1915, Fayette Co., TX. Education: 8th grade and GED, Radhost School and La Grange High School, TX. Enlisted in U.S. Army Corps during WWII, Mar. 17, 1942,

San Antonio, TX. Attained rank of Cpl. Theater of Operations: EAME. Battles: Utah Beach, Normandy, Ardennes, France, Rhineland, Central Europe. Military Occupation: Light truck driver and light machine gunner. Decorations: EAME Campaign Medal and Good Conduct Medal. Honorably discharged Oct. 19, 1945. Married Minnie Hoelscher; three daughters: Carolyn Sumbera Meiners, Jane Sumbera Campbell, Marlene Sumbera Pazderny. Mechanic for 35 years. Musician (drummer) with several Central Texas bands for 32 years, longest tenure with the Ray Baca Band of Fayetteville, TX. Died July 6, 1981; burial La Grange, TX. Submitted by daughter Carolyn Meiners of La Grange, TX.

Supak, Lenton, son of Henry and Vlasta Supak, was born June 30, 1929, in El Campo, TX. Graduated from El Campo High School in 1948, received B.S. in 1952 from SWTS in San Marcos, M.S. in 1959 from A&I in Kingsville. Inducted on Jan. 22, 1954 in Houston and served during the Korean War. Served two years of active duty and four years inactive duty. Served as chief computer and radio operator for the 9th AAA Guided Missile Battery at San Francisco, CA. This unit served to protect the city in case of attack. Received the Good Conduct Medal. Discharged Dec. 31, 1961. Retired after coaching and teaching math for 35 years. Hobbies: fishing and gardening. Home of record: Palacios, TX.

Surovcak, John J., son of Joseph and Theresa Surovcak, Sr., was born July 28, 1895, Fayetteville, TX. Enlisted WWI, U.S. Army Corps, Ft. Sam Houston, TX, May 17, 1917. Attained rank of Musician, 3/C, HQ Co., 57th Inf. Theater of Operations: American. Played clarinet in U.S. Army Corps Military Band. Medals: Good Conduct, WWI Victory, among others. Honorably discharged Apr. 4, 1919. Died Nov. 12, 1965; interred at Catholic Cemetery, Sealy, TX. Submitted by daughter, Betty Surovcak Melnar, Home of record: Houston, TX.

Surovcak, Joseph, Jr., son of Joseph and Theresa Surovcak, Sr. (they were farmers), was born Jan. 6, 1892, Fayetteville, TX. Enlisted in the U.S. Army Corps, Bellville, TX, June 24, 1918, age 26. Attained rank of Pvt., 34th Co., 165th Deport Brigade. American Expeditionary Forces, European Theater. Honorably discharged Nov. 29, 1918, Camp Travis, San Antonio, TX. Married Annie Kutra, Feb. 17, 1919, Frydek, TX, St. Mary's Catholic Church; six children. Died June 29, 1969, V.A. Hospital, Houston, TX. Submitted by daughter, Bertha Surovcak Sanders. Home of record: Clute, TX.

Surovik, Johnnie Jerry, son of Frank J. and Frances Surovik, was born on May 31, 1927, at Caldwell, Burleson Co., TX. Attended New Tabor School, Caldwell, and graduated from Caldwell High School. Enlisted in Caldwell, TX, and entered active duty on Dec. 22, 1945, at Camp Roberts, CA. Stationed at Army Air Force Training Command from Apr. 22–Oct. 5, 1946 as Radio Mechanic RAF, Scott Field, IL; Radio Repairman Aircraft Equipment, Scott Field, from Oct. 14–Dec. 21, 1946. Stationed at Davis Monthan AFB, Tucson, AZ from Dec. 22, 1946–Dec. 21, 1948. Attained rank of Sgt. Entered ready reserves on June 17, 1949, and was discharged on Mar. 7, 1953 USAR. Graduated from Dow Martin School of Radio Arts in Hollywood, CA, on May 2, 1952. Worked for KTXC radio station in Big Spring, TX; Czech Polka program at El Campo, TX, radio station; and KTLW radio station in Texas City, TX. Went to work for KGUL-TV in Galveston, TX as a cameraman, in 1956. Died in an automobile accident between LaMarque and Houston, TX, on Apr. 17, 1957.

Susil, Charles Joe, son of John and Mary Susil, was born Jan. 15, 1905, Val, Klobouky, Czechoslovakia (now Czech Republic). Education: Live Oak Catholic School, Ellinger, TX. Enlisted U.S. Army Corps, Feb. 1941, Houston, TX. Stationed at Camp Bowie, Brownwood, TX. Attained rank of Pvt., with Co. G, 143rd Inf., 36th Div. Honorably discharged June 3, 1941. Killed in an accident, Aug. 30, 1941; buried at Forest Park Cemetery, Houston, TX. Submitted by Emily Thoede of Houston, TX.

Susil, Johnnie Jerome, son of John and Mary Susil, was born Aug. 30, 1920, Columbus, Colorado Co., TX. Education: St. Joseph Catholic School, Frelsburg, TX, John Marshall Jr. High, Houston, TX. Worked at Southern Pacific Shop, Houston, TX, prior to enlisting in U.S. Army Corps at Houston, TX. Theater of Operations: EAME. Medals: EAME Campaign, WWII Victory, Good Conduct, and others. Honorably discharged Jan. 1946. Killed in automobile accident, June 12, 1947. Buried Forest Park Cemetery, Houston, TX. Submitted by Emily Thoede, Houston, TX.

Svacek, Arnold A., son of Mr. and Mrs. Victor Svacek, West, TX. Entered Army, 1937. Served during WWII in Pacific, attaining rank of Pfc. Awards: AP Ribbon w/1 BSS, GCM. Discharged 1945.

Svacek, John J., son of Mr. and Mrs. Victor Svacek, West, TX. Entered Army, 1942, attained rank of Sgt. Trained in Alabama, GA and CA. Discharged 1944.

Svacek, Raymond R., son of Mr. and Mrs. Victor Svacek, West, TX. Entered Army, 1940. Attained rank of Sgt. Served in E.T. Awards: EAME w/1 BSS, GCM, AD, and Victory Ribbon. Discharged 1943.

Svacina, Albin, West, TX, WWII veteran, PRISONER OF WAR.

Svadlenak, Stanfield S., son of Mr. and Mrs. John Svadlenak, Taylor, TX. Education: University of Texas. Enlisted U.S. Army Corps, 1941; basic training, Camp Wallace, TX. Theater of Operations: Asiatic-Pacific. Served in Philippines and Japan. Medals: American Defense, Asiatic-Pacific Theater Campaign w/2 BSS, Philippine Liberation, Combat Inf. Badge, Good Conduct, WWII Victory, ribbons. Attained rank of 1st Sgt. prior to honorable discharge, 1945. Married Hazel Rubbins, NM.

Svaton, Arnold Ernest, son of Frank and Angelina Svaton, was born Mar. 20, 1913, Caldwell, Burleson Co., TX. Education: Caldwell, TX, Schools. In National Guard, 36th Div., before enlisting in U.S. Army Corps, several years prior to WWII. Stationed in Marfa, TX. Theater of Operations during WWII: EAME. Served in Sicily in July 1943. Member of General Patton's 7th Army Rangers Div. Medals: Purple Heart, Silver Star, WWII Victory, National Defense. Attained rank of Tech 5/C. WOUNDED IN ACTION in Italy. Died Jan. 1, 1982, of heart attack. Buried at Caldwell, TX. Submitted by Frank Joseph Svaton, Jr.

Svaton, Frank Joseph, Jr., son of Frank and Angelina Svaton, was born June 17, 1918, Caldwell, Burleson Co., TX. Graduated Caldwell High School. Served in National Guard, 36th Div., before WWII. Theater of Operations: Asiatic-Pacific. Attained rank of Tech 5/C. Ft. Sam Houston, TX. Entered U.S. Army Corps, Feb. 19, 1942, TX. Honorably discharged Oct. 2, 1945. WOUNDED IN ACTION at Saipan during enemy bombing. Also took part in Marshall Islands Campaign. Married Rose Elizabeth, who saw her husband in a *March of Times News* film at Metropolitan Theater in Houston, TX, showing the invasion of Saipan. Medals: Asiatic-Pacific Campaign w/3 BSS, Good Conduct, WWII Victory. Home of record: Houston, TX.

Svehlak, August J., III, Granger, TX. WWII veteran. Member, American Legion Post No. 282, Granger, TX.

Svetik, Robert L., son of Ladislav A. Svetik and Mary Krenek, was born Oct. 25, 1940, in Angleton, TX. Attended Brazosport High School at Freeport. Enlisted in the U. S Air Force at Freeport, TX, during the Viet Nam Conflict. Attained the rank of Airman 1/C. Awards: Good Conduct Medal, and others. Separated from service on Sept. 15, 1963, at Luke AFB, Glendale, AZ. Home of record: Sugarland, TX.

Svetlik, Ludvik J., son of Emil Svetlik and Annie Otto, was born on Aug. 7, 1917, at Hallettsville, Lavaca Co., TX. Attended rural school through the seventh grade. Enlisted in the Air Force on Oct. 14, 1941, at Ft. Sam Houston, San Antonio, TX. Attended Airplane Mechanic School and received diploma on Apr. 25, 1942, at Keesler

Field, MS. Received certificate of completion of Glenn Martin Service Training School for B-26s in May 1942. Entered Aviation Cadet school and received wings at Deming, NM, in July 1943 as Bombardier. Entered the European Theater of Operations at the end of 1943, with the 100th Bomb Group and flew 31 missions over Germany in the B-17 Bomber, including the Schienfurt raid on ball-bearing plants, also the shuttle mission from England to Russia to Italy and back to Britain, and the D-Day mission over Normandy. Received the Air Medal, the Distinguished Flying Cross, and three OLC and European Theater of Operation Medal w/2 Battle Stars. Honorably discharged Sept. 1945. Rank: First Lt. Joined the reserves in 1952 and was discharged with rank of Capt. in 1958. Married Ann L. Brogger at Sacred Heart Catholic Church in Hallettsville, TX, in Sept. 1943. Died Feb. 11, 1965, at the age of 47.

Svinky, Richard V., was born Sept. 23, 1919, Austin Co., TX. Served in U.S. Army Corps during WWII. Attained rank of Pfc., Signal Corps. Died Dec. 3, 1945; buried St. Mary's Catholic Cemetery, Frydek, Austin Co., TX.

Svoboda, Adrian Leonard "Ed," son of Joseph G. Svoboda and Rose E. Kozisek, was born on Dec. 11, 1939, at David City, NE. Attended St. Mary's High School, David City, NE, St. Benedict's College, Atchison, KS, St. Thomas Seminary, Denver, CO, and Central Michigan University (off Campus Masters Program), Mt. Clemens, MI. Enlisted at Omaha, NE on May 3, 1963, and served in the Viet Nam Conflict as Lt. Col. USAF. Flew C-141 support missions, 1968-1972. Medals: Bronze Nakhom Phanom, Thailand 1972-1973, BSS, MSM, Air Medal, AF Commendation, Small Arms Marksmanship, Combat Readiness, AF Longevity, National Defense Service, Viet Nam Service Medal, AF Outstanding Unit Award with Valor device, Republic of Viet Nam Gallantry Cross, and Republic of Viet Nam Campaign Medal. Served as Squadron Commander, 86th Military Airlift Squadron, Travis AFB, CA (141). Attended Air Command and General Staff College, 1976-77. Stationed Osan AB, Korea 1966-67. Home of record: Richardson, TX.

Svoboda, Daniel J., son of Jerry and Vera Svoboda of Taylor, TX, was born July 10, 1917, in Taylor, Williamson, TX. Education: Taylor High School. Enlisted U.S. Army Corps, July 23, 1935, at Fort Sam Houston, TX; basic training, Ft. Sam Houston, TX; additional training, Camp Maxey, TX, Camp Swift, TX. Rank: CWO, 2nd Inf. Div., 102nd Inf. Div. and 8th Armored Div. Battles: Rhineland, France, Holland, Germany, Czechoslovakia, Central Europe. Medals: EAME Medal with two BSS, American Campaign Medal, American Defense Service Medal, WWII Victory Medal, and BSS Medal. Discharged Jan. 9, 1946.

Svoboda, Jim, son of Anton and Agnes Svoboda, was born May 6, 1916. Enlisted in Houston, TX. Served overseas in Naples Foggia GO 33 WD 45 Rome Arno, Southern France, Rhineland, Central Europe. Received the Distinguished Unit Badge, EAME Campaign Medal with five BSS, and one Bronze Arrowhead, Good Conduct Medal, American Defense Medal, Combat Infantryman's Badge. Discharged July 27, 1945. Home of record: Pasadena, TX.

Svoboda, Joe, West, TX. WWII veteran, U.S. Navy.

Svojger, Joseph, Jr., son of Joseph Svojger, Sr. and Rose Obal Svojger, was born on Feb. 21, 1919, at Fort Worth, TX. Graduate of Polytechnic High School, Fort Worth, TX, 1939. Enlisted in the U.S. Army in Jan. 1941 in Fort Worth, and went overseas in July 1942. Served in the European Area in WWII as Cpl., Company B, 16th Inf., 1st Inf. Div., and fought in Africa, Sicily,

Normandy, France, Germany and Belgium. WOUNDED IN ACTION in Germany in Dec. 1944. Received the Silver Star, BSS for Gallantry in Action, and Purple Heart Medal w/2 OLC. First reported MISSING IN ACTION, then reported to have been KILLED IN ACTION, Belgium on Jan. 19, 1945. Buried in United States Military Cemetery, Henri-Chapelle, Belgium, and later brought back to the U.S. and interred at Mt. Olivet Cemetery in Fort Worth, TX. After being wounded in Germany, he was awarded the Purple Heart and the Silver Star on Christmas Day, 1944. The citation reads in part: "For gallantry in action in the vicinity of LaLande, Normandy, France, Aug. 1, 1944. Leaving a position of safety and crossing an area vulnerable to enemy attack, Cpl. Svojger placed casualties into a vehicle and at the risk of his life drove over heavily bombed roads to an aid station. His prompt and gallant action was instrumental in preventing heavy loss of life." During the Battle of the Bulge, in Jan. 1945, Joe and a companion left a position of safety to reach casualties, again sacrificing his life for service beyond the call of duty in caring for the wounded. His companion was killed immediately and it showed that he made every effort to carry the boy back. Both bodies were found some distance away. This accounted for his being reported missing in action, as it took some time until the bodies were found. The citation received from the President of the United States says, "In grateful memory of Joseph Svojger, Jr., who died in the service of his country in the European Area, Jan. 19, 1945. He stands in the unbroken line of patriots who have dared to die that freedom might live and grow and increase its blessings, freedom lives, and through it he lives in a way that humbles the undertakings of most men." signed by Franklin Delano Roosevelt, President of the United States. Submitted by Joseph's sister, Rose, Home of record: Ft. Worth, TX.

Svrcek, Alfons, West, TX. WWII veteran, PRISONER OF WAR.

Svrcek, Emil J., son of John Svrcek and Frances Stolar, was born Apr. 21, 1912, Fayetteville, TX. Graduated from LaGrange High School and Durham College, Dallas, TX. Enlisted in WWII, Seabees, SF/1 U.S. Navy. Died Aug. 2, 1979; buried LaGrange Cemetery, TX. Submitted by niece Evelyn Vecera, Bellaire, TX.

Svrcek, Joe F., son of Jan Lev/John Leo Svrcek and Filomena/Philomena Grmela, was born Mar. 19, 1917, at West, TX. Attended high school and business college. Went to school in Cottonwood, TX, Waco Academy, and National School of Business in Waco, TX. Enlisted at the Recruiting Station, Fort Worth, on Feb. 6, 1941, prior to WWII. Volunteered for service in the Philippine Islands. Assigned to anti-aircraft. Served in the Asiatic-Pacific Theater of Operations. Participated in the Philippine Islands Campaign (Defense of Battan and Corregidor) and Antisubmarine Campaign, G Battery, 60th Coast Artillery, AA. Anti-Aircraft Battery assisted in control of enemy aircraft on Bataan Peninsula until Apr. 8, 1942. Returned to Corregidor and fought until the fall of Corregidor on May 6, 1942. Rank: Staff Sgt. WOUNDED IN ACTION on May 5, 1942, at Fort Mills, Corregidor, and later taken prisoner by the Japanese forces. Remained a PRISONER OF WAR for 40 months. Awards: WWII Victory Medal, Good Conduct Medal, Purple Heart, BSS, Ex-Prisoner of War, Distinguished Unit Badge w/2 Oak Leaves, Philippine Defense w/1 Star, American Defense w/1 BSS, Asiatic Campaign w/2 BSS, Victory Ribbon, one Service Stripe, seven Overseas Stripes, and Philippine Defense Ribbon. Discharged from service on June 29, 1946, at Ft. Sam Houston, TX. Married Mary Mynarcek; two girls, two boys: Frank, Bernadette, Rosemarie, Benjamin. Home of record: West, TX.

Svrcek, John Cyril, son of John Svrcek and Frances Stolar, was born July 2, 1919, Fayetteville, TX. Education: LaGrange, TX, and University of Texas, Austin, majored in Pharmacy. Enlisted in U.S. Navy, Houston, TX, 1942. Motor Machinist's Mate, V-6, USS Sc664 USNTS, San Diego, CA. Ratings: AS, MM2s, MoMM2c, MoMMLC. 26 months sea duty. Honorably discharged Nov. 7, 1945, Camp Wallace, TX. Died Dec. 5, 1972; buried La Grange, TX. Submitted by Evelyn Vecera.

Svrcek, Ludwig, son of Frank Svrcek and Mary

Michalsky, was born Aug. 19, 1912, Fayetteville, TX. Drafted during WWII, Feb. 3, 1941, Ft. Sam Houston, TX. Assigned to 103rd Div., Medical Corp. Theater of Operations: EAME. Battles: Central Europe, Battle of the Bulge. Medals: EAME Campaign Medal, among others. Honorably discharged at Ft. Sam Houston, from 45th Div, Home of record: Fayetteville, TX.

Swinky, Joseph, served Feb. 1943–Dec. 1945, U.S. Army Corps, during WWII.

Swinky, Richard, served Nov. 1941–Oct. 1945, U.S. Army Corps.

Swinky, Willie L., served Dec, 1941–May, 1945, U.S. Army Corps.

Sykora, A. L., son of Mr. and Mrs. William Sykora, Rose, TX. Entered Seabees, during WWII, 1943, attaining rank of PO 1/C. Served Asiatic-Pacific Theater. Awarded AP and PL Ribbons. Discharged 1946.

Sykora, August C., was born Aug. 22, 1898. Served in the U.S. Armed Forces in 902nd QM AVN Co. Died Jan. 27, 1970. Buried in St. Mary's Cemetery, West, TX.

Sykora, Charles V., Waco, McLennan Co., TX. Military Veteran.

Sykora, Dennis Justin, son of Justin Sykora and Leona Fishback, was born Nov. 29, 1959, Yoakum, TX. Enlisted in USMC, Oct. 1978. Honorably discharged Jan. 1983. Married Charlene Ferro, Oct. 3, 1981; divorced, 1988: one daughter: Dayleen. Industrial Mechanic, Bloomington, TX. Home of record: Bloomington, TX.

Sykora, George J., was born Apr. 23, 1918. Served in U.S. Army during WWII, 354th In. 89 Inf. Div. Died Mar. 26, 1945. Buried in St. Mary's Cemetery, West, TX.

Sykora, Ignac J., son of Ignac Sykora and Annie Kubala, was born Jan. 5, 1904, Mt. Calm, Hill Co., TX. Education: St. Mary's Catholic School, West, TX. Enlisted in U.S. Army Air Corps, Oct. 26, 1942, Waco, TX. Attained rank of Pfc. Honorably discharged 1943. Married Albina Vrba, Jan. 22, 1942. Died Oct. 3, 1976, West, TX. Submitted by Eveline Lenart of Abbott, TX.

Sykora, Joseph Bernard, was born Aug. 20, 1914, Mt. Calm, Hill Co., TX. Education: Mt. Calm and Mesquite, TX, elementaries. Served in WWII. Married Vlasta Sophie Parlas; one son: Joseph. Submitted by Sister Cornelia M. Knezek, SSCJ, of Amarillo, TX.

Sykora, Joseph W., son of Ignac Sykora and Annie Kubala, was born Mar. 22, 1917, West, TX. Education: St. Mary's Catholic School, West, TX. Enlisted in U.S. Army Corps during WWII. Theater of Operations: EAME. Served in England, France, Germany. WOUNDED IN ACTION and taken PRISONER OF WAR. Honorably discharged at end of WWII. Attained rank of Pfc. Medals: BSS, Purple Heart, EAME Campaign. Carpenter, Painter. Died Nov. 25, 1987, Houston, Harris Co., TX. Buried at Memory Gardens Cemetery, Corpus Christi, TX. Submitted by Eveline Lenart of Abbott, TX.

Sykora, Justin, Jr., son of Justin Sykora, Sr., and Leona Fishback, was born Jan. 8, 1946, Yoakum, TX. Enlisted in U.S. Navy, Sept. 1966. Honorably discharged Dec. 10, 1969. Married Annie Mae Kovar of Ganado, TX, Sept. 12, 1970; three children: Justin III, Frank, Justine. Fireman-Paramedic. Home of record: Stafford, TX. Submitted by Eveline Lenart of Abbott, TX.

Sykora, Pete, served in U.S. Armed Forces during

WWI. Rank of Pvt. Died in service. Listed on St. Martin's Church, Tours, TX, Memorial.

Sykora, Peter V., son of Mr. and Mrs. Alois Sykora, West, TX. Entered Navy in 1943. Attained rank of SKV 2/C, during WWII. Served in Hawaii. Discharged 1945.

Sykora, Petra "Peter," son of John Sykora and Johanna Baca, was born Dec. 18, 1887, Bordovicich, Moravia, Czechoslovakia. Immigrated with parents to West, TX. Enlisted in U.S. Army Corps during WWI. Attained rank of Pfc. Vojina 64 Pluhu, Pechoty-S.S., 64th Inf. KILLED IN ACTION, France, Nov. 9, 1918. Buried St. Mary's Catholic Cemetery, West, TX. Submitted by Eveline Lenart of Abbott, TX.

Sykora, Robert, son of Justin Sykora and Leona Fishback, was born Oct. 15, 1958, Corpus Christi, TX. Enlisted in USMC, May 1977. Honorable discharge Oct. 1982. Employed in construction.

Sykora, Stanley A., son of Mr. and Mrs. Charlie Sykora, West, TX. Entered Army in 1941. Served during WWII, European Theater, attaining rank of T/Sgt. Awards: EAME w/4 Stars, Amer. Def., AT and GCM. Discharged 1945.

Synatzske, Charlie A. H., son of Mr. and Mrs. Aug. Synatzske, Taylor, TX. Education: Taylor High School. Enlisted U.S. Navy, 1942. Basic training, San Diego, CA. Theater of Operations: Asiatic-Pacific. Served in invasions of Wake, Marshalls, Guam, Gilberts, Saipan. Medals: Asiatic-Pacific Theater Campaign Medal w/BSS, WWII Victory Medal. Attained rank of MM 2/C prior to honorable discharge, 1945.

Talasek, Frankie Edward, son of John William Talasek and Emilie Barbara Sodek, was born Oct. 18, 1930, in Temple, TX. Attended St. Mary's Parochial School in Taylor and graduated from Taylor High School. Enlisted in the U.S. Air Force on Feb. 22, 1949, prior to the Korean Conflict. Served at Sheppard AFB, Wichita Falls, TX; Brooks Air Base, San Antonio, TX; Elmenndorf Air Base, Anchorage, Alaska; Perrin Air Base, Denison, TX: Wheellis Air Base, Tripoli, Libya; and Medina Air Base, San Antonio, TX. Separated from service on Oct. 10, 1960. Rank: Staff Sgt. Married Belen Rincon; six children: David Scott, Denise Carol Laurence, Diana Lynn, Stewart (deceased), Daniel Edward, and Francis Joseph. Died Dec. 31, 1982, and is interred in St. Mary's Cemetery at Taylor, TX.

Tallas, Bennie Cecil, son of Tomas Ed and Josefa Manak Tallas, Granger, TX, was born June 4, 1924. Graduate of Friendship High School. Enlisted in U.S. Army Air Corps, 1941; basic training, NE; additional training, CO, NM, MS, FL. Theaters of Operations: Asiatic-Pacific, CBI. Served in India, China, Guam, Saipan. Awards: Air Medal w/OLC, Distinguished Flying Cross, Asiatic-Pacific Theater Campaign Medal w/4 BSS, CBI Theater Campaign Medal, Good Conduct Medal, WWII Victory Medal, Ribbons. Achieved rank of T/Sgt. prior to honorable discharge, 1945. Died Jan. 12, 1987; buried Holy Cross Catholic Cemetery, Granger, TX.

Tallas, Jerry Edward, son of Tom Tallas and Jossie, was born May 18, 1921, at Taylor, TX. Enlisted in the U.S. Marine Corps, during World War II. Served with the Occupational Forces in Japan and attained the rank of Pfc. Awards: Good Conduct Medal. Discharged Aug. 10, 1946, at the First Separation Company, Marine Corps Base, San Diego, CA. Home of record: Taylor, TX.

Tallas, John Cecil, son of Bennie Cecil and Josie Mary Paternostro Tallas, was born Sept. 28, 1947, in Bryan, Brazos Co., TX. Education: Noel, MO, High School, New York University, graduated 1977, B.S., Aeronautics, Embry Riddle Aeronautical University, Datona Beach, FL, graduated 1979, and M.S., Counseling and Psychology, Troy State University at Dothan, AL, graduated 1992. Branch of service: U.S. Army. Rank: Lt. Col. (Retired). Military Occupation: Armor Crewman, Warrant Officer Aviator, Infantry Officer, and Aviation Branch Aviator. Theater of Operations: Southeast Asia, Republic of Viet Nam, two tours of duty. Served in five separate campaigns. Medals: Bronze Star w/1 OLC, Meritorious Service w/2 OLC, Army Commendation w/1 OLC, Army Good Conduct, National Defense Service, Humanitarian Service w/2 OLC, Armed Forces Reserve, Army Service Ribbon, Republic of Viet Nam Campaign, Master Army Aviator Badge, Air Assault Badge, Air Medal w/Numeral 15, Viet Nam Service w/1 Silver Star, Navy Commendation, Sea Service Deployment Ribbon, Republic of Viet Nam Civil Actions, Unit Citation Badge, Republic of Viet Nam Cross of Gallantry w/ Palm, Unit Citation Badge. Discharged May 31, 1990. Married Mary Catherine Blankenship; four children: Steven, Tami, Ray and John C. Jr. Home of record: Enterprise, AL.

Technik, Julius Charles, son of Ambrose Technik and Agnes Borak, was born in Moulton, TX, on May 20, 1919. Education included Komensky Public School and Southwestern State of San Marcos, Masters in Education. Enlisted in the Army Aug. 14, 1941. Served in the European Theater of Operations. Battles: Battle of England, Normandy, Northern France, Ardennes, Rhineland. Participated in Central Europe Ground Combat.

Awarded the American Defense Ribbon, European African Middle Eastern Ribbon, and the Good Conduct Medal. Discharged Oct. 26, 1945. Rank: Sgt., Gun Commander. Retired after teaching school for thirty years.

Tesar, Alphonse Timothy, son of John Tesar and Mary Novak, was born on Aug. 12, 1915 at Sweet Home, TX. Enlisted in the U.S. Army at Ft. Sam Houston, TX, during WWII. Served in the European, African, and Middle Eastern Theater of Operations and participated in the Naples-Foggia, North Apennines, Po Valley and Rome-Arno Campaigns. WOUNDED IN ACTION. Awards: Purple Heart, European African Middle Eastern Campaign Medal, Good Conduct Medal, and Combat Infantryman Badge. Separated from service on Oct. 6, 1945. Died Dec. 21, 1987.

Tesar, Fred, son of Albert Tesar and Hedwig, was born Jan. 26, 1910, Granger, TX. Education: Friendship, TX, Elementary School. Enlisted Mar. 4, 1942, Camp Wolters, TX, during WWII. Theater of Operations: EAME. Battles: Naples-Foggia, Rome-Arno, Southern France, Rhineland and Central Europe. Medals: Purple Heart GO #6 Hq 95 Evac Hosp Mar. 10, 1944, EAME Theater Ribbon w/5 BBS, Meritorious Unit Award GO #364 7th Army Aug. 4, 1945, Bronze Arrowhead, Good Conduct Medal. WOUNDED IN ACTION, Feb. 7, 1944, Italy. Honorably discharged Oct. 18, 1945, Camp Wolters, TX. Married Flossie Dolezalek Svrcek, Dec. 21, 1949, Durant, Bryan, OK; two daughters: Joyce Lynn Tesar Moore and Karen Sue Tesar Swift, three grandchildren: Grover Dwayne Moore, Gregory Franklin Moore, Amy Lynn Swift Thompson. Died Apr. 14, 1972, Wilson N. Jones Hospital, Sherman, TX; buried Cedarlawn Memorial Cemetery, Sherman, TX, Apr. 17, 1972. Lovingly submitted in her grandfather's memory by granddaughter, Amy Lynn Swift Thompson of Allen, TX.

Tirk, Anthony, Jr., son of Mr. and Mrs. Anthony Tirk/Tyrek (immigrants from Czechoslovakia), of Colleyville, was born June 4, 1917, Ft. Worth, TX. Education: Grapevine, TX, public schools, graduated Texas A&M College, 1939. Enlisted in the U.S. Army Air Corps, 1940. Received wings, Stockton, CA, July 1941. Upon going overseas, had flown on more than 44 missions. Awards: Distinguished Flying Cross, Purple Heart, Silver Star, and Air Medal w/8 OLC. Rank: Lt. Col. MISSING IN ACTION, Mar. 11, 1944, serving w/12th Air Force, later listed KILLED IN ACTION, Mar. 11, 1944, due to anti-aircraft barrage between Venice and Padova, Italy. Submitted lovingly in his memory and honor by his sister, Lydia Tirk Alholm of Colleyville, TX.

Tirk/Tyrek, Lydia, daughter of Mr. and Mrs. Anthony Tirk/Tyrek (immigrants from Czechoslovakia), of Colleyville, was born Apr. 30, 1920, Ft. Worth, TX. Attended high school in Grapevine, TX, graduated from N. Texas State Teachers College in 1942. Taught school for a brief period; enlisted in the WAVES (Navy) in Nov. 1943. Took basic training at Hunter College, NY. Assigned and stationed Washington, DC, as personnel supervisor of a barracks of 112 WAVES. Honorably discharged Aug. 1946. Rank: Chief. Entitled to wear WWII Victory Medal and American Campaign Medal. Upon leaving service, married Roy Leonard Alholm; two sons: Roy Leonard, Jr. and Anthony Alholm. Home of record: Colleyville, TX.

Tobola, Charles J. "Charlie," son of Charles R. Tobola and Veronica Kupchak, was born Aug. 18, 1918, in Schulenburg, TX. Attended grade school and high school in Penelope, TX. Enlisted in the U.S. Army Corps at Hillsboro, TX, on Mar. 1, 1941. Served in both the Asiatic-Pacific and the European, African, and Middle Eastern Theaters of

Operations aboard the USS *General Bliss,* during WWII. Attained the rank of Master Sgt. Separated from service Sept. 22, 1945. Married Mary; three children: two girls and a boy. Employed by Mobil Oil Company. Retired after 35 years. Home of record: Beaumont, TX.

Tobola, Henry A., son of Jim Tobola and Mary Marek, was born July 3, 1922, at West, TX. Attended St. Mary's School, West, TX, High School, and Hillsboro Junior College. Enlisted in the U.S. Army Air Corps at Dallas, TX, during WWII. Served in both the American and European, African, and Middle Eastern Theaters of Operations. Attained the rank of Staff Sgt. Decorations: American Campaign Medal, European-African-Middle Eastern Campaign Medal w/2 campaign stars, Good Conduct Medal, WWII Victory Medal, one Service Stripe, and four Overseas Service Bars. Discharged Dec. 16, 1945, at Ft. Sam Houston, TX. Home of record: Grand Prairie, TX.

Tobola, Ludwik L., son of Mr. and Mrs. Jim Tobola, West, TX. Entered AAF, 1942. Trained at Kelly Field, TX, Camp Luma, NM, and MO. Attained rank of S/Sgt. Awards: GCM, WWII Victory Ribbon, and American Theater Ribbon. Discharged 1945.

Tobolka, Edward J., son of Mr. and Mrs. Ed Tobolka, Granger, TX. Enlisted U.S. Army Corps, 1946. Basic training, Camp Callan; additional training, Ft. Ord, CA, Ft. Lewis, WA, Ft. Bragg, NC. Served in ETO. Medals: ETO Campaign Medal w/2 BSS, WWII Victory Medal. Attained rank of Cpl.

Tobolka, Jerome L., son of Mr. and Mrs. Ed Tobolka, Granger, TX. Enlisted U.S.Army Corps, 1946. Basic training, Ft. Sam Houston, TX. Rank: Pvt.

Tobolka, Julius A., son of Mr. and Mrs. Ed Tobolka, Granger, TX. Enlisted Merchant Marines, 1941. Basic training, St. Petersburg, FL; additional training, Havana, Cuba, Alameda, CA. Served in Atlantic, Mediterranean, Red Sea, Persian Gulf.

Tomanek, Victor Joseph, son of Joseph John Tomanek and Anna Zelena, was born Dec. 19, 1918, Gilliland, TX. Completed Gilliland, TX, High School. Enlisted Jan. 29, 1942, U.S. Army Corps, Camp Wolters, TX, during WWII. Served in the Asiatic-Pacific Theater of Operations (Aleutian Islands Campaign and Alaska). Medals: Asiatic-Pacific Campaign w/1 BSS, Good Conduct, and WWII Victory. Discharged Oct. 19, 1945, Sheppard Field, TX. Married Lydia Elizabeth Fojtik, 1948; seven children. Farmer and Lone Star Gas employee (retired). "Wonderful father and family man. It is people like this who served their country, their community and their family, that have made this country great." Died on Feb. 19, 1985; buried Moore Memorial Gardens, Arlington, TX. Submitted by son, R. Tomanek, Arlington, TX.

Tomek, Charlie J., son of Frank Tomek, Sr. and Annie Czarnesky, was born on Oct. 14, 1920, in Cameron, Milam Co., TX. Attended Marak Catholic School, St. Monica Catholic School, Elm Ridge Public School, and Yoe High School in Cameron. Enlisted in the U.S. Army on Feb. 12, 1941, at Ft. Sam Houston, TX. Served during WWII in the European, African, and Middle Eastern Theater of Operations as a member of Battery C (Heavy machine gunner and Chief of Ammo Section), 38th Field Artillery, 2nd Inf. Div. (Indian Head). Participated in the Normandy, Northern France, Ardennes: Alsace, and Rhineland Campaigns. At the Invasion of Normandy, Battle of St. Lo, Hill 192, Battle of Brest, and the Battle of the Bulge. At Pilsen, Czechoslovakia when the war ended in Europe. Awards: the American Defense Service Medal, European African Middle Eastern Campaign Medal w/4 Campaign Stars, and the Good Conduct Medal. Separated from service on Oct. 3, 1945, at Ft. Sam Houston, TX. Home of record: Cameron, TX.

Tomek, Frank J., Jr., son of Frank Tomek, Sr. and Annie Czarnecky, was born Aug. 19, 1916, in Cameron, TX. Received his education at Elm Ridge, Cameron, and USF GED. Enlisted in the Air Force at Fort Bliss, July 15, 1935, with Troop B, 8th Cavalry. Rank: M/Sgt. Theater of Operations: Alaskan Air Command, MAAG Italy, and

Far East Material Command, Japan. Medals: National Defense Service, Good conduct w/4 OLC, Commendation Ribbon and AFLSA w/5 Bronze OLC. Retired Feb. 28, 1959, at Wiesbaden AB, Wiesbaden, Germany, and took a civil service job in Heidelberg for ten years with the Army. Upon returning to VA, worked in civil service for the Navy until Mar. 31, 1984, when he retired with a total of 47 years with the U.S. Government. Home of record: Virginia Beach, VA.

Tomek, Jerry F., son of Frank Tomek, Sr. and Annie Czarnesky, was born on Sept. 7, 1925, in Cameron, Milam Co., TX. Attended Elm Ridge Public School, St. Monica's Catholic School, and Yoe High School at Cameron. Enlisted in the U.S. Navy on Oct. 8, 1942 at Houston, TX, during WWII. Served in the Asiatic-Pacific Theater of Operations in the Kula Gulf aboard the USS *Helena*. MISSING IN ACTION July 6, 1943, when the USS *Helena* was torpedoed and sunk in the Kula Gulf during an engagement with enemy ships. Status was changed to KILLED IN ACTION, details not known, on Aug. 10, 1945.

Tonn, Leon F., son of Mr. and Mrs. Fred Tonn, Walburg, TX. Education: Georgetown High School. Enlisted U.S. Army Corps; basic training, Ft. Warren, WY. Theater of Operations: American. Medals: ATO Campaign, WWII Victory. Attained rank of T/4 prior to honorable discharge. Married Ottis Schonerstedt.

Tonn, Norbert A., son of Mr. and Mrs. Adolph Tonn, Jarrell, TX. Education: Theon High School. Enlisted in U.S. Army Corps, 1942; basic training, Camp Wolters, TX; additional training, Ft. Bragg, NC. Theater of Operations: EAME. Served in England, Africa, Sicily, France, Belgium, and Germany. Medals: Good Conduct, EAME Theater Campaign w/8 BSS, one Bronze Arrowhead, WWII Victory, Ribbons. Attained rank of T/5 prior to honorable discharge, 1945.

Trcalek, Bennie F., son of B. K. and Annie Trcalek, was born Dec. 10, 1920, Caldwell, TX. Graduate of Texas A&M. Received commission as 1st Lt. at A&M. Enlisted in U.S. Army Corps, Ft. Knox, KY. Theater of Operations: EAME. Fought in the Battle of the Bulge. WOUNDED IN ACTION, Luxembourg. Lost left eye. Disabled American Veteran. Medals: BTO Ribbon, Purple Heart, EAME Campaign, WWII Victory. Honorably discharged 1945. Died Oct. 7, 1987. Submitted by Edwin L. Hlavaty, Caldwell, TX.

Trcalek, John W., son of John Trcalek and Helen Zalobny, was born on Apr. 22, 1913, in Caldwell, TX. Attended Caldwell High School. Enlisted in the service on Feb. 27, 1941, at Caldwell. Served during WWII for 41 months in the Asiatic-Pacific Theater of Operations and participated in campaigns at Guam and Siapan. Awards: Asiatic-Pacific Campaign w/2 campaign stars, and Good Conduct. Separated from service on Oct. 28, 1945. Home of record: Caldwell, TX.

Trcka, Alfred, WWII veteran, of Granger, TX.

Trlica, Johnny D., U.S. Navy: USN Trng and Dist Center, Pers. O., San Diego, CA. WWII veteran of Granger, TX.

Trlica, Ray, U.S. Navy: Corps. Evac. Hosp. No. 1. WWII veteran, of Granger, TX.

Trlica, William "Willie," son of Mr. and Anna Hofferek, was born Nov. 4, 1894, in Kovar, TX. Enlisted in the U.S. Army at Cion, TX, during WWI, 1917–1918. Served in France and Germany as a member of the American Expeditionary Forces. Member of SPJST Lodge 20, Granger, TX. Died Feb. 2, 1961.

Trojacek, Anton L., son of Anton Trojacek and Barbora Cvach, was born Dec. 24, 1873, Ennis, TX. Education: Lone Oak School, Creechville,

TX. Enlisted U.S. Army Corps, Sept. 1897, at age of 23 years and nine months. Had brown eyes, dark hair, dark complexion, 6'2" in height. Rank: Pvt. 2/C, Demobilization Detachment. Discharged May 1, 1919, Camp Travis, Ft. Sam Houston, TX. Married June 21, 1919, Otilie Petrash of Ennis, TX. She died Sept. 14, 1932. Married Olga Sulc in 1936. Died May 5, 1963, Ennis, TX; buried at St. Joseph's Cemetery. Submitted by Sylvia J. Laznovsky, Ennis, TX.

Trojacek, Bob Henry, son of Willie D. Trojacek and Bozena Jarolimek, was born Jan. 31, 1926, Ennis, TX. Graduated Ennis, TX, High School. Enlisted Mar. 28, 1944, Camp Wolters, TX, in U.S. Army Corps. Served in England, France, Holland, Belgium and Germany as an Army Automatic Rifleman, with Co. F, 311th Inf. Battles: Ardennes, Rhineland, Central European. Medals: Presidential Unit Citation, Good Conduct, WWII Victory Ribbon, EAME Theater Ribbon w/3 BSS, Purple Heart. wounded IN ACTION. Honorably discharged Apr. 11, 1946, Camp Chaffee, AR. Married Aug. 6, 1949, Lillian Mary Zabojnik, of Ennis, TX; three children. Died Dec. 3, 1990.

Trojacek, Emil F., son of Joe M. and Mary J. Trojacek, was born on July 22, 1916, near Ennis, TX, at Telico. Graduated from high school and attended Southwest Aeronautical Institute at Dallas, TX. At the time of induction, owned and operated a country grocery store in Telico. Inducted in the service at Ft. Sill, OK, on Dec. 1, 1941. Served in the Asiatic-Pacific Theater of Operations. Participated in campaigns in New Guinea. KILLED IN ACTION Dec. 31, 1942. Awarded the Purple Heart posthumously. Interred in St. Joseph's Cemetery at Ennis, TX.

Trojacek, Frank, son of Joseph J. Trojacek and Mary Bobalik, was born Feb. 15, 1922, in Ennis, TX. Attended school at Crisp, TX. Served during WWII in the Asiatic-Pacific Theater of Operations as member of Headquarters Co., 1st Bn., 27th Inf. Attained the rank of Technical Sgt. Awards: Asiatic-Pacific Campaign, Good Conduct, WWII Victory, Army of Occupation, and two Overseas Service Bars. Separated from service Aug. 1, 1946, at Ft. Sam Houston, TX. Home of record: Dallas, TX.

Trojacek, George Frank, son of Frank W. Trojacek and Antonia Honza, was born June 17, 1924, Ennis, TX. Education: St. John's Catholic, Telico, and Central High Schools. Drafted into U.S. army Corps, Mar. 15, 1943; trained at Camp Claiborne, LA. Assigned to Co. A, 1636th Engineering Construction Bn., attached to 2nd Cavalry, as a Bridge Carpenter. Theater of Operations: EAME. Battles: England, France, Normandy, Luxembourg, Norway, Philippines, Japan, Northern France, Ardennes, Rhineland, Battle of Bulge. Medals: EAME Campaign w/3 BSS, Asiatic Pacific Campaign, Philippine Liberation Ribbon, Good Conduct, Meritorious Unit Award, and WWII Victory. Assigned to the front lines in Luxembourg during Christmas, 1944. Honorably discharged Jan. 1946, Camp Fannin, TX. Farmed for a brief time, then, was with Ennis *Daily News* 42 years. Married Agnes Novak; they are retired. Home of record: Kaufman, TX. Submitted by Sylvia J. Laznovsky.

Trojacek, Frank W., son of Anton Trojacek and Barbora Cvach, was born on June 17, 1895, in Ennis, TX. Education: Lone Oak School, Creechville, TX. Enlisted in the U.S. Army at Dallas, TX, Aug. 28, 1918, during WWI. Was serving at San Antonio, TX, as a member of the 67th Balloon Corps when the Armistice was signed. Separated from service shortly thereafter. Married Antonie Honza on Nov. 10, 1919; four children. Died Aug.

9, 1964, Ennis, TX; buried at St. Jospeh's Cemetery. Submitted by Sylvia J. Laznovsky, Ennis, TX.

Trojacek, John L., son of John W. Trojacek and Cecilia Kudrna, was born Aug. 16, 1920, Ennis, TX. Completed seventh grade, Mote School, Ennis, TX. Enlisted in U.S. Air Force, Sept. 28, 1942, Dallas, TX, during WWII. Theater of Operations: EAME. Served in AZ, NJ, North Africa, Sicily, Italy, France. Medals: Good Conduct, WWII Victory, EAME Campaign w/7 BSS. Battles: Africa, Sicily, Italy, France. Attained rank of T-5 Cpl. Assigned to 12th Air Force Ser. Command, truck mechanic. Honorably discharged Oct. 12, 1945. Occupations: house moving, trucking, row mach. and mfg. Retired in 1983. Married Lillie Vlk (deceased), 1945; three children: Pauline Trojacek Gajdica, John W. Trojacek, Elizabeth Trojacek Slovak; one granddaughter: Jennifer Slovak. Married Evelyn Vitovsky in 1983. Home of record: Garland, TX.

Trojacek, John W., son of Joseph Trojacek and Anna Cvach, was born Dec. 1, 1895, Crisp, TX. Completed third grade, Crisp, TX. Enlisted Apr. 1918, Ennis, TX. Served with the American Expeditionary Forces in TX, NM, and France. Medals: WWI Victory, and others. Attained rank of Pfc., Co. A, 109th Ammunition Train, 34th Div., truck driver. Honorably discharged July 1, 1919. Married Cecilia Kudrna; three children: John L. Trojacek, Adell Trojacek Vlk, Mary Trojacek Kucera. Died Jan. 22, 1968. Submitted in loving memory of his father by son John L. Trojacek.

Trojacek, Leo Charlie, son of Charlie Trojacek and Mary Taraba, was born Sept. 7, 1928, at Telico, TX. Attended school at Telico and Ennis High School. Enlisted in the U.S. Army on Feb. 7, 1952, at Dallas, TX, during the Korean Conflict. Served in Korea. Participated in operations in two campaigns, and attained the rank of Cpl. Awards: Good Conduct Medal, National Defense Service Medal, and Korean Service Medal w/2 campaign stars. Discharged Mar. 17, 1954, at Ft. Bliss, TX. Married Helen Kopecky on Dec. 14, 1946. Home of record: Dallas, TX.

Trojacek, Viola D., daughter of Willie D. Trojacek and Bozena Jarolimek. Graduated Ennis, TX, High School. Attended San Antonio College. Enlisted Feb. 15, 1945, Dallas, TX. Basic and medical training, Ft. Oglethorpe, GA. Served in U.S. Army Medical Corps, stationed at Military Hospital, McKinney, TX, and William Beaumont Hospital, El Paso, TX. Attained rank of Tech Sgt. At El Paso, TX, was in charge of transferring all patients from the hospital to other Army hospitals. Honorable discharge Jan. 19, 1947. Married Aug. 10, 1946, Minor Pierce, who also served in Army Medical Corps; four children, and also have grandchildren. Home of record: Plano, TX. Submitted by Sylvia J. Laznovsky, Ennis, TX.

Trumbull, Harold Luther, was born May 18, 1912. WWII veteran. T/Sgt., US Air Force. Died Sept. 3, 1955; buried Holy Cross Catholic Cemetery, Granger, TX.

Tschoerner, Bennie A., son of Mr. and Mrs. Frank Tschoerner, Jarrell, TX. Education: Southwestern University. Enlisted U.S. Navy, 1945; basic training, San Diego, CA. Additional training, Chicago, IL, Gulfport, MS, Corpus Christi, TX. Attained rank of AETM 3/C prior to honorable discharge. Married Marie Simek.

Tschoerner, Edwin Richard, son of Felix Rudolph Tschoerner and Louise Mary Kubala, was born Oct. 11, 1922, Jarrell, TX. Education: Theon County School, 1935-1938; Graduate, Jarrell High School, 1941. Enlisted U.S. Navy Seabees, Dec. 21, 1942. Attained rank of Coxswain. Basic training, Camp Bradford, VA; additional training, Peary, VA. Theater of Operations: Asiatic-Pacific. Served in Guadalcanal and Okinawa. Medals: Asiatic-Pacific Theater Campaign w/BSS, WWII Victory, ribbons. Military Occupation: Stevedore, loaded and unloaded ships. Bombed and shot at by the Japanese during tour of duty. Honorably discharged Nov. 22, 1945. Married Martha Theresa Sladecek; one daughter: Elsie Faye Tschoerner Lynch. Civilian Occupation: Power Plant Control Room Operator until retirement, Dec. 30, 1984. Hobby: gardening. Home of record: Austin, TX.

Tschoerner, Gustav G., was born Aug. 20, 1894. Enlisted in U.S. Army Corps about 1918, during WWI. Rank: Musician, 3/C. Honorably discharged. Married Albina Karkoska; three children: Agnes, Raymond, Wilbert. Civilian Occupation: Farmer. Died Feb. 13, 1963; buried Corn Hill, Williamson Co., TX.

Tschoerner, John F., son of Emil Tschoerner and Emilie Karkoska, was born Mar. 7, 1923, Corn Hill, Williamson Co., TX. Enlisted in U.S. Naval Reserve about 1941; served during WWII. Attained rank of S-1. Died Apr. 29, 1956; buried Corn Hill, Williamson Co., TX.

Tschoerner, William F., son of Mr. and Mrs. Albert Tschoerner, Jarrell, TX. Enlisted U.S. Army Corps, 1942; basic training, Ft. Knox, KY. Theater of Operations: EAME. Served in Africa. Captured, PRISONER OF WAR, 10 months in Italy. Broke out of prison in 1944, reached America with help of Polish troops. Attained rank of Pfc. prior to honorable discharge in 1944.

Tucek, Frank J., son of Mr. and Mrs. J. H. Tucek, Taylor, TX. Enlisted U.S. Army Corps, 1943; basic training, Ft. Sill, OK. Additional training, Ft. Ord, CA. Theater of Operations: Asiatic-Pacific. Served in New Caledonia, Fiji, New Guinea, Philippines. Medals: Good Conduct, APO w/2 BSS, Philippine Liberation, ribbons. Attained rank of Sgt. prior to honorable discharge, 1946.

Turek, Edwin A., son of Mr. and Mrs. Andrew Turek, Thrall, TX. Education: Treadwell High School. Enlisted in service, 1942; basic training, Camp Cooke, CA. Additional training, Ft. Jackson, SC, NY, IN. Theater of Operations: European. Served in France, Germany, Austria. Medals: Good Conduct, ETO w/2 BSS, WWII Victory, Ribbons. Attained rank of T/4 prior to honorable discharge, 1945.

Tydlacka, Floyd F., son of Mr. and Mrs. Joseph Tydlacka, West, TX. Attended West schools. Entered Navy 1943; served on USS *Pecos*, in Asiatic-Pacific Theater of Operations. Attained rank of EM 3/C. Awards: AT, AP w/8 stars, PL w/2 stars, and WWII Victory Ribbon w/1 star. Discharged 1945.

Tydlacka, Rudolf, served Jan. 1943–Sept. 1945, U.S. Army Corps, during WWII.

Tyll, Alfonz, was born Aug. 5, 1896. WWI veteran. Died Dec. 26, 1965; buried at Calvary Catholic Cemetery, Granger, TX.

Tyll, Frank, served in U.S. Armed Forces during WWI, 1917–1918. Member of SPJST Lodge 20, Granger, TX.

Tyll, Slava, was born Feb. 12, 1905. Pvt., U.S. Army Corps during WWII. Died Aug. 24, 1973; buried Calvary Catholic Cemetery, Granger, TX.

Tyll, Walter L., was born Oct. 31, 1906. Cpl., U.S. Army Air Corps during WWII. Died Aug. 4, 1972; buried Calvary Catholic Cem., Granger, TX.

Tyrek/Tirk–See Tirk.

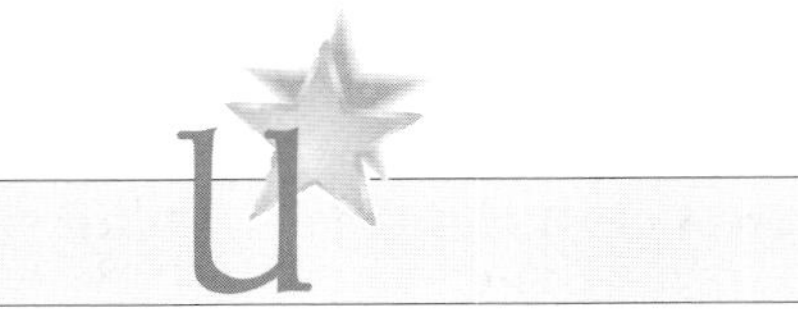

Urban, Henry, son of Mr. and Mrs. P. Urban, West, TX. Entered Army in 1940; served during WWII. Discharged 1943, having attained rank of Pfc. Married Christine Picha.

Urbanek, Albin E., son of Anton F. Urbanek and Emily Vitek, was born Feb. 21, 1928, Taylor, Williamson Co., TX. Education: Coupland High School; Tyler Jr. College, 1950; Indiana Technical College, 1953. Enlisted Feb. 16, 1946, U.S. Army Corps, Ft. Sam Houston, TX. Attained rank of Sgt. Theater of Operation: Pacific: Nagoya and Tachicawa, Japan, Far Eastern Air Force. Medals: Army of Occupation–Japan, WWII Victory, Asiatic-Pacific Campaign. Military Occupation: Aircraft Radio Operator Mechanic. Honorable discharge Jan. 11, 1949. Civilian occupation: Retired Systems Engineer, retired July 1, 1993. Married Mary Chrisie Smith; two children: Jonathan and James. Hobbies: fishing, hunting, traveling. Home of record: Tampa, FL.

Urbanek, Alex J., son of Mr. and Mrs. Frank Urbanek, Taylor, TX. Education: Taylor High School. Enlisted U.S. Army Air Corps, 1942; basic training, Daniel Field, GA. Theater of Operations: European. Served in England, France, Belgium, Germany. Medals: Good Conduct, WWII Victory, ETO w/2 BSS, ribbons. Attained rank of Sgt. prior to honorable discharge, 1945.

Urbanek, Allen J., son of Anton F. and Millie Vitek Urbanek, Taylor, TX. Graduate of Tyler High School. Enlisted U.S. Army Air Corps, 1944; basic training, TX. Additional training, WI, NC. Served in Italy.

Urbanek, Anthony F., son of Anton F. and Millie Vitek Urbanek, was born Feb. 20, 1933, at Taylor, Williamson Co., TX. Tyler, TX; graduated St. Mary's High School, Taylor, TX, 1951. Enlisted in US Army May 18, 1956, at Georgetown, TX. Basic training at Ft Hood, TX; graduated from Army Medical Service School, Ft. Sam Houston, TX. Stationed at Ft. Monmouth, NJ. Discharged May 17, 1958, as a Pfc. Married Gloria Ann Egbert; four children: Karen, Laura, Janice, and Mark. Address of record: Spring Lake Hts., NJ.

Urbanek, Anton F., son of John Urbanek and Francis Zak, was born Sept. 20, 1895, Taylor, Williamson Co., TX. Education: Tyler School. Enlisted May 26, 1917, U.S. Army Corps, Taylor, TX. Artillery Man. Theater of Operations: European. Battles: American Expeditionary Force in France, WWI. Served with 132nd Field Artillery Battery C, 36th Div.. Medals: WWI Victory, EOT Campaign, WWI Armistice Day. Honorable discharge, Apr. 17, 1919. Self-employed. Enjoyed fishing and hunting. Married, nine children: Sybil Urbanek Gola, Mary Urbanek Gola, Elizabeth Urbanek Roberts, Allen, Albin, Lee, Anthony, Millie, Siegmond. Died Mar. 22, 1970; buried St. Mary's Catholic Cemetery, Taylor, TX. Submitted by Allen J. Urbanek, Taylor, TX.

Urbanek, Ben J., son of Charles J. Urbanek and Annie H. Kaspar, Taylor, TX. Education: Taylor High School. Enlisted U.S. Army Corps, 1942; basic training, Camp Robinson, AR; additional training, LA, IL, IN. Theater of Operations: European. Served in England. Medals: Good Conduct, European Theater Campaign; ribbons. Attained rank of Cpl. prior to honorable discharge. Married Eileen Rielly, Manchester, England.

Urbanek, Charles John, son of Charles J.

Urbanek and Annie H. Kaspar, was born Feb. 23, 1937, Taylor, Williamson Co., TX. Education: Tyler Country School; St. Mary's Catholic School, Taylor TX, 1954 graduate. Enlisted 1954, Taylor, TX, Texas National Guard. Tank gunner. Theater of Operations: Berlin callup active 10 months, and Ft. Polk, LA. Medals: standard. Honorable discharge, 1962. Employed by Alcoa as general mechanic. Married, four children: Ramona L., Gary W., Mark S., Brenda Urbanek Harrison. Hobbies: hunting and fishing. Home of record: Thrall, TX.

Urbanek, Daniel T., son of Mr. and Mrs. Joe Urbanek, Taylor, TX. Enlisted U.S. Army Corps, 1942; basic training, OK; additional training, TX. Theater of Operations: European. Served in Africa, Italy, France. WOUNDED IN ACTION, Italy, 1944. Medals: Good Conduct, ETO w/3 BSS, Purple Heart w/1 OLC, Combat Infantry Badge, Presidential Citation, WWII Victory, Ribbons. Attained rank of Sgt. prior to honorable discharge, 1945.

Urbanek, Douglas Raymond, son of Allen J. and Mary Ann Gola. Born July 20, 1952, at Taylor, Williamson Co., TX. Graduated from Taylor High School, 1970. Enlisted in U.S. Army Nov. 29, 1972, in San Antonio, TX. Basic and advanced training at Ft. Polk, LA. Infantry Indirect Fire Crewman. Served in Europe. Decorations: National Defense Service, Expert Hand Grenade, Marksman-M16. Honorable Discharge, Ft. Dix, Nov. 15, 1974. Married Rebecca Lynn Pokorny; three children: Michelle Renee, Jennifer Nicole, and Laura Lynn. Residence of record: Taylor, TX.

Urbanek, Frank J., son of Mr. and Mrs. Frank Urbanek, Taylor, TX. Education: Coupland High School. Enlisted U.S. Navy, 1944; basic training, San Diego, CA; additional training, Camp Davisville, RI. Theater of Operations: Asiatic-Pacific. Served in HI.

Urbanek, James, son of Albin E. Urbanek and Mary Chrisie Smith, was born about 1965, of Taylor, Williamson Co., TX. Education: Clark High School, Manila, Philippine Islands, 1983. Enlisted in U.S. Army Corps, Special Forces, Nov. 1983, Tampa, FL. Attained rank of Sgt. Communications, Army Rangers. Theater of Operations: ETO and Panama. Still in service. Won Soldier of the Year Award. Married Victoria Worrel; children: Jamie, Christina, Chad. Hobbies: fishing, hunting, parachuting. Information submitted by father Albin E. Urbanek, Tampa, FL.

Urbanek, Jerome C., son of Mr. and Mrs. Charles Urbanek, Taylor, TX. Graduate, Taylor High School. Enlisted U.S. Army Corps, 1945; basic training, Ft. Lewis, WA; additional training, Fitzsimmons General Hospital, Denver, CO. Served during WWII.

Urbanovsky, Alphonse, of West, TX. WWII veteran. S/Sgt., U.S. Army Air Corps. Served in England.

Urbanovsky, Daniel Frank, Jr., son of Daniel Urbanovsky, Sr. and Lydia Maresh, was born July 6, 1926, West TX. Education: St. Mary's Catholic elementary school and West, TX, High School. Enlisted in U.S. Armed Forces, July 10, 1944, West, TX. Attained rank of S 1/C. Theater of Operations: Asiatic-Pacific. Honorably discharged July 3, 1946. Married Lillian Bezdek. Home of record: West, TX.

Urbanovsky, Daniel Frank, son of Vincent and Rozina Urbanovsky, was born on July 21, 1893, in West, McLennan Co., TX, the oldest of twelve children. Completed fourth grade at St. Mary's Catholic School, West, TX. Taught the photography business at age 22, by a friend. Inducted into the U.S. Army on May 27, 1918, West, TX, during WWI. Attained the rank of Pvt. Trained at Camp MacArthur, Waco, TX, and served in France as a member of the American Expeditionary Forces. Fought in the trenches, being slightly WOUNDED IN ACTION at the Battle of St. Michel. Honorably separated from the service on Apr. 9, 1919. Married Lydia Maresh. Died on Oct. 4, 1971, and is interred in St. Mary's Catholic Cemetery, West, TX.

Urbanovsky, Eddie V., (also listed in Army records as Eddie V. Urbanofsky), son of Vincent Urbanovsky, Sr. and Anna Gerik Urbanovsky, was born March 23, 1895, on parents' farm, eight miles east of Fayetteville, TX. Education: County Line School #80, near the Colorado Co. line. Completed the sixth grade, which was as far as the school went at that time. Enlisted in the U.S. Army during WWI at La Grange, TX, Aug. 7, 1918, going to Camp Travis, TX. While on manuevers in the U.S., was accidentally gassed with a number of other soldiers, and was sick a long time. Honorably discharged July 22, 1919, having attained the rank of Pfc. Married Annie Zaskoda, and lived in Fayetteville, TX. Hobbies: fishing in fresh water or in the Gulf; hunting deer and possum. Died Oct. 16, 1964; buried in the Fayetteville Catholic Cemetery. Lovingly submitted by sister Frances Sinsel, and niece Helen Mikus.

Urbanovsky, Ernest, J., was born Oct. 21, 1915. Served in the U.S. Army during WWII. Attained rank of TEC. Died June 15, 1990; buried St. Mary's Catholic Cemetery, West, TX.

Urbanovsky, Joseph T., was born Apr. 14, 1908. Served in U.S. Army during WWII as S/Sgt. Died Dec. 25, 1991; buried at St. Mary's Catholic Cemetery, West, TX.

Urbanovsky, Laddie John, son of Edward F. Urbanovsky and Mary A. Pustejovsky, was born Apr. 3, 1926, in Abbott, TX. Attended the Abbott schools. Enlisted July 12, 1944, at Camp Wolters, TX; basic training at Ft. Riley, KS in the horse cavalry; advanced training at Fort Ord and Camp Anza, CA. Sent to Northern India by way of Melbourne, Austrialia, and Bombay. Decided to make army a career. Sent to Fort Dix, N.J. by way of Suez Canal and Gibraltar. Rank: S/Sgt. Duty stations included Fort Sam Houston, TX, Fort Whitier, AK, Hokkaido, Japan, Czech Language School in Monterrey, CA, Kaiserslaughter, Germany, Fort Lewis, WA, Bangkok, Thailand, and Fort Campbell, KY. Medals: Army Commendation, Good Conduct w/3 Clasps, Victory, American Theater, South Pacific. Retired Feb. 28, 1966.

Urbanovsky, Raymond Andrew, son of John Urbanovsky and Josefina Sykora, was born on Nov. 11, 1901, in West, McLennan Co., TX. Grandparents were Frank and Karolina Fajarek Urbanovsky who arrived in Texas from Verovice, Moravia, in 1872. Attended schools in West, TX; St. Mary's Seminary, LaPorte, TX; Toby's Business College, Waco, TX, graduated 1921. Inducted into U.S. Army, Aug. 30, 1942, Dallas, TX, during WWII. Stationed at Camp Wolters, TX, and worked in the Finance Office as a Company Clerk in Reception Center. Assigned to Headquarters and Headquarters Co. Also performed duties as Troop Escort for recruit assignment transports being shipped out to Chicago, IL. Discharged Mar. 19, 1943, having passed the maximum age limit for active duty personnel. Financial Secretary of Supreme Lodge of the SPJST Fraternal Order in Fayetteville, TX. Retired in 1973. Died Dec. 27, 1988. Home of record: Temple, TX. Submitted by daughter Dorothy Urbanovsky Stiff, whose home is Clearwater, FL.

Urbanovsky, Robert Eugene, son of Vince L. Urbanovsky and Mary A. Kasmiersky, was born Feb. 4, 1945, Fayetteville, TX. Graduate of St. John's High School, Fayetteville, TX. Enlisted Aug. 3, 1964, Houston, TX, U.S. Army Corps. Basic training, Ft. Polk, LA. Airborne course, Ft. Benning, GA, Mar. 25, 1965. Member of famous "Green Berets," 1st Bn., Co. A, 26th Infantry. Sent to Viet Nam Sept. 25, 1965. Became member of 1st Inf. Div. Viet Nam, the Blue Spaders, who participated in many battles starting Jan. 17, 1966. Robert's group was part of Operation Silver City, a "search and destroy" mission north of Phu Loi, which started Mar. 9, 1966. The battle ended on Mar. 22, 1966, but because the group was not relieved or notified, they kept fighting, and as a result, Robert and many more were KILLED IN

ACTION two days after the battle ended. Medals: Purple Heart, United States Military Merit, Gallantry Cross w/Palm from the Government of the Republic of Viet Nam. Buried in St. John's Catholic Cemetery, Fayetteville, TX. Submitted by mother Mary Urbanovsky of Fayetteville, TX.

Urbis, Harry J., son of Mr. and Mrs. Joe Urbis, born Oct. 6, 1917, West, TX. Education: West High School, Hill County Junior College. During WWII, entered Naval Air Force. Served as Seaman 1/C, head of Ship Service Dept. Stationed at Waldron Field, Corpus Christi, TX. Discharged 1945. Married Rosalee Smajstrla. Buried in St. Mary's Catholic Cemetery, West, TX.

Urbish, Frank W., son of Mr. and Mrs. Frank W. Urbish, Taylor, TX. Education: St. Mary's High School. Enlisted U.S. Army Air Corps, 1943; basic training, TX; additional training: CA, AZ, NM, SC, NE, IL, IN. Theater of Operations: European. Medals: ETO w/3 BSS, Air Medal, BSS, WWII Victory, ribbons. Married Dorothy Candor.

Vacek, John R., son of John J. Vacek and Mary Prazak, was born Aug. 27, 1918, East Bernard, TX. Education: Holy Cross Catholic School and East Bernard, TX, High School; University of Texas, Austin, TX, B.S. in Pharmacy, Jan. 1942. Enlisted in U.S. Army Corps, Ft. Sam Houston, San Antonio, TX, Apr. 1, 1942. Theater of Operations: China-Burma-India (CBI); Battles: Burma-Assam Road, 14th Evacuation Hospital, 1943-44; attending Merrills Marauders and Chinese Army: 1945, 198th St. Hospital; Decca, India, Kurmitula Air Field attending to Hump Pilots from C-54s. Given a direct commission, 1944, on Burma-Assam Road. Rank: 1st Lt. Left New York July 9, 1943, on SS *West Point* and returned Dec. 24, 1945, to New York aboard S.S. *McRae*. Home of record: Dickinson, TX.

Vacek, Sylvester Sam, son of John J. Vacek and Marie Prazak, was born Dec. 16, 1916, East Bernard, TX. Education: Holy Cross School, East Bernard, TX, High School, University of Texas at Austin, graduated 8/28/39. Enlisted in U.S. Army Corps, Recruiting Station, Houston, TX, Oct. 28, 1942. Theater of Operations: EAME. Assigned to 209th Finance Section, Station 114, ETO. Medals: American Theater Campaign; EAME Campaign; Good Conduct; WWII Victory Ribbon; one Service Stripe; Marksman Carbine Badge; U.S. Army Finance Insignia. Honorable discharge Feb. 12, 1946, Ft. Sam Houston, TX. Married Josephine; two children: Joanne and Samuel. Retired from Exxon. Hobbies: growing pineapples, grafting plants such as pecans, peaches, plums, pears, and world travels. Home of record: Wharton, TX.

Vaclavik, Emil Lucas, son of John A. Vaclavik and Hermiona Pavliska, was born Aug. 17, 1912, Floresville, TX. Attended Pecosa School. Served in U.S. Army Corps. Stationed Camp Hann, CA, and Ft. Lewis, WA. In 40th Inf. Div, 160 Inf Com D. Rank: T/4. Theater of Operations: Asiatic-Pacific. Medals: Asiatic-Pacific Campaign w/3 BSS, Philippine Liberation w/1 BSS, Good Conduct, Combat Infantry Badge, WWII Victory, one service stripe, six overseas service bars. Battles: Bismarck, Archipelago, Sou Philippines Liberation, Luzon GO 33 WD 45. Military occupation: cook. Honorably discharged Dec. 5, 1945. Married Laura Mae Weid, Sept. 17, 1947; three children: David Emil, Dale John, Amelia. Home of record: El Campo, TX.

Vaculik, Jerry, son of Mr. and Mrs. Joe Vaculik, was born Oct. 21, 1922. Worked for the Highway Department, and was drafted in Mar. 1944. Buried in the Praha Cemetery.

Vaja, Albert Jim, son of Alois Vaja and Anna Sebek, was born Dec. 11, 1923, in Houston, TX. Completed high school. Enlisted in the service at Houston, TX, on Nov. 7, 1942, during WWII, to be an aircraft mechanic in the U.S. Air Corps at Ellington Air Base. However, was sent to an air base at Eagle Pass, TX, and assigned to the 1046th Guard Squad, a Military Police Detachment, for 18 months. Assigned to the European, African, and Middle-Eastern Theater of Operations on Feb. 26, 1944. Spent 14 months in England and later was transferred to an Infantry unit in England for training. Spent four months in France and Germany. Decorations include the European African Middle Eastern Campaign Medal. Discharged from service on Nov. 16, 1945, at Camp Polk, LA. Home of record: Houston, TX.

Vajdak, Henry Louis, son of Henry Vajdak and Annie Sefcik, was born Nov. 17, 1936, Rogers, TX. Education: Snook School, graduated high school,

1954. Enlisted U.S. Navy, Dec. 5, 1958. Basic training, San Diego, CA. Electrician's Mate School, Great Lakes Naval Base, Waukegan, IL. Assigned to Aircraft Carrier USS *Franklin D. Roosevelt* CVA 42, whose home port was Mayport, FL. Made annual six-month cruises to Mediterranean Sea. In the latter part of enlistment, Cuban Missile Crisis took place. Achieved rank of Electrician's Mate 2/C. Honorably discharged Dec. 10, 1962. Married Darlene Suehs; three children: Randy, Steven, and Kell. Hobbies: hunting and fishing. He and his brother are in business of operating a cotton and grain farm. Home of record: Snook TX.

Vajdak, Scott Wayne, son of Walter Vajdak and Marcia, was born July 26, 1971, Brenham, TX. Education: K-12, Snook, TX, 1976 through 1989. Enlisted as E-2, 1989, U.S. Army Corps. Stationed at Ft. Leonardwood, MO, for basic training, then sent to Ft. Bliss, TX for remainder of enlistment. Trained as mechanic on Hawk Air Defense Missile System; sent back to school for upgrade training on system during Desert Storm. Honorably discharged on Sept. 10, 1993. Home of record: Somerville, TX. Submitted by parents, Walter and Marcia Vajdak.

Vajdak, Walter Marvin, son of Henry Vajdak and Annie, was born July 21, 1940, Temple, TX. Graduated Snook, TX, High School. Enlisted in U.S. Navy, May 14, 1962, Bryan, TX. Attained Rank ADJ2 (Aviation Machinist Mate). Boot training in San Diego, CA. "A" School in Memphis, TN. Served with VT-22 (Training Squadron) doing maintenance and repair on F9F Cougars. Honorably discharged May 13, 1965, Kingsville, TX. Married Marcia; two children: Denise and Scott. Farms cotton and grains. Enjoy outdoors, hunting, fishing, and flying. Attend Hope Evangelical Free Church in Bryan, TX. Home of record: Somerville, TX.

Valchar, Jerry Edward, son of Jerry Joe Valchar and Annie Malinovsky, was born Dec. 13, 1917, Oakland, TX. Education: Oakland High School and Blinn Junior College, Brenham, TX, Accounting. Enlisted Dec. 11, 1941, Houston, TX, U.S. Army Corps. Theater of Operation: North Africa-CBI; attained rank of Staff Sgt. Decorations: American Theater Campaign Medal, EAME Campaign Medal, Asiatic Pacific Campaign Medal w/1 BSS, WWII Victory Medal, GCM, Marksman Rifle Sharpshooter Medal. Honorably discharged, Camp Fannin, TX, Dec. 10, 1945. Home of record: Temple, TX.

Valcik, John Hus, son of Josef and Bozena Valcik, was born Nov. 8, 1914, Dallas, Dallas County, TX. Education: UTA, Pre-Med, Baylor College of Medicine, Dallas, TX. Earned college tuition by playing the violin, an instrument he loved throughout his long and productive life. Enlisted in the U.S. Navy, 1941, Dallas, TX. Served as Commander in regular Navy until 1946. In Gilbert Offensive. In charge of many ships' hospitals during WWII. Received approximately 25 medals, but labels have been lost with time. Lifetime member of USNR. After discharge, encouraged by J. T. Darwin, M.D., to help with his large medical practice. Was a driving force behind the building of Decatur Community Hospital. Participated for 35 years in Czechoslovakian Orchestra, playing regularly on Czech Day at the State Fair of Texas. Upon his demise, both Texas House and Senate sent resolutions to his family in his honor. Submitted lovingly by his widow, Elizabeth, in his memory. Home of record: Decatur, TX.

Valek, George Charles, son of Frank Edward Valek (born 1889, Ennis, TX, died 1938) and Emily Vrla (born 1887, Luskovice, Moravia, died 1924) was born Sept. 2, 1911, S.E. of Ennis, TX. Four brothers and one sister: William, Frank, Joe, Raymond, Emily. Education: St. John Nepomucene and Ennis High School, graduated 1929; Texas A&M, B.S. and Master of Education. Commissioned as 2nd Lt., U.S. Army Corps, May 28, 1934. 1st military duty: CCC Camp, Nov. 1, 1935–May 1, 1936.

Texas Power and Light as cost-estimator of rural power lines, June 1, 1936–June 1, 1939. Worked at Standard Tilton Milling Co. (American Beauty Flour) on July 3, 1939, as diesel engine operator, later as chief elec. engr. Called to active duty, Ft. Sill, OK, 1st Lt., Mar. 20, 1941, Ft. Knox, KY, 1st Armored Div, Co. A, 69th Armored Reg. Sailed from NY, May 30, 1942, landing in N. Ireland, then Liverpool, England. Initial landing Nov. 11, 1942, at Mers-El-Kebir (Oran) Algiers, N. Africa, battlefield conditions. Maktar, Mateur, Faid Kasserine, Bizerte, and on to Tunis for a Victory Parade. Battlefield promotion to Capt., and Command of Co. C, Ord-Maint., 1st Armored Div. Landed in Naples, Italy, Nov. 27, 1942, at Anzio Beachhead, May 7, 1944. Left Anzio, June 6, invasion of Europe. Arrived Dallas, TX, July 15, 1944. Served as training officer S-3. Promoted to Maj., Oct. 4, 1946. Stationed at New Brunswick, promoted to Lt. Col., Aug. 6, 1953. Retired from Active Reserve, Sept. 2, 1971. Retired from Standard-Tilton-Conagra, Mar. 1, 1974. Medals: American Defense, American Theater, EAME w/4 BSS, WWII Victory, four BSS, one Bronze Spear (initial invasion). Met Justine Pavlicek, Nov. 1936; married Dec. 27, 1938, St. John Nepomucene, Bomarton, TX; children: Harlis Wright and Carolyn Valek Wright, Richard Staight and Kathleen Valek Staight. Since retirement, refinished old furniture valued at $10,000 from homes of parents. President, Catholic Czech Club in Dallas, TX, 1976-81, President Czech Catholic Union of Texas (KJT#111) 1978 and 1982-86. Home of record: Dallas, TX.

Valek, Joe Edward, son of Frank Edward Valek (born 1889, Ennis, TX, died 1938) and Emily Vrla (born 1887, Luskovice, Moravia, died 1924), was born Dec. 17, 1916, Ennis, TX. Enlisted in U.S. Army Air Corps, Dallas, TX, Jan. 19, 1942. Gunnery School, Tyndal Field, FL. Theater of Operation: Southwest Pacific. Battles: New Guinea, Bismarck Sea, Dutch East Indies, Philippine Islands, Okinawa. Medals: Good Conduct, Asiatic Pacific (9 Battle Stars), three Presidential Citations, Philippine Liberation, Machine Gun, and Carbine Sharpshooter Expert. WOUNDED IN ACTION: left leg and broken ankle, in parachute jump in Australia. During tour of duty, made parachute jump and two crash landings, one in WV and one in New Guinea. Honorably discharged Oct. 2, 1945, San Antonio, TX. Home of record: Mesquite, TX.

Valenta, Adolph Edward, son of Joe Valenta and Mary Vecera, was born Jan. 21, 1895, Corn Hill, TX. Attended schools in Corn Hill, TX, and St. Mary's in LaPorte, TX. Enlisted in U.S. Army Corps, May 28, 1917, Taylor, TX. Attained rank of Pfc. Assigned as mechanic of Battery D, 132nd Field Artillery, in American Expeditionary Forces. Served overseas in France. Honorably discharged with excellent character, on Apr. 10, 1919, Camp Bowie, TX, reason, demobilization. Rank: Sgt. Married Louise Knapek of Corn Hill, TX; five daughters, three sons. Lifetime Farmer. Died Sept. 10, 1988; interred in Holy Trinity Cemetery, Jarrell, TX. Submitted by A. M. Hrncir of Round Rock, TX.

Valenta, Daniel M., son of Mr. and Mrs. Frank Valenta, Schwertner, TX. Education: Bartlett High School. Enlisted U.S. Army Corps during WWII, 1945. Basic training, Camp Hood; additional training, Indianapolis, IN. Theater of Operations: American. Served in U.S.A. Rank: Pvt.

Valenta, Frankie J., son of Mr. and Mrs. Frank Valenta, Schwertner, TX. Education: Schwertner school. Enlisted U.S. Army Corps, 1942. Basic training, Camp Claiborne, LA. Theater of Operations: European. Served in France, Germany, Central Europe. Medals: ETO Campaign w/4 BSS, Good Conduct, WWII Victory, ribbons. Attained rank of Tec. 4 (Sgt.) prior to honorable discharge, 1945.

Valenta, Joe I., son of Mr. and Mrs. Frank Valenta, Schwertner, TX. Education: Bartlett High School. Enlisted U.S. Navy, 1943, basic training, San Diego, CA. Additional training, San Francisco, CA, Treasure Island, CA. Theater of Operations: Asiatic-Pacific. Served aboard USS *Proteus* in Guam, Midway, Japan. Attained rank of BM 2/C.

Valenta, Marcus Anthony, born July 26, 1905, Sweet Home, TX. Commissioned Chaplain's Corps, Feb. 1933. Called to Active Duty in U.S. Army Reserve during national emergency, 1940. Assigned to Hawaiian Dept., Dec. 7, 1941, at Pearl Harbor. Participated in Invasion of Okinawa, Easter Sunday, Apr. 1, 1945. Largest air and sea invasion in history of world. WWII ended Aug. 15, 1945. Remained in Reserve until Aug. 1965, with 32 years of U.S. Army Corps service. Appointed pastor of St. Philip, El Campo and St. John, Taiton, on Apr. 1, 1946. Transferred to Praha, TX. on Sept. 15, 1954.

Valerian, Henry John, son of Joe Valerian and Mary Sodolak, was born June 30, 1923, Sealy, Austin Co., TX (Frydek Rural Area). Education: grammar school, Bernard Prairie, TX. Enlisted Oct. 23, 1942, San Antonio, TX, USMC Reserve. Theater of Operations: Asiatic-Pacific. Battles: Tarawa Atoll, Gilbert Islands, Nov. 24, 1943 to Dec. 8, 1943, Tinian, Marianas Islands, Aug. 2, 1944 to Aug. 10, 1944, WWII. Medals: Sharp Shooter Badge, Presidential Citation w/3 Stars, Rifleman Expert Badge. Honorably discharged Oct. 31, 1945. Married Georgia Svoboda; children: Lawrence, Henry Jr., Patrick, Charlene Valerian Brietzke, Judy Valerian Zapalac. Hobbies: bingo, hunting, fishing, sports. Home of record: Wallis, TX.

Valigura, George M. F., son of Martin F. Valigura and Mary Drozd, was born July 18, 1924, Moulton, TX. Enlisted in U.S. Army Corps, Sept. 27, 1948, Fort Sam Houston, TX. Basic training, Camp Wolters, Mineral Wells, TX. Left for overseas, Oct. 27, 1944. Served in England, France, Belgium, Holland, and Germany. Medals: WWII Victory Ribbon, GCM, American Theater Ribbon, EAME Theater Ribbon, and three BSS. Battles: Rhineland, Ardennes, Central Europe. Served as cook in garrison and field kitchens, supervised other personnel in keeping kitchen sanitary, kept records of supplies, served as Tech 5 or T-Cpl. for Co. K, 290th Inf. Reg. during WWII. Honorably discharged Mar. 25, 1946. Died Jan. 30, 1982; interred at St. Joseph's Catholic Cemetery, Moulton, TX. Submitted in loving memory by his widow, Annie Valigura of Moulton, TX.

Valigura, Raymond M., son of Paul F. Valigura and Vinie, was born Apr. 28, 1923, Caldwell, TX. Education: High School. Enlisted in U.S. Army Corps, WWII, Ft. Sam Houston, TX. Attained rank of Tech Sgt. Theater of Operations: EAME. Battles: WWII–Germany, France-Africa. Medals: WWII Victory Ribbon w/2 BSS, BSS, Combat Infantry Badge, Good Conduct. Served under General Patton, 1944 to end of WWII. Honorably discharged Mar. 1946. Home of record: Caldwell, TX. Submitted by Edwin L. Hlavaty.

Valusek, John J., son of John Valusek and Albina Macik, was born on Nov. 28, 1917, Snook, Burleson Co., TX. Entered U.S. Army Corps, Nov. 29, 1943, Houston, TX. Basic training at North Camp Hood, TX. Assigned to England, took advanced training in the 101st Air Borne Div. Fought Northern France, Rhineland, Ardennes Central Europe. Medals: WWII Victory Ribbon, Purple Heart w/1 OLC, EAME Ribbon w/5 BSS, Combat Infantry Badge ACTM. WOUNDED IN ACTION. Honorably discharged Nov. 26, 1945, as Pfc., Military Police Detachment A, Service Command Unit #1748, Camp Carson, CO. Home of record: Texas City, TX.

Vana, Augustine C., son of Mr. and Mrs. Fred Vana, West, TX. Attended West High School. Entered Navy 1943 during WWII. Attained rank of S 1/C. Served in Asiatic-Pacific Theater of Operations. Awards: GCM, WWII Victory, and AT Ribbons. Discharged 1946,.

Vana, George J., son of Mr. and Mrs. Fred Vana, West, TX. Graduated grammar school. Entered Army, 1937. Served in U.S.A. Died at Ft. Warren, WY, where he trained.

Vana, Henry, of West, TX. WWII veteran.

Vana, Leo, West, TX. WWII veteran, U.S. Navy.

Vana, Oswald, entered the U.S. Navy during WWII. Theater of Operations: EAME. Served on USS *Savannah* in the Mediterranean. Served in N. Africa, Sicily, Italy. Attained rank of FCCP Officer.

Vana, Theophil Leo, son of Mr. and Mrs. Fred Vana, West, TX. Attended West High School. Entered Navy in 1941; served during WWII. Served on USS *Kingsbury* APA 177. Rank: CEM.

Vanecek, Dan F., son of George J. Vanecek, Sr. and Mary Drozd, was born Aug. 16, 1931, Sinton, TX. Education: Sinton and Granger public schools, graduated high school, Granger, TX. Enlisted in U.S. Army, Sept. 1952, San Antonio, TX. Theater of Operations: Korea. Military Occupation: Construction Engineer. Spent winter of 1953 on construction of bridge (8 months total) over Imjim River. Honorably discharged July 1954. Married Sybil M. Gola; six children: Sue, Peggy, Jeana, Barby, Tim, and Tom. Self Employed Upholsterer. Hobbies: models and art. Home of record: Taylor TX.

Vanecek, George J., Jr., son of George J. Vanecek, Sr. and Mary Drozd, was born 1922, Granger, TX. Education: completed eighth grade, Sinton, TX, public schools. Enlisted in U.S. Air Force, 1941, during WWII. Rank: Sgt. Motor Pool. Battles: Normandy Invasion. Medals: EAME Campaign w/BSS, WWII Victory, among others. Honorably discharged 1945. Married Margie David; four children: Larry, Ronnye, Richy, Miselle. Employed as carpenter until retirement in 1992. Hobbies: modeling and art. Home of record: Taylor, TX. Submitted by brother Dan Vanecek, Taylor, TX.

Vanecek, George J., Sr., son of John Vanecek and Elisabeth Martinka, was born in 1902, Granger, TX. Completed sixth grade, Granger, TX. Enlisted in the Texas National Guard, 1941, Sinton, TX. Attained rank of Mess Sgt. Honorably discharged 1946. Farmer, retired 1975. Married Mary Drozd; six children: George, Helen, Dan, Sybil, John, Tim. Deceased 1993. Buried at Granger, TX. Submitted by son, Dan F. Vanecek of Taylor, TX.

Vanecek, Jerome Daniel, son of Emmett Frank Vanecek and Johanna "Janie" Baca, was born July 21, 1911, at Rogers, TX. Education: elementary school, Seaton, TX. Inducted into the U.S. Army Corps, Ft. Sam Houston TX, Apr. 2, 1942. Theater of Operations: American. Investigator, MP unit. Attained rank of Sgt. Medals: Good Conduct, WWII Victory, American Campaign. Honorably discharged May 12, 1946. Self-styled artist, painted landscapes in his spare time. Married Marie; one daughter Gladys Vanecek Truas. Worked for the Ethyl Corp. Died Aug. 8, 1976, of a heart attack in a Pasadena Hospital. Services held at Forest Park, Lawndale; interred in Pasadena, TX.

Vanecek, Joe George, son of Emmett Frank Vanecek and Johanna "Janie" Baca, was born Dec. 19, 1922, Rogers, TX. Education: Williamson and Bell County grade schools, Salado, Lost Prairie and Troy, TX. Enlisted 1943, during WWII, at Ft. Sam Houston, TX. Stationed there Jan. 20, 1943 through Sept. 9, 1945. EAME, 19 months in Italy. Medals: Sharpshooter Carbine, Good Conduct, EAME Campaign w/8 BSS, Distinguished Unit Badge w/1 OLC, Lapel Button (ruptured duck). Married Verta Mae. Hobbies: hunting, fishing, and playing dominoes. Home of record: Bulverde, TX. Submitted by sister, Mary Vanecek Millender of Temple, TX.

Vanecek, John, son of George J. Vanecek, Sr. and Mary Drozd, was born 1941, Sinton, TX. Graduated Granger High School. Enlisted 1959, USAF. Honorably discharged in 1963. Rank: Sgt. Hobby: photography. Occupation: design. Married Melinda Rhoades; one daughter Melyne. Home of record: Houston, TX. Submitted by brother, Dan Vanecek, Taylor, TX.

Vanecek, John C., Jr., son of John C. Vanecek, Sr. and Pauline A. Mueller, was born on Sept. 9, 1948, in Granger, TX. Attended schools in Taylor and graduated from Taylor High in 1967. Enlisted in the U.S. Air Force at San Antonio, TX, during the Viet Nam Conflict. Served as a weapons mechanic in CO, FL, Spain, and Turkey. Attained the rank

of Staff Sgt. prior to his separation from the service in Dec. 1971. Decorations include the National Defense Service Medal, Good Conduct Medal, and Marksmanship Ribbon. He is pursing a career as an Insurance Agent. Hobbies: hunting and fishing. Married Suzanne Huser. Home of record: Granger, TX.

Vanecek, John Charles, Sr., son of Emmett Frank Vanecek and Johanna "Janie" Baca, was born Nov. 2, 1920 in Seaton, Bell Co., TX. Attended elementary school in Salado, TX. Enlisted in the U.S. Army Air Corps at Ft. Sam Houston, TX on Sept. 11, 1942, during WWII. Served in the EAME Theater of Operations as an Ammunition Supply Tech, 554th Bomb Sqdn, 386th Bomb Group, 9th Air Force. Attained the rank of Staff Sgt. Participated in air offense operations in Normandy, Northern France, and the Rhineland. Decorations: Good Conduct Medal, EAME Campaign Medal, Distinguished Unit Badge, Meritorious Service Citation, WWII Victory Medal. Separated from service on Sept. 10, 1945. Auto mechanic until retirement in Nov. 1985. Hobbies: hunting, working crossword puzzles, fishing, garage sales, and flea markets. Married Pauline Miller; two children: Janie Vanecek Mucha and John Charles Vanecek, Jr., three grandchildren. Home of record: Georgetown, TX.

Vanecek, Michael Henry, son of Paul Lewis Vanecek and Agnes Klepac, was born July 15, 1952, Sinton, TX. Sinton H.S. graduate, Denver Plumbing Tech. Enlisted Ft. Sam Houston, TX, U.S. Air Force. Theater of Operations: Korea. Medals: Air Force Plumbing Tech, GCM. Attained rank of S/Sgt. Honorably discharged July 24, 1979, Loring AFB, ME, and Denver, CO. Died Nov. 27, 1985.

Vanecek, Paul Lewis, son of John J. Vanecek and Rosalia Martinka, was born July 25, 1920, Granger, TX, Education: 7 years. Enlisted USAF at Ft. Sam Houston, TX. ETO, Bomb Group 405th DRS, ground crew (kept bombers in air). Medals: Airplane Mechanic and Tech Medal, and GCM. Honorably discharged Nov. 19, 1945, Sheppard AFB, Wichita Falls, TX. Rank: Pfc. Had three sons and two brothers in service. Home of record: Sinton, TX.

Vanecek, Paul T., son of Paul Lewis Vanecek and Agnes Klepac, was born July 18, 1950, Sinton, TX. Education: Sinton High, Sinton, OK, Ft. Sill, OK, Ft. Polk, LA. Enlisted in U.S. Army Corps Reserves, Sinton, TX. Theater of Operations: USA. Achieved rank of Cpl., E-4. Corpus Christi Army Depot, TX. Medals: NDSM, Expert–Rifle, Letter of Achievement–Track Vehicle Mechanic, Letter of Achievement–Small Engines. Honorable discharge, Aug. 24, 1976, Sinton, TX. Home of record: Corpus Christi, TX.

Vanecek, Tim, son of George J. Vanecek, Sr. and Mary Drozd, was born 1936, Sinton, TX. Education: Sinton Elementary; Granger, TX, High School. Enlisted in USAF, 1955. Rank: Sgt. Honorably discharged 1963. Employed in air craft repair. Hobby: flying. Died Sept. 30, 1983, at 47 years of age. Interred in Granger, TX. Submitted by his brother, Dan F. Vanecek of Taylor TX.

Vanecek, William Victor, son of Frank Vanecek and Johanna "Janie" Baca, was born May 28, 1916, Rogers, TX. Education: Oscar and Seaton grade schools, Bell Co., TX. Entered service in Abilene TX, during WWII, about 1942. Quartermaster cook in the U.S. Army, stationed in AK. Hobbies:

hunting, fishing, and cooking. Honorably discharged in TX. One son: William L. Vanecek, Galveston. Died Feb. 12, 1971; buried in Dickinson, TX. Submitted lovingly in his honor and memory by sister Mary Vanecek Millender of Temple, TX.

Vanek, Anton L., Jr., Granger, TX. WWII veteran. Member, American Legion Post No. 282, Granger, TX.

Vanek, Edwin J., son of Joe F. Vanek and Mary Tylich, was born Feb. 6, 1921, Schulenburg, TX. Education: Velehrad and Moravia, TX. Drafted into U.S. Army Corps, during WWII, Sept. 22, 1942, Lavaca Co., TX. Stationed at Ft. Sam Houston, TX, and Camp Gruber, OK. Assigned 88th Div., Battery A, 913th Field Artillery Bn. Theater of Operations: EAME–North Africa and Italy. Battles: Rome-Arno, North Apennines, Po Valley, Italy. Medals: Good Conduct, EAME Campaign Ribbon, and WWII Victory. Home of record: San Antonio, TX.

Vanek, Edwin Louis, West, TX. WWII veteran. Served in U.S. Army Corps from 1945 until 1947.

Vanek, Frankie John, son of Joe F. Vanek and Mary Tylich, was born Oct. 4, 1935, Moravia, Lavaca Co., TX. Education: Schulenburg High School and Victoria College, TX, Enlisted in Army National Guard, May 1, 1958, El Campo, TX. Attained rank of SP5-E5. Received honorable discharge, Apr. 30, 1964. Home of record: El Campo, TX.

Vanicek, Johnnie Henry, son of John and Albina Vanicek, was born Sept. 25, 1918, Bell Co., TX. Education: Lost Prairie School. Entered U.S. Army Corps, 1943, Ft. Sam Houston, TX. Trained at Camp Hood, TX. Rank: Pfc. Served in Okinawa and Hokkaido, Japan. Medals: WWII Victory, Asiatic-Pacific Theater Campaign, and others. Honorable discharge, 1945, Ft. Sam Houston, TX. Married Lydia Klinkovsky; three children and grandchildren, in Temple, TX. Died Dec. 3, 1979, V.A. Hospital, Temple, TX; buried in Seaton Cemetery, Temple, TX.

Vanzura, Bill, West, TX. WWII veteran, U.S. Navy.

Vanzura, Larry, of West, TX. WWII veteran, U.S. Army Corps.

Vanzura, Rudolph L., was born Mar. 17, 1898. Served in U.S. Armed Forces during WWI at IBM HV AA REGT CAC. Attained rank of Pfc. Died Nov. 23, 1966. Buried in St. Mary's Cemetery, West, TX.

Vasek, Julius P., son of Peter Vasek and Emma Kubicek (brother of Jerome, Martha and George), was born Oct. 21, 1919, St. John's Community, near Schulenburg, Fayette Co,, TX. Education: St. John's Parochial School, St. John's, TX. Entered U.S. Army Corps, May 18, 1942, Ft. Sam Houston, TX. Received training at Camp Wolters, TX, Camp Meade, MD. Rank: Staff Sgt. Theater of Operations: EAME. Fought in Battle of Brennan. Squad Leader, 1st Armored Div. under Gen. Mark Clark. Sent to North Africa, Sicily and Italy. WOUNDED in Northern Italy on April 23, 1945, and died soon after. Military funeral services were conducted on Friday, Dec. 10, 1948, with interment in the St. John's Cemetery. Medals: Purple Heart posthumously, Good Conduct, EAME. Very talented in drawing. Remembered as a true patriot who gave his life for his country. Submitted lovingly in his honor and memory by niece Barbara Vasek Snowden, of Pasadena, Texas.

Vaudak, Jerry Charlie, son of Frank Vaudak and Rosalie Kadlecek, was born Jan. 26, 1909, Merle, TX. Education: Snook public school. Drafted Feb. 26, 1942, Camp Wolters, TX, U.S. Army Corps. Assigned to Battery B, 793 Anti-aircraft Artillery, Automatic Weapons Bn. Theater of Operation: Asiatic-Pacific. Battles: Aleutians Islands and Eastern Mandates. Medals: Asiatic-Pacific Theater Campaign w/BSS, Good Conduct, WWII Victory. Attained rank of Pfc. prior to honorable discharge, Oct. 29, 1945. Died Dec. 4, 1964. Submitted by Lee Roy Cervenka, Lake Jackson, TX.

Vavra, Harold L., son of Mr. and Mrs. Vavra, enlisted Nov, 1950, TX, U.S. Marines, attained rank of Corporal, honorable discharge, Oct, 1953.

Vavra, Herbert A., son of Mr. and Mrs. Vavra, enlisted in U.S. Army Corps, Oct, 1950, TX, U.S. Army Corps, TX, attained rank of Pfc. Honorably discharged Sept. 1952.

Vavra, James Arnold, son of P. W. "Pete" Vavra and Leach "Sis" Deggs (both parents deceased in West, TX), was born Jan. 12, 1921, Dallas, TX. Completed West High School. Enlisted in Waco, TX, in U.S. Navy, July 3, 1940. Served during WWII. Boot camp, San Diego, CA. Boarded USS *Saratoga* at Long Beach, CA, transferred to USS *Idaho*, BB43 (battleship) for four years, to USS *Chicago*, CA136, then USS *Quincy*. Honorably discharged July 11, 1946, Camp Wallace, TX, after 64 months sea duty. Served in Atlantic and Pacific Ocean, from Iceland to the Aleutian Islands, the Philippine Islands, South Pacific, Australia, Hong Kong, Shanghai, into Tokyo Bay for signing of peace treaty. Boatswain's Mate First Class when discharged. WOUNDED IN TRAINING (serving country). Medals: American Defense, American Area Campaign, Asiatic-Pacific Area, WWII Victory, China Service, European-African-Middle Eastern, Good Conduct, Occupation Service. Home of record: Lakewood, NJ. Submitted by A. C. and Richard Vavra.

Vavra, Richard J., son of P. W. "Pete" Vavra and Leach "Sis" Deggs (both parents deceased, West, TX), was born July 28, 1925, Ross, McLennan Co., TX. Education: elementary and high schools at Ross and West, TX, A half year at Texas A&M. Enlisted in TX in U.S. Navy during WWII, Dec. 7, 1943. Attained rank of Seaman First Class (Radio Operator). Trained at San Diego, CA, at Oceanside, CA, as member of 286th Joint Assault Signal Corp (JASCO), then aboard USS *Neville* and USS *American Legion*, USS *Colorado* (BB45) (battleship, USS *Sitkoh Bay* (CVE86), USS *Golden City* APA169) as passenger. Served as radio operator at the airstrip on Eniwetok Island of Marshall Islands from Dec. 24, 1945, to Apr. 13, 1946. Also stationed at Coronado Naval Base, San Diego, CA, and TADCEN, Camp Elliott, CA. seven months overseas. Served in Iceland and South Pacific. Medals: Asiatic-Pacific, American Defense, and WWII Victory Ribbons, GCM, North Atlantic Ribbon. Honorably discharged May 6, 1946, Camp Wallace, TX. Home of record: West, TX. Submitted by Richard and A.C. Vavra.

Vavra, William Robert, son of P. W. "Pete" Vavra and Leach "Sis" Deggs (both parents deceased in West, TX), was born Jan. 5, 1919, Dallas, TX, education: elementary and junior high at Ross, TX. Enlisted in U.S. Navy, during WWII, Nov. 23, 1940, Dallas, TX. USN Training Station, San Diego, CA. Served aboard the USS *Idaho*, BB43 (battleship), USS *Menefee*, APA 202, USS *Dayton*, CL 105, in North Atlantic, Philippine Area, South Pacific. Medals: WWII Victory, American Defense, GCM, Asiatic-Pacific w/3 stars. Advanced to Boatswain's Mate 2/C, when honorably discharged Dec. 11, 1946, Boston, MA. Married Pauline Bafford. Home of record: Lakewood, CA. Submitted by Richard and A. C. Vavra.

Vecera, Edwin Paul, son of Frank Vecera and Anna Srubar, was born Sept. 16, 1924, Austin, Travis Co., TX. Enlisted U.S. Army Corps, July 26, 1944, Ft. Sam Houston, TX. Heavy Machine Gunner 605, 1st Cavalry Div. Campaigns include Liberation of S. Philippines, Luzon 00 105 WD 45. Medals: Combat Infantryman Badge, Asiatic Pacific Theater Campaign Ribbon w/2 BSS, Philippine Liberation Campaign Ribbon w/1 BSS, GCM, Army Occ. (Japan), Victory Ribbon, three Overseas Service Bars. Honorably discharged Aug. 10, 1946. Home of record: Bellaire, TX.

Vecera, Eugene A., was born Aug. 26, 1951, Weimar, Colorado, TX. Commissioned a 2nd Lt. through U.S. Army Corps ROTC, Adjutant General Corps, University of Houston, 1973. B.A., History; Univ. of NE, M.A., Education. Citizen sol-

dier, combined both civilian and military career. In reserves, served as asst. adjutant, 1st Inf. Trng. Brig., Ft. Polk, LA, 5th Bn., 57th Air Defense Artillery, Ft. Bliss, TX. Professional management officer, Army Personnel Ctr., St. Louis, MO. Staff projects at Military Personnel Ctr., Washington, DC, Forces Command HQ, Atlanta, GA, 5th Army HQ, San Antonio, TX. Currently assigned as Personnel Services Officer, 311th Corps Support Command. Medals: Meritorious Service, Army Commendation w/2 OLC, Army Achievement w/2 OLC, National Defense Service Ribbon w/Star, Army Service Ribbon, Reserve Overseas Service Ribbon, Reserve Forces Service Ribbon. Rank: Maj. Married Julie; children: Jeramie and Victoria. Home of record: Los Angeles, CA.

Velek, Edwin A., son of Albert and Francis Velek, was born Aug. 18, 1919, Gonzales Co., TX. Education: high school and two years of university. Enlisted Ft. Sam Houston, TX, Apr. 15, 1941, U.S. Army Air Corps. Theater of Operations: European for three and a half years; Normandy Invasion with the 148th AAA, 1st Army, 9th Air Force. Medals: American Defense Service, EAME Campaign w/2 BSS, and GCM. Honorably discharged Oct. 21, 1945. Home of record: Houston, TX.

Vernon, Louis A. (changed about 1920 from Vrana, Ludwig A.), son of Cyril Vrana and Marie Spaniel, was born about 1898, Moravia, Lavaca Co., TX. Education: Moravia, TX, elementary school. Enlisted Dec. 10, 1917, Camp Bowie, Ft. Worth, TX, in U.S. Army Corps. Honorably discharged Apr. 1, 1919. Prior to military service, worked as a telegrapher, Dallas, TX. After discharge, married Ola Mae Bristow, a widow with three children. Lived in Dallas, TX, where they operated a furniture factory until early 1930s. Five children were born to them: Louis Anthony (died at age 2), Ruth Helen, Marc Anthony, Mary Louise, and Martha Joan. Died Apr. 3, 1970, Kerrville, TX. Submitted by nephew William "Bill" Vrana of Corpus Christi, TX.

Veselka, Adolph A., was born Oct. 30, 1921. Served in U.S. Army during WWII. Died Nov. 30, 1990. Buried in St. Mary's Cemetery, West, TX.

Veselka, Charlie Henry, was born Nov. 20, 1894. Served as Pvt. in U.S. Army during WWI. Died Oct. 5, 1989. Buried in St. Mary's Cemetery, West, TX.

Veselka, Ernest G., son of Jim J. Veselka and Emily Kyselka, was born Dec. 10, 1922, in West, TX. Attended S. Bosque Elementary and LaVega High School in Bellmead, TX. Entered the Marines in Waco, TX, 1942. Trained in San Diego, CA. Rank: Tech Sgt. Served in the South Pacific. Battles: Marshall Islands, Gilbert Islands, and Ellice Islands. Medals: Asiatic-Pacific Campaign w/3 BSS, Good Conduct, American Theater of Operations Ribbon, WWII Victory Ribbon. Discharged Nov. 1945 at El Toro, CA. Married Dalores Ann Len. He had six brothers who served together and came home alive from overseas duty. Home of record: Waco, TX.

Veselka, George E., son of Jim J. and Emily Kyselka, was born Feb. 18, 1925, in West, TX. Attended S. Bosque High and LaVega High School in Bellmead. Joined the Air Force, 1944, in Waco, TX. Served in European Theater, Italy. Rank: Staff Sgt. Received an Air medal w/2 OLC, EAME Ribbon, AT Ribbon, and WWII Victory Ribbon. Discharged Nov. 1945 in FL. Home of record: Waco, TX.

Veselka, Henry Emil, son of Jim J. Veselka and Emily Kyselka, was born Oct. 26, 1917, West, TX. Attended schools in West and Elk, TX. Enlisted in the Army at San Antonio, TX, 1941. Trained at Knox, KY. Rank: T-5. Theater of Operation:

EAME–French Algiers, Morocco, and Europe. Battles: Naples-Foggia, Rome-Arno, Africa, and Italy. Medals: American Defense, Good Conduct, and EAME Campaign w/4 BSS. Discharged June 30, 1945. Married Agnes Clara Snider. Died Oct. 30, 1979, in West, TX. Buried at St. Mary's Catholic Cemetery.

Veselka, Jerome "Jerry," son of Jim J. Veselka and Emily Kyselka, was born Mar. 1, 1928, West, TX. Attended schools in Speegleville High, LaVega, and South Bosque. Entered the Navy in Waco, TX, 1945. Trained in San Diego, CA. Served in the U.S. and Pacific on USS *Kermit Roosevelt*. Served in China and Japan. Awarded Asiatic-Pacific Ribbon. Discharged Aug. 6, 1946, at Camp Wallace, TX. Rank: Seaman 2/C. Died Mar. 18, 1969, in Waco, TX. Buried at Memorial Park, Waco, TX.

Veselka, John Mack, was born Jan. 13, 1893. Served in U.S. Army during WWI. Died Apr. 9, 1988. Buried in St. Mary's Cemetery, West, TX.

Veselka, Joseph, son of Mr. and Mrs. John Veselka, was born Sept. 1, 1916, near West, TX. Attended Cottonwood School. Entered the Army in Aug. 1942 at Camp Wolters, and trained at Camp Kearns, UT. Rank: Pfc. Served in Europe. Discharged in Jan. 1946. Medals: WWII Victory Ribbon, GCM, AT Ribbon, and EAME Ribbon. Married Willie Mae Pavelka. Died in 1989; buried, St. Mary's Catholic Cemetery. Home of record: West, TX.

Veselka, Louis, son of Jim J. Veselka and Emily Kyselka, was born Oct. 16, 1919, West, TX. Attended schools in LaVega High School in Bellmead, TX. Entered the Army at San Antonio, TX, 1942. Rank: Sgt. Theater of Operations: Asiatic-Pacific. Fought in the Aleutian Islands, France, and Battle of the Bulge in Germany. Received Combat Infantry Badge, American Defense, and APE TO medals and ribbons w/2 Battle Stars, WWII Victory Ribbon. Discharged Nov. 12, 1945, at Tyler, TX. Married Martha Rejcek. Home of record: Waco, TX.

Veselka, Raymond J., son of Mr. and Mrs. R. W. Veselka, attended LaVega School. Entered U.S. Navy, 1945. Trained in San Diego, CA. Served on USS *Okinawa*. Honorably discharged in 1946, with rank of CM 3/C.

Veselka, Robert R., son of Mr. and Mrs. R. W. Veselka, attended LaVega School. Entered U.S. Navy, 1946. Rank: S2/C. Trained at Camp Peary, VA. Served in U.S.A.

Veselka, Victor V., son of Jim J. Veselka and Emily Kyselka, was born Dec. 31, 1914, in Terrell, TX. Attended St. Mary's Catholic School and public schools in West, TX. Joined the U.S. Army Corps, 1940, Waco, TX. Trained at Camp Bowie, TX, Camp Blanding, FL, and Camp Edwards, MA. Rank: Pfc. Served in the N. African and Italian Campaigns. Fought in several battles in Europe. Received the EAME with BSS, Division Blue Bar, Combat Infantry Badge, Good Conduct and Purple Heart medals, American Theater Ribbon, and WWII Victory Ribbon. WOUNDED IN ACTION, Italy, 1944. Discharged Oct. 3, 1945, Camp Livingston, LA. Died in 1961 in West, TX. Buried at St. Mary's Catholic Cemetery, West, TX.

Vesely, Henry Louis, son of John Vesely and Marie Gregurek, was born July 4, 1929, Ganado, Jackson Co., TX. Completed 10 years at White Hall School, Ganado, TX. Enlisted in USMC, July 27, 1948, San Antonio, TX. Received basic training in San Diego, CA. Stationed at Barstow, CA, including Nebo and

Yermo Camps, Alameda, CA, Camp Pendleton, CA. Participated in operations against enemy forces in South and Central Korea. Medals: Korean Service, GCM, Purple Heart, United Nations Service. WOUNDED IN ACTION, Sept. 12, 1951. Served one year involuntary enlistment. Honorably discharged with rank of Sgt., July 26, 1952, Marine Barracks NAATC, Naval Air Station, Corpus Christi, TX. Home of record for Henry L and Frances Vesely, Ganado, TX.

Viktorin, Jerry O., son of Mr. and Mrs. F. J. Viktorin, Jarrell, TX. Education: Arkansas University ASTRP. Enlisted U.S. Army Air Corps during WWII, 1943. Basic training, Sheppard Field, TX; additional training. Lowery Field. Honorable discharge, 1945. Rank: Aviation Cadet.

Vilim, Herbert William, Jr., son of Herbert William Vilim, Sr. and Loretta Stapelton, was born Apr. 5, 1920, Chicago, IL. Received Masters of Education and Superintendent of Schools Certificate in TX. Entered the U.S. Army and served in the Asiatic-Pacific Theater of Operations as an Instructor. Rank: Sgt. Was the first instructor the Armed Forces Institute sent overseas. Taught, by mail, members of all services (Army, Air Corps, Navy, and Marines). Discharged from service on Feb. 6, 1946, at Brisbane, Australia, at own request, to visit with 65 families of relatives. Visited and lived with relatives for nine months. Returned to U.S. Feb. 1947, aboard last American passenger ship to visit Australia for ten years. Stayed one year in Chicago, IL, and moved permanently to San Antonio, TX, for its climate.

Vinklarek, Emil, retired Catholic priest from Schulenburg, TX., is active in many areas. He has poems published in *Threshold of a Dream* by the National Library of Poetry under his pen name, Padre V. While a chaplain in the Armed Forces near the end of WWII, had to break the news to mothers of fallen soldiers. Response to seeing their grief was the poem, "Gold Star Mother." After Gulf War ended, he made the poem public. Home of record: Schulenburg, TX.

Visviki, Charlie, served three years, U.S. Army Corps, during WWII.

Visviki, Joe, served three years, U.S. Army Corps, during WWII.

Vitek, Aug F., son of Mr. and Mrs. Joe Vitek, Granger, TX. Education: Granger High School. Enlisted U.S. Army Corps, 1941. Basic training, Ft. Sam Houston, TX. Additional training, Ft. Sill, OK, Camp Roberts, CA. Discharged 1943.

Vitek, Henry E., son of Mr. and Mrs. Aug Vitek, Granger, TX. Enlisted U.S. Army Air Corps, 1940. Basic training, Brook Field; additional training at Chanute Field. Theater of Operations: Asiatic-Pacific. Served in Netherlands, E. Indies, Philippines. Medals: Asiatic-Pacific Theater Campaign w/4 BSS, WWII Victory, ribbons. Attained rank of M/Sgt. prior to honorable discharge, 1945. Home of record: Granger, TX. Member, American Legion Post No. 282, Granger, TX.

Vitek, J. V. "Peanut," WWII veteran of Granger, TX.

Vitek, Joe, son of Mrs. A. Demek, West, TX. Attended West High School. Entered Navy, 1944, during WWII. Attained rank of S 1/C. Trained in San Diego. Served in Hawaii, Solomons, and W. Carolines. Awards: AP Ribbon w/2 Battle Stars. Discharged 1945.

Vitek, Joe A., son of Mr. and Mrs. Aug Vitek, Granger, TX. Education: Texas University and Southwestern University. Enlisted in U.S. Navy, 1942. Trained at Southwestern University and Cornell University, Hollywood, FL. Rank: Ensign. Served in Asiatic-Pacific Theater of Operations. USS *Queens* APA 103.

Vitek, Louis, served in U.S. Armed Forces during WWI, 1917–1918. Member of SPJST Lodge 20, Granger, TX,

Vittek, Charles, son of Anton Vittek and Justina Cevnycuk, was born Oct. 27, 1920, Taylor, Williamson Co., TX. Education: Rices Crossing School, GED High School. Enlisted Aug. 29, 1942, Ft. Sam Houston, TX, U.S. Army Air Corps. Attained rank of Sgt. Power Turret and Gun Sights. Theater of Operations: European. Served in England, Europe. Medals: WWII Victory, EOT Campaign w/BSS. Honorable discharge, Dec. 4, 1945. Married Ruth Fisher. auto body mechanic. Hobby: gardening. Home of record: Austin, TX.

Vittek, Julius T., son of Anton Vittek and Justina Cevnycuk, was born Dec. 21, 1929, Taylor, Williamson Co., TX. Education: Hutto, TX, High School, 1947; credits from University of MD. Enlisted in U.S. Air Force, Oct. 27, 1948, Lackland AFB, TX. Attained rank of CM/Sgt. Airborne Electronics Instructor. Eight years overseas, including Okinawa, Japan, Saipan, Germany, Norway, Greece, England. Traveled throughout

48 of the 50 states. Retired from military Dec. 31, 1974. Civilian occupation: Sonar Electronics. Married Anna Marie Urbanek; two children: Monica and Mark. Hobbies: ham radio, electronics. Home of record: Austin, TX.

Vlk, Joe Raymond, son of Joseph Vlk and Anna Krajca, was born Aug. 8, 1921, Ennis, TX. Education: Lone Oak and St. John, Ennis, TX. Enlisted in U.S. Army, Ennis, TX, Oct. 13, 1942. Served in ETO. Medals: GCM, two battle stars, citation for outstanding work, and ETO Ribbon. Honorably discharged Dec. 5, 1945, Camp Fannin, Tyler, TX. Home of record: Dallas, TX.

Voelkle, Billy J., Jarrell, TX. Graduate of Waco High School. Enlisted U.S. Navy, 1944. Basic training, San Diego, CA; additional training, Gulfport, MS, Richmond, VA. Served during WWII in Philippines and Japan. Married Elba Dean Woodward, Jarrell, TX.

Vojtek/Woytek *see* Paul Woytek. Vojtek is original spelling.

Vojtek, Calvin John, son of Fred Frank and Anna Vojtek, was born May 24, 1930, Harris Co., TX. Educated through 12th grade. Drafted, Houston, TX. Theater of Operation: Korean War. Honorably discharged Feb. 1953. Home of record: Cypress, TX.

Volcik, Adolph L., son of Mr. and Mrs. Frank Volcik, attended Ross School. Entered U.S. Army Corps, 1943; trained at Camp Roberts and Camp Stoneman, CA. Rank: Pfc. Served in Australia, Good Enough Islands, Netherlands, East India, Morotia. WOUNDED IN ACTION in Netherlands. Awarded two BSS, GCM, and Combat Infantry Badge. Honorably discharged in 1945. Married Willie Mae Kocian.

Volcik, Albert Tom, son of Mr. and Mrs. Frank Volcik, attended West Elementary. Entered U.S. Navy, 1946. Trained in San Diego, CA. Attained rank of SF 2/C. Served in Emaru, Guam, Okinawa, aboard USS *Cetus*. Awarded AP Ribbon, AT Ribbon, Okinawa Campaign Ribbon, and WWII Victory Ribbon. Honorably discharged, 1945.

Volcik, Edwin, West, TX, military veteran.

Volcik, Edwin V., son of Mr. and Mrs. Frank Volcik, attended Ross School. Entered U.S. Army Corps, 1940. Trained at Ft. Clark, Ft. Sam Houston, Ft. Bliss, TX, Camp Young, CA, VA, and NY. Rank: S/Sgt. Served in Africa, Sicily and Italy. Awarded AD Ribbon, Campaign Medal with six BSS, Silver Star, Purple Heart, and GCM. WOUNDED IN ACTION, Italy, 1944. Honorably discharged, 1945.

Volcik, Eugene Charles, son of Paul Volcik and Mary Palla, was born Apr. 21, 1928, Smithville, TX. Graduated Smithville, TX, High School, 1945, University of Texas College of Pharmacy, 1952. Enlisted in U.S. Navy, Austin, TX, about 1945. Attained rank of Seaman 1/C. Theater of Operations: EAME. Boot camp, San Diego, CA. Served on USS *Huntington*, July 1946–Dec. 1947, USS *Albany*, Dec. 1947–Feb. 1948. Medals: EAME, European Occupational Area, WWII Victory, Good Conduct, EAME Campaign. Honorably discharged Feb. 18, 1948. Married Viola Stiteler, 1953; children: Charlie, Wayne, Mary. Presently (1993) a pharmacist. Plan to semi-retire Feb. 17, 1994. Hobby: collect very old newspapers (some about 200 years old), and headline newspapers. Honors: Served as president, Capital Area Pharmaceutical Assoc.; co-president, LBJ High School; Elder and Deacon in Trinity Presbyterian Church. Had the honor of being lay preacher at the 120th celebration of First Presbyterian Church in Smithville, TX. Home of record: Austin, TX.

Volcik, John, son of Frank Volcik and Mary Raaz Volcik Bartosh of Hallettsville, TX, was born June 24, 1910, Lemonville, TX. Education: El Campo High School, El Campo, TX. Lived on farm two miles east of El Campo for 30 years. Was mechanic, pilot, and flew his private plane. Veteran of WWII,

drafted Apr. 16, 1942. Served as Military Police Cpl. in Service Command in Ft. Worth, Tarrant Co., TX. Honorably discharged Oct. 2, 1945. Died at Grand Saline Hospital, mass at St. Peter's Catholic Church at Mineola, said by cousins, Fr. Paul Raaz of San Antonio and Fr. John Rohman. Interred at Hope Family Cemetery, Mineola, TX. Submitted by sister Mary Stehno.

Volcik, Julius Rudolph "Joe," son of Paul Volcik and Mary Palla, was born Dec. 10, 1919, Smithville, TX. Graduated 1938, Smithville, TX, High School. Enlisted U.S. Navy, 1942, Houston, TX. Attained rank of Gunnersmate 2/C. Shipped to U.S. Naval Training Station for boot camp, later to U.S. Navy Landingcraft School, San Diego, CA. Theater of Operations: American, EAME, CBI. Battles: Guadalcanal, Tulagi, Munda, Rendova, Vell La Vella, Green Islands, Solomon Islands, Bougainville, Emiru, Mariannas Islands at Guam, Tinnian, Saipan. Medals: American Campaign w/Foreign Service, Asiatic Pacific Campaign w/4 BSS, Presidential Unit Citation, CBI Campaign, Good Conduct, WWII Victory. WOUNDED IN ACTION. Injured while aboard ship, loading Thompson Machine Guns on Tinian Island, not serious. Attended Advanced Gunnersmate School, Washington, D.C. Had honor of marching in Franklin D. Roosevelt Funeral Procession, then to Dam Neek, VA, as anti-aircraft gun instructor, to San Francisco for overseas duty, boarded Aircraft Carrier USS *Bogue* to HI, from Hawaii on APD USS *Yokes* to Guam to guard Japanese prisoners of war, then to China on carrier, USS *Antietam* to Tsingtao, China. Stayed in transit aboard the following ships: Cruiser USS *Alaska*, USS *Montauk,* USS *Zaurak* to Taku, China, Arrived Shanghai, China, USS *Basilan*, Shanghai, China to Nagasaki, Japan, on to Hawaii to Seattle, WA, Seattle to San Diego on USS *Lacerta*, San Diego to Camp Wallace for honorable discharge, Jan. 19, 1946. 22 months of duty was spent on USS LST 398 in Solomon Islands and Marianas Islands, one trip to Auckland, New Zealand for war damage LST 398 in battle on Vella La Vella Island. LST 398 lost five dead, 21 wounded, Vella La Vella Island. Married Gladys Mae Ryza; two children, Stephen M. and Donna J. Retired from Missouri-Kansas Railroad Co., Oct. 31, 1984 w/46 years of service. Home of record: Denison, TX.

Volcik, Walter, son of Paul Volcik and Mary Palla, was born Dec. 18, 1924, of Smithville, TX. Graduated Smithville High School, Voc. Ag. three years, special training course for SW Bell. Enlisted, U.S. Navy, San Antonio, TX. Boot camp, Ft. Ord, CA; further training at Oceanside, CA. Rank: Coxswain (T). Unit was used in the filming of *The Fighting Seabees* with John Wayne. Boarded USS *Moremant Port,* and sailed to Pearl Harbor, HI. Unit helped rescue sailors off LSTs that exploded in West Loch. From Pearl Harbor into invasion of Peleliu. Landed marines on Peleliu, then moved into Ulithi Islands on USS *Clay* to get ready for future invasions. Medals: American Theater of Operations w/Ribbon, Asiatic-Pacific Theater Campaign w/1 BSS, WWII Victory. Honorably discharged Jan. 13, 1946. Was a self-educated, observant person who was friendly and liked by all who knew him. Married; one daughter, Pamela Volcik Gardner, and one grandson, Joshua Gardner. Died Apr. 24, 1985. Submitted by sister Bessie Volcik Bradshaw, Smithville, TX.

Volek, Johnnie J., WWII veteran. Member, American Legion Post No. 282, Granger, TX.

Volek, Paul Milton, son of John Volek and Francis Simcik, was born Aug. 14, 1924, in Taylor, TX. Education: Moravia Elementary School. Enlisted, U.S. Navy, Mar. 16, 1943, during WWII. Served Asiatic-Pacific Theater of Operations, Gunner's Mate, with rank of Seaman 1/C. Campaigns: Saipan, Palaus, Pearl Harbor, Fiji, Canton, Pago, Guadalcanal, Manila, Tawi, aboard USS *Pocompe*. Honorably discharged Dec. 1945. Civilian Occupation: Taylor ISD bus driver/janitor until retirement in Mar. 1989. Hobbies: fishing, building bird houses, dancing, playing accordion. Married Delores Cervenka; two children: Mervin and Danny. Home of record: Taylor, TX.

Volney, Darwin C., Granger, TX. U.S. Navy: USS *Sub Chaser 632*. WWII veteran.

Volny, Willie, served in U.S. Armed Forces during

WWI, 1917–1918. Member of SPJST Lodge 20, Granger, TX.

Vonasek, Frank F., was born Jan. 18, 1917. Served in U.S. Army, WWII, attained rank of Sgt. Died Jan. 1, 1981. Buried in St. Mary's Cemetery, West, TX.

Vrabel, Tim J., Bartlett, TX. WWII veteran. Member, American Legion Post No. 282, Granger, TX.

Vrana, Albert C., son of Mr. and Mrs. R. Vrana. Entered Army 1944, during WWII. Attained rank of Cpl. Served in England, France and Germany. Awards: EAME Ribbon w/2 BSS, GCM, and Victory Ribbon. Discharged 1945.

Vrana, Albert F., son of Mr. Vrana and Mrs. Christine Vrana, Granger, TX. Enlisted in U.S. Army Corps, 1945. Basic training, Camp Fannin. Served in Germany. WWII veteran. Member, American Legion Post No. 282, Granger, TX.

Vrana, Edwin, son of Mr. and Mrs. August Vrana, West, TX. Entered Army, 1942. Attained rank of Pfc. WOUNDED IN ACTION, Germany. PRISONER OF WAR, Germany, 2½ years. Received Purple Heart. Married Esther Pavlas.

Vrana, Inocence Frank, was born Feb. 1893. Served in U.S. Army, WWI, as a Pvt. Died Apr. 18, 1963. Buried in St. Mary's Cemetery, West, TX.

Vrana, Joseph Pete, II, son of Josef R. Vrana and Marie A. Cmerek, was born Mar. 27, 1932 in Williamson Co., TX. Attended Palacky School and Sts. Cyril & Methodius School in Granger, TX. Enlisted in the U.S. Army on Mar. 17, 1953, at Ft. Sam Houston, TX, during the Korean Conflict. Served in Korea as member of the 38th Inf. Reg. Decorations: Korean Service Medal, UN Service Medal, and National Defense Service Medal. Separated from service on July 13, 1954. Married Laura Ann Neidig; six children: Joseph III, Michael, Raymond, Steven, Marvin, and Carolyn. Farmer in the Granger area. Enjoys playing the accordion. Member, American Legion Post No. 282, Granger, TX. Home of record: Granger, TX.

Vrana, Leo Raymond, son of Ignac Bohuslav Vrana and Emilie Olsovsky, was born Mar. 21, 1921, in Moravia, TX. Graduated from Robstown High School in 1938. Enlisted in the Navy, 1940, Houston, TX. After basic, was assigned to battleship USS *California*. Attended the Naval (New Construction) Gunnery School, Washington, DC. Was aboard the USS *California* at Pearl Harbor when Japanese attacked on Dec. 7, 1941. The USS *California* took two aerial torpedo hits, two 500-pound bomb hits, and "abandon ship" was given. Fortunately, most aboard swam ashore. From Jan. to Oct. 1942, approximately 500 of the original crew members remained assigned to the USS *California*, raising the ship, removing, with dignity, the bodies of deceased shipmates, performing a general ship cleanup, and getting her ready for sea. The USS *California* arrived at Bremerton Naval Ship Yard, WA, in Oct. 1942, was modernized, and sailed back to the Pacific to avenge herself. After several campaigns, including one in the Philippines in which she was hit by a kamikaze, she steamed into Tokyo Bay to cover the 6th Army landing and occupation of Japan in Aug. and Sept. 1945. Leo's entire WWII tour was served aboard the USS *California*, in both the American and Asiatic-Pacific Theaters of Operations, participating at Pearl Harbor, Midway, Leyte, Luzon, Lingayen Gulf, and Okinawa Gunto. Attained rank of Turret Capt. 1/C. Medals: American Campaign, Asiatic-Pacific Campaign w/campaign star, Philippines Liberation Ribbon w/3 campaign stars, and Pearl Harbor Congressional Commemorative, 50th Anniversary, 1991. Discharged Nov. 14, 1946. Married Henrietta Barbara Prochaska on Apr. 15, 1947; four children: Suzanne, Mary, Stephen, and Gregory. Joined father in construction business in 1947 in the Corpus Christi area. After father retired in 1957, managed the business until retirement in 1987. Member of the USS *California* Association, Pearl Harbor Survivors Association, and the Veterans of Foreign Wars. Home of record: Corpus Christi, TX.

Vrana, Ludwig A./Vernon, Louis A. (changed name about 1920)

Vrana, William, son of Emil Vrana and Albina Peter (daughter of Mikolos Peter of Frenstat, Czechoslovakia) and Anna Blahuta, was born June 22, 1914, Moravia, Lavaca Co., TX. Education: Moravia Elementary and Rural High, 1921-31, Schulenburg High, 1934-35, University of Texas, 1935-39, B.A. in geology. Enlisted Jan. 24, 1944,

Ft. Sam Houston, TX. Assigned to U.S. Army Signal Corps. Basic training, Camp Kohler, CA, then took course in AM and FM radio repair and maintenance at Ft. Monmouth, NJ, course in rigger school (antenna const.), Camp Crowder, MO. After WWII ended, assigned to Ft. Meyer, Washington, DC, and the WAR booster radio station at Alexandria, VA, with the 2506th Service Command Unit, 17th Signal Service Co. Medals: American Theater Campaign Ribbon, Good Conduct, WWII Victory Ribbon. Honorably discharged May 3, 1946, Ft. Sam Houston, TX. Prior to military service, employed as civil service with International Boundary Commission, El Paso, TX, and with U.S. Army Corps of Engineers, Houston, TX. After service, with Tenneco as geologist, Houston office (May 1946–Dec. 1953). Exploration manager for Tenneco in Corpus Christi (Jan. 1954–June 1960). Self-employed consulting geologist until present. Married Joyce Raasch, native of Houston, TX, in 1942; two sons. Home of record: Corpus Christi, TX.

Vrazel, Ervin F., son of Frank and Mary Vrazel.

Vrazel, Joseph N., born in Breslau, Texas, served in France.

Vrazel, Lawrence Louis, son of Louis and Frances Vrazel, was born July 18, 1923, in Gonzales, TX. Served in the US Air Corps. Died Sept. 24, 1988.

Vrazel, Norbert B., son of Joseph and Viola Vrazel. Born Feb. 23, 1922 in Yoakum, TX. Education: Yoakum High School and University of Wisconsin. Enlisted in US Navy, Sept. 1, 1942, in Houston, TX. Served in the Atlantic Theater of Operations. Medals: American Theater, and Good Conduct. Discharged Aug. 1954. Address of record: Yoakum, TX.

Vrazel, Phillip, born 1917.

Vrazel, Raymond A., son of Joseph and Viola Vrazel, was born in Yoakum, TX. Attended Yoakum High School and the Merchant Marine Academy.

Vrba, Albert A., son of Mr. and Mrs. Joe Vrba. Attended West High School. Entered Army 1940. Served during WWII, and attained the rank of Cpl. Served in Central Europe, Normandy, Ardennes, and Rhineland. WOUNDED IN ACTION, Belgium. Awards: Purple Heart, five BSS, one Service Stripe, GCM, two overseas Bars and ET Ribbon. Discharged 1945.

Vrba, Alfred L., Tours, TX, WWII veteran. Battles: Belgium. WOUNDED IN ACTION.

Vrba, Alphonse, West, TX, WWII veteran.

Vrba, Anton W., Leroy, TX. Entered Army 1939. Served during WWII as a Pvt. in Ireland, England, Wales, Belgium, France, and Germany. WOUNDED IN ACTION, France, 1944. Awards: Purple Heart, GCM, ET Ribbon w/3 Battle Stars, AD Ribbon. Discharged 1945.

Vrba, Daniel Louis, son of Bill Vrba and Olga Stepan, was born Sept. 29, 1931, West, McLennan Co., TX. Graduated from West High, 1948, received B.S. from University of Houston, 1960, Doctor of Jurisprudence in Law, University of Houston, 1964. Enlisted in USAF, Waco, TX, Jan. 3, 1951. Theater of Operations: Lackland AFB, TX,

Sheppard AFB, TX, Chanute AFB, IL, Ellington AFB, TX, Pepperell AFB, St. John's, Newfoundland, Ernest Harmon AFB, Stephenville, Newfoundland, Thule AFB, Greenland, St. Anthony

Distant Early Warning Station, St. Anthony, Newfoundland and Goose AFB, Goose Bay, Labrador. Ribbons: Good Conduct, National Defense (Korean War). Survived plane crash at St. Anthony's, Newfoundland, during take-off from the water in an S.A. 16 amphibious plane, July 30, 1954. Honorably discharged Oct. 1954. Married Sally Kronenwetter of York, PA; four children: Elaine, Alan, Cynthia, Warren. Attorney-at-law, Houston, TX. Home of record: Houston, TX.

Vrba, Della, is a Registered Nurse, graduated Providence Hospital School of Nursing, Waco, TX. Served in the Nurse Corps during WWII in England, ET.

Vrba, Frank J., of Tours, TX. WWII veteran. Theater of Operations: Asiatic-Pacific. Served in South Pacific.

Vrba, James Mathews, III, son of James Mathews Vrba, Jr. and Anna Louise Criswell, was born Nov. 5, 1936, Tulsa, OK. Educated: Briscoe Elementary, Stonewall Jackson Jr. High, Lamar High, Houston, TX, Texas A&M, graduated 1960, College Station, TX, B.S. physical education. Active duty 1960. Transportation School, Primary Helicopter School, and Aviation School. Rank: 2nd Lt, Transportation Corps. Assigned to 544th Transportation Detachment, Ft. Knox, KY, then, 45th Transportation Co. in Korea, Ft. Benning, GA, 11th Air Assault Div., instructor pilot, Primary School, Ft. Wolters, TX. Duty in Viet Nam with the 167th Trans. Detach. Returned to Viet Nam 1967, C.O., 150th Trans. Detach. Rank: Capt. KILLED IN ACTION Jan. 31, 1968, at Vinh Long Airfield in the Mekong Delta area. Commission as Maj. came through while still listed as MISSING IN ACTION. Buried with full military honors at Mineral Wells, TX. Medals presented posthumously to his widow: Silver Star, Air Medal w/10 OLC, BSS w/1 OLC, Purple Heart. The Silver Star Citation stated "for gallant actions during a mortar and ground attack on Vinh Long Airfield, Republic of Viet Nam. on Jan. 31, 1968. During the attack, Major Vrba discovered that several of the defensive bunkers were in possession of the enemy. He made his way to the command bunker and attempted to establish communications with the primary command post. Here, he was fatally wounded by enemy small arms fire, before communications could be established. Though unsuccessful in his main objective, Major Vrba stopped the main advance of enemy forces by his unparalleled leadership and daring actions." The Air Medal and 10 Oak Leaf Clusters were presented for numerous helicopter air strikes during the period of Aug. 1, 1967 through Dec. 21, 1967. In Aug. 1969, a hangar at the U.S. Army Transportation Center at Ft. Eustis, VA, was designated Vrba Hangar, and a bronze plaque was placed on the hangar. Married; one child: James IV, who married Adella Anne Miller. They have two children: Jamie Lea and Taylor Mathews Vrba.

Vrba, Jerry V., was born Apr. 4, 1909. Served in U.S. Navy during WWII with rank of AMM. Died Dec. 8, 1986. Buried in St. Mary's Cemetery, West, TX.

Vrba, Louis, Tours, TX, veteran, U.S. Navy.

Vrba, Raymond, of West, TX. WWII veteran, U.S. Army Corps, 910th Field Artillery Battalion.

Vrla, Arnold M., son of Frank B. Vrla and Mary R. Kudrna, was born Jan. 16, 1920, Ennis, TX. Graduated: Ennis Public School, 1936, Draughon's Business College for two and a half years. Enlisted at Kelly Field, San Antonio, TX, U.S. Army Air Corps, during WWII. Achieved rank of Staff Sgt. Theater of Operation: China-Burma-India. Medals: Battle of Madagascar, CBI Theater Campaign, Good Conduct. "Our Air Corps Squadron did major overhaul on airplane engines and I was the administrative clerk in Squadron Headquarters." Honorable discharge, Ft. Sam Houston, TX, 1946. Home of record: Dallas, TX.

Vrla, Henry J., son of Mr. Vrla and Josie Jelinek, was born Oct. 5, 1913, Ennis, TX. Education: Bardwell, TX, Enlisted Camp Wolters, Mineral Wells, TX, during WWII, U.S. Army Corps Achieved rank of Tec 5. Inf. basic training 521-Radar Apr. 846. Battles: Rome Arno, North Apennines, Po Valley Go33 WD45. Medals:

WWII Victory Ribbon, American Theater Campaign, one Service Stripe, five overseas service bars w/3 BSS. Honorable discharge Nov. 11, 1945, Ft. Sam Houston, TX. Died July 23, 1956. Submitted by Mrs. Joe F. Vrana, Ennis, TX.

Vybiral, Bennie Joseph, son of Mr. and Mrs. Ben Vybiral, was born Apr. 25, 1926, Buckholts, TX. Graduated from Yoe High School, Cameron, TX. Enlisted U.S. Navy, Naval Training Center, San Diego, CA. American Theater of Operations. Achieved rank of AS, S2/C. Honorable discharge, June 1946. Home of record: Bryan, TX.

Vydrzal, Stan, son of Dominik and Mary Vydrzal, was born Oct. 10, 1920, Cistern, TX. Attended Robbins School. Enlisted in Houston, TX. Served in the European Theater from Sept. 15, 1943, to July 26, 1945, in Normandy, Rhineland, Ardennes, and Central Europe in the 101st Airborne Div., Co. E, 327th Glider Inf., "The Screaming Eagles." Rank: Pfc. WOUNDED IN ACTION June 1944 in France when an amphibious jeep rolled over on him, requiring immediate surgery which was done on the ground under a tent. WOUNDED IN ACTION again Oct. 1944 in Holland when a shell burst in his foxhole, killing his buddy, and requiring 16 stitches in his own head. Medals: American Service w/3 Stars, Good Conduct, WWII Victory, Purple Heart w/2 OLC, Automatic Rifleman, Combat Infantryman Badge, Presidential Unit Citation, Bronze Service Arrowhead (Holland), Bronze Service Arrowhead (France), Distinguished Unit Badge (Belgium), Distinguished Unit Badge (France), Belgium Fourragere (Action at Bastogne, Dec. 1944 and Coast of France Invasion of Europe, June 1944). Discharged Nov. 9, 1945. Died Aug. 3, 1958. Buried with full military honors in Oak Hill Cemetery, Smithville, TX.

Vyoral, Charlie John, Sr., son of Bartos Vyoral and Mary, was born Apr. 29, 1919, Eastgate, TX. Education: Wolfe Island School, Dayton, TX. Enlisted in San Antonio, TX, during WWII, U.S. Army Corps. Attained rank of Pfc. Theater of Operations: EAME, American. Fought in England, France, Germany. Medals: Marksman in Pistol, Rifle, Machine Gun. Medals: WWII Victory, American Defense, Good Conduct, EAME Campaign w/2 BSS. Honorably discharged from Camp San Luis Obispo, CA. Married Margaret Kovalcik, Nov. 19, 1946; three children: Patricia, Charlie John Jr., Melinda, six grandchildren. Bought farm in 1947, raised cotton, corn, milo, rice, beans, and cattle. Now retired. Home of record: Dayton, TX.

Vyvial, Adolph, son of Frank Vyvial and Annie Fojt. Completed sixth grade, Little Kentucky School, Ganado, TX. Enlisted Dec. 9, Houston, TX, U.S. Army Air Corps. Cpl., 887th Chemical Co. Air Operations Siapan. Theater of Operations: Asiatic-Pacific. Medals: Presidential Citation, GCM. Honorably discharged Oct. 11, 1945, Ft. Bliss, TX. Home of record: Ganado, TX.

Vyvial, Allen, son of Frank Vyvial and Annie Fojt, was born June 5, 1926, Louise, TX. Education: high school and two years A&M. Enlisted U.S. Army Corps, San Antonio, TX, during WWII. Theater of Operation: Pacific. Attained rank of Pfc. Medals: numerous small arms expert marksmanship, Pacific Theater, 33rd Army Div. Command, USMP, GCM, one overseas bar. Attended U.S. Adjutant's General School, Custodian Correctional School, Ft. Oglethorpe, GA. Honorably discharged Nov. 27, 1946, Ft. Sam Houston, TX.

Vyvial, Arnold, son of John Joseph Vyvial and Thersa, was born Jan. 31, 1922, Ft. Bend Co., TX. Education: Richmond High School, TX. Enlisted Naval Recruiting Station, Houston, TX, June 25, 1942. Theater of Operations: EAME. USNOB, Palermo, Sicily, AATB Arzew, Algeria, USS LST SSI. Rank: Motor Machinist Mate 2/C. Honorable discharge Dec. 22, 1945. Married Dorothy Strickland

Vyvial; children: Larry Arnold and Rodney Joe. Worked 43 years with Texas Highway Dept. Very active in Ft. Bend Czech Heritage Society. Died Mar. 9, 1993, Richmond, TX; buried Greenlawn Cemetery, Richmond, TX. Submitted in loving memory by his widow, Dorothy Strickland Vyvial, of Rosenberg, TX.

Vyvial, Edward John, son of Frank Vyvial and Annie Fojt, was born Feb. 28, 1916, Louise, Wharton Co., TX. Completed seventh grade at Little Kentucky School. Enlisted in Edna, TX, U.S. Army Corps, during WWII. Basic training, San Antonio, TX. Assigned to 349th Inf., 88th Div. Theater of Operations: Europe. Battles: Italy, Poe Valley. KILLED IN ACTION Oct. 16, 1944. Interred in the American Memorial Cemetery, Florence, Italy. Achieved rank of Pvt. Posthumously awarded the Purple Heart. Submitted by Clois A. Gresham, Ganado, TX.

Vyvial, Elgin W., son of Frank Vyvial and Annie Fojt, was born Dec. 20, 1929, Louise, Wharton County, TX. High school graduate. Enlisted in USMC, Feb. 3, 1949, Galveston, TX. Served in Korea–capturing and securing Seoul, Sept. 21, 1950 to Oct. 7, 1950; Wonson-Hungnam-Chosin Campaign, Korea, Oct. 26, 1950 to Dec. 7, 1950. Medals: GCM, Korean Service w/2 Battle Stars, United Nations Ribbon. Honorably discharged Feb. 2, 1952. Home of record: La Marque, TX.

Vyvjala, Bernard F., son of August Vyvjala and Anastasia Tupa, was born June 5, 1933, Flatonia, TX. Graduated from Flatonia High, and North Texas State College in Denton. Enlisted in U.S. Army Corps about 1952, Houston, TX. Rank: Specialist 3/C. Medals: Rifle Marksmanship, and Good Conduct. Honorably discharged Dec. 13, 1956. Home of record: Houston, TX.

Vyvlecka, Frank Charles, son of Joseph and Adella Kreneck Vyvlecka, was born Dec. 23, 1931, Jourdanton, TX. Graduated from Jourdanton High. Enlisted in U.S. Army Corps, Aug. 4, 1953, at Ft. Sam Houston, TX. Basic training, Ft. Bliss, El Paso, TX. Rank: Cpl., 1514 Radar Operator, 2nd Army Div., Fort Devens, MA., Det #5, 1170th SU Organization HQ Btry 76th FA BN, 76th RCT. Honorably discharged June 6, 1955. Medals: National Defense Service, Good Conduct. Married Maureen Reynolds on April 21, 1956; four children: Kevin, Barry, Sheila, and Kathleen, six grandchildren. Owns and runs a machine shop in Jourdanton, TX.

Vyvlecka, Joe J., son of Joseph and Adella Kreneck Vyvlecka, was born Mar. 21, 1929, Jourdanton, TX. Graduated from Jourdanton High. Enlisted in U.S. Army Corps, January 4, 1951, at Ft. Sam Houston, TX. Basic training, Ft. Hood, TX. Assigned to 2nd Armd. Div., 124th Army Ordinance Maint. Bn., Bad-Kreuznach, Germany. Honorably discharged December 18, 1952. Medals: Army Occupation, Good Conduct. Raised family, owned, and operated a dairy in Jourdanton, TX.

Vyvlecka, Robert Lee, son of Joseph and Adella Kreneck Vyvlecka, was born Oct. 9, 1930, Jourdanton, TX. Graduated from Jourdanton High. Enlisted in U.S. Army Corps, July 10, 1951, at Ft. Sam Houston, TX. Basic training, Camp Roberts, CA. Assigned to USAR Engr., Korea, COB 151st Engr. G-BN-APO301. Honorably discharged August 14, 1953. Rank: Sgt. (E-5). Medals: Korean Service w/2 BSS, United Nations Service. Married Janet Havrda, Schulenburg, TX, Apr. 27, 1957; five children: Robert, James, Kenneth, Diane, and Carrie, 15 grandchildren. Home of record: Davis, CA.

Wachsman, Estelle Ann Necker, see Estelle Ann Necker.

Wagner, Alphonse W., son of Chas. S. Wagner and Emily Kocian, was born July 21, 1925, Shiner, Lavaca Co., TX. Education: Evergreen School, St. Ludmila's Academy. Enlisted Nov. 12, 1943, USMCR, San Antonio, TX. Medals: Expert Rifleman, WWII Victory, and others. Honorably discharged July 2, 1946, Camp LeJeune, NC. Active in the Hallettsville community for many years. Member of American Legion, Lions Club, and Knights of Columbus. Married Joyce Rother: six children, 14 grandchildren. Employed by Ford Motor Company as Parts Manager for over 40 years. Hobbies: chasing elk in Colorado Mountains with sons. Home of record: Hallettsvile, TX.

Walla, Adolph, was born Dec. 4, 1907. Served in the U.S. Army. Died Jan. 12, 1975. Buried in St. Mary's Cemetery, West, TX.

Walla, Albin J., was born Feb. 19, 1910. Served in U.S. Marine Corps with rank of Sgt. Died Oct. 6, 1989. Buried in St. Mary's Cemetery, West, TX.

Walla, Frank, was born Dec. 4, 1907. Served in U.S. Army. Died Jan. 12, 1975. Buried in St. Mary's Cemetery, West, TX.

Walla, Marshall C. Jr., son of Marshall C. Walla, Sr. and Martha Marie Wenkler, was born Dec. 8, 1942, in Houston, TX. Education: Sam Houston High School and Texas A&M. Enlisted in Houston, TX, and served as a Capt. in the 3rd Corps Area, Tay Ninh, Viet Nam. Medals: BSS 'Valor' (2), Air Medal, Viet Namese SVC, Viet Nam Campaign, Good Conduct, National Defense. Discharged Aug. 24, 1970, at El Paso, TX. Member of the Confederate Air Force–flies as a co-pilot on a B-25. Home of record: Houston, TX.

Watzlavick, Aug J. A., son of Raymond J. Watzlavick and Sophie M. Knietz, was born Jan. 18, 1914, Yoakum, TX. Education: St. Rose of Lima School, Schulenburg, TX; Schulenburg High School; College of Pharmacy–Ph. G , University of Texas, Austin; School of Medicine, M.D., University of Texas, Galveston, TX; Santa Rosa Hospital, San Antonio, TX, Internship and Residency. Enlisted in U.S. Army Corps, July 9, 1943, Houston, TX. Attained rank of Pfc. Honorably discharged Mar. 1, 1946, Galveston, TX. Commissioned as 1st Lt., July 2, 1947, U.S. Army, Ft. Sam Houston, TX. Honorably discharged Oct. 2, 1947, Ft. Sam Houston, TX. Married Leona Mazoch; two children: Thomas Raymond and Nancy Jane. Member MAC/AUS (Reserve), July 30, 1942 to Mar. 23, 1943, 2nd Lt. Home of record: Schulenburg, TX.

Watzlavick, Joseph D. "Joe," son of R. J. Watzlavick and Sophie Kneitz, was born Aug. 4, 1918, Oakland, TX. Graduated University of Texas, Austin, TX, B.S. Geology. Enlisted Ft. Sam Houston, assigned 8th USAF and 9th USAF. Navigator, B-26 Bombers, 86 combat missions over France, Belgium, Holland, Germany. Medals: Air w/11 clusters, Distinguished Flying Cross w/1 OLC. Honorable discharge, Dec. 1945. Home of record: Bellaire, TX. Submitted by Evelyn Vecera, Bellaire, TX.

Wavra, John, of New Ulm TX. WWII veteran. Shot down returning from Ploesti Oil Fields. PRISONER OF WAR for over a year. Married Josephine.

Wavra, Rubin Thomas, son of John and Josephine Wavra, was born Dec. 10, 1922, New Ulm, TX. Education: New Ulm Elementary and Columbus High School, TX. Enlisted in Houston, TX, WWII, U.S. Army Air Corps. Theater of Operations: North Africa, Mediterranean, European. Battles: Ploesti, Vienna, Graz Ovieder-

Neinstedt, Marseilles, Toluene, Vernier, Constanta, Trieste, Zagreba. Medals: Purple Heart, Distinguished Service Cross, Air Medal w/2 OLC, North African Campaign, Mediterranean Campaign, European Campaign, seven Campaign Stars, WWII Victory Ribbon. WOUNDED IN ACTION. Honorable discharge Sept. 21, 1945. Father, John Wavra, was a POW for over a year, returning from Ploesti Oil Fields. Home of record: Houston, TX.

Wentrcek, Edward T., Granger, TX. Served in the U.S. Navy during WWII. Member, American Legion Post No. 282, Granger, TX.

Wentrcek, Ernest Alvin, Jr., son of Ernest and Billie Wentrcek, was born Feb. 19, 1948, in Bryan, TX. Education: Stephen F. Austin High School, Bryan; Sam Houston State University (B.S.), University of Central Texas (Masters), Texas A&M University (doctoral work). Sworn in at Houston, TX, June 9, 1969, and assigned to HQ Material Command of Europe-Zweibrucken, West Germany. Rank: Sgt. (E-5) with military clearance: NATO Top Secret. Discharged Jan. 19, 1972. Occupation is Director of Juvenile Services, Brazos Co., TX, and college instructor (sociology). Married Ginger Young Wentrcek; one child: Kristin Michelle. Hobbies: collecting political campaign items and genealogical research. Home of record: Bryan, TX.

Wentrcek, Ernest Alvin, Sr., son of Frank and Vlasta Wentrcek, was born Feb. 7, 1928, in Shiner, TX. Attended Kings Highway School, Wheelock, TX, Stephen F. Austin High School, Bryan, TX, and Texas A&M. Inducted into the Army in Houston, TX, Apr. 20, 1946, and served in the Army Reserves from Oct. 1947 until Oct. 1950, when he was called back to active duty for the Korean War as Sergeant (E-5). Released from active duty Oct. 30,1951. First tour of duty was served in the Army Medical Administrative Corps, stationed at the Army/Navy Hospital in Hot Springs, AR. Second tour of duty was at Advanced Army Finance School in St. Louis. Then stationed at Camp Polk, LA. Home of record: Bryan, TX.

Wentrcek, Marvin J., WWII veteran of Granger, TX.

Wentrcek, Roy, served in U.S. Army Corps, WWII. Hometown: Granger, TX.

Wokaty, Augustine V., son of Anton Wokaty, Sr. and Magdalean Kubecker, was born May 13, 1897, Wokaty, Milam Co., TX. Education: North Ulm, Milam Co., TX. Enlisted in U.S. Navy, July 8, 1918, during WWI, Dallas, TX. Released from active duty, Feb. 3, 1919 at Naval Training Camp, San Diego, CA. Married Matilda Marak. Died June 23, 1955, Corpus Christi, TX. Interred at Seaside Memorial Park, Holy Rosary Section, Corpus Christi, TX. Submitted by Mr. and Mrs. Leon A. Seidenberger, Corpus Christi, TX.

Wokaty, Daniel M., son of Daniel M. Wokaty and Della Mae Kramer, was born May 26, 1936, Waco, McLennan Co., TX. Education: Waco High School, TX. Enlisted 1956, USMC, San Antonio, TX. Theater of Operations: Korea and Viet Nam. Battles: Viet Nam. Medals: Navy Accommodation, Purple Heart, Navy Achievement, Civil Action: President Unit Citation, Meritorious Unit, Good Conduct, National Defense, Korea Service Citation, Marine Expeditionary, Viet Nam Service, Viet Nam Cross Gallantry, Viet Nam United Nations, Viet Nam Campaign, Expert Rifle and Pistol. WOUNDED IN ACTION. Honorably discharged Apr. 30, 1978, after 22 years. Employed by Northwest Transport Service. Married Francia Andres; three daughters: Michell, Jennifer, Kathrine. Hobbies: hunting, fishing, camping. Home of record: Hewitt TX.

Wokaty, Eugene A., son of Augustine V. Wokaty and Matilda Marak. Education: St. Anthony's School, Cameron, TX, Elizabeth St. School, Corpus Christi, TX, Corpus Christi Academy, TX.

Enlisted in U.S. Army Corps, TX. Theater of Operations: Korea. Rank: Pfc. KILLED IN ACTION Jan. 17, 1953, Korea. Interred in Seaside Memorial Park, Wokaty Plot, Holy Rosary Section, Corpus Christi, TX. Submitted by Mr. and Mrs. Leon A. Seidenberger, Corpus Christi, TX.

Wolf, Cyril J., Blanco, TX. WWII veteran. Member, American Legion Post No. 282, Granger, TX.

Wolf, Cyril S., son of Mr. and Mrs. J. P. Wolf, Granger, TX. Graduate, Granger High School. Enlisted U.S. Navy, 1942, during WWII. Basic training, San Diego, CA. Theater of Operations: Asiatic-Pacific, American. Served in Pacific. Medals: Asiatic-Pacific Theater Campaign w/BSS, American Theater Campaign, Philippine Liberation, WWII Victory Medal, Ribbons. Attained rank of MoMM 1/c prior to honorable discharge, 1945. Served aboard USS P.C. 1591. Member, American Legion Post No. 282, Granger, TX. Home of record: Granger, TX.

Wolf, Daniel J., Granger, TX. WWII veteran. Member, American Legion Post No. 282, Granger, TX.

Wolf, Gilbert A., son of Mr. and Mrs. Oscar Wolf, Granger, TX. Enlisted U.S. Army Corps, 1942, basic training, Camp Swift. Theater of Operations: American, European. Medals: ETO w/4 BSS.

Wolf, Peter Paul, son of Mr. and Mrs. J. P. Wolf, Granger, TX. Enlisted U.S. Army Air Corps, 1941; basic training, Brooks Field, TX. Theater of Operations: American. Attained rank of Cpl. prior to honorable discharge, 1945.

Wolfe, Antone John, Jr., son of Anton Carol Wolf and Teresa Hecl, was born May 2, 1920, Bryan, Brazos Co., TX. Education: Smetana School, Brazos Co., TX, Rye School, Brazos Co., through seventh grade. Member of KJT No. 44, Bryan, TX, before joining Army. Mother, Tracy Hecl Wolf, immigrated from Czechoslovakia to Cornhill, TX, married, and moved to Bryan, TX. Enlisted in U.S. Army Corps, Dec. 23, 1941, Ft. Sam Houston, San Antonio, TX. Attained rank of Pfc. Theaters of Operation: American and EAME, Asiatic-Pacific. Medals: American Theater Campaign, EAME Campaign w/1 BSS, Asiatic Pacific Campaign w/1 BSS, GCM, WWII Victory, Aleutian Islands, Northern France. Honorably discharged Nov. 12, 1945, Camp Fannin, TX.

Wolfe, Anton Michael, son of Antone John Wolfe, Jr. and Magdalene D. Wolfe, served in the military in peacetime.

Wostarek, John, son of Joe Wostarek and Amalia Pavlicek, was born in the New Ulm, TX, area. Served with the American Expeditionary Forces in France, during WWI, as a member of the U.S. Army. Interred in the Sts. Peter and Paul Cemetery in Frelsburg, TX.

Woytek, Antone, entered Army, 1940, West, TX. Attained rank of Cpl. Served in Italy. PRISONER OF WAR in Germany for 18 months. Awards: two Battle Stars, GCM, and ET Ribbon. Discharged 1945.

Woytek, Jerry, entered service during WWII, 1943, Waco, TX. Served as Pfc. in S. Pacific. Awards: GCM and AP Ribbon. Discharged 1944.

Woytek, Marvin Edmond, son of Paul Woytek and Selma Quitta, was born Mar. 21, 1931, Hallettsville, TX. Education: Vsetin School, TX, through eighth grade. Enlisted Oct. 29, 1952, in U.S. Army Corps, Gonzales, TX. Theater of Operations: Far East. Engaged in Korean Conflict, shooting 105 Howitzer. Medals: Korean Service w/1 BSS, United Nations Service, National Defense Service. Honorably discharged Aug. 20, 1954. Assigned to Army Reserve for six years. Submitted by Marvin Woytek, Hallettsville, TX.

Woytek, Paul, son of Pavel Vojtek and Anna Sebesta, was born Feb. 5, 1890, Hallettsville, TX. Education: grammar school, Vsetin, TX. Enlisted in Hallettsville, TX, WWI, U.S. Army Corps, July 15, 1918. Pvt., Co. K, 9th Inf., with American Expeditionary Forces. Theater of Operations: Europe (France), Battles: Meuse-Argonne, France. Honorably discharged Aug. 22, 1919. Died Apr. 6, 1976. Submitted by Marvin Woytek, Hallettsville, TX.

Woytek, Raymond J., son of Jim Woytek and Tillie Barabas, was born May 21, 1923, Holland,

TX. Grandparents: John R. and Paulina Valchar Woytek, Joe and Augina Kunz Barabas. Attended Holland High School (1941) and Nixon Clay Commercial College (1946). Enlisted at Fort Sam Houston, TX, on Mar. 22, 1943. Rank: Sgt., 150th Engineer Combat Bn., 3rd Army, European Theater. Fought in the Battle of the Bulge, and Luxembourg. WOUNDED IN ACTION. Medals: Presidential Unit Citation and Purple Heart. Home of record: Round Rock, TX.

Wysocki, Joseph, son of Mr. and Mrs. Wysocki, was born Aug. 15, 1915. Enlisted in TX during WWII, in U.S. Army Corps. Died Apr. 4, 1985; buried St. Mary's Catholic Cem., Frydek, Austin Co., TX.

Wysocki, Steve, son of Mr. and Mrs. Wysocki, was born Dec. 22, 1918. Enlisted in U.S. Army during WWII. Rank: Pvt. Died May 8, 1988; buried St. Mary's Catholic Cem., Frydek, Austin Co., TX.

Zabojnik, Emil L., son of Louis M. Zabojnik and Miss Malota, was born May 14, 1933, in Ennis, TX. Attended St. John's School at Ennis. Inducted into the U.S. Army at Ft. Sam Houston, TX, during the Korean Conflict. Served in Alaska and attained the rank of Pfc. Separated from service in 1955 at Ft. Bliss, TX. Home of record: Ennis, TX.

Zabransky, George J., son of Adolph Zabransky and Louise Ermis, was born on Feb. 23, 1923 at Schulenburg, TX. Attended Schulenburg High School. Entered the Army on Nov. 19, 1943, Ft. Sam Houston, TX. Trained at Fort Knox, KY, Camp Bowie, and Camp Barkley, TX. Attained rank of Cpl. Served in the European area in the 495th Armd. Field Artillery, 12th Armd. Div. in the Battle of the Bulge–Rhine River–Colmar–Danube River. Medals: European Theater of Operations w/3 BSS, Army of Occupation, WWII Victory Ribbon, American Theater Campaign Ribbons, Good Conduct, and Presidential Citation. Discharged June 8, 1946, at Fort Sam Houston, San Antonio, TX. Married Vi Zabransky; three children: Mike, Sandra Zabransky Ashworth, Deborah Zabransky Thurmond; six grandchildren. Retired from Cameron Iron Works. Home of record: Houston, TX.

Zahirniak, Ernest G., son of Willie Zahirniak and Annie Cepak, was born Sept. 11, 1923, in West TX. Attended school at West. Enlisted in the U.S. Army at Ft. Sam Houston, TX, during WWII. Assigned to the European, African, and Middle Eastern Theater of Operations, 36th Div. Attained the rank of Staff Sgt. Participated in the Normandy, Northern France, Ardennes:Alsace, Rhineland, and Central Europe Campaigns. D-Day participant at the Normandy Invasion. WOUNDED IN ACTION three times: Teeth shot out of his mouth on Aug. 13, 1944, and gunshot wounds in Dec. 1944 and on Mar. 29, 1945. Went from the Normandy beaches on D-Day through France, Belgium, Germany, and into Czechoslovakia, when WWII ended in Europe. Decorations include the BSS Medal, Purple Heart w/2 OLC, and European-African-Middle Eastern Campaign Medal w/5 campaign stars. Discharged June 29, 1945. Home of record: West, TX.

Zahirniak, Harry, of West, TX. WWII veteran, PRISONER OF WAR.

Zahirniak, Larry P., son of Mr. and Mrs. Fred Zahirniak, West, TX. Entered Army in 1940, attained rank of Pfc. Served in Africa and Italy. PRISONER OF WAR, Germany, for 19 months. Awards: ET, AD, and Victory Ribbon. Discharged 1945.

Zahirniak, Patrick J., son of Senior Master Sgt. Robert W. and Mrs. Zahirniak, was born Jan. 10, 1967, Bunker Hill AFB, IN. Education: high school and MCC College. Enlisted Feb. 1988, Waco, McLennan Co., TX, U.S. Army Corps. Rank: E-5, Sgt.. Locations served: Ft. Leonard Wood, MO, CA, Mass., TX, Saudi Arabia, Iraq. Battles: Desert Shield and Desert Storm. Medals: Army Commendation, Campaign Medals. Still on active duty, helicopter mechanic. Submitted by father Robert W. Zahirniak. Home of record: West, TX.

Zahirniak, Robert W., son of Willie and Annie Zahirniak, was born July 29, 1930, West, TX. High school education. Enlisted in U.S. Army Air Corp, June 2, 1948, Waco, TX. Locations served: Japan, Korea, Bermuda, Thailand, Indiana, OH, TX, NY. Battles: Korea, two tours; Viet Nam. Medals: Japanese Occupation, Korean Service, U.N. Medal; Viet Nam Service,; GCM, Air Force Commendation. Retired Aug. 1, 1975, as Senior Master Sgt., after 27 years of active duty. Occupation: utility Operator-master mechanic at M&M Mars. Retired after 17 years. Home of record: West, TX.

Zajicek, Charles, son of George and Rosalie Zajicek, was born about 1896. Served in WWI. Died in France on Dec. 14, 1918, and is buried there.

Zajicek, Charlie Carl, son of John Zajicek and Marie Toninger, was born Oct. 1, 1914, in

Holland, Bell Co., TX. Graduated from Vilas, TX, High School in 1933. Enlisted in the U.S. Army on Aug. 26, 1941, at Ft. Sam Houston, TX. Served in the Asiatic-Pacific Theater of Operations, during WWII, as a motor boat operator with the 65th Engineers. Attained the rank of Technical Sgt. Participated in operations throughout the Pacific including the North Solomons, Luzon, and Guadalcanal. At Pearl Harbor during the Japanese air attack on Dec. 7, 1941. Decorations include the American Defense Service Medal, Asiatic-Pacific Campaign Medal, Good Conduct Medal, Philippine Liberation Ribbon, and Meritorious Unit Commendation Award. Died on Mar. 15, 1950; interred at Val Verde, Milam Co., TX.

Zajicek, David Bruce, son of Johnnie and Alice Zajicek, was born on Oct. 15, 1945, at Ganado, Jackson Co., TX. Education included two years of college. Attained the rank of Specialist 4. Served in the Viet Nam Theater of Operation. Received the National Defense Service Medal, the Republic of Viet Nam Campaign Medal, Expert Rifle, and Viet Nam Service Medal w/1 BSS. Discharged Oct. 15, 1971. Home of record: Sugarland, TX.

Zajicek, Gene Allen, son of Johnnie and Alice Zajicek, was born Apr. 21, 1944, at Ganado, Jackson Co., TX. Education included six years of college. Enlisted at Houston, TX; served with USS *Ranger* CVA-61 RVAH-9. Achieved the rank of E-5. Received the National Defense Medal, Viet Nam Medal, and Good Conduct Medal. Home of record: Warrenton, VA.

Zajicek, Johnnie, son of George and Rosalie Zajicek, was born on Feb. 26, 1917, at Ganado, Jackson Co., TX. Attended school through the eighth grade. Enlisted at Fort Sam Houston and attained the rank of Pfc. Served in the European Theater of Operations and fought in Rhineland GO33WD45. WOUNDED IN ACTION and received the Purple Heat Medal, Combat Infantry Badge, Expert Rifle, Good Conduct, and American Theater Victory Medals. Discharged Nov. 20, 1945. Died on Aug. 7, 1985.

Zajicek, Raymond Douglas, son of Johnnie and Alice Zajicek was born on Jan. 22, 1943, at Ganado, Jackson Co., TX. Graduated from high school. Enlisted at Houston, and attained the rank of Specialist 4/C. Received the Expert Rifle and Good Conduct Medals. Discharged July 28, 1965. Home of record: Ganado, TX.

Zajicek, Raymond Lewis, son of John Zajicek and Marie Toninger, was born in Holland, Bell Co., TX, on July 18, 1918. Graduated from high school at Rogers, TX, in 1936 and attended Texas A&M College. Enlisted in the U.S. Army on Apr. 3, 1941, at Ft. Sam Houston, TX. Served in the European, African, and Middle Eastern Theater of Operations during WWII as a communications installer and repairman. Served in Africa in Algeria, Morocco, and Tunisia; and in Europe in England, Ireland, Scotland, and Italy. Participated in the Naples-Foggia, Rome-Arno, Northern Apennines, and Po Valley Campaigns. Worked personally for General Eisenhower when he was Commander of Allied Forces in Africa, and also for General Mark Clark when he was Commander of 5th Army in Italy, installing communications equipment in their offices. Decorations: European-African-Middle Eastern Campaign Medal w/4 campaign stars, American Defense Service Medal, Good Conduct Medal, and Presidential Unit Citation. Separated from service on Oct. 24, 1945. Married Estha Ann Dusek; two children: Jimmy Gene, and Terry Ann Zajicek Fuchs. Engaged in ranching and growing pecans. Home of record: Holland, TX.

Zak, Vernon Albert, son of John Zak and Albina Woytek, was born Jan. 16, 1923, Rabb Switch, Lavaca Co., TX. Education: Rab Switch School, east of Hallettsville, TX. Enlisted at Ft. Sam

Houston, TX. Attained rank of Pfc. in U.S Army Corps. Theater of Operations: European. Assigned to 547th AAA AW Bn., 95th Inf. Div., ETO. Battles: Metz, Germany. Honorably discharged, 1946. Married Vicki Holy, 1953; children: Vernell and David. Retired in 1988 from San Bernard Electric Co-op, with 34 years of service. Home of record: Temple, TX.

Zalesak, John Joseph, son of Charles Zalesak and Frances Pavlicek, was born Feb. 26, 1922, Sealy, TX. Education: Guardian Angel Catholic School and Wallis High School. Inducted into U.S. Army, Dec. 31, 1942, Ft. Sam Houston, San Antonio, TX. Basic training, Camp Wallace, TX, and Ft. Bliss, TX, as a gunner—putting in lead and elevation, giving the command to fire, and estimating the range for a target. Landed in France on D-Day. Campaigns: Ardennes, Rhineland, Central Europe, Northern France, and the Battle of the Bulge. Medals: EHMA Ribbon Arrowhead, OPGA, GCM, American Theater Ribbon, WWII Victory Medal Ribbon. Slightly WOUNDED; honorably discharged Nov. 21, 1945, Camp Bowie, TX. Married Margaret in 1946; seven children, 18 grandchildren, two great-grandchildren. Home of record: Crosby, TX.

Zalesky, Bernard Tom, son of Joe Zalesky and Mary Biskup, was born May 20, 1928, at Cameron, TX. Education: Curry Public School, Yoe High School. Inducted in the U.S. Army on Nov. 30, 1950, during the Korean Conflict. Served in Korea. Participated in three campaigns, and attained the rank of Technical Cpl.Decorations include the Korean Service Medal w/3 campaign stars, and United Nations Service Medal. Separated from service at Ft. Hood, TX, on Sept. 6, 1952. Married; two children: Thomas, and Sherry Lynn Zalesky Vansa. Home of record: Cameron, TX. Portions submitted by Emil Zalesky, including picture.

Zalesky, Emil Antone, son of Joe Zalesky and Mary Biskup, was born July 18, 1917, Cameron, TX. Education: St. Monica's Catholic, and Curry Public Schools. Enlisted at Ft. Sam Houston, TX. Achieved Rank of Tech. 5. Fought in Pacific Theater of Operations. Battles: Aleutian, Philippines, Ryukyus. Medals: Asiatic-Pacific Campaign Medal w/3 BSS and one Bronze Arrowhead, Philippine Liberation Ribbon w/2 BSS, GCM, American Defense Service Medal, one service stripe, four overseas service bars. Honorably discharged Nov. 30, 1945. Married Ann Hosek; one daughter: Dolores Zalesky Fisher. Home of record: Cameron, TX.

Zapalac, George H., son of Mr. and Mrs. Henry Zapalac, West, TX. Entered Navy 1942. Attained rank of SK 1/C. Served in Admiralty. Awards: Victory, and AP ribbons. Discharged 1946.

Zapalac, Henry, son of Joseph Zapalac and Anna Vykukal of West, TX, was drafted in 1918 and served in France during WWI. Home of record: West, TX.

Zapalac, James C., son of James M. Zapalac and Sophia Rek, was born Oct. 29, 1920, El Campo, TX. Education: El Campo High School, TX, Memphis State Graduate School, Memphis, TN. Commissioned a Lt., U.S. Navy, Houston, TX. Theater of Operations: Pacific Ocean. Medals: American Defense, American Theater, Asiatic-Pacific Campaign, WWII Victory, National Defense. Retired Aug. 1, 1967. Home of record: Millington, TN.

Zapalac, Jerry D., son of Mr. and Mrs. Lud. Zapalac, West, TX. Attended West High School. Entered Navy, 1944, attained rank of SF 3/Cf. Trained at LCS. Discharged 1946.

Zapalac, John Frank, son of Joseph Zapalac and Anna Vykukal, was born on July 31, 1893, in West, TX. Completed fifth grade. Inducted on Oct. 7, 1917, into U.S. Army Corps from West, TX. Served in the 36th Div., 111th Engineers. Fought with AEF in France: St. Michiel Offensive from Sept. 12-18, 1918, and in the Meuse-Argonne Offensive from 9-26-18 to 11-18-18. Promoted to Musician 2/C. Played the clarinet and saxophone in the Armed Forces Band. Recalled time the military band played music for

General Pershing. WWI was not all music, though. When outfit reached the front lines, the musical instruments were put in the bus, and guns and packs were issued. One time he and some soldiers were on the back of a Model T truck that accidentally drove to the front lines. The Germans spotted them and began shooting. They drove in a zigzag pattern and made it to a wooded area. Fortunately, no one was hurt. Another time, the food supplies got lost and they did not eat for three days. Honorably discharged June 18, 1919. Joined the Texas State Guard and served until he became disabled. Died Nov. 30, 1987, after a lengthy illness. Buried in St. Mary's Catholic Cemetery, West, TX. Submitted by widow, Bettie Zapalac, Abbott, TX.

Zapalac, Lillian M., daughter of Mr. and Mrs. Henry Zapalac, West, TX. Attended West High School. Graduated Providence Hospital School of Nursing. Entered Army Nurse Corps in 1945 during WWII, as an R.N. Commissioned 2nd Lt. Served in General Hospital, Ft. Sam Houston. Awards: Victory, and A.T. Ribbons. Discharged 1946.

Zarosky, Clement L., was born Nov. 12, 1895, Cameron, Milam Co., TX. WWI, Pvt., Btry. B, 132 FA36 Div. Married Annie L. Died Nov. 2, 1960; buried at Sts. Cyril & Methodius Catholic Cemetery, Marak, TX.

Zaruba, Richard, served in U.S. Army Corps, during WWII.

Zaskoda, Dominik, son of Frank and Anna Zaskoda, was born on Dec. 30, 1909, at El Campo, TX. Attended school through the eighth grade. Enlisted at Fort Sam Houston. Served at Luzon, Southern Philippines. Battles: Bismarck Archipelago, Luzon, Southern Philippines. WOUNDED IN ACTION. Medals: Good Conduct, Purple Heart. Discharged Oct. 2, 1945. Home of record: Louise, TX.

Zaskoda, Havel F., son of Peter G. Zaskoda and Frances Wostarek, was born in the El Campo, TX area. Served in the Asiatic-Pacific Theater of Operations in the U.S. Navy aboard the USS *Milller*, during WWII. Home of record: Sealy, TX.

Zaskoda, Rudolph C., was born in Nada, TX. Served during the Korean Conflict in the U.S. Navy aboard the USS *Wiltsie*.

Zaskoda, Valerian J., son of Peter G. Zaskoda and Frances Wostarek, was born in El Campo, TX. Served in the Asiatic-Pacific Theater of Operations in the U.S. Navy aboard the USS *Florican*, during WWII.

Zatopik, Elo, West, TX, military veteran.

Zavodny, Aug Joe Lee, son of Joseph Zavodny and Lydia Bartos, was born Nov. 17, 1921, Cyclone, Bell Co., TX, in a family of eight children. Schooling at Cyclone, TX. Was a farmer. Entered U.S. Army Corps, Nov. 9, 1942, Ft. Sam Houston, TX. Trained at Ft. Riley, KS, and Camp Maxey, TX. Rank: Cpl. Arrived in England, Nov. 1943. After six months intensive training, debarked on Omaha Beach, France, June 12, 1944, six days after the Invasion of Normandy. Was in battle four months. KILLED IN ACTION, Sept. 24, 1944, Battle of the Bulge, Belgium, age 23. In Nov. 1947, his body arrived in Rogers, TX, by train with an escort. Buried at St. Joseph's Catholic Cemetery, Cyclone, TX—the 4th generation alongside his parents, grandparents and great-grandmother. Medals: Expert Rifleman, Expert Machine Gunner and Pistol, GCM, EAME w/Bronze Battle Stars, and Purple Heart. Submitted by Lillian B. Mikulec, Buckholts, TX.

Zavodny, Jerry, son of Joseph Zavodny and Lydia Bartos, was born Nov. 18, 1913, Meeks, Bell Co., TX, third child of eight. Enlisted in Army Air Corps, Nov. 9, 1942, Ft. Sam Houston, San Antonio, TX. Trained and served at AAB Jefferson Barracks, MO, AAB, Salt Lake City, UT, AAB Herrington, KS, AAB Alamogordo, NM, AAB Charleston, SC. Basic training and Airplane Mechanic School at Kessler Field, MS. Received GCM Medal. Honorably discharged Feb. 18, 1946, Tyler, TX. Married Mollie Porubsky, 1939, who died in 1971. Married Louise (Marek)

Psencik; two stepsons, four step-grandchildren. Engaged in ranching, farming, and general merchandise business at Red Ranger, Bell Co., TX. Home of record: Rogers, TX. Submitted by Lillian B. Mikulec, Buckholts, TX.

Zboril, Robert, served Oct, 1942–Apr, 1944, in U.S. Army Corps, during WWII.

Zboril, Rudolph "Rudy" J., son of Rudolph Zboril and Vincencia Ondra, was born Dec. 15, 1915, Frydek, Austin Co., TX. Education: St. Mary's Catholic School, Frydek, Mixville Public School. Enlisted in U.S. Army Corps during WWII. Assigned to First Cavalry Div. Member of the 8th Engineers Sqdn. Served in South Pacific for 30 months. Medals: Asiatic-Pacific Theater Campaign w/5 BSS, Philippine Liberation Ribbon w/2 BSS, WWII Victory. Honorably discharged. Married Anne Siska, Feb. 9, 1942; four children: Wilbert, Rudolph, Vincencia Zboril Lloyd, Bernadette Zboril Weatherford. Died Nov. 21, 1993, buried St. Mary's Cemetery, Frydek, TX.

Zbranek, Alfred James, son of Frank V. and Mary Hattie Zbranek, was born June 18, 1930, El Campo, TX. Education: Jones Creek School, El Campo ISD, Garwood ISD, TX. Enlisted in U.S. Navy at Houston, TX, 1948. Served with 1st Marine Div., First Marine Reg., Second Bn., Dog Co. Theater of Operation: Korean War. Battles: Wonson area, Hangyang area, Heart Break Ridge. WOUNDED IN ACTION twice: June 10, 1951, Wia-Hangyang area, and Sept. 13, 1951, Wia-Kajon-Ni area. Medals: two Purple Hearts, Korean Service w/OLC, United Nations Service Ribbon and Medal. Home of record: East Bernard, TX.

Zbranek, Henry, Granger, TX. WWII veteran. Member, American Legion Post No. 282, Granger, TX. Deceased.

Zbranek, Joe R., son of Mr. and Mrs. Joe J. Zbranek, Granger, TX. Education: Granger High School. Enlisted U.S. Army Corps, 1942; basic training, Ft. Sam Houston, TX. Additional training, Camp Wallace, Ft. Crockett, San Jacinto, Sabine Pass. Theaters of Operation: American, Asiatic-Pacific. Served in Florida Island, Eimeria, Luzon. Medals: ATO, A-PO w/2 BSS, Philippine Liberation, Good Conduct, WWII Victory, ribbons. Attained rank of Cpl. prior to honorable discharge, 1945.

Zbranek, Johnnie A., son of Mr. and Mrs. Joe J. Zbranek, Granger, TX. Education: Granger High School. Enlisted U.S. Army Corps, 1942; basic training, Ft. Sam Houston, TX. Additional training, Camp Davis, NC. Theater of Operations: Asiatic-Pacific. Served in New Guinea, Philippines. Medals: A-PO, Philippine Liberation, Good Conduct, Ribbons, WWII Victory. Attained rank of Pfc. prior to honorable discharge, 1946.

Zbranek, Larry, West, TX, WWII veteran.

Zbranek, Louis H., son of Frank Rudolph Zbranek and Mary David, was born July 6, 1937, Granger, Williamson Co., TX. Education: high school, Granger, TX, GED. Enlisted May 23, 1956, San Antonio, TX, U.S. Navy. Attained rank of DC 2/C, damage controlman, shipfitter, carpenter. Theater of Operations: South Pacific, Taiwan Straits, Sea Japan, 1958-59, Philippine Sea on Cruiser USS *Saint Paul* CA-73, and USS *Marshall* DDE 676, Mediterranean Sea on USS *Springfield* U-G 7, and USS *Franklin Roosevelt* CVA 42, 1960-64. Awarded two Good Conduct Medals. Honorable discharge, Aug. 4, 1964. Married Janie Cepcar; one daughter: Kathy Lynn Zbranek. Hobbies: fishing, hunting, Lotto. Home of record: Pflugerville, TX .

Zelenevitz, Louis Dominic, son of Mr. Zelenevitz and Mrs. Frances Zelenevitz, Dime Box, TX, was born 1907. Education: Dime Box School. Enlisted U.S. Navy, 1944; basic training, San Diego, TX. Theater of Operations: Asiatic-Pacific. Served aboard USS *Kenneth Whiting* A.V. 14, in Saipan, Peleliu, Okinawa, Japan. Medals: Asiatic-Pacific Theater Campaign w/2 BSS, American Theater, WWII Victory, Ribbons. Attained rank of S 1/C prior to honorable discharge, 1943. Married Milady Marie Kenchern, Granger TX. Died 1982; buried Holy Cross Catholic Cemetery, Granger, TX.

Zernicek, Alois D., son of Josef Zernicek and Mary Sliva, was born Nov. 9, 1927, at Frydek, TX. Enlisted in the U.S. Army on May 9, 1946 at Bay City, TX, shortly after the end of WWII. Served in the Asiatic-Pacific Theater of Operations with the Occupational Forces in Japan as a member of the 695th Engineer Base Equipment Co. Separated from service on Oct. 30, 1947, at Ft. Lewis, WA. Enlisted again in the U.S. Army and served two tours in Viet Nam during the Viet Nam Conflict: Mar. 30, 1967-June 12, 1969, and Feb. 21-Sept. 3, 1971. Worked as a material storage specialist and subsistence supply specialist. Decorations include

the Army of Occupation Medal, WWII Victory Medal, National Defense Service Medal, Viet Nam Service Medal, Viet Nam Campaign Medal, Viet Nam Gallantry Cross w/Palm, Meritorious Unit Commendation, and Good Conduct Medal (4th award). Retired from service on Mar. 27, 1975, at Ft. Eustis, VA with the rank of Staff Sgt. (received a medical discharge) after 18 years of service. Married Margaret Eugenia Crawley (a descendant of John Hancock) on Oct. 17, 1969; one son: Joseph John. Died in Wadsworth, TX, on June 27, 1977. Interred at St. Joseph's Cemetery, Petersburg, VA.

Zernicek, Emil A., son of Josef Zernicek and Mary Sliva, (1st of 14 children), was born Apr. 14, 1919, at Waller, TX. Inducted in the U.S. Army during WWII at Houston, TX, on Sept. 18, 1942. Assigned to the 5th Ind. Hq. 102nd Inf. Div. Qualified as a Sharp Shooter. Member of Co. H, 406th Inf. Rank: Pvt. Honorably discharged Nov. 2, 1943, at Shreveport, LA. Married Irene Julia Archer on Oct. 19, 1945; two sons: Emil Joseph and George Paul. Irene died Dec. 1953 of rheumatic fever. Married Delores Catherine Cerny on July 5, 1959, at Bay City, TX; four children: Priscilla Irene, Janice Inez, Stephen James, and Mark Alan. Died July 1, 1977; interred in the Cedarville Cemetery in Bay City, TX.

Zernicek, Emil John, son of Joseph Zernicek and Emilie Tannich, was born Jan. 19, 1885, in Ammannsville, TX. Enlisted in the U.S. Army, during WWI. Served with the American Expeditionary Forces in France. Reenlisted for another six months, saw action in France, and was KILLED IN ACTION on a French battlefield on Oct. 8, 1918, at the age of 33. Body was sent home to be buried in Frydek Catholic Cemetery on Sept. 5, 1921. Grave marker gives the information that Emil was a Pfc. in the 141 Inf., 36 Div.

Zernicek, Frank, son of Josef Zernicek and Mary Sliva, was born Aug. 14, 1917, Frydek, Austin Co., TX (1 of 14 children). Inducted in the Army at Bay City on Jan. 30, 1941. Pfc., assigned to 36th Div., Co. C, 143rd Inf. as a salvage technician in Europe. Battles: Rome-Arno. Decorated with a Silver Star by Gen. Mark Clark in 1944 for service on an Italian battlefield. He and another soldier crawled through a mine field while being exposed to enemy fire to drag two wounded men to safety. Sent back to the States in 1944 and became an Airman Recruit. Sent to the Asiatic-Pacific Theater in July 1945, and returned in Nov. Discharged in Dec. at Fort Sam Houston, TX. Medals: American Defense Service, American Theater Campaign, EAME Campaign w/1 BSS, Asiatic-Pacific Theater Campaign, Philippine Liberation Campaign, Good Conduct, Victory Ribbon, and Combat Infantryman Badge. Discharged at Ft. Sam Houston, TX, Dec. 12, 1945. Returned to Bay City and was an oil field laborer. Died on Feb. 27, 1962, and was buried in the Cedarvale Cemetery in Bay City.

Zernicek, Josephine Agatha, twin daughter of Josef Zernicek and Mary Sliva, was born May 6, 1923, at Sealy, TX. Attended St. Mary's Catholic School at Frydek, TX. Enlisted in the U.S. Army WACs at Ft. Crockett, Galveston, TX, on July 24, 1944, during WWII. Served in the American Theater of Operations as a member of the WAC Detachment, 4136th Army Air Force Base Unit as an auto equipment operator. Received a hardship discharge on June 14, 1944, so she could care for her youngest brother, George Zernicek, who was suffering from Hodgkin's Disease. Married Brice P. Green who worked for Amoco until retiring; nine children: Jerry Lynn (from Brice's previous marriage), Brice P., Jr., Mary Louise, Jean Helen Green Vanek (deceased), William Joseph "Bill," Henry John, A. F. "Punky", Barbara Ann, and Thomas James "Jimmy." Brice is also a twin and they are the grandparents of three sets of twins among their 20 grandchildren. Home of record: Palacios, TX.

Zernicek, Louise Imelda, twin daughter of Josef Zernicek and Mary Sliva, was born May 6, 1923, in Sealy, TX, one of 14 children. Attended St. Mary's Catholic School at Frydek, TX. Enlisted July 24, 1944, in the U.S. Army WACs at Ft. Crockett, Galveston, TX, during WWII. Served in the American Theater of Operations as a member of

WAC Detachment #1852, Service Command Unit. Decorations include American Theater Campaign and Good Conduct Medals. Discharged at Fort Sam Houston, on Dec. 16, 1945. Married Wid Wright Sewad in Beaumont, on Sept. 9, 1948; twelve children: Wid Wright Jr., Elizabeth Ann, Henry Wayne, Paul Richard, Lloyd Raymond, Mary Kathleen, Jane Ella and Thomas Alois. Home of record is Dutch Mills, AR.

Zernicek, Ludwig J., son of Josef Zernicek and Mary Sliva, was born Jan. 20, 1925, Sealy, TX. Family moved from Frydek area near Sealy to Bay City area in the late 1930s. Entered the Army Mar. 11, 1943. Rank: Pfc., horse-breaker, Camp Atterbury, IN, Medical Bn., 10th Mt. Div. In Europe, was stationed in the Apennines Valley of Italy. Served 2 years, 9 months, 11 days before discharge. Medals: Good Marksmanship M-16, Victory, AT Ribbon, EAME Theater Ribbon w/2 BSS, Good Conduct. After war, married Lillian Gertrude Culver, May 8, 1948; six children: Ludwig Lawrence, Michael Harry, Joseph Francis, Anthony Christopher, Thersia Mary, and Lillian Ann. Daughters served with the Armed Forces during the Viet Nam Conflict.

Zernicek, Vaclav A., son of Joseph Zernicek and Emilie Tannich, was born Oct. 7, 1892, in Ammannsville, TX. Parents moved to a Czech community south of Waller in the 1890s and then to Frydek, Austin Co., TX, in 1916. Helped on family farm until drafted. Inducted into the U.S. Army, during WWI. His unit and period of service are unknown. Details of his service records are not known, but he did return home. After the war he was very sick from effects of yellow fever he caught while enlisted. When well, he continued to help his parents on the family farm. Died Sept. 29, 1938; buried in the Frydek Catholic Cemetery.

Zernicek, Willie, son of Ludwig Anton Zernicek and Mary Skarpa, was born Sept. 25, 1920, at Frydek, TX. Inducted into the U.S. Army on Aug. 23, 1944, at Houston, TX, during WWII. Served in the Asiatic-Pacific Theater of Operations and participated in the Luzon Campaign as a member of Co. G, 129th Inf. Decorations: Asiatic-Pacific Campaign Medal with campaign star, WWII Victory Medal, Good Conduct Medal, Philippine Liberation Ribbon, and Philippine Independence Ribbon. Discharged Oct. 29, 1946, at Ft. Sam Houston, TX.

Zernicek, Willie, son of Josef Zernicek, Sr. and Emelia Zernicek, was born Sept. 25, 1920, in Frydek, TX. Inducted in the Army Aug. 23, 1944, at Houston, TX. Rank: Tech 4. Served as an auto mechanic with Co. G, 129th Inf. in the Philippines on Luzon. Decorations include Combat Infantryman Badge, Asiatic-Pacific Campaign w/1 BSS, Philippine Liberation w/1 BSS, Philippine Independence, Good Conduct, WWII Victory Medal, and two Overseas Service Bars. Discharged Oct. 29, 1946, at Fort Sam Houston, TX.

Zernick, Lillian Ann, daughter of Ludwig J. Zernick and Lillian Gertrude Culver, served during the Viet Nam Conflict.

Zernick, Thersia Mary, daughter of Ludwig J. Zernick and Lillian Gertude Culver, served in the Viet Nam Conflict.

Zett, Albert R., military service veteran. Home of record: Ovilla, TX.

Zett, Ben J., son of Rudolph Emil Zett and Albina Pustejovsky, was born Apr. 13, 1914, in Granger, TX. Attended Taylor High School and also attended Houston Barber College. Enlisted in the U.S. Army Air Corps in 1939 at Kelly Field in San Antonio, TX. Assigned to the Asiatic-Pacific Theater of Operations during WWII. Participated in military operations in New Guinea and in the Philippines. Participated in the Berlin Air Lift. Decorations include the American Defense Service Medal, Asiatic-Pacific Campaign Medal w/2 BSS, Philippine Liberation Ribbon with BSS, Good Conduct Medal, BSS, and WWII Victory Medal. Separated from service on Oct. 31, 1956, rank of T/Sgt. Married Mary Roznovsky. Is a farmer in the Granger area. Member, American Legion Post No. 282, Granger, TX. Home of record: Granger, TX.

Zett, Christopher P., was born 1916. WWII veteran. Died 1992; buried Holy Cross Catholic Cemetery, Granger, TX.

Zett, Christopher Rudolph, son of Rudolph Emil Zett and Albina Pustejovsky, was born May 25, 1916 in Granger, Williamson Co, TX. Education: Granger, TX. Enlisted in U.S. Navy at Navy Recruiting Station, Houston, TX, June 11, 1940, prior to WWII. Basic training, San Diego, CA. Assigned to USS *Utah* as water tender. USS *Utah* was assigned to the Asiatic-Pacific Theater of Operations and was sunk during the Japanese air attack on Pearl Harbor on Dec. 7, 1941. Served on USS *Flusser* which was also sunk. In naval operations in Australia, Guadalcanal, New Guinea and New Britain Admiralties. WOUNDED IN ACTION. Medals: Silver Star, A-P Campaign Medal, Purple Heart, American Defense Medal. Separated from service Aug. 12, 1944. Part time farmer/fisherman. Married Anita Streich; three children: Ronnie, Clifford, and Lester. Died Mar. 4, 1992; interred in the Holy Cross Catholic Cemetery, Granger, TX.

Zett, Daniel Frank, son of Rudolph Emil Zett and Albina Pustejovsky, Granger, TX. Education: Granger High School. Enlisted U.S. Army Corps, 1942; basic training, Ft. Sam Houston, TX. Rank: Pvt. Discharged 1943. Married Edith Rychlik.

Zett, Emanuel, WWII veteran of Granger, TX.

Zett, Frank David, son of Frank B. Zett and Myrtle Beard, was born Apr. 6, 1949. Attended St. Edwards High School in Austin, and graduated from A. S. Johnson High School in Austin in 1968. Enlisted in the U.S. Air Force at Austin, TX, during the Viet Nam Conflict. Served in the Viet Nam area as a B-52 crewman conducting combat air operations from Okinawa, Japan, and Guam. At the opening of the Fairlord AFB in England in 1979. Was also one of the first crew members to receive schooling and to be assigned to the B-1B Bomber at Dyess AFB, TX. He has also participated in Crash Recovery and Investigation of aircraft accidents. Decorations include the Air Force Meritorious Service Medal w/3 OLC, Air Force Outstanding Unit Medal w/2 OLC, Air Force Good Conduct Medal w/6 OLC, National Defense Service Medal, Viet Nam Service Medal, Air Force Short Tour Ribbon, Air Force Long Tour Ribbon, Air Force Longevity Ribbon w/4 OLC, and Republic of Viet Nam Campaign Medal. Retired from service on Oct. 31, 1990, with the rank of Master Sgt. Employed as truck driver/mechanic. Married Linda S. Marshall; two sons: John D. and Christopher K. Frank is a member of the Knights of Columbus, Council 2163. Home of record: Abilene, TX.

Zett, Lester J., served in U.S. Armed Forces since WWII. Buried Holy Cross Cemetery, Granger, Williamson Co., TX.

Zett, Methodius, WWII veteran of Granger, TX.

Zett, Ralph William, son of Rudolph Emil Zett and Albina Pustejovsky, was born Aug. 25, 1918 in Granger, TX. Graduated from Granger High School in 1937 and subsequently attended Draughon's Business School in Dallas, TX. Enlisted in the U.S. Navy at Houston, TX, on July 1, 1942, during WWII. Basic training, San Diego, CA. Served in the Asiatic Pacific Theater of Operations as Chief Storekeeper, Supplies and Ordnance. Attained the rank of CSK. Participated in naval operations at New Hebrides, Guam, and Okinawa. Decorations include the Asiatic-Pacific Campaign Medal, American Campaign Medal, Good Conduct Medal, and the WWII Victory Medal. Separated from service on Feb. 2, 1946. Employed by Texas Power and Light Company as an ACR Clerk until retirement in Aug. 1983. Hobbies: hunting and fishing. Married Alice Mary Naizer; two children: Marla Rachel Zett Prcin and Thomas Earl Zett. Home of record: Taylor, TX.

Zett, Thomas Earl, son of Ralph W. Zett and Alice

Mary Naizer, was born Aug. 29, 1958, in Taylor, TX. Graduated from Taylor High in 1976. Received B.S. (Marketing) from Texas A&M University in 1980, and earned Masters (Logistics) at the Florida Institute of Technology in 1988. At graduation from Texas A&M University was commissioned a 2nd Lt. in the Ordnance Corps and entered active duty in Aug. 1980. Served in Europe and at the White Sands Missile Range in Operations/Security, ORSA, S-1/Adjutant, and Command positions before entering the U.S. Army Reserves in 1990. Currently assigned to the 75th Div. (Exercises) at Houston, TX, with the rank of Maj. Decorations include Meritorious Service Medal, Army Achievement Medal, National Defense Service Medal, Army Service Medal, Overseas Ribbon, Army Reserves Overseas Training Ribbon, and the Airborne Badge. Was a Distinguished Military Student/Graduate at Texas A&M University and Honor Graduate at the Army Ordnance Officer Advance Course. Married Rebecca Kay Walker; two children: Jennifer Lynn and Elizabeth Ann. Employed as an office manager. Hobbies: hunting, fishing, and bike riding. Home of record: Houston, TX.

Zett, William J., WWII veteran of Granger, TX.

Zett, Zigmund A. "Zik," was born Sept. 19, 1916. WWII veteran. Died Mar. 20, 1983; buried at Calvary Catholic Cemetery, Granger, TX.

Zhanel, Frank, son of Anton and Mary Zhanel, was born Apr. 12, 1919, in Ennis, TX. Attended Village Creek School. Frank entered the Army on Feb. 13, 1942. His Theater of Operation was Europe. Staff Sgt. Zhanel served with Co. C, 36th Armed Infantry. Regiment, 3rd Armed Division., First Army. He was WOUNDED IN ACTION and his list of medals include Combat Infantry Badge, BSS, Purple Heart with two OLC, EAME with five BSS and two Unit Citations. He was honorably discharged Sept. 27, 1945 and home of record is Ennis, TX.

Zhanel, Joe Thomas, son of Thomas Zhanel and Hermina Zabojnik (immigrants from Brezuvky, Moravia), was born on Apr. 8, 1925, Creechville community of Ennis, TX. Entered the Army on July 12, 1943, and received training at Camp Wolters, TX. Rank: Pfc. Served with the 175th Inf. Reg., 29th Div. WOUNDED IN ACTION twice in France: June 29, 1944, and Aug. 27, 1944. WOUNDED IN ACTION a third time in Germany on Oct. 14, 1944. Received a Purple Heart each time. KILLED IN ACTION. On Feb. 24, 1945, in Germany, was fatally wounded by stepping on a land mine. Died the next day on Feb. 25, 1945. Services were conducted by a Catholic chaplain of the U.S. Army. Buried in Plot J, Row 11, Grave 15, of the American Military Cemetery in the Netherlands in the village of Margraten, where 8,301 of our military dead and 1,722 missing are listed on two walls of the Court of Honor at the cemetery entrance. Two nephews visited the grave in 1976.

Zhanel, John J., son of Anton and Mary Zhanel, was born June 24, 1916 in Ennis, TX. Attended Village Creek School. Enlisted in the Army in Jan. 1941, at Camp Bowie, TX. Rank: Pfc. Theaters of Operation: North Africa and Italy. Medals: Good Conduct, Purple Heart, and EAME. MORTALLY WOUNDED IN ACTION Nov. 30, 1943, in San Pietro, Italy, and died Apr. 21, 1944, in Crile General Hospital in Cleveland, OH.

Zhanel, Stanley Frank, son of Thomas Zhanel and Hermina Zabojnik, was born on Feb. 15, 1927 at Ennis, TX. Attended St. John Catholic School in Ennis, TX. He entered the Army in Dallas, and served in the Korean War. PFC Zhanel received his discharge on Sept. 7, 1951 at Fort Sill, Oklahoma. He died on June 16, 1976.

Zhanel, Stanley K., son of Anton and Mary

Zhanel, was born Nov. 21, 1923, in Ennis, TX. Attended Central High School. Entered the Army on Jan. 18, 1943, at Dallas, TX. Rank: Tech Fifth Grade. Served in Central Europe and in Czechoslovakia with Co. B, 782nd Tank Bn. Received the American Theater Campaign, EAME Campaign w/1 BSS, Good Conduct, and WWII Victory Medals. Discharged Feb. 8, 1946. Died Aug. 13, 1981.

Zich/Zichacek, Carl William, son of Ladislav Zichacek and Helen Kotas, was born on Aug. 4, 1916, at Fort Worth, TX. Attended school through the eighth grade, and night school for four years to learn the carpentry trade. Entered the service at Dallas. Received training at Camp Wolters. Served in the South Pacific, New Guinea, Netherlands, East Indies, Philippines, Okinawa, and Japan. Sgt. Zich received Mechanic Badge, Drivers Badge, Asiatic-Pacific Campaign Medal w/4 BSS, Philippine Liberation Ribbon w/2 Bronze Medals, Overseas Medals, four Victory Ribbons, Good Conduct Medal, four Hash Stripes. Discharged at Fort Sam Houston in Oct. 1945. Married; daughter was born while he was serving in New Guinea and was 2½ years of age when he first saw her. Worked for the same construction firm for 48 years. Served as president and trustee of SPJST, worked as appraiser and salesman for Slavonic Mutual First Insurance, and was active in church and community work. Home of record: Fort Worth, TX.

Zidek, Louis B., son of Anton M. Zidek and Sofhie Vincek, was born Aug. 19, 1890. Enlisted in U.S. Navy, fought in WWII. Theater of Operations: Asiatic-Pacific. Medals: Congressional Medal of Honor for operations on Leyte, Luzon, Okinawa, Gunto, and the Aleutians, Philippine Liberation Ribbon w/2 stars, for Leyete and Luzon operations, EAME Ribbon w/1 BSS for African Operation, American Defense Medal, American Campaign Ribbon w/3 stars, Good Conduct Medal, Asiatic-Pacific Medal w/4 stars. Died Apr. 20, 1974; buried Sunset Memorial Park, San Antonio, TX. Submitted by A. Kulach, Austin, TX.

Zimmerhanzel, Paul Peter, Sr., son of Joe Jacob Zimmerhanzel and Agnes Mares, was born June 29, 1925, Cistern, Fayette Co., TX. Education: Flatonia and Longbranch, TX (Taylor, Williamson Co., TX area). Enlisted Nov. 11, 1943, Ft. Sam Houston, TX, U.S. Army Corps. Attained rank of Sgt. Military Occupation: Artillery Section Chief 864. Theaters of Operation: American, Asiatic-Pacific, EAME. Battles: Central Europe. Medals: American Theater Campaign, EAME Theater Campaign w/BSS, Asiatic-Pacific Theater Campaign and Ribbon, Good Conduct, WWII Victory, Ribbons. Honorable discharge Apr. 3, 1946. Married Beatrice Zett, two children: Paul Peter Jr., Cheryl Elizabeth Zimmerhanzel Scruggs. Occupation: marketing, ranching. Retired Jan. 1, 1990. Hobbies: hunting and fishing. Home of record: Taylor, TX.

Zmolek, Jerry E., son of Joseph A. Zmolek and Mary T. Janku, was born Oct. 21, 1932, New Waverly, Walker Co., TX. Graduated Ennis High School, TX. Enlisted in Texas Air National Guard, Hensley Field. Assigned to 181st Ftr. Bmr. Sqdn. Enlisted in USAF at Dallas Air Force Recruiting Office, Dallas, TX. Maintained P-51 (mustangs) airworthy during Korean Conflict with 181st Fighter Bomber Sqdn. Flight Engineer on the B-25 Mitchel Bombers from 1953 to 1957. Honorable discharged from 181st Ftr Bmr Sq, Jan. 10, 1953, from USAF, Feb. 10, 1957. Since 1957, has been employed with airlines and still enjoys being around airplanes. Home of record: Ferris, TX.

Zrubek, Arnold John, son of Arnold T. Zrubek and Angela Bohac, was born in Granger, Williamson Co., TX. Education: Granger High School. Enlisted in U.S. Air Force. Now retired. Married Jeanette Seggern; two children, both in military: Brenda Zrubek Ford and Brian Patrick Zrubek.

Zrubek, Brenda Renee, daughter of Arnold John Zrubek and Jeanette Seggern, was born in Granger, Williamson Co., TX. Education: Taylor High School, TX. Enlisted U.S. Armed Forces, still in military, as is husband, Bryan Ford. Two children.

Zrubek, Brian Patrick, son of Arnold John

Zrubek and Jeanette Seggern, was born in Williamson Co., TX. Education: Granger, TX High School. Enlisted in U.S. Air Force.

Zrubek, Edwin J., son of Mr. and Mrs. Frank Zrubek, Granger, TX. Education: Circleville School. Enlisted U.S. Army Corps, 1942, during WWII. Basic training, Camp Robinson, AR. Additional training, Ft. McPherson, GA. Theater of Operations: Asiatic-Pacific, American. Medals: Good Conduct, Asiatic-Pacific Theater Campaign, ATO, WWII Victory, Ribbons. Attained rank of Sgt. prior to honorable discharge, 1946. Member, American Legion Post No. 282, Granger, TX. Home of record: Granger, TX.

Zrubek, Emil, Granger, TX. WWII veteran. Member, American Legion Post No. 282, Granger, TX.

Zrubek, Jerome R., Granger, TX. WWII veteran. U.S. Navy: USS P.C.E. 877.

Zurek, Joseph, served in U.S. Armed Forces during WWI, 1917–1918. Member of SPJST Lodge 20, Granger, TX.

Zurovetz, Albert I., was born Sept. 19, 1934. Pfc. LOST AT SEA, Chon Harbor, Korea. Died Jan. 21, 1954. Marker erected at Calvary Catholic Cemetery, Granger, TX.

Zurovetz, Daniel H., son of Mr. and Mrs. George Zurovetz, Granger, TX. Enlisted U.S. Army Corps, 1943. Basic training, Camp Callan, CA. Additional training, Ft. Ord, CA. Theater of Operations: Asiatic-Pacific. Served in Hawaii, Philippines, Okinawa, Korea. Medals: Good Conduct, Philippine Liberation w/1 Star, Asiatic-Pacific Theater Campaign w/2 BSS, WWII Victory, Ribbons. Attained rank of T/5 prior to honorable discharge, 1946.

Zurovetz, Elias J., served in U.S. Armed Forces since WWII. Disabled American Veteran, Veteran of Foreign Wars. Buried Holy Cross Cemetery, Granger, Williamson Co., TX.

Zurovetz, Jesse A., son of Julius Zurovetz and Louise Kubala, was born Nov. 28, 1931, Corn Hill, Williamson Co., TX. Enlisted in U.S. Army Corps about 1949. Attained rank of Sgt. Honorably discharged. Civilian occupation: farmer. Died Apr. 29, 1974. Buried Corn Hill, TX.

Zurovetz, Johnnie C., son of Mr. and Mrs. John Zurovetz, Granger, TX. Education: Granger and Palacky schools. Enlisted in U.S. Army Air Corps, 1942. Basic training, Roswell, NM; additional training, Kearns, UT. Theater of Operations: Asiatic-Pacific. Served in Hawaii, Marshalls, Palau, Marianas. Medals: Good Conduct, Asiatic-Pacific Theater Campaign w/2 BSS, WWII Victory, ribbons. Attained rank of Cpl. prior to honorable discharge, 1945.

Zvolanek, Bob, military service veteran. Home of record: Dallas, TX.

Zvonek, Adolph J., son of Rudolph M. Zvonek and Mary Walla, was born Feb. 26, 1917, Plum, Fayette Co, TX. Education: La Grange High School, Sam Houston State University, Huntsville, B.S., 1948. Taught school in Plum for four years. Enlisted July 14, 1942 in U.S. Army at La Grange, TX. Rank: S/Sgt. Served in the Southwest Pacific Theater of Operation in New Guinea. Participated in the Invasion of Luzon Philippines on Jan. 9, 1945, and served with the Occupation Forces in Tokyo, Japan. Medals: American Theater Campaign, Asiatic-Pacific Campaign w/3 BSS, Philippine Liberation Ribbon w/1 BSS, Good Conduct, Victory Ribbon, one Service Stripe, and two Overseas Service Bars. Discharged Dec. 10, 1945, at Fort Sam Houston, San Antonio, TX. Taught agriculture to Army veterans in Taylor, from 1948 to 1954. Since 1954 has been in the residential building business and developer of residential subdivisions in Taylor, TX. Home of record: Taylor, TX.

Zvolanek, Bohumil A., son of Joe Zvolanek and Anna, was born Mar. 14, 1909, Libun, Czechoslovakia. Attained college education in Czechoslovakia. Married Ann Tupy. Enlisted in U.S. Army Corps, Dallas, TX, Dec. 29, 1942, during WWII. Served in EAME Theater of Operations overseas 15 months. Medals: EAME Campaign Ribbon w/2 BSS, American Campaign, and WWII Victory, Good Conduct. Honorably discharged Dec. 1, 1945, Ft. Bliss, El Paso, TX. Home of record: Dallas, TX.